WWW.RAABE.DE

Sekundarstufe II

RAAbits Englisch

Impulse und Materialien für die kreative Unterrichtsgestaltung

Inhalt:

Brexit: success or failure? – Über den Brexit diskutieren (ab Kl. 10)
Ihre Lernenden setzen sich mit Bildern, Texten und einem Video zum Thema auseinander, um sich die Kontroverse vor Augen zu führen.

Nigerian coming-of-age stories – Interkulturelle Kompetenzen entwickeln (S II)
In der Reihe untersuchen die Schülerinnen und Schüler unterschiedliche Textsorten und lernen so die Lebenswelt Heranwachsender in Nigeria kennen.

The impact of social media – Medien kritisch betrachten (Kl. 9–11)
Neben der Anwendung sozialer Medien reflektieren die Lernenden ihr eigenes Konsumverhalten und analysieren dessen Einfluss auf sich selbst und auf die Gesellschaft.

Impressum

RAAbits Englisch
Ausgabe 2/2023

ISSN: 0946-5308 / 0946-5294
ISBN: 978-3-8183-0025-8 / 978-3-8183-0026-5

Das Werk, einschließlich seiner Teile, ist urheberrechtlich geschützt. Es ist gemäß § 60b UrhG hergestellt und ausschließlich zur Veranschaulichung des Unterrichts und der Lehre an Bildungseinrichtungen bestimmt. Die Dr. Josef Raabe Verlags-GmbH erteilt Ihnen für das Werk das einfache, nicht übertragbare Recht zur Nutzung für den persönlichen Gebrauch gemäß vorgenannter Zweckbestimmung. Unter Einhaltung der Nutzungsbedingungen sind Sie berechtigt, das Werk zum persönlichen Gebrauch gemäß vorgenannter Zweckbestimmung in Klassensatzstärke zu vervielfältigen. Jede darüber hinausgehende Verwertung ist ohne Zustimmung des Verlages unzulässig und strafbar. Hinweis zu §§ 60a, 60b UrhG: Das Werk oder Teile hiervon dürfen nicht ohne eine solche Einwilligung an Schulen oder in Unterrichts- und Lehrmedien (§ 60b Abs. 3 UrhG) vervielfältigt, insbesondere kopiert oder eingescannt, verbreitet oder in ein Netzwerk eingestellt oder sonst öffentlich zugänglich gemacht oder wiedergegeben werden. Dies gilt auch für Intranets von Schulen und sonstigen Bildungseinrichtungen. Die Aufführung abgedruckter musikalischer Werke ist ggf. GEMA-meldepflichtig.

Für jedes Material wurden Fremdrechte recherchiert und ggf. angefragt.

Dr. Josef Raabe Verlags-GmbH
Ein Unternehmen der Klett Gruppe
Rotebühlstraße 77
70178 Stuttgart
Telefon +49 711 62900-0
Fax +49 711 62900-60
meinRAABE@raabe.de
www.raabe.de

Redaktion: Juliane Thon, Kathrin Olßon, Anna Müller
Satz: pagina GmbH, Tübingen
Bildnachweis Titel: © Craig Hastings/Moment
Korrektorat und Lektorat: Ellen Black
Druck: Uslugi Wydawniczo-Poligraficzne Paper&Tinta; Nadma, Polen

Gedruckt auf chlorfrei gebleichtem Papier

Mai 2023

Liebe Lehrerin, lieber Lehrer,

immer wieder belegen Studien, dass es negative Korrelationen zwischen der Nutzung sozialer Medien und der mentalen Gesundheit gibt. Dennoch sind soziale Medien allgegenwärtig und aus unserer Gesellschaft nicht mehr wegzudenkenden. Viele Nutzende wissen wenig über die möglichen Auswirkungen ihres Nutzungsverhaltens, andere wiederum sind sich zwar über die negativen Folgen bewusst, schaffen es dennoch nicht, ihren Konsum zu reduzieren.

Dass soziale Medien auch positive Aspekte aufweisen und hierfür vor allem das individuelle Nutzungsverhalten ausschlaggebend ist, wird in einem Artikel aus The Guardian thematisiert, der die Grundlage für unsere Einheit **Studying articles on the impact of social media – Soziale Medien kritisch betrachten** bildet. Anhand des Textes setzen sich Ihre Lernenden der Klassen 9 bis 11 kritisch mit dem Thema *„social media"* auseinander, erarbeiten den relevanten Wortschatz und beziehen Stellung.

In unserer Unterrichtsreihe **Nigerian coming-of-age stories – Anhand unterschiedlicher Textsorten interkulturelle Kompetenzen entwickeln** lernen Ihre Schülerinnen und Schüler der Sekundarstufe II anhand eines Films, einer Kurzgeschichte und eines Romanauszugs die Lebenswelt Heranwachsender in Nigeria unter dem Einfluss westlicher Kultur(en) kennen. Dabei erweitern sie ihre interkulturelle Kompetenz und trainieren die Analyse unterschiedlicher Textsorten.

Nach dem Referendum über den sogenannten Brexit im Jahr 2016 und dem EU-Austritt des Vereinigten Königreichs am 31. Januar 2020 ist vieles durch das am 24. Januar 2020 unterzeichnete Austrittsabkommen geregelt. Doch schon bald nachdem MP Rees-Mogg zum Minister for Brexit Opportunities and Government Efficiency (bis Februar 2022) ernannt wurde, stellte sich die Frage nach dem Erfolg des Brexits. In unserer zweiten Reihe für die Sekundarstufe II **Brexit: success or failure? – Über den Brexit und seine Konsequenzen diskutieren** setzen sich die Lernenden mit dem Thema mithilfe von Bildern, Texten und einem Video auseinander.

In unserer Reihe **Interviewing graduates – Ein jahrgangsstufenübergreifendes Projekt** nutzen Sie die fremdsprachliche Kompetenz Ihrer Oberstufenschülerinnen und -schüler, um den Unterstufenschülerinnen und -schülern eine motivierende Kommunikationssituation zu bieten. In diesem Projekt entwickeln die Lernenden der Unterstufe Interviewfragen sowie kurze Präsentationen für die Oberstufenschülerinnen und -schüler und wiederholen dabei ausgewählte Grammatikbereiche. Auch die angehenden Abiturklassen profitieren von dem Projekt, indem sie ihre Antworten adressatengerecht formulieren und ihr Sprachbewusstsein im Umgang mit Fehlern der Jüngeren üben.

Bei inhaltlichen Anmerkungen, Wünschen und Rückfragen zum Produkt erreichen Sie uns unter J.Thon@raabe.de und 0711-62900-91.

Wir wünschen Ihnen viel Freude mit unseren Unterrichtsreihen und einen schönen Frühling.

Ihre Redaktion Englisch

Folgen Sie uns auf Instagram, Facebook und Twitter unter @RAABEVerlag

Einsortierungsanleitung

Bitte sortieren Sie die enthaltenen Einheiten wie folgt in Ihren Ordner ein:

Themenbereich Einheit	Bitte diese Seiten einfügen
I.C.5.2 Studying articles on the impact of social media – Soziale Medien kritisch betrachten (Klassen 9–11)	komplett
II.C.3.5 Nigerian coming-of-age stories – Anhand unterschiedlicher Textsorten interkulturelle Kompetenzen entwickeln (Klassen 10–13) **	komplett
III.B.13 Interviewing graduates – Ein jahrgangsstufenübergreifendes Projekt (Klassen 6 und Klassen 11–13)	komplett
V.278 Brexit: success or failure? – Über den Brexit und seine Konsequenzen diskutieren (ab Klasse 10) **	komplett

Hinweis: Alle Einheiten, Zusatzmaterialien sowie eine aktuelle Inhaltsübersicht finden Sie auch in Ihrem **Online-Archiv** im RAABE-Webshop. Loggen Sie sich unter www.raabe.de mit Ihren Kundendaten in Ihr Webshop-Konto ein. Wenn Sie noch kein Konto haben, melden Sie sich unter meinraabe@raabe.de, um Ihre Zugangsdaten zu erhalten.

Themenvorschau

In den folgenden Lieferungen erwarten Sie u. a. diese Themen:

Ghost Boys – **Auseinandersetzung mit Polizeigewalt gegen Schwarze (Kl. 8/9) (August 2023)**
Durch die Perspektive der Romanfiguren lernen die Schülerinnen und Schüler Diskriminierungs- und Rassismuserfahrungen Schwarzer Jugendlicher in den USA des 21. Jahrhunderts kennen.

Abiturrelevante Themen anhand der Netflix-Serie *„Explained"* erarbeiten (S II) (August 2023)
Die Materialien eignen sich zur Wiederholung und Vertiefung von Themen aus den Bereichen *„Science and technology"* und bieten zahlreiche Impulse zum Trainieren der Sprechfertigkeit.

The African American experience: Film in a Box (S II) (November 2023)
In der Reihe lernen die Schülerinnen und Schüler die Geschichte der *African Americans* näher kennen, indem sie eine Präsentation zu einem Film des Genres *„Black Cinema"* vorbereiten.

(Änderungen vorbehalten)

I.C.5.2

Lektüren, Lieder, Sachtexte – Non-Fictional Texts

Studying articles on the impact of social media – Soziale Medien kritisch betrachten (Klassen 9–11)

Martina Angele

Die Nutzung sozialer Medien ist ein wesentlicher Bestandteil der heutigen Lebenswelt. Daher ist das Thema „*Consequences of social media use*" ein wichtiges Element im Englischunterricht. Die Lernenden reflektieren ihr Konsumverhalten von sozialen Medien und analysieren dessen Einfluss auf sich selbst und auf die Gesellschaft. Während der inhaltlichen Erarbeitung des Themas trainieren sie ihre Lese-, Hör-Seh-Verstehens- und Sprechkompetenz sowie ihre Urteilsfähigkeit.

KOMPETENZPROFIL

LearningApps - interaktive Lernbausteine

Klassenstufe:	9–11
Dauer:	ca. 4–8 Unterrichtsstunden
Kompetenzen:	1. Sprechen: austauschen, präsentieren, argumentieren; 2. Hör-Seh-Verstehen: einem Video Informationen entnehmen; 3. Leseverstehen: Sachtexte lesen und verstehen; 4. Schreiben: einen *comment* schreiben
Medienkompetenzen:	Suchen, Verarbeiten und Aufbewahren (1); Produzieren und Präsentieren (3); Schützen und sicher agieren (4); Problemlösen und Handeln (5); Analysieren und Reflektieren (6)
Thematische Bereiche:	*social media, media awareness, informative/argumentative texts, having a voice, the individual in society*
Material:	*Mentimeter, LearningApps*, Zeitungsartikel aus The Guardian

Fachliche Hinweise

Wissenschaftliche Studien belegen, dass es **negative Korrelationen** zwischen der Nutzung von **sozialen Medien** und der **mentalen Gesundheit** gibt. Seit der Einführung von Smartphones um das Jahr 2000 hat sich vor allem die psychische Gesundheit junger Menschen stetig verschlechtert. Dennoch sind soziale Medien ein aus der Gesellschaft nicht mehr wegzudenkendes und **allgegenwärtiges Phänomen**. Viele Nutzende wissen wenig über die möglichen Auswirkungen ihres Nutzungsverhaltens, andere wiederum sind sich zwar der negativen Folgen bewusst, schaffen es dennoch nicht, den Konsum zu verringern. Dass soziale Medien auch positive Aspekte aufweisen und hierfür vor allem das konkrete individuelle **Nutzungsverhalten** ausschlaggebend ist, wird in einem Artikel aus The Guardian thematisiert, der die Grundlage für die Einheit bildet. Anhand des Textes setzen sich die Lernenden kritisch mit dem Thema *„Social media"* auseinander, erarbeiten den relevanten Wortschatz und beziehen Stellung.

Zum Thema *„Consequences of social media use"*

Die immer weiter ansteigende Nutzung sozialer Medien hat weitreichende **Folgen** für ihre Nutzer und Nutzerinnen. Die meisten Menschen verwenden soziale Medien täglich und nutzen die vielfältigen **Vorteile** für private und berufliche Zwecke. Personen von überall können miteinander kommunizieren und sich gegenseitig vernetzen und **austauschen**. Dabei können Gedanken, Bilder und Videos in Echtzeit im Netz geteilt werden und Menschen mit ähnlichen **Interessen** werden schnell und einfach zusammengebracht. Auch von Unternehmen werden die sozialen Medien genutzt – für Marketing oder Online-Handel. Dadurch wird ihr **Profit** gesteigert. Neben den vielen Vorteilen werden die **Nachteile** gerade unter Jugendlichen unterschätzt. **Cybermobbing** und **Hacking** ist in den letzten Jahren gravierend angestiegen und betrifft nicht nur Schulen, sondern auch Unternehmen und Privatpersonen. Private Daten sind im Internet nicht sicher und werden vermehrt von Hackern gestohlen und beispielsweise zu Werbezwecken eingesetzt. Darüber hinaus werden falsche Informationen und Gerüchte schneller verbreitet. Durch die ansteigende **Informationsflut** wird es immer schwieriger zwischen Fakten und sogenannten *„fake news"* zu differenzieren. Ein weiterer Nachteil liegt darin, dass sich Menschen kontinuierlich mit ihren Mitmenschen vergleichen, was zu ernsthaften gesundheitlichen Problemen und zu einer Art **Abhängigkeit** nach dem „Onlinesein" führen kann. Der Zeitungsartikel *„'Phones are like a scab we know we shouldn't pick': the truth about social media and anxiety"*, die Grundlage für diese Unterrichtseinheit, erläutert die genannten Themen und macht auf die Probleme durch soziale Medien aufmerksam.

Didaktisch-methodische Hinweise

Zur Lerngruppe und den curricularen Vorgaben

Diese Unterrichtseinheit richtet sich an die Klassen 9–11 des Gymnasiums. Entsprechend sind die Materialien auf die Niveaustufe A2/B1 gemäß dem Gemeinsamen Europäischen Referenzrahmen für Sprachen aufbereitet worden. Bereits in Klasse 9 wird kompetenzorientiert für die Kursstufenarbeit vorbereitet. Textkompetenz, Sprechkompetenz, Hörkompetenz und Schreibkompetenz werden in vereinfachter Form erworben und progressiv ausgeweitet. Die Klassen 9 und 10 konzentrieren sich dabei auf informative Texte, Bildbeschreibungen, Diskussionen und das Schreiben von argumentativen Texten. Ebenfalls wird mit *having a voice* die Meinungsbildung der Schülerinnen und Schüler gefördert. Klasse 11 vertieft die genannten Themen mit Schwerpunkten auf *The individual in society, The world of work, The media – tool, drug, manipulator, friend.*

Zum Aufbau der Unterrichtseinheit

Die Bearbeitung des Artikels „'Phones are like a scab we know we shouldn't pick': the truth about social media and anxiety" (M 3) steht im Mittelpunkt dieser Unterrichtseinheit und wird durch vorbereitende sowie weiterführende Aufgaben eingerahmt. Die Materialien M 1–M 6 bauen aufeinander auf und sollten zusammen eingesetzt werden. Eine *pre-reading activity* (M 1) führt die Lernenden zum Ausgangsartikel (M 3) hin. Mithilfe von M 5 und M 6 werden das Textverständnis und die Wortschatzkenntnis gesichert. Die Materialien M 7–M 11 beinhalten weiterführende Aufgaben. Durch die Arbeit mit dem Artikel als Textgrundlage wird die Lesekompetenz der Lernenden gefördert. Auch die Hörverstehens- sowie die Sprechkompetenz werden mittels der Arbeit mit Videos und anhand von Diskussionsaufgaben erweitert. Abgerundet wird die Unterrichtseinheit durch das Üben der Schreibkompetenz der Schülerinnen und Schüler in M 10.

Zur Differenzierung

Um eine Differenzierung zu gewährleisten, gibt es Materialien auf dem Niveau A2. Für **lernschwächere** Schülerinnen und Schüler sind unterstützende Materialien zusammengestellt. Die Lernenden erhalten **Tipps** und **Hilfestellungen** für die Bildanalyse (M 2), für die Textarbeit (M 4), für die Durchführung von Diskussionen (M 9), sowie für das Verfassen eines *comment* (M 11). Außerdem können Vokabelübungen und *useful words/phrases* zur Bewältigung der Aufgaben verwendet werden. Die Differenzierung wurde auch für **stärkere** Schüler und Schülerinnen umgesetzt. Die zusätzlichen spielerischen Übungen in *LearningApps* (M 6) werden von den Lernenden bearbeitet, die zeitlich vor ihren Mitschülern und Mitschülerinnen die vorherigen Aufgaben bewältigt haben.

Zur Erweiterungsmöglichkeit

Da die Schülerinnen und Schüler vielfältige Arbeitsmöglichkeiten haben und Dank der unzähligen Berührungspunkten zwischen sozialen Medien und den Lernenden, kann diese Unterrichtsreihe für verschiedene Klassen und Niveaustufen eingesetzt und dementsprechend angepasst werden.

Zum Einsatz der Materialien im digitalen Unterricht

Auch digital lässt sich diese Unterrichtseinheit problemlos durchführen. Neben **Mentimeter** stehen den Lernenden Aufgaben in digitaler Version mit **LearningApps** zur Verfügung. Unter folgendem Link sind sie zu einer Kollektion zusammengefasst, abrufbar und stehen Ihnen kostenlos zur Verfügung: https://learningapps.org/watch?v=p5h8tespn23. Wenn Sie die Kollektion oder einzelne Apps ansehen und bearbeiten wollen, verwenden Sie folgenden Link: https://learningapps.org/display?v=p5h8tespn23. Unter „ähnliche Kollektion erstellen" gelangen Sie zur Bearbeitung der Kollektion – mit einem weiteren Klick auf die Einzelapp können Sie auch diese bearbeiten. Nutzen Sie zum Teilen der Einzellinks mit den Lernenden den Link unter „Teilen" und den automatisch generierten QR-Code.

Medienkompetenzen (KMK)

(1) Suchen, Verarbeiten und Aufbewahren: zielgerichtete Internetrecherche durchführen (**M 8**)
(3) Produzieren und Präsentieren: Erstellung einer PowerPoint (**M 10**)
(4) Schützen und sicher agieren: Risiken und Gefahren der digitalen Umgebung erarbeiten (**M 1**, **M 3**, **M 5**, **M6**, **M 7**, **M 8**, **M 10**)
(5) Problemlösen und Handeln: *LearningApps* als digitales Werkzeug nutzen (**M 5–M 7**)
(6) Analysieren und Reflektieren: Kritische Bewertung von Posts aus sozialen Netzwerken/Fake News (**M 1**)

Mediathek

Lehrwerksbezug

Eine Anknüpfung der Einheit ist an folgende Lehrwerke/*Units* möglich:

- Access Band 5, Unit 4, „Connecting in Englisch", Cornelsen.
- Green Line 5, Unit 1–3 (*informative texts*, Bildbeschreibung, sich austauschen, *argumentative texts*, *having a voice*), Klett.
- Context, „Finding One's Place – the Individual in Society", „The World of Work", „The Media – Tool, Drug, Manipulator, Friend?", Cornelsen.
- Green Line Oberstufe, Unit 3, „The Media", Klett.
- Pathway Advanced, „Modern Media – Social, Smart and Spying?", Westermann.
- Camden Town Oberstufe, Theme 1 „A society of screens", Theme 3 „Global challenges", Westermann.

Weiterführende Internetseiten

- https://www.theguardian.com/commentisfree/2021/dec/27/2021-reporting-harm-social-media-online
  In diesem Text geht es um Gefühle, die durch *social media* erzeugt werden. Der Vergleich mit anderen und das eigene Selbstbewusstsein stehen im Fokus des Artikels.
- https://www.theguardian.com/society/2020/nov/16/one-in-five-children-in-england-and-wales-experienced-online-bullying-in-2019
  Das Thema des Artikels ist das Mobbing im Internet und die daraus resultierenden Konsequenzen für Jugendliche.
- https://www.bbc.com/future/article/20180104-is-social-media-bad-for-you-the-evidence-and-the-unknowns
  In diesem Artikel werden das Pro und Contra von *social media* diskutiert.
- https://www.webroot.com/us/en/resources/tips-articles/computer-security-threats-hackers
  Wie Hacker vorgehen und wie man sich davor schützen kann, ist das Thema dieses Artikels.
- https://cybersecurityventures.com/hackerpocalypse-cybercrime-report-2016/
  In diesem Zeitungsartikel wird diskutiert, wieviel die Cyberkriminalität jährlich kostet.

[letzte Abrufe: 31.03.2023]

Auf einen Blick

1. Stunde

Thema: Talking about your social media use

M 1 **Pre-reading activity – Describe and discuss /** sich über die eigene Handynutzung und einen Videoclip austauschen (EA, PA, UG)

M 2 **The striking features … – The four-step analysis /** wichtige Aspekte der Bildbeschreibung wiederholen (EA/PL/UG)

Benötigt: ☐ Beamer/Whiteboard/Tablets oder Smartphones für das Öffnen der Links

2./3. Stunde

Thema: Working out the consequences of social media from a newspaper article

M 3 **Social media and anxiety – Reading a newspaper article /** einen Zeitungsartikel lesen (EA/UG)

M 4 **Skimming, scanning, taking notes – How to work with texts /** Aspekte der Arbeit mit informativen Texten wiederholen (EA/PL/UG)

M 5 **What did you understand? – Reading comprehension /** das Leseverstehen überprüfen (EA, GA/UG)

M 6 **Let's practise! – Focus on words /** den Wortschatz zum Text erarbeiten (EA, PA/UG)

Benötigt: ☐ Textmarker zur Bearbeitung von M 3
☐ Tablets oder Smartphones zur Bearbeitung der *LearningApps*

4. Stunde

Thema: Viewing the downsides of social media

M 7 *The Social Dilemma* **– Watching and understanding a video /** einem Video wichtige Informationen zu den Schattenseiten der sozialen Medien entnehmen (EA, UG)

Benötigt: ☐ Beamer/Whiteboard bzw. Tablets/Smartphones für die Präsentation des Videos und die Bearbeitung der *LearningApps*

5./6. Stunde

Thema: Different perspectives on social media

M 8 **Is social media a blessing or a curse? – Table talk /** die positiven und negativen Seiten der sozialen Medien aus verschiedenen Perspektiven diskutieren (GA)

M 9	**Let's review – How to discuss /** wichtige Aspekte zur Teilnahme an einer Diskussion wiederholen (EA/PL/UG)
Benötigt:	☐ Flexibel bewegbare Tische und Stühle für die Gruppenarbeiten und den *table talk*

7./8. Stunde

Thema:	Writing about the consequences of social media
M 10	**Pros and cons – Writing about social media /** mithilfe eines Zeitungsartikels einen *comment* verfassen (EA); eine Präsentation vorbereiten und vorstellen (GA)
M 11	**How to write a comment – Tips and useful words/phrases /** Aspekte zum Schreiben eines *comment* wiederholen (EA/PL/UG)
Benötigt:	☐ Tablet oder Computer für die Erstellung und Vorstellung der Präsentationen ☐ ggf. ZM PowerPoint Presentation für M 10

Minimalplan

Bei Zeitmangel können die wichtigsten Inhalte innerhalb der folgenden vier Stunden erarbeitet werden:

2./3. Stunde	Working out the consequences of social media from a newspaper article	M 3–M 6
5./6. Stunde	Different perspectives on social media	M 8–M 9

Zusatzmaterial im Online-Archiv bzw. in der ZIP-Datei

ZM PowerPoint Presentation   Eine PowerPoint-Präsentation als Musterlösung (M 10)

Erklärung zu den Symbolen

 Dieses Symbol markiert differenziertes Material. Wenn nicht anders ausgewiesen, befinden sich die Materialien auf mittlerem Niveau.

 einfaches Niveau   mittleres Niveau   schwieriges Niveau

 Zusatzaufgaben    digitales Endgerät    *LearningApps*

Pre-reading activities – Describe and discuss

M 1

Practise and improve your speaking skills by talking about your phone and social media use.

Tasks

1. Guess how much time you spend on your phone. Check your phone for the actual time you spend on it and share your total screen time.
2. Get together in pairs. Describe and analyse the picture.

© Mauritius Images/Alamy

3. Talk about your use of your smartphone and social media and answer the following questions.
   a) Did your screen time show that you spend more time on social media than you had guessed?
   b) On which app do you spend the most time and for what purpose?
   c) Do you compare yourself or your life with what you see from other people's lives on their social media accounts?
   d) Do you feel uncomfortable or odd when your battery dies or when you forget your phone?
4. When spending time on social media, you cannot avoid being influenced. Look at the list of some of the most successful influencers in Germany: https://raabe.click/TopInfluencers [last access: 31/03/2023]. Discuss the following questions with your partner.
   a) Which accounts do you follow?
   b) What is the main content they share? What is positive/negative about their content?
   c) Would you like to be them? Why (not)?
5. Watch the video *Are you living an Insta lie? Social media vs. reality.*
   https://raabe.click/InstaLie [last access: 31/03/2023]
   Which issue does the clip address? Can you relate?
   Reflect your own social media behaviour critically. With reference to the issue shown in the clip, are you sometimes living an Insta lie? Complete the following sentences beginnings:
   a) The clip addresses the issue that …
   b) Regarding my own social media behaviour …

M 2 The striking features … – The four-step analysis

When describing what people are doing in a picture, always use the **Present Progressive**. Remember the **four-step analysis**:

1. **Introduction**

   Your introduction should answer the following questions:
   - What type of image is it? – Why was it drawn/taken?
   - Where is the picture/photo from? – Who made it and when?
   - What does the image/photo show?

drawing	© Liliane Oser	pencil charcoal ink drawing	portrait caricature cartoon
painting	© Ulrike Bahl	watercolour oil	portrait landscape still-life
photograph	© Thinkstock/iStockphoto	black and white colour photograph	portrait landscape

2. **Description**

   Look at the picture carefully, then describe it systematically:
   - from the centre to the corners – from the foreground to the background – from left to right – from top to bottom

   Remember to look at details:
   - the setting (place and time) and/or the situation – the quality of the picture (clear or blurred, realistic or abstract …) – the striking features of the objects – the characters, e.g. their appearance and body language (facial expressions, gestures, postures)

   > **Useful phrases**
   > This is a picture/drawing/photo/an image of …; on the right/left …; at the top/bottom …; in the middle … in the foreground/background …; … you can see … ; … the people are …; the date of the picture seems to be … because …; the most important thing for the artist is …

3. **Analysis**

   Your analysis should answer the following questions:
   - Does the image transport a message/have an intended effect?
   - Which pictorial elements are used to get the message across/to produce the effect?
   - How do the different elements interact?

4. **Evaluation**

   Your evaluation should answer the following questions:
   - Do you think that the image is effective in getting the message to the target group?
   - Does it use suitable means for doing so?
   - What effect does the image have on you?

Social media and anxiety – Reading a newspaper article   M 3

Find out more about the impacts of social media and phone use.

Tasks

1. Skim the newspaper article for an overview. Highlight the main ideas.
2. Read the article carefully. Look up words you do not understand in a dictionary. Write the words and their explanations down.
3. Underline keywords.
4. Take notes to help you understand and remember the content.

"Phones are like a scab[1] we know we shouldn't pick[2]": the truth about social media and anxiety

[…] Most people think that phones are a bad thing for anxiety[3]. Parents, in particular, believe phones are terrible for the mental health of children, teenagers and young adults.

5 So, what is the truth? […] I felt I had to get to the bottom of the relationship between phones and anxiety. And to be honest, it doesn't look great. Since smartphones came out in around 2000, there has been a steady decline in the mental health of young people. […] What I have observed clinically is that rather than being the cause of the problem per se[5], phones seem to act as a catalyst[6] to our emotions. This can be a positive thing, when it

10 allows us to connect with friends and family; share happy news; photos or jokes. It also allows marginalised[7] communities to find each other.

However, humans are wired[8] to foresee danger and our minds can quickly spiral from an initial trigger to create catastrophic, wholly imaginary circumstances, which our bodies respond to as though they are true. In your head this goes something like: "Some of my

15 friends are meeting without me > they don't want me there > they don't really like me > nobody really likes me > I am fundamentally unlovable and will die alone."

The phone contributes[9] to this in a number of different ways. First it allows us to know our friends are meeting without us. There was something in "ignorance is bliss[10]" and now there is no ignorance. We know, and we get to sit on our sofa […] and compare our inside

20 worries, our worst sides, our ugliest self, with endless, perfectly curated[11] versions of other people's lives. And guess what? That makes us anxious[12] and unhappy.

Our phone is like a scab we know we shouldn't pick. We know it is making us feel bad seeing our rich friend on a weekend trip away with her gorgeous partner; we know we should put our phone down and go and do something constructive and positive […]. Look,

25 there is someone on Instagram with a perfect bathroom and a beautiful body showing us what we should be doing, and we are just sitting around scrolling – no wonder no one wants to hang out with you. In this way, your phone can trigger a second round of self-judgment[13] about how lazy or worthless you are.

The phone intensifies a comparison culture that can leave you feeling not good enough in

30 every single aspect of life: not thin enough; not successful enough; not tidy or organised enough; not living in a nice enough home; not well-read[14] or smart enough.

And while research into the effects of this on mental health is in its infancy[15], there is particularly damning[16] research in relation to viewing photos of perfect bodies, which is shown to increase body dissatisfaction, with a link to eating disorders. Even when we

35 know the images are doctored[17], and even when they are shown in relation to fitness, they still impact[18] on body dissatisfaction.

So some of the questions I ask my patients about their phone use are:

Are you using your phone to connect to people or to compare to people? The former is positive for mental health but the latter will likely increase anxiety.

Is there a tipping point[19] where phone use changes from positive to negative? Do you notice this tipping point? And can you put your phone away then? My experience suggests[20] it is just at this point that the phone is at its most magnetic.

Is your phone getting in the way of you doing things which are positive for mental health? Phone use is perhaps at its most damaging when it gets in the way of sleeping, eating regularly, being outside and moving your body, all of which are important for wellbeing. Research suggests that there may be a sweet spot[21] with mobile phone use, after which the screen stops being helpful or fun and starts having a negative impact on wellbeing. An analogy[22] to drinking is helpful: a couple of glasses of red wine can be relaxing; a bottle a night is not so helpful. And like with drinking, some people find it difficult to stop just at the point when they should.

So if you are experiencing anxiety, think about your phone use – think about how much time you spend on it and on what kind of content. Readdressing this might be one important key in unlocking a less anxious life.

Phone and internet use is best when it is in line with our other values rather than taking us away from them. [...]

© by Tara Porter found at The Guardian: https://www.theguardian.com/lifeandstyle/2022/may/22/phones-are-like-a-scab-we-know-we-shouldnt-pick-the-truth-about-social-media-and-anxiety [last access: 31/03/2023]

---

1 **scab:** a dry, rough protective crust that forms over a cut or wound during healing – 2 **(to) pick:** (to) detach and remove sth. from where it is growing – 3 **anxiety (about/over sth.):** the state of feeling nervous or worried that sth. bad is going to happen – 4 **(to) get to the bottom of sth.:** (to) find out the real cause of sth., especially sth. unpleasant – 5 **per se:** meaning "by itself", used to show that you are referring to sth. on its own – 6 **a catalyst for sth.:** a person or thing that causes a change – 7 **(to) marginalize (AE):** (to) prevent from participating fully in social, economic and political life because of a lack of access to rights, resources and opportunities – 8 **(to) be wired to do sth.:** metaphorical meaning (to) be programmed to do sth. because of the way the human brain works – 9 **(to) contribute to sth.:** (to) be one of the causes of sth. – 10 **bliss:** extreme happiness – 11 **curated:** selected, organised, and presented – 12 **anxious:** feeling worried or nervous – 13 **self-judgment:** the act of judging oneself, e.g. one's character, looks, qualities, actions – 14 **well-read:** having a lot of knowledge from reading widely/ knowledgeable – 15 **infancy:** the early stage in the development/the state or period of babyhood or early childhood – 16 **damning:** very critical, showing that so. is wrong or guilty – 17 **(to) doctor:** (to) change the content or appearance of (a document or picture) in order to trick so.; (to) falsify – 18 **(to) impact on:** (to) have influence on so./sth – 19 **tipping point:** the time/point at which a change or an effect cannot be stopped – 20 **(to) suggest:** (to) produce an idea in the mind; (to) mention an idea for other people to consider – 21 **sweet spot:** optimum point – 22 **analogy:** a comparison between one thing and another

Skimming, scanning, taking notes – How to work with texts

Here are relevant tips on how to work with texts.

Task
Have a look at the strategies and explanations. Make sure you understand everything.

Reading strategies
Comprehension is an important aspect of reading and an active part to understand and extract meaning for better overall awareness. By learning reading strategies, you can improve your reading comprehension abilities and make reading easier and more enjoyable.
There are two components of reading comprehension:
- text comprehension (using the language to develop an awareness of what the meaning is behind the text) and
- vocabulary knowledge (to understand the language being used).

Please observe the following reading comprehension strategies:
1. Improve your vocabulary.
   Read as much as possible to improve your ability to guess what a word means in a certain context. Make a list of unfamiliar words as you read and look them up in the dictionary.
2. Come up with questions about the text you are reading.
   Ask questions about the text while you are reading to get a further insight into the text and its meaning. You can also make notes.
3. Look for the main idea.
   Find out the main idea of each paragraph. If a paragraph is very short, you can also summarise two paragraphs. Ask yourself: What is the author's main point in this paragraph?
4. Re-read the text to ensure understanding.
   If you finish a sentence or paragraph and you do not understand what it was trying to convey, take the time to re-read it until you do. Read more slowly the second time and look up definitions for any words you don't know the meaning of.
5. Read aloud.
   Reading aloud forces you to slow down and gives you more time to process what you are reading.
6. Do not memorise.
   You do not need to memorise every word present in the passage or every specific point. Understanding the flow, structure and the main points in the passage should be your priority.
7. If you have to answer questions about a passage (or the text in general), do not read the passage first.
   Always go through the questions first and then the passage. This will prepare you to focus on the things you need to look for in the passage.
8. Do not spend time on words or text passages that you cannot comprehend at first.
   If you are struggling with passages, for example, in an exam, make sure you have the patience to skip such a passage. Focus on the ones that you can manage. Go back to the tricky passages later.

Skimming = going through a text quickly and getting the gist (identifying its main ideas)

First, look at a text before you analyse it in detail or when there is no chance to look at the text in detail.

1. Look at illustrations, pictures, keywords, headings etc. to get an idea of the content of the text.
2. Read the first and the last sentence of each paragraph – one of them usually states the main idea. The very last sentence of the text often contains a summary.
3. Summarise the text in your own words. If you are able to do this without a problem, your skimming was probably successful.

> **Look out for headings, pictures and keywords and do not read every word, concentrate on beginnings and ends of paragraphs as well as keywords.**

Scanning = going through a text quickly and finding particular details

Only one part of the text is interesting because you have to answer particular questions on it. Also, you have to compare only particular aspects in selected texts.

1. Think of keywords or phrases that might be useful to search for when looking for the information you need.
2. Move quickly down the page and stop when you find a keyword or phrase. Read the part where you found it. Then continue scanning the text.

> **Headings and pictures give you an idea of what to expect from a text. What questions would you want the text to answer? Look out for relevant keywords. Read that part of the text carefully and underline or mark the text if possible. Take notes if necessary.**

Marking up a text

1. As you read the text, bear in mind what information you are looking for. You may want to read the task/question again.
2. When you find the relevant information in your text, mark it by underlining, highlighting or circling the relevant words or passages. Mark only keywords.
3. Finally, add headings or keywords in the margin or summarise passages with short phrases or sentences.

Taking notes

1. Decide what you want to note down, e.g. for a summary or for a comparison.
2. Read the text and underline or mark it, if possible. Use systematic markings, symbols and abbreviations that you recognise when you look at them later on.
3. Skim the text to extract the most important headings (or questions) and keywords from the text for the gist. Write them down and add your own comments.
4. If you need more detailed information for some aspects, add comments.

> **Use simple language for your notes and avoid copying words without understanding them properly. Structure your notes.**

What did you understand? – Reading comprehension

M 5

Check your understanding of the text.

Tasks

1. Tick the correct completions. Give evidence from the text by providing the line(s) and the first and last words of the quotation. You can also complete this task online as a *LearningApp*: https://learningapps.org/watch?v=pf0m7o3pk23

    a) Since smartphones came out …
       - ☐ 1) young people increasingly struggle with mental health issues.
       - ☐ 2) young people are happier than before.
       - ☐ 3) nothing really changed regarding youngster's mental health.

       Quotation: _____
       _____
       line(s): _____

    b) Using smartphones …
       - ☐ 1) definitely causes mental health issues.
       - ☐ 2) per se is not the problem, but the way we use it can be one.
       - ☐ 3) is falsely accused to have the potential to be bad for our mental health.

       Quotation: _____
       _____
       line(s): _____

    c) Phone use …
       - ☐ 1) can be positive up to a certain point but beyond it can be damaging.
       - ☐ 2) creates a positive body image.
       - ☐ 3) is in no connection to eating disorders.

       Quotation: _____
       _____
       line(s): _____

2. Are these statements true or false? Tick the correct box and correct the wrong statement(s) in your exercise books. Write down the lines from the text. You can also complete this task online as a *LearningApp*: https://learningapps.org/watch?v=pf7i0ff7c23

Statement	True	False
a) When used for socialising and making friends, for example, smartphones can be good for one's mental health.		
b) Smartphones encourage a culture of comparison which can lead to the feeling that we are never good enough and, thus, negatively affect our mental health.		

Statement	True	False
c) Comparing yourself to others on social media does not affect your body image if you are aware that the images are posed and edited.		
d) The underlying problem with smartphones is that they tend to magnetise us the most when we pass the point where it is still good for us to use them.		

3. Complete the sentences in your own words. Give evidence from the text by providing the line(s)
   a) Using smartphones per se is not the problem, but as they act like a catalyst to our emotions …

   _____

   b) Smartphones are like a scab we know we shouldn't pick because …

   _____

   c) Phone use can be compared to drinking alcohol because …

   _____

4. Match the terms in the box with the graph which is putting phone use in relation to its benefits for our mental health. You can also complete this task online as a *LearningApp*: https://learning apps.org/watch?v=p3zz2vn2n23

   > using it to compare oneself with others – using it to connect with other people – sweet spot – particularly hard to stop using

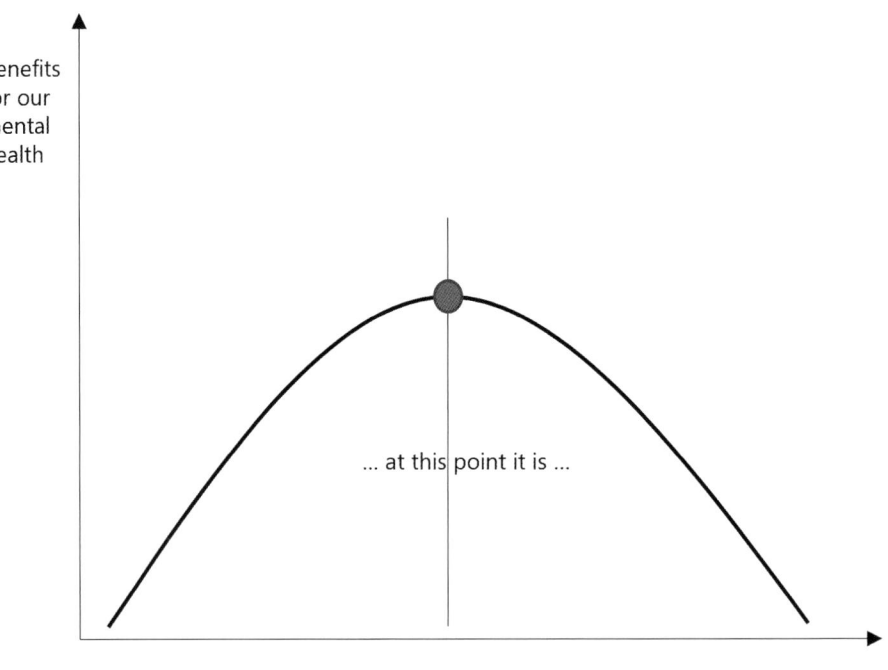

Let's practise! – Focus on words

M 6

Increase your word power.

Tasks

1. Solve the crossword puzzle by filling in the boxes with the English translation of the German words below. You can also complete this task online as a *LearningApp*: https://learningapps.org/watch?v=pfbywiszn23

> a) Angst/Unruhe – b) geistige Gesundheit (*two words*) – c) gepolt (sein, etwas zu tun) –
> d) vergleichen – e) Unzufriedenheit – f) manipuliert/bearbeitet – g) Kipppunkt (*two words*) –
> h) Einfluss

Solution: ▢ ▢ ▢ ▢ ▢ ▢ ▢ ▢ ▢
         1 2 3 4 5 6 7 8 9

> The solution word is a very important keyword regarding the use of phones and social media: we need to use our phones and social media with … not only of its benefits but especially of its potential dangers.

2. Complete the following sentences with words in the box. Use the right form. You can also complete this task online as a *LearningApp:* https://learningapps.org/watch?v=pj8fyfmza23

   marginalise – intensify – sweet spot – eating disorders – curate – anxiety – tipping

   a) Generally speaking, using our phones is neither only beneficial nor totally harmful for our mental health. There is a certain point up to which using our phones can be beneficial but beyond it, phone use can lead to severe mental health issues like _____ .

   b) A negative aspect about social media and phone use is that it _____ the phenomena called "comparison culture", as we constantly compare ourselves and our lives to _____ content we see online.

   c) Being confronted with perfect bodies all the time when scrolling through social media content can lead to dissatisfaction with our own bodies, which is in connection to _____ .

   d) A positive influence on our mental health can be achieved through the use of social media and mobile phones if the main purpose of its use is to connect with other people, which is for example particularly important for members of _____ groups.

   e) A particularly challenging problem of phone use is putting it down at the point where use turns from benefiting to harming our wellbeing. This point is called the _____ or _____ point.

3. Write well-formed sentences using the following words.
   a) we – scab – much – phone – overlong – know – them – we – spend – time – pick – be – not – like – should – because – on – too – hurt – our – use – phone – compare – with – pick – it – just
   b) wellbeing – they – from – use – sleep – keep – eat – if – phones – our – us – move – harm – our – and
   c) of – never – cause – other – picture – with – compare – good – lives – constant – ourselves – doctored – of – people's – can – a – feeling – be – enough

Extra: When you have finished early, work with two more *LearningApps* to practise your vocabulary skills and knowledge about phone use and social media:
Find the words: https://learningapps.org/watch?v=pjsy5x6p323
Quiz: https://learningapps.org/watch?v=p3bkgr34323

The Social Dilemma – Watching and understanding a video

Improve your listening and viewing comprehension skills.

Tasks

Watch the trailer of the Netflix documentary-drama *The Social Dilemma*:
https://raabe.click/TheSocialDilemma [last access: 31/03/2023]
Then complete the tasks.

1. What is the trailer about? Write down the topic.

   _____

2. Watch the beginning again (0:00–1:10 min.) and tick the correct box. Are the statements true or false?
   You can also complete the task as a *LearningApp*: https://learningapps.org/watch?v=p9vzkofhk23

Statement	True	False
a) The location of users is crucial for search results on Google.		
b) Only a few actions on the Internet are recorded.		
c) Psychology is employed to influence user behaviour.		
d) Many people interpret admiration on social media as real.		
e) Social media has no psychological impact on the current generation.		

3. Watch the rest of the trailer again (1:10–2:18 min.) and tick the correct completion(s).
   You can also complete the task as a *LearningApp*: https://learningapps.org/watch?v=p5ka6otdj23
   a) Facebook affects …
      ☐ 1) user behaviour with their permission.
      ☐ 2) nobody.
      ☐ 3) user behaviour subconsciously.
   b) Fake news spread …
      ☐ 1) faster than true news.
      ☐ 2) four times faster than true news.
      ☐ 3) six times faster than true news.
   c) Technology creates …
      ☐ 1) a sense for real world issues.
      ☐ 2) a lack of face-to-face interaction.
      ☐ 3) a feeling of loneliness.

> **You don't know the words?**
> Practise your vocabulary with *LearningApps*:
> https://learningapps.org/watch?v=pf25pkaot23

M 8

Is social media a blessing or a curse? – Table talk

Improve your speaking skills.

Tasks

1. Form four groups of 3 or 4 people. Each group will work with a specific profile that they will represent later in the table talk.

Group 1: Influencer Lisa	Group 2: Gamer Nick
– 22 years old – Influencer – Earns a lot of money on social media and loves her followers – Prefers self-presentation on the Internet	– 20 years old – Student – Enjoys playing computer games – Cannot relate to the hype surrounding social media
Group 3: Dad Daniel	**Group 4: Teenager Trixie**
– 50 years old – Salesman – Father of 14-year-old teenager – Does not want his son to have a mobile phone and to participate in a "fake" digital world – Perceives the Internet as a threat	– 16 years old – Student – Uses social media in her free time to communicate with friends, play games and for following celebrities and posting

2. In your group:
   - Collect information and construct arguments you will use in the table talk.
   - Write down your key statement and arguments to support it.
   - Prepare to represent your profile in the discussion.
3. The table talk:
   - Perform the table talk. Discuss the issue through the perspective of your role.
   - Let the teacher (or a classmate) moderate the discussion.

> **Remember the following rules of social interaction:**
> Do not interrupt each other. Stay friendly and calm. Each argument is equal and important. Listen carefully to each other and write down the arguments given by the other side.

4. Copy the grid. Write down arguments for the corresponding parties, using notes from the table talk.

Social media can be a blessing because …	Social media can be a curse because …

Let's review – How to discuss

M 9

Use this page to help you remember how to take part in a discussion.

Tasks

Read the phrases and make sure you understand them. You may use this page as a cheat sheet.

Giving your opinion	Asking for somebody´s opinion	Holding the floor
− In my view/opinion … − I think/believe … − If you ask me … − I´d say (that) … − Personally speaking, … − The way I see it …	− What is your opinion? − What do you have to say about that? − How about you? − What do you think about …? − What would you say if we …?	− Just let me finish. − Do you mind? You'll get your turn in a moment. − Can I just finish this point?
Agreeing with somebody	**Disagreeing with somebody**	**Being certain … or not so certain**
− That's right/correct. − That's a good/great idea. − That is definitely true. − I am of the same opinion. − That's exactly what I think. − That's my opinion, too. − It makes sense to me.	− I partly agree, but … − I'm afraid I have to disagree. − I disagree with what you are saying. − No, that's not right/true.	− I'm quite certain about this. − Absolutely./Definitely. − I know for sure that … − I may be wrong, but I think … − That's a weak/strong argument.
Taking the floor	**Asking for clarification**	**Making suggestions**
− Excuse me, can I just say something about that? − Excuse me, can/may I come in here, please?	− What exactly do you mean by …? − Could you explain that point? − Tell us a bit more about … − Can you give us an example of …?	− Let's … − What about …? − Why don't we …? − I think we should … − We could … − How about …? − I suggest …

Rules for your discussion

1. Respect the others.
2. Ask to clarify information instead of criticising immediately.
3. Be actively involved in the discussion.
4. Listen to the others and let them finish speaking.
5. Avoid derogatory comments.
6. Talk in the first person and not in general terms.
7. Take problems and occurring troubles seriously.
8. Look at your discussion partner.
9. Stick to facts and keep it factual.
10. Remember to have fun!

M 10

Pros and cons – Writing about social media

Prepare to write a comment. Then state your opinion on social media in a comment.

Tasks

1. Read the article and highlight important aspects.
2. Copy the grid below. Identify and collect the main arguments for and against social media in the text. Remember to write down the lines where you found the argument.

cons	pros

3. Write a comment on an aspect of social media, for example on the question *Is social media bad?* – use arguments from task 2.
4. Create a PowerPoint presentation on the topic *Social media use*. Include general information, what you have learnt so far and also your personal experiences. Focus on the effects of social media use and find solutions to reduce the negative impact on people's mental health. Present it in class.

Soziale Medien: Fluch und Segen zugleich

[…] Soziale Medien spielen heute eine wesentliche Rolle für die psychische Gesundheit. Speziell unter Jungen sind sie allgegenwärtig, ein wesentlicher Teil von Beziehungsarbeit findet mittlerweile digital statt – von der Anbahnung von Kontakten über deren Festigung
5 bis zu Abbrüchen. Wer mit anderen Personen in Verbindung stehen will, muss neben dem persönlichen Kontakt zunehmend auch digital greifbar sein.

Welche Vorteile und Möglichkeiten in digitaler Kommunikation stecken, erlebten während der Pandemie auch zahlreiche Menschen, denen die Nutzung sozialer Netzwerke aus eigener Erfahrung noch fremd war. Durch Lockdowns, Isolation, Quarantäne und die Reduzierung physischer Kontakte wurden sie von einem Tag auf den anderen zum größten Fenster nach außen – auch für zahlreiche ältere Menschen.

Ausgegrenzte Personen oft nur online erreichbar

Mit Interesse beobachtete das auch Johanna Grüblbauer, die Studiengangsleiterin für Medienmanagement an der Fachhochschule St. Pölten. Dort hatte man bereits vor der Pandemie Pilotprojekte und Versuche gestartet, um Ältere in den digitalen Raum zu locken. Dort würden zahlreiche Vorteile warten, etwa um neue Kontakte zu knüpfen oder Einsamkeit zu lindern, beispielsweise mit Online-Kartenspielrunden.

Grüblbauer zufolge seien digitale Kommunikationsmittel speziell während der Lockdowns „ein absoluter Vorteil" gewesen, ebenso wie „das generationenübergreifende Denken, dass man diese Technologien von Jung bis Alt verwendet, um auch Anschluss für diejenigen herzustellen, die diese Technologie zuvor noch nicht genutzt haben".

Sobald der Zugang zu sozialen Medien hergestellt ist, liegt ein weiterer enormer Vorteil in deren einfacheren Verfügbarkeit. Am Smartphone ist es jederzeit und von jedem Ort aus möglich, mit anderen in Verbindung zu treten und Fotos oder Videos zu teilen. Zudem fällt es digital auch deutlich leichter, Hilfe anzunehmen. Diese Erfahrung machte man auch in zahlreichen sozialen Einrichtungen, unter anderem in der Suchtberatung. Kurt Fellöcker, der Studiengangsleiter für Suchtberatung an der Fachhochschule St. Pölten: „Über die digitalen Medien ist es möglich, zu Menschen zu gelangen, die sonst kaum von sich aus in Kontakt treten würden. Das haben wir zum Beispiel in der Jugendintensivbetreuung gesehen."

Digitale Welt schuf neue Ängste

Digitale Medien – ob Online-Computerspiele, soziale Medien oder Streamingplattformen – sind vor allem wegen ihrer problemlosen Verfügbarkeit auch geeignet, um psychische Abhängigkeiten zu erzeugen. Davon betroffen können alle Altersgruppen von Kindern bis Älteren sein.

Mittlerweile stark verbreitet sind jedenfalls Ängste, die im Zusammenhang mit der ständigen Verfügbarkeit von neuen Inhalten und Interaktion sind. Ein Beispiel dafür ist die in medienpädagogischen und psychologischen Kreisen bekannte Angst „FOMO" („Fear of missing out", übersetzt also „Sorge, etwas zu verpassen"; Anm.). Das Phänomen beschreibt eine zwanghafte Angst, entweder eine soziale Interaktion, eine besondere Erfahrung oder ein anderes befriedigendes Ereignis zu versäumen und nicht mehr auf dem Laufenden zu sein.

Integrierte psychologische Tricks erzeugen Abhängigkeit

Von Phänomenen wie diesen und hochaktiven Nutzerinnen und Nutzern, die von frühmorgens nach dem Aufstehen bis spätabends vor dem Schlafengehen online möglichst aktiv sind, profitieren die dahinterstehenden Unternehmen. Die Anbieter sozialer Medien verfolgen das Ziel, ihre Mitglieder zu möglichst viel Online-Interaktion zu motivieren. Die Währung dabei sind Klicks.

Dazu arbeiten die Firmen mit psychologischen Tricks „und haben verschiedene Möglichkeiten eingebaut, wie man dort positive Bestätigung bekommt, die ähnlich auf Menschen wirkt wie manche Drogen oder andere Substanzen. Das löst in den Betroffenen dann natürlich ein Befriedigungsgefühl bzw. ein Belohnungsgefühl aus, nach dem man infolge immer wieder sucht", so der Sucht- und Präventionsexperte Fellöcker.

Johanna Grüblbauer zufolge machen Belohnungsmechanismen jedoch nur einen Teil des psychischen Drucks aus, den soziale Medien aufzubauen fähig sind. Kein Medium war je schneller und unmittelbarer als das Internet, insofern wird auch die zeitliche Unmittelbarkeit ausgenützt, um Nutzerinnen und Nutzer aktiv online zu halten. „Ein Beispiel, das jeder kennt, ist WhatsApp. Die Häkchen, die uns anzeigen, ob unsere Nachrichten schon angekommen sind und bereits gelesen wurden, bauen einen gewissen Druck auf, dass wir innerhalb einer gewissen Zeitspanne antworten."

Onlinesucht: Wenn Vorteile zum Nachteil werden

Soziale Medien können also beides: Einerseits erwarten Nutzerinnen und Nutzer in den digitalen Räumen Erlebnisse und Eindrücke, die positive Gefühle vermitteln und Kontakt zu anderen ermöglichen, andererseits können sie auch psychischen Leidensdruck aufbauen bzw. verstärken.

Nach Ansicht des Suchtexperten Fellöcker können soziale Medien in seltenen Fällen sogar suchtähnliches Verhalten provozieren. „Es besteht die Gefahr, dass man in die Nutzung ‚hineinkippt' und dabei vergisst, andere realere, analoge Formen der Kommunikation zu verwenden, weil es zum Teil leichter ist, die digitale Bindung zu halten als persönliche Kontakte." In besonders schweren Fällen könne die Abhängigkeit so zwanghaft werden, dass Entwicklungsverzögerungen auftreten, „was sich daran zeigt, dass die Persönlichkeitsentwicklung ab einem gewissen Punkt stoppt."

Forderung nach mehr Medienkompetenz

Vorbeugen kann man dem laut Experten mit ausreichend persönlichen Kontakten. Bei guter sozialer Einbettung überwiegen in der digitalen Kommunikation die positiven Effekte gegenüber den Schattenseiten. Allerdings gilt es speziell im Umgang mit Kindern und Jugendlichen, die Schattenseiten nicht zu negieren und genau hinzusehen. Fellöcker zufolge sollten dann die Alarmglocken schrillen, wenn man sich realer sozialer Interaktion immer mehr entzieht und sie durch digitale Kommunikation ersetzt. „Wenn man ein Treffen mit Freunden absagt, weil einen die Vorstellung stresst, ein paar Stunden nicht online zu sein und die realen Freundschaften darunter leiden, gilt es auf jeden Fall genauer hinzusehen." Soziale Medien an sich seien aber weder gut noch böse. Ob ihre positiven oder negativen Eigenschaften überwiegen, entscheidet das Nutzungsverhalten und damit jeder Mensch für sich. Aus diesem Grund pochen sowohl die Medienfachfrau als auch der Suchtexperte auf Prävention und Aufklärung – beginnend bereits bei den Jüngsten. Johanna Grüblbauer hält einen gesunden Zugang zum digitalen Raum samt digitaler Medienkompetenz heute mittlerweile „zu den wesentlichsten Anforderung", die Kinder und Jugendliche für ihre Zukunft erwerben müssen. „Daher gehören die wesentliche Themen aus dem Bereich digitaler Technologien in meinen Augen auch fix in den Stundenplan".

© by Veronika Berger, found at ORF: https://noe.orf.at/stories/3122070/25 [last access: 31.03.2023]

Vocabulary help:

curse: der Fluch – **blessing:** der Segen – **mental health:** die psychische Gesundheit – **ubiquitous:** allgegenwärtig – **relationship work:** die Beziehungsarbeit – **pandemic:** die Pandemie – **quarantine:** die Quarantäne – **numerous:** zahlreich – **card game round:** die Kartenspielrunde – **cross-generational:** generationsübergreifend – **availability:** die Verfügbarkeit – **(to) get in touch:** in Verbindung treten – **social facility:** die soziale Einrichtung – **addiction counseling:** die Abhängigkeitsberatung – **youth care:** der Jugendschutz – **dependency:** die Abhängigkeit – **compulsive:** zwanghaft – **substance:** die Substanz – **feeling of satisfaction:** das Gefühl der Zufriedenheit – **period of time:** die Zeitspanne – **digital space:** digitaler Raum – **developmental delay:** die Entwicklungsverzögerung – **personal development:** die Persönlichkeitsentwicklung – **financial support:** die finanzielle Unterstützung – **media literacy:** die Medienkompetenz – **space access:** der Zugang zum digitalen Raum

How to write a comment – Tips and useful words/phrases

M 11

Refresh your memory on how to write a comment.

Task
Use these tips and useful phrases when writing your comment.

What is a comment?
A written comment expresses your personal opinion on a certain topic or issue. It is a common means used in media to state one's point of view to the readership in a more or less critical way. Make notes first and structure your thoughts systematically before starting to write.

1. **Introduction**
   Make some introductory remarks in which you, for example, raise a question or refer to a current problem. The introduction should clarify your topic/concern.

2. **Main part: Your arguments**
   State, demonstrate and describe the positive and negative effects of a topic/situation. Support your view of the situation by providing examples. You can refer to or quote famous people or experts on this matter or relate it to other comparable issues. Emphasise the argument by referring to further/future consequences.

3. **Conclusion**
   Conclude your comment by giving your personal view of the situation/problem. Strategically, it is smart to relate your final remarks to your introduction in order to finally wrap up the topic and make your point.

Useful words

- **Connectives:** although, as … as …, as well, because, but, even if, however, in order to, in spite of, not … either, not until, provided that, since, so that, therefore, unless, whereas, while
- **Adverbs of comment:** actually, after all, apparently, basically, fortunately, frankly, in fact, in my opinion, naturally, unfortunately, obviously, of course, perhaps, possibly, probably, sadly
- **Adverbs of degree:** very, absolutely, almost, at all, at least, completely, drastically, extremely, hardly, most of all, particularly, quite, rarely, rather, really, utterly, virtually
- **Structuring phrases:** both … and …, consequently, secondly, furthermore, in the end, it is true that … but …, last but not least, on the one hand … on the other hand …, on top of that
- **Linking words:** additionally, moreover, furthermore, again, further, then, besides, correspondingly, similarly, regarding, although, otherwise

Useful phrases

- Opponents of this idea claim/maintain that …
- Those who disagree / are against these ideas may say / assert that …
- Some people may disagree with this idea, …
- Some people may say that …; however, …
- They claim that … since …
- The main/first/most important advantage of …

Hinweise und Erwartungshorizonte

1. Stunde

Hinweise (M 1 und M 2)

Ziel von **M 1** und **M 2** ist es, die Schülerinnen und Schüler mit dem Thema der Unterrichtseinheit vertraut zu machen und gegebenenfalls Vorkenntnisse zu aktivieren.

Differenzierungshinweis (M 2)

M 2 dient lernschwächeren Lernenden als Hilfestellung bei der Bildanalyse. Es bietet sprachliche Unterstützung in Form von Redewendungen sowie Hilfestellungen für die Bildbeschreibung und -interpretation.

Digitalhinweis (M 1)

Die Umfrage in *task 1* kann über *Mentimeter* (www.mentimeter.com) erfolgen. Sie erstellen sich zuerst einen Account, loggen sich ein und gehen an der Seite auf die drei Striche der Menüleiste. Dort wählen Sie „*my presentations*" aus und können dann eine neue Präsentation erstellen. Sobald Sie präsentieren, wird schon gesagt, wie sich die Schülerinnen und Schüler einloggen können (auf www.menti.com mit dem Code, der dann dort erscheint.) Sie zeigen dann im Unterricht die Präsentation, und was die Schüler und Schülerinnen schreiben, erscheint dann.

Erwartungshorizont (M 1)

1. Individual contributions. For example:
   I often/seldom/never spend time on my phone because …
2. Individual results. Students might mention the following aspects:
   The picture conveys the message that social media has a magnetising effect on us. The dominant figure in the middle of the picture is like a magnet. The woman in the phone is using a magnet that represents social media to communicate. It appears that she is commanding the other participants in the cartoon to come to her as they are walking in line towards her. The others might all be holding their smartphones in their hands and seem to be using different social networks. By putting the magnet in the foreground and using the woman as a representative who is commanding and attracting the other people, the cartoon effectively illustrates the impact our phones and social media have. By illustrating a phone as the commander of the people in line, the cartoonist criticises the magnetising effect of social media use in a meaningful way.
3. Individual results. For example:
   a) Yes, I thought I had spent two hours per day on social media. Actually, I spent around four hours on social media every day. / No, I guessed correctly. / No, I spent an hour less on social media than I had guessed.
   b) I spend a lot of time on Instagram/Twitter/TikTok … because I do not want to miss out on anything / I communicate with my friends over social media.
   c) Yes, I compare myself with others and want what they have. / No, social media is fake anyway.
   d) Yes, I feel like I am going to miss out on something when my battery dies. / No, I feel relieved when I forget my phone because I feel like then I am free.

4. Individual results. For example:
   a) I follow Pamela Reif and Andre Hamann. / I do not follow any of those influencers because I do not think they share their real lives.
   b) They share positive content about fitness, food and great pictures of their lives and themselves.
   c) I would like to be like them because they are good looking, have great lives, are popular and can have everything they want. / I do not want to be like them because they do not have any privacy / because what they post is fake / because they live with a lot of pressure.
5. Individual results. For example:
   a) The clip addresses the issue that …
      social media often does not reflect the truth of people's lives, but rather a carefully selected, perfect version of it. In some cases, this does not represent the reality at all, but is a so-called "Insta lie". We influence each other with this. When we see the posts of others, we also want to publish posts that will get many likes but do not represent our reality.
   b) Regarding my own social media behaviour …
      I should spend less time on social media and not let influencers manipulate me so much. When I post a picture, my thought is how many people will like it – I want to post the reality instead of "Insta lies".

Hinweise (M 3–M 6)

2./3. Stunde

Ziel der Materialien **M 3–M 6** ist es, anhand des The Guardian Artikels das Thema „*Social media and anxiety*" zu erschließen und das Leseverstehen zu überprüfen.

Differenzierungshinweis
Lernschwächere Lernende nutzen das Material „*Skimming, scanning, taking notes – How to work with texts*" (**M 4**). Es bietet Unterstützung zum systematischen Lesen, Bearbeiten und Markieren von Texten sowie zum Verfassen von Notizen. **Schnelle** Lernende können mit den beiden *LearningApps* in der Zusatzaufgabe auf **M 6** zur Überprüfung des erarbeiteten Textinhalts gefördert werden.

Erwartungshorizont (M 3)

1.–3. Individual results. For example:

   "Phones are like a scab we know we shouldn't pick": the truth about social media and anxiety

   […] Most people think that phones are a bad thing for anxiety. Parents, in particular, believe phones are terrible for the mental health of children, teenagers and young adults.
5 So, what is the truth? […] I felt I had to get to the bottom of the relationship between phones and anxiety. And to be honest, it doesn't look great. Since smartphones came out in around 2000, there has been a steady decline in the mental health of young people. […] What I have observed clinically is that rather than being the cause of the problem per se, phones seem to act as a catalyst to our emotions. This can be a positive thing, when it
10 allows us to connect with friends and family; share happy news; photos or jokes. It also allows marginalised communities to find each other.
   However, humans are wired to foresee danger and our minds can quickly spiral from an initial trigger to create catastrophic, wholly imaginary circumstances, which our bodies

respond to as though they are true. In your head this goes something like: "Some of my friends are meeting without me > they don't want me there > they don't really like me > nobody really likes me > I am fundamentally unlovable and will die alone."

The phone contributes to this in a number of different ways. First it allows us to know our friends are meeting without us. There was something in "ignorance is bliss" and now there is no ignorance. We know, and we get to sit on our sofa […] and compare our inside worries, our worst sides, our ugliest self, with endless, perfectly curated versions of other people's lives. And guess what? That makes us anxious and unhappy.

Our phone is like a scab we know we shouldn't pick. We know it is making us feel bad seeing our rich friend on a weekend trip away with her gorgeous partner; we know we should put our phone down and go and do something constructive and positive […]. Look, there is someone on Instagram with a perfect bathroom and a beautiful body showing us what we should be doing, and we are just sitting around scrolling – no wonder no one wants to hang out with you. In this way, your phone can trigger a second round of self-judgment about how lazy or worthless you are.

The phone intensifies a comparison culture that can leave you feeling not good enough in every single aspect of life: not thin enough; not successful enough; not tidy or organised enough; not living in a nice enough home; not well-read or smart enough.

And while research into the effects of this on mental health is in its infancy, there is particularly damning research in relation to viewing photos of perfect bodies, which is shown to increase body dissatisfaction, with a link to eating disorders. Even when we know the images are doctored, and even when they are shown in relation to fitness, they still impact on body dissatisfaction.

So some of the questions I ask my patients about their phone use are:

Are you using your phone to connect to people or to compare to people? The former is positive for mental health but the latter will likely increase anxiety.

Is there a tipping point where phone use changes from positive to negative? Do you notice this tipping point? And can you put your phone away then? My experience suggests it is just at this point that the phone is at its most magnetic.

Is your phone getting in the way of you doing things which are positive for mental health? Phone use is perhaps at its most damaging when it gets in the way of sleeping, eating regularly, being outside and moving your body, all of which are important for wellbeing. Research suggests that there may be a sweet spot with mobile phone use, after which the screen stops being helpful or fun and starts having a negative impact on wellbeing. An analogy to drinking is helpful: a couple of glasses of red wine can be relaxing; a bottle a night is not so helpful. And like with drinking, some people find it difficult to stop just at the point when they should.

So if you are experiencing anxiety, think about your phone use – think about how much time you spend on it and on what kind of content. Readdressing this might be one important key in unlocking a less anxious life.

Phone and internet use is best when it is in line with our other values rather than taking us away from them. […]

© by Tara Porter found at The Guardian: https://www.theguardian.com/lifeandstyle/2022/may/22/phones-are-like-a-scab-we-know-we-shouldnt-pick-the-truth-about-social-media-and-anxiety [last access: 31/03/2023]

4. Individual results. For example:
   - line 29: feeling of not being good enough
   - lines 9–11: positive, e.g., Facebook, Twitter, Instagram, …
   - lines 29–31: Are more discussions about fairness and tolerance needed?
   - lines 40–43: As the usage of a phone is a kind of status symbol in today's society the tipping point might be difficult to find.
   - lines 32–34: Who could help? How could those teenagers be helped?
   - line 38: Phones are also required in many fields of today's society: online banking, booking procedures, personal documents …

Erwartungshorizont (M 5)

1. a) 1) "since" … "people"; lines 6–7 – b) 2) "What" … "emotions"; lines 8–9 – c) 1) "Research" … "wellbeing"; lines 46–47
2. a) true (lines 9–11) – b) true (lines 29–30) – c) false: Comparing yourself to others on social media can affect your body image even if you are aware that the images are posed and edited. (lines 34–36) – d) true (lines 40–42)
3. Individual results. For example:
   a) … they can be both: a good and a bad thing, depending on our mood and how we use it. If we mainly use it to connect with other people, using our phones can be good for our mental health. But sometimes, we create fake scenarios in our heads and spiral into negative thoughts when we see posts of our friends going out or if we compare ourselves too much with the lives of other people. (lines 9–11; 19–36)
   b) … we somehow know that they can harm our mental health and hurt us, but still, we cannot resist to use our phones. This can be like opening a healing wound again. (lines 22–24)
   c) … just like with alcohol: it can be fun to consume, but it can also be dangerous. The sweet spot of consuming alcohol as well as using our phones is highly individual and differs from person to person. There is a tipping point, from which onward the consumption is more harmful than helpful, but it is very hard to realise that point and then to put down our phones. Just like some people do not feel the point when they should stop drinking, and they will feel bad as a result (lines 40–50).
4. Individual results. For example:

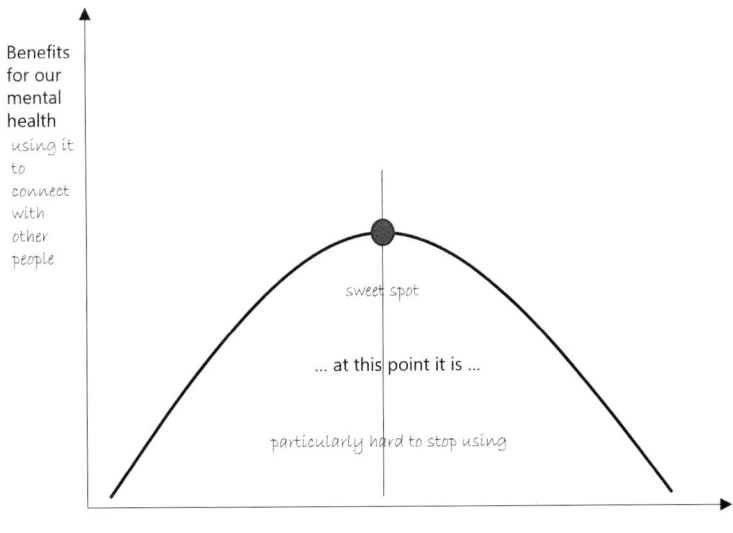

Erwartungshorizont (M 6)

1. a) anxiety – b) mental health – c) wired – d) compare – e) dissatisfaction – f) doctored – g) tipping point – h) impact
   solution: awareness
2. a) anxiety – b) intensifies; curated – c) eating disorders – d) marginalised – e) sweet spot; tipping
3. a) Overlong phone use is compared with picking scabs: we know we should not pick them because it hurts, just like spending too much time on our phones.
   b) If using our phones keeps us from sleeping, eating and moving, they harm our wellbeing.
   c) Constantly comparing ourselves with doctored pictures of other people's lives can cause a feeling of never being good enough.

4. Stunde

Hinweise (M 7)

Das **Ziel** von **M 7** ist es, das Hör-Seh-Verstehen der Lernenden zu fördern. Es werden weitere Aspekte des Themenfelds „*Social media*" beleuchtet.

Differenzierungshinweis
Lernschwächere Lernende üben die relevanten Vokabeln mit einer *LearningApp*.

Erwartungshorizont (M 7)

1. Individual results. For example:
   The video is about social media and its dangers. The bad influences on society are highlighted. / The video is a film from Netflix, which focuses on several social media platforms and shows how users are being manipulated.
2. a) true – b) false – c) true – d) true – e) false
3. a) 3) – b) 1) – c) 2)

5./6. Stunde

Hinweise (M 8 und M 9)

Das **Ziel** von **M 8** und **M 9** ist es, die Sprechkompetenz der Lernenden zu fördern. Die Lernenden nehmen einen Perspektivenwechsel vor und diskutieren und evaluieren die gewonnenen Erkenntnisse der vorherigen Stunden.

Differenzierungshinweis (M 9)
Lernschwächere Lernende können auf **M 9** zurückgreifen, in der wichtige Aspekte zur Diskussionsführung wiederholt werden. Es dient auch als Spickzettel während der Diskussion.

Erwartungshorizont (M 8)

1.–3. Individual results.
4. Individual results. For example:
   Social media can be a blessing because …
   - it connects people from all over the world easily; there are no boundaries in the digital world.

- people can share their thoughts and opinions with the world; it brings people together, who share similar interests (community).
- people present themselves in the best light.
- the option of profit for private persons and companies exists.
- you can express your opinion and have an impact.

Social media can be a curse because …
- it goes hand in hand with cybermobbing and hacking.
- it can cause addiction, especially teenagers are the main target. Effects of addiction range from isolation and unproductivity to depression.
- fake news, gossip and rumours can spread faster.
- people compare themselves with others. This can lead to serious health problems.
- private information and data are not secure (data tracking).

Hinweise (M 10 und M 11)

7./8. Stunde

Das **Ziel** von **M 10** und **M 11** ist es, zuerst einen *comment* zu schreiben und schließlich die gewonnen Informationen aus dieser Unterrichtseinheit in einer Präsentation zusammenzuführen und mit den eigenen Erfahrungen zu ergänzen.

Differenzierungshinweis

Lernschwächere Schülerinnen und Schüler können für *task 3* (M 10) bei Bedarf auf **M 11** zurückgreifen, die eine Anleitung zum Erfassen eines *comment* sowie *useful phrases* and *words* aufweist.

Erwartungshorizont (M 10)

1. Individual results.
2. Individual results. For example:

cons	pros
– psychological dependencies are easily created (lines 31–33)	– find and maintain relationships quickly and easily (lines 23–25)
– anxiety arises due to the constant availability of new content and interaction (FOMO) (lines 35–41)	– access to the outside world for isolated people (lines 9–11)
– companies work with psychological tricks so that people are online as often as possible (lines 45–48)	– alleviate loneliness of older persons (lines 15–17)
– psychological pressure through reward mechanisms and temporal immediacy (lines 49–50 and 56–59)	– possible to connect with others and share photos or videos at any time and from any place (lines 23–24)
– can provoke addiction-like behaviour (lines 65–66)	– it is easier to accept help digitally (lines 4–5)
– may lead to developmental delays (lines 69–70)	– positive feelings are conveyed (lines 61–62)

3. Individual results.
4. Individual results. An example can be found in the online archive (*ZM PowerPoint Presentation*). Students might mention the following aspects:
   - Introduction:
     - Social media and the Internet are connected to each other. They play an enormous role in today's global communication.
     - Social media has made communication very easy and inexpensive.
     - Communication and transport is faster and more reliable.
     - Social media delivers up-to-date news, information and other important issues within a few seconds all around the world (Facebook, Instagram, Twitter, YouTube …)
   - The positive impact of social media:
     - convenient communication
     - opportunity to share feelings and opinions
     - enhance education
     - fostering business growth and promotion
     - advertising
     - increase sales
     - better living standards as the world gets closer
     - search for important news or information
   - The negative impact of social media:
     - fake profiles and relationships
     - spreading of rumours
     - addiction to social media
     - anxiety and depression
     - cyberbullying
     - cultural aggression
   - Conclusion: In the present world, we cannot imagine our lives without social media. It has spread into many areas of existence, such as professional life, personal life and family life. We should be more conscious of social media's security measures and more careful with personal information. The use of social media should not affect one's personal life or the life of others.

II.C.3.5

Landeskunde – The English-Speaking World

Nigerian coming-of-age stories – Anhand unterschiedlicher Textsorten interkulturelle Kompetenzen entwickeln (S II)

Dirk Beyer

Welche Themen beschäftigen nigerianische Jugendliche in ihrem Alltag? Was sind typische Elemente in der nigerianischen Literatur? Und wie unterscheidet sich die Lebenswelt der Lernenden von der nigerianischer Jugendlicher? Die *Nigerian coming-of-age story* ist in Nordrhein-Westfalen Abiturthema. In der vorliegenden Unterrichtsreihe setzen sich Ihre Schülerinnen und Schüler anhand eines Films, einer Kurzgeschichte und eines Romanauszugs mit der Lebenswelt Heranwachsender in Nigeria unter dem Einfluss westlicher Kultur(en) auseinander. Dabei erweitern sie ihre interkulturelle Kompetenz und trainieren die Analyse unterschiedlicher Textsorten.

KOMPETENZPROFIL

Klassenstufe:	Q1/Q2 (G8), 12/13 (G9)
Dauer:	3–12 Unterrichtsstunden
Kompetenzen:	1. Lesen: literarische Texte verstehen und Textdeutungen entwickeln; 2. Interkulturelle kommunikative Kompetenz; 3. Hör-Seh-Verstehen: einem Film zentrale Informationen entnehmen
Thematische Bereiche:	*Nigeria* (Landeskunde, Themen und Motive nigerianischer Literatur), *coming-of-age, growing up, global challenges, identity in a diverse world, individual and society*
Medien:	*LearningApps,* Video(link)s
Zusätzlich benötigt:	Film „*Nigerian Prince"* (2018) von Faraday Oroko (Netflix)

Fachliche Hinweise

Das Thema „*Nigeria*" im Englischunterricht der Oberstufe

Unter dem Titel „*Voices from the African Continent: Focus on Nigeria*" erhielt das Thema „Westafrika" ab dem Jahr 2021 Einzug ins englische **Zentralabitur** vieler Bundesländer. Mit Nigeria wird der Bezug zu einem Land hergestellt, das sich seit Beginn seiner Unabhängigkeit von Großbritannien im Jahr 1960 bis heute im Wandel befindet und durch politische, soziale und religiöse Instabilität gekennzeichnet ist. Die aktuellen Richtlinien für die Sekundarstufe II in Nordrhein-Westfalen sowie die Richtlinien und Vorgaben für das **Abitur in Nordrhein-Westfalen** ab 2021 verorten Nigeria als **Rahmenthema postkolonialer Literatur**, das die Lebenswirklichkeiten in einem weiteren anglophonen Kulturraum beschreibt. Im Mittelpunkt stehen dabei die Alltagswirklichkeiten und Zukunftsperspektiven junger Erwachsener sowie ihre politischen, sozialen und kulturellen Wirklichkeiten. Die Oberstufenlernenden bauen in diesem Zusammenhang grundlegendes **soziokulturelles Orientierungswissen** auf. Ebenso spielen **globale Herausforderungen** und **Zukunftsvisionen** des Landes eine wichtige Rolle. Im Schwerpunkt geschieht dies durch die (literarische) Textarbeit, die die Lernenden mittels interkulturell-kommunikativen Kompetenzaufbaus zu interkulturellem Verstehen und Handeln befähigt.

(Nigerian) Coming-of-age stories

Coming-of-age-Geschichten spielen besonders beim Übergang von der Sekundarstufe I in die Oberstufe eine wichtige Rolle. Das Übertreten Jugendlicher ins junge Erwachsenenalter sowie die damit verbundenen Prozesse der Selbstfindung und Identitätsentwicklung werden durch die Erzählungen textbezogen analysiert und mit **persönlichen Erfahrungen** der Schülerinnen und Schüler verbunden. Durch das Lesen nigerianischer Jugenderzählungen (hier im erweiterten Begriff als Filmsequenzen, Kurzgeschichte und Romanauszug) entnehmen die jugendlichen Schülerinnen und Schüler **kulturell-relevante Themen** und stellen persönliche Bezüge her. Sie nehmen **Konflikte** anderer Länder und Kulturen wahr (M 1–M 3 „*Nigerian Prince*" und M 7–M 9 „*The Girl with the Louding Voice*") und erfahren wichtige **Hintergründe zur Lebensweise**, zu den Problemen sowie zur Landeskunde Nigerias (M 4–M 6 „*Collector of Memories*" und M 10). Im Hinblick auf den Aspekt des Fremdverstehens ermöglichen *coming-of-age*-Erzählungen nicht nur die Möglichkeit zur **Perspektivübernahme**, sondern erlauben gleichzeitig wichtige Grenzerfahrungen.

Zu den ausgewählten Filmen und Texten

Der Netflix-**Film „*Nigerian Prince*"** von 2018 ist ein erfolgreicher Actionthriller des amerikanisch-nigerianischen Regisseurs Faraday Okoro. Er beschreibt die Geschichte des amerikanisch-nigerianischen Teenagers Eze, der von seiner Mutter zu Verwandten ins nigerianische Lagos geschickt wird. Dort soll er den nigerianischen Lebensstil sowie seine Wurzeln kennenlernen.

Die ***coming-of-age short story* „*Collector of Memories*"** von Joshua Chizoma erschien 2021 in der Anthologie „*The Hope, the Prayer, the Anthem*". Der junge nigerianische Nachwuchsautor Chizome, der für den Caine Prize nominiert wurde, beschreibt hierin die Geschichte einer jungen Frau, die im nigerianischen Hinterland bei einer Pflegefamilie aufwächst. Die Erzählung aus der Ich-Perspektive ermöglicht eine persönliche Betroffenheit bei den Leserinnen und Lesern und baut die interkulturelle Kompetenz aus, indem Bezüge zwischen nigerianischen und westlichen (Text)-Elementen hergestellt werden können.

Abi Darés Debüt-**Roman „*The Girl with the Louding Voice*"**, der 2020 erschien, wurde zum New York Times-Bestseller und war für den Desmond Elliot Prize für Neuautorinnen nominiert. Der *coming-of-age*-Roman erzählt die Geschichte Adunnis, eines 14-jährigen nigerianischen Mädchens, das in Armut aufwächst. Um das Geld für die Familie und seinen Alkoholkonsum aufzutreiben, wird Adunni von ihrem Vater verkauft und zwangsverheiratet. Von ihrem neuen Ehemann vergewaltigt, flieht sie nach Lagos und versucht sich ein neues Leben in der Großstadt aufzubauen. Sie kommt bei einer nigerianischen Großindustriellen unter, die sie als Hausmädchen einstellt und mehrfach misshandelt. Adunni erkennt schnell, dass Bildung und Wissen ihre einzige Möglichkeit für eine gute Zukunft sind. Mit der Unterstützung einer neu gewonnenen Freundin bewirbt sich die Protagonistin um ein Stipendium, das ihre Eintrittskarte in eine neue (bessere) Zukunft werden soll.

Didaktisch-methodische Hinweise

Zur Lerngruppe und den curricularen Vorgaben

Kernlehrpläne und Bildungspläne aller Bundesländer betonen die Bedeutung der Schulung und Ausbildung **interkultureller Kompetenz**. Das Erleben, Erfahren, Betrachten und kritische Reflektieren anderer Kulturen sowie das Herstellen **inter- und transkultureller Bezüge** wird von der Erprobungsstufe bis hin zur allgemeinen Hochschulreife sukzessive aufgebaut. Die vorliegenden Materialien sind überwiegend für den Unterricht der gymnasialen Oberstufe konzipiert, in welchem nicht nur die Themen *„Growing-up"* und *„Global Challenges"*, sondern in manchen Bundesländern auch das Thema *„Nigeria"* als postkoloniales Land feste Bestandteile der Lehrpläne darstellen. Vorwissen zum Thema *„Nigeria"* ist nicht notwendig. Die Aufgabenformate zum globalen und detaillierten Lese- und Hör-Seh-Verstehen entsprechen den curricularen Standards und eignen sich insbesondere für den Einsatz in Grundkursen sowie leistungsschwächeren Leistungskursen.

Zu den inhaltlichen Schwerpunkten der Unterrichtsreihe

Der inhaltliche Schwerpunkt der Reihe liegt auf dem Kennenlernen und Erfahren einer erweiterten, fremdsprachlichen Bezugskultur am Beispiel Nigerias (Zentralabitur Nordrhein-Westfalen). Einerseits erarbeiten die Schülerinnen und Schüler wesentliche **soziale und wirtschaftliche Herausforderungen** (zum Beispiel Korruption, Gewalt, mangelnde Bildung und Armut) sowie **landeskundliche Hintergründe**, **Einzelschicksale junger Erwachsener** und mögliche Zukunftsperspektiven, andererseits erfahren sie, wie nigerianische Jugendliche und junge Erwachsene mit diesen Herausforderungen umgehen, welche **Copingstrategien** sie nutzen und welche Aussichten sie in ihrem Leben erwarten. Auf diese Weise schulen die Lernenden ihr (inter)kulturelles Verständnis.
Die vorliegende Unterrichtseinheit besteht aus insgesamt zehn Materialien, die sich vier Themenkomplexen widmen. Anhand von **M 1–M 4** untersucht die Lerngruppe den bekannten **Blockbuster „Nigerian Prince"**. Neben einer kurzen inhaltlichen Einführung mithilfe des **Trailer**s, analysieren die Lernenden ausgewählte **Filmauszüge** sowie eine **Filmrezension** mit der sie den Film abschließend reflektieren.
Im Anschluss erarbeiten die Schülerinnen und Schüler die **Kurzgeschichte „Collector of Memories"** (**M 5** und **M 6**). Durch die *coming-of-age story* erhalten sie einen Einblick in typische Alltagssituationen Nigerias und nehmen Teil am Leben und Schicksal der jungen Protagonistin. Um eine weibliche Hauptfigur geht es auch in Abi Darés **Bestsellerroman *„The Girl with the Louding Voice"*** (**M 7–M 9**). Der Schwerpunkt der Materialien umfasst neben einer Heranführung an den Inhalt des Romans, das Thema „Bildung". In **M 10** lernen die Schülerinnen und Schüler durch einen **Zeitungsartikel** das aktuelle Nigeria, die Sicht von Teenagern und jungen Erwachsenen auf ihre Zukunft sowie die Zukunft des Landes kennen.

Mögliche Alternativen oder Erweiterungsmöglichkeiten

Streamingdienste wie beispielsweise Netflix bieten derzeit eine große Auswahl an sogenannten Nollywood-**Filmen** an, die ähnliche Themen wie der Film *„Nigerian Prince"* beinhalten. Auch die Kurzgeschichte *„Collector of Memories"* kann gegen andere **Kurzgeschichten** zum Thema *„Coming-of-age in Nigeria"* substituiert oder ergänzt werden. Hier bieten sich beispielsweise Texte von C. N. Adichie, Helon Habila und Sefi Atta an. Ähnliches gilt für den Romanauszug von Abi Daré. Das Schicksal junger Erwachsener wird in vielen Romanen junger, nigerianischer Autorinnen und Autoren thematisiert, welche häufig Anknüpfungspunkte zur westlichen Welt thematisieren und auf diese Weise für deutsche Schülerinnen und Schüler erfahrbar sind. Beispiele für solche **Romane** beziehungsweise Romanauszüge sind unter anderem die Texte von Chibundu Onuzo, Olumide Popoola, Chigozie Obioma, C. N. Adichie, Toni Kann und Tehu Cole.

Lehrwerksbezug
- Context Oberstufe (Cornelsen): Chapter 1, „Finding Your Place – The individual in society"
- Green Line Oberstufe (Klett): Kapitel 1 „Identity in a diverse world"
- Green Line Oberstufe (Klett): Kapitel 8 „Nigeria"

Mediathek

Primärliteratur

▶ **Daré, Abi:** The Girl with the Louding Voice. Sceptre-Verlag. London, 2020.
Der Roman dient als Grundlage für M 7 bis M 9 und eignet sich auch als Ganzschrift für den Englischunterricht der Oberstufe.

Sekundärliteratur

▶ **Beyer, Dirk:** Arbeitsblätter mit *LearningApps* erstellen. In: Teaching Compendium – Digitale Tools im Literaturunterricht. Ernst Klett Sprachen. Stuttgart, 2022. S. 13–15.
Das Werk beschreibt unterschiedliche digitale Tools und deren Verwendung im fremdsprachlichen Literaturunterricht. Übersichtlich werden die jeweiligen Tools ins Unterrichtsgeschehen eingebettet, die Methode erklärt und fachdidaktisch legitimiert.

▶ **Beyer, Dirk:** Coming of age the Nigerian way. Der Fremdsprachliche Unterricht Englisch 2020 (166). S. 41–47.
Der Fachartikel argumentiert für eine verstärkte Einbeziehung unterschiedlicher nigerianischer *coming-of-age*-Geschichten in den Englischunterricht. Er benennt sowohl Beispiele als auch mögliche methodische Herangehensweisen.

▶ **Beyer, Dirk:** Voices of Africa – Nigeria. Teacher's Guide. Ernst Klett Sprachen. Stuttgart, 2020.
Die Lehrerhandreichung zum Student Reader *„The Bigger Picture – focus on Nigeria"* bietet zu einer unterrichtsbezogenen Textauswahl unterschiedliche methodische Herangehensweisen, die sowohl digitale als analoge Möglichkeiten eröffnen.

▶ **Beyer, Dirk:** The Nigerian coming-of-age novel: Ansätze zur transkulturellen Literaturdidaktik. In: Bartosch, Roman et al.: Interkulturelles Lernen im Englischunterricht: Fokus Nigeria – Themen, Texte und Aufgaben. Klett-Kallmeyer-Verlag. Hannover, 2020. S. 183–205.
Der Fachartikel liefert eine sinnvolle und prägnante Zusammenfassung der transkulturellen Literaturdidaktik und beinhaltet fachdidaktische Grundlagen und methodische Herangehensweisen.

Weiterführende Internetseiten

- https://padlet.com/dienst5_9_4_94/voices-from-the-african-continent-nb1c9utj970r [letzter Abruf: 31.03.2023]
In dem Padlet finden sich Links mit Hintergrundinformationen über Nigeria, seine Geschichte und seine Gegenwart.
- https://www.sueddeutsche.de/kultur/abi-dare-nigeria-maedchen-mit-der-lauternen-stimme-1.5423073 [letzter Abruf: 31.03.2023]
- https://www.deutschlandfunkkultur.de/abi-dare-das-maedchen-mit-der-lauternen-stimme-geschichte-100.html [letzter Abruf: 31.03.2023]
Rezensionen von Darés Roman *„Girl with the Louding Voive"* aus der Süddeutschen Zeitung und vom Deutschlandfunk Kultur, die sich zum Beispiel für eine Mediationsaufgabe im Unterricht einsetzen lassen.

Auf einen Blick

1./2. Stunde

Thema: *Nigerian Prince* I: Nigerian teenagers in film

M 1 **Discover the film *Nigerian Prince* – Watching the trailer /** den Film anhand seines Trailers kennenlernen, typische Trailer-Merkmale bestimmen (EA) und Hintergrundinformationen auf den Film übertragen (EA, PA, UG)

M 2 **Nigerian and Western elements – Analysing the film /** ausgewählte Filmszenen analysieren und typische nigerianische und westliche Elemente identifizieren (EA, GA)

Benötigt:
☐ digitale Endgeräte zum Ansehen des Trailers
☐ Laptop/Tablet mit Netflix-Zugang und Beamer/Whiteboard zum Ansehen des Films

3. Stunde

Thema: *Nigerian Prince* II: intercultural conflicts

M 3 ***Nigerian Prince*: An intercultural coming-of-age story? – Background info /** interkulturelle Konflikte, ihre Merkmale und Entstehung erarbeiten (PA) und auf den Protagonisten des Films übertragen (GA); Interviews zum Thema „Interkulturelle Konflikte" vorbereiten und durchführen (EA, PA)

Hausaufgabe: Einen Blogeintrag aus Ezes Sicht schreiben

4. Stunde

Thema: *Nigerian Prince* III: film review

M 4 **The reception of *Nigerian Prince* – Reading a film review /** eine Filmkritik zum Film „Nigerian Prince" lesen und verstehen (EA); zur Kritik Stellung beziehen (EA) und weitere Hintergründe zum „Nigerian Prince Scam" anhand eines Videos diskutieren (UG, PA)

Hausaufgabe: Eine Filmrezension über „Nigerian Prince" schreiben

Benötigt: ☐ ggf. digitale Endgeräte für die Bearbeitung in *LearningApps*

II.C.3.5 Landeskunde – The English-Speaking World ▶ Nigerian coming-of-age stories

5./6. Stunde

Thema: *Collector of Memories* I: comprehension

M 5 ***Collector of Memories* – Understanding a Nigerian short story /** eine nigerianische *coming-of-age short story* lesen und das Textverständnis anhand unterschiedlicher Aufgabenformate sichern (EA, PA); erste nigerianisch-kulturelle Textelemente erkennen (EA)

Benötigt: ☐ ggf. digitale Endgeräte für die Bearbeitung in *LearningApps*

7./8. Stunde

Thema: *Collector of Memories* II: typical cultural elements

M 6 ***Collector of Memories:* A typical Nigerian short story? – An Internet research /** arbeitsteilig Hintergrundinformationen zu typischen nigerianischen Elementen in der Literatur online recherchieren (PA), die Ergebnisse präsentieren (PA, PL) und auf die Kurzgeschichte übertragen (EA); die Inhalte einer Dokumentation über Aberglauben in Nigeria mit der Kurzgeschichte vergleichen (EA)

Benötigt: ☐ digitale Endgeräte für die Internetrecherche und das Abspielen des Videos

9. Stunde

Thema: *The Girl with the Louding Voice* I: context

M 7 ***The Girl with the Louding Voice* – Putting an extract into context /** anhand eines Videos das Thema „Bildung" in Nigeria rekapitulieren (PL); einen Auszug aus dem *coming-of-age*-Roman lesen und diesen kontextualisieren (EA); den Romanauszug mit der Kurzgeschichte vergleichen (EA) und die Sprache im Roman analysieren (EA)

Benötigt: ☐ digitale Endgeräte für das Abspielen des Videos

10. Stunde

Thema: *The Girl with the Louding Voice* II: education

M 8 ***The Girl with the Louding Voice* – What does education mean to Adunni? /** weitere Hintergründe zum Thema „Bildung" anhand eines Zitats und eines Sachtexts erarbeiten (PL, EA); die Bedeutung von Bildung für die Protagonistin anhand von Romanauszügen analysieren (EA)

11. Stunde

Thema: *The Girl with the Louding Voice* III: the author

M 9 ***The Girl with the Louding Voice* – Watching an interview with the author /** anhand eines Videos Informationen über die Protagonistin Adunni und die Autorin Daré sammeln (EA); autobiografische Elemente im Roman identifizieren (PA), den Stellenwert des Romans diskutieren (PL)

Benötigt: ☐ digitale Endgeräte für das Abspielen des Interviews

12. Stunde

Thema: Online article: Nigerian teenagers today

M 10 ***What are Nigerian teenagers up to These Days?* – Reading a newspaper article /** einen Onlineartikel lesen und verstehen (EA); die Gemeinsamkeiten und Unterschiede zwischen nigerianischer und deutscher Jugendkultur anhand eines Venn-Diagramms herausarbeiten (GA)

Minimalplan

Die drei thematischen Bausteine der Unterrichtsreihe kann die Lehrkraft unabhängig voneinander einsetzen. Dadurch ergeben sich drei thematisch-inhaltliche Schwerpunkte:

Baustein 1: *Nigerian Prince* – Analysing a Nollywood film   **M 1–M 4**
Baustein 2: *Collector of Memories* – A Nigerian short story   **M 5–M 6**
Baustein 3: *The Girl with the Louding Voice* – Excerpt from a Nigerian novel   **M 7–M 9**

Erklärung zu den Symbolen

	Dieses Symbol markiert differenziertes Material. Wenn nicht anders ausgewiesen, befinden sich die Materialien auf mittlerem Niveau.

	leichtes Niveau		mittleres Niveau		schwieriges Niveau
	Zusatzaufgaben		Alternative		Selbsteinschätzung

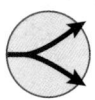

Discover the film *Nigerian Prince* – Watching the trailer

M 1

The film *Nigerian Prince* was released in 2018. It is an American-Nigerian bilingual suspense thriller. The viewers get an inside view of typical Nigerian places like Lagos as well as typical elements of Nigerian culture like food and traditions.

> **Info box: About the film *Nigerian Prince***
>
> **The plot of the film**
> The film *Nigerian Prince* is about the young and stubborn American-Nigerian teenager Eze who is sent to Nigeria by his mother against his will. In Nigeria, he is supposed to experience his family's roots and explore his identity. But Eze does not like Nigeria and longs to return to the USA. To collect money for a return ticket, he teams up with his criminal Nigerian cousin Pius, a Nigerian prince scammer. Both try to scam unsuspecting foreigners to get money for Eze's ticket back to the USA.
>
> **The Nigerian prince scam ("419 scam")**
> The title of the film, *Nigerian Prince*, refers to a typical Nigerian form of fraud – the "Nigerian prince scam", also known as the Nigerian Criminal Code "419 scam". Here, a person receives a letter or an email that offers a huge financial reward, if a smaller amount of money is sent to cover certain "expenses" like banking fees and administrative costs first. The scammers will continue to ask for money to gain personal profit.

Tasks

1. Read the info box. Then watch the trailer of *Nigerian Prince*: https://www.youtube.com/watch?v=0L7HpCW7mkU [last access: 31/03/2023] [min. 02:13]
   While watching, tick the conventions used in the trailer.
2. Watch the trailer for a second time and make notes on the following questions. Compare your answers with those of a partner.
   a) What do you learn about the two protagonists, Eze and Pius?
   b) How is the Nigerian prince scam presented in the trailer?

> **Trailer conventions**
> ☐ There is an emotional beginning.
> ☐ The protagonist is introduced.
> ☐ The setting is introduced.
> ☐ The title of the film is shown.
> ☐ The trailer uses different scenes to show beginning, middle and ending.
> ☐ There are short conversations between the characters.
> ☐ The trailer shows the official beginning of the film.
> ☐ The trailer builds to a climax and stops (= cliff-hanger technique).
> ☐ The final shot has a lasting effect on the audience.
> ☐ There is a person telling the character's story (= voice-over technique).

M 2 — Nigerian and Western elements – Analysing the film

Nigerian Prince is an American-Nigerian film combining typical elements of Nigerian culture with elements of the American (Western) world. Both clash when Eze, the American-Nigerian protagonist, is sent from his American home to stay with his Nigerian aunt in Lagos.

Info box: Elements of Western culture in Nigeria
Nigeria is Africa's most populated country. It became independent in 1960. Before its independence, it was occupied by British forces and became a British protectorate in 1901. Due to the strong Western influence, Nigeria's official language (in addition to more than 250 ethnic groups and their own languages and dialects) is English. Many Nigerians have used this connection to the Western world as well as their language skills to leave Nigeria and immigrate to America to become part of the Western world and its way of life.

Tasks

1. Watch the three scenes from the film *Nigerian Prince*. Contrast Eze's situation in the USA with his situation in Nigeria. While watching, make notes on what is typical Nigerian versus what is typical American (Western) in the scenes.

Scene [time]	Typical Nigerian	Typical American (Western)
Eze at the airport [min. 3:50–8:30]		
Eze at his aunt's place [min. 8:50–12:40]		
Welcome to Lagos [min. 24:00–28:00]		

2. In groups of three to four students, discuss the following question:
   Why is Eze unhappy in Nigeria and cannot cope with his aunt or cousin's way of life?
3. Watch the whole film and focus on the Internet scam elements.

Nigerian Prince: An intercultural coming-of-age story? – Background info

M 3

Growing up with two cultural worlds can affect a teenager's development and lead to conflicts. In the film *Nigerian Prince,* these conflicts are shown in various situations between the protagonist Eze and his American-Nigerian mother and Nigerian aunt.

> **Info box: Teenagers and intercultural conflicts**
>
> Children who grow up with parents who are foreign-born are often straddling two cultures – that of their parents, and that of their peers. This can be both an amazing opportunity and a struggle for a child as she develops her own identity. It also presents opportunities and challenges for parents.
>
> 5   All parents hope that their children succeed and thrive in the world. All parents have moments where they worry about their children. There are many universal parenting issues, and there are many issues that are intensified when two cultures are involved. […] Research has shown […] that children go through a process of individuation during their adolescent years. This is true for the general population and carries extra
>
> 10 weight for children growing up with two cultures. This is the period of a child's life where she's more likely to drift away from his/her culture of origin.
>
> Source: https://momentousinstitute.org/blog/how-to-help-kids-navigate-two-cultures [last access: 31/03/2023] (text abbreviated for didactic reasons)

Tasks

1. Read the background information on intercultural conflicts of teenagers growing up with two cultures. With a partner, identify two to three examples of intercultural conflicts shown in the film *Nigerian Prince*.
   Tip: Focus on the interactions between Eze and his mother and aunt.
2. Read Eze's (suggested) inner thoughts and feelings in the thought bubbles below.
   In groups of four, discuss whether the thoughts and feelings are realistic.
3. **Expert task:** Interview classmates who grew up with more than one culture. Prepare the interview by noting down questions about their experiences and feelings. Compare their experiences to Eze's situation in Nigeria.
4. Write a blog entry from Eze's perspective about his first days in Nigeria.

Thought bubbles:
- I am American, not Nigerian!
- My mum does not understand anything!
- Life in America is much easier and better!
- How can my aunt and cousin live here?

Pictures: © simplehappyart/iStock/Getty Images Plus

M 4 The reception of *Nigerian Prince* – Reading a film review

Nigerian Prince has been a successful film showing Nigeria and its capital city Lagos from the perspective of an American-Nigerian teenager. The feature debut of American-Nigerian director Faraday Okoro shows convincing acting and some of Nigeria's most common social problems.

Film review: *Nigerian Prince*
By Owen Gleiberman

An American teenager goes on a trip to Nigeria, only to learn that he's trapped in a scavenger nation where life is a matter of who scams who.

We've all seen movies – like "Beirut," with Jon Hamm – in which a trouble-shooting agent or foreign correspondent has to make his way through a scavenger nation that's a nest
5 of danger and instability and corruption. "Nigerian Prince" is one of those movies, except that the central character is no spy. He's a surly American teenager named Eze (Antonio J. Bell), who arrives in the sprawling Nigerian capital of Lagos to spend four weeks with his aunt. Or so he thinks. His mother flew him over there so he could soak up his Nigerian heritage, which sounds innocent enough, until you learn that she cancelled his return
10 ticket the moment he arrived. Eze isn't just visiting – he's trapped. In a place with spotty electricity, hamburgers that taste like dog food, and people you can't trust.

His first morning there, his Aunt Grace (Tina Mba) throws a bucket of water on him when he won't get out of bed, and then she warns him that the next time it will be boiling water. (She sounds like she means it.) For a drama that's all about a middle-class kid from the U.S.
15 visiting the land of his ancestors, "Nigerian Prince" is no scrappy travelogue – it's closer to a YA version of "Midnight Express."

The movie was directed by the New York-based Nigerian-American filmmaker Faraday Okoro, and it's the first feature to have been completed with a grant from the Tribeca Film Festival's Untold Stories program (in collaboration with AT&T). The first thing to say about
20 "Nigerian Prince" is that Okoro makes good on that backing. He creates a drama with a vivid and personalized sense of locale (the streets are alive), and he shows us how the characters emerge from it – like Pius (Chinaza Uche), a hustler with a grin of devastating sincerity, or Grace, played by Tina Mba with a scary stern fierceness that she somehow normalizes. Grace's threatening personality grows right out of the harshness of Nigeria, a
25 place where everyone is scrambling for cash, and you're either toiling away at a dead-end job or have joined the underground culture of scam artists.

Pius, who is Eze's cousin, has been a scammer for years, a role he wears lightly, even though it means his existence is controlled by Smart (Bimbo Manuel), an officer in the country's nefarious police force who is basically a gang leader in uniform. Nigeria, as
30 this movie presents it, is a nation of law and disorder. And Eze has to find a way out. It's not just that the place is dangerous; we can see how the corruption saps his spirit. Yet he forms a connection with Pius, who could use a fellow hustler and promises to get Eze onto a plane out of the country. If this were a more sentimental movie, both young men might get what they were going for. As it is, only one does, leaving the other in the dust.

35 There's one terrific scam sequence in "Nigerian Prince" (the title, in fact, refers to a classic scam). Pius goes to the hotel room of a businessman and tries to sucker him into the "black money" scam, which involves hundred-dollar bills coated with black paint, which can be removed by an expensive array of chemicals, which the mark has to pay for, and that's the scam (since the bills are just construction paper). Everything about this sequence is

40 terrific, including the surprise that caps it. Yet "Nigerian Prince" would have been better if we saw more of this stuff. Okoro has bent over backwards not to make the poverty-row version of a glib crime thriller, but he shouldn't have bent so far.

That said, his refusal to provide us with the usual suspenseful payoffs creates its own disquieting social resonance. He's saying that there's no catharsis to this life – no ultimate
45 score that lends it all meaning. It's the scrambling-rat version of a hand-to-mouth existence. And any illusion of camaraderie is just another scam.

Source: https://variety.com/2018/film/reviews/nigerian-prince-review-1202982837/ [last access: 31/03/2023]

Tasks

1. Read the film review. Look up words and phrases you do not know yet in a (online) dictionary. You can also use the vocabulary aid for help.

2. *Comprehension:* Read the film review again and tick the correct end of the sentences a)–e).
   https://learningapps.org/watch?v=p04jcefpa23
   a) According to the author *Nigerian Prince* is a film about …
      ☐ a spy making his way through a scavenger nation.
      ☐ an American teenager making his way through a scavenger nation.
      ☐ a foreign agent in Nigeria.
   b) The name of the actor playing the role of Eze is …
      ☐ Faraday Okoro
      ☐ Pius Garba
      ☐ Antonio J. Bell
   c) The author writes that Okoro creates …
      ☐ a lively drama with authentic characters.
      ☐ a thriller with unrealistic characters.
      ☐ a boring setting with convincing characters.
   d) In the film, Nigeria is portrayed as a nation …
      ☐ struggling with foreigners.
      ☐ of disorder.
      ☐ with inhabitants sticking to the law.
   e) The film is …
      ☐ extremely sentimental.
      ☐ has no fantastic scam scene.
      ☐ socially disquieting.

3. *Comprehension:* Complete the sentences a)–e). https://learningapps.org/watch?v=pwqa4msdk23
   a) The film was directed by Faraday …
   b) "Black money" involves hundred-dollar bills coated with black …
   c) The genre of *Nigerian Prince* can be called a crime …
   d) The director of the film says there is no … to life.
   e) The film provides the viewer with no suspenseful …

4. *Vocabulary*: Match the English terms on the left with their corresponding definition on the right.
https://learningapps.org/watch?v=py1hd4yit23

1. ancestor	a) so. who collects things people have thrown away or left behind
2. heritage	b) lecture or motion picture describing a journey
3. grant	c) causing damage or destruction
4. hustler	d) person from whom one is descended (e.g. parents)
5. (to) soak up sth.	e) causing worry
6. devastating	f) sth. that is handed down or belongs to one by reason (e.g. of birth)
7. scavenger	g) extremely wicked, villainous
8. glib	h) to enjoy sth. as much as possible
9. nefarious	i) reaching over a big area
10. sprawling	j) an amount of money given to a person or organisation for a special purpose by another organisation
11. disquieting	k) thoughtlessly, superficially
12. travelogue	l) a person who employs fraudulent or unscrupulous methods to obtain money

5. Comment on the film review. With which aspects do you (not) agree?
6. Watch the extract from the TV show *The Simpsons* dealing with a Nigerian Prince scam. In class, comment on Moe's behaviour:
https://www.youtube.com/watch?v=HcMYZmPKThw [last access: 31/03/2023] [min. 0:47]
7. Discuss the question below with a partner and make notes on your results:
Why do so many people fall into the trap of the Nigerian Prince Scam every year?
8. Write your film review for the film *Nigerian Prince*.

Collector of Memories – Understanding a Nigerian short story

M 5

Collector of Memories is a story by Joshua Chizoma and was nominated for the Caine Prize shortlist in 2022. The Caine Prize is an important literary award for the best short story by African writers.

> **About the author:** Joshua Chizoma is a Nigerian writer. His works have been published or forthcoming in Prairie Schooner, AFREADA, Entropy Magazine, Kalahari Review, Prachya Review and elsewhere. His story, *A House Called Joy*, won the 2018 Kreative Diadem Prize in the Flash fiction category. Chizoma was shortlisted for the 2021 Afritondo Short Story Prize and won the 2020 Awele Creative Trust Short Story Prize. He is an alumnus of the 2019 Purple Hibiscus Creative Writing Workshop taught by Chimamanda Adichie.

Tasks

1. Read the first part of the short story. Look up words you do not know yet in a (online) dictionary.
2. *Comprehension:* Put the following events from the first part of *Collector of Memories* into their chronological order by writing the numbers 1 to 8 on the lines.
   https://learningapps.org/watch?v=pcieegrxt23
   ____ polytechnic
   ____ Aunty Rhoda
   ____ Regina and mother's fight
   ____ a baby is found
   ____ dating Chike
   ____ a lost key
   ____ mother is ill
   ____ a mother-daughter talk
3. *Vocabulary:* Match the English terms on the left with their German equivalent on the right.
   https://learningapps.org/watch?v=psgjsup1c23

1. abandoned	a) das Waschmittel
2. infraction	b) höflich, zuvorkommend
3. detergent	c) verformbar
4. indignity	d) die Schürze, der Kittel
5. decipherable	e) grässlich, schrecklich
6. (to) pepper so. with sth.	f) der Regelverstoß, das Vergehen
7. pinafore	g) der/die Analphabet/in
8. dire	h) kindlich, kindisch
9. illiterate	i) entzifferbar, entschlüsselbar
10. malleable	j) jmd. mit etw. übersäen
11. puerile	k) die Beleidigung, die Demütigung
12. courteous	l) verlassen, verstoßen

4. Skim through the extract of the short story again. Sum up important information about the protagonist Chibusonma by making notes next to the text.

5. What is typical Nigerian in the story? Match the Nigerian elements in *Collector of Memories* with their definition. https://learningapps.org/watch?v=pw2ejr2q523

Nigerian elements
Ramsey Nouah
Super Story
UTME
harmattan cold
JAMB
Cabin Biscuit
Ankara dress

Definition
colourful African-Nigerian fashion
Nigerian university entrance exam
Nigerian actor and director
Nigerian entrance exam for tertiary-level institutions
Nigerian television series
Nigerian plain hard sweet biscuit
West African season between end of November and March

6. How could the story continue? Note down ideas for a possible ending of the story.

Ideas for an ending of the story:

Extract from the short story *Collector of Memories* by Joshua Chizoma	Notes:
Mother made me a collector of memories. She taught me that we carry our histories in sacks tied around our necks, adding to their burdens as years lengthen our lives. Each time she told me about the night she found me, she added to my collection. We'd be in the middle of watching a movie and she'd go, 'Do you know you did not cry the first two weeks I brought you home? I was so scared you were dumb.' Or, 'I can't believe you like custard now. As a baby, you only tolerated pap, hot pap like this that did not even burn your throat.' She'd then launch into a narrative punctuated by laughter, pausing only to confirm some detail from her sisters or to disagree with them over one. Over the years, I learned that she found me on a new year's eve, right about the time the harmattan cold was just picking up, but not boil-water-even-for-doing-dishes freezing yet. That I was wearing a yellow pinafore, swaddled in a blanket that smelled of talcum powder, and that there'd been two different earrings in my ear lobes. I also learned that she found me in an empty carton – a Cabin Biscuit box, she added later. She reached into the air to pluck those memories whenever she wanted to throw jabs at me about my skin, or my face, or my penchant for eating Cabin Biscuits. However, the first time we had that heart to heart, it had been because of a fight she had with our neighbour, Regina. We lived in a compound where the houses were spread so far apart as though to pretend it wasn't a public yard. The two-bedroom bungalows squatted in a semi-circle, huddled together like American football players before take-off. It surprised everyone that the landlord who'd had the good sense to build each bungalow separately, would then do something as foolish as making the toilets, shared one to three bungalows, communal. The toilets were often the cause of quarrels. The fights were about who did not flush the toilets well (and left it for their slaves to flush abi?[1]) or who used only one sachet of detergent to improperly wash the toilet (shey those of us that wash with two sachets na fool we be?[2]) or who lost the shared key and was taking their time replacing it. This last reason was the cause of the fight between Mother and Regina. Regina's son had lost their own key. They'd asked us for ours and had been sharing it with us before the boy, a whole twelve-year-old dimkpa[3], lost our own key too. Mother had had to suffer the indignity of asking our other neighbour for their key any time we wanted to use the toilet. That day, she made me practically run from school because she was pressed. When we got home, she was about to grab the key when she remembered that it had still not been replaced. Instead of going to ask our other neighbour for theirs, she headed for Regina's house, her handbag still slung over her shoulder. Regina's church's house fellowship was in full swing when my mother knocked. The tenants had had meetings about these evening fellowships because the attendees sometimes forgot that Regina's parlour was neither their church auditorium nor soundproof. That day, Regina first sent out her	

Extract from the short story *Collector of Memories* by Joshua Chizoma

45 son to tell my mother to come back later. When Mother refused, she came out herself.
She wore the face of someone who was being courteous on the pain of death. 'Ah, neighbour. What is this thing that cannot wait for me to finish listening to God's word?' she asked, retying her wrapper laboriously.
50 My mother told her she was sorry to interrupt but that she wanted to collect money for the new key.
'Ah, I no get plenty money here. In the evening na me go come find you. Abeg, no vex.'[4]
But Mother insisted. She was firm and malleable at the same time, using the
55 tone she used when telling the obnoxious parents of her pupils that, no, she would not go to their house to conduct lessons for their children, they'd have to come to hers. And it worked, because Regina went in and came out with the money scrunched up in her fist. Perhaps, it was the way Regina gave her the money, almost throwing it at her, that my mother had had to clap the air
60 to catch the notes. Or maybe it was not really the money that was peppering her, maybe my mother just wanted to be petty, because as she turned to leave, she gave as a parting shot:
'Do I blame you? Is it not because I am sharing a compound with an illiterate like you?'
65 'Don't even come for me. O gini di[5]? Who does not know children make mistakes?' Regina shouted.
My mother could not have aimed her punch lower. Everyone in the compound knew Regina's story and how she'd clawed her way from poverty.
'If your world is complete, go and fetch water with a basket na. Nonsense
70 and nonsense.'
'It is okay,' her church members said. They were standing on her verandah; an emergency recess had been called, no doubt.
'Leave me. Every time she will be carrying face for somebody like say na she better pass. She thinks we do not know her shameful secret. If I open this my
75 mouth for her eh, she will pack out of this compound.'
When my mother heard this, she dropped her bag and every pretence of civility with it.
'You see that thing you want to say, you must say it today oo[6].'
She clapped her hands together and came to stand in front of Regina, pushing
80 her breasts onto her face.
'E pass say I pick child for gutter? E pass am? Oya, talk na?'[7]
Regina did not respond. She was probably too shocked to. Even I had not expected the drama to take such a swift turn.
'Good. I think say you no dey[5] fear.' My mother turned around then and
85 saw me. Her face became a mélange of conflicting emotions: anger, shame, remorse. But anger won. She grabbed me and said, 'Who asked you to follow me?' Although she hadn't asked me not to.
That night she bristled with anger, and even grading papers did not help. Eventually, she dropped the pen and called me to her side.

Extract from the short story *Collector of Memories* by Joshua Chizoma	Notes:

'Chibusonma, come here,' she said.

I walked over from the sofa to the single chair she was sitting on. She shifted and I squeezed in with her. She stroked my arm, and I could feel the flames within her tempering, losing their rage.

Aunty looked up from her phone, and Chidinma paused the movie she was watching, trapping Ramsey Nouah's face on the screen. 'It is better you hear it from my mouth,' she began.

***

It was one of those things you knew. The way yes was yes and no was no. They were definites, and I could hold them to my breast, my history. That night, my mother did not romanticize the idea that I was an abandoned child she had picked up. She said it in a matter-of-fact way, like she was teaching me to memorize numbers, like she wanted me to know just for the sake of it. As I grew older and recognized that bricks and sticks sometimes are no match for words, I was grateful. Because after that day I realized how things could shape-shift if you had no sight. Snide remarks and snarky jokes found context and became decipherable. But because my mother did not burden my story with the weight of shame, I had none to spare. Even beyond that, I was hemmed in on every side by love, from my mother and her two sisters. Their love cushioned the effect of the taunts from the other children, fashioned me an armour that bricks and sticks and words could not penetrate.

Rhoda, whom everyone called Aunty, was the oldest and had a hairdressing salon. Her sisters did not go to her shop. They said her hands were 'painful', although they made sure it was only the walls of our house that heard them say so. She loved 'living' and was the one who bought the TV and paid for the light bill. Each time the bill came, she'd divide the sum and remind her sisters each morning to contribute, placing her share on the centre table so 'everyone could see she had done her part'. Seven out of ten times she'd eventually go to pay it herself, gaining monopoly over the TV remote and daring anyone to change the channel even when she fell asleep watching Super Story.

Chidinma, the middle child, sold recharge cards and phone accessories. She was the most generous of the three, the one with the least savings too. They used to say, 'Except Chidinma does not have, that's why she will not give you. If she has money and you have a need, forget it.'

Mother was a primary four teacher. She taught the class for years, even when she got her teacher's training certificate, even when she got a university degree through distance learning. She refused to leave for another class. Her name was Florence, but most people knew her as 'Aunty Primary Four'.

Mother mothered me exclusively when it came to meting out punishment. Her sisters would tally all my infractions, waiting for her return so they'd bear witness. At the end my mother would respond, 'You mean she was this stupid, and you did not beat her?' incredulity lacing her tone, after which she'd drag me close and give me a whooping herself. But apart from this area,

Extract from the short story *Collector of Memories* by Joshua Chizoma

135 the three sisters fed me their different flavours of motherhood. It usually was Aunty who bought me clothes and made my hair every weekend. Saturday evenings she'd bring out the kitchen stool to our corridor, spread her legs, and trap my body within her warmth. Sometimes it was a whole family affair, with Mother shining a torch and Chidinma separating and handing
140 out the attachments. I did not have the luxury of protesting her painful hand. It was enough that I debuted a new hairstyle each Monday morning. Pain was a small price to pay.

Chidinma bought me the UTME form for the polytechnic I ended up going to. I'd written JAMB the first time and failed. When I wrote it for the second time
145 and failed again, Mother did not say anything. I knew she was beginning to think that the first failure was not a fluke. I passed the third time with a small margin, and Chidinma bought me a form for the polytechnic.

That day, she called me to her shop, brought out the papers, and in a voice that entertained no arguments said, 'Fill this thing, my friend.'
150 I stared at the paper on the table. None of my friends went to the polytechnic. Who would? University students were the *shit*. They returned home only during the holidays, bamboo stalk thin and sporting lingo that included 'projects' and 'lectures' and 'handouts'. They got away with many things, especially those who went to schools with ear-famous names like the
155 University of Ibadan and the University of Nigeria. Plus, everybody and their nannies knew that it was the 'not-so-bright' students who settled for the polytechnic.

I considered my options for a while. They weren't many.

'I am going to live off-campus. I will not be going from the house,' I said.
160 'Okay,' Chidinma replied. We both understood it was a bargain. That was a compromise she could take to her sisters.

***

I started dating Chike in my final year, four years ago. He was a customer care agent at a mobile phone company and had once helped me do a SIM
165 card welcome back. Chike was affable and took the job of being a nice person very seriously. He was the kind of person who would never refuse going the extra mile but complained while doing the task. Good-natured complaints about how it was taking his time or how he was tired, in such a way that it was not really grumbling, seeming almost like a normal conversation.
170 I moved in with him after graduation. By that time, I had spent so many weekends at his place that the one time I did not come home on a Monday, Mother did not bother asking me what happened. It was like a natural occurrence, like night giving birth to day or weeds sprouting in the rainy season. One day I was living with my mother and her two sisters, the next I
175 was going from Chike's house to the bank where I worked.

Every time he mentioned marriage, I packed my bags and went to Binez hotels down the street. The manager knew me and usually assigned me the one room with good netting on the door. Chike always came for me after two days or so; the longest he'd stayed without me was seven days. The last time

Extract from the short story *Collector of Memories* by Joshua Chizoma	Notes:
180 he came to pick me, he had been dripping with righteous anger and asked me whether it was not time to stop my childishness. Whenever I think of it, I wonder if I hadn't moved in with Chike, if my attention hadn't been consumed by that puerile drama we were intent on performing, whether the events that followed afterwards would have been 185 different. Whether I would have caught my mother's sickness earlier, or more appropriately, traced its root and found its cure. But like a hen, I took my eyes off Mother for a minute – such that I was unaware of how dire things were at home the Friday Aunty and Chidinma visited me at work – and a kite swooped in. 190 That day, I was wearing a new Ankara dress. Chidinma sat on a plastic chair in the reception area and Aunty came to stand before me, speaking to me in snatches while I attended to customers. In between clearing withdrawal slips and receiving deposits, Aunty managed to tell me to come by the house in the evening for an urgent matter and I was able to feign that the most 195 pressing thing then was the zip of the new dress cutting into my back, and not the scary reality of what it meant for my aunts to visit me at my place of work to summon me home. *Source:* https://www.afritondo.com/afritondo/collector-of-memories [last access 31/03/2023] (shortened for didactic reasons)	

1 **abi?:** right? – 2 **shey those of us that wash with two sachets na fool we be?:** Are people who wash with two sachets fools? – 3 **dimkpa:** (Nigerian Igbo language) brave person – 4 **In the evening na me go come find you. Abeg, no vex:** I'll visit you in the evening. Please don't be angry – 5 **O gini di?:** What is it? – 6 **oo:** highlights the importance of the statement – 7 **E pass say I pick child for gutter? E pass am? Oya, talk na:** Did somebody say that I found the child in the gutter? Did I find it there? Come on, talk now – 8 **dey:** they

7. Read the end of the story: https://www.afritondo.com/afritondo/collector-of-memories [last access 31/03/2023] Compare your ideas with the actual ending of the story.
8. *Comprehension*: Tick the correct ending of the sentences a)–e).
   https://learningapps.org/watch?v=p0r7ywa8k23
   a) Chibusonma was taken away from …
      ☐ her father   ☐ her grandmother   ☐ her mother
   b) The protagonist's birth mother is described as …
      ☐ friendly   ☐ crazy   ☐ too old
   c) Chibusonma's family thinks Chibusonma's foster mother is …
      ☐ cursed   ☐ poisoned   ☐ being robbed
   d) Chibusonma and Chike's relationship can be described as …
      ☐ perfect   ☐ difficult   ☐ pure friendship
   e) Chibusonma's birth mother …
      ☐ forgives her foster mother   ☐ wishes her foster mother to die   ☐ does not talk to her.
9. Discuss the questions a)–c) about the short story in groups of three to four students:
   a) What does the beginning of the story, "we carry our histories in sacks tied around our necks, adding to their burdens as years lengthen our lives" mean?
   b) Which role does education play for a) Chibusonma and b) Chibusonma's (foster) mother?
   c) Why is it so difficult for the protagonist to feel loved?

M 6

Collector of Memories: A typical Nigerian short story? – An Internet research

The short story *Collector of Memories* represents typical Nigerian cultural elements. Here, you will find background information that will help you to understand the short story better.

Research team 1: Lack of education and illiteracy

Because many Nigerian children and teenagers do not attend school on a regular basis and quite a lot of public institutions are unorganised, approximately 10.5 million children are not able to read and write properly nor can they do maths. In addition to this, corruption has an enormous influence on Nigeria's educational system. Many teachers are neither well educated nor well paid. Highly qualified teachers are rare and not very well paid either. The curriculum of many public schools is out-dated and private tuition is expensive and only affordable by a very small part of Nigerian people.

© peeterv/Getty Images/E+

Useful links for your research:
- https://baysplanet.org/nigeria-is-careless-about-child-illiteracy-and-heres-what-we-know/
- https://leadership.ng/that-report-on-illiteracy-level-in-nigeria/

Research team 2: Social inequality

Nigeria is home to some of the richest and of the poorest people on earth. The country's economic inequality has reached extreme levels, despite being the largest economy in Africa. The country has an expanding economy with abundant human capital and the economic potential to lift millions out of poverty. The combined wealth of Nigeria's five richest men – $ 29.9 billion – could end extreme poverty at a national level, yet 5 million people face hunger. More than 112 million people are living in poverty in Nigeria, yet the country's richest person would have to spend $ 1 million a day for 42 years to exhaust his/her fortune.

© marisa Arregui/iStock/Getty Images Plus

Useful links for your research:
- https://www.oxfam.org/en/nigeria-extreme-inequality-numbers
- https://leadership.ng/social-inequality-threat-to-nigerias-existence-gov-fayemi/

Research team 3: Witchcraft and Juju

Many Nigerian people believe in the supernatural. Therefore, witches, witchcraft, superstition, and Juju – a spiritual belief system using amulets and spells as religious practice – are often portrayed in Nigerian literature as well as Nigerian films. According to that belief system, Juju spells can be used in a good or bad way. Juju can help people, or it can be used in a nefarious and destructive way.

© Britannicus84/iStock/Getty Images Plus

Useful links for your research:
- https://www.bbc.com/news/world-africa-50742414
- https://cultureready.org/blog/encountering-different-beliefs-nigeria-and-witchcraft

Tasks

1. Work in pairs: read the info box assigned to you with an example of a typical cultural element in Nigerian literature. Gather additional background knowledge by doing Internet research on your topic.

2. Be ready to give a 3-minute presentation of your results to the other pairs and add their findings to your notes.

3. Have a close look at the short story *Collector of Memories* again. Where and how are the three cultural elements represented? Copy the table below and take notes.

Nigerian cultural elements	References in *Collector of Memories*
Lack of education and illiteracy	
Social inequality	
Witchcraft and Juju	

4. Watch the short documentary *A child accused of witchcraft* by UNICEF: https://www.youtube.com/watch?v=MOF4-iGoetw [last access 31/03/2023] [min. 03:18]

   Compare and contrast its content to the short story. What are similarities and what are differences between the documentation and the short story?

M 7

The Girl with the Louding Voice – Putting an extract into context

The Girl with the Louding Voice is Abi Daré's first novel. It is about a teenage girl living in a world of child-marriage, abuse, social inequality and sexism looking for a chance to find "her own voice" and a better life.

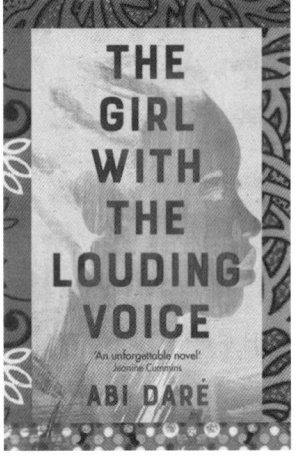

© Hodder & Stoughton Ltd   © Penguin Random House

***The Girl with the Louding Voice* – a short summary**
Adunni is a 14-year-old girl who lives with her poor family in a small village close to Lagos. She would like to get an education, but her family does not have enough money to pay for school or university fees. To earn some money for the family, Adunni's father sells her as a bride to a much older man who lives with his other two wives in a big house close to Adunni's village. Morufu – her new husband – rapes her and she runs away to Lagos. There she is employed by a rich lady called "Big Madam" who abuses her and uses her as a slave to do the household. Adunni meets a nice lady and tries to get an education with her help.

The Girl with the Louding Voice **by Abi Daré** (extract from Chapter 1)

This morning, Papa call me inside the parlour. He was sitting inside the sofa with no cushion and looking me. Papa have this way of looking me one kind. As if he wants to be flogging[1] me for no reason, as if I am carrying shit inside my cheeks and when I open mouth to talk, the whole place be smelling of it. "Sah[2]?" I say, kneeling down and putting
5 my hand in my back. "You call me?" "Come close," Papa say.
I know he want to tell me something bad. I can see it inside his eyes; his eyesballs have the dull[3] of a brown stone that been sitting inside hot sun for too long. He have the same eyes when he was telling me, three years ago, that I must stop my educations. That time, I was oldest of all in my class and all the childrens was always calling me "Aunty."
10 Jimoh, one foolish boy in the class was laughing me one day as I was walking to sit on my table. "Aunty Adunni," Jimoh was saying, "Why are you still in primary school when all your mates are in secondary school?" I know Jimoh was wanting me to cry and be feeling bad, but I look the devil-child inside his eyes and he look me back. I look his upside-down triangle shape head, and he look me back. Then I sticked my out my tongue and pull my
15 two ears and say, "Why are you not inside bicycle shop when your head is like bicycle

seat?" The class, that day, it was shaking with all the laughters from the childrens, and I was feeling very clever with myself until Teacher Shola slap her ruler on the table three times and say: "Quiet!"

20 It was when I was getting more better in my Plus, Minus and English that Papa say I must to stop because he didn't have moneys for school fees. I tell you true, the day I stop school, and the day my Mama was dead is worst day of my life. […] Papa make noise with his throat and lean on the wood back of the sofa with no cushion. The cushion have spoil because our last born Kayus, he have done too many piss inside it. Since the boy was a baby, he been pissing as if it is a curse. The piss mess the cushion, so Mama make Kayus to
25 be sleeping on it for pillow. We have a Tee-Vee[3] in our parlour; it didn't work. […] We even putting small flower vase on top it, a crown on the prince head. When we have visitor, Papa will be doing as if it is working and be saying, "Adunni, come and put evening news for Mr Bada to watch." And me, I will be responding, "Papa, the remote controlling, it have missing." Then Papa will shake his head and say to Mr Bada, "Those useless children, they
30 have lost the remote control again. Come, let us sit outside, drink and forget the sorrows of our country, Nigeria."

Source: Daré, A. (2020): The Girl with the Louding Voice. UK: Hodder & Stoughton. P.3/4. (abbreviated for didactic reasons)

1 **(to) flog so.:** to beat so. with a whip or a stick to punish the person – 2 **sah:** sir (Nigerian Pidgin English) – 3 **dull:** not clear or bright – 3 **Tee-Vee:** TV (short for television) in Nigerian Pidgin English

Tasks

1. Nigeria is Africa's most successful economy. Unfortunately, a lot of Nigerian children, teenagers and adults are still uneducated and are not part of that success.
    a) Talk to a partner: based on your knowledge give possible reasons why education is difficult to achieve for many Nigerians.
    b) Watch the short documentary *Getting kids back to school in northern Nigeria* by DW The 77 Percent:
    https://www.youtube.com/watch?v=hahxW8jYMwU [last access 31/03/2023] [min. 03:25]
    Take notes on how rural northern Nigeria tries to improve its education.
2. Read the summary of the novel *The Girl with the Louding Voice*. Then read the extract of the novel and sum up the information about Adunni and her family.
3. With a partner, use your background knowledge about Nigeria to discuss the following statement of Adduni's father:
    "Come, let us sit outside, drink and forget the sorrows of our country, Nigeria."
4. Compare the extract from the novel with the short story *Collector of Memories*.
5. **Expert task:** Read the extract of the novel again and focus on its language. Identify typical elements of "Nigerian English".

M 8

The Girl with the Louding Voice – What does education mean to Adunni?

Infobox: Education in Nigeria
One in every five of the world's out-of-school children is in Nigeria. Even though primary education is officially free and compulsory, about 10.5 million of the country's children aged 5–14 years are not in school. […] Getting out-of-school children back into education poses a massive challenge. Gender, like geography and poverty, is an important factor in the pattern of educational marginalization. […] The education deprivation in northern Nigeria is driven by various factors, including economic barriers and socio-cultural norms and practices that discourage attendance in formal education, especially for girls. Ensuring educational provision in predominantly rural areas and the impact of insurgency in the northeast present significant challenges. In north-eastern and north-western states, 29 percent and 35 percent of Muslim children, respectively, receive Qur'anic education, which does not include basic skills such as literacy and numeracy. The government considers children attending such schools to be officially out-of-school. Source: https://www.unicef.org/nigeria/education [last access 31/03/2023]

novel extracts	comment
"My mama say education will give me a voice. I want more than just a voice, Ms. Tia. I want a louding voice," I say. "I want to enter a room and people will hear me even before I open my mouth to be speaking. I want to live in this life and help many people so that when I grow old and die, I will still be living through the people I am helping." (pp. 263/64)	
"Now I know that speaking good English is not the measure of intelligent mind and sharp brain. English is only a language, like Yoruba and Igbo and Hausa. Nothing about it is so special, nothing about it makes anybody have sense." (p. 287)	
"That day, I tell myself that even if I am not getting anything in this life, I will go to school. I will finish my primary and secondary and university schooling and become teacher because I don't just want to be having any kind voice ... I want a louding voice." (p. 23)	
"When I walk away from the library, I don't close the door. I leave it open for the spirit in all the books to be following me." (p. 310)	
"Why will I fill up the world with sad childrens that are not having a chance to go to school? Why make the world to be one big, sad, silent place because all the childrens are not having a voice?" (p. 59)	

Source: Daré, A. (2020): The Girl with the Louding Voice. UK: Hodder & Stoughton. Pp. 263/64, p. 287, p. 23, p. x and p.59

Tasks

1. In class, comment on the Nigerian proverb, "It takes a whole village to raise a child", and point out its relevance for the novel *The Girl with the Louding Voice*.
2. Read the text about education in Nigeria by UNICEF and explain: **a)** Why are Nigerian girls more disadvantaged than boys? **b)** What are possible reasons why one out of five out-of-school children worldwide lives in Nigeria?
3. Read the extracts from the novel and comment on the value of education for Adunni.

The Girl with the Louding Voice – Watching an interview with the author

M 9

Abi Daré, the author of the *The Girl with the Louding Voice*, is an educated Nigerian born woman. With her debut novel and New York Times bestseller, Daré aims at speaking up for Nigerian women and supporting the fight against poverty and child-marriage in Nigeria.

> **About the author:** Abi Daré grew up in Lagos, Nigeria and has lived in the UK for eighteen years. She studied law at the University of Wolverhampton and has an M.Sc. in International Project Management from Glasgow Caledonian University as well as an MA in Creative Writing at Birkbeck University of London. *The Girl with the Louding Voice* won The Bath Novel Award for unpublished manuscripts in 2018 and was also selected as a finalist in 2018 The Literary Consultancy Pen Factor competition. Abi lives in Essex with her husband and two daughters, who inspired her to write her debut novel.
>
> Source: https://www.goodreads.com/book/show/50214741-the-girl-with-the-louding-voice [last access 31/03/2023]

© Picture: Dudley Council/Wikimedia cc by sa 2.0

Tasks

1. Read the short biography of Abi Daré in the box. Then watch the interview with the author: https://www.youtube.com/watch?v=jIQOPneQDco [last access 31/01/2023] [min. 04:01]
   While watching, decide whether the statements a)–e) are true or false:

	Statement	True	False
a)	Adunni's father talks to her about the importance of education.		
b)	Adunni's "voice" helps her to become a part of Nigeria's society.		
c)	The protagonist focuses on helping other people and herself.		
d)	Author Abi Daré sees education as an everlasting investment in her future.		
e)	Abi Daré uses education as a weapon for herself and her family.		

2. With a partner, answer the questions a) and b):
   a) How is the protagonist Adunni described by the author?
   b) What were Daré's main intentions to write the novel?
3. Discuss in class: A novel set in Nigeria dealing with education and academic support is important for Nigerian readers and readers of Nigerian origin.

M 10

What are Nigerian Teenagers up to These Days? – Reading a newspaper article

Nigerian teenagers and teenage culture have undergone an incredible change in the last decade. Still connected with some traditional values, globalisation has had an influence on the process of growing-up in Nigeria.

© Wirestock/iStock/Getty Images Plus

© DragonImages/iStock/Getty Images Plus

What are Nigerian Teenagers up to These Days?
by BellaNaija Features
In ancient Nigeria, becoming a teenager meant you were now a big man/woman and you were already 'ripe' for marriage. This meant that you would be expected to start owning your farm, know how to haggle[1] in the marketplace, know how to take care of the home, your spouse and children. Everyone looked forward to becoming adults – independent
5 and free from the shackles[2] of their parents' instructions.
But it is not so today, especially now that there's education (which takes the most part of your teenage years) and youngsters dream of having white-collar jobs. The economy is also less promising than it was in the past, so today's youths want to *hit it big* before starting a family. Who can blame them? *Nobody likes suffering.*
10 With the advent of technology, the world becoming one global village and many people embracing liberalism, freedom of expression and so on. Our teenagers are now going haywire!!! Before, kids used to fear their parents – real fear (sprinkled with small love). If you are in a public place, every part of your parent's face means something. If they raise their eyebrows or squint their eyes, immediately your brain will send a signal to your
15 body to behave. The worst part of it is if you go visiting and the host is offering you all sorts of things. Once you look at your mum and she says *"collect it"* but her lips are twitching, her eyes are blinking and she's smiling menacingly[3], you will just respect yourself and lie that your stomach is full.
But now, these kids will just clock 18 *peren*[4] and start "Oh mum, I'm no longer a kid, I'm
20 now a big boy" *Big wetin?* If you meet a typical Nigerian parent, they will remind you that as long as you're still under their roof and eating their food, you are not big. If you're not careful *sef,* this reminder will be accompanied by slaps and *konks*[5]. *Big for where?*
[…]
Our teenagers are no longer the timid "my daddy says I should be a doctor" ones anymore.
25 In today's world, they are doing amazing things – especially with technology.
Today's teenagers have moved from the traditional 'go to school, be in the science or commercial department (don't forget that the arts are for the *olodos*[6]) and then become a Doctor, Engineer or Banker.' Teenagers are better exposed and have more knowledgeable

dreams. It is common to hear teenagers say things like "I want to be a dancer, an artist, a
writer, a tech guru, a graphics designer" and so on. That's because with technology comes
new job roles, better enlightenment, and creativity. What's more? You get to have fun
while doing your dream job. Our teenagers have noticed this and can't wait to tap into this.
We also have the overzealous[7] teenagers. The *"I don't want to work for anybody. I'm going
to be a CEO and establish my own business"* ones. When these teenagers are talking,
adults will just be *yinmu-ing*[8], knowing fully well that they will soon wake up to smell the
coffee.

So what are Nigerian teenagers up to?

Some are hiding at the back of the house rapping. They have J.Cole and M'I's albums
and they are *jamming* to it *big time.* With music being one of Nigeria's biggest and most
successful exports, many of our teenagers want to become musicians. You can find them
writing Simi's lyrics in a book or memorizing so they can later sing it in the bathroom.

Our teenagers want to become footballers, they would have loved painting, but they are
not sure if artists in Nigeria are making any money. But footballers? They make *badt*
money. The goal is not to play for Nigeria, or maybe they can just start from Nigeria and
get signed by bigger clubs in the long run.

Some of our teenagers are also painting their faces and preparing to be supermodels. The
most Beautiful Girl in Nigeria goes home with millions of naira while the best graduating
students get a laptop at most (and that's if it is not *audio laptop*). So legs – check, skin –
check, brain – check and every other thing – check. Our teenagers are good to go.

On a more serious note, Nigerian teenagers are doing amazingly well. Unlike many Nigerian
youths, these teenagers have, from an early age, made a decision on what they want to
do and in some cases, they already know how to get what they want. Our teenagers are
making video games, apps, animations, speaking up against injustice and lending their
voices to the many wrongs in our society.

You cannot help but envy their boldness, zeal, and the ferocity of their dreams. They are
shutting out all societal expectations and carving a path for themselves.

They are starting out early – very early and it is soothing to realize that many of them
know what they are doing. […]

Source: https://www.bellanaija.com/2019/11/what-are-nigerian-teenagers-up-to-these-days/ (21 November 2019) [last access 31/03/2003] (abbreviated for didactic reasons)

1 **(to) haggle:** feilschen, handeln – 2 **shackle:** die Fessel – 3 **menacingly:** bedrohlich – 4 **peren:** Nigerian beads – 5 **konk:** a hit on so.'s head with one's knuckles – 6 **olodo:** a dull or stupid person – 7 **overzealous:** showing too much energy or enthusiasm – 8 **yinmu-ing:** twitching

Tasks

1. *Comprehension:* Read the newspaper article about teenagers in modern Nigeria and decide whether the following statements are true or false.
   https://learningapps.org/watch?v=p6b3xvc4323

	Statement	True	False
a)	In ancient Nigeria, many teenagers already had children.		
b)	Academic success is important for many young Nigerians today.		
c)	Many Nigerians stay with their parents till the age of 30.		
d)	There has been a major change from traditional to modern values in Nigeria.		
e)	Modern Nigerian music is also very famous in other countries.		

2. *Vocabulary:* Match the English terms on the left with their corresponding definition on the right.
https://learningapps.org/watch?v=pu4qyom3k23

1. (to) carve
2. timid
3. ancient
4. naira
5. (to) go haywire
6. spouse
7. (to) raise
8. (to) jam

a) to stop working properly
b) a person's husband or wife
c) to cut into wood or stone to make sth.
d) to play music informally together with others without practising
e) to lift sth. up
f) very old, from an old time
g) shy and nervous, easily scared
h) Nigerian currency

3. Copy the Venn diagram below onto a sheet of paper. In groups of four, have a close look at the article again and fill in the diagram: What is typical for Nigerian teenagers (left circle). Add what is typical for German teenagers (right circle). Identify elements both teenage cultures have in common and write them into the middle.

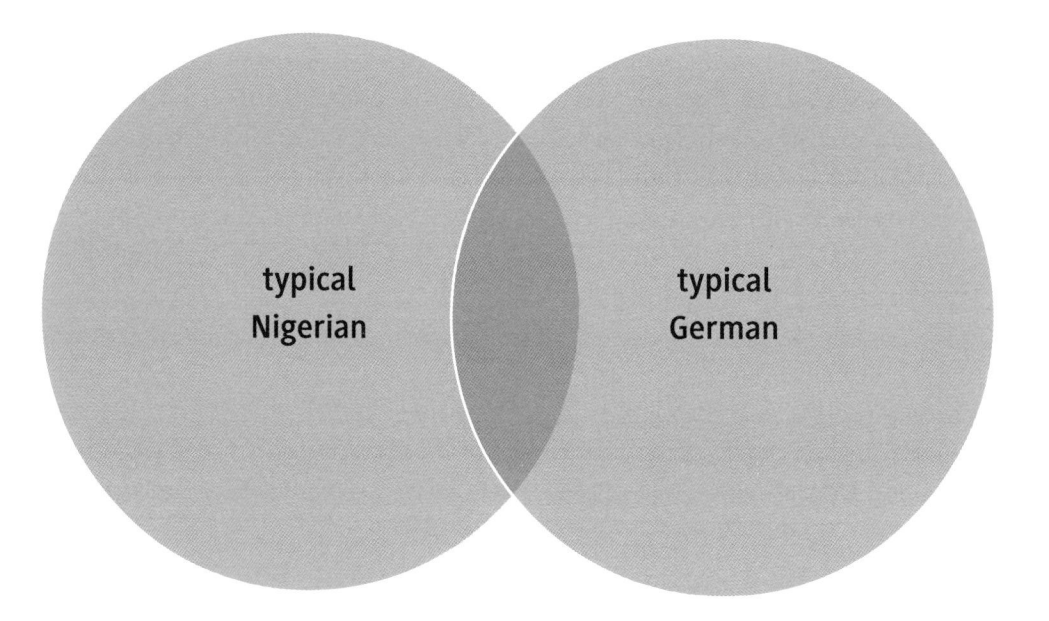

typical Nigerian | **typical German**

Hinweise und Erwartungshorizonte

Hinweise (M 1 und M 2)

1./2. Stunde

Ziel: Die Schülerinnen und Schüler lernen erste Inhalte des Films *„Nigerian Prince"* anhand des Filmtrailers kennen. Sie vergleichen die neue Heimat des Protagonisten Eze, Nigeria, mit den USA und vollziehen die Gefühle und Konflikte des Protagonisten nach.

Didaktisch-methodische Hinweise (M 1)

Der Filmtrailer fungiert als **Einstieg** in die Unterrichtsreihe und bahnt einen ersten Zugang zum Film *„Nigerian Prince"* an. Die Lehrkraft geht vor dem ersten Anschauen und nachdem die Lernenden die **Infobox** (*task 1*) gelesen haben im Unterrichtsgespräch auf die **Zweideutigkeit des Filmtitels** ein. Der Begriff steht, neben seiner wörtlichen Bedeutung, für eine in Nigeria weitverbreitete Form des Internetbetrugs. Hierbei fordern Betrügerinnen und Betrüger unter falscher Identität Geld für spezielle Leistungen und Investitionen ein, tauchen jedoch nach einer Anzahlung mit dem Geld unter. Anhand des Trailers erfahren die Schülerinnen und Schüler erste wichtige Details über die Situation des Protagonisten Eze und dessen unterschiedlichen Lebensbedingungen in den USA und Nigeria. Da Eze sich in einem ähnlichen Alter wie die Lernenden befinden dürfte, wird ein hohes Identifikationspotenzial geschaffen. Gleichzeitig wiederholen und vertiefen die Schülerinnen und Schüler ihr Grundlagenwissen über Filmtrailer, indem sie typische **Trailer-Merkmale** identifizieren und ihr Hör-Seh-Verstehen sichern.

Sicherung (M 1)

Über ihre Ergebnisse aus der *while-viewing task 2 a)* tauschen sich die Schülerinnen und Schüler anhand der *think-pair-share* Methode aus.

Den Abschluss der Unterrichtsstunde bildet ein Rückbezug zum Filmtitel und den damit verbundenen Internetbetrug, indem die Lernenden anhand der Hintergrundinformationen zum Scam 419 (siehe Infobox) das Verhalten der Figuren im Trailer thematisch einordnen (*task 2 b*).

Digitalhinweis (M 2)

Der Film *„Nigerian Prince"* wird über den **Onlinestreaming-Dienst Netflix** präsentiert. Da erfahrungsgemäß mindestens jede/r zweite Lernende über einen Netflix-Zugang verfügt, sehen die Schülerinnen und Schüler die Filmauszüge entweder über ihre privaten Zugänge oder im Klassenzimmer über den Zugang der Lehrkraft an. Sollte die Lehrkraft kein Netflix-Konto besitzen, ist es möglich, kurzfristig und unkompliziert online ein Netflix-Konto ab ca. 4,99 Euro pro Monat einzurichten. Das Konto bringt keine vertragliche Bindung mit sich und ist monatlich online kündbar.

Hausaufgabe

Die Lernenden schauen den Rest des Films zu Hause an und legen ihren Fokus dabei auf den Internetbetrug (*task 3*).

Erwartungshorizont (M 1)

1.
- ☐ There is an emotional beginning.
- ✓ The protagonist is introduced.
- ✓ The setting is introduced.
- ✓ The title of the film is shown.
- ✓ The trailer uses different scenes to show beginning, middle and ending.
- ✓ There are short conversations between the characters.
- ☐ The trailer shows the official beginning of the film.
- ✓ The trailer builds to a climax and stops (= cliff-hanger technique).
- ✓ The final shot has a lasting effect on the audience.
- ✓ There is a person telling the character's story (= voice-over technique).

2. a)

Eze	• Nigerian American teenage boy visiting his aunt and cousin in Nigeria • does not have a return ticket to fly back home • is in a bad mood, does not want to be in Nigeria • tries to help his cousin doing illegal things to buy a ticket back to the USA • has a conflict with his mother and his aunt • dislikes Nigeria; thinks of himself as "only" an American
Pius	• is Eze's cousin • a fraud (Nigerian scammer) • has problems with the Nigerian police • is in danger, needs money • receives help from his cousin Eze to get back his money

b)
- Eze's cousin Pius is involved in various Nigerian Prince online scams.
- Pius has problems with the Nigerian police due to his illegal activities.
- Eze would like to help Pius and also try to be a Nigerian scammer to get money for his flight back to the USA.

Erwartungshorizont (M 2)

1.

Scene [time]	Typical Nigerian	Typical American (Western)
Eze at the airport [min. 3:50–8:30]	– Eze has to pay money to get his luggage (bribe). – Nigerian corruption, illegal – less corruption with white American/Australian people	– passport control: Eze is American-Nigerian and can go to Nigeria without difficulties – Australian way of dealing with situations (UN guy)

Scene [time]	Typical Nigerian	Typical American (Western)
Eze at his aunt's place [min. 8:50–12:40]	– power-out, lack of electricity, „high-people" arrange that – Eze has to share a bed/room with his aunt → lack of privacy – no Internet in his aunt's house – aunt = professor (has her own "big" house)	– Eze has his own room (privacy) – modern technology: Apple computer and Internet access – his mother works in a hospital (seems to be well paid)
Welcome to Lagos [min. 24:00–28:00]	– typical Nigerian city – merchants, hawkers in the streets – colourful – crowded streets – Internet café with anti-scam-sign – slow Internet connection – Eze's cousin is an Internet scammer (illegal job) – Nigerian food – Igbo states – Igbo land	– use of social media – online shopping – Nigerian food (hamburgers) versus American food (hamburgers)

2.
- Eze's time in Nigeria is very different from his life in the USA.
- lack of luxury and comfort (electricity, Wi-Fi connection, American food etc.)
- lack of privacy (has to share a room/bed with his aunt)
- he was forced to go to Nigeria by his mother → he is angry with his mother for making him visit his aunt
- Lagos' streets are dirty and crowded.
- lack of democracy and too much corruption (e.g. scene at the airport)
- Eze cannot stand Nigeria and its culture and feels unhappy, annoyed and angry.

Hinweise (M 3) 3. Stunde

Ziel: Die Schülerinnen und Schüler setzen sich mit den Konflikten Jugendlicher, die mit verschiedenen Kulturen aufwachsen, anhand eines Sachtexts auseinander und übertragen ihr Wissen auf den Protagonisten Eze.

Einstieg

Die Lernenden, die inzwischen den vollständigen Film als Hausaufgabe angesehen haben, fassen im Unterrichtsgespräch zusammen, wie der **Internetbetrug** im Rest des Films dargestellt wird. Dabei äußern sie auch begründet ihre Meinung zum Ausgang des Films.

Die Lehrkraft leitet zum Stundenthema über, indem sie die Schülerinnen und Schüler nach den

Unterschieden zwischen ihrer eignen und der nigerianischen Kultur fragt. Anschließend lesen die Lernenden die Infobox über interkulturelle Konflikte bei Teenagern.

Tipp
M 3 eignet sich gut, um das Thema „Jugendliche aus der nigerianisch-amerikanischen Diaspora" zu bearbeiten, kann aber auch auf weitere Bereiche, zum Beispiel *Hispanic Americans* übertragen werden.

Hinweis zur Differenzierung
Schnellarbeitende Schülergruppen sammeln in der **expert task** in einem Interview Erfahrungen ihrer Mitschülerinnen und Mitschüler zum Thema, fassen diese zusammen und setzen sie mit dem Protagonisten des Films in Bezug.

Hausaufgabe
Die Lernenden verfassen einen Blogbeitrag aus Ezes Sicht (**task 4**).

Erwartungshorizont (M 3)

1.
   - Eze has problems to adapt to the "lack of luxury" in Nigeria (no own room, no Wi-Fi, problems with electricity)
   - airport: Eze faces corruption due to his dark skin colour
   - Eze would like to become a Nigerian prince scammer to solve his problems and because he thinks people in Nigeria solve their problems "differently".
   - Eze's mother thinks he is American Nigerian, but Eze thinks of himself as American.
2. Individual answers
3. Individual interview results
4. <u>Example for a blog entry</u>:

   Everything is different here in Nigeria: dirty streets, no sufficient electricity, corruption and no private living space. But how am I supposed to manage without reliable Wi-Fi? How am I supposed to fit into a society that is corrupt and supports illegal activities like scamming? And how can I survive on hamburgers that do not even taste close to those at home?

   I need to go back home to the USA as soon as possible! These circumstances might work for Nigerians but not for me: I was not born here. I identify as American and am used to a different standard and way of life. I cannot even deal with my own aunt's mentality. To me, she almost seems crazy and does not accept my privacy at all. How could my mother make me live with her?! I am so angry at her for sending me to filthy Nigeria. If she wanted me to experience my heritage, she should have let me stay in the USA. That's where I come from, that's where I fit in. At least most of the time … One good thing is: nobody here is interested in the colour of my skin. I also understand my mother and her way of bringing me up better now that I have seen where she comes from. The only really good thing is that I am getting along fine with my cousin Pius, although I wish he would finally start an honest life …
   Eze

Hinweise (M 4)

4. Stunde

Ziel: Die Schülerinnen und Schüler untersuchen eine Filmkritik, die Bezug auf wichtige Themen des Films *„Nigerian Prince"* sowie auf dessen internationalen Erfolg nimmt.

Einstieg
Zwei oder drei Lernende lesen im Plenum ihren **Blogeintrag (M 3, *task 4*)** vor, den sie als Hausaufgabe verfasst haben. Die Lehrkraft und die Lerngruppe geben ihnen ein Feedback, ob darin alle wesentlichen Gedanken und Gefühle Ezes plausibel aus Sicht der Figur dargelegt sind.

Digitalhinweis
Die Aufgaben zur Überprüfung des Leseverstehens liegen digital und kostenlos in *LearningApps* vor und sind mit Konto bearbeitbar („ähnliche App erstellen" anklicken):
https://learningapps.org/display?v=p04jcefpa23
https://learningapps.org/display?v=pwqa4msdk23
https://learningapps.org/display?v=py1hd4yit23

Sachhinweis – Auszug aus der Serie *„The Simpsons"*
Um den weitreichenden Effekt des *Nigerian Prince Scams* und dessen mediale Repräsentation im westlichen Raum zu verstehen, sehen die Lernenden in ***task 4*** einen kurzen Auszug aus der U.S.-amerikanischen Kultserie *„The Simpsons"* an. Hierin berichtet der etwas einfältige Barinhaber Moe dem Protagonisten Homer Simpson, dass er auf einen nigerianischen Internetbetrug hereingefallen ist und auf diese Weise eine große Menge Geld verloren hat. Hierbei wird das Klischee eines Geschädigten aufgezeigt, dessen einfache Lebensweise ein typisches Merkmal für Betrugsopfer darstellt. Moe handelt aus Geldgier und mangelndem Einkommen und erhofft sich durch die Onlinegeldüberweisung finanziellen Profit und somit ein besseres Leben.

Didaktisch-methodischer Hinweis
Die Lehrkraft setzt ***task 6*** entweder als Recherche- oder als Tempoaufgabe ein: In Partner- oder Kleingruppenarbeit diskutieren die Schülerinnen und Schüler mögliche Gründe für das Investieren von Geld in (fragwürdige) Internetgeschäfte. Sie müssen sich hierzu in die Rolle der nigerianischen Mittelklasse hineinversetzen und aus der Sicht eines Scam-Geschädigten argumentieren.

Erwartungshorizont (M 4)

1. Individual results
2.
   a) According to the author, *Nigerian Prince* is a film about *an American teenager making his way through a scavenger nation*.
   b) The name of the actor playing the role of Eze is *Antonio J. Bell*.
   c) The author writes that Okoro creates *a lively drama with authentic characters*.
   d) In the film, Nigeria is portrayed as a nation *of disorder*.
   e) The film is *socially disquieting*.
3. a) Okoro – b) paint – c) thriller – d) katharsis – e) payoffs
4. 1. d) – 2. f) – 3. j) – 4. l) – 5. h) – 6. c) – 7. a) – 8. k) – 9. g) – 10. i) – 11. e) – 12. b)

5. Individual results
6.
- Moe falls for a Nigerian prince scam: he invested a big amount of money and lost everything.
- He thinks he is emailing with a real Nigerian person (prince) due to his bad grammar and language.
- Moe is a simple-minded person and easy to convince.
- Homer does not understand the situation, too → showing the audience how easy "some people" can be deceived by the scam.

7.
- Nigerian prince scam: 419 scam
- illegal transfer of money → usually introduced via mail, fax or email
- most common Nigerian fraud
- people who are not skeptical of Nigerian people asking for money transfer large amounts of money
- many Nigerian people do not have much money, are poor or in desperate need for something → they are quite naïve and uneducated

8. Individual results

5./6. Stunde

Hinweise (M 5)

Ziel: Die Schülerinnen und Schüler setzen sich mit einer authentischen nigerianischen Kurzgeschichte auseinander, indem sie diese in einem ersten Schritt lesen und ihr Textverständnis sichern.

Einstieg
Die Lehrkraft präsentiert zunächst nur den **Titel** der Kurzgeschichte, *„Collector of Memories"*. Die Lerngruppe stellt im Plenum Überlegungen an, worum es in der Kurzgeschichte gehen könnte. Am Ende der Doppelstunde findet in *task 9 a)* ein Rückbezug zum Einstieg statt.

Digitalhinweis
Die Aufgaben zur Überprüfung des Leseverstehens liegen digital und kostenlos in *LearningApps* vor und sind mit Konto bearbeitbar („ähnliche App erstellen" anklicken):
https://learningapps.org/display?v=pcieegrxt23
https://learningapps.org/display?v=psgjsup1c23
https://learningapps.org/display?v=pw2ejr2q523
https://learningapps.org/display?v=p0r7ywa8k23

Didaktisch-methodischer Hinweis
Da die (Kurz-)Geschichte relativ umfangreich ist, wurde sie zur Entlastung der Lernenden stellenweise gekürzt und in zwei Teile unterteilt.

Erwartungshorizont (M 5)

1. Individual results

2. <u>1</u> a baby is found – <u>2</u> a lost key – <u>3</u> Regina and mother's fight – <u>4</u> a mother-daughter talk – <u>5</u> Aunty Rhoda – <u>6</u> polytechnic – <u>7</u> dating Chike – <u>8</u> mother is ill

3. 1. l) – 2. f) – 3. a) – 4. k) – 5. i) – 6. j) – 7. d) – 8. e) – 9. g) – 10. c) – 11. h) – 12. b)

4. <u>Summarised information about the protagonist</u>: first person narrator of the story; "foster girl"; was found in a carton by her foster mother on New Year's Eve; lives with her foster mother and her two aunts in a small house; visits school; not very good at school; studies and later works at a bank; difficult for her to form a proper relationship with her boyfriend; does not know her complete/real story

5. **Ramsey Nouah:** Nigerian actor and director – ***Super Story***: Nigerian television series – **UTME:** Nigerian university entrance exam – **harmattan cold:** West African season between the end of November and March – **JAMB:** Nigerian entrance exam for tertiary-level institutions – **Cabin Biscuit:** Nigerian plain hard sweet biscuit – **Ankara dress:** colorful African-Nigerian fashion

6. Individual results
7. Individual results

8. a) her mother – b) crazy – c) cursed – d) difficult – e) forgives her foster mother

9. <u>Possible solution</u>:
   a) Effect (mainly negative) of past experiences (sacks) which have a stressing effect on people.
   b) Chibusonma: less important, more interested in relationships/partnership, staying at home rather than leaving for university; Chibusonma's (foster) mother: important, she wants the best for her daughter.
   c) Foster child, has difficulties bonding with people, she does not know about her biological mother.

Hinweise (M 6)

7./8. Stunde

Ziel: Um die kulturellen Aspekte und Konflikte der Kurzgeschichte besser zu verstehen, erarbeiten die Schülerinnen und Schüler in einem zweiten Schritt typische Elemente und Themen nigerianischer Literatur.

Didaktisch-methodischer Hinweis
Die Lehrkraft steigt mit einer **Frage** in die Unterrichtsstunde ein, die die Lernenden im Plenum beantworten:
- *Is the short story* Collector of Memories *typical Nigerian? Give reasons.*

Erwartungshorizont (M 6)

1./2. <u>Lack of education and illiteracy</u>: many Nigerian children do not attend schools regularly; public schools are badly funded and, therefore, unorganised and not well equipped (e.g. no desks, textbooks or toilets); the school curricula are mostly outdated; teachers are often badly qualified; even highly qualified teachers are not well paid; private schools are too expensive for most families; in rural areas, most families cannot even afford to send their children to public schools or prefer their children to work in order to contribute to the family income → increase in child trafficking, child labour and early marriages (43 percent of girls are married at the age of 18); 10.5 million Nigerian children cannot read or write properly; Nigeria has the world's largest number of illiterate children.

Social inequality: the social gap between rich and poor is especially high in Nigeria, although Nigeria's economy is expanding; Nigerian economy is the biggest in Africa; the combined wealth of Nigeria's wealthiest five persons could end extreme poverty in Nigeria; more than 112 million people live in poverty in Nigeria; up to 79 percent of rural labour force are women, but they are five times less likely to own land than men; there are enough resources but corruption leads to an unequal distribution of the resources.

Witchcraft and Juju: many Nigerians believe in the supernatural; Juju (= a spiritual belief system using amulets and spells) spells can be used for good or bad reasons; each ethnic group in Nigeria has a word for wizards and witches; many believe that witchcraft can cause poverty, infertility and diseases; witchcraft is officially forbidden by law and punishable by a jail term; the media often reports about people who are supposed to be wizards or witches; there are still public events associated with witchcraft taking place in Nigeria, especially Christians protest against those events; witchcraft is also used by people to make money; many children are accused of witchcraft and cast out by their families; witchcraft and Juju are also often represented in Nigerian literature and films → lately witchcraft became popular through media → lead to more accusations among children, women and elderly people

3.

Nigerian cultural elements	References in the short story
Lack of education and illiteracy	− the neighbour Regina is an "illiterate" (l. 63) − although the protagonist's foster mother is a teacher (l. 126), they cannot afford a better life − the protagonist failed JAMB two times (ll. 144/145) − "university students were the *shit*" (l. 151) − she has many prejudices about educated people (l. 151 ff.)
Social inequality	− shared toilet (l. 25 ff.) − lack of quality of living (the protagonist shares a two-room bungalow with her mother and two aunts although all three women work, and her mother even studied and is a qualified teacher) − Regina "clawed her way from poverty" (l. 78) − the protagonist was abandoned as a baby out of poverty "child for gutter" (l. 81), she was found in an empty carton box (l. 15)
Witchcraft and Juju	− the foster mother is supposed to have been cursed by the protagonist's birth mother − her illness "is spiritual" − the curse is taken from the foster mother

4.

similarities	differences
– the birth mother of the short story's protagonist and the girl from the documentary are both accused of witchcraft – both females are accused of having made someone ill – both are vulnerable (orphan girl and woman suffering from a mental illness) – both find support (the girl at UNICEF and the birth mother at church and with her family; she also receives medical support for her dementia) – the people who accused both females of witchcraft are not punished even though there are laws that forbid such accusations – beliefs in witchcraft are widespread	– the girl from the documentary is still a minor while the birth mother of the protagonist is a grown-up – the girl was abandoned by her family and threatened to be killed; the birth mother of the protagonist lives with her brother and his family – many children are accused of witchcraft

Hinweise (M 7)

9. Stunde

Ziel: Die Schülerinnen und Schüler erweitern ihre literarischen und interkulturellen Kompetenzen, indem sie einen Auszug aus dem Bestsellerroman „*The Girl with the Louding Voice*" lesen und mehr über die Lebens- und Bildungssituation nigerianischer Jugendlicher, insbesondere von Mädchen, erfahren.

Einstieg

Die Lernenden knüpfen an ihr Vorwissen aus den vorangegangenen Unterrichtsstunden an, indem sie sich zu zweit über das Bildungswesen in Nigeria austauschen (***task 1 a***) und sich anschließend anhand eines Videos Beispiele notieren, wie die Bildungssituation in Nigeria verbessert werden könnte (***task 2 a***).

Sachhinweis

In ***task 3*** wenden die Lernenden sowohl die Inhalte aus dem Romanauszug als auch ihr Vorwissen aus M 5 und M 6 über typische nigerianisch-kulturelle Elemente an. Diese beziehen sie auf ein **Zitat** aus dem Roman („*Come, let us sit outside, drink and forget the sorrows of our country, Nigeria.*"). Daré spricht hierbei die wirtschaftlichen und sozialen Probleme bestimmter Bevölkerungsgruppen und deren Auswirkung auf Familien und ihre Strukturen an. Dies sind Bedingungen, unter denen viele nigerianische Kinder und Jugendliche aufwachsen und von denen ihr Leben entscheidend geprägt wird. Adunnis Vater ist alkoholabhängig, weil er unter den schlechten Bedingungen seines Landes leidet. Die Familie hat finanzielle Probleme, nur einen beschränkten Zugang zu Bildung und Adunnis Mutter ist jung verstorben. All diese Faktoren sind mögliche Gründe für den „Verkauf" der eigenen Tochter.

Achtung

Soll der thematische Baustein „*The Girl with the Louding Voice* – Excerpt from a Nigerian novel" unabhängig von den anderen beiden Bausteinen (siehe Minimalplan auf Seite 8) eingesetzt werden, streicht die Lehrkraft *task 5*.

Hinweis zur Differenzierung

In der **expert task** untersuchen schnellere oder lernstärkere Schülerinnen und Schüler das „*Nigerian English*" des Romanauszugs, das auf jugendliche Leserinnen und Leser in Wort und Schrift zunächst oftmals befremdlich wirken kann, da es von gewohnten sprachlichen Feinheiten und sprachlicher Korrektheit abweicht. Nach einem ersten Kontakt durch die Filmszenen aus „*Nigerian Prince*" (siehe M 1–M 3), lenken sie ihre Aufmerksamkeit auf sprachliche Diversitäten im Textauszug von Darés Roman.

Erwartungshorizont (M 7)

1. a) Many people cannot afford to send their children to school, the Nigerian school system is not funded properly (teachers are not highly qualified and not well paid, schools lack equipment)
   b) foundations, raising awareness about the importance of education in rural areas, letters to parents to encourage them to send their children to school, free basic education, improving transport to school

2. <u>Information about Adunni and her family</u>: Adunni lives with her siblings and father in a small house in a rural area. Adunni's father often hits her. Adunni had to stop her education due to financial reasons. Her mother died some time ago. Adunni's father drinks a lot of alcohol and seems to be desperate about their family and financial situation.

3. <u>Discussion of the statement</u>: The political, economic and social situation of Nigeria is difficult: corruption and violence; brain drain as well as a lack of education in lower social classes; lack of support for lower social classes; political instability; high rate of illiterate people → Adunni's father and family suffer from Nigeria's social, economic and educational problems; Adunni had to leave school despite the fact that she wanted to be educated; Adunni's father is desperate because he does not have a job and, therefore, plans on selling his daughter; he drinks a lot of alcohol to forget his and his family's problems.

4. <u>Comparison</u>: both protagonists grow up (partly) without their birth mothers; both girls do not come from wealthy backgrounds; while Adunni is abused by her father, husband and employer, Chibusomna grows up in a loving family; Adunni is not allowed to get an education although education is very important to her; Chibusomna is allowed to go to school and get an education, but education is not her main goal, she even thinks poorly about students; both stories are told by a first-person narrator; the language used in the extract from the novel reflects Adunni's lack of education, the language in the short story is much more elaborated

5. <u>Typical elements of "Nigerian English"</u>: third-person-singular "s" is missing: "Papa call me […]", "Papa say […]", "[…] he want to tell […]"; prepositions/articles etc. are missing (elliptic sentences): "[…] boy in the class was laughing me […]", "We even putting small flower […]"; wrong plural forms: "educations", "childrens"

Hinweise (M 8)

10. Stunde

Ziel: Die Schülerinnen und Schüler setzen sich mit einem Problem der nigerianischen Gesellschaft, dem Mangel an schulischer (Aus)Bildung und dem daraus resultierende Analphabetismus, auseinander und übertragen dieses auf Romanauszüge und die Situation der Protagonistin.

Didaktisch-methodischer Hinweis

Die Lernenden kommentieren im Plenum das bekannte nigerianische Sprichwort und beziehen es auf den Auszug aus *„The Girl with the Louding Voice"* (**task 1**), den sie aus der vorangegangenen Unterrichtsstunde kennen.

Erwartungshorizont (M 8)

1. Comment on the Nigerian proverb: an entire community of people is needed to help a child growing up in a good way; children feel connected through community; to educate a child is not easy and needs a lot of energy and support; parents and adults as role models; Adunni's situation shows that her village, family and the society she lives in have let her down; the circumstances in which she grew up could have been more supportive especially when it comes to education

2.
   a) Why Nigerian girls are more disadvantaged than boys: socio-cultural norms, Muslim girls often have to stay home to fulfil their "traditional tasks"

   b) Possible reasons why one out of five out-of-school children live in Nigeria: economic barriers, socio-cultural norms, difficulties of transport (many Nigerian children live far away from school, parents do not own cars), parents and families do not value education, children and teenagers have to focus on other jobs and do not have time to go to school (housework duties, farming, caring for younger siblings etc.)

3. Comment on the value of education for Adunni:

novel extract	comment
"My mama say education will give me a voice. […]"	– Adduni's mother values the importance of education – louding voice: Adduni will be able to speak up (for herself) – she wants to become a "real and valuable" person and live her own life – she wants to help and support other people
"Now I know that speaking good English is not […]."	– everybody can speak English or be taught to speak English – the language of the colonisers and the West is not better than Nigerian languages – people speaking English are not automatically more intelligent – a language is not (only) a question of intelligence

novel extract	comment
"That day I tell myself that even […]."	– school and education are very important – Adunni desperately wishes to get an education – teachers are very educated people to Adunni – only educated people have "a real and louding" voice
"When I walk away from the library, I […]."	– importance of books – access to books = access to knowledge – "spirit of knowledge"
"Why will I fill up the world with sad childrens that […]."	– reference to the bad education system of Nigeria – many children are illiterate and do not have the chance to get an education – no education = no voice

11. Stunde

Hinweise (M 9)

Ziel: Anhand eines Interviews mit der Autorin Abi Daré erarbeiten die Schülerinnen und Schüler Hintergrundinformationen zum Inhalt und der Entstehung des Romans, aber auch zur aktuellen Situation Nigerias sowie der enormen Bedeutung von Bildung und Ausbildung.

Einstieg
Die Lernenden überlegen im Plenum, was die **Intention der Autorin** Abi Daré gewesen sein könnte, ihren Roman *„The Girl with the Louding Voice"* zu schreiben.

Sachhinweis – Interview mit Abi Daré
Daré beschreibt in dem Interview *„Inside the Book: Abi Daré ('The Girl with the Louding Voice')"* mit dem Verlag Penguin Random House unter anderem ihren eigenen biografisch-akademischen Werdegang und nennt ihre (alleinerziehende) Mutter als ihr Vorbild. Darés Roman beinhaltet autobiografische Elemente: Darés Mutter vermittelte ihr die gleichen Werte, die auch Adunni von ihrer Mutter vermittelt bekommt: *„Everything can be taken from you, except your education."*
Das YouTube-Video ist hier abrufbar https://www.youtube.com/watch?v=jIQOPneQDco und hat eine Spielzeit von 04:01 Minuten. Das Interview ist in sehr guter Tonqualität verfügbar, sodass der Inhalt für die Schülerinnen und Schüler gut verständlich ist.

Erwartungshorizont (M 9)

1. <u>Statements</u>: a) false; b) true; c) true; d) true; e) false
2.
   a)
   – a 14-year-old spirited girl
   – getting an education gives Adunni (a louding) voice
   – desires to go for something good
   – Adunni needs the help and support of other people
   – Adunni believes in the good things and attitudes of people

b)
- autobiographical elements:
Adunni's mother has a similar opinion about education as Daré's mother → "people can't take away your education".
- in the author's opinion, an education opens doors and makes people listen to you; to her, an education is the most powerful weapon a person can have → Daré could be aiming at pointing out the importance of education to her readers (in similar situations)

3.
- Nigeria is a country of contrast, a few very rich people, but many poor people.
- Education can support people to fulfil their (Nigerian) dream(s).
- Education allows people to move from one social class to another.
- Adunni raises herself from a difficult life to a happy and fulfilled way of life
  → The novel could inspire people in similar situations to get an education
  → The novel could nurture people's hope for better living conditions
  → The novel can raise awareness to the problem in Nigeria and other countries.

Hinweise (M 10)

11. Stunde

Ziel: Diese Unterrichtsstunde schließt die Unterrichtsreihe ab, indem mithilfe eines Zeitungsartikels der Bogen zum Alltag nigerianischer Teenager heute gespannt wird. Die Schülerinnen und Schüler lernen die wirtschaftlichen Fortschritte und Änderungen in der Wertevorstellung kennen und stellen interkulturelle beziehungsweise transkulturelle Bezüge zu ihrer eigenen Kultur her.

Einstieg
Die Lehrkraft steigt mit dem Titel des Onlineartikels ein. Die Lernenden spekulieren im Plenum zur im Titel aufgeworfenen Frage.

Digitalhinweis
Die Aufgaben zur Überprüfung des Leseverstehens liegen digital und kostenlos in *LearningApps* vor und sind mit Konto bearbeitbar („ähnliche App erstellen" anklicken):
https://learningapps.org/display?v=p6b3xvc4323
https://learningapps.org/display?v=pu4qyom3k23

Methodisch-didaktischer Hinweis
Der Onlineartikel ist sprachlich etwas anspruchsvoller, da er neben einigen komplexen Wörtern und Kollokationen ebenso Phrasen des nigerianischen Englisch verwendet. Um die sprachliche Komplexität des Textes besser erfassen zu können, dienen die *tasks 1* und *2* als sprachlich-inhaltliche Sicherung. Vokabelannotationen unterhalb des Texts dienen als zusätzliche Hilfestellung.

Erwartungshorizont (M 10)

1. a) True, b) True, c) False, d) True, e) True
2. 1. c) – 2. g) – 3. f) – 4. h) – 5. a) – 6. b) – 7. e) – 8. d)

3. Possible solutions:

Typical Nigerian	Both	Typical German
- recent development from starting a family as a teenager to career before family - education takes up most part of teenage years - many teenagers dream of "white-collar jobs" - technology and globalisation leads to liberalism and freedom for teenagers - teenagers are more independent from their parents' influence - new job possibilities due to advances in technology - new jobs in technology mean that teenagers can combine their dream job and their passion/hobbies - other new jobs: artist, dancer, footballer, (rap) musicians, model - speak up against wrongs in society - shut out parental and societal expectations - are ambitious - start early to follow their dreams	- globalised: want to connect through social media - would like to do more creative jobs in technology, media or sports - wish to do something valuable in life - speak up against wrongs in society	- technology plays a huge role in their lives - health and sustainability are important to them - huge pressure to perform/be successful - family becomes more and more important again - globalised: want to see the world/connect through social media - aim to do something valuable in life - work-life-balance is important - many teenagers would like to go abroad and see the world before higher education and jobs start - speak up against societal problems (e.g. climate change)

V.279

Unterrichtsmagazin

Brexit: success or failure? – Über den Brexit und seine Konsequenzen diskutieren (ab Klasse 10)

Waltraud Feger

© Craig Hastings/Moment

Brexit und kein Ende! Nach dem Referendum 2016 und dem EU-Austritt des Vereinigten Königreichs am 31. Januar 2020 ist vieles durch das am 24. Januar 2020 unterzeichnete Austrittsabkommen geregelt. Doch schon bald nachdem MP Rees-Mogg zum *Minister for Brexit Opportunities and Government Efficiency* (bis Februar 2022) ernannt wurde, stellte sich die Frage nach dem Erfolg des Brexits. Heute, nach einer verheerenden Bilanz des EU-Austritts, wird schon gelegentlich die Frage gestellt, ob der *exit* von Brexit kommen wird. Die Lernenden setzen sich mit Bildern, Texten und einem Video zum Thema auseinander, um sich die Kontroverse vor Augen zu führen.

KOMPETENZPROFIL

LearningApps - interaktive Lernbausteine

Klassenstufe:	ab Klasse 10
Dauer:	5 Unterrichtsstunden inkl. LEK
Inhalt:	*British society, politics, democracy, history*
Kompetenzen:	1. Lese- und Schreibkompetenz: Zeitungsartikel lesen und verstehen, (kreative) Texte schreiben, Bildmaterial beschreiben/interpretieren; 2. Hör-Seh-Verstehen: einem Kurzvideo zentrale Informationen entnehmen; 3. Sprechkompetenz: sich über Abbildungen austauschen, abstrakte Begriffe und Einflussfaktoren diskutieren; 4. Interkulturelle Kompetenz: Sachwissen zum Austritts Großbritanniens aus der Europäischen Union erwerben und demonstrieren

Fachliche Hinweise

In dieser Einheit geht es um einen Rückblick auf den Austritt Großbritanniens aus der Europäischen Union (Brexit) und die Auswirkungen auf die Gegenwart unter dem Blickwinkel der **Versprechungen und gegenwärtigen Realität**. Die Tatsache, dass jetzt – sieben Jahre nach dem Referendum – ein weiterer Brexit-Minister ernannt wurde, spricht Bände über den komplizierten Austritt aus der EU. Ein weiteres Indiz ist der Titel: *Minister for Brexit Opportunities and Government Efficiency*. Die enthaltenen Texte (auch die in der Klausur), das Video und das Bildmaterial stellen Boris Johnson und den ehemaligen Brexit-Minister Rees-Moog auf den Prüfstand und hinterfragen den Erfolg des Brexit.

Zum Brexit und zur aktuellen Situation

Eingeleitet vom damaligen Premierminister David Cameron, findet im Juni 2016 ein **Referendum** statt, bei dem 52 Prozent der teilnehmenden Briten für den **EU-Austritt** Großbritanniens stimmen. Cameron, der sich für einen Verbleib in der EU aussprach, tritt zurück und Theresa May wird neue Premierministerin. Die Brexit-Befürworter machten dem britischen Volk einige **Versprechungen**: Größerer Wohlstand, florierender Handel, Einschränkung der Migration. Etwa ein Jahr später, im März 2017, reicht London den **Austrittsantrag** ein. Es folgt eine **zweijährige Frist** (bis Ende März 2019), in der die Brexit-Bedingungen ausgehandelt werden sollen. 2018 einigt sich die britische Regierung auf einen Entwurf des Austrittsvertrags, der von der EU verabschiedet wird. Das Londoner Unterhaus lehnt den Vertrag aber drei Mal ab. Im März 2019 stimmen die Abgeordneten für eine **Verlängerung der Brexit-Frist**: Zunächst auf den 12. April 2019 und kurz vor Ablauf der Frist auf den 31. Oktober 2019. Nach Rücktritt von May als Vorsitzende der Konservativen und Regierungschefin, wird Boris Johnson Premierminister, der mit Großbritannien **mit oder ohne Deal** am 31. Oktober die EU verlassen will. Nachdem Johnson die Mehrheit im Parlament verliert, folgt eine chaotische Phase. Am 17. Oktober schließen das Parlament und die EU eine neue Brexit-Vereinbarung, der Brexit wird erneut auf **Ende Januar 2020** verschoben. Im Dezember 2019 gewinnen Johnsons Tories die absolute Mehrheit bei den Parlamentswahlen. Ein Gesetz über den EU-Austritt wird beschlossen, die EU stimmt zu. Am 31. Januar 2020 tritt Großbritannien aus der EU aus. Es folgen die Verhandlungen zu einem **Handelsabkommen**, die von der Corona-Pandemie unterbrochen werden, Johnson möchte aber keine Verlängerung der Verhandlungen. Nachträglich stellt er das beschlossene Brexit Abkommen in Frage und möchte einseitige Änderungen vornehmen, was von der EU kritisiert und rechtlich nachverfolgt wird. Ein „No Deal" steht wieder im Raum, auch weil die EU Zugeständnisse in Handel und Fischerei fordert. Nach zehn Monaten Verhandlung einigen sich Johnson und EU-Kommissionspräsidentin Ursula von der Leyen schließlich auf ein Handelsabkommen.

Was sind die **Auswirkungen** des Brexits? Der Brexit schadete dem Land massiv: Einschränkung der Wirtschaft und Stillstand des Handels. Der entstandene Schaden wird auf 4 % des Bruttosozialproduktes geschätzt. Der „Schutz" der Insel vor Migranten läuft angesichts der weiterhin hohen Ströme an Flüchtlingen über den Ärmelkanal ins Leere. Das Gesundheitssystem steht so schlecht dar wie noch nie. Fast 60 % der Briten sehen den Brexit laut Umfragen als Fehler an.

Didaktisch-methodische Hinweise

Im Vordergrund der Unterrichtsreihe steht die Förderung der **interkulturellen Kompetenz** bezüglich des Austritts Großbritanniens aus der Europäischen Union und die **kommunikativen Kompetenzen**. Sie ist abgesehen von einigen Analyse- und Diskussionsaufgaben ab Klasse 10 einsetzbar.

Die Materialien können als Einheit oder einzeln verwendet werden. Die Einheit kann wie folgt gegliedert werden:

1. **Hinführung zum Thema** mittels Fotos und deren zeitlicher Einordnung. Aktivierung von Vorkenntnissen zum Thema „Brexit" (M 1)
2. **Aufarbeitung des Hintergrunds** des Brexit mit Hilfe eines Erklärvideos und Hinführung zum gegenwärtigen Stand (M 2).
3. **Erarbeitung der aktuellen Situation** anhand von zwei Guardian Artikel: *„Brexit one year on [...]"* stellt die von Vorteilen geprägten Erwartungen an den Brexit und die Situation ein Jahr nach EU-Austritt gegenüber. Der Artikel *„Six years on [...]"* beleuchtet die Konsequenzen des Brexit 6 Jahre nach der Abstimmung. Ergänzt werden die Artikel mit einer Karikatur.
4. **LEK:** Die LEK besteht aus einem aktuellen Guardian Artikel sowie einem Mediationsartikel aus der Neue Zürcher Zeitung, die die Fragen stellen, wie erfolgreich der Brexit war und welche Folgen sichtbar geworden sind. Sie deckt alle Anforderungsbereiche ab. Die Mediationskompetenz der Lernenden wird in dieser Reihe vorausgesetzt.

Hinweise zum digitalen Einsatz

Einige der Aufgaben liegen zur interaktiven Bearbeitung in *LearningApps* vor. Das Hör-Seh-Verstehen in M 2, die Vokabelaufgabe in M 3 sowie die Wortschatzarbeit und eine der Leseverstehensaufgaben in M 4 können von den Lernenden digital bearbeitet werden.

Differenzierungshinweis

Die Materialien bieten mehrere Differenzierungsmöglichkeiten. Leistungsschwächeren Lernenden stehen in den Materialien Vokabelunterstützung sowie Zusatzinformationen als Tipp zur Verfügung. Des Weiteren können leistungsstärkere Lernenden die Wortschatzarbeit zu Beginn der Erarbeitung der Artikel auslassen.

Mediathek

Sekundärliteratur

▶ Martill, Benjamin and Uta Staiger: Brexit and Beyond, Rethinking the Futures of Europe, UCL Press, London, 2018) available to download free: www.ucl.ac.uk/ucl-press [letzter Abruf: 17.01.2023]
  Eine Zusammenstellung von wissenschaftlichen Aufsätzen, die von Experten und Expertinnen geschrieben wurden. Es dient als zusätzliches Hintergrundwissen für die Lehrkraft.

Weiterführende Internetseiten

▶ https://assets.publishing.service.gov.uk/government/uploads/system/uploads/attachment_data/file/1054643/benefits-of-brexit.pdf [letzter Abruf: 17.01.2023]
  Eine Studie zum Thema *"The Benefits of Brexit [...]"*. Am Ende wird festgehalten, dass schon einige Chancen des Brexits wahrgenommen wurden und dass weitere umgesetzt würden.

▶ https://eulawanalysis.blogspot.com/2022/02/hunting-benefits-of-brexit.html?msclkid=c7ef3ce9b7e811ecb02063f7ea63dd56 [letzter Abruf: 17.01.2023]
  Eine Studie von Jacques Delors, der zu einem negativen Fazit kommt. Die Studie enthält zudem interessante Kommentare, die zusätzlich im Unterricht eingesetzt werden können.

Auf einen Blick

1. Stunde

Thema: Warming-up to the topic: *Brexit*

M 1 **Talking about Brexit – A pictorial approach /** anhand von Bildmaterial zum Brexit und dem Referendum in das Thema einsteigen (PA/PL)

Hausaufgabe: Einen Blogbeitrag zum Thema Brexit schreiben (Aufgabe 3)

Benötigt: ☐ ggf. digitale Endgeräte für die Recherche (Tipp)

2. Stunde

Thema: EU Referendum explained

M 2 **Brexit for non-Brits – An introduction /** Video verstehen und sich mit wichtigen Aspekten auseinandersetzen (EA); kreatives Schreiben: einen Kommentar zum Video verfassen (PA) und Brexit erklären (EA)

Hausaufgabe: Recherche eines weiteren Videos (Aufgabe 6)

Benötigt: ☐ Abspielmöglichkeit für das Video
☐ ggf. digitale Endgeräte für die Bearbeitung in *LearningApps*

3. Stunde

Thema: Frustration over negative Brexit results

M 3 ***Brexit one year on: So, how's it going?* /** Vokabelaufgabe bearbeiten (EA oder PA); Zeitungsartikel verstehen und analysieren (EA); einen fiktiven Kommentar diskutieren (PA)

Hausaufgabe: Einen Social Media-Beitrag kommentieren (Aufgabe 6)

Benötigt: ☐ ggf. digitale Endgeräte für die Bearbeitung in *LearningApps*

4. Stunde

Thema: Brexit has not yet been done

M 4 ***Six years on, the cold reality of Brexit is hitting Britain* /** Text verstehen (EA/PA), Wortschatz erarbeiten (EA); Cartoon analysieren (EA/PA/PL)

Hausaufgabe: Einen *comment* zum Erfolg/Misserfolg vom Brexit schreiben (Aufgabe 5)

Benötigt: ☐ Dokumentenkamera/Beamer/Whiteboard für Projektion des Cartoons
☐ ggf. digitale Endgeräte für die Bearbeitung in *LearningApps*

5. Stunde

M 5 **Lernerfolgskontrolle /** einen Text verstehen, analysieren und kommentieren, eine Mediationsaufgabe bearbeiten (EA)

Talking about Brexit – A pictorial approach

M 1

Use these pictures and cartoons to look back on Brexit and its referendum.

Tasks

Work with a partner.

1. Talk about the photos/cartoons. Look for clues to find out which one/s was/were taken before the referendum. Discuss with a partner.
   TIP: You may use this information and the timeline: https://raabe.click/BrexitTimeline [last access: 17.01.2023]
2. Choose one picture/cartoon. Be prepared to describe it and present your ideas in class.
3. Write a blog entry on Brexit in which you take up an important aspect you came across during the class discussion.

Photo: Jon Worth

© Lenscap Photography/Shutterstock

© Foxys Graphic/Shutterstock

© CartoonStock

© Chris Riddell/The Observer

M 2 — Brexit for non-Brits – An introduction

You do not really remember what Brexit is all about? This video will refresh your memory.

Tasks

1. Work with the video. Read the sentences in task 2 before you start watching. Watch the video, perhaps at reduced speed (0,75).
   TIP: Use the vocabulary and information in the boxes for help.
   The Guardian: *EU referendum explained: Brexit for non-Brits*: https://raabe.click/BrexitExplained
   You can do task 2 and task 3 as a *LearningApp* as well:
   https://learningapps.org/watch?v=pzb21k8f523

> **Vocabulary: literally:** wörtlich – **detached:** separated, removed – **physically:** here: rein äußerlich – **(to) head for:** (to) go into the direction of – **(to) invoke:** (to) conjure up, heraufbeschwören – **(to) surrender:** (to) declare defeat – **overbearing:** domineering, arrogant – **bloodthirsty:** blutrünstig – **rematch:** here: another war – **(to) benefit:** (to) be useful, sth. does good – **consequential:** important, with many consequences – **ballot box:** die Wahlurne

> **Information: Barack Obama:** former American President (2009–2017) – **IMF:** Internationaler Währungsfonds – **Emma Thompson:** renowned British actress – **Nigel Farage:** former member of the European Parliament and member of the UK Independence Party, one of the founders of the Brexit Party – **Marine Le Pen:** member of the French Parliament, head of the right-wing extremist Rassemblement Party – **Michael Caine:** renowned British actor – **Boaty McBoatface:** an expensive polar scientific research ship whose name (first meant as a joke) was confirmed by an online poll

2. True or false? Answer the questions.

Statements	True	False
a) This video explains how the Queen negotiates with the EU.		
b) On 23 June 2016, British voters decided on leaving the EU.		
c) The country was totally united in its wish to quit the EU.		
d) There was a feeling of being dominated by the Europeans.		
e) Some of the remainders remembered their victory after the WWII but would rather not fight again with the Europeans.		
f) They said the single market was a good idea but leaving it would be better.		
g) Johnson and Farage are prominent and respectable remainders.		
h) The then Mayor of London, Boris Johnson and Nigel Farage are called an "eccentric cast of characters".		
i) Marine Le Pen and Michael Caine are both Scots.		
j) RRS Boaty McBoatface is an expensive scientific research ship.		

3. Read the split statements. Then watch the video one more time and match the corresponding halves.

1	It was argued the single market would be at risk,		a	as Britain is no longer attached to the rest of Europe.
2	The British were undecided,		b	concerning the name of the polar scientific research ship.
3	The decision may be similarly important, as the one opinion poll		c	whose fight they did not want to be repeated or be involved with.
4	But on 23 June 2016, the British had to decide,		d	of the European continent – with Britain still a part of it – about 8000 years ago.
5	All of them were of the opinion this decision		e	favour of remaining in the EU or leaving the EU.
6	Today's reality being quite different,		f	as some wanted to leave to take up glorious times of the empire.
7	Lots of important people were in		g	if they left the European Union.
8	This video starts off with the geological development		h	if they go it alone or if they stay put.
9	Those who wanted to stay reminded the others of WWII,		i	(leave or remain) was most crucial for their whole generation.

4. Creative writing: YouTube offers comments on the video. Here is one of them:
   "Sorry, I don't like this video – even though it's by The Guardian, a serious paper – but this video is not serious. The title, EU referendum explained: Brexit for non-Brits, is misleading, as the comment is rather superficial and mocking. The comparison between the Second World War and a match ("… as glorious as the Second World War was for Britain, it's probably best we don't have a rematch") is disgusting. I don't like the colloquial and emotional language. The same goes for labelling Farage ("serial EU hater") and Trump. From Ian"
   With a partner, study the making, e. g., the animation and wording of the video and then comment on Ian's entry.

5. Imagine while staying with the family of your American penfriend, her sister Chris (12 years) asks whether you can explain to her what Brexit stands for. Against the background of the video, clarify this topic for her. Use simple words and short sentences, so that Chris can understand your explanation.

6. Find another video on Brexit and present what it says to the class.

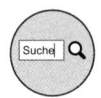

M 3

Brexit one year on: So, how's it going?

Those promised rewards[1] for Britain of leaving the EU should surely be with us by now. What have been the costs and gains[2] of 'taking our country back'?

On New Year's Day, the UK will have been fully out of the European Union for a year: out of its political and legal structures, out of its single market[3], out of its customs union[4].

This was what Boris Johnson and Michael Gove – who led the Leave campaign – had wanted. No awkward[5] halfway house[6] like Theresa May had negotiated[7]. No Brexit light[8]. Out completely. Gone. Brexit well and truly done.

It was only with a clean break, they told us, that the UK could unleash[9] its full potential, and wrestle[10] free from the chains of EU regulation and bureaucracy.

Liberated, we could take back control of our borders, our money, our laws. We could look outwards to the world in a new age of discovery, striking trade deals[11] far away from the EU, creating fresh levels of prosperity[12] for Global Britain. So, a year on, how is it all going? The resignation last weekend of Lord Frost, the minister overseeing Brexit, gave a clue[14] that all was not entirely well. "Brexit is now secure … the challenge for the government now is to deliver on the opportunities it gives us. You know my concerns about the current direction of travel," Frost told the Prime Minister in his resignation letter.

There are suggestions from some in government that Frost – a Brexit purist[15] […] – came to suspect Johnson had no real plan, no real detailed idea of how to make Brexit work beyond slogans and soundbites[16].

He was also frustrated at the deadlock[17] over Northern Ireland. A year into Brexit proper, the UK is still at loggerheads[18] with the EU over the Northern Ireland protocol that Frost and Johnson themselves negotiated and hailed[19] as a good way to solve difficult border problems, as part of the withdrawal agreement[20].

Whatever issues were riling[21] Frost the most, delivering on Brexit promises is proving a lot harder than making them had been.

What is clear is that, initially at least, Brexit is making us poorer. It has contributed to labour shortages in many business sectors as EU workers have returned home.

There are grievances[22] that run deep in specific sectors that were promised much and got almost nothing. Fishermen feel betrayed[23]. […] Small businesses, which export to the EU, have been hit by extra costs and paperwork.

The extent[24] of economic damage from Brexit has been made clear by the Office for Budget Responsibility[25], which predicts that leaving the EU will reduce our long-term GDP[26] by around 4 %, compared to a fall of around 1.5 % that will be caused by the pandemic.

Rather than boosting our trade, Brexit is holding it back. Goods exports[27] were down 14 % year on year in the third quarter of 2021 according to the Office for National Statistics, with both exports to the EU and non-EU destinations suffering[28]. […]

Our latest Opinium poll[29] shows that over 60 % of people now think Brexit has either gone badly or worse than they expected. It also found that 42 % of people who voted Leave in 2016 had a negative view of how Brexit had turned out so far.

Getting Brexit done was the easy bit. Proving it was worth it and for the good is turning out to be far more difficult.

Source: Helm, Toby: "Brexit one year on: so how's it going?" in The Guardian. 25 Dec 2021. Found at: https://www.theguardian.com/politics/2021/dec/25/brexit-one-year-on-so-hows-it-going [last access: 09/02/2023]

1 **reward:** prize, die Belohnung – 2 **gain:** profit – 3 **single market:** der Binnenmarkt (innerhalb der EU) – 4 **customs union:** die Zollgemeinschaft – 5 **awkward:** difficult – 6 **halfway house:** here: der Kompromiss – 7 **(to) negotiate:** (to) broker, deal with – 8 **Brexit light:** compared to a 'light' product, 'not a quality' Brexit – 9 **(to) unleash:** (to) let loose, free – 10 **(to) wrestle:** (to) struggle – 11 **(to) strike a deal:** (to) come to an agreement – 12 **prosperity:** being successful and thriving – 13 **resignation:** official announcement to quit – 14 **clue:** hint – 15 **purist:** so. who adheres strictly and often excessively to a tradition – 16 **soundbites:** brief and catchy comments – 17 **deadlock:** standstill – 18 **(to) be at loggerheads:** (to) disagree with, (to) have different opinions – 19 **(to) hail:** (to) welcome, (to) acclaim – 20 **withdrawal agreement:** das Austrittsabkommen – 21 **(to) rile:** (to) annoy – 22 **grievance:** complaint – 23 **(to) betray:** (to) cheat, (to) deceive – 24 **extent:** scale, size – 25 **Office for Budget Responsibility:** die Abteilung für Budgetverantwortung – 26 **GDP:** das Bruttoinlandsprodukt, BIP – 27 **goods exports:** exports of wares – 28 **(to) suffer:** (to) be badly afflicted – 29 **poll:** survey, inquiry

> **Information**: **Michael Gove**: MP – **Leave campaign:** campaign for a 'leave' vote in EU referendum: end supremacy of EU law, take control, invest in NHS & science – **Theresa May**: Prime Minister after Cameron and before Johnson – **Lord Frost**: Brexit Minister who resigned in December 2021 – **Opinium poll**: agency that publishes predictions

Tasks

1. Before you work on the article brush up your vocabulary. Match the words with their translation or their synonym. You can do this task as a *LearningApp* as well:
   https://learningapps.org/watch?v=p6286v2v323
   You can do the exercise with your partner if you want to.

customs union		die Zollgemeinschaft
(to) be at loggerheads		das Austrittsabkommen
awkward		complaint
(to) negotiate sth.		der Stillstand
deadlock		(to) disagree very strongly
grievance		etw. aushandeln
withdrawal agreement		der Rücktritt
GDP/Gross Domestic Product		das Bruttoinlandsprodukt/BIP
liberated		difficult
resignation		beitragen
(to) betray		(to) cheat, (to) deceive
suggestion		(to) be set free
(to) contribute		proposal, recommendation

2. Mr. Helm is interviewed against the background of his article. Write down the questions to his answers.

   a) _____
   Johnson and Gove were in charge of the campaign whose aim was Brexit and leaving the EU.

   b) _____
   The British were promised that the UK could take back their borders, their money, their laws and could create new levels of prosperity.

c) _____
Lord Frost wrote that Brexit was secure but did not yet deliver on the opportunities.

d) _____
They thought that Frost suspected Johnson to have no real plan or idea of how to make Brexit work.

e) _____
That there was a deadlock over Northern Ireland, as his and Johnson's NI protocol did not solve the border problems.

f) _____
Brexit is making the British poorer, it has contributed to labour shortages and EU workers leaving the UK.

g) _____
Fishermen felt betrayed, small businesses had extra costs and paperwork.

h) _____
The Office for Budget Responsibility recognises damage and predicts a reduction of around 4 % of GDP.

i) _____
Trade is damaged, exports were 14 % down, while exports to the EU and non-EU destinations are impacted, too.

j) _____
According to the recent opinion poll, a majority of 60 % think Brexit turned out badly or worse than they had expected.

3. Which stylistic/rhetorical/linguistic devices does the writer use and to what avail?

stylistic device	quotation	function
alliteration		
allusion		
anaphora		
antithesis		
euphemism		
hyperbole		
image		

stylistic device	quotation	function
irony		
leitmotif		
metaphor		
parallelism/ enumeration/climax		
personification		
repetition		
rhetorical question		
simile		

4. Against the background of task 3, point out how the stylistic/linguistic/rhetorical devices contribute to bringing across the message of the text.
5. Recently, several papers and TV hosts asked their readers and spectators to give a very personal account of their ideas of Brexit being a success or failure. Here is one opinion. Discuss it with your partner and say what you think of its contents and its choice of words.

> To my mind, Brexit seems to be working pretty successfully in breaking up the relations among the four nations of the UK and with our nearest neighbours in the EU.
> Where I live, much perfectly good agricultural land is being sold off for housing as the landowners can no longer get the workers to grow our vital foodstuff.
> Brexit is making us accustomed to food and medical shortages.
> It seems to be most effective in destroying our NHS which, I guess, it is being cut up in order to sell it to US corporates.
> The destruction of our standards of living and the increases of our cost of living seems to be progressing well.
> So, yes, I think that for those who plan to destroy the UK, Brexit is going pretty well!

6. Comment on an entry for social media where a reader has called Johnson "a cheerleader for Brexit".

M 4 — Six years on, the cold reality of Brexit is hitting Britain

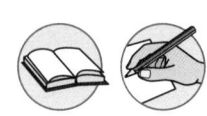

Séamus Boland, Mel Wood, Steven Lorber […] examine the consequences of Britain leaving the EU.

Reading about Brexit and its emerging[1] realities on the sixth anniversary of the UK voting to leave the EU (Brexit is making cost of living crisis worse, new study claims, 22 June), I was reminded of the Hans Christian Andersen story *The Emperor's New Clothes*. Here, the weavers persisted[2] with the lie that they were creating the most fantastic set of clothes for the emperor. He believed them, despite the fact that there was no evidence of their existence. So certain was he of this false narrative that he led a public procession celebrating their wearing [these new clothes], only for a child to say: "He's got nothing on."

[…] the businesses, farmers, fishers and scientists of Britain are now realising the horrible truth: Brexit was a fraud[3] of giant proportions. Disconnecting from its neighbouring and biggest trading partner was always foolish and, in economic terms, suicidal[4].

The weavers of Brexit convinced voters that they would get their sovereignty[5] back, even though they never lost it. They spun stories[6] of incredible wealth generated from all sorts of magic trade deals, even though former British leaders such as Winston Churchill and Margaret Thatcher were exponents[7] of a Europe that would make trade its central theme and that, along with a suite of rights-based initiatives based on proper human values, would outlaw[8] war from within for future generations.

At least, the emperor finally realised his folly[9]. It's time the British people realised the same sooner rather than later.

Séamus Boland *Ballycumber, County Offaly, Ireland*

On the sixth anniversary of the Brexit vote[10], a reminder of some of the points made by the Vote Leave campaign[11]: If we vote leave, we can create a fairer, more humane immigration system. We can have a friendlier relationship with the EU based on trade. We'll be free to trade with the whole world. We send more than £350m to the EU every week – enough to build a modern hospital every week of the year. Heaven forbid[12] that we were lied to, or did I just miss something?

Mel Wood *Dublin*

Labour is going to "improve, not scrap[13]" the Brexit deal, says David Lammy (Report, 23 June). May I suggest an area for improvement? We took our border terrier to the vet[14] last week in preparation for a holiday in the EU. At a cost of almost £200, we received a complex 10-page "Animal health certificate for the non-commercial movement to a member state from a third country of dogs …" with some 22 official veterinary stamps. This was unnecessary before Brexit – and, if a Labour government were willing to approach discussions with the EU constructively, is hardly likely to be considered necessary now. For the future, the vet's practical advice was to bypass the certificate and associated costs by obtaining[15] a pet passport issued in the EU. Oh, that we humans could choose to take a similar approach.

Steven Lorber *London*

Would any of the Boris Johnson cheerleaders who praise his "leadership" on Ukraine and close relationship with its president, Volodymyr Zelenskiy, care to explain why they maintain their disdain[16] for the EU despite the clear advantages that Ukraine sees in becoming a member?

Ian Arnott *Peterborough*

Source: Letters by Séamus Boland, Mel Wood, Steven Lorber and Ian Arnott: "Six years on, the cold reality of Brexit is hitting Britain" in The Guardian. 27 Jun 2022. Found at:
https://www.theguardian.com/politics/2022/jun/27/six-years-on-the-cold-reality-of-brexit-is-hitting-britain
[last access: 09/02/2023]

1 **(to) emerge**: (to) turn up – 2 **(to) persist**: (to) continue to lie – 3 **fraud**: swindle, deceit – 4 **suicidal**: wanting to kill yourself, likely to lead to death – 5 **sovereignty**: die Souveränität, Eigenständigkeit – 6 **(to) spin stories**: (to) think up stories – 7 **exponent**: here: so. who supports sth. – 8 **(to) outlaw**: (to) make illegal – 9 **folly**: craziness – 10 **Brexit vote**: survey of the public on Brexit – 11 **Vote Leave campaign**: Motto der Kampagne: Wählen Sie "Raus aus der EU" – 12 **heaven forbid**: Gott bewahre! – 13 **(to) scrap**: (to) get rid of – 14 **vet**: colloquial for veterinary – 15 **(to) obtain**: (to) get – 16 **disdain**: a feeling of contempt for so. or sth. regarded as inferior or unworthy

> **Information: Hans Christian Anderson**: Danish writer of fairy tales – **Winston Churchill**: Prime Minister 1940 – 1945; 1951–1955 – **Margret Thatcher**: Prime Minister 1979–1990 – **We send more than £350m to the EU every week**: slogan on Johnson's battle bus to make people vote "Leave the EU"

Tasks

1. Expand your vocabulary. Fill in the gaps of the grid which contains words from the text. You may use your mobile phone.
   You can do this task as a *LearningApp*: https://learningapps.org/watch?v=pz7rj0s4k23

noun	noun (person)	verb
narration, narrative		
		(to) create
weaving		
	campaigner	
construct, construction		
		(to) believe
		(to) lose
deal		
	voter	
		(to) improve

2. Read the article. Show your comprehension of the text by matching the correct parts of the sentences. You can also do this task as a *LearningApp*:
https://learningapps.org/watch?v=pfo2jdhjk23

Here, the weavers persisted with the lie that	they were creating the most fantastic set of clothes.
He believed them, despite the fact that	there was no evidence of their existence.
He led a public procession celebrating their wearing these new clothes	only for a child to say: „He's got nothing on."
Scientists of Britain are now realising the horrible truth;	Brexit was a fraud of giant proportions.
The weavers of Brexit convinced voters that they would get	their sovereignty back, even though they never lost it.
This was unnecessary before Brexit – and, if a Labour government were willing to approach	discussions with the EU constructively, it is hardly likely to be considered necessary now.
The vet's practical advice was to bypass the certificate	and associated costs by obtaining a pet passport issued in the EU.
They spun stories of incredible wealth	generated from all sorts of magic trade deals.
If we vote leave, we can create a fairer,	more humane immigration system.
On the sixth anniversary of the Brexit vote, a reminder	of some of the points made by the Vote Leave campaign.

3. Answer the questions. Compare your results with a partner.
   a) At what does the writer hint in his headline?

   _____

   b) What is the result – according to a recent study – after 7 years of Brexit?

   _____

   c) The writer is reminded of a well-known fairy tale. What is it about?

   _____

   d) Who are the people who had been made believing in the Brexit opportunities and why?

   _____

   e) What is – in their opinion – the most foolish mistake in the British economy?

   _____

   f) Why were PM Churchill and PM Thatcher in favour of working with Europe?

   _____

g) To what conclusion does Boland come at the end of his comparison with the fairy tale?

h) Why does Mel Wood quote slogans from the Leave campaign?

i) What does Steven Lorber's story about his dog teach us about Brexit?

j) What is Ian Arnott's point?

4. Work with the cartoon. Think – pair – share: Work alone. Then, compare your results with a partner. Present your ideas in class.
   a) Describe the cartoon.
   b) Analyse it. Include the political issues and views concerning Brexit and PM Johnson.
   c) Say what the text and the cartoon have in common. Consider the textual and visual features of the cartoon and the rhetorical devices of the text.

© Chris Riddell/The Observer

Information: Rwanda immigration policy: illegal immigrants are sent by plane to Rwanda, Africa, where they are processed – **Cost of living crisis:** energy and food have become more expensive – **I got Brexit done:** originally "get Brexit done", a slogan Johnson and his party used in the run-up of the election in 2019 – **Party gate:** this was a crisis because it was leaked that Johnson had several parties during lockdown – **Levelling up:** a policy of the Tories started in 2019 which aims at reducing the mainly economic imbalances between areas and social groups across the UK – **Civil service efficiency:** a blow at his paper "The benefits of Brexit" and Rees-Mogg's title: Minister for Brexit opportunities and government efficiency

5. Write a comment on the following question: Was/is Brexit a success or a failure?

M 5 Lernerfolgskontrolle

Part A: *Three years after Brexit, where is the new golden age that they promised us?*

At 11 pm on the last day of January, it will be precisely three years since the UK departed the European Union, an anniversary that prompts me to ask: how are you enjoying the "new golden age"? […]

You will remember his claim that the subs[1] paid to the EU only had to be redirected to the NHS[2] to transform it into a world-envied[3] health service. Strike[4] one. What we actually have is a collapsing NHS. Another of their boasts was that the UK would "take back control" of its borders. Strike two. Unmanaged migration is not falling, but rising. The most critical promise was that the economy would roar like a liberated lion just as soon as the UK was "unshackled"[5] from the "sclerotic"[6] EU. Strike three. The UK is the sick man of the G7, the only member with an economy that is still smaller than it was before the pandemic. […] Quitting has not been empowering[7] but enervating[8]. […] The self-harms[9] inflicted by Brexit also include the suppression of investment and shortages of workers in key sectors. Nothing in the Brexit prospectus[10] has survived contact with reality. […]

Some of the advocates[11] for the project now recognise that it has failed and have begun to admit as much. Alex Hickman, a business adviser at Number 10 during the Johnson premiership, recently wrote: "Those of us who backed Leave[12] must acknowledge that Brexit isn't working… It is not clear to most people what Brexit is actually for." Some of the champions of Brexit can see it has been a disaster, but can't publicly admit it – a category that includes members of the cabinet. […]

David Cameron walked off the job rather than try. Theresa May spent three miserable years pursuing a mirage[13]. Boris Johnson lied that he had an "oven-ready deal" and then repudiated[14] the agreement he had himself negotiated. Liz Truss sold herself to her party on the basis that she knew where to find the end of the rainbow containing the pot of mythical Brexit treasure. Her excursion to la-la land[15] was so ruinous that she became the briefest prime minister in our history. […] The national mood has become one of Bregret[16]. Pollsters[17] report that those who think Brexit has had a negative impact outnumber those who reckon it positive by more than two to one. Six years on from the referendum, a chunky[18] segment of those who supported Leave are suffering buyer's remorse[19]. A rising majority of the public now say that it was wrong to leave the EU. […] That's a disappointment to those who think that what the UK should really be asking itself is whether there is a way to turn back the clock and return to an EU we should never have left. Another product of Bregret is that pollsters now report that a majority of the public say that, given the choice, they would like to rejoin. There's a vanishingly[20] slight chance of that happening in the foreseeable future because, even supposing that the EU would welcome us back, the politics of negotiating re-entry and then holding another referendum are so incredibly difficult. The sad and cruel truth is that strategic blunders[21] as colossal as Brexit can't be corrected easily or swiftly. Some mistakes have to be paid for over many years. This, alas[22], is the UK's fate. Not a golden age, but ages of regret. [566 words]

Source: Andrew Rawnsley: Three years after Brexit, where is the new golden age that they promised us? In The Guardian. 22 Jan 2023. Found at https://www.theguardian.com/commentisfree/2023/jan/22/three-years-after-brexit-where-is-the-new-golden-age-that-they-promised-us [last access: 09/02/2023]

1 **subs:** subsidies; die Subventionen – 2 **NHS:** National Health Service – 3 **(to) envy:** beneiden – 4 **strike:** der Treffer, Schlag – 5 **unshackled:** befreit, ungebunden – 6 **sclerotic:** erstarrt, verhärtet – 7 **empowering:** constructive, creative – 8 **enervating:** schwächend – 9 **self-harm:** die Selbstverletzung – 10 **prospectus:** here: die Werbeschrift – 11 **advocate:** here: der Befürworter/die Befürworterin – 12 **Leave:** the referendum campaign, so called by the Tories: Vote Leave – 13 **mirage:** illusion – 14 **(to) repudiate:** verleugnen, dementieren – 15 **la-la land:** musical romance (2016), maybe a metaphor for people pursuing their dreams – 16 **Bregret:** Brexit regret; Brexit bereuen, nachtrauern – 17 **pollster:** der Meinungsforscher/die Meinungsforscherin – 18 **chunky:** very big – 19 **buyer's remorse:** the sense of regret after a purchase – 20 **vanishing:** verschwindend – 21 **blunder:** serious mistake – 22 **alas:** unfortunately

> **Information**
>
> **Prime Ministers belonging to the Conservative Party:** David Cameron (2010–2016); Theresa May (2016–2019); Boris Johnson (2019–2022); Liz Truss (September 2022–October 2022); Richi Sunak (since October 2022) – **the new golden age:** promise given by the Conservative Party before the referendum in which the voters were to decide whether to leave the European Union – his claim: refers to Jacob Rees-Mogg, former Minister for Brexit opportunities and government efficiency – **the sick man:** in the late 1990s, Germany was called the sick man of Europe because of its failing economy – **Brexit prospectus:** paper by the Johnson government: "The benefits of Brexit: How the UK is taking advantage of leaving the EU", January 2022 – **the end of the rainbow:** metaphor for wanting something that is impossible to obtain

Tasks
1. Outline Rawnsley's view on Brexit and its present prospects. *(Comprehension)*
2. Analyse how the author's special use of language presents his views. *(Analysis)*
3. Choose one the following tasks:
3.1. Discuss the following questions: Why do you think Great Britain has left the EU? What did it expect and why does the writer speak of a disappointment? *(Evaluation: comment)*
3.2. Having won an award as political commentator of the Observer, Rawnsley gives an interview to the media on the main issues of his job and his latest research on Brexit. Against the background of the article, write the interview considering the work done in class on Brexit. Find at least 4 questions and 4 answers. *(Evaluation: re-creation of text)*

Part B: Mediation: *[...] Tagelanger Megastau lässt Briten mit dem Brexit hadern*

[...] Wieder zeigt sich: Probleme auf der Insel können viele Ursachen haben, aber durch den Brexit wird es meistens noch schlimmer.

Viele Staus zu Ferienbeginn sind normal, aber dieser hier ist besonders. Seit Freitag finden sich Tausende Briten in kilometerlangen Autoschlangen wieder, manche von ihnen für
5 mehr als zehn Stunden. Der Stillstand herrscht im Südosten Englands, bei der Zufahrt auf den Fährhafen von Dover und den Autoverlader des Eurotunnels in Folkestone. Der Fährhafen rief zeitweilig den Ausnahmezustand aus. Der Autoverlader wurde am Sonntag vom Automobilverband AA zum «Hotspot der Ferienhölle» erklärt.

Die BBC hat einen Live-Blog eingerichtet, in dem unter anderem der dreifache Familienvater
10 Manesh Luthra zu Wort kommt. Am Samstagmorgen um 4 Uhr fuhr die Familie von Essex im Nordosten Londons los. Um 5 Uhr 45 erreichte sie den Eurotunnel-Terminal. Für 7 Uhr 50 hatten sie den Zug für die halbstündige Fahrt unter dem Ärmelkanal gebucht. Stattdessen saßen sie fest. [...]. Es habe keine Informationen gegeben, keine Unterstützung, keine Versorgung. Erst um 22 Uhr am Samstagabend kam die Familie in Frankreich an.

Eine Kolonne von 320 Kilometern

Doch nicht nur Personenwagen stehen im Stau. Auf den Straßen reihten sich auch Lastwagen kilometerlang aneinander. Manche Autobahnen wurden zu Stellplätzen umfunktioniert, auf denen am Sonntag noch 600 Lastwagen auf ihre Weiterreise warten mussten. Die Sperrungen vergrößerten das Chaos für Personenwagen auf den verbliebenen Schnellstraßen. Der Hafen von Dover teilte am Sonntagmittag mit, er habe bisher an diesem Wochenende 72 000 Passagiere abgefertigt, was einer Verkehrskolonne von umgerechnet mehr als 320 Kilometern entspreche.

Die Diskussion über die Ursachen hält britische Medien und die Politik in Atem. Es war bekannt, dass an diesem Wochenende viel los sein würde: Vergangene Woche begannen vielerorts die Schulferien. Und das erste Mal seit zwei Sommern können die Briten, die oft von Corona-Restriktionen im In- und Ausland zurückgehalten wurden, für die wichtigsten Ferien des Jahres frei die Insel verlassen. [...]

Sofort wird über den Brexit diskutiert

Wie bei vielen britischen Problemen ist auch hier eine Diskussion darüber entbrannt, ob der Brexit für den Schlamassel verantwortlich sei. Das neue Reiseregime [Reiseregelung], das seit Anfang 2021 mit dem Ende der EU-Personenfreizügigkeit gilt, wird schließlich jetzt zum ersten Mal im großen Stil auf die Probe gestellt.

Die üblichen Reflexe funktionieren zuverlässig: Die konservative britische Regierung verortete die Hauptschuld für das Chaos bei der französischen Grenzpolizei. Deren Beamte sind nämlich auch in Dover im Einsatz und kontrollieren noch auf britischem Boden die Papiere der Reisenden, die sich durch den Ärmelkanal auf den Weg machen. Im Gegenzug sind britische Beamte in Calais stationiert – zum Beispiel, um illegale Einwanderer abzufangen, bevor sie auf der Insel ankommen [...]

Allerdings hat der Brexit einen Effekt, der die gegenwärtigen Probleme verschärft: Jede Grenzkontrolle dauert nun länger als früher. [...]

Source: Triebe, Benjamin: Frankreich – so nah und doch so fern: Tagelanger Megastau lässt Briten mit dem Brexit hadern. In Neue Zürcher Zeitung. Found at https://www.nzz.ch/panorama/grossbritannien-riesiger-stau-vor-dover-schuert-brexit-debatte-ld.1695039 [last access: 09/02/2023]

Task

Imagine, you are staying with your friend in London. His/her parents want to drive you home, but you think it is too much and you would rather take a plane. Then, you find an article from a Swiss paper and read it. You inform your hosts by summing up the essentials and talk them out of the trip to Germany. (*Mediation*)

Hinweise und Erwartungshorizonte

Hinweise (M 1)

1. Stunde

Ziel ist es, dass die Schülerinnen und Schüler anhand von Cartoons und Bildern in das Thema einsteigen und ihr Vorwissen aktivieren. Sie äußern sich **mündlich und schriftlich** zu Bildern/Cartoons.

Methodische Hinweise

Als **Einführung** in das Material wird die **Karikatur 3. Reihe links** verwendet. Die Lernenden beschreiben das Bild und versprachlichen die Botschaft: Große Gefahr für Großbritannien steht bevor, da der Wagen (die britische Regierung) von den Klippen zu fallen droht mit darinsitzenden Politikern, die in verschiedene Richtungen steuern. Besonders gefährlich sieht das Gefährt selbst aus, da es aus zwei Vorderteilen besteht. Nach Erarbeitung der Bilder/der Karikaturen werden die Ergebnisse **gesichert**, indem die Lernenden einen Cartoon oder ein Bild (ausgenommen des Einstiegscartoons) auswählen und es im Plenum vorstellen.

Differenzierungshinweis

Sollten die Lernenden mit dem Thema nicht vertraut sein, dient der Link (https://raabe.click/Brexit Timeline) als Orientierungshilfe und Unterstützung bei der Einordnung der Bilder/Cartoons.

Hausaufgabe

Aufgabe 3 kann als Hausaufgabe gegeben werden, in der die Lernenden einen Blogbeitrag schreiben, der interessante Informationen aus der Klassendiskussion aufgreift.

Erwartungshorizont (M 1)

1./2.

image	topic/image	clue; before or after the referendum	what happened and why?
1. row	Johnson's battle bus	"vote leave" written on the bus, used before the referendum	The inscription, "We send …" is a lie that was placed there to deceive the people or to make them vote in favour of Brexit.
2. row, left	British newspaper front pages on the eve of 23 June 2016	on the eve of the EU referendum front pages, used before the referendum	controversial banners, often inviting readers to vote or not to vote "leave" = Brexit
2. row, right	map of the European Union	map shows the UK (in red) is not in the EU, used after the referendum	The UK has left the EU; the countries bordering UK are painted in blue

image	topic/image	clue; before or after the referendum	what happened and why?
3. row, left	Brexit cliff edge	cartoon shows Brexiteers and Remainers (Theresa May /Nigel Farage) in 2019, used after the referendum	Dover cliff edge, the car with politicians heading for the abyss symbolising different opinions on which way to take, seemingly undecided
3. row, right	All aboard Boris Johnson's lying-bus	cartoon shows Johnson's picture on the bus; text reads "I've taken back control"; in the bus sheep symbolising Tory cabinet members, used after the referendum	After his cabinet reshuffle, Johnson and his cabinet head for the sunlit uplands, meaning "a happy future", which is a figure of speech used by Churchill

3. Individual results. Example:
   Hello!
   We looked at the images and decided to do some research on the ones which deal with Johnson's buses. The first one, Boris's battle-bus for the referendum, is a photo and gives evidence of a lie. The false assertion invites voters to believe that the EU has exploited Britain. The imperative "vote leave" was meant to bring about a change and give money to their "NHS instead". "Let's fund" and a second "let's take back" are meant to remind voters that they are together in one "boat" against the EU. While the real battle-bus is red and the inscription in white, the cartoon bus is mainly in blue with Johnson's portrait on the front of the bus. Behind the glass, there are heads of many sheep and on the left two more sheep are about to get on the already crowded bus. Behind the windscreen there is a small sign saying, "Tory cabinet". The inscription on the bus says, "Boris the lying bus". While the real bus had the inscription, "Let's take back control", the blue bus now says, "I've taken back control". Both buses have these slogans on the side. It is a clear sign that they belong together, and that Johnson is in charge now, which is true when he says in the speech bubble, "All aboard for the sunlit uplands". Boris is going to take those sheep-like ministers and MPs into a bright future with "Brexit done" and "levelling up". In the front portrait, Boris seems to be smiling but his droopy eyelids express dishonesty.
   The cartoonist disagrees with Boris's "sunlit uplands" as an enormous cloud of exhaust gases shows up behind the bus and forecasts difficult times.
   This is our interpretation. Are there any questions or comments?
4. Individual results.

2. Stunde

Hinweise (M 2)

Ziel ist es, dass die Schülerinnen und Schüler anhand **eines Videos** das Thema im Detail erarbeiten und ausgewählte Aspekte sowie dessen Rezeption kommentieren.

Sachlicher Hinweis
Das Video in **M 2** präsentiert weitere Einzelheiten zum Brexit und macht die Materie – mittels Landkarten und „Handpuppen" – in witziger Form leicht verständlich.

Differenzierungshinweis

Leistungsschwächere Lernende schauen das Video in reduzierter Geschwindigkeit und mit Untertitel an. Sie nutzen außerdem die Unterstützung durch das Vokabular.

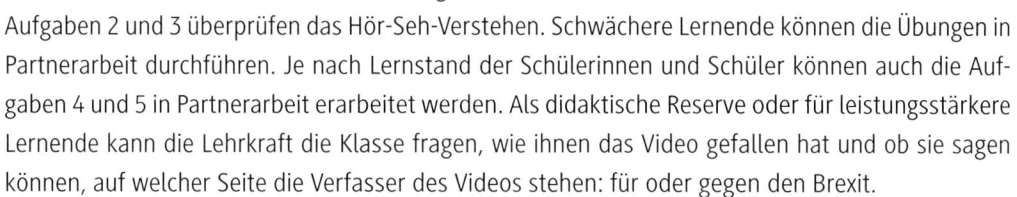

Aufgaben 2 und 3 überprüfen das Hör-Seh-Verstehen. Schwächere Lernende können die Übungen in Partnerarbeit durchführen. Je nach Lernstand der Schülerinnen und Schüler können auch die Aufgaben 4 und 5 in Partnerarbeit erarbeitet werden. Als didaktische Reserve oder für leistungsstärkere Lernende kann die Lehrkraft die Klasse fragen, wie ihnen das Video gefallen hat und ob sie sagen können, auf welcher Seite die Verfasser des Videos stehen: für oder gegen den Brexit.

Digitalhinweis

Die Aufgaben zur Überprüfung des Hör-Seh-Verstehens liegen digital und kostenlos in *LearningApps* vor und sind mit Konto bearbeitbar („ähnliche App erstellen" anklicken): https://learningapps.org/display?v=pzb21k8f523

Hausaufgabe

Aufgabe 6 kann als Hausaufgabe gegeben werden, in der die Lernenden weitere Videos recherchieren und am Anfang der nächsten Stunde vorstellen.

Erwartungshorizont (M 2)

1./2.

Statements	True	False
a) This video explains how the Queen negotiates with the EU.		x
b) On 23 June 2016, British voters decided on leaving the EU.	x	
c) The country was totally united in its wish to quit the EU.		x
d) There was a feeling of being dominated by the Europeans.	x	
e) Some of the remainders remembered their victory after the WWII but would rather not fight the Europeans again.	x	
f) They said the single market was a good idea but leaving it would be better.		x
g) Johnson and Farage are prominent and respectable remainders.		x
h) The then Mayor of London, Boris Johnson and Nigel Farage are called an "eccentric cast of characters".	x	
i) Marine Le Pen and Michael Caine are both Scots.		x
j) RRS Boaty McBoatface is an expensive scientific research ship.	x	

3. 8d; 6a; 4h; 2f; 9c; 1g; 7e; 5i; 3b.
4. Individual results. Example:

   Hello Ian,

   You are right in saying that an explanation should not sound like a mockery. But as it is meant to be "for non-Brits", there seems to be a wink, as the British are often fond of showing a stiff upper lip. It may be aimed at students who prefer some humorous or playful approach, especially for such a serious topic like Brexit. This is also true for the funny animation; e. g. Margret Thatcher's jaw being moved like that of a puppet to make fun of politicians. Although the video's animation seems to be from the early days of filming, the message is clear and effective, especially the one at the end about RRS Boaty McBoatface. Even if the comparison between WWII and a match is going too far, the general approach is amusing and students and other will understand it as such.

Regards, John and Betty

5. Individual results. Example:

Well, Chris, this is not easy to explain, as even the politicians do not fully understand this topic. But I'll try! Let's start with the term itself. Brexit is a blend of **BR**ITAIN and **EXIT,** meaning Britain leaves the European Union. This union has a very large parliament in Brussels and representatives from all member states. They look upon themselves as a union with a free market without border controls. Britain was a member of the European Union. But after 40 years, the British wanted to leave as they felt being treated badly by its rules. As all contracts had to be changed and border check points needed to be established, the resulting chaos and turmoil had to be overcome. And this is not the end of the list of difficulties.

6. Individual results.

3. Stunde

Hinweise (M 3)

Ziel des Materials ist es, dass die Lernenden den aktuellen Brexit-Stand anhand einer inhaltlichen und analytischen Textbetrachtung erschließen.

Methodische Hinweise

Als **Einstieg** in den Zeitungsartikel dient eine Vokabelaufgabe zur Entlastung. Erst im nächsten Schritt erfolgt eine Aufgabe zum Textverständnis, die anspruchsvoll ist und in Partnerarbeit erarbeitet werden kann. Sie beinhalten auch einen **Perspektivenwechsel**. Um die Lernenden bei der Textanalyse zu unterstützen, arbeiten die Lernenden mit vorgegebenen **Stilmitteln** in einer Tabelle, finden diese im Text und bestimmen ihre **Funktion**. Daraufhin ziehen die Schülerinnen und Schüler ein Fazit und analysieren die **Botschaft** des Textes. Die dabei aktivierten Fähigkeiten werden dann angewendet, wobei es um eine Analyse eines **ironisch/sarkastischen Kurztextes** geht.

Digitalhinweis

Der Vorentlastung des Vokabulars dient die sehr einfache *LearningApp*, bei der die Lernenden auch einiges erraten können: https://learningapps.org/display?v=p6286v2v323

Hausaufgabe

Aufgabe 6 kann als Hausaufgabe gegeben werden. Darin kommentieren die Lernenden einen Eintrag auf Social Media, in dem Johnson "*a cheerleader for Brexit*" genannt wird.

Erwartungshorizont (M 3)

1.

customs union	die Zollgemeinschaft
(to) be at loggerheads	(to) disagree very strongly
awkward	difficult
(to) negotiate sth.	etw. aushandeln
deadlock	der Stillstand

grievance	complaint
withdrawal agreement	das Austrittsabkommen
GDP/Gross Domestic Product	das Bruttoinlandsprodukt/BIP
liberated	(to) be set free
resignation	der Rücktritt
(to) betray	(to) cheat, (to) deceive
suggestion	proposal, recommendation
(to) contribute	beitragen

2.
a) Who was in charge of the Leave campaign and what was its aim?
b) What promises were made to the British people for a "positive" vote?
c) In how far does the resignation of Lord Frost – the former Brexit minister – hint at some grievances against Brexit?
d) What did some of Frost's colleagues suggest about other motives of his resignation?
e) What else was a source of frustration to Frost?
f) What can be said about the first consequences of Brexit?
g) How did Brexit effect some important sectors?
h) What can be said about the influence of Brexit on the British economy?
i) What influence does Brexit have on trade?
j) What do the British people say about the success of Brexit?

3.

stylistic device	example/quotation	function
alliteration	beyond slogans and soundbites	to emphasise the writer's disappointment
allusion	Brexit <u>light</u>	indirect reference to a product with less fat → irony
anaphora	We could take back control We could look outwards	sentences starting with the same words underline the positive outlook
antithesis	… the costs and gains of taking our country back … delivering on Brexit promises is proving a lot harder than making them had been … … Getting Brexit done was the easy bit … Proving it … to be far more difficult … … were promised much and got almost nothing … rather than boosting our trade, Brexit is holding it back …	working with contrasts improves the understanding of the problem

stylistic device	example/quotation	function
euphemism	a clue that all was not entirely well	using polite expressions instead of unpleasant ones
hyperbole	Brexit is now secure … the challenge … the world in a new age discovery, striking trade deals … levels of prosperity	an exaggeration making sth. sound better → not true or why does he step down? Why are people poorer than before Brexit?
image	the UK is still at loggerheads with the EU	appealing to the reader's imagination: UK and EU fighting
irony	Gone. Brexit well and truly done. Those promised rewards for Britain of leaving EU should surely be with us by now.	saying the opposite of what he means
leitmotif	Brexit and its negative results: Brexit going badly.	the topic with its negative repercussions recurs throughout the article
metaphor	… to wrestle free from the chains of EU regulation …	poetic comparison without using 'like' or 'as'
parallelism/ enumeration/climax	UK … fully out of the EU … out of its political …, out of its single market, out of its customs union no real plan … no real detailed idea …	repeating identical/similar words to put emphasis on the facts
personification	with both exports to the EU and non-EU destinations suffering	exports are looked upon as suffering from a disease like humans
repetition	Johnson had no real plan, no real detailed idea of how to make Brexit	deliberately using words more than once
rhetorical question	headline: Brexit one year on: So, how's it going?	a question to which the answer is obvious or not possible or not expected
simile	no awkward halfway house like Theresa May had negotiated	comparison using 'like' or 'as'

4. Individual results. Example:
   The journalist uses that special tongue-in-cheek device to reveal his sarcastic undertone concerning Brexit, which is a kind of leitmotif, and which is taken up by "UK and the EU … best of enemies". Using denials/negations combined with emotional words – here light, truly – draw the readers'/spectators' attention to the fact that there is more "interesting stuff" to come. His ridiculing undertone using words like "clean break, liberated, unleash its full potential" together with a metaphor "wrestle free from the chains of EU regulation …" reveal the writer's intention of

criticising the government and the Prime Minister. The anaphora "we could take back" "we could look forward" together with the conditional highlight the improbability of the promises coming true. This is outshone by the climax "fresh levels of prosperity for Global Britain", which sounds full of mockery since the contrast (loss and poverty) is the actual reality. The next paragraph provides evidence of a failing Brexit as the Brexit minister, Lord Frost, explains that "delivering on the opportunities" of Brexit has not yet been achieved. Another potential reason for Frost's resignation is the failure of the Northern Ireland protocol. While comparing reality and Brexit promises, the writer uses comparatives. Other facts are negative as well: promised much – got almost nothing; fishermen betrayed etc. The writer is aware of the negative results of Brexit. Apart from quoting the effects of Brexit on special sectors, he highlights the resignation of the Brexit minister as evidence of Brexit's failure.

5. Individual results. Example:

The writer seems to affirm the question whether Brexit was successful. But the reader finds quite the contrary like a bleak outlook: the possible breakup of the union. When commenting on the situation in England, the writer is negative about his own surroundings, as farmers run out of farmhands. The consequences are the shortage of food and medical supplies. The NHS is on its way to be "cut up" and "sold off". To him, the standard and cost of living is going down. The writer uses words such as "destroy" and "destruction", which he uses especially in his conclusion. The reader is aware that the comment is ironic when the positive statement of "successful" is turned round by using it with a negative implication. The writer is obviously concerned about the situation since he reveals his personal experience, which is negative and full of forebodings. His colloquial style and his repetitions of "destroy" are meant to be a wake-up call for the reader and/or politicians.

6. Individual results.

Hinweise (M 4)

4. Stunde

Ziel des Materials ist es, dass die Schülerinnen und Schüler einen Text erarbeiten sowie einen Cartoon analysieren und dadurch den aktuellen Brexit-Stand erschließen.

Methodische Hinweise

Als **Einstieg** in das Material projiziert die Lehrkraft den Cartoon aus Aufgabe 4 bereits an die Wand. Die Lernenden beschreiben ihn, sammeln erste Assoziationen, im Unterrichtsgespräch werden die Vokabeln semantisiert. Die Erarbeitung des **Textes** beginnt erneut mit einer Vokabelaufgabe und erfolgt daraufhin in **Partnerarbeit**. Im Anschluss wird der Einstiegscartoon noch einmal näher betrachtet, analysiert und auf den Text bezogen.

Digitalhinweis

Aufgaben 1 und 2 liegen zur interaktiven Bearbeitung in *LearningApps* vor. Sie sind kostenlos verfügbar sowie mit Konto bearbeitbar („ähnliche App erstellen" anklicken):
https://learningapps.org/display?v=pz7rj0s4k23
https://learningapps.org/display?v=pfo2jdhjk23

Hausaufgabe

Aufgabe 5 kann als Hausaufgabe gegeben werden. Hier üben die Lernenden, in einem Kommentar die eigene Meinung zum Erfolg/Misserfolg des Brexit auszudrücken.

Erwartungshorizont (M 4)

1.

noun	noun (person)	verb
narration, narrative	narrator	(to) narrate
creation	creator	(to) create
weaving	weaver	(to) weave
campaign	campaigner	(to) campaign
construct, construction	constructor	(to) construct
belief	believer	(to) believe
loss	loser	(to) lose
deal	dealer	(to) deal
vote	voter	(to) vote
improvement	improver	(to) improve

2.

Here, the weavers persisted with the lie that	they were creating the most fantastic set of clothes.
He believed them, despite the fact that	there was no evidence of their existence.
He led a public procession celebrating their wearing these new clothes	only for a child to say: „He's got nothing on."
Scientists of Britain are now realising the horrible truth;	Brexit was a fraud of giant proportions.
The weavers of Brexit convinced voters that they would get	their sovereignty back, even though they never lost it.
This was unnecessary before Brexit – and, if a Labour government were willing to approach	discussions with the EU constructively, it is hardly likely to be considered necessary now.
The vet's practical advice was to bypass the certificate	associated costs by obtaining a pet passport issued in the EU.
They spun stories of incredible wealth	generated from all sorts of magic trade deals.
If we vote leave, we can create a fairer,	more humane immigration system.
On the sixth anniversary of the Brexit vote, a reminder	of some of the points made by the Vote Leave campaign.

3.
a) He thinks Brexit is a disappointment although the expectations were running high.
b) According to the study, the cost of living has worsened.
c) The emperor is talked into believing that his new (non-existing) clothes are extraordinary.
d) Businessmen, farmers, fishermen and scientists are aware of the Brexit failure. They were deceived by some Brexiteers.
e) Forsaking their neighbours and stopping trading with them is – according to them – even suicidal.
f) They had in mind to boost trade, human values and to outlaw war.
g) Similarly to the emperor's realisation of his folly, Boland hopes the British would understand that they were deceived by the Brexiteers.
h) He makes fun of them by saying ironically, "Heaven forbid that we were lied to" since all the slogans proved to be untrue.
i) Because of Brexit, the procedure of taking a dog abroad is costly and a terrible bureaucratic paper chase.
j) While referring to the obvious friendship between Johnson and Zelenskiy, Arnott ironically points at their disagreement on the EU: Johnson wants out and Zelenskiy wants in.

4. Individual results. Example:
Both the text and the cartoon deal with promises and lies by the government and by Boris Johnson. The interesting imagery points at the complicated political implications in 10 Downing Street as the 'weavers' of the fairy tale become the 'weavers of Brexit' who 'spun stories'. Inventing stories seems to be Johnson's main occupation, as his crown 'Liar' reveals. The cartoon shows a connection with Andersen's fairy tale: if you take away Johnson's "cover-ups", it boils down to the naked truth: almost obscene with his private parts covered by a bottle of champagne. Its inscription hints at an operation Johnson dubbed "Operation Save Big Dog". This was an attempt to hold on to power by sacking many members of his staff, in a bid to deflect blame from himself and the parties during lockdown. However, the bottle and the tumbler in Johnson's hand reveal his predisposition towards alcoholism. Going in the same direction is the small note's text addressed to former PM Margaret Thatcher asking her whether he can sack Sue Gray, whom he had put in charge with the investigation into party gate. Obviously, he has dumped that idea as the scrunched-up letter lies on the floor and, of course, Thatcher died already in 2013. The cartoonist combines Johnson's imagined clothes with his scandals characterised by superlatives (magnificent, eye-catching, exquisitely embroidered etc.) and gives him a small crown with the inscription LIAR. Looking closely at Johnson's policies, we understand that they are "a fraud of giant proportions". This is also true for the Rwanda policy. Already 120 million pounds have been paid to the Rwandan government, but because of protests, the initiative was adjourned. Several groups of the population (e.g. farmers, fishermen, scientists lied to by Brexiteers) are hit hard by the cost-of-living crisis. Johnson's boast, "I got Brexit done", again is a lie because Brexit does not work as all four commentators say. Then there is his slogan "civil service efficiency cuts" which has a double meaning. It may be a reference to the Big Dog initiative when he fired lots of his staff, but it could also mean "cuts in efficiency". The reader can find a similar outcome in Mel Wood's comment referring to slogans from the Leave campaign. He ironically pretends to be unsure about it while questioning his own awareness of foul play. Boland finishes his disillusioned views with a final advice. The British should admit that they were deceived. Arnott asks Johnson's fans and admirers ("cheerleaders") to explain the discrepancy between Johnson's and Zelenskiy's friendship and their different attitudes towards the EU. Lorber talks about a strange experience of customs bureaucracy concerning his

dog. He wishes for the British to have an EU passport to bypass lengthy customs controls. That is what Johnson's father did: he acquired French citizenship and got himself a French passport.
5. Individual comments.

Hinweise (LEK)

5. Stunde

Methodische Hinweise

Part A

1. Grundkompetenz: *Comprehension*
   In der ersten Aufgabe geht es um die richtige Wiedergabe des Textes mit eigenen Worten. Im Mittelpunkt des Interesses steht Rawnsleys offene oder versteckte Kritik am Brexit und der Politik der *Conservative Party*.

2. Grundkompetenz: *Analysis*
   Eine sprachliche und inhaltliche Analyse ist wertvoll, damit die Absicht des Autors durchschaut wird. In dem Text geht es nicht nur um den Brexit, sondern auch um Fehler der *Conservative Party* und deren Premierminister und -ministerinnen. Allerdings sagt Rawnsley das nirgends, auch der Name der Partei wird in diesem Auszug nicht genannt. Die Frage ist: Wie schafft der Schreiber es, dass man die Fakten genau im Gedächtnis hat und auch genau weiß, worum es geht. Die Antwort darauf heißt: rhetorische Stilmittel, die Rawnsley einsetzt, um Klarheit zu schaffen.

3.1. Grundkompetenz: *Evaluation, comment*
   Da der gedankliche Hintergrund zur Bearbeitung dieser Frage stark abhängig ist von der im Unterricht behandelten Brexit-Thematik, kann man hier die Hürde nicht zu hoch legen. Andrew Rawnsley spricht drei wichtige Themen an, nämlich *NHS, border control (immigration)* und *failing economy*. Darüber hinaus müsste man noch wissen, dass viele Briten und Britinnen auf die Tricks und Lügen der Tories hereingefallen sind.

3.2 Grundkompetenz: *Evaluation, re-creation*
   Mit den Informationen des Zeitungsartikels sowie auf Basis des vorhandenen Wissens (aus den Unterrichtsstunden) beweisen die Lernenden Ihre Kompetenzen im Kreativen Schreiben. Das Zielformat ist ein Interview mit dem Autor des Zeitungsartikels. Die Lernenden müssen in dem Perspektivwechsel also die Einstellung des Autors einfließen lassen.

Part B

Grundkompetenz: *Mediation*
Der Zieltext ist eine kurze Information im Gespräch mit den Eltern eines englischen Freundes oder einer englischen Freundin, die die wichtigsten Einzelheiten aus dem Artikel zusammenfasst. Aspekte, die herausgestellt werden sollten, sind: lange Autoschlangen vor der Abfertigung an der Grenze in Dover. Der Brexit ist schuld. Mehrere Stunden Wartezeit, daher besser keine Autoreise.

Erwartungshorizont (LEK)

1. In the headline, the reader is warned to come across a rather controversial topic as Brexit and "the new golden age" will not match, not even after three years. The author comes up with three key sections of British life that have not improved. On the contrary, the NHS is "collapsing". The banner on Johnson's battle bus "Take back control" is far from reality as even more migrants arrive in GB. The shrinking British economy reveals the lie of the "golden

age". Leaving the EU is a "self-inflicted harm" with which the business world has been hit as well. Rawnsley sums it up saying that everything that has been promised does not meet reality. The writer then turns to Brexit supporters and opposers that may confess to Brexit's failure, but some former supporters would not admit it in public. And Rawnsley highlights that this would also be true for some cabinet members.

All prime ministers dealing with Brexit unsuccessfully cannot get away with it and are punished by Rawnsley: Cameron seems unable to face the job, May could not deliver, Johnson lied and turned down his own agreement while Liz Truss – living in a cloud-cuckoo-land – was not down to earth and had to step down.

Rawnsley turns to the general public who admit that Brexit was not worth it. Their mood has become "Bregret" according to pollsters. Some even feel like returning to the EU, but the author is realistically negative about it because – in the long run – it may be much too difficult with negotiations and a referendum.

At this point, the writer takes up the headline's main idea of "the new golden age" and admits that there is no such thing; rather, "ages of regret".

2. The rhetorical question in the headline promises a firework of arguments and contrasts: Brexit → promise → the new golden age? The subtitle – taken from the article further down – comes up with the devastating answer, "Nothing in the prospectus has survived contact with reality". At the beginning of the extract, the writer attacks one of the main culprits, Jacob Rees-Mogg, the minister for Brexit opportunities and government efficiency, who claimed to use the money directly for the NHS which went to the EU before Brexit. Rawnsley then turns to the three main disasters, which he calls "strikes" with a double meaning. Number one: the "world-envied health service" is collapsing. The author works with contrasts to make his point, as everything that was okay before Brexit is now crumbling as in number 2: the control of British borders is failing. Number 3: the British economy is at a terrible low. He sums this up using the contrasts "empowering versus enervating". He carries on with a different kind of contrast when looking at groups of people with different opinions before and after Brexit calling it a "disaster" or is "not working". The same goes for his comment on "Leave" supporters "suffering from buyer's remorse" which is somehow funny and a metaphor for people regretting having supported Brexit. He sums up the situation by using the new blend "Bregret" = Brexit + regret. Rawnsley is very outspoken concerning the last conservative PMs when qualifying May with a "mirage", Liz Truss being in "la-la land" and getting at Johnson's lies and blaming him for having had second thoughts about an agreement of his own making. Having said that one does not have any doubts about the writer's stance and views by the sheer mass of negative qualifiers (disaster, colossal blunders, the sick man, ruinous, self-harms, mistakes), Rawnsley's view on Brexit becomes totally clear, as not one positive aspect turns up. But Rawnsley is not naïve and asks for a retrial. He is just giving in to "ages of regret".

3.1 Individual results. Example:

I think, most of the people were taken in by the Tories who kept repeating that the UK had to pay too much money to the EU and that they could save the NHS by putting that money into the NHS instead. Well, it has turned out that it has not materialised as the author says. One of the main ideas for leaving the EU was to be in control of British affairs. They felt being manipulated or "losing their sovereignty". The British did not want to be told by the EU how many migrants to take. Thus, the Tories promised they would stop the influx, but reality is different as many more arrived after Brexit. The British wanted their economy to prosper, but after they had left the EU, the problems became really alarming concerning Northern Ireland and the fishing industry clashing with the French etc. But then, the government tried to cover up by pretending that it was the pandemic that was responsible for the failing economy. As a conclusion, everything that had been promised before Brexit turned out to be impossible to obtain. That is why Bregret characterises the situation properly. Yes, it is above all a disappointment, especially because this situation cannot be mended easily, as the writer points out at the end of the article.

3.2. Individual results. Example:

J. Congratulations, Mr. Rawnsley, how do you feel now that another award is yours?

R. Thank you for coming. Of course, it feels great, and my family is very pleased, too.

J. Am I right, you have been working on that never ending topic of Brexit again?

R. Correct. I did some research because these days there is a lot of fake news which is difficult to eliminate.

J. Absolutely, tell our audience to what your findings are? Was Brexit worth it?

R. Definitely not. But we must live with it. We have reached a point of no return.

J. I wish you would think again. But thank you for your time, Mr. Rawnsley.

R. Thank you. My pleasure.

4. Individual results. Example:

I'm sorry to tell you that driving me home is not such a good idea, but I truly appreciate your offer to give me a ride. The point is – and has been for weeks now – there is chaos in Dover. According to this article there are extremely long queues. Cars and lorries have to wait for hours on end. There is an example of a family that had to wait for more than ten hours. "Why?", you might ask. It is because of Brexit and the now necessary controls take much longer to process people and cars. Stamps are necessary and there is not enough personnel to do the job. My dear friends, to be honest, I would rather take a plane to spare you the chaos in Dover. It was so great to stay with you, and I really enjoyed our time together. All of us getting stranded in a giant queue would be a poor ending of an otherwise wonderful experience. What do you think?

WWW.RAABE.DE

RAABE,
KLASSE SCHULE

Sekundarstufe II

RAAbits Englisch

Impulse und Materialien für die kreative Unterrichtsgestaltung

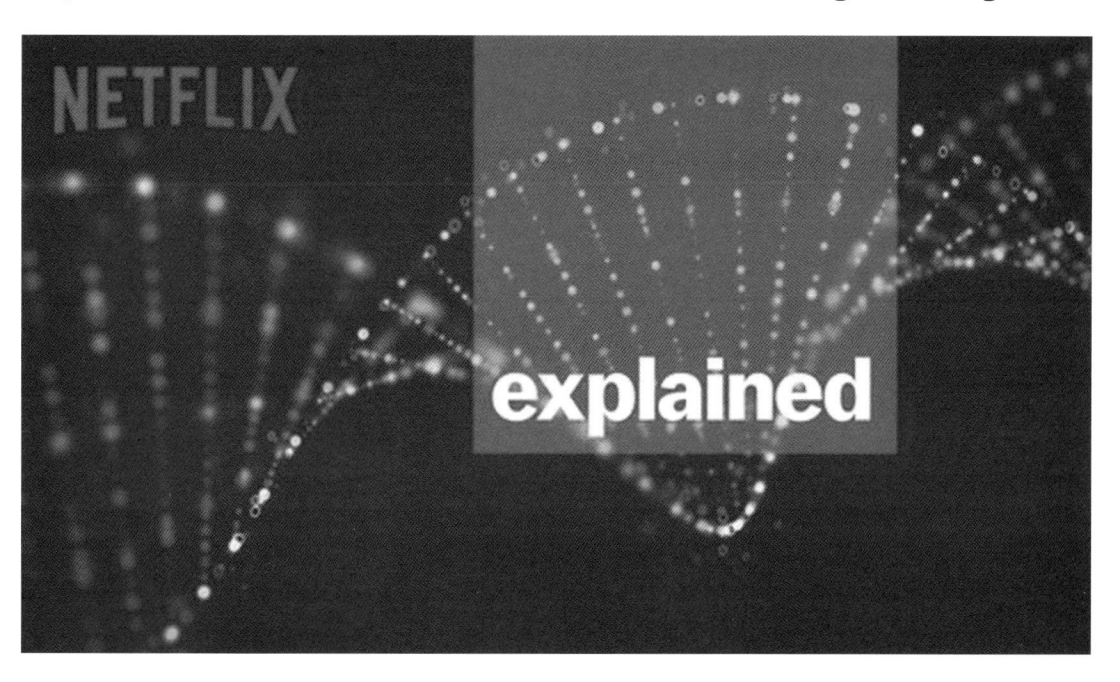

Inhalt:

Abiturrelevante Themen anhand der Netflix-Serie „Explained" erarbeiten (S II)
Worin liegen die globalen Herausforderungen des 21. Jahrhunderts? Die Oberstufenlernenden setzen sich anhand der Doku mit diesen auseinander und trainieren ihre Sprechkompetenz.

Who is Charles III? – Auseinandersetzung mit einem Monarchen (ab Kl. 10)
Ihre Lernenden gehen dieser Frage unter anderem nach, indem sie Bilder und das Video einer Rede Charles' analysieren sowie aktuelle Artikel über ihn und die Monarchie untersuchen.

Impressum

RAAbits Englisch
Ausgabe 3/2023

ISSN: 0946-5308 / 0946-5294
ISBN: 978-3-8183-0025-8 /978-3-8183-0026-5

Das Werk, einschließlich seiner Teile, ist urheberrechtlich geschützt. Es ist gemäß § 60b UrhG hergestellt und ausschließlich zur Veranschaulichung des Unterrichts und der Lehre an Bildungseinrichtungen bestimmt. Die Dr. Josef Raabe Verlags-GmbH erteilt Ihnen für das Werk das einfache, nicht übertragbare Recht zur Nutzung für den persönlichen Gebrauch gemäß vorgenannter Zweckbestimmung. Unter Einhaltung der Nutzungsbedingungen sind Sie berechtigt, das Werk zum persönlichen Gebrauch gemäß vorgenannter Zweckbestimmung in Klassensatzstärke zu vervielfältigen. Jede darüber hinausgehende Verwertung ist ohne Zustimmung des Verlages unzulässig und strafbar. Hinweis zu §§ 60a, 60b UrhG: Das Werk oder Teile hiervon dürfen nicht ohne eine solche Einwilligung an Schulen oder in Unterrichts- und Lehrmedien (§ 60b Abs. 3 UrhG) vervielfältigt, insbesondere kopiert oder eingescannt, verbreitet oder in ein Netzwerk eingestellt oder sonst öffentlich zugänglich gemacht oder wiedergegeben werden. Dies gilt auch für Intranets von Schulen und sonstigen Bildungseinrichtungen. Die Aufführung abgedruckter musikalischer Werke ist ggf. GEMA-meldepflichtig.

Für jedes Material wurden Fremdrechte recherchiert und ggf. angefragt.

Dr. Josef Raabe Verlags-GmbH
Ein Unternehmen der Klett Gruppe
Rotebühlstraße 77
70178 Stuttgart
Telefon +49 711 62900-0
Fax +49 711 62900-60
meinRAABE@raabe.de
www.raabe.de

Redaktion: Juliane Thon, Kathrin Olßon
Satz: pagina GmbH, Tübingen
Bildnachweis Titel: © Figure: Netflix
Korrektorat und Lektorat: Ellen Black
Druck: Uslugi Wydawniczo-Poligraficzne Paper&Tinta; Nadma, Polen

Gedruckt auf chlorfrei gebleichtem Papier

August 2023

Liebe Lehrerin, lieber Lehrer,

Trockenheit, Dürre und Waldbrände – der Sommer 2022 zählt in Europa seit den Wetteraufzeichnungen zu den wärmsten Sommern. Auch 2023 sind in Deutschland Hitzerekorde geknackt worden und in Teilen Europas wie zum Beispiel in Spanien herrschte sogar Wasserknappheit. Mit diesen und weiteren globalen Herausforderungen des 21. Jahrhundert setzen sich Ihre Schülerinnen und Schülerinnen in unserer Oberstufenreihe **Talking about ecological, technological and social challenges – Abiturthemen anhand der Netflix-Serie *„Explained"* erarbeiten** auseinander. Diese werden anhand der populären Dokumentation erarbeitet und diskutiert. Dabei steht sowohl die Festigung des Hör-Seh-Verstehens, als auch Sprechkompetenz im Fokus.

Auch in unserer zweiten Reihe **Living for the future: Focus on sustainability – Merkmale nachhaltigen Lebens erörtern** geht es um den verantwortungsvollen Umgang mit Ressourcen und die Folgen der Umweltverschmutzung und des Klimawandels. Ihre Lernenden der Klassen 7 bis 10 erwerben anhand unterschiedlicher Textarten die Sachkompetenz, in Zukunft nachhaltig zu agieren. Dabei schulen sie schwerpunktmäßig ihr Leseverstehen und ihre Hör-Seh-Kompetenz.

Mit aktuellen gesellschaftlichen Herausforderungen beschäftigen sich Ihre Mittelstufenschülerinnen und -schüler in unserer Unterrichtseinheit **Jewell Parker Rhodes' *Ghost Boys* – Sich anhand des Bestsellers mit den Themen „Rassismus" und „Polizeigewalt" in den USA auseinandersetzen**. Ihre Lernenden erleben die Probleme durch die Perspektive der jugendlichen Protagonisten. Dabei üben sie anhand abwechslungsreicher analytischer und kreativer Schreibaufgaben, literarische Ganzschriften zu untersuchen. In angeleiteten Internetrecherchen erschließen sie außerdem selbstständig wichtige Hintergrundinformationen zur Geschichte der USA und des Civil Rights Movements.

Ihre Schülerinnen und Schüler ab Klasse 10 nehmen in unserer Unterrichtsreihe **British monarchy: Who is Charles III? – Auseinandersetzung mit einem kritischen Monarchen** den britischen König Charles III genauer unter die Lupe. Dabei gehen sie nicht nur der Frage nach, wer Charles eigentlich ist, sondern auch, ob er seiner Aufgabe als König gewachsen ist. Hierzu untersuchen sie Charles' Rolle in den Medien, indem sie Bilder und das Video einer Rede analysieren sowie u. a. einen aktuellen Artikel über die Besonderheiten Charles' lesen.

Bei inhaltlichen Anmerkungen, Wünschen und Rückfragen zum Produkt erreichen Sie uns unter J.Thon@raabe.de und 0711-62900-91.

Wir wünschen Ihnen viel Freude mit unseren Unterrichtsreihen und einen erfolgreichen Schulstart.

Ihre Redaktion Englisch

Folgen Sie uns auf Instagram, Facebook und Twitter unter @RAABEVerlag

Einsortierungsanleitung

Bitte sortieren Sie die enthaltenen Einheiten wie folgt in Ihren Ordner ein:

Themenbereich Einheit	Bitte diese Seiten einfügen
I.C.1.34 Jewell Parker Rhodes' *Ghost Boys* – Sich anhand des Bestsellers mit den Themen „Rassismus" und „Polizeigewalt in den USA" auseinandersetzen (Klassen 8–10)	komplett
II.C.8.7 Talking about ecological, technological, and social challenges – Abiturthemen anhand der Netflix-Serie *„Explained"* erarbeiten (Klassen 10–13) **	komplett
V.280 British monarchy: Who is Charles III? – Auseinandersetzung mit einem kritischen Monarchen (ab Klasse 10) **	komplett
V.281 Living for the future: Focus on sustainability – Merkmale nachhaltigen Lebens erörtern (Klassen 7–10)	komplett

Hinweis: Alle Einheiten, Zusatzmaterialien sowie eine aktuelle Inhaltsübersicht finden Sie auch in Ihrem **Online-Archiv** im RAABE-Webshop. Loggen Sie sich unter www.raabe.de mit Ihren Kundendaten in Ihr Webshop-Konto ein. Wenn Sie noch kein Konto haben, melden Sie sich unter meinraabe@raabe.de, um Ihre Zugangsdaten zu erhalten.

Themenvorschau

In den folgenden Lieferungen erwarten Sie u. a. diese Themen:

The African American experience: Film in a Box (S II) (November 2023)
In der Reihe lernen die Schülerinnen und Schüler die Geschichte der Afroamerikaner:innen näher kennen, indem sie eine Präsentation zu einem Film des Genres *„Black Cinema"* vorbereiten.

ChatGPT: Discussing the pros and cons of artificial intelligence (ab Kl. 10) (November 2023)
Die Lernenden setzen sich anhand aktueller Zeitungsartikel mit den positiven und negativen Aspekten der revolutionären Erfindung auseinander und entwickeln eine eigene, kritische Meinung.

Heartstopper **– Die Graphic Novel und die Serie vergleichen (Kl. 8–10) (November 2023)**
Der Umgang mit Diversity stellt einen wichtigen Fokus der Unterrichtsreihe dar. Zudem wird der Umgang mit Fernsehserien und Graphic Novels als multimodales Textgenre geschult.

Reading Sarfraz Manzoor's *Greetings from Bury Park* – Abiturtraining (S II) (Februar 2024)
Anhand eines innovativen Lesetagebuchs und abwechslungsreicher Methoden wie der Strukturlegetechnik oder eines Lerntempoduetts erschließen die Lernenden die Memoiren.

(Änderungen vorbehalten)

II.C.8.7

Landeskunde – Science, Technology and Environment

Talking about ecological, technological and social challenges – Abiturthemen anhand der Netflix-Serie „*Explained*" erarbeiten (S II)

Maike Bümmerstede

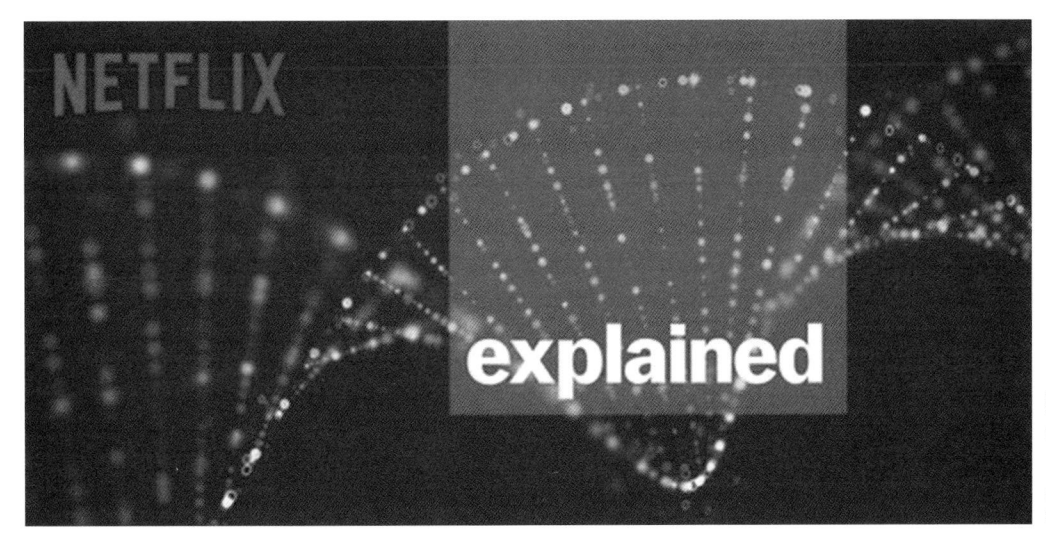

© Figure: Netflix

Wie wird sich die globale Wasserkrise auf unser Leben auswirken? Wie sieht der Fleischkonsum der Zukunft aus? *Genome-editing* am Menschen – Fluch oder Segen? In dieser Unterrichtseinheit setzen sich Ihre Schülerinnen und Schüler mit globalen Herausforderungen des 21. Jahrhunderts auseinander, die sie anhand der Netflix-Dokumentation *„Explained"* erarbeiten und diskutieren. Dabei festigen die Lernenden schwerpunktmäßig sowohl ihr Hör-Seh-Verstehen als auch ihre Sprechkompetenz.

KOMPETENZPROFIL

LearningApps - interaktive Lernbausteine

Klassenstufe:	11/12 (G8), 12/13 (G9)
Dauer:	2–13 Unterrichtsstunden + LEK
Kompetenzen:	1. Hör-Seh-Verstehen: einer Dokumentation zentrale Informationen entnehmen; 2. Sprechkompetenz: ökologische, technologische und soziale Herausforderungen beschreiben, Lösungsansätze diskutieren und dazu Stellung beziehen; 3. Medienkompetenz: eine Internet-Recherche durchführen
Thematische Bereiche:	*ecological challenges, science and technology, world of work, social challenges*
Material:	digitale Kreuzworträtsel als Wortschatzsicherung (*LearningApps*), Vorschlag für eine mündliche Prüfung im Tandemformat
Zusätzlich benötigt:	Dokumentarreihe *„Explained"* (2018 und 2019) von Ezra Klein und Joe Posner (Netflix)

Fachliche Hinweise

Zu den globalen Herausforderungen des 21. Jahrhunderts

Im 21. Jahrhundert stehen wir zahlreichen globalen Herausforderungen gegenüber, die mit enormen **ökologischen**, **technologischen** und **sozialen Problemen** einhergehen und unsere Lebensweise langfristig verändern werden. Der **Klimawandel** und seine verheerenden Folgen, einschließlich extremer Wetterbedingungen und **Naturkatastrophen**, stellen eine immer größer werdende Bedrohung für unseren Planeten und die Menschheit dar. Gleichzeitig sind Kriege und Konflikte in vielen Teilen der Welt an der Tagesordnung, Ressourcen werden knapper und der Wandel der globalisierten Welt schafft strukturelle Veränderungen, an die wir uns stetig anpassen müssen.

Die COVID-19-Pandemie hat unser Leben und unsere Gesellschaft grundlegend verändert und uns vor neue Herausforderungen gestellt. Sie hat uns gezeigt, wie anfällig wir als globale Gemeinschaft sind und wie wichtig es ist, gemeinsam Lösungen zu finden.

Auf der anderen Seite bieten **neue Technologien** wie **künstliche Intelligenz** oder **Gentechnik** Chancen. Bereits jetzt erleichtern sie unser Leben in vielen Bereichen und haben das Potenzial, den Herausforderungen unserer Zeit mit nachhaltigen Lösungsansätzen zu begegnen. Gleichzeitig bergen diese Technologien auch die Gefahr, Ungleichheit zu fördern und werfen ethische und moralische Fragen auf.

Diese Themen sind gerade für junge Menschen von besonderer Relevanz. Aufgabe der Schule ist es auch, mit den Jugendlichen über Zukunftsängste ins Gespräch zu kommen, fundiertes Wissen zur Verfügung zu stellen und mögliche Lösungsansätze zu diskutieren.

Zur Netflix-Serie „Explained" und der Auswahl der Folgen

Die US-amerikanische **Dokumentarreihe** „Explained" beschäftigt sich mit einigen der oben genannten Themen, liefert fundierte und **gut recherchierte Fakten**, die auf anschauliche und unterhaltsame Weise präsentiert werden und bietet viele **Anregungen zur Diskussion**. Die erste Staffel der Reihe, die von Ezra Klein und Joe Posner mit Vox Media produziert wird, wurde im Jahr 2018 auf dem Streaming-Dienst Netflix veröffentlicht. Namhafte Persönlichkeiten wie die Schauspielerin Emma Stone und der Schauspieler Christian Slater moderieren die Episoden. Die Wochenzeitschrift Die Zeit lobt die leichte Zugänglichkeit der Folgen: „[Sie] beschreiben dennoch selbst ein so komplexes Thema wie Genom-Editierung anschaulich, dank leicht verständlicher Aussagen ausgewiesener Fachleute. Besser und moderner hat Bildungsfernsehen lange nicht ausgesehen."[1]

In der vorliegenden Unterrichtseinheit findet die Lehrkraft Materialen zu den folgenden vier Episoden: „The World's Water Crisis", „The Future of Meat", „Designer DNA" und „Why Women Are Paid Less".

„The World's Water Crisis"

Die Episode handelt von der Wasserkrise, mit der viele Länder auf der ganzen Welt aktuell konfrontiert sind. Die Dokumentation beleuchtet, wie die weltweite **Wasserknappheit** verheerende **Auswirkungen** auf die Gesellschaft, die Wirtschaft und die Umwelt hat. Es wird aufgezeigt, wie sich die Wasserknappheit auf verschiedene Teile der Welt auswirkt, insbesondere auf die Länder Afrikas, Asiens und Südamerikas. Die Folge zeigt, wie der **Klimawandel**, das **Bevölkerungswachstum** und der Anstieg des Wasserbedarfs durch die **Landwirtschaft** und **Industrie** zur globalen Wasserknapp-

---

[1] Peitz, Dirk; https://www.zeit.de/kultur/film/2018-05/explained-netflix-vox-youtube-dokumentation-show-konkurrenz?utm_referrer=https%3A%2F%2Fwww.google.de%2F [letzter Abruf: 07.05.2023]

heit beitragen. Da hier insbesondere auf den enormen Wasserverbrauch in der Fleischproduktion eingegangen wird, lässt sich die Folge gut mit der Folge „*The Future of Meat*" verknüpfen.

„The Future of Meat"
Die Folge beleuchtet, wie sich die **Fleischindustrie** über viele Jahrzehnte entwickelt und gewandelt hat und wie sich der **steigende Fleischkonsum** auf Menschen und Umwelt auswirkt. Es wird gezeigt, wie die traditionelle Fleischindustrie mit der steigenden Nachfrage nach Fleisch, insbesondere in Schwellenländern, nicht mithalten kann und zu einer ernsthaften Bedrohung für die Umwelt wird. Es wird deutlich: Die Fleischindustrie muss sich grundlegend wandeln und nachhaltige Lösungen müssen dringend entwickelt werden.
Im zweiten Teil beschäftigt sich die Dokumentation mit neuen Technologien, die eine umweltfreundliche und **nachhaltige Fleischproduktion** versprechen. Es wird diskutiert, welche **Vor**- und **Nachteile** Alternativen wie zum Beispiel im Labor gezüchtetes Fleisch haben und wie sie die Fleischindustrie revolutionieren könnten.

„Designer DNA"
In der Folge geht es um **Gentechnologie** und **synthetische Biologie**. Die Dokumentation zeigt, wie moderne Technologien es ermöglichen, das Erbgut von Lebewesen gezielt zu verändern und neue Organismen zu schaffen, die unseren Bedürfnissen und Wünschen entsprechen. Die Entwicklung von **CRISPR** (ein molekularbiologisches Verfahren, um einen DNA-Strang an einer vorgegebenen Stelle zu durchschneiden und zu verändern) war ein entscheidender Schritt im Feld der Gentechnologie und ist vielversprechend, wenn es zum Beispiel darum geht, in Zukunft bestimmte Erbkrankheiten zu heilen beziehungsweise von vorneherein zu vermeiden.
Die Folge macht aber auch deutlich, dass wissenschaftlicher Fortschritt auch bedeutet, dass die Gesellschaft mit ganz neuen **ethischen Fragen** konfrontiert wird; zum Beispiel bezüglich möglicher **Auswirkungen** auf die Umwelt und die Gesellschaft sowie die **Missbräuche** der Technologie.

„Why Women Are Paid Less"
Die Folge geht dem Thema des **Gender Pay Gap**, also des geschlechtsspezifischen Lohngefälles, auf den Grund. Zunächst wird die aktuelle Situation mit der Situation in den 1950er und 1960er Jahren verglichen und es werden **Ursachen** aufgezeigt, die das Lohngefälle bedingt haben, beziehungsweise immer noch bedingen. Es wird deutlich, dass trotz einer Verbesserung der Stellung der Frau in der Arbeitswelt noch nicht von **Chancengleichheit** gesprochen werden kann.
Im zweiten Teil untersucht die Dokumentation mögliche **Lösungsansätze** und Maßnahmen. Anhand der Beispiele Island und Ruanda wird aufgezeigt, dass es durchaus möglich ist, den Gender Pay Gap zu verringern und die Situation der Frauen zu verbessern.

Didaktisch-methodische Hinweise

Zum Aufbau der Unterrichtseinheit

Die Unterrichtseinheit gliedert sich in drei Teile und lässt sich je einem Themenfeld zuordnen.

Die Arbeitsblätter können als komplette Unterrichtseinheit eingesetzt werden. Die einzelnen Folgen bieten sich aber auch zur Wiederholung oder Erweiterung schon unterrichteter Themen an und können unabhängig voneinander zum Einsatz kommen.

In allen vier Episoden geht es um Herausforderungen, denen die Gesellschaft im 21. Jahrhundert gegenübersteht. Daher wird als **Einstieg** zunächst der **Begriff „global challenge"** näher betrachtet. Im Anschluss daran werden folgende **drei Themenfelder** erarbeitet:

1. *Ecological challenges*: „The World's Water Crisis", „The Future of Meat"
2. *Technological challenges*: „Designer DNA"
3. *Social challenges*: „Why Women Are Paid Less"

Zu den methodischen Schwerpunkten

Da die Unterrichtseinheit unter anderem der Vorbereitung auf die mündliche Abiturprüfung dient, kommen Methoden zum Einsatz, die insbesondere die Sprechfertigkeit fördern. Das geschieht zum Beispiel in Form von *Think-Pair-Share*-Aufgaben, Partner- und Projektarbeit.

Es werden dabei Materialien eingesetzt, die für die Förderung der Sprechfertigkeit geeignet sind und zudem häufig als **Sprechimpulse** in mündlichen Prüfungen zur Anwendung kommen, zum Beispiel **Diagramme (M 4, M 12** und **LEK)** und **Cartoons (M 9)**. Zudem stellen die Schülerinnen und Schüler an vielen Stellen den **Bezug zur eigenen Lebensrealität** her, zum Beispiel durch einen **Fragebogen** zum Wasserverbrauch **(M 2)** und zum eigenen Fleischkonsum **(M 6)**. Diese Formate eignen sich zum einen gut, um sich in Partnerarbeit auszutauschen, zum anderen ist es für Lernende oft leichter und motivierender, sich zu Sachverhalten zu äußern, die sie persönlich betreffen. Auf diese Weise werden abstrakte und komplexe Themen greifbarer und spannender.

Lernschwächere Schülerinnen und Schüler werden durch gezielte **Vokabelvorentlastung** und *useful phrases* nach dem Prinzip des *Scaffolding* unterstützt.

Zur Lerngruppe und den curricularen Vorgaben

Die ausgewählten Folgen der Serie *„Explained"* eignen sich zum einen zur Erarbeitung **abiturrelevanter Themen**. Die Episoden *„The World's Water Crisis"* und *„The Future of Meat"* lassen sich gut in eine Unterrichtsreihe zur Lehrplaneinheit *„Ecological challenges"* einbetten. Die Folge *„Designer DNA"* passt gut in den Themenbereich *„Science and technology"*, die Folge *„Why Women Are Paid Less"* knüpft an den Bereich *„World of work"* an.

Zum anderen eignen sich die Materialien besonders zur **inhaltlichen Vertiefung** und für die **Vorbereitung** auf die **mündliche Abiturprüfung**. Aufgrund der Kürze der einzelnen Episoden (Spielzeit zwischen 15 und 20 Minuten) lassen sie sich gut in den Unterricht integrieren. Sie liefern fundierte Fakten, die anschaulich erklärt werden und bieten Anregung zur weiteren Diskussion und zur Entwicklung eigener Ideen, wie man den dargestellten Herausforderungen unserer Zeit begegnen könnte.

Die Materialien eignen sich zum Einsatz in einem Grundkurs oder Leistungskurs, auch zur Vertiefung von Inhalten oder zur Wiederholung vor der Abiturprüfung.

Hinweise zum digitalen Einsatz

Die **Wortschatzarbeit (M 7**, **M 11** und **M 14)** wird von den Lernenden digital bearbeitet.

Lehrwerksbezug

Eine Anknüpfung an die aktuellen Lehrwerke der Oberstufe ergibt sich durch den Bezug zu den Themen „*Science and technology*", „*World of work*" und „*Ecological issues*"
- Challenge 2 (Klett) Englisch für die Jahrgangsstufen 1 und 2: Kapitel 1 „*Ecological Issues*", Kapitel 2 „*Science and Technology*" und Kapitel 8 „*The World of Work*"
- Green Line (Klett) Oberstufe, Nordrhein-Westfalen, Kapitel 9 „*Global Challenges*", Kapitel 10 „*Ecological Challenges*" und Kapitel 11 „*Science and Vision of the Future*"
- Green Line (Klett) Oberstufe, G8, Kapitel 8 „*Science and Utopia*"

Medienkompetenzen (KMK)

(1) Suchen, Verarbeiten und Aufbewahren: zielgerichtete Internetrecherche durchführen (**M 8, M 11**)

(3) Produzieren und Präsentieren: Erstellung einer PowerPoint (**M 5, M 8**)

(5) Problemlösen und Handeln: *LearningApps* als digitales Werkzeug nutzen (**M 4, M 7, M 11, M 14**)

Mediathek

Netflix-Serie „*Explained*"
- Klein, Ezra; Posner, Joe (Produzenten): Explained. Staffel 1. Vox Media. USA 2018.
- Klein, Ezra; Posner, Joe (Produzenten): Explained. Staffel 2. Vox Media. USA 2019.
  Das Streamen der Serie ist über einen Netflix-Account möglich. Ein monatlich kündbares Basis-Abonnement kostet 7,99 € (Stand Juli 2023). Weitere Informationen finden Sie auf der offiziellen Netflix-Website: www.netflix.com.
  Zudem können die einzelnen Folgen über die Netflix-App heruntergeladen und offline gezeigt werden.

Weiterführende Internetseiten
- https://www.footprintnetwork.org/resources/footprint-calculator/ [letzter Abruf: 26.07.2023]
  Hier finden sich Informationen zu den Themen „Nachhaltigkeit", „Umweltschutz" und „Klimawandel". Besucherinnen und Besucher der Seite können ihren ökologischen Fußabdruck berechnen.
- https://www.britishcouncil.org/climate-connection/get-involved/resources-school-teachers [letzter Abruf: 26.07.2023]
  Aktivitäten und Materialien zum Thema „Nachhaltigkeit und Klimawandel" vom British Council
- https://www.pbslearningmedia.org/resource/lesson-plan-gene-editing-and-crispr/lesson-plan-gene-editing-and-crispr/ [letzter Abruf: 26.07.2023]
  Eine Unterrichtseinheit zum Thema CRISPR und Gentechnologie
- https://www.youtube.com/watch?v=R_mQMZ2kV4Y&ab_channel=BobBlume-Netzlehrer [letzter Abruf: 26.07.2023]
  Informatives Video mit Tipps zum Thema „Präsentieren"

Auf einen Blick

1. Stunde

Thema: Global challenges in the 21st century: An introduction

M 1 **Talking about global challenges – A picture stimulus /** Bilder zum Thema *„Global challenges"* beschreiben (PA) und eine Mindmap erstellen (EA)

2./3. Stunde

Thema: Environmental challenges: Water crisis I

M 2 **Our most precious resource – Talking about water consumption /** sich anhand eines Rankings mündlich über das Thema *„Water consumption"* austauschen und Annahmen formulieren (PA/UG)

M 3 *Explained: The World's Water Crisis* – **Understanding an episode /** Inhalte einer Dokumentation verstehen und wiedergeben (EA)

Benötigt: ☐ Laptop/Tablet mit Netflix-Zugang und Beamer/Whiteboard zum Ansehen der Folge

4./5. Stunde

Thema: Environmental challenges: Water crisis II

M 4 **How much water is needed to produce our food? – Describing a graph /** ein Diagramm beschreiben und analysieren (PA) sowie mögliche Lösungen diskutieren (UG)

M 5 **Creating awareness – The UNICEF Dirty Water Vending Machine Campaign /** den Inhalt eines Videos verstehen und wiedergeben (EA); eine eigene Umwelt-Kampagne entwickeln und umsetzen (GA)

6./7. Stunde

Thema: Environmental challenges: Meat consumption I

M 6 **How much meat do you eat? – A questionnaire /** den eigenen Fleischkonsum mit einem Fragebogen reflektieren (EA) und mit anderen vergleichen (PA)

M 7 *Explained: The Future of Meat* – **Understanding an episode /** Inhalte einer Dokumentation verstehen und wiedergeben (EA)

Benötigt: ☐ Laptop/Tablet mit Netflix-Zugang und Beamer/Whiteboard zum Ansehen der Folge

8./9. Stunde

Thema:	Environmental challenges: Meat consumption II
M 8	**The Beyond Burger or cultured meat: What will the future look like? – A project** / eine Internetrecherche über nachhaltige Lebensmittel durchführen und die Ergebnisse präsentieren (GA)

10./11. Stunde

Thema:	Technological challenges: Genetic engineering
M 9	*Choose your child's talent* – **Describing and analysing a cartoon** / eine Karikatur beschreiben und analysieren (PA)
M 10	*Explained: Designer DNA* – **Understanding an episode** / Inhalte einer Dokumentation verstehen und wiedergeben (EA)
M 11	**Genetic engineering: A blessing or a curse? – A panel discussion** / eine Internetrecherche durchführen (GA), eine Podiumsdiskussion vorbereiten (GA) und durchführen (PL)
Benötigt:	☐ Laptop/Tablet mit Netflix-Zugang und Beamer/Whiteboard zum Ansehen der Folge

12./13.

Thema:	Social challenges: Gender pay gap
M 12	**Talking about the gender pay gap – Describing and analysing a diagram** / ein Diagramm beschreiben und untersuchen; über mögliche Ursachen diskutieren (PA)
M 13	*Explained: Why Women Are Paid Less* – **Understanding an episode** / Inhalte einer Dokumentation verstehen und wiedergeben (EA)
M 14	**Introducing a women's quota – Reading an article** / die Inhalte eines Zeitungsartikels verstehen und wiedergeben (EA); über die Vor- und Nachteile einer Frauenquote diskutieren (PA/GA)
Benötigt:	☐ Laptop/Tablet mit Netflix-Zugang und Beamer/Whiteboard zum Ansehen der Folge

Lernerfolgskontrolle

LEK	Global challenges – Oral mock exam

Minimalplan

Die Materialien zu den drei Themenschwerpunkten lassen sich auch unabhängig voneinander einsetzen. Die Bearbeitung lediglich einer der drei Netflix-Episoden ist problemlos möglich.

M 1 Talking about global challenges – A picture stimulus

What are the global challenges we are facing in the 21st century?

© www.colourbox.com

Tasks

1. With a partner, describe the pictures.
2. Find a heading for each picture. Which global challenges do they represent?
3. What do you already know about the issues represented by the pictures?
4. Which of these issues is the most worrisome for you? Give reasons.
5. Name other global challenges we are facing today. Describe in which way they affect your everyday life.
6. *Working with words*: Create a mind map. Write down key words which are connected to the topic *Global challenges of the 21st century*. Include your ideas.

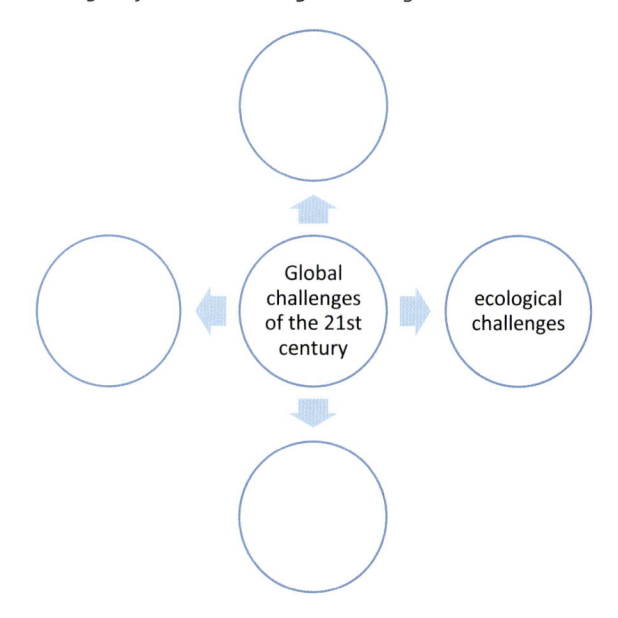

Our most precious resource – Talking about water consumption

M 2

Let's have a look at water consumption in average German households and your own water consumption.

Warm-up

Finish the sentence.

Water is _____.

Tasks

1. Which activities do you think use the highest amount of water? Which activities use the least amount of water? Rank the activities from the table below. Guess how much water the average consumer in Germany used per day in 2021.

	activity	ranking
	taking a shower/bath	
	watering the garden/cleaning the house	
	food and drinks	
	washing the dishes	
	flushing the toilet	
	doing the laundry	

2. Compare and contrast your results with a partner. Are the ranking and your guesses similar or different? Give reasons for your assumptions.
3. Share your results in class. Ask your teacher for the answers. What do you find surprising and why?

Language support: dialogue

Making assumptions
- I think/assume/suppose that …
- It is (not) very likely that …
- Probably, …
- It is safe to assume that …

Talking about amounts and numbers
- the majority of the population …
- only a low amount of water …
- a high amount of water …
- the average consumer …

Agreeing with your partner
- I think you are right.
- I totally/partly agree with you.

Disagreeing with your partner
- I disagree with you.
- Do you really think so?

Expressing your opinion
- I find it surprising that …
- I didn't expect that …

M 3 — *Explained*: The World's Water Crisis – Understanding an episode

Water is a precious resource and water scarcity is a problem that can have significant impacts on human health, economic development and the environment. The thought-provoking Netflix documentary *The World's Water Crisis* takes the audience on a journey around the world, to explore the causes of the water crisis, its impact on local communities and the potential solutions that could help tackle this urgent issue.

Pre-watching activities

1. *Working with words:* Match the expressions a)–i) with their corresponding definitions in the table below.

a) liquid freshwater	b) groundwater	c) gallon
d) irrigation	e) surface water	f) (to) drain
g) drought	h) arid	i) aquifer

definition	letter
1. any type of water that is above ground, including rivers, lakes, wetlands etc.	
2. having little or no rain	
3. to make something empty or dry by removing the liquid from it	
4. a layer of rock or soil that can take in and hold water	
5. naturally occurring water with very low concentrations of salt	
6. a long period of time when there is little or no rain	
7. the practice of supplying water to an area of land through pipes or canals so that crops will grow	
8. water that is found under the ground in soil, rocks etc.	
9. a unit for measuring liquid; in the USA it is equal to about 3.8 litres	

2. *Speaking:* With a partner, discuss the following questions. Make guesses and write down your answers.
    a) How much water is there on earth?
    b) How much of this water is liquid freshwater?

3. Watch the documentary until minute 3:10. Compare your answers with the information provided in the documentary. Note down the correct answers to the questions above.

While-watching activities

Watch the complete documentary and work on the tasks below.

1. Tick the correct statements.

   A. Mexico City …

      a) … was originally built on an island in the middle of a lake.
      b) … has a problem with water scarcity because it is in an arid area.
      c) … pumps water from water deposits, so-called aquifers, that lie underground.
      d) … collects and uses rainwater to supply its inhabitants with drinking water.
      e) … has a problem with sinking houses, which has been caused by pumping groundwater.

   B. Which of the following statements about water consumption are correct?

      a) Humans need to drink around two gallons of water per day.
      b) We use around three gallons of water when we flush the toilet.
      c) More than 90 percent of our water is used in agriculture and industry.
      d) The majority of the water in a bottle of Coca Cola is not the water that you actually see in the bottle.
      e) You need 2,500 litres of water to produce one cup of coffee.

2. Note down keywords.

   a) Explain why meat has such a high amount of so-called "embedded water".

   b) Outline why huge companies grow crops in arid places.

3. Finish the sentences using information from the documentary.

   a) If water had a higher price …

   b) Possible disadvantages of putting a higher price on water are …

M 4   How much water is needed to produce our food? – Describing a graph

How much water is needed to produce vegetables or eggs? Find out!

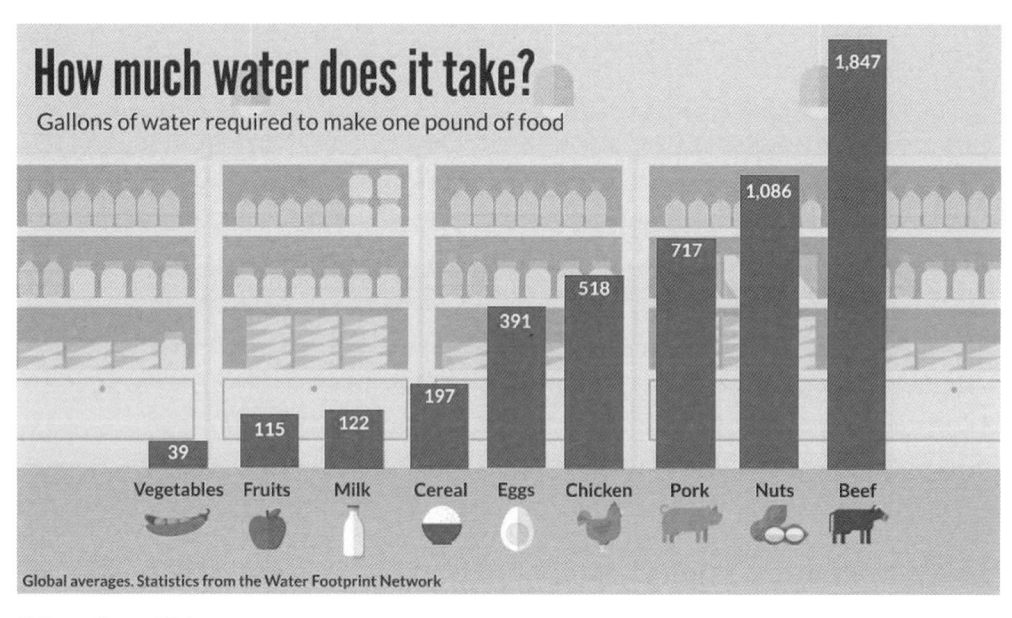

How much water does it take?
Gallons of water required to make one pound of food

- Vegetables: 39
- Fruits: 115
- Milk: 122
- Cereal: 197
- Eggs: 391
- Chicken: 518
- Pork: 717
- Nuts: 1,086
- Beef: 1,847

Global averages. Statistics from the Water Footprint Network

© Figure: Denver Water

Tasks

1. *Speaking:* With a partner, describe and analyse the information presented in the graph. Relate it to the documentary *The World's Water Crisis*.
   Tip: You may use the phrases in the box below.

Language support: describing a graph

Description
- The bar chart "...", published by ... shows ...
- Each bar represents ...
- ... the highest amount of water ...
- ... the least amount of water ...
- ... much more water than ...

Analysis
- The figures clearly show that ...
- It is striking that ...
- This leads to the assumption that ...
- All in all, one can say that ...

---

2. *Speaking*: What can you do to reduce your water usage in your everyday life and help conserve this resource? Include your knowledge about personal water consumption as well as about water usage by industries. Come up with at least five suggestions.

Creating awareness – The UNICEF Dirty Water Vending Machine Campaign

M 5

What is Guerrilla Marketing and how does UNICEF use it to create awareness for the water crisis?

Info box
Guerrilla marketing is an advertisement strategy in which a company uses surprise and/or unconventional interactions in order to promote a product or service. It is a type of publicity. The term was popularised by Jay Conrad Levinson's 1984 book *Guerrilla Marketing*. Guerrilla marketing uses multiple techniques and practices in order to establish direct contact with potential customers. One of the goals of this interaction is to cause an emotional reaction in the clients, and the ultimate goal of marketing is to induce people to remember products or brands in a different way than they might have been accustomed to.   *Source: Wikipedia*

Tasks

1. Watch the video *Guerrilla Marketing Example – UNICEF Dirty Water Vending Machine Campaign*:
   https://www.youtube.com/watch?v=Ug5OdN3QpJI&ab_channel=CreativeGuerrillaMarketing
   [last access: 24/07/2023]
   Answer the questions below. Take notes while watching the video.
   a) Explain UNICEF's dirty water campaign. What aim does UNICEF want to achieve with this campaign?
   b) How did the people in the street react to the dirty water vending machine? Describe.
2. *Speaking:* With a partner, discuss this question:
   Do you think that this form of advertising is effective? Why (not)? Give reasons.
3. *Creating a water scarcity campaign*: In small groups, create a water scarcity campaign to motivate other students to save water. Your campaign should aim to raise awareness about the importance of water conservation and encourage other students to take action to conserve water in their daily lives.

How to plan your campaign
a) Brainstorm ideas for your campaign. Consider the following questions: • What message would you like to convey to your target audience?   • What type of campaign will be most effective (e.g., posters, videos, events)?   • What actions can students take to conserve water?   b) Develop a detailed plan for your campaign.   c) Execute your campaign.   d) Evaluate the effectiveness of your campaign.   • Was your message clear and effective?   • Did you reach your target audience?   • Did your campaign motivate students to take action to conserve water?

M 6

How much meat do you eat? – A questionnaire

Reflect on your meat consumption.

Questionnaire: Meat consumption

© www.colourbox.com

1. How often do you eat meat?

   a) everyday
   b) at least three times a week
   c) once a week
   d) once or twice a month
   e) very rarely
   f) never, I am vegetarian/vegan

2. Where do you and your family normally buy your meat?

   a) at a supermarket
   b) at the butcher's
   c) at an organic grocery store
   d) I do not buy meat.
   e) other: _____

3. On a scale from 0–10: How much are you interested in reducing your meat consumption?

   not interested   somewhat interested   highly interested

   0 → 10

4. Which of the following factors could motivate you to eat less meat?

   a) health reasons
   b) environmental reasons
   c) ethical reasons
   d) other: _____

5. Which of the following reasons prevent you from reducing meat in your diet?

   a) Meat contains important nutrients.
   b) I like the taste of meat just too much.
   c) There are no delicious vegetarian alternatives.
   d) A meat-based diet is cheaper.
   e) Other reasons (please specify): _____

6. Which of the following meat alternatives have you heard of or tried? Do you know any other meat substitutes?

   a) tofu
   b) seitan
   c) tempeh
   d) other: _____

Tasks

1. Answer the questions from the questionnaire.
2. Compare your answers with a partner.

Explained: The Future of Meat – Understanding an episode

M 7

Find out more about meat consumption, its consequences and alternatives.

Pre-watching activities

1. In the sentences a)–d) the numbers are missing. Discuss them with a partner, then fill in the gaps using the following numbers.

| 455 million | one billion | 24,000 | quadrupled |
| 23 billion | doubled | 1.5 billion | |

a) Every ten seconds, humans kill _____ animals for food.

b) The global population has more than _____ in the last 50 years. In the same period of time, the amount of meat we produce has more than _____.

c) There are now _____ pigs, _____ cows and _____ chickens on this planet.

d) By 2050, global meat production is expected to increase to _____ tons.

2. Watch the intro of the documentary *Explained: The Future of Meat* and check whether your guesses were correct. Which of the numbers do you find surprising or worrisome? Give reasons.

While-watching activities

1. Watch the documentary until minute 9:30. Tick whether the following statements are true or false. Correct the false statements on a sheet of paper.

statement	true	false
a) Humans have always consumed meat.		
b) Some of the nutrients that meat contains are not easy to find in plant-based products.		
c) Meat consumption did not only change human's bodies, but also had an impact on social structures.		
d) If you compared a chicken from the 1950s to a chicken nowadays, it would look more or less the same.		
e) The top meat-eating countries can be found on the African continent.		
f) Meat consumption is increasing considerably in industrialised countries.		
g) Meat is one of the most efficient ways to feed people.		

2. Watch the second part of the documentary and answer the following questions. Take notes while watching.

   a) Which characteristics should meat alternatives have to be able to compete with real meat products?

   b) Why does the "Impossible Burger" taste like a real burger?

   c) What is cultured meat or cell-based meat? What are its advantages and disadvantages?

Post-watching activity: discussion

1. Explain the following quotation from the documentary.

   > "People think of corn and beef as natural. They are not natural, of course. They are highly domesticated products."

2. Work in small groups and discuss the following questions.
   a) What do you think will the future of meat look like?
   b) Which of the meat alternatives presented in the documentary offer sustainable solutions for the future?
   c) Report your ideas to the class.

Working with words

Revise the new vocabulary with the help of a crossword:
https://learningapps.org/view31165411

The Beyond Burger or cultured meat: What will the future look like? – A project

M 8

Info box

Since 2009, the Sustainable Foods Summit has been covering major sustainability developments in the food industry. How are sustainability schemes and eco-labels evolving in the food industry? With growing proliferation in labels, what are the prospects for a single sustainability standard for food products? What is the future outlook for plant-based foods? What developments are occurring in sustainable ingredients? How can food & beverage firms move towards circularity? How can operators close their material loops? Such questions are regularly addressed at this international series of summits.

Source: Ecovia Intelligence, https://sustainablefoodssummit.com/europe/about/ [last access: 26/07/2023]

© gorodenkoff/iStock/Getty Images Plus; Denise Taylor

Task

You are part of the marketing team of a food company that focuses on innovative and sustainable meat alternatives. You have developed a new product that is sustainable, affordable and tastes great. You are going to present your new product at the *Sustainable Foods Summit* in Amsterdam. Work in small groups and prepare a presentation in which you promote your product. Follow these steps:

- **Step 1:** Go online and find information about companies that sell innovative meat alternative products. In your group, choose a company and a product that you would like to promote.
- **Step 2:** Prepare a presentation that promotes your product. Make sure you include the following aspects:
  - Introduction to the company and product
  - Explanation of the product's sustainability features
  - Explanation of the product's taste and how it compares to real meat
  - Conclusion and call to action for consumers to test the product
- **Step 3:** Present your product in class.
- **Step 4:** Decide in class which product is the most convincing one.

Helpful links for your online research

- https://allthingsbugs.com/
- https://www.hey-planet.com/
- https://mosameat.com/
- https://www.beyondmeat.com/de-DE/products/the-beyond-burger
- https://impossiblefoods.com/

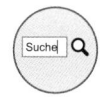

How to give a presentation

Here are some tips for a successful presentation.

1. **Division of work**
   Each group member should participate in the presentation and be responsible for a specific aspect of the presentation. For example, one member could be responsible for the introduction of the company, while another student could explain the sustainability features of the product.
2. **Visual aids**
   Prepare visual aids such as charts, graphs and images to help support your presentation.
3. **Preparation**
   Practise your presentation as a group to ensure that it is polished and professional. Be prepared to answer questions about the product and its features.

M 9 *Choose your child's talent* – Describing and analysing a cartoon

Task

Speaking: Work on your own and take notes. Then discuss your ideas with a partner.
- Describe the cartoon. Focus on important details.
- Explain the message of the cartoon.
- Evaluate the cartoon and give your personal opinion.

© Bold Business/Dusan Reljic

Describing and analysing cartoons

- Use the *Present Progressive Tense* to describe people's actions.
- *Be precise* and use phrases such as, in the foreground, next to, in the lower right-hand corner etc.
- The cartoonist pursues a specific *goal*, e.g., he/she wants to criticise people or institutions, he/she wants to entertain people by making fun of a public figure, he/she wants to convey a quite serious message …
- Cartoonists use certain *techniques* to make a point, such as exaggeration, irony, symbols, stereotypical representations, wordplay …

Explained: Designer DNA – Understanding an episode

M 10

Designer DNA – scientific feat or terrifying social experiment?

Warm-up
Which of the following technological developments is the most worrisome for you?
- artificial intelligence
- surveillance technology
- genetic editing/genetic engineering

Work on your own and make notes. Discuss your ideas with a partner, then report your ideas to the class.

Pre-watching activity
In small groups, have a look at the following words. Explain the meanings of the words. If you are unsure, look them up in a monolingual (online) dictionary.

DNA	human genome	germline	enhancement
in vitro fertilisation	genetic trait	therapy	plastic surgery

While-watching activities
Watch the documentary *Explained: Designer DNA* and work on the following tasks.

1. Tick the correct answers.
    CRISPR ...

    a) ... is a technology that has been applied for several decades.
    b) ... is an immune system found in viruses.
    c) ... operates with enzymes that act like scissors and cut DNA.
    d) ... can be used in every living organism.
    e) ... has already been used to change the genome of an embryo.

2. Fill in the missing words.

Somatic cells are most of the body's cells, e.g., _____ (1). These cells do not pass their _____ (2) to their offspring. Germline cells, on the other hand, are _____ (3). These cells pass their _____ (4) to future generations. If you make changes in _____ (5), you ultimately affect the human population.

For that reason, _____ (6) editing is much more controversial than _____ (7) editing.

3. Answer the following questions. Note down key words.
   a) What is the difference between therapy and enhancement? Why has the line between these two areas become fuzzy in recent decades?

   b) What is preimplantation genetic diagnosis (PGD)? What is it used for?

   c) What are the downsides of genetic technology?

Genetic engineering: A blessing or a curse? – A panel discussion

M 11

Working with words

Revise the new vocabulary with the help of this crossword:
https://learningapps.org/view31165681

Tasks

1. *Speaking*: Explain the following quotations. Use your own words.

"The idea that we are all sick, that I 'suffer' from dwarfism ... No, I live with dwarfism. I don't suffer, I suffer from how society treats me."

Rebecca Cokley, disability-rights activist
Source: Explained: Designer DNA (Netflix)

"There's already a lot of active research going on using the CRISPR technology to fix diseases like Duchenne muscular dystrophy or cystic fibrosis or Huntington's disease. They're all diseases that have known genetic causes, and we now have the technology that can repair those mutations to provide, we hope, patients with a normal life."

Prof. Jennifer A. Doudna, U.S.-American biochemist
Source: https://www.brainyquote.com/quotes/jennifer_doudna_754103

© Pictures: IronChefBatman, https://en.wikipedia.org/wiki/Rebecca_Cokley#/media/File:Cokley_Headshot.jpg, via Wikimedia Commons Cmichel67, CC BY-SA 4.0 https://de.wikipedia.org/wiki/Jennifer_A._Doudna#/media/Datei:Jennifer_Doudna_in_2021_by_Christopher_Michel_(cropped).jpg, via Wikimedia Commons

2. *Panel Discussion:* You are going to have a panel discussion with the topic *Genetic engineering – a blessing or a curse?*

   The participants are
   - Prof. Jennifer A. Doudna, one of the discoverers of CRISPR gene editing technology
   - Rebecca Cokley, the director of the Disability Justice Initiative at the Center for American Progress
   - John Harris, a theologian who specialises in bioethics *and*
   - Jessica Long, a Paralympic swimmer and 29-time medalist.

Work in small groups and prepare for the discussion. Each group will be assigned one panelist, there will be one group that is going to prepare the part of the host.

Rules for the discussion

- **Be respectful:** Do not use language that may be perceived as derogatory, offensive or discriminatory.
- **Listen attentively:** Listen attentively to the ideas and perspectives of others without interruption.
- **Stick to the topic:** Keep the discussion focused on the issues related to the topic being discussed.

Preparation

a) Go online and find information about your panelist. What is his/her attitude towards genetic engineering? Write down arguments that support his/her position.
b) Come up with at least three questions that you could ask the other participants.
c) Select one spokesperson who is going to represent your ideas in the panel discussion.
   <u>If you prepare the role of the host:</u> Prepare questions that you will ask the panelists during the discussion. Your questions should be clear, thought-provoking, and designed to spark a meaningful conversation among the participants.

Prof. Jennifer A. Doudna • U.S.-American biochemist • one of the first women who received the Nobel Prize in science • pioneering work in gene editing	**Rebecca Cokley** • U.S.-American disability rights activist • was born with achondroplasia[1] a cause of dwarfism • served as an appointee in the administration of President Obama
Helpful link https://www.theguardian.com/science/2017/jul/02/jennifer-doudna-crispr-i-have-to-be-true-to-who-i-am-as-a-scientist-interview-crack-in-creation	**Helpful link** https://www.washingtonpost.com/opinions/if-we-start-editing-genes-people-like-me-might-not-exist/2017/08/10/e9adf206-7d27-11e7-a669-b400c5c7e1cc_story.html
John Harris • British bioethicist and philosopher • one of the founders of the International Association of Bioethics • supports gene editing	**Jessica Long** • Russian-American Paralympic swimmer from Baltimore • has won 29 medals • because of fibular hemimelia[2] her lower legs were amputated when she was a baby
Helpful link https://www.theguardian.com/science/2015/dec/02/why-human-gene-editing-must-not-be-stopped	**Helpful link** https://inspiremykids.com/jessica-long-the-only-disability-in-life-is-a-negative-attitude/

© Pictures: IronChefBatman, CC BY-SA 4.0 https://de.wikipedia.org/wiki/Jennifer_A._Doudna#/media/Datei:Jennifer_Doudna_in_2021_by_Christopher_Michel_(cropped).jpg, via Wikimedia Commons Cmichel67; CC BY-SA 4.0 https://en.wikipedia.org/wiki/Rebecca_Cokley#/media/File:Cokley_Headshot.jpg, via Wikimedia Commons; Arienette22, CC BY-SA 3.0 https://en.wikipedia.org/wiki/John_Harris_%28bioethicist%29#/media/File:John_Harris_(2008).jpg, via Wikimedia Commons; Saulo Cruz, CC BY 2.0 https://de.wikipedia.org/wiki/Jessica_Long#/media/Datei:Jessica_Long.jpg, via Wikimedia Commons

*1 **Achondroplasie:** eine genetische Erkrankung, die eine Form des Kleinwuchses verursacht. Sie wird durch eine Mutation des für die Regulation des Knochenwachstum verantwortlichen Gens bedingt – 2 **fibulare Hemimelie:** eine seltene angeborene Erkrankung, bei der das Wadenbein (Fibula) teilweise oder vollständig fehlt oder unterentwickelt ist. Das betroffene Bein ist daher kürzer als das gesunde Bein. Die Ursache ist nicht bekannt.*

Talking about the gender pay gap – Describing and analysing a diagram

M 12

Have you already heard about the gender pay gap? Let's have a close look at some facts and figures.

Gender pay gap

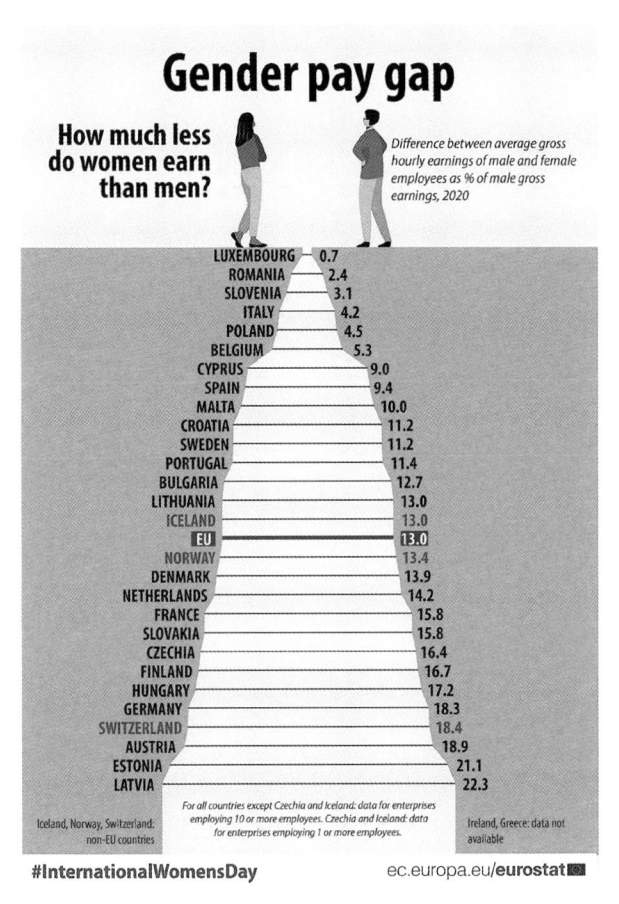

How much less do women earn than men?

Difference between average gross hourly earnings of male and female employees as % of male gross earnings, 2020

Country	%
LUXEMBOURG	0.7
ROMANIA	2.4
SLOVENIA	3.1
ITALY	4.2
POLAND	4.5
BELGIUM	5.3
CYPRUS	9.0
SPAIN	9.4
MALTA	10.0
CROATIA	11.2
SWEDEN	11.2
PORTUGAL	11.4
BULGARIA	12.7
LITHUANIA	13.0
ICELAND	13.0
EU	13.0
NORWAY	13.4
DENMARK	13.9
NETHERLANDS	14.2
FRANCE	15.8
SLOVAKIA	15.8
CZECHIA	16.4
FINLAND	16.7
HUNGARY	17.2
GERMANY	18.3
SWITZERLAND	18.4
AUSTRIA	18.9
ESTONIA	21.1
LATVIA	22.3

For all countries except Czechia and Iceland: data for enterprises employing 10 or more employees. Czechia and Iceland: data for enterprises employing 1 or more employees. Iceland, Norway, Switzerland: non-EU countries. Ireland, Greece: data not available.

#InternationalWomensDay ec.europa.eu/eurostat

© Figure: EC Europe/Eurostat

Language support: describing a diagram

Description
- The diagram shows …
- The lines in the middle represent …
- The numbers on the right indicate …
- To the left of the lines, you can see …
- Women in the EU earn on average …
- Across the EU, the gender pay gap differs widely, …

Analysis
- The figures clearly show that …
- It is striking that …
- The numbers suggest that …

Tasks

1. *Speaking:* With a partner, describe and analyse the information presented in the diagram. You may use the phrases in the box above.
2. *Speaking:* With 18.3 percent, Germany had one of the highest pay disparities between men and women in the EU in the year 2020. Do you find these numbers surprising? What might be possible reasons? With a partner, come up with ideas and make notes. Then share your ideas in class.

M 13 — *Explained: Why Women Are Paid Less* – Understanding an episode

Why does the pay gap persist despite changing norms in recent decades?

Pre-watching activity

In small groups, have a look at the following words. Explain the meanings of the words. If you are unsure, look them up in a monolingual (online) dictionary.

gender pay gap	maternity leave	paternity leave	female quota
primary caregiver	breadwinner	promotion prospects	CEO

While-watching activities

Watch the documentary *Explained: Why Women Are Paid Less* and work on the following tasks.

1. Which of the following statements about the gender pay gap in the 1950s are correct? Tick the correct answers.

   a) The number of women in the workforce was very low.
   b) Most women stayed at home even though, on average, they had a similar level of education.
   c) Around 70 percent of the women who worked were in the educational sector.
   d) It was already illegal for employers to offer jobs only to men. Nevertheless, it was a common practice.
   e) The gender pay gap was also connected to a set of cultural norms about gender roles that persisted in society.

2. Explain what has changed in recent decades. Take notes.

3. Explain what has *not* changed. What is the "heart" of the pay gap in society today? Take notes.

4. Explain how Rwanda and Iceland have managed to almost close their pay gaps? Take notes.

Introducing a women's quota – Reading an article

M 14

A women's quota – the solution to the problem?

Germany agrees 'historic' mandatory boardroom quota for women

Germany's coalition government will introduce a mandatory[1] quota for the number of women working as senior management in the country's listed companies, in a move hailed[2] as a "historic" step towards sexual equality in German boardrooms[3]. In a deal agreed on Friday evening by Angela Merkel's
5 Christian Democrats and their junior partner the Social Democrats, management boards with more than three members must include at least one woman, reversing a voluntary system that critics argue has failed to achieve the required shift towards gender equality.

Franziska Giffey, Germany's federal minister for women, said: "This one
10 breakthrough is historic. We are putting an end to women-free boardrooms in large companies. We are setting an example for a sustainable, modern society. We are exploiting all of our country's potential so that the best in mixed teams can be more successful. Because nothing is done voluntarily, and we need guidelines to move forward."

15 The move comes after recent research found the representation of women in senior management in German companies was lagging behind peers in rival major economies.

Women make up 12.8% of the management boards of the 30 largest German companies listed on the blue-chip Dax index[4], according to a September survey
20 by the Swedish-German AllBright foundation[5]. The figure compares with 28.6% in the US, 24.5% in the UK and 22.2% in France, the study said.

The research also stated that Dax companies were losing women in senior positions, while there had been a rise in "the number of Dax companies without a single woman on the board from six companies in the previous year to 11
25 currently".

However, forcing large companies to act is likely to anger some in German business, who have been arguing that the move is an unjustified interference in private enterprise.

The coalition deal will also compel[6] a minimum quota of 30% of women on
30 supervisory boards[7] for companies where the federal government holds a majority shareholding.

The government added that a further quota would also be introduced for "corporations under public law", such as health insurance companies and pension and accident insurance institutions as well as the Federal Employment Agency.[8]

Source: Goodley, Simon: Germany agrees 'historic' mandatory boardroom quota for women. In: The Guardian 22 November 2020; found at:
https://www.theguardian.com/business/2020/nov/22/germany-agrees-historic-mandatory-boardroom-quota-for-women [last access: 26/07/2023]

1 **mandatory:** obligatory, binding – 2 **(to) hail:** (to) praise – 3 **boardroom:** a room where the people who control the company have their meetings – 4 **companies listed on the blue-chip Dax index:** *börsenorientierte Unternehmen* – 5 **AllBright Foundation:** a foundation that aims to empower and support women in their professional and personal lives – 6 **(to) compel:** (to) force so. to do sth. – 7 **supervisory board:** *der Aufsichtsrat* – 8 **Federal Employment Agency:** *die Bundesagentur für Arbeit*

While-reading activities

1. Skim the text and find out what the following numbers refer to.

| a) 12.8% | b) 24.5% | c) 30% | d) more than 3 | e) 11 |

2. Read the text thoroughly and work on the following tasks. Write complete sentences and use your own words.

a) Explain what the Christian Democrats and the Social Democrats agreed on.

b) Outline in which way this breakthrough is historic, according to Franziska Giffey.

c) Explain why the introduction of a women's quota might anger some business people.

Post-reading activity

In pairs or small groups, discuss the pros and cons of a women's quota as a solution to the gender pay gap. Also discuss some alternative solutions to the gender pay gap. Are there any other policies or approaches that could be more effective or more acceptable?

Working with words

Revise the new vocabulary with the help of this crossword:
https://learningapps.org/watch?v=pypjsnukj23

Global challenges – Oral mock exam

LEK

Topic: Global challenges in the 21st century
Student A – The growing global hunger for meat

MONOLOGUE

Prepare a five-minute talk about the topic *The growing global hunger for meat*. Use the scheme below as a starting point:

1. Describe and analyse the diagram below.
2. Explain in which way meat consumption is problematic for the environment.

Daily meat consumption per person, 2020

Daily meat consumption is shown relative to the expected EU average of 165g per person in 2030. This projection comes from the livestock antibiotic scenarios from Van Boeckel et al. (2017).

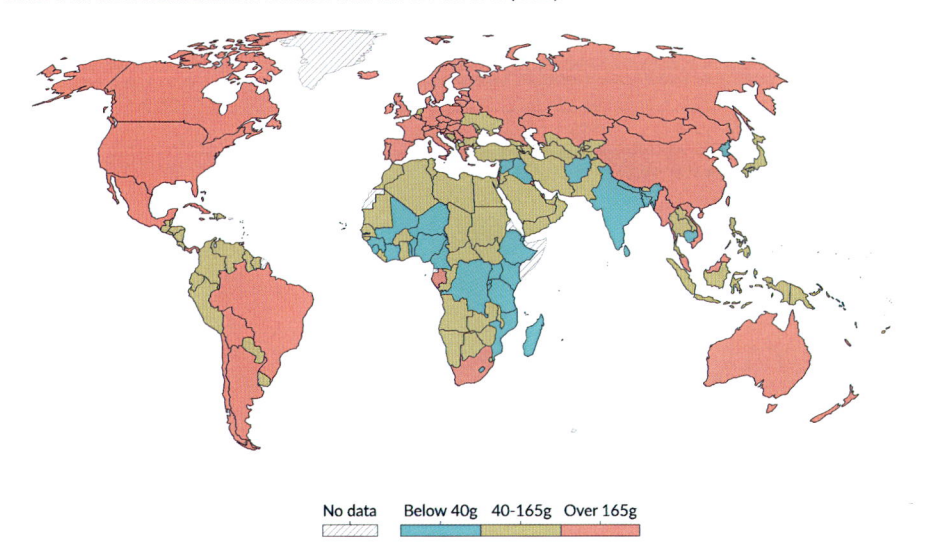

No data · Below 40g · 40-165g · Over 165g

Source: Food and Agriculture Organization of the United Nations   OurWorldInData.org/antibiotic-resistance-from-livestock • CC BY
Note: Data shows per capita meat supply, which does not subtract consumer waste. Actual meat consumption will be lower than these figures.

© Map: Our World in Data/ cc by

DIALOGUE

Be prepared to discuss the following question in-depth:

Which environmental and social challenges are we facing in the 21st century and which solutions might help us to solve these problems in the future?

Topic: Global challenges in the 21st century
Student B – The global water crisis

MONOLOGUE

Prepare a five-minute talk about the topic *The global water crisis*. Use the chart as a starting point:
1. Describe and analyse the chart below.
2. Outline some factors that contribute to water scarcity.

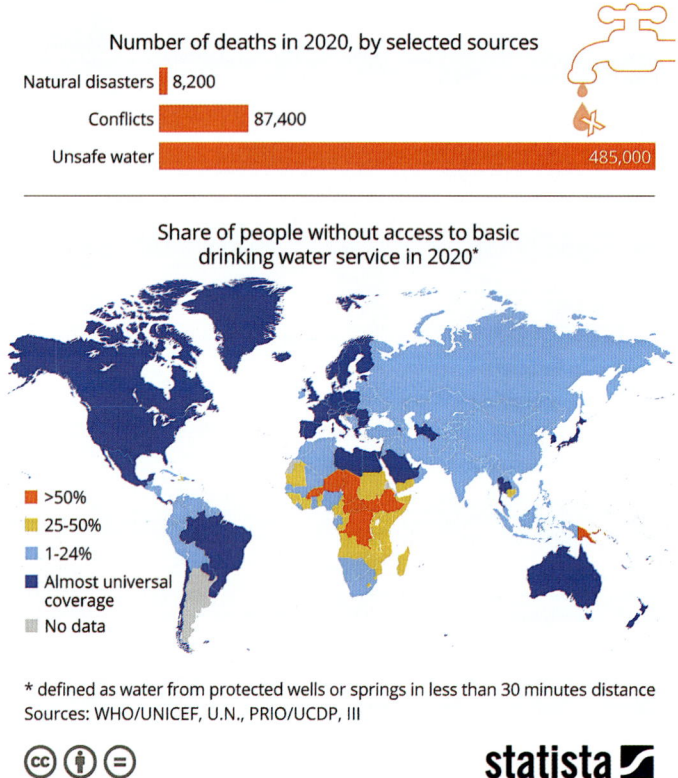

Unsafe Water Kills More People Than Disasters and Conflicts

Number of deaths in 2020, by selected sources
- Natural disasters: 8,200
- Conflicts: 87,400
- Unsafe water: 485,000

Share of people without access to basic drinking water service in 2020*
- >50%
- 25-50%
- 1-24%
- Almost universal coverage
- No data

* defined as water from protected wells or springs in less than 30 minutes distance
Sources: WHO/UNICEF, U.N., PRIO/UCDP, III

statista

© Map: Statista

DIALOGUE

Be prepared to discuss the following question in-depth:
Which environmental and social challenges are we facing in the 21st century and which solutions might help us to solve these problems in the future?

Hinweise und Erwartungshorizonte

Hinweise (M 1)

1. Stunde

Ziel: In allen vier ausgewählten Folgen der Dokumentarreihe „*Explained*" geht es um Herausforderungen, denen die Menschen im 21. Jahrhundert gegenüberstehen. Daher beschäftigen sich die Schülerinnen und Schüler als **thematischen Einstieg in die Unterrichtsreihe** anhand von Bildimpulsen zunächst mit dem Begriff „*global challenges*". Anschließend ordnen sie ihre Ideen in Form einer Mindmap den Kategorien „ökologische", „technologische" und „soziale" Herausforderungen zu.

Erwartungshorizont (M 1)

1./2.
Picture one shows a forest that is on fire. In the background, one can see flames, clouds of smoke and burnt trees. In the foreground, one can see trees which have not caught fire yet.
A possible heading could be *Devastating wildfires*.
In **picture two**, one can see a branch of an apple tree with fruits hanging on it. On the left-hand side, next to the branch, there is a hand wearing a white, medical glove. The hand is holding a syringe which contains a red liquid. The person is injecting the red substance into the apple. The picture conveys the idea of scientific innovation in food production. A possible heading could be *GMOs – curse or blessing?*
Picture three shows a beach that is covered with garbage. The sand is barely visible, as it is covered with piles of plastic bags, discarded bottles, cans and other trash that has been left behind or dumped into the ocean. In the background, crystal clear blue water is visible.
The beach is surrounded by lush green vegetation. A possible heading could be *Man-made destruction of paradise*.
In **picture four**, one can see a group of protesters who are participating in a demonstration. In the centre of the picture, a woman is holding up a sign which says, "[We] need a change". In the background, one can see another sign which says "No!" They could be advocating for various issues, such as social justice, climate change or political change. In the foreground, one can see a policeman who is trying to prevent the protesters from advancing further. A possible title could be *Citizen empowerment* or *The power of collective action*.

The pictures refer to the following global challenges:
– **Climate change** and the consequences linked to global warming, such as extreme-weather events, droughts, melting ice caps, rising sea levels etc.
– Scientific innovations, such as **genetic engineering** and its possible impacts on living organisms, food, and the human body
– The environmental impact of human activity, particularly the careless disposal of waste, and the problem of **plastic waste** in the oceans
– **Social injustice**, **racism, and inequality**; the importance of social activism and the role of peaceful protests in bringing about positive change

3.–5. Individual results.

6. Mindmap: Musterlösung:

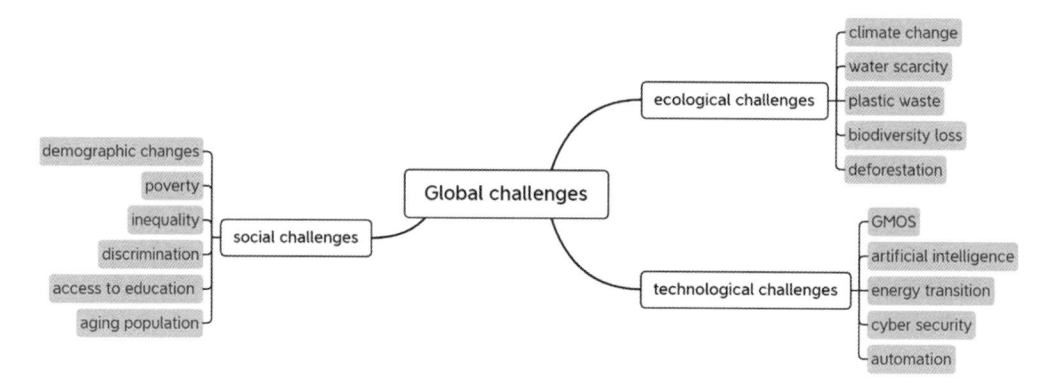

```
                                    ┌─ climate change
                                    ├─ water scarcity
                      ecological ────┼─ plastic waste
                      challenges     ├─ biodiversity loss
                                    └─ deforestation
demographic changes ─┐
poverty ─────────────┤
inequality ──────────┼─ social ── Global challenges
discrimination ──────┤   challenges
access to education ─┤
aging population ────┘              ┌─ GMOS
                                    ├─ artificial intelligence
                      technological ─┼─ energy transition
                      challenges    ├─ cyber security
                                    └─ automation
```

2./3. Stunde

Hinweise (M 2 und M 3)

Ziel: Hier sensibilisieren sich die Schülerinnen und Schüler hinsichtlich des Themas „*Water crisis*", indem sie einen Bezug zur eigenen Lebensrealität herstellen. Nach der Hinführung zum Thema erfolgt die inhaltliche Erarbeitung anhand der Kurzdokumentation „*The World's Water Crisis*" aus der Netflix-Reihe „*Explained*".

Hinweis zur Differenzierung

Ein *Language Support* (**M 2**) dient als Hilfestellung zum mündlichen Austausch für schwächere Lerngruppen. Die Aufgaben in **M 3** stellen eine Mischung zwischen **geschlossenen Aufgabentypen** (*true/false statements*, *tick the correct answers*) und anspruchsvolleren, **offenen Aufgaben**, die in Stichworten zu beantworten sind, dar. Auf diese Weise gelingt es auch lernschwächeren Schülerinnen und Schülern, das Material zumindest anteilig zu bearbeiten und im Abschluss darüber ins Gespräch zu kommen.

Erwartungshorizont (M 2)

1. Ranking: taking a shower/bath (1) – flushing the toilet (2) – doing the laundry (3) – washing the dishes (4) – watering the garden/cleaning the house (5) – food and drinks (6)
   In 2021, the average consumer in Germany used 129 liters per day.
   source: https://de.statista.com/infografik/5609/wofuer-wir-wasser-verbrauchen/
2. Individual results.
3. Example: I find it surprising that the average consumer uses such a large amount of water. I think, one reason might be that many people are unaware of the quantity of water they use in their homes daily, and some common activities can result in excessive water consumption. For instance, taking long showers, leaving the tap running while brushing teeth or shaving and using older, less efficient appliances can contribute to high water usage. This is an issue of concern, and it is important to find ways to reduce our water consumption.

Erwartungshorizont (M 3)

Pre-watching activities
1. Words and their definitions: 1. e), 2. h), 3. f), 4. i), 5. a), 6. g), 7. d), 8. b), 9. c)
2. Individual results.

3. a) 326 trillion gallons (gallon= 3.7 litres)
   b) 1% is liquid freshwater.

While-watching activities
1. Correct statements: A. a), c), e) – B. b), c), d)
2. Keywords:
   a) You need huge amounts of water to grow cattle feed, e.g., it takes 510 litres of water to grow just one kilogram of alfalfa, a common cattle feed. An average cow eats about 12 kilograms of cattle feed per day.
   b) Farmers hardly pay anything for the water they use. Water is priced like there will always be enough of it and there is no incentive to save water.
3. Finished sentences:
   a) If water had a higher price, ... farmers would not grow crops that require huge quantities of water in very arid areas. / ... farmers would stop using very inefficient irrigation methods. / ... governments would be willing to invest the money to repair the water infrastructure.
   b) Possible disadvantages of putting a higher price on water are ... that the price of consumer goods would skyrocket, and industries might collapse. / ... small farmers might be affected much more than big companies. / ... the higher price on water would have the greatest impact on the poor.

Hinweise (M 4 und M 5)

4./5. Stunde

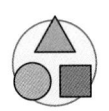

Ziel: Die Schülerinnen und Schüler setzen sich anhand einer Grafik vertiefend mit dem Thema „Water crisis" auseinander, indem sie auch ihren eigenen Wasserverbrauch reflektieren und diskutieren. Anschließend lernen sie exemplarisch, wie Menschen auf das Thema „Wasserknappheit" aufmerksam gemacht werden können und wie ein Bewusstsein dafür geschaffen werden kann, dass Handlungsbedarf besteht.

Hinweis zur Differenzierung (M 4)
Eine *wordbank* mit „*useful phrases*" erleichtert es den Lernenden, sich mündlich zu der Grafik zu äußern.

Sachhinweis – UNICEF-Kampagne *Dirty Water Vending Machine* (M 5)
Guerilla Marketing ist eine Werbestrategie, die auf unkonventionelle, teilweise schockierende Weise die Aufmerksamkeit potenzieller Kundinnen und Kunden auf sich zieht. Wie Guerilla Marketing funktionieren kann, wird anhand der *Dirty Water Vending Machine*-Kampagne von UNICEF aufgezeigt. In einem Video sieht man, wie Flaschen mit ungenießbarem, dreckigem Trinkwasser in einem Automaten zum Verkauf angeboten werden. Ziel ist nicht der Verkauf dieser Flaschen. Vielmehr will die Organisation darauf aufmerksam machen, dass viele Menschen in Entwicklungsländern keinen Zugang zu sauberem Trinkwasser haben.

Erwartungshorizont (M 4)

1. The bar chart titled *How much water does it take?* displays the amount of water required in gallons to produce one pound of food for various food types. The blue bars represent each food type, including vegetables, fruits, milk, nuts, beef, eggs, chicken, and pork. The chart highlights

that beef is the most water-intensive food to produce, requiring 1,847 gallons of water per pound. Nuts are the second-most water-intensive food, requiring 1,086 gallons of water per pound. On the other hand, vegetables require the least amount of water, with only 39 gallons of water needed per pound of food, followed by fruits with 115 gallons per pound.

Eggs and chicken require a moderate amount of water to produce, with 391 and 518 gallons of water per pound of food, respectively. Pork is also relatively water-intensive, requiring 717 gallons of water per pound of food. The data from the chart suggests that a plant-based diet is much more sustainable in terms of water usage compared to a meat-based diet.

2. Individual results.

Erwartungshorizont (M 5)

1. a) UNICEF's „dirty water" campaign aims to raise awareness about the issue of access to clean water in developing countries, particularly among children. The campaign highlights the fact that millions of children worldwide are forced to drink contaminated water, which can result in serious illnesses and even death. The campaign uses a variety of strategies such as advertisements, social media and fundraising initiatives to spread awareness and encourage people to take action.
   b) The campaign was quite successful. A lot of people were willing to donate money to support UNICEF.
2. Individual results.
3. Individual results.

6./7. Stunde

Hinweise (M 6 und M 7)

Ziel: In der Doppelstunde steht das Thema „*Meat consumption*" im Fokus, das inhaltlich an das vorherige Thema „Wasserkrise" anknüpft. Mit einem Fragebogen werden die Schülerinnen und Schüler für das Thema sensibilisiert und reflektieren ihren eigenen Fleischkonsum. Anschließend erfolgt die inhaltliche Erarbeitung des Themas anhand der Kurzdokumentation „*The Future of Meat*" aus der Dokumentarreihe „*Explained*".

Tipp (M 6)

Anschließend an die Auswertung der Fragebögen in Partnerarbeit kann im Plenum auch schon eine Diskussion über mögliche Alternativen angeregt und über die Inhalte der Episode „*The Future of Meat*" spekuliert werden:
– *What could future meat consumption be like?*

Digitalhinweis (M 7)

Die Aufgaben zur Überprüfung des Wortschatzes liegen digital und kostenlos in *LearningApps* vor und sind mit Konto bearbeitbar („ähnliche App erstellen" anklicken):
https://learningapps.org/31165411

Hinweis zur Differenzierung (M 7)

Durch den Einsatz geschlossener und offener Aufgabentypen wird erneut sichergestellt, dass auch lernschwächere Schülerinnen und Schüler die Arbeitsaufträge bewältigen können.

Erwartungshorizont (M 6)

Individual results.

Erwartungshorizont (M 7)

Pre-watching activities
1. a) 24,000; b) doubled, quadrupled; c) one billion pigs, 1.5 billion cows, 23 billion chickens; 455 million
2. Individual results.

While-watching activities
1. a) false; correction: Early humans had a diet based on fruits, seeds and leaves.
   b) true
   c) true
   d) false; correction: The chicken from the 1950s would be smaller, skinnier and would resemble a pigeon. Chickens today grow four to five times bigger (thanks to antibiotics and selective breeding).
   e) false; correction: The top meat-eating countries can be found in North and South America, in Europe and Australia.
   f) false; correction: Meat consumption is stagnating in industrialised countries while it is going up sharply in emerging economies.
   g) false; correction: Meat is one of the least efficient ways to feed people.

2. Answers to the questions:
   a) Meat alternatives should be delicious, they should taste like meat, deliver proteins and iron and should be accessible and affordable.
   b) The company patented a way to synthesised heme iron in a lab, a component that gives meat its distinct flavour.
   c) Cultured meat is meat grown in a laboratory. You need a cell culture taken from the body of an animal, and the cells need a growth medium to grow.
   Advantages: uses about half the energy of beef production, needs small amounts of land and water, produces less greenhouse gas emissions
   Disadvantages: it only kind of tastes like meat, it is still very expensive to produce, it is difficult to imitate the structure of real meat, people might find it disgusting

Post-watching activity
1. The quotation refers to the fact that a huge amount of the products that we eat are not natural. Animals have been manipulated by humans for hundreds of years through selective breeding, the use of drugs and antibiotics and, more recently, through artificial insemination and growth hormones.
2. Individual results.

8./9. Stunde

Hinweise (M 8)

Ziel: Hier setzen sich die Schülerinnen und Schüler in einer Internetrecherche mit Fleischalternativen auseinander und bewerten diese hinsichtlich der Faktoren Nachhaltigkeit, Nährstoffe und Kosten. Die Lernenden wählen in ihrer Gruppe passende Informationen aus, strukturieren diese und teilen sie in Form einer Präsentation mit der Klasse.

Hinweis zur Differenzierung
Zur Unterstützung der Internetrecherche sind Webseiten einiger Produzenten aufgelistet, die bereits Alternativen zu konventionellen Fleischprodukten auf den Markt gebracht haben. Im Arbeitsauftrag ist die Struktur der Präsentation vorgegeben, zudem enthält der Kasten *How to give a presentation* weitere Hinweise zur Arbeit in der Gruppe.

Tipp
Gegebenenfalls kann das Projekt als kleiner Wettbewerb gestaltet werden und die Lerngruppe stimmt darüber ab, welches Produkt das überzeugendste ist.

Erwartungshorizont (M 8)

Siehe Kriterien für die Präsentation (M 8, Seite 18)

10./11. Stunde

Hinweise (M 9–M 11)

Ziel: In der Doppelstunde erarbeiten die Schülerinnen und Schüler die Inhalte der Episode „*Designer DNA*", beleuchten die Thematik aus verschiedenen Blickwinkeln und beziehen Stellung.

Einstieg (M 9)
Um in das Thema einzusteigen, beschreiben und analysieren die Lernenden den **Cartoon (M 9)** mit dem Titel *Choose your child's talent* von Dusan Reljic. Mithilfe des Cartoons wird der recht komplexe und anspruchsvolle Inhalt der Episode vorentlastet.

Didaktisch-methodischer Hinweis (M 10)
Da die Schülerinnen und Schüler die Begriffe (*pre-watching activity*), die für das Verständnis der Episode „*Designer DNA*" notwendig sind, eigenständig recherchieren, sollte ein Internetzugang vorhanden sein. Zudem sollte die Lehrkraft anschließend im Plenum klären, ob die Begriffe wirklich verstanden wurden.

Digitalhinweis (M 11)
Die Aufgaben zur Überprüfung des Wortschatzes liegen digital und kostenlos in *LearningApps* vor und sind mit Konto bearbeitbar („ähnliche App erstellen" anklicken):
https://learningapps.org/31165681

Erwartungshorizont (M 9)

In the cartoon *Choose your child's talent* by Dusan Reljik a young couple with a dog is depicted standing in front of a shop window that is decorated with babies in cradles. Each cradle indicates the talents that the babies will possess in their future lives. So, the parents can decide whether their child should become an athlete, a politician, a music genius etc. At the top of the cartoon, a speech bubble reads, "Do we want a tech tycoon or a tax lawyer?" The cartoonist uses exaggeration to bring across his message. The cartoon humorously criticises the concept of "designer babies" or the practice of genetically modifying embryos to create desired physical or intellectual traits. It highlights the potential ethical and societal implications of such practices and the potential for creating a world of genetically modified humans who are not diverse and unique anymore.

Erwartungshorizont (M 10)

Warm-up
Individual results.

Pre-watching activity
DNA: the chemical material in the cells of animals and plants that carries genetic information; **human genome:** complete set of genes in a cell of a human; **germline:** population of a multicellular organism's cells that pass on their genetic material to the progeny; **enhancement:** a synonym of 'improvement'; **in vitro fertilisation:** process of fertilisation where an egg is combined with sperm outside the body, in vitro ("in glass"); **genetic trait:** a genetically determined characteristic; **therapy:** a medical treatment that is normally following a medical diagnosis; **plastic surgery:** an operation that is used to alter or improve the physical appearance of a person.

While-watching activities
1. Correct answers: c), d)
2. Missing words: (1) blood cells, skin cells, brain cells; (2) DNA; (3) sperm and egg cells; (4) DNA; (5) germline cells; (6) germline gene editing; (7) somatic gene editing
3. Answers to the questions:
   a) therapy: treat diseases; enhancement: give advantages to people who are healthy
      The line between these two areas has become fuzzy because there is no agreement on which genetic conditions need to be fixed and there is no clear definition of what a disease is.
   b) Cells from an embryo created through IVF are removed and tested for genetic diseases. Embryos without diseases can be selected and implanted in the woman's womb.
   c) Downsides of genetic technology:
      – It can narrow the range of human variation.
      – Individual choices may influence the demography of a country.
      – Ethical questions arise: are we allowed to judge whether a life is valuable or not? Does a person with a disability have a less valuable life?
      – The technology is not available to everyone: unequal access to healthcare, only rich people will benefit.
      – The idea that the genes of a certain ethnic group are superior is dangerous (eugenics).

Erwartungshorizont (M 11)

1. **Quotation 1 – Rebecca Cokley:** Cokley's statement challenges the common perception that people with disabilities are inherently „sick" or „suffering". Cokley, who lives with a form of dwarfism, points out that her condition is not something to be pitied or seen as a source of suffering. Rather, the challenges she faces come from the way society treats her.
Quotation 2 – Prof. Jennifer Doudna: Doudna highlights the potential of CRISPR technology to address genetic diseases. Diseases such as Duchenne muscular dystrophy or Huntington's disease are caused by specific genetic mutations that have been identified. In the past, there were few options to treat these diseases. The new technology offers hope for patients with these genetic diseases to lead a normal life.
2. Individual results.

12./13. Stunde

Hinweise (M 12–M 14)

Ziel: In dieser Doppelstunde, geht es um gesellschaftliche Herausforderungen, insbesondere um die Benachteiligung von Personengruppen in der Arbeitswelt. Exemplarisch wird dies am geschlechtsspezifischen Lohnunterschied (*gender pay gap*) aufgezeigt. Nachdem sich die Lernenden mit der Problematik beschäftigt haben, geht es um mögliche Lösungsansätze.

Hinweis zur Differenzierung (M 12)
Das spontane Beschreiben eines Diagramms bereitet vielen Lernenden Schwierigkeiten, da ein spezifischer Wortschatz dazu notwendig ist. Eine *wordbank* mit nützlichen Ausdrücken erleichtert ihnen den mündlichen Austausch.

Sachhinweis (M 14)
Der Artikel „*Germany agrees 'historic' mandatory boardroom quota for women*" aus dem Guardian knüpft inhaltlich an die Grafik (M 12) an: Im europäischen Vergleich bewegt sich Deutschland im unteren Drittel die Gehaltsunterschiede zwischen Männern und Frauen betreffend. Um die Geschlechtergleichstellung in Führungspositionen zu stärken, führte die damalige Regierung im Jahr 2021 das Führungspositionen-Gesetz[1] ein. Dadurch soll eine Frauenquote von mindestens 30 Prozent in den Aufsichtsräten börsennotierter Unternehmen erreicht werden.

Digitalhinweis (M 14)
Die Aufgaben zur Überprüfung des Wortschatzes liegen digital und kostenlos in *LearningApps* vor und sind mit Konto bearbeitbar („ähnliche App erstellen" anklicken):
https://learningapps.org/display?v=pypjsnukj23

Erwartungshorizont (M 12)

1. <u>Description of the diagram</u>: The diagram *Gender pay gap – How much less do women earn than men?* shows the income differences between male and female employees in various European

---

[1] Vgl. Bundesministerium für Familie, Senioren, Frauen und Jugend, https://www.bmfsfj.de/bmfsfj/themen/gleichstellung/frauen-und-arbeitswelt/quote-privatwitschaft/mehr-frauen-in-fuehrungspositionen-in-der-privatwirtschaft-78562 [letzter Abruf: 02.04.2023]

countries in 2020. The right side of the chart indicates the percentage difference between what women earned per hour and what men earned. The corresponding countries are shown on the left. The lines in the middle provide a visual representation of the gender pay gap. The gender pay gap varies significantly across the EU, including non-EU countries such as Iceland, Norway, and Switzerland. It ranges from 0.7% in Luxembourg to 22.3% in Latvia. On average, women earned 13% less than men in 2020. It is noteworthy that Germany's gender pay gap is much higher than the EU average at 18.3%. This suggests that women are still underrepresented in high-paying positions and industries and that more work needs to be done to close the gap and ensure that women receive fair and equal pay for their work.
2. Individual results.

Erwartungshorizont (M 13)

Pre-watching activity

gender pay gap: the difference between the average earnings of men and women in the workforce; **maternity leave:** a period of time that a woman takes off from work before and after giving birth to a child; **paternity leave:** a period of time that a man takes off from work before and after the birth of a child; **female quota:** a regulation imposed by the government that requires a certain percentage of women to be represented in a particular field or position, the purpose of implementing a female quota is to enhance the representation of women in areas where they are underrepresented; **primary caregiver:** a person who takes on the primary responsibility for the care of another person, mostly a child or an elderly adult; **breadwinner:** a person who earns the main income for their household; **promotion prospects:** career advancement opportunities; **CEO:** short for Chief Executive Officer, the highest-ranking executive in a company

While-watching activities

1. Correct statements: a), e)
2. What has changed: Women are as well educated as men and hold powerful positions, discrimination has become illegal, and women work in jobs that in the past were considered typically male jobs.
3. What has *not* changed: Women are still expected to raise children. Even working mothers spend many hours on childcare (nine hours more than their male counterparts). The "heart" of the pay gap lies in the discrimination against women with children.
4. Rwanda: Due to social tensions between different ethnic groups and a genocide that targeted Tutsi and moderate Hutu people in 1994, almost one million people were killed in Rwanda. As a result, women made up 60–70% of the remaining population, which forced them to take on roles traditionally reserved for men. Women took on jobs such as military and police officers among others. Since then, the Rwandan Constitution guarantees equal rights for both men and women.
Iceland closed their gender pay gap by implementing family-friendly policies and enacting laws to ensure gender equality in the workplace. In 1975, a grassroots movement led by women protested in the streets of Iceland demanding equal rights and opportunities. This movement brought attention to the gender pay gap and helped push for change. In the 1980s, Iceland guaranteed maternity leave to women. However, it was not until the year 2000 that Iceland introduced a law that made it obligatory for fathers to take parental leave. This leave could not be transferred to the mother and had to be used or it was lost. As a result, 97% of fathers in Iceland now take paternity leave, and for companies, it makes no difference anymore.

Erwartungshorizont (M 14)

While-reading activities

1. a) 12.8%: share of women in management boards of the 30 largest German companies listed on the blue-chip Dax index
   b) 24.5%: share of women in management boards of the largest listed companies in the UK
   c) 30%: minimum quota of women on supervisory boards for companies where the federal government holds a majority shareholding according to the new coalition deal
   d) more than 3: management boards with more than three members must include at least one woman, according to the deal
   e) 11: number of Dax companies without a single woman on the board in 2020 (when the article was published)

2. a) The coalition agreed on the introduction of a compulsory quota for the number of women working in management positions in listed companies. Management boards that have more than three members must include one woman. Furthermore, they agreed on a minimum quota of 30% of women on supervisory boards.
   b) According to Franziska Giffey, this step is historic because it will make women-free boardrooms in large companies impossible. She adds that this is the basis of a modern society where men and women have equal opportunities to participate in all areas of life. Since changes will not happen voluntarily, it is important to provide guidelines in order to achieve more equality.
   c) Some people argue that the government should not interfere in private enterprises.

Post-reading activity

<u>Pros and cons of a women's quota</u>:

pros	cons
– Increases gender diversity in leadership positions, which can bring different perspectives and approaches to decision-making – Provides equal opportunities for women to hold leadership positions – Helps to close the gender pay gap by increasing the number of women in higher-paying jobs – Can inspire and empower young women to pursue leadership roles	– Can be seen as unfair to male candidates who may be more qualified or experienced for a particular job – may create tension among employees who feel that female colleagues are only in leadership positions due to the quota – may encourage companies to hire less qualified women to meet the quota rather than finding the best candidate for the job

Hinweise (LEK)

Die für die vorliegende Unterrichtsreihe ausgewählten Episoden aus *„Explained"* eignen sich insbesondere auch zur **Vorbereitung auf die Abiturprüfung**, da verschiedene Lehrplanthemen exemplarisch behandelt werden. Es bietet sich daher an, die Inhalte als Grundlage für eine **mündliche Prüfung** heranzuziehen.

Bei der Lernerfolgskontrolle handelt es sich um eine Prüfung im **Tandem-Format**, das heißt die Lernenden erhalten eine kurze Vorbereitungszeit, in der sie zu ihrem Thema und ihren Materialien einen **fünfminütigen Vortrag** vorbereiten. In der sich daran anschließenden **Dialogphase** diskutieren die beiden Prüfungskandidatinnen oder -kandidaten zu einem vorgegebenen Themenbereich.

Hier stehen Materialien aus dem gleichen Themenbereich zu zwei unterschiedlichen Aspekten zur Verfügung. Auf diese Weise können die Prüfungskandidateninnen und -kandidaten auf der Grundlage ihrer Materialien in der zweiten Phase in die Diskussion starten.

Die erste Aufgabe bezieht sich auf die Episode *„The Future of Meat"*, die zweite Aufgabe knüpft an die Episode *„The World's Water Crisis"* an. Beide Aufgaben lassen sich gut über die Problematik *„Water scarcity"* miteinander verbinden. In der Dialogphase diskutieren die Prüflinge auch mögliche Lösungsansätze. Dazu greifen sie auf die Inhalte beider Episoden zurück. Die Aufgabe ist sehr offen formuliert, sodass der Dialog von den Lernenden gestaltet werden kann.

Erwartungshorizont (LEK)

Student A – The growing global hunger for meat

1. The chart illustrates the daily meat consumption per person in various countries worldwide in 2020. The countries are represented by distinct colours on the chart: red represents meat consumption over 165g per day, brown represents meat consumption between 40 and 165g per day, and blue represents meat consumption less than 40g per day.

   The most remarkable feature of the chart is the African continent, where the least amount of meat is consumed, with most countries falling in the blue and brown categories. In contrast, North America, Europe, Russia, China, and Australia have the highest meat consumption, with nearly all areas falling in the red category. India has meat consumption patterns similar to those found in many countries on the African continent, while South America has a mixed pattern, with some countries in the red category and others in the brown category. It is noteworthy that meat consumption has increased significantly in emerging economies such as China. The growing income levels in these countries have resulted in increased demand for meat, as it is seen as a symbol of wealth and status. This has led to an increase in the consumption of meat in these countries in recent years.

2. Meat consumption can have a significant impact on the environment. It requires large amounts of water and land, while contributing to deforestation, and greenhouse gas emissions. Furthermore, meat production requires large amounts of resources, including water, land and energy. With global population growth and increasing demand for meat, these resources may become increasingly limited in the future.

Student B – The global water crisis

1. The chart with the title *Unsafe Water Kills More Than Disasters and Conflicts* illustrates the number of deaths caused by different sources in the year 2020, with a focus on the impact of unsafe water. At the top of the chart there are three bars representing the number of deaths

caused by natural disasters, conflicts and unsafe water. The first bar shows that 8,200 people died due to natural disasters, the second bar shows that 87,400 people died due to conflicts, and the third bar reveals that 485,000 people died due to unsafe water. Below the bar chart there is a world map representing the percentage of people who lacked access to basic drinking water service in 2020. The map uses three colours to highlight the level of access to water in different countries. The countries highlighted in blue had access to water, while those highlighted in yellow had limited access. The countries highlighted in orange had an access of less than 50%. It is not surprising to note that the majority of industrialised countries had unlimited access to water, while nearly all countries with limited or very limited access can be found on the African continent. This emphasizes the pressing need to improve access to clean water in these countries, as unsafe water is a major cause of death and disease worldwide.

2. Factors contributing to water scarcity: climate change (more frequent droughts and water shortages in some regions); Population growth: as the global population continues to grow, the demand for water is increasing; Agricultural practices: agriculture is one of the largest consumers of water, and inefficient irrigation methods can result in wasteful water usage by farmers; Industry: the production of goods requires vast quantities of water.

V.280

Unterrichtsmagazin

British monarchy: Who is Charles III? – Auseinandersetzung mit einem kritischen Monarchen (ab Klasse 10)

Waltraud Feger

© IMAGO/i Images

Ist Charles III der Rolle des Königs von Großbritannien gewachsen? Bevor er König wurde, fiel der Monarch unter anderem durch öffentliche Meinungsäußerungen zu kontroversen politischen Themen wie zum Beispiel dem Umweltschutz auf. In einer konstitutionellen Monarchie wie der britischen jedoch hat der Monarch eine rein repräsentative Aufgabe und überlässt politische Fragen der Regierung. In den vorliegenden Unterrichtsmaterialien gehen Ihre Schülerinnen und Schüler der Frage nach, was den britischen König ausmacht und wofür er steht. Dabei setzen sie sich auch mit Charles' Rolle in den Medien auseinander, indem sie Bilder und das Video einer Rede analysieren sowie einen aktuellen Artikel über die Besonderheiten Charles' lesen.

KOMPETENZPROFIL

LearningApps - interaktive Lernbausteine

Klassenstufe:	ab Klasse 10
Dauer:	ca. 1–5 Unterrichtsstunden + LEK
Kompetenzen:	1. Hör-Seh-Verstehen: Bildern und einem Kurzvideo zentrale Informationen entnehmen; 2. Leseverstehen: einen Zeitungsartikel verstehen; 3. Schreiben: schriftliche Kommentare verfassen
Thematische Bereiche:	*British monarchy, British society, British values*

Fachliche Hinweise

Im Vordergrund dieser Unterrichtsreihe steht die Förderung der Lernenden bezüglich historisch wichtiger Aspekte Großbritanniens und dessen **Zukunft**. Hierbei fällt auf, dass nicht nur **Harry** und seine Frau **Meghan Kritik** an der königlichen Familie äußern, sondern auch die Bevölkerung **Proteste** anmeldet, die einerseits Harrys Vorwürfe bezüglich Rassismus und Mobbing aufgreifen und andererseits mit dem Aufruf **#notmyKING** eine „richtige Demokratie" mit einem vom Volk gewählten Staatsoberhaupt fordern. Auch das **Commonwealth** scheint zu bröckeln, da immer mehr Staaten Eigenständigkeit fordern. Nach dem Tode von Queen Elizabeth weigerte sich Australien von nun an Charles' Konterfei auf seine Geldscheine zu drucken. Die kanadische Provinz Québec hat – aufgrund von Protesten – den Schwur auf den britischen Souverän freigestellt. Ein anderes Problem hat einerseits mit den **Medien**, andererseits mit Charles selbst zu tun. In Harrys Buch „*Spare*" und in seinen Interviews äußert er sich kritisch zur königlichen Familie. Hinzu kommt die Netflixserie „*The Crown*", die die neunziger Jahre und somit die **Eheprobleme** von Charles und Diana thematisiert. Dies wirkt sich ebenfalls wenig förderlich auf Charles' Popularität aus. Dasselbe gilt auch für Camilla Parker Bowles, mit der er zu der Zeit eine Affäre hatte. Experten und Expertinnen gehen davon aus, dass das **Image** der königlichen Familie – auch wegen Prince Andrews Fehltritt – erneut Schaden nimmt. Hinzu kommt, dass König Charles Ende Februar 2023 in Misskredit geriet, als er die EU-Präsidentin zum Tee auf Schloss Windsor empfing. Am selben Tag hatte sie zusammen mit Premierminister Sunak ein Abkommen unterzeichnet – das sogenannte *Windsor Framework* – das Handelserleichterungen für Nordirland mit sich bringt und das das *NorthernIreland Protocol*, das zum Brexit erforderlich war, außer Kraft setzt. Die Lernenden befassen sich mit den Geschehnissen und beschäftigen sich daher unter anderem mit der Frage nach dem Fortbestand der konstitutionellen Monarchie.

Didaktisch-methodische Hinweise

Diese ein- bis fünfstündige Unterrichtsreihe mit dem sich anschließenden Klausurvorschlag und einem Test ist zum Einsatz in der Oberstufe gedacht. Hier kann sie im Unterricht der Sekundarstufe II, im Grund- und Leistungskurs, als Einheit, aber auch in einzelnen Kapiteln behandelt werden. Sie bietet sich auch für den Einsatz in einer leistungsstarken Klasse 10 an.

Zu den curricularen Vorgaben

Alle Lehrpläne der Bundesländer fordern die Behandlung der Entwicklung der britischen Gesellschaft. Der Lehrplan des Landes NRW sieht das Thema „Das Vereinigte Königreich im 21. Jahrhundert – Selbstverständnis zwischen Tradition und Wandel: *Tradition and change in politics and society: the UK in the European context*" vor. Dazu gehört auch die Einführung von Charles III in sein Amt und seine Krönung am 6. Mai 2023.

> Eine Anknüpfung an das Thema „*Great Britain and the Monarchy*" ist mit allen gängigen Lehrwerken der Klassen 9–13 möglich, so wie in folgenden Lehrwerken/*Units*:
> - *Pathway Advanced*, 2022: „The Duke of Sussex (Prince Harry): The Power of the Invisible Role Model"
> - *Pathway Advanced*, Schöningh 2015: „The U.K. between Tradition and Modernity"
> - *Context*, Cornelsen 2022, Chapter 4: „The UK – between Tradition and Change"
> - *Green Line Oberstufe*, Klett 2022: „Tradition and change in the UK"

Zur Erweiterungsmöglichkeit

Eine interessante Erweiterungsmöglichkeit besteht darin, einen längeren **Artikel** portionsweise, beispielsweise eine Seite je Lernenden, als **Referatsthemen** zu verteilen. Ein geeigneter Artikel ist *„What kind of King will Charles III be?"* von The Guardian, zu dem eine Audio-Datei zur Verfügung steht (37:32 min.): https://www.theguardian.com/uk-news/2014/nov/19/-sp-what-kind-king-will-prince-charles-be [letzter Aufruf: 25.07.2023]. Der aus dem Jahre 2014 stammende Artikel, befasst sich mit der Eigenschaft von König Charles, die für sein Amt nachteilig ist, nämlich seine Kritikbereitschaft, die der Autor als „Einmischen" bezeichnet. Ähnliches sagt ein weiterer Autor im Artikel *„Prince Charles will not be silenced when he is made king, say allies"*, der sich ebenfalls für diese Aufgabe anbietet: https://www.theguardian.com/uk-news/2014/nov/19/becoming-king-not-silence-prince-charles-allies [letzter Aufruf: 25.07.2023].

Mediathek

Bücher

- **Murphy, Philip:** „*Monarchy and the end of Empire: The House of Windsor, the British Government and the Post-war Commonwealth*". Oxford University Press, Oxford 2013.
  Diese genaue, ausführliche Studie untersucht das Dreiecksverhältnis zwischen der britischen Regierung, dem Königshof und dem modernen Commonwealth seit 1945. Besondere Aufmerksamkeit widmet Murphy der Rolle des Monarchen.
- **Prince Harry Windsor**: „*Spare*". Random House, London 2023.
  Prinz Harrys Buch, dessen Ghostwriter J. R. Moehringer ist, erzeugte viele Diskussionen. In der Ich-Form verfasst, liest sich der Band wie ein Roman. Folgende Themen werden dabei unter anderen aufgegriffen: Streitigkeiten zwischen Harry und William, die auch zu Handgreiflichkeiten führten, Camilla, der Tod ihrer Mutter Diana, Harrys Beziehungen und die Tötung von 25 Taliban.

Weiterführende Internetseiten

- Podcast: *„Prince Harry's memoir: why has 'spare' gone rogue?"* (37:21 min.)
  https://www.theguardian.com/news/audio/2023/jan/11/prince-harry-memoir-why-has-spare-gone-rogue-podcast
  Dieser Podcast beschreibt den Medienrummel um das Buch, auch schon vor seinem Erscheinen. Der Podcast ist besorgt wegen der Wirkung der ausführlichen Beschreibung, die vor sehr intimen Enthüllungen nicht haltmacht.
- Podcast: *„What's the future of the Commonwealth under King Charles III?"* (23 min.)
  https://www.bbc.co.uk/programmes/w3ct39tl
  Nach dem Tode von Queen Elizabeth II ist Charles III das Oberhaupt des *Commonwealth of Nations*. Die Frage stellt sich: Wird das Commonwealth unter seiner Führung gedeihen oder schrumpfen? Eine sehr aktuelle Fragestellung. Experten und Charles III selbst kommen hier zu Wort.
- YouTube-Video: *„King Charles III: A Modern Monarch"* (42 min.)
  https://www.youtube.com/watch?v=WpFuTCZ05p4
  Dies ist eine gut zusammengestellte Fernsehsendung mit über 2 Millionen Aufrufen und über 2000 Kommentaren. Thema ist der Lebensweg Charles' III mit vielen historischen Aufnahmen und einem guten Kommentar und vorhandenem Transkript.

[letzte Aufrufe: 25.07.2023]

Auf einen Blick

1. Stunde

Thema:	Warming up to the topic: Prince/King Charles
M 1	**Some highlights of Charles' life – Working with pictures /** sich über Charles III und seine Familie austauschen (PA, UG, EA)
Hausaufgabe:	Ein Foto auswählen, schriftlich einordnen und vorstellen (*task 2*)
Benötigt:	☐ digitale Endgeräte für die Recherche

2. Stunde

Thema:	After the Queen's death, Charles takes over
M 2	**King Charles' first speech to the Parliament – Working with a video /** König Charles' Rede erarbeiten (PA, UG, EA)
Benötigt:	☐ Hausaufgabe aus M 1 ☐ Internetzugang und digitale Endgeräte zum Abspielen des Videos und zur Bearbeitung der *LearningApp*

3. Stunde

Thema:	Prince Charles, heir to the throne for a lifetime
M 3	**Who is King Charles III – Working with an article /** Aufgaben zum Textverstehen und zur Grammatik bearbeiten (EA, PA, GA)
Benötigt:	☐ Bild 1 von M 1 ☐ Internet und digitale Endgeräte zur Bearbeitung der *LearningApp*

4. Stunde

Thema:	Impact of Harry's Book *Spare*
M 4	**The beginning of the end? – Discussing Prince Harry's book /** Aufgaben zum Textverständnis und kreative Aufgaben zum Thema bearbeiten (PA, UG, EA)
Hausaufgabe:	Einen Artikel auswählen und vorstellen (*task 5*)
Benötigt:	☐ Internet und digitale Endgeräte zur Bearbeitung der *LearningApp* und für die Recherche

5. Stunde

Thema:	The unconstitutional King Charles?
M 5	**An impartial king? – Talking about Ursula von der Leyen's visit /** Aufgaben zum Textverständnis und kreative Aufgaben bearbeiten (EA, PA)
M 6	**Charles III – A multiple choice test /** das Erlernte überprüfen (EA/GA)
Benötigt	☐ Bild 2 von M 1
	☐ Internet und digitale Endgeräte zur Bearbeitung der *LearningApp* (M 6)
	☐ ZM 1 LEK in Klassenstärke

Minimalplan

Die Zeit ist knapp? Folgende Materialien der Unterrichtsreihe kann die Lehrkraft unabhängig voneinander einsetzen. Dadurch ergeben sich folgende Schwerpunkte:

Getting to know King Charles III	M 1 und M 3
King Charles' speech	M 2
King Charles and the future	M 2, M 4 und M 5

Hinweise zum Online-Archiv bzw. zur ZIP-Datei

Alle Materialien des Beitrags finden Sie im Online-Archiv als Word-Dokumente. So können Sie die Materialien gezielt bearbeiten und sie auf die Lerngruppe abstimmen.

Zusätzlich im Online-Archiv bzw. in der ZIP-Datei

ZM 1 LEK	eine Lernerfolgskontrolle zur Analyse eines Artikels und dem Verfassen einer Mediation

Erklärung zu den Symbolen

Dieses Symbol markiert differenziertes Material. Wenn nicht anders ausgewiesen, befinden sich die Materialien auf mittlerem Niveau.

einfaches Niveau	mittleres Niveau	schwieriges Niveau
Zusatzaufgaben	Alternative	Selbsteinschätzung

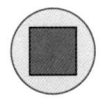

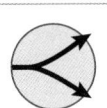

M 1   Some highlights of Charles' life – Working with pictures

What do you already know about the British king?

❶ ❷ ❸ ❹

© Anwar Hussein/Kontributor/WireImage; © Lorna Roberts/Shutterstock; © Chris J. Ratcliffe/Getty Images; © IMAGO/i Images

Tasks

1. With a partner, work with the photos ❶ to ❹:
   a) Describe the photos.
   b) Speculate which of the photos were taken when Charles was still Prince of Wales and which ones were taken when he was already King. Give reasons.
   c) Choose one of the photos and research online about the occasion of the picture.
   d) Prepare a three-minute presentation about your findings.
2. Choose a photo of Charles III from a German newspaper or social media and cut or print it out. Prepare a short, written presentation with background information about the occasion to be shown in a gallery walk in class.

King Charles' first speech to the Parliament – Working with a video

M 2

Find out what Charles III said in his first speech to Parliament.

Vocabulary

address of condolence: *die Beileidsbekundung* – **touchingly:** *rührend* – **(to) encompass:** *erfassen* – **pattern:** here: *das Verhaltensmuster* – **I cannot help but ...:** *Ich komme nicht umhin ...* – **(to) dedicate so. to sth.:** *sich mit Leib und Seele etwas verschreiben* – **commitment:** *das Engagement, die Verpflichtung* – **betterment:** *der Wertzuwachs* – **ancient:** *very old* – **this great hall:** Westminster Hall, a historic building built in 1097, it is big enough for all the members of the House of Commons and the House of Lords – **reminder:** *die Erinnerung, die Mahnung* – **tangible:** *precise, concrete* – **late:** here: *verstorben* – **(to) commemorate sth.:** *an etw. erinnern* – **silver jubilee:** 25th anniversary of accession – **sundial:** *die Sonnenuhr* – **golden jubilee:** 50th anniversary of accession – **stained glass window:** *das Bleiglasfenster* – **diamond jubilee:** 60th anniversary of accession – **poignant:** *ergreifend* – **(to) unveil:** *enthüllen* – **unprecedented:** *noch nie da gewesen* – **platinum jubilee:** 70th anniversary of accession – **(to) house:** here: *unterbringen* – **progress:** here: *die Prozession* – **span:** *die Zeitspanne* – **(to) pledge:** *geloben* – **(to) maintain:** (to) support – **vow:** *oath* – **unsurpassed:** *unübertroffen* – **devotion:** *die Hingabe* – **counsel:** *der Ratschlag* – **(to) be resolved:** (to) be determined – **faithful:** *gewissenhaft*

Tasks

Watch the video: https://raabe.click/CharlesSpeechParliament (03:45 Min.) [last access: 25/07/2023].

1. *Comprehension:* Answer the questions a)–d).
   a) Why does King Charles address the members of Parliament?

   b) What has obviously happened shortly before his speech?

   c) What was "unprecedented" about Queen Elizabeth?

   d) What are the promises he makes to his audience?

   For further practice do the task in *LearningApps*:
   https://learningapps.org/watch?v=pqy6qk0xj23

2. *Comprehension:* Watch the video for a second time and complete the sentences a)–e).
   a) To Charles, Elizabeth II was _____
   b) "I cannot help but feel _____"
   c) "Parliament is the living and breathing instrument _____"
   d) "The great bell of Big Ben, one of the most powerful _____"
   e) "We gather today in remembrance of the remarkable _____"

3. Imagine you read the following comment below the video of Charles' speech on YouTube:
   MonaMonarchy: *Sorry, Charles, I cannot believe your vow of being 'faithful' following a vow. Diana will never be forgotten!*
   With a partner, discuss the comment.
4. Write your own YouTube comment in which you react to MonaMonarchy's comment.
5. *Analyse:* Which stylistic devices does King Charles use in his speech and to what avail?

Stylistic device	Quotation	Function
alliteration		
allusion		
anaphora		
antithesis		
hyperbole		
image		
leitmotif		
metaphor		
climax parallelism		
personification		
repetition		

6. Listen to Charles' speech again. Describe how he feels about his late mother.

Who is King Charles III – Working with an article

M 3

His life, his opinions, his hobbies – find out more about Charles III.

King Charles III – a man who's never done things by the book

At the age of 73 and after spending 70 years as heir to the throne, he has now become King.

King Charles III has never been one to do things by the book[1]. At the age of 73 and after spending 70 years as heir to the throne, he has now become King. As a senior member of the royal family and eldest son of Queen Elizabeth II, the former Prince of Wales has been compelled[2] to devote his life to service and uphold[3] many long-standing traditions. Following the death of the Queen, Charles III automatically succeeded the throne, but will not be formally proclaimed King until an Accession Council[4] is held at St James's Palace in London on Saturday. While he might be following in the footsteps of his mother, if his public life thus far is anything to go by[5], Charles could take steps to modernise the monarchy even more after he is crowned.

Commitment[6] to the environment

Far ahead of the mainstream, Charles has campaigned for environmental awareness[7] since the 1980s and in 2021 unveiled[8] a hugely ambitious[9] project. The Nature Capital fund[10] seeks to raise[11] £ 7.5 bn from businesses to invest in sustainable[12] initiatives around the world. A keen[13] gardener, he became interested in organic farming[14] […], later co-authoring a book on the topic and founding organic food brand[15] Duchy Originals, sales of which go to the Prince of Wales's Charitable Fund[16].

Marrying a second time

Usually, the royal family does everything it can to keep romantic scandals under wraps[17], but in 1994, Charles admitted[18] in a television interview that he had been unfaithful to Diana, Princess of Wales, whom he married in 1981. He said that the marriage had already 'irretrievably[19] broken down' by the time the affair began. Charles and Diana divorced in 1996, a year before Diana was killed in a car crash in Paris. Charles and Camilla Parker-Bowles rekindled[20] their relationship and were married at Windsor Castle in 2005, with Camilla becoming the Duchess of Cornwall.

On her Platinum Jubilee[21] in February 2022, the Queen expressed her 'sincere wish' that Camilla would become Queen Consort[22] when Charles became King – and that wish has now been granted, as is shown on the official royal website.

Outspoken about architecture

While he may want to modernise the royal family, it's safe to say Charles is not a fan of modern architecture, once famously describing a proposed extension[23] to London's National Gallery as a 'monstrous carbuncle[24] on the face of a much-loved friend'. Preaching his building preservation[25] gospel overseas, he helped set up the National Trust for Canada, which is committed to protecting historic urban areas, and is patron[26] of an organisation working on the conservation of Orthodox monasteries[27] in Romania, where he owns a house.

Sharing his love of gardening

Nowadays, gardening is a very trendy hobby, but Charles was way ahead[28] of the curve[29]. He was mocked by the press for admitting in an interview in 1986: "I just come and talk to the plants, really – very important to talk to them. They respond."

45 It seems Charles could see the funny side, though. Asked in 2013 on the BBC's Countryfile[30] whether he still conversed[32] with his greenery[31], he said: "No, now I instruct[32] them instead. You can't make a joke, can you really, without people taking you seriously – it always comes back to haunt[35] you."

(562 words)

Source: Katie Wright, Todd Fitzgerald: https://www.manchestereveningnews.co.uk/news/uk-news/king-charles-iii-man-whos-24972706 [last access: 25/07/2023]

> 1 **(to) do things by the book:** *dem Formalen Genüge tun* – 2 **(to) be compelled:** (to) be forced – 3 **(to) uphold:** (to) support – 4 **accession council:** *der Thronbesteigungsrat* – 5 **if his public life thus far is anything to go by:** *wenn man nach seinem bisherigen öffentlichen Leben urteilt, könnte Charles ...* – 6 **commitment:** *das Engagement, die Verpflichtung* – 7 **awareness:** *das Bewusstsein* – 8 **(to) unveil:** (to) show, (to) announce – 9 **ambitious:** *ehrgeizig* – 10 **fund:** *der Anlagefond* – 11 **(to) raise:** *aufbringen, bereitstellen* – 12 **sustainable:** *nachhaltig* – 13 **keen:** eager, enthusiastic – 14 **organic farming:** *der biologische Anbau* – 15 **brand:** *die Marke, das Produkt* – 16 **charitable fund:** *der Wohltätigkeitsfond* – 17 **under wraps:** secret – 18 **(to) admit:** (to) agree that sth. is true – 19 **irretrievable:** *unwiederbringlich* – 20 **(to) rekindle:** *wiederaufleben* – 21 **Platinum Jubilee:** *das 70-jährige Jubiläum* – 22 **Queen Consort:** *die Königin, die Gemahlin des Königs* – 23 **extension:** an added part (to a building) – 24 **carbuncle:** *die Eiterbeule* – 25 **(to) preach his building preservation:** here: *das "Glaubensbekenntnis" zur Erhaltung von Gebäuden predigen* – 26 **patron:** here: *der Schirmherr* – 27 **monastery:** *das Kloster* – 28 **way ahead:** *weit voraus* – 29 **curve:** here: *die Welle* – 30 **Countryfile:** series of the BBC: here: *"Landleben"* – 31 **(to) converse:** (to) have a conversation – 32 **greenery:** here: *das Grünzeug* – 32 **(to) instruct:** (to) give orders – 33 **(to) haunt:** *verfolgen, heimsuchen*

Prince Charles – A timeline of his life

1948	Prince Charles is born as the first child to Prince Philip, Duke of Edinburgh and Princess Elizabeth, daughter to King George VI.
1950	Charles' sister Anne is born to Princess Elizabeth and Prince Philip.
1952	King George VI dies and is succeeded by Charles' mother Princess Elizabeth, who becomes Queen Elizabeth II.
1953	Charles' great-grandmother, Queen Mary, dies.
1953	Elizabeth II is crowned in Westminster Abbey.
1958	Prince Charles is created Earl of Chester and Prince of Wales.
1960	Charles' brother Andrew is born to Queen Elizabeth II and Prince Philip.
1964	Charles' brother Edward is born to Queen Elizabeth II and Prince Philip.
1967	Charles leaves school with six O levels and two A levels.
1967	Charles attends Trinity College, Cambridge to study anthropology, archaeology and history.
1968	Charles moves to Aberystwyth, Wales, to study Welsh history and the Welsh language.
1969	Charles is invested as Prince of Wales at Caernarfon Castle.
1970	Charles leaves university with two Bachelor of Arts degrees.
1971	Charles starts training as a jet pilot.
1974	Charles qualifies as a helicopter pilot and joins Naval Air Squadron on HMS Hermes.
1981	Charles marries Diana Frances Spencer.
1982	William is born to Prince Charles and Princess Diana.
1984	The second son Henry, known as Harry, is born to Prince Charles and Princess Diana.
1986	The marriage between Charles and Diana is broken. Charles turns to Camilla.

1992	In Parliament, PM Major announces that Charles and Diana are to separate.
1996	Lady Diana and Prince Charles' marriage is formally dissolved.
1997	Charles' former wife Lady Diana Spencer is killed in a car crash in Paris.
1997	Queen Elizabeth is criticised for remaining in Scotland rather than returning to London because of Diana's death.
1997	Queen Elizabeth makes a public broadcast commenting on Diana and expressing her feelings.
2002	Charles' grandmother, Queen Mother, dies at the age of 101.
2005	Prince Charles and Camilla Parker-Bowles' engagement is announced.
2005	Prince Charles and Camilla Parker Bowles marry.
2006	Queen Elizabeth celebrates her 80th birthday.
2011	William, eldest son of Prince Charles, marries Catherine Middleton at Westminster Abbey.
2013	George, the first son to William and Catherine, is born.
2015	Charlotte is born to William and Catherine.
2015	Queen Elizabeth becomes the longest reigning British monarch, surpassing Queen Victoria.
2018	Louis, William and Catherine's third child, is born.
2018	Prince Harry marries Meghan Markle at St. George's chapel, Windsor.
2019	Charles' grandson Archie Harrison is born to Meghan and Prince Harry in London.
2020	Prince Harry and his wife announce they will step back from Royal duties and will not receive public funding.
2021	Charles' granddaughter Lilibet (Lili) Diana is born to Meghan and Prince Harry in California, USA.
2022	Charles represents his mother and delivers the Queen's speech at the state opening of Parliament.
2022	At the Queen's Platinum Jubilee, Charles represents his mother at all events.
2022	8th September: Queen Elizabeth II dies at Balmoral Castle. Charles becomes King after the Queen's death.
2022	9th September: Charles delivers his first address as King on TV.
2022	19th September: King Charles III and Camilla Queen Consort attended the funeral services for Elizabeth II.
2022	13th October: King Charles has his first weekly audience with PM Liz Truss at Buckingham Palace. At the age of 73 and after spending 70 years as heir to the throne, he has now become King.

Tasks

1. *Comprehension:* Read the article and the statements about the text a)–k). Decide whether they are true or false by ticking the right box.

Statements	True	False
a) The Prince of Wales has been compelled to devote his life to the Anglican Church.		
b) After the Queen's death, Charles automatically succeeded the throne.		
c) After he will be crowned, he will take steps to modernise the monarchy.		

Statements	True	False
d) Since the 1990s, Charles has campaigned for environmental awareness.		
e) A scandal came into the open when Prince Charles declared he had betrayed Diana.		
f) Charles was interested in organic farming and wrote a book on it.		
g) Charles met his former lover Camilla and married her in 2005.		
h) Charles and Diana divorced in 1996. A year later, Diana died in a car accident in Paris.		
i) Charles hates modern architecture but did approve of the new extension to the National Gallery.		
j) In 2022, the Queen wanted Camilla to become "Queen Consort".		
k) Charles being fond of gardening was mocked by the press and took revenge.		

For further practice, do this extra task in *LearningApps*:
https://learningapps.org/watch?v=psbpjwpia23

2. *Grammar:* Put the verbs in the conditional sentences a)–h) into the correct form.

   a) If Edward VIII had not abdicated, his brother George _____ (not to take) over and _____ (not to become) George VI.

   b) Elizabeth would not have been crowed in 1953, if her father _____ (not to die) so early.

   c) Charles III _____ (to have) a peaceful coronation in May 2023, if his sons calm down.

   d) If Elizabeth had stayed childless, that _____ (to be) the end of the royal Windsors.

   e) If Harry _____ (not to reveal) so many private stories in his book, he would be liked more by his family.

   f) If Harry _____ (to have) enough money, Meghan and he would not care for leaving California forever.

   g) If Charles' sister Anne had been born first, she _____ (to become) Queen Anne II.

   h) Charles III said he would be happy if Camilla _____ (to be crowned), too.

3. The death of Queen Elizabeth has caused many people to reflect on monarchy in British society. 13 percent of British people are critics of the monarchy and therefore are against Charles' coronation. Imagine you read an entry on social media with the hashtag and caption #NotMyKing. Against the background of the article and the timeline of Charles' life, write a comment in which you state whether you are in favour of Charles' reign or not. Give reasons.

The beginning of the end? – Discussing Prince Harry's book   M 4

Have you heard of Prince Harry's book *Spare*? Let's talk about it.

Prince Harry's book could be 'beginning of end' for royals,
warns Charles['] biographer

Catherine Mayer says anger over racism, misogyny and wealth in the royal family can undermine public consent for a monarchy

The "absolutely catastrophic" implications[1] of attacks on the behaviour of the royal family in the new memoir[2] from the Duke of Sussex are being ignored,
5 according to Catherine Mayer, the royal analyst[3] and biographer of King Charles. Early publication of the Spanish edition of *Spare*[4] has put the focus on personality clashes, some of it fed by the royal publicity machine[5], and this could threaten the constitutional monarchy, whether or not the British public is calling for such a change, Mayer believes.

10 "It is possibly something that will mark the beginning of the end of the monarchy, and that is what we should discuss. It is important, given the lack of trust in the state at the moment and an upsurge[6] in rightwing[7] politics. Members of the royal family have become our proxies[8] for anger about racism, misogyny[9] and wealth. This is, after all, an institution that stands for inequality, so there are huge things
15 at stake[10]."

Mayer, whose book *The Heart of a King* was subject to similar pre-publication[11] security leaks[12] and distortion[13] when it came out in 2015, argues[14] that fundamental questions raised by Harry [...] are being dodged[15]. Accusations of bullying[16], racism and misogyny, as well as the class distinctions[17] shored up[18] by
20 the monarchy, will eventually combine to undermine the basis of the consent[19] by which the royal family rule, if they are not addressed, she predicts.

"There is a general misapprehension[20] that this is a light story about a British tourist attraction. The polarisation[21] on both sides of the row is styled[22] as a defence of the monarchy, but it's not that," said Mayer. "This is not just a celebrity[23]
25 knockabout story[24]. What we are talking about is the status of a significant[25] institution of state[26], with significant powers and significant taxpayer funding[27], so whether you are pro- or anti-monarchy, it deserves to be considered seriously."

[...] The prospects for reconciliation[28] were remote[29] even before the book, Mayer said, "but there is a strong incentive for King Charles to initiate[30] some kind of
30 truce[31] – this is bringing back the fallout[32] from his first marriage and questions about Queen Camilla are resurfacing[33] already."

Mayer notes that the alleged[34] racism, bullying and image manipulation inside the institution[35] are not being examined. Left alone[36], they have the power to dissolve faith in the idea of a hereditary[37] head of state.

35 [... "]The whole family is meant to be an idealised reflection of the British people themselves and Harry's marriage to Meghan made the job much easier," she said. "The failure[38] of that project is absolutely catastrophic for the royal family."

The emotional impact of the new book gains extra weight when Harry tells Bradby[39] about his feeling of numbness[40] following the sudden death of his
40 mother, Diana, Princess of Wales in 1997: "I cried once, at the burial[41], and you know I go into detail about how strange it was and how actually there was some

guilt that I felt and I think William felt as well, by walking around the outside of Kensington Palace[42] ... Everyone thought and felt like they knew our mum, and the two closest people to her, the two most loved people by her, were unable to show any emotion in that moment."

(560 words)

Source: Vanessa Thorpe: https://www.theguardian.com/uk-news/2023/jan/08/harrys-book-end-of-monarchy-royal-biographer [last access: 25/07/2023]

---

1 **implication**: effect, impact – 2 **memoir**: *die Lebenserinnerungen* – 3 **analyst**: here: *die Biografin* – 4 ***Spare***: title of Prince Harrys memoir, written together with a ghostwriter, published on 10 January 2023, accidently already available on 5 January in Spain, title *Reserve/Spare* refers to Harry having been the second in line for the throne after William – 5 **royal publicity machine**: sensational papers and other media – 6 **upsurge**: *der steile Anstieg* – 7 **rightwing**: here: *rechtspopulistisch* – 8 **proxy**: *der Stellvertreter* – 9 **misogyny**: *die Frauenfeindlichkeit* – 10 **(to) be at stake**: *auf dem Spiel stehen, es geht um ...* – 11 **pre-publication**: *die vorzeitige Veröffentlichung* – 12 **security leak**: *die Sicherheitslücke* – 13 **distortion**: *die Verzerrung* – 14 **(to) argue**: (to) give reasons – 15 **(to) be dodged**: (to) be pushed aside – 16 **bullying**: *das Mobbing* – 17 **class distinctions**: *die Klassenunterschiede* – 18 **(to) be shored up**: *gestützt werden* – 19 **consent**: *die Zustimmung, die Billigung* – 20 **misapprehension**: *das Missverständnis, die falsche Auffassung* – 21 **polarisation**: here: *die Unverwechselbarkeit* – 22 **(to) be styled**: here: (to) be called – 23 **celebrity**: *die Berühmtheit* – 24 **knockabout story**: *die Schmierengeschichte* – 25 **significant**: important, considerable – 26 **institution of state**: *die staatliche Einrichtung* – 27 **taxpayer funding**: *die Finanzierung durch den Steuerzahler* – 28 **reconciliation**: *die Versöhnung* – 29 **remote**: far away – 30 **(to) initiate**: (to) cause sth. (to) begin – 31 **truce**: *der Waffenstillstand* – 32 **fallout**: bad results – 33 **(to) resurface**: (to) come to the surface again – 34 **alleged**: *angeblich* – 35 **the institution**: name for the Royal family, the same as "the firm" – 36 **left alone**: here: *ganz zu schweigen davon* – 37 **hereditary**: here: *mit ererbtem Titel* – 38 **failure**: *das Scheitern* – 39 **Bradby**: Tom Bradby, a famous journalist and author – 40 **numbness**: *die Erstarrung* – 41 **burial**: *die Beerdigung* – 42 **Kensington Palace**: London residence of Prince Charles and Princess Diana

---

Tasks

First, read the article. Then do the tasks.

1. Fill in the gaps. Look at the text again to find the words you need.

   Catherine Mayer, King Charles' _____, warned against the dangerous _____ of Prince Harry's new book (*Spare*), because its content threatens the _____ _____. Due to the insecure political situation because of rightwing politics and lack of trust, the British monarchy is at _____. The book coming up with stories of bullying, racism and misogyny together with class _____ will promote resentment among the people. The controversy is not meant to defend the _____, but it is an attack on the Royal family and this concerns the _____ as well. Mayer is of the opinion that Charles has to find a way to _____ the family, but this is not easy as there are more problems to cope with: negative fall-out from Charles' _____

_____ and _____ about Queen Camilla. Mayer is aware that racism, _____ and _____ _____ in the Royal family have not been addressed. But on the whole, because of all that, people might have second thoughts about their _____ _____ _____ who had not been elected by them but is a hereditary _____.

For further practice, do this extra task in *LearningApps*:
https://learningapps.org/watch?v=pjp3gb6dt23

2. Work with a partner. Prepare a role play. Read the role cards and decide who is the father and who is his daughter/son. This is the situation: at home in the living room, the Browns – father, mother and their daughter/son – have been watching the evening news which had been reporting on Prince Harry's new book and on some of its shocking topics. While Mrs Brown is more interested in her new copy of the magazine *Woman*, Mr Brown and his daughter/son have a discussion and are of different opinions concerning Harry and his tell-all book. Present it in class.

> **Role card 1: Mr Brown**
> You are the family father – aged 52 – working as a train conductor. You are a loyal voter of the Labour Party, a good family man, liberal, and harmonious in your relationship with your wife and daughter/son and always open to other views. While you used to admire Queen Elizabeth, you now view the new King with scepticism, as you have never forgiven him for how he treated poor Diana and his affair with Camilla. On the one hand, you are shocked because of the revelations made by Harry. On the other hand, you cannot understand why Harry is giving away so much information to the public that should remain confidential. You say, "He (Harry) does not understand how privileged he is. One doesn't do this to one's own family".

> **Role card 2: Susan/Evan**
> You are Mr Brown's 20-year-old daughter/son, and you enjoy engaging in discussions about topics turning up in the news like politics or the Royal family with your father. While your father strongly believes in the ideas of the Labour Party, you have a far more open-minded approach to new aims in politics, but you are – like your mother – a strong supporter of the Royal family and the monarchy as a whole.

3. Against the background of the newspaper article, write a comment for a newspaper answering the question, "Should the monarchy go?"
4. Choose a photo on the topic in a German newspaper or on social media and prepare a short statement in class.
5. Find a German article on a similar topic on the difficulties the Royal family is facing and prepare a short presentation. Present it in class.

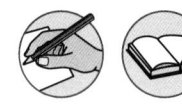

M 5 — An impartial king? – Talking about Ursula von der Leyen's visit

Who invited the EU president Ursula von der Leyen to tea?

How No 10 sweetened up the EU president with a royal cup of tea

European Commission president and 'passionate anglophile' Ursula von der Leyen met the king after NI trade deal agreed

When King Charles III ascended[1] the throne, the new monarch is said to have accepted he would have a changed role with less freedom to intervene[2] in politics.

5 But he had reckoned[3] without the Windsor framework[4].

It was a moment with a distinctly royal flavour – sealed[5] at the Windsor Guildhall [...].

As Ursula von der Leyen took to the podium, a painting of the young Queen Elizabeth was at her left shoulder. [...] Later, Von der Leyen sealed a historic
10 moment by taking tea with Charles [...].

Outraged Tory Brexiters[6] and the Democratic Unionist party[7], including the former first minister[8] Arlene Foster, condemned Sunak's judgment in involving the monarchy in such a controversial[9] political moment. Even Labour MPs questioned the constitutional implications[10].

15 But among those in the room, there were subtle hints[11] this was not something entirely at the instigation[12] of the prime minister. Von der Leyen has always described herself as passionate anglophile with a love for British history and – it was hinted – a personal desire to meet Charles.

[...] No 10 insisted that the royal connections were entirely coincidental[13], not
20 intended [...] to suggest the deal had a seal of approval[14] from the king.

Buckingham Palace's own announcement [...] said that the king was acting on "the government's advice" and that their discussions would feature[15] a "range of topics".

No 10's line was the opposite – that it was a decision for Buckingham Palace. "It's
25 not uncommon for his majesty to accept invitations to meet certain leaders – he has met President [Andrzej] Duda [of Poland] and President Zelenskiy recently. He is meeting with the president of the EU today."

[...] Foster, who led the DUP during the negotiations[16] for Theresa May and Boris Johnson's Brexit deals, tweeted[17]: "I cannot quite believe that No 10 would ask
30 HM the king to become involved in the finalising[18] of a deal as controversial as this one.["]

"It's crass[19] and will go down very badly[20] in NI. We must remember this is not the king's decision but the government, who it appears are tone-deaf[21]."

The Labour MP Chris Bryant said it was a "terrible mistake from the government
35 – we should never bring the monarchy into political disputes".

Sammy Wilson, the DUP's chief whip[22], was also deeply critical of the timing of the meeting, saying it risked "dragging[23] the king into a hugely controversial political issue".

The former cabinet minister Jacob Rees-Mogg [told GB News] "I think the sovereign
40 should only be involved when things have been completed and accepted," [...].

"The king gives assent[24] to acts of parliament when parliament has agreed, he doesn't express his view on acts of parliament when they are going through the process[25]. I think the same applies[26] – that his majesty should not be involved until there is full support for this agreement."

45 But with the deal done[27], with warm words from Von der Leyen for "dear Rishi" and a promise of a fresh era[28] of relations with the EU, the tea at Windsor Castle took place despite the protestations. […]

(519 words)

Source: Jessica Elgot https://www.theguardian.com/uk-news/2023/feb/27/kings-meeting-ursula-von-der-leyen-outcry-monarchy-northern-ireland *[last access: 25/07/2023]*

---

1 **(to) ascend the throne:** (to) become king – 2 **(to) intervene:** (to) become involved – 3 **(to) reckon:** (to) expect sth. to happen – 4 **Windsor framework:** a post-Brexit agreement which was signed on the 27 February 2023 by PM Rishi Sunak and EU-President von der Leyen – 5 **(to) seal:** here: (to) sign, *besiegeln* – 6 **Tory Brexiters:** conservative supporters of Brexit – 7 **Democratic Unionist Party (DUP):** national conservative party in Northern Ireland – 8 **first minister:** here: leader of Northern Ireland – 9 **controversial:** *strittig* – 10 **implications:** *die Konsequenzen, die Verwicklungen* – 11 **subtle hints:** *der subtile Hinweis, die Andeutung* – 12 **instigation:** *die Veranlassung* – 13 **coincidental:** *zufällig* – 14 **approval:** agreement, consent – 15 **(to) feature:** here: (to) have – 16 **negotiation:** *die Verhandlung* – 17 **(to) tweet:** (to) enter short information on the social media platform Twitter – 18 **(to) finalise:** (to) finish the last part – 19 **crass:** *krass* – 20 **(to) go down badly:** *nicht gut ankommen* – 21 **tone-deaf:** *schwerhörig, taub* – 22 **chief whip:** a leader in a political party with several functions – 23 **(to) drag:** *ziehen, schleifen* – 24 **assent:** *die Einwilligung* – 25 **(to) be going through the process:** here: while they are debating the issue – 26 **(to) apply:** here: *zutreffen* – 27 **the deal done:** here: the contract being signed – 28 **era:** *die Ära*, a new period of time in history

---

Tasks

First, read the article. Then, do the tasks.

1. Read the split sentences below.
    a) Match the corresponding halves by drawing lines.
    b) Put the sentences in the correct order. Start with E.

A.	Later, von der Leyen sealed a historic	(1)	judgment in involving the monarchy.
B.	There were subtle hints this was not	(2)	bring the monarchy into political disputes.
C.	Buckingham Palace's own announcement said	(3)	connections were entirely coincidental.
D.	I cannot quite believe that No 10 would ask the king	(4)	moment by taking tea with Charles.
E.	The new monarch is said to have accepted the	(5)	that the king was acting on "the government's advice".
F.	I think the sovereign should only be involved	(6)	there is full support for this agreement.
G.	His majesty should not be involved until	(7)	would have a changed role with less freedom.
H.	Outraged Tory Brexiters condemned Sunak's	(8)	something entirely at the instigation of the PM.
I.	No 10 insisted that the Royal	(9)	to become involved in the finalising of a deal.
J.	Chris Bryant said we should never	(10)	when things have been completed and accepted.

2. Study the text and the quotations in the grid below. Decide who said what according to the article. Tick off the right boxes.

Quotations	Foster	Tory Brexiteers	Wilson	Bryant	Labour MPs
never bring the monarchy into political disputes					
condemned Sunak's judgment in involving the monarchy					
dragging the king into a hugely controversial political issue					
king ... in the finalising of a deal as controversial as this one					
questioned the constitutional implications					

3. Work with a partner. Imagine a student starting a career as a journalist was given the task to study the article. Read his notes in the table. Tick his notes that are not in the article.

the student's notes	not in the article
a) King Charles is ready for the new job	
b) "Windsor framework" is a paper planned by Charles	
c) von der Leyen arrived in Windsor to finalise the contract	
d) "Windsor framework" is about how to deal with illegal immigrants	
e) a lot of MPs are against the meeting of the EU chief and Charles	
f) constitutional monarchy is never to interfere in political issues	
g) von der Leyen was invited by the king to have tea with him	
h) a Labour MP said it was a terrible mistake from the government	
i) because of protests, the meeting did not take place	

4. Work with a partner. Discuss the quotation, "'Heads will roll': Anger at King Charles' meeting with EU boss Ursula von der Leyen".
   Write a short critical entry for a blog on the internet on the topic of the quotation.
   Source: Stanley Adams https://ukdaily.news/heads-will-roll-anger-at-king-charles-meeting-with-eu-boss-ursula-von-der-leyen-362037.html [last access: 25/07/2023]

5. Work with a partner. Imagine a journalist wrote a comment with the headline "The King was wrong to offer an unconstitutional tea to the EU president von der Leyen".
   Against the background of the article, find out what she/he means by "unconstitutional tea" and why she/he thinks that the king was wrong.
   Write an interview with her/him.
   Present your interview in class.

Charles III – A multiple choice test

M 6

What do you remember?

Task

Tick the correct answer/completion. You can also do this task as a competition with your classmates or against the system in *LearningApps*: https://learningapps.org/watch?v=pb9t4288523

1. On which occasion was the photo taken with the Royal family on the balcony?

a) on Prince Philip's birthday	
b) at Prince Charles' marriage	
c) on Queen Elizabeth's official birthday	

2. Where did King Charles address all members of Parliament for the first time?

a) in Buckingham Palace	
b) in Westminster Hall	
c) in Parliament	

3. What was the main topic of Charles' address to all members of Parliament?

a) the death of Queen Elizabeth II	
b) Charles' coronation	
c) Camilla's becoming Queen consort	

4. Shortly before the Queen's death the British had celebrated the Queen's jubilee. Which one was it?

a) the golden jubilee	
b) the diamond jubilee	
c) the platinum jubilee	

5. At the end of that extract of his speech, King Charles promised …

a) to reform the country and the monarchy.	
b) to serve the country and its people in the same way as his mother did.	
c) to stop Harry and Meghan from upsetting people.	

6. One article talks about Charles' favourite topics and hobbies. Which are they?

a) The Royal Marine and the Royal Air Force.	
b) Environment, architecture and gardening.	
c) Literature and artificial intelligence.	

7. Why are Harry and Meghan so much in the limelight (*Rampenlicht*)?

a) They have given another interview about their lives at Buckingham Palace.	
b) They are having a second child.	
c) Harry has published a tell-all memoir.	

8. Why does Harry's book infuriate most people? Because …

a) he is using foul language.	
b) he does not go into details about all scandals.	
c) he is giving away too much of indiscreet behaviour of his family.	

Hinweise und Erwartungshorizonte

1. Stunde

Hinweise (M 1)

Ziel ist es, den Schülerinnen und Schülern anhand von Bildern Charles III vorzustellen und Vorkenntnisse zu aktivieren.

Methodische Hinweise

Als **Einstieg** dient das Foto, das Mitglieder der königlichen Familie auf dem Balkon des Buckingham Palace zeigt. Die drei weiteren Fotos auf M 1 verdeckt die Lehrkraft während der Bildpräsentation im Plenum. Die Lernenden werden die abgelichteten Personen voraussichtlich leicht identifizieren können, da die britische Königsfamilie unter anderem durch die Netflix-Serie „*The Crown*", die Veröffentlichung der Memoiren Prinz Harrys und seine Netflix-Dokumentation sowie den Tod der Queen medial auch für jüngere Leute präsent ist.

Zunächst äußern sich die Lernenden spontan im Plenum zu dem Foto. Daraufhin stellt die Lehrkraft inhaltliche Fragen:

– *How can you be sure that Charles is still Prince of Wales when the photo on the balcony was taken?*
– *Which occasion is shown?*

Als **Hausaufgabe** wählen die Lernenden ein weiteres Foto aus dem Leben von Charles aus, das sie kurz schriftlich einordnen und vorstellen (*task 2*).

Erwartungshorizont (M 1)

1. a) ❶ The first photo shows an open horse-drawn carriage carrying Prince Charles and Lady Diana Spencer. They are on their way to St Paul's Cathedral in London for their wedding on 29 July 1981. Princess Diana is dressed in a white wedding gown and Prince Charles is attired in a ceremonial uniform. The couple is smiling at the crowd.

   ❷ The second photo shows the Royal family on the balcony of Buckingham Palace during the Trooping the Colour ceremony for Queen Elizabeth's birthday in June 2015. It is a colourful picture as the Royals, especially the men in their colourful uniforms, are clad festively. Also, the balcony's rail is embellished with a red front fairing. It is a day of celebration: the Queen's official birthday (her actual birthday falls on 21 April). It is a tradition that every year all regiments parade at different locations in London. The ceremony concludes with a flypast by the Royal Air Force, which is watched by the Royals on the balcony. Finally, the national anthem is played.

   ❸ The third photo captures the moment when an anti-monarchy protester is being escorted away from the Houses of Parliament on 12 September in 2022, just before King Charles' first address to Parliament. Six policemen and policewomen can be seen accompanying the protester, who is wearing a chequered shirt. He holds up a poster bearing the slogan "Not My King".

   ❹ The fourth photo shows King Charles and Queen Camilla dressed in formal evening attire during the reception in honour of the South African president on 12 December 2022 at Buckingham Palace. A smiling King Charles is wearing a tailcoat and a lot of decorations and medals. Queen Camilla is standing beside him dressed in a blue evening gown with complimentary jewellery, a diadem with blue jewels (sapphires) and a matching necklace.

b) The first two photos depict Charles in his role as Prince of Wales, the last one shows him as king. The third one captures a moment when King Charles is on his way to deliver a speech in Parliament.

c/d) Examples for short presentations on two of the pictures:

❶ Although the wedding between Charles and Diana, who was very popular with British people, was often referred to as "a fairy tale wedding" or "the wedding of the century" and was watched on television by 750 million people, their marriage did not result in lasting happiness. The couple separated in 1992 and was divorced in 1996. Dozens of books were published about Charles' and Diana's relationship as well as the love triangle involving Charles, Diana and his former mistress Camilla Parker Bowels.

Diana died in 1997 in a car crash in Paris while being pursued by paparazzi just one year after the divorce. She left behind her two teenage sons, William and Harry. More facts about the marriage between her and Charles can be found on https://raabe.click/CharlesDiana [last access: 25/07/2023].

❸ The anti-monarchy protester signals the growing unrest and anti-monarchy sentiments. Australia removes the image of the British sovereign from its currency notes and in Québec, another region within the Commonwealth, is abolishing the oath on the British sovereign.

2. Individual results.

Hinweise (M 2)

2. Stunde

Ziel ist es, dass die Schülerinnen und Schüler den Anfang der Rede des englischen Thronfolgers vor den Abgeordneten des britischen Unter- und Oberhauses inhaltlich erarbeiten.

Einstieg

In einem *gallery walk* betrachten die Lernenden die Bilder, die ihre Mitschülerinnen und Mitschüler als **Hausaufgabe (M 1, *task 2*).** ausgewählt und schriftlich präsentiert haben. Anschließend nennen sie im Plenum das Bild, das sie am meisten interessiert/berührt/beeindruckt hat und begründen ihre Meinung.

Mit einem Rückgriff auf die Ergebnisse von **M 1** gelingt es den Schülerinnen und Schülern, einen Zugang zum Stundenthema zu finden: Der neue König hält seine erste Rede vor allen Vertreterinnen und Vertretern des Volkes (Unter- und Oberhaus) in der Westminster Hall.

Sachhinweis

In dem Ausschnitt aus Charles' erster Rede vor dem britischen Parlament thematisiert er den **Anlass der Rede**, den Tod seiner Mutter, dankt den Abgeordneten für ihre Beileidsbekundungen anlässlich des Todes seiner Mutter, erwähnt Queen Elizabeths Verdienste und ihre Vorbildfunktion für Charles und legt das Versprechen ab, ihrem Vorbild zu folgen.

Methodische Hinweise

Da der König – dem Anlass angemessen – langsam spricht, ist die Rede für die Lernenden gut zu verstehen. Dennoch sollten die Schülerinnen und Schüler vor dem ersten Hören die Vokabelangaben durchlesen und diese während des Hörens vor sich haben. In lernschwächeren Gruppen empfiehlt es sich, die Untertitel einzuschalten, da die *tasks 2* und *3* zum Hör-Seh-Verstehen genaue Angaben verlangen. Hinzu kommt, dass die Schülerinnen und Schüler in *task 5* die **rhetorischen Figuren** aus der Rede untersuchen. Es empfiehlt sich, für diese Aufgabe den Zugang zum Transkript zu ermöglichen, das auf YouTube rechts vom Video über das Menü (drei Punkte anklicken) angeboten wird.

Digitalhinweis

Eine Zusatzaufgabe zur Verständnissicherung können die Schülerinnen und Schüler mit *LearningApps* erarbeiten. Unter folgendem Link ist die Übung kostenlos verfügbar und mit Konto bearbeitbar: https://learningapps.org/display?v=pqy6qk0xj23

Erwartungshorizont (M 2)

1. a) He thanks both Houses of Parliament for their addresses of condolences.
   b) Queen Elizabeth II, his mother, has died.
   c) Her last jubilee marked her 70 years in office, which no other ruler had reached.
   d) Like his mother, he will maintain the principles of constitutional government and serve his country and his people.
2. a) To Charles, Elizabeth II was his beloved mother and "a pattern to all princes living".
   b) "I cannot help but feel the weight of history which surrounds us."
   c) "Parliament is the living and breathing instrument of our democracy."
   d) "The great bell of Big Ben, one the most powerful symbols of our nation throughout the world."
   e) "We gather today in remembrance of the remarkable span of the Queen's dedicated service to her nations."
3./4. Individual results. Example for a reaction to a YouTube comment:

   You have a point there. Charles' behaviour towards Diana, while having an affair with Camilla, displayed a lack of sensitivity and care. I agree, having married Camilla does not seem to be the right thing to do neither to his sons nor to the public. Recently, we all could see the scandal in the Netflix series *The Crown*. However, it is possible that Charles is now more conscious of the public watching him. We may be able to trust him now to do the right thing – as he has promised in his speech.

5.

Stylistic device	Quotation	Function
alliteration	**re**memberance of the **re**markable span	to emphasise his point
allusion	the late queen's **progress** from Buckingham Palace to the cathedral	an indirect reference to the funeral cortege
anaphora	**We** see the construction ... **We** see all around us ...	to emphasise a positive outlook on his reign and the future
antithesis	I cannot help ... which surrounds **us** ... which reminds **us**	use of contrasts to improve the understanding of the importance of history, democracy and monarchy
hyperbole	The **great** bell of Big Ben, one of the **most powerful** symbols of our nation **throughout the world**.	to remind the audience of Britain's history, tradition and power

Stylistic device	Quotation	Function
image	duty which with **God's help**	to appeal to the imagination of the audience and underline his devotion and humbleness with regard to his office
leitmotif	The late **majesty**, my mother, the **Queen**	Charles' matter in hand, following her in the same spirit
metaphor	feel the **weight** of history	to show his awareness of the importance of history and his own role in it
climax parallelism	**which** surrounds us ... and **which** reminds us	to emphasise the presence of history and his mother's legacy
personification	the **living** and **breathing instrument** of our democracy	to depict democracy as vital and lively
repetition	Jubilee, the Queen	to stress the late Queen's importance

6. Charles' feelings towards his late mother: he seems to love his mother: "beloved mother", "darling late mother"; Charles shows great respect for her long reign and accomplishments: "remarkable span of the Queen's dedicated service", "unsurpassed devotion", "example of selfless duty"

Hinweise (M 3)

3. Stunde

Ziel ist es, dass die Schülerinnen und Schüler mittels einer Zeitskala und eines Zeitungsartikels das Leben von Charles kennenlernen, um die Ereignisse rund um seine Krönung besser einordnen und beurteilen zu können.

Methodische Hinweise

Die Lehrkraft zeigt als **Bildimpuls** erneut das erste Foto aus M 1, das Prinz Charles und Diana zeigt. Mithilfe des Bildes aktivieren die Lernenden ihr **Vorwissen** über den **Scheidungsskandal** des Thronfolgers. Sodann erfolgt die Überleitung zum Artikel: „*Let's find out how a British newspaper depicts the divorce scandal and the new king*".
Am Ende der Unterrichtsstunde sammelt die Lehrkraft die fertiggestellten *comments* ein. Zwei bis drei *comments* werden zu Beginn der Folgestunde vorgelesen und im Plenum diskutiert.

Digitalhinweis

Eine Zusatzaufgabe zur Verständnissicherung können die Schülerinnen und Schüler mit *LearningApps* erarbeiten. Unter folgendem Link ist die Übung kostenlos verfügbar und mit Konto bearbeitbar: https://learningapps.org/display?v=psbpjwpia23

Erwartungshorizont (M 3)

1. a) false – b) true – c) false – d) false – e) true – f) false – g) true – h) true – i) false – j) true – k) true
2. a) If Edward VIII had not abdicated, his brother George would not have taken over and would not have become George VI.
   b) Elizabeth would not have been crowed in 1953, if her father had not died so early.
   c) Charles III will have a peaceful coronation in May 2023, if his sons calm down.
   d) If Elizabeth had stayed childless, that would have been the end of the royal Windsors.
   e) If Harry had not revealed so many private stories in his book, he would be liked more by his family.
   f) If Harry had enough money, Meghan and he would not care for leaving California forever.
   g) If Charles' sister Anne had been born first, she would have become Queen Anne II.
   h) Charles III said he would be happy if Camilla was crowned, too.
3. Individual results. Example of a comment:

   If you look at Charles' timeline and the article, you can understand that his life has not been all smiles – especially his life in the limelight – with paparazzi chasing him.

   The article emphasises Charles' apprenticeship as the heir to the throne, following in the footsteps of his mother, and expresses hope that he might modernise the monarchy. However, there is a dark chapter in Charles' life. His infidelity towards his first wife Diana has led people to question his honesty. Nevertheless, it is possible that he has changed for the better since he has married his former lover.

   Charles' hobbies and beliefs, the environment and gardening, has endeared him to many. This will not be true for his outspokenness regarding modern architecture.

   To my mind, it would have been better if the Queen had already passed the crown to William. Not only because of Charles' age, but also because Prince William and his wife could have offered a fresh start with a clean reputation, instilling a positive outlook for the British monarchy.

4. Stunde

Hinweise (M 4)

Ziel von M 4 ist es, dass die Lernenden die Einschätzungen von Catherine Mayer, der Biographin von König Charles, kennenlernen und reflektieren.

Sachhinweis

Da Catherine Mayer 2015 eine Biografie von Prinz Charles veröffentlichte, ist davon auszugehen, dass sie die Situation, nach der Veröffentlichung von Harrys Buch „Spare", gut einschätzen kann. Inhaltlich geht es in „Spare" unter anderem um schwerwiegende Vorwürfe gegenüber einigen Familienangehörigen, die Rassismus, Mobbing und Frauenfeindlichkeit belegen. Der von den gravierenden Vorwürfen ausgehende Imageschaden kann die konstitutionelle Monarchie in Gefahr bringen.

Methodische Hinweise

Als **Hausaufgabe** wählen die Lernenden einen auf Deutsch geschriebenen Artikel, der ein ähnliches Thema aufweist. Zu Beginn der nächsten Stunde stellen die Lernenden ihre Artikel kurz vor (*task 5*).

Digitalhinweis

Eine Zusatzaufgabe zur Verständnissicherung können die Schülerinnen und Schüler mit *LearningApps* erarbeiten. Unter folgendem Link ist die Übung kostenlos verfügbar und mit Konto bearbeitbar: https://learningapps.org/display?v=pjp3qb6dt23

Erwartungshorizont (M 4)

1. Catherine Mayer, King Charles' biographer, warned against the dangerous implications of Prince Harry's new book (*Spare*), because its content threatens the constitutional monarchy. Due to the insecure political situation because of right-wing politics and lack of trust, the British monarchy is at risk. The book coming up with stories of bullying, racism and misogyny together with class distinctions will promote resentment among the people. The controversy is not meant to defend the monarchy, but it is an attack on the Royal family and this concerns the taxpayer as well. Mayer is of the opinion that Charles has to find a way to reconcile the family, but this is not easy as there are more problems to cope with: negative fall-out from Charles' first marriage and questions about Queen Camilla. Mayer is aware that racism, bullying and image manipulation in the Royal family have not been addressed. But on the whole, because of all that, people might have second thoughts about their head of state who had not been elected by them but is a hereditary monarch.

2. Individual results. For example:
   Susan: This is terrible, isn't it? The Sun has commented that no Royal has ever been so "nasty" to his own family. This is a real bombshell! How could he do this?
   Mr Brown: Absolutely! He is being unfair to his family in many ways. But perhaps Meghan is pushing him, seeking revenge for that racist question about their baby's "colour of skin".
   Susan: You have a point there. However, we should not forget their financial situation. As they are no longer "working royals", their apanage has been stopped. I think, the Daily Mail wrote that Harry received $20 million for *Spare*.
   Mr Brown: Selling out your family for such a sum, incredible! But what will Charles say? His image is really crumbling. Not only is Harry publicly challenging him, but also the Netflix series *The Crown* is delving into the details of his marriage to Diana. Oh, I really do not like him. He did not deserve this beautiful woman whom he betrayed with Camilla.
   Susan: You are right there. I would not want to be in his shoes right now. This scandal does not align well with the coronation.
   Mr Brown: That is what I have been saying all along: the Royals are nothing more than parasites. Look at Andrew – such a terrible person. The queen was right to strip him of his titles. Let's abolish the monarchy and let's have a real democracy with a president elected by the people. I'm sure Keir Starmer and the Labour Party will lead the way to success in this regard.
   Susan: I would not go that far. I still believe in the queen ... sorry, I mean the king and the monarchy ...
   Mr Brown: Let's hear what your mum says. I think she is a strong supporter of the royals. Mary, Susan and I want to know with whose side you're on – Harry's or the royal family's?

3. Individual results. For example:
   Should the monarchy be abolished? Well, yes, I think so. Queen Elizabeth was a good queen

and fulfilled her duties. However, with a new king, there is an opportunity for change because the system seems outdated, especially the Commonwealth.

Having said that, one might think of other aspects that should "go" as well. Charles, for instance, is quite old and his right to be king and head of state is based solely on inheritance rather than proving his capabilities through democratic means. In true democracies leaders are chosen through elections. Why shouldn't we do the same? Then there is the financial aspect. The media has repeatedly said that the Queen was one of the richest women in the world, and the fact that she does not pay any taxes remains a mystery. Consequently, Charles is very rich, and he and the other Royals get a lot of money from the state to which they are entitled. At times like ours with inflation high and low wages, this great discrepancy does not go down well with the people. And there is another point. Prior to the publication of Harry's book, the British were proud of their Royals perceiving them as idealised representation of a family. However, with the release of the book, people are shocked as the carefully crafted image begins to crumble. Let's wait and see what the future holds.

4./5. Individual results.

5. Stunde

Hinweise (M 5)

Ziel von M 5 ist es, den Protest vieler Politiker den Schülerinnen und Schülern nachvollziehbar zu machen, der sich im Vorfeld zu Ursula von der Leyens Empfang bei König Charles erhob.

Sachhinweis

Der **Brexit** aus dem Jahre 2020 bezeichnet den Austritt Großbritanniens aus der EU, in der sie seit 1973 gewesen war. Der Austritt ist für viele negative Konsequenzen verantwortlich, von denen Nordirland und die Republik Irland am meisten betroffen waren. Dabei geht es vor allem um die Handelsbeziehungen, die nach dem Brexit wieder Zollkontrollen und sehr viel Bürokratie erforderlich machten. PM Boris Johnson war in Nachverhandlungen nicht erfolgreich, jedoch sein Nachfolger, Rishi Sunak, konnte das folgenschwere Northern Ireland Protocol durch das **Windsor Framework** – nach Verhandlungen mit der EU – ersetzen. Die Unterzeichnung des Abkommens am 27.02.2023 hatte Sunak bewusst nach Windsor verlegt, um einerseits den Namen und die Absegnung durch den König zu suggerieren, obwohl dies nicht den Tatsachen entspricht und verfassungswidrig ist. Schon im Vorfeld zu von der Leyens Reise nach England entbrannte eine Kontroverse bezüglich der Frage, ob der König sie empfangen darf oder nicht.

Die **Verfasserin** des **Artikels** ist eine preisgekrönte Journalistin, die politische Editorin bei The Guardian ist und über die folgenden Themen berichtet: die britische Regierung, Parlament und Whitehall. Es gab viele Kommentare zu den Vorfällen, deren Überschriften die Aufregung scheinbar belächelten, wie zum Beispiel „*A storm in a Windsor teacup*" und „*How No 10 sweetened up the EU president with a royal cup of tea*". Aber die Situation ist alles andere als hier angedeutet, denn man liest auch: „*Heads will roll*". Der Grund ist die Annahme, dass König Charles seine Kompetenzen überschritten habe. Der **gewählte Artikel** geht der Frage nach, wer für die Einladung der EU-Chefin verantwortlich ist. Interessant ist, dass man nicht auf Sunaks Aussage zurückgreift, sondern nur auf seinen Sprecher oder den Kommentar von „*No 10*", was die Journalistin im Titel umsetzt. Dies gilt auch für Charles, der sich durch die Bekanntgabe des Buckingham Palast vertreten lässt. Es bleibt also offen, wer sie eingeladen hat. Offensichtlich muss die **Klärung schwierig** sein. Die Journalistin weist mit dem Satz „*No 10's line was the opposite*" darauf hin, dass man sich gegenseitig die **Schuld** gibt.

Erwartungshorizont (M 5)

1. E. (7) – A. (4) – H. (1) – B. (8) – I. (3) – C. (5) – D. (9) – J. (2) – F. (10) – G. (6)
2.

Quotations	Foster	Tory Brexiteers	Wilson	Bryant	Labour MPs
never bring the monarchy into political disputes				X	
condemned Sunak's judgment in involving the monarchy	X	X			
dragging the king into a hugely controversial political issue			X		
king … in the finalising of a deal as controversial as this one	X				X
questioned the constitutional implications					

3. Not in the article: b), d), g), i)
4. Individual results. For example:
   Hi everyone,
   Frankly, we think it is nonsense to make a fuss about the king having tea with the EU president. If he can meet other heads of states, why not the EU president? Ok, you might say that is because of the constitutional monarchy, the sovereign is expected to stay out of political matters. However, Charles did not interfere, as the contract had already been signed. You might say that some hurdles still remain, such as approval from the Parliaments of Britain and Northern Ireland. Well, I don't see any harm in the royal tea talk. And the phrase "Heads will roll" seems quite ridiculous to take literally, unless we were living in the time of the French Revolution … What do you think?
5. Individual results. For example:
   Interviewer: Hello, RJ! I'm from Radio 4. Can I ask you some questions regarding your recent article in The Sun?
   RJ: Yes, of course. Go ahead.
   Interviewer: Could you explain to us why you believe King Charles was wrong, as stated in your headline "The King was wrong to offer an unconstitutional tea to the EU president von der Leyen".
   RJ: That's a simple question. The monarch is not supposed to interfere in politic affairs.

Interviewer: This is not as simple a question as it might seem. Did the king actually interfere in politics?
RJ: Well, he did involve himself by inviting the EU president to Windsor castle.
Interviewer: On the contrary, he couldn't have interfered since the contract had already been signed.
RJ: You have a point there. However, this contract is not fully finalised as the parliaments of Britain and Northern Ireland have to agree to this deal.
Interviewer: Alright, but how could Ms von der Leyen influence the MPs of Britain and Northern Ireland?
RJ: I feel cornered. Nevertheless, our constitution dictates that the monarch should stay away from political matters.
Interviewer: Now I got you, as there isn't a written constitution like in Germany. In Britain, it is tradition that guides us.
RJ: I concede defeat! You are right. I'll never again accuse King Charles of crossing the line again.
Interviewer: I would prefer if you didn't make that promise, as this is just the beginning for King Charles. I remind you of Prince Charles and his history of criticism. I'm quite sure there is more to come. Let's wrap it up here. Thank you for your time.
RJ: Thank you for having me.

Hinweise (M 6)

Ziel ist es, dass die Lernenden das neu Erlernte durch den Multiple-Choice-Test überprüfen und somit Wissenslücken aufdecken.

Digitalhinweis

Der Test liegt digital als motivierendes Pferderennen-Spiel in *LearningApps* vor, bei dem die Lernenden gegeneinander, oder gegen das System, antreten können. Unter folgendem Link ist die Übung kostenlos verfügbar und mit Konto bearbeitbar: https://learningapps.org/display?v=pb9t4288523

Erwartwungshorizont (M 6)

1. b) – 2. b) – 3. a) – 4. c) – 5. b) – 6. b) – 7. c) – 8. c)

WWW.RAABE.DE

RAABE
KLASSE SCHULE

Sekundarstufe II

RAAbits Englisch

Impulse und Materialien für die kreative Unterrichtsgestaltung

Inhalt:

K. Brown Jackson: The first Black female U.S. Supreme Court justice (Kl. 10–13)
In der Kurzeinheit erwerben die Lernenden Orientierungswissen zu dem historischen Ereignis und reflektieren seine Bedeutung für die gesellschaftspolitische Entwicklung in den USA.

McManus: *One of Us Is Lying* – Auseinandersetzung mit Stereotypen (ab Kl. 10)
Die Schülerinnen und Schüler brechen anhand handlungsorientierter Aufgaben Stereotype auf. Zudem lösen sie das *murder mystery* u. a. anhand eines *investigation boards*.

Realistic simulations to improve communicative skills (Kl. 8–11)
Die Materialien zu den sechs angebotenen Simulationen fördern die kommunikative Kompetenz Ihrer Lernenden auf motivierende Weise in realitätsnahen Unterrichtssituationen.

Impressum

RAAbits Englisch
Ausgabe 1/2023

ISSN: 0946-5308 / 0946-5294
ISBN: 978-3-8183-0025-8 / 978-3-8183-0026-5

Das Werk, einschließlich seiner Teile, ist urheberrechtlich geschützt. Es ist gemäß § 60b UrhG hergestellt und ausschließlich zur Veranschaulichung des Unterrichts und der Lehre an Bildungseinrichtungen bestimmt. Die Dr. Josef Raabe Verlags-GmbH erteilt Ihnen für das Werk das einfache, nicht übertragbare Recht zur Nutzung für den persönlichen Gebrauch gemäß vorgenannter Zweckbestimmung. Unter Einhaltung der Nutzungsbedingungen sind Sie berechtigt, das Werk zum persönlichen Gebrauch gemäß vorgenannter Zweckbestimmung in Klassensatzstärke zu vervielfältigen. Jede darüber hinausgehende Verwertung ist ohne Zustimmung des Verlages unzulässig und strafbar. Hinweis zu §§ 60a, 60b UrhG: Das Werk oder Teile hiervon dürfen nicht ohne eine solche Einwilligung an Schulen oder in Unterrichts- und Lehrmedien (§ 60b Abs. 3 UrhG) vervielfältigt, insbesondere kopiert oder eingescannt, verbreitet oder in ein Netzwerk eingestellt oder sonst öffentlich zugänglich gemacht oder wiedergegeben werden. Dies gilt auch für Intranets von Schulen und sonstigen Bildungseinrichtungen. Die Aufführung abgedruckter musikalischer Werke ist ggf. GEMA-meldepflichtig.

Für jedes Material wurden Fremdrechte recherchiert und ggf. angefragt.

Dr. Josef Raabe Verlags-GmbH
Ein Unternehmen der Klett Gruppe
Rotebühlstraße 77
70178 Stuttgart
Telefon +49 711 62900-0
Fax +49 711 62900-60
meinRAABE@raabe.de
www.raabe.de

Redaktion: Juliane Thon, Kathrin Olßon, Anna Müller
Satz: pagina GmbH, Tübingen
Bildnachweis Titel: © Adam Schultz/White House Photo/public domain
Korrektorat und Lektorat: Ellen Black
Druck: Uslugi Wydawniczo-Poligraficzne Paper&Tinta; Nadma, Polen

Gedruckt auf chlorfrei gebleichtem Papier

Februar 2023

Liebe Lehrerin, lieber Lehrer,

als in den USA der 83-jährige liberale Richter Stephen Breyer Anfang 2022 seinen Rückzug zum Sommer ankündigte, löste Präsident Joe Biden sein Wahlversprechen ein, die erste schwarze Frau für den Supreme Court zu nominieren. Nach erfolgreicher Bestätigung durch den Senat wurde Ketanji Brown Jackson am 30.06.2022 als 116. Richterin am U.S. Supreme Court vereidigt. Die Ernennung Jacksons ist ein bedeutender Schritt hin zu mehr Diversität und ein Meilenstein in der Geschichte der USA. In unserer Kurzeinheit **Ketanji Brown Jackson: The first Black female U.S. Supreme Court justice – Orientierungswissen zum historischen Ereignis erwerben** reflektieren die Oberstufenschülerinnen und -schüler die Bedeutung des Ereignisses vor dem Hintergrund gesellschaftspolitischer Entwicklungen in den USA.

In unserer zweiten Unterrichtseinheit für die Sekundarstufe II, **Karen M. McManus: *One of Us Is Lying* – Auseinandersetzung mit Stereotypen anhand des Kriminalromans**, setzen sich die Lernenden mit dem abiturrelevanten Thema *„Individual and society"* auseinander. Anhand handlungsorientierter Aufgaben zum Roman trainieren sie, Stereotype aufzubrechen und gesellschaftliche Phänomene und Sachverhalte multiperspektivisch zu betrachten. Zudem beschäftigen sie sich immer wieder mit der Lösung des Kriminalfalls, indem sie beispielsweise ein *investigation board* erstellen oder die Tatverdächtigen befragen.

Im Fokus unserer Materialsammlung **Realistic simulations to improve communicative skills – 6 Simulationen für den flexiblen Einsatz im Unterricht** steht die kommunikative Kompetenz der Mittel- und Oberstufenschüler:innen. Die Materialien der angebotenen sechs Simulationen sind handlungsbezogen, lernendenorientiert sowie kommunikationsfördernd und motivieren die Lernenden zum Austausch in realitätsnahen Unterrichtssituationen.

Die Klassen 8/9 erleben in unserer Reihe **The novel *The Absolutely True Diary of a Part-Time Indian* – Den Roman durch ein Lesetagebuch erarbeiten** mal lachend, mal eher weinend, aber vor allem die humorvollen Cartoons bewundernd, den konfliktreichen Alltag des Reservatlebens aus der Perspektive eines jugendlichen *Native American*. Durch die Gestaltung eines Lesetagebuchs setzen sich die Schülerinnen und Schüler auf kreative Weise mit den Themen des Romans auseinander.

Bei inhaltlichen Anmerkungen, Wünschen und Rückfragen zum Produkt erreichen Sie uns unter J.Thon@raabe.de und 0711-62900-91.

Wir wünschen Ihnen viel Spaß mit unseren Unterrichtseinheiten und einen guten Start ins neue Halbjahr!

Ihre Redaktion Englisch

Folgen Sie uns auf Instagram, Facebook und Twitter unter @RAABEVerlag

Einsortierungsanleitung

Bitte sortieren Sie die enthaltenen Beiträge wie folgt in Ihren Ordner ein:

Themenbereich Beitrag	Bitte diese Seiten herausnehmen	Bitte diese Seiten einfügen
I.C.1.33 The novel *The Absolutely True Diary of a Part-Time Indian* – Den Roman durch ein Lesetagebuch erarbeiten (Klassen 8/9)		komplett
II.B.2.27 Karen M. McManus: *One of Us Is Lying* – Auseinandersetzung mit Teenager-Stereotypen anhand des Kriminalromans (ab Klasse 10)**		komplett
V.277 Realistic simulations to improve communicative skills – 6 Simulationen für den flexiblen Einsatz im Unterricht (Klassen 8–11)		komplett
V.278 Ketanji Brown Jackson: The first Black female U.S. Supreme Court justice – Orientierungswissen zum historischen Ereignis erwerben (Klassen 10–13)**		komplett
** Diese Beiträge sind nur in den Lieferungen für die S I/II und für die S II enthalten.		

Hinweis: Alle Einheiten und Zusatzmaterialien stehen Ihnen zusätzlich als PDF und editierbare Word-Dateien zur Verfügung. Diese finden Sie in Ihrem persönlichen **Online-Archiv**. Loggen Sie sich unter www.raabe.de mit Ihren Kundendaten in Ihr Webshop-Konto ein. Wenn Sie noch kein Konto haben, melden Sie sich unter meinraabe@raabe.de, um Ihre Zugangsdaten zu erhalten.

Themenvorschau

In den folgenden Lieferungen erwarten Sie u. a. diese Themen:

Brexit: Success or failure? – Über die Konsequenzen des Brexits diskutieren (S II) (Mai 2023)
Ihre Schülerinnen und Schüler untersuchen Texte und Videos zum Thema, um sich eine fundierte eigene Meinung bilden zu können, die sie abschließend diskutieren.

Living in two worlds: Nigerian coming-of-age stories (S II) (Mai 2023)
Durch Filme, Romane und Kurzgeschichten setzen sich die Lernenden mit den Herausforderungen des Heranwachsens nigerianischer Jugendlicher unter westlichem Kultureinfluss auseinander.

Ghost Boys **– Polizeigewalt gegen Afroamerikaner untersuchen (Kl. 8/9) (August 2023)**
Durch die Perspektive der Romanfiguren lernen die Schülerinnen und Schüler Diskriminierungs- und Rassismuserfahrungen Schwarzer Jugendlicher in den USA des 21. Jahrhunderts kennen.

(Änderungen vorbehalten)

Literatur – Novels

Karen M. McManus: *One of Us Is Lying* – Auseinandersetzung mit Stereotypen anhand des Kriminalromans (ab Klasse 10)

Anne-Kathrin Weisbrod

© Boris Zhitkov / Getty Images

Wer hat Simon während des Nachsitzens in der Schule getötet? Glaubt man den Stereotypen, die seine vier überlebenden Mitschülerinnen und Mitschüler verkörpern, dürfte der Fall bereits gelöst sein – oder vielleicht doch nicht? In der vorliegenden Unterrichtseinheit lernen Ihre Schülerinnen und Schüler anhand handlungsorientierter Aufgaben, Stereotype aufzubrechen und gesellschaftliche Sachverhalte multiperspektivisch zu betrachten. Zudem beschäftigen sie sich immer wieder mit der Lösung des Kriminalfalls in dem populären Jugendroman, indem sie beispielsweise ein *investigation board* erstellen.

KOMPETENZPROFIL

Klassenstufe:	ab Klasse 10
Dauer:	14–16 Unterrichtsstunden + LEK
Kompetenzen:	1. Leseverstehen: eine Ganzschrift lesen und verstehen; 2. Sprachmittlung: einen deutschen Text in eine englische E-Mail mitteln; 3. Interkulturelle Kompetenz und Multiperspektivität: Stereotype hinterfragen; 4. Medienkompetenz: kritischer Umgang mit sozialen Medien
Inhalt:	*Individual and society, stereotypes, identity, growing up, relationships, murder mystery,* Jugend-Kriminalroman
Medien:	*reading quizzes*
Zusätzlich benötigt:	Roman *„One of Us Is Lying"* von Karen M. McManus

Fachliche Hinweise

Zur Autorin Karen M. McManus und ihrem Werk
Die US-Amerikanerin Karen M. McManus wurde 1969 in Massachusetts, USA geboren und studierte Englisch und Journalismus. Seit 2017 ist sie auch als Jugendbuchautorin tätig. Ihr **bekanntester Roman „One of Us Is Lying"**, veröffentlicht 2017, besetzte Monate lang Platz eins der **New York Times-Bestsellerliste**. Er wurde **2021** vom amerikanischen Streamingdienst Peacock als **Fernsehserie** aufbereitet.

Zum Inhalt von „One of Us Is Lying"
„One of Us Is Lying" ist ein **Jugend-Kriminalroman**, der multiperspektivisch aus Sicht der vier verdächtigten Schülerinnen und Schüler erzählt wird. An der Bayview High müssen fünf Schülerinnen und Schüler nachmittags beim Lehrer Mr. Avery nachsitzen – **Bronwyn** (*the geek*), **Addy** (*the princess*), **Nate** (*the criminal*), **Cooper** (*the jock*) und **Simon** (*the outcast*). Doch anders als sonst verlassen nur vier von ihnen den Klassenraum lebend, denn Simon stirbt in Folge einer allergischen Reaktion. Zunächst wird der Vorfall als Unfall eingestuft, was sich ändert, als in einem anonymen TumblR-Post behauptet wird, Simons Tod sei geplant gewesen und sein Mörder oder seine Mörderin habe ihm beim Sterben zugesehen. Darauf erfolgen **polizeiliche Ermittlungen** in deren Fokus die vier überlebenden Nachsitzerinnen und Nachsitzer stehen. Da alle vier ihr eigenes dunkles **Geheimnis** haben, hat somit jede/r von ihnen auch ein Motiv, denn Simon wollte am nächsten Tag einen großen Skandal auf seiner **Gossip-App** *About That* veröffentlichen.

Zu den Themen in „One of Us Is Lying"
Der Roman bietet sowohl wegen seiner Erzählstruktur (**Multiperspektivität**), als auch aufgrund seiner Themen wie zum Beispiel „*stereotypes*", „*prejudices*" und „*social media*" viele Ansatzpunkte für den Unterricht, da die Themen auch die Lebenswelt der Schülerinnen und Schüler betreffen. Auch die im Roman dargestellten Freundschaften und Beziehungen sowie Schulprobleme bieten ein hohes Identifikationspotenzial für Jugendliche.

Didaktisch-methodische Hinweise

Zur Lerngruppe und den curricularen Vorgaben
Die vorliegende Reihe wurde bereits im Präsenzunterricht sowohl mit einem Leistungskurs als auch mit einem Grundkurs des zweiten Semesters durchgeführt. Der Roman kann jedoch bereits **ab Klasse 10** eingesetzt werden, da er sich inhaltlich gut an Themen wie „*identity*", „*growing up*" und „*relationships*" anschließen lässt. Er kann auch an eine Unterrichtseinheit zum Thema „*(social) media*" anknüpfen.

In der **Oberstufe** kann die Lektüre im Rahmen des in Berlin/Brandenburg vorgegebenen **Semesterthemas „Individuum und Gesellschaft"** eingesetzt werden. „One of Us Is Lying" eignet sich insbesondere auch zur **Kompetenzfestigung**. Im Rahmen der Einheit können die Lernenden ihre **interkulturelle Kompetenz** trainieren. Dies bietet sich insbesondere deshalb an, weil die Behandlung des Romans mit seinem multiperspektivischen Erzählansatz dabei helfen kann, in der Gesellschaft existierende **Vorurteile abzubauen**. Dies kann unter anderem durch das im Roman bereits angelegte Vornehmen von **Perspektivwechseln** und die Analyse von Lebensverhältnissen sowie unterschiedlicher Standpunkte geschehen. Dies wird zusätzlich durch die in der Reihe inkludierten **handlungsorientierten Aufgabenformate** unterstützt. Außerdem bietet der Roman den Schülerinnen und Schülern Anlass, sich vor dem Hintergrund ihrer eigenen Lebensrealität mit den Erlebnissen, Emotionen und entgegengebrachten Vorurteilen der Hauptfiguren kritisch auseinanderzusetzen. Des Weiteren kann die Lektüre einen Beitrag zur Festigung der **Lesekompetenz** leisten, da im Rahmen der Reihe verschiedene **Lesestrategien** angewandt werden. Zusätzlich ist es möglich, die Reihe zur Festigung der **Medienkompetenz** zu nutzen, da die zentrale Rolle von Tumblr und der Gossip-App *About That* im Rahmen des Romans hierfür Anlass bieten.

Zum Leseprozess

Die Unterrichtseinheit stützt sich auf folgende Textausgabe: **McManus, Karen M.**: One of Us Is Lying. Delacorte Press. New York 2017. ISBN: 978-1524714680. Preis: ca. 7,79 Euro.
Der Umfang der Lektüre (**368 Seiten**) ist nicht zuletzt aufgrund der Romanform ab Klasse 10 problemlos zu bewältigen. Das **sprachliche Niveau** ist dem der Schülerinnen und Schüler angemessen, und unbekannte oder schwierige Begriffe können meist durch den Kontext erschlossen werden. Die Lernenden lesen *„One of Us Is Lying"* sukzessive als **Begleitlektüre zu der vorliegenden Unterrichtsreihe**. Dabei lesen sie als **Hausaufgabe** zwischen einem und höchstens vier Kapiteln. Ihren Lesefortschritt und ihr Textverständnis überprüfen die Schülerinnen und Schüler regelmäßig mithilfe der *reading quizzes* (ZM 1), die sich als Download im Online-Archiv bzw. der Zip-Datei befinden. Als **Differenzierung** in lernschwächeren Kursen kann die Lehrkraft außerdem vor der Lektüre die Schülerinnen und Schüler auf einen oder zwei tatverdächtige Romanfiguren aufteilen, sodass diese beim Lesen alle wesentlichen Informationen zu der oder den ihnen zugeteilten *suspects* notieren. Vorbereitend auf die erste Unterrichtsstunde der Reihe lesen sie das erste Kapitel des Romans und bearbeiten das *reading quiz 1*.

Zu den didaktisch-methodischen Schwerpunkten der Unterrichtsreihe

Die Fähigkeiten zur Perspektivübernahme, zum Selbst- und Fremdverstehen sind wesentliche Voraussetzungen und Momente des sozialen und gesellschaftlichen Handelns, sie entwickeln sich jedoch nur unzureichend, wenn sie nicht explizit in Jugendlichen gefördert werden.[1] Hierzu soll die Unterrichtsreihe einen Beitrag leisten, auch, indem sie gezielt versucht, Stereotype zu dekonstruieren. Methodisch und strukturell basiert die Reihe auf der Grundidee des **Leseprozesses** als **Interaktion**, die insbesondere die **Schülerorientierung** und somit auch **schüleraktivierende Methoden** anstrebt. Dieser Zugang ermöglicht gleichzeitig eine ideale Förderung der interkulturellen Kompetenz, da die Veränderungen, die im Leben der vier Schülerinnen und Schüler nach dem Tod Simon Kellehers auftreten, auch eine Herausforderung für die eigene Lebenswelt der Lesenden darstellen und sie somit in der Lage sind, ihnen neue Einsichten in ihr Selbst- und Weltverständnis zu eröffnen. Deshalb spielt die **imaginative**, **kreative** und **gestaltende Mitwirkung** der Lernenden bei allen in der Einheit Anwendung findenden Methoden eine große Rolle.[2] So finden sich die Schülerinnen und Schüler beispielsweise in die Rolle der polizeilichen Ermittlerinnen und Ermittler ein und erstellen ein *investigation board* (**M 2** und **M 11**), übernehmen die Rolle von Journalistinnen und Journalisten, die in einer **Reportage (M 6)** über den Fall berichten oder erstellen **Jahrbuchseiten (M 8)** für die Romanfiguren, um eine **Charakterisierung** vorzubereiten.

---

[1] Vgl. Bergmann, Klaus: *Multiperspektivität. Geschichte selber denken,* S. 48 f.
[2] Vgl. Nünning/Surkamp: *Englische Literatur Unterrichten. Grundlagen und Methoden,* S. 13.

KMK-Medienkompetenzen im Überblick

Medienkompetenzen (KMK)
(1) Suchen, Verarbeiten und Aufbewahren: zielgerichtete Internetrecherche durchführen (**M 7**)
(3) Produzieren und Präsentieren: Erstellung einer eigenen Nachrichtensendung (**M 6**)
(4) Schützen und sicher agieren: Risiken und Gefahren der digitalen Umgebung erarbeiten (**M 5**)
(6) Analysieren und Reflektieren: Kritische Bewertung von Posts aus sozialen Netzwerken / Fake News (**M 5**)

Lehrwerksbezug

Thematische Anknüpfungspunkte der Reihe sind an folgende Lehrwerke/Units möglich:
- *Cornelsen: Access 10; Unit 3 „How do you become you?"*
- *Cornelsen: Context Oberstufe, Chapter 1 „Finding One's Place – the individual in society"*
- *Westermann: Camden Town Oberstufe; Units 1 and 2 „A society on screens: The digital age"* und *„Identity – Finding your place"*

Mediathek

Sekundärliteratur

▶ **Bergmann, Klaus:** Multiperspektivität: Geschichte selber denken. Wochenschau Verlag. Schwalbach 2008.
Fachliteratur zur Förderung der Multiperspektivität im Unterrichtsfach Geschichte. Das Werk bietet darüber hinaus auch viele fächerübergreifende Anregungen zur Förderung der Multiperspektivität und des Fremdverstehens durch den Einsatz von Jugendliteratur.

▶ **Nünning, Ansgar; Surkamp, Carola:** Englische Literatur unterrichten 1. Grundlagen und Methoden. Klett/Kallmeyer. Seelze-Velber 2006.
Fachdidaktische Grundlagen, auf denen die Gestaltung der vorliegenden Unterrichtsreihe basiert. Das Werk enthält weitere Anregungen zur Vertiefung.

Filme und Serien

▶ **Hughes, John:** *„The Breakfast Club"* (1985)
Der Jugendfilm eignet sich insbesondere zum Vergleich der Anfangssequenz von Film und Lektüre und der verwendeten Schüler- und Schülerinnen-Stereotypen.

▶ **Saleh, Erica:** *„One of Us Is Lying"* (2021)
Die Serie basiert auf dem gleichnamigen Roman. Sie ist in acht Episoden unterteilt und in Englisch auf Peacock zu streamen. Seit Juni 2022 läuft auf RTL+ die deutschsprachige Version.

Internetseiten

▶ https://bildungsserver.berlin-brandenburg.de/fileadmin/bbb/unterricht/unterrichtsentwicklung/Individualisierung_des_Lernens/text_production_sek_II_web.pdf [letzter Abruf: 04.01.2023]
Die Broschüre bietet Anleitungen, Beispiele und Selbsteinschätzungsbögen für die Produktion verschiedener Textsorten und stellt eine Orientierungshilfe für Schülerinnen und Schüler dar.

Auf einen Blick

Vor der ersten Unterrichtsstunde der vorliegenden Reihe haben die Schülerinnen und Schüler das erste Kapitel der Lektüre „*One of Us Is Lying*" gelesen sowie das erste *reading quiz* (ZM 1) hierzu bearbeitet.

1. Stunde

Thema:	An introduction – The genre and the main characters
M 1	***One of Us Is Lying* – A closed-circle mystery?** / Kennenlernen des literarischen Genres und der Figuren-Stereotypen (EA); Entwickeln von Standbildern der Figurenkonstellation (GA/PL)
Homework:	*Read the second chapter of* One of Us Is Lying *and do reading quiz 2.*
Benötigt:	☐ ggf. Beamer/Whiteboard

2. Stunde

Thema:	The exposition
M 2	**Conducting a crime investigation – Creating a plan** / Erstellen eines Ermittlungsplans; Formulieren erster Hypothesen zum Tathergang; Präsentieren des Plans in einer *poster presentation* (EA/GA/PL)
Homework:	*Based on your knowledge from the first two chapters of* One of Us Is Lying, *make a list of information that a good investigator might already have about the case.*
Benötigt:	☐ ggf. Beamer/Whiteboard

3./4. Stunde

Thema:	Narrative perspectives and change of perspective
M 3	**Who tells the story? – The matter of perspectives** / Erarbeiten der Bedeutung von Erzählperspektiven und der Multiperspektivität (PL/EA); Übertragen des Anfangs vom dritten Kapitel in eine neue Perspektive (EA)
Homework:	*Read the third chapter of* One of Us Is Lying *and do reading quiz 3.*
Benötigt:	☐ ggf. Beamer/Whiteboard

5. Stunde

Thema:	A mediation
M 4	**Writing a mediation about PTSD – Skill file and practice /** Einführen in die Sprachmittlung; Lesen eines deutschen Artikels und Wiedergeben des Textinhalts auf Englisch in einer E-Mail (EA)
Homework:	*Read chapters four to six of* One of Us Is Lying *and do reading quiz 4.*
Benötigt:	☐ ggf. Beamer/Whiteboard

6. Stunde

Thema:	The media I – The role of social media
M 5	**The impact of social media – Disucssing pros and cons /** Auseinandersetzen mit der eigenen Verwendung sozialer Medien und Vergleichen mit der im Roman dargestellten (EA/UG); Erarbeiten eines Vorschlags zum verantwortlichen und positiven Umgang mit sozialen Medien anhand eines Videos (EA)
Homework:	*Collect information that you would like to include in a TV news report on the events at Bayview High.*
Benötigt:	☐ ggf. Beamer/Whiteboard ☐ Internet zum Abspielen des YouTube-Videos

7./8. Stunde

Thema:	The media II – A news report
M 6	**Witnesses and motives – Creating an on-site TV report /** Sammeln von Kriterien eines guten Nachrichtenbeitrags (GA/PL); Umsetzen der Kriterien in Form eines eigenen Berichts über die Ereignisse an der Bayview High (EA/GA)
Homework:	*Read chapters seven to ten of* One of Us Is Lying *and do reading quiz 5.*
Benötigt:	☐ ggf. Beamer/Whiteboard

9./10. Stunde

Thema:	The role of high school stereotypes
M 7	**Stereotypes: harmful or harmless? – An essay /** Beschäftigen mit gängigen Stereotypen (EA/UG); Auseinandersetzen mit ihren Vor- und Nachteilen anhand eines *comments* und eines *essays* (EA)
Homework:	*Read chapters eleven to 13 of* One of Us Is Lying *and do reading quiz 6.*

Benötigt:	☐ ggf. Beamer/Whiteboard
	☐ Internetzugang für den Test und die Onlinerecherche

11. Stunde

Thema:	The characters of the novel I – High school stereotypes
M 8	**Defying stereotypes – Creating a yearbook entry /** Annähern an die vier Protagonisten aus stereotypischer und persönlicher Perspektive anhand der Gestaltung zweier Jahrbuchvarianten (EA/PA/UG)
Homework:	*Read chapters 14 to 17 of* One of Us Is Lying *and do reading quiz 7.*
Benötigt:	☐ ggf. Beamer/Whiteboard
	☐ evtl. Smartphones/Kameras
	☐ ggf. Requisiten zur Darstellung der Figuren auf den Fotos

12. Stunde

Thema:	The characters of the novel II – A characterisation
M 9	**Who are you? – Writing a characterisation /** Sammeln von Vorwissen zu den Figuren (GA) und passende Wortschatzarbeit (EA); Verfassen einer Charakterisierung (EA)
Homework:	*Read chapters 18 and 19 of* One of Us Is Lying *and do reading quiz 8. Finish writing the characterisation.*
Benötigt:	☐ ggf. Beamer/Whiteboard

13. Stunde

Thema:	Change of perspective
M 10	**Hot seat – The characters in interview /** Übernahme der Perspektive einer Figur (EA); Stellungnahme zu Handlungsmotiven der Figuren in einer *hot seat activity* (GA/PL)
Homework:	*Read chapters 20 to 23 of* One of Us Is Lying *and do reading quiz 9.*
Benötigt:	☐ ggf. Beamer/Whiteboard

14./15. Stunde

Thema:	Summing up the case I – Investigation board
M 11	**The state of the investigation – Creating an investigation board /** Hineinversetzen in die Rolle des Ermittlerteams und Lösen des Falls (EA/GA/PL)
Homework:	*Read chapters 24 to 27 of* One of Us Is Lying *and do reading quiz 10*.
Benötigt:	☐ ggf. Beamer/Whiteboard ☐ Materialien für das Erstellen des *investigation boards*

16. Stunde

Thema:	Summing up the case II – Newspaper article
M 12	**Investigative journalism – Writing an article /** Verfassen eines investigativen Zeitungsartikels zum Fall Simon Kelleher (EA)
Homework:	*Read the rest of* One of Us Is Lying.
Benötigt:	☐ ggf. Beamer/Whiteboard

Lernerfolgskontrolle

LEK	**Writing a newspaper article and a mediation /** Zusammenfassen und Analysieren eines Textausschnitts; Verfassen eines Zeitungsartikels und einer Mediation (EA)
Benötigt:	☐ Wörterbücher

Minimalplan

Bei Zeitknappheit können die Schülerinnen und Schüler den Roman während einer der Schulferien lesen. Lesebegleitend würden sie dann die Aspekte für die Charakterisierung sammeln und die Charakterisierung verfassen (M 1, *task 1 b)* und M 9). Der Zeitungsartikel (M 12) könnte bei Zeitmangel zur abschließenden Hypothesenbildung fallengelassen werden. Die Lehrkraft entscheidet dann abhängig vom Kenntnisstand der Lerngruppe, ob der Artikel aus der Klausur entfällt.

Hinweise zum Online-Archiv bzw. zur ZIP-Datei

Alle Materialien des Beitrags finden Sie im Online-Archiv als Word-Dokumente. So können Sie die Materialien am Computer gezielt bearbeiten und sie auf Ihre Lerngruppe abstimmen.

Zusätzlich im Online-Archiv bzw. in der ZIP-Datei:

ZM 1 Reading quizzes
ZM 2 Skill file: writing an essay – An essay organiser
ZM 3 Vocabulary list – Using linking words

One of Us Is Lying – A closed circle mystery?

M 1

Who is who – and who did it?

Tasks

1. Read the definition of a traditional closed circle mystery in the box below.
   a) Based on what you know from the first chapter of *One of Us Is Lying*, how does the novel (not) fit the criteria of a closed circle mystery? Give reasons for your opinion.
   b) Who are the suspects in Simon Kelleher's collapse? What are their names and what do you know about them from the first chapter? Collect the information in a grid.

© Boris Zhitkov / Getty Images

> **Closed circle of suspects**
> Closed circle mysteries are a subgenre of detective fiction that prominently features a closed circle of suspects as a literary device and plot element.
> This type of story requires a specific setting: the location of the crime (usually a murder) is typically remote or isolate; thus, only the people present at the crime scene at the time of
> 5 the incident could have committed the crime. Since limited access of outsiders is an essential element to the genre, the stories are often set on a ship, train, an island, at a remote country house or isolated village where outsiders are rare.
> These locations enable the investigator or detective to quickly establish a limited number of suspects, all of whom have credible means, motives and opportunities. After having identified
> 10 his/her small circle of suspects, the detective is now tasked with eliminating the innocents from his pool of possible murderers, gradually narrowing down the pool of people.
> In some closed circle mysteries, the author further supports the notion of a limited circle of suspects by making it inescapable. This is sometimes achieved by making locations inaccessible. Accompanying circumstances that enable further isolation might be: weather conditions, no
> 15 communication with the outside world, roads blocked, bridges collapsing etc.
> The golden age of this genre was in the pre-World-War-II era and would often feature upper-class settings as well as suspects.

2. In groups of five: Create a freeze frame in which you show the relationship between the five students at detention. Reflect their characters in their gestures, body language and facial expressions.
   Be able to explain your choice of positioning and your reasons for portraying the characters the way you did.
3. At one point during detention, Simon claims that the others are "walking teen-movie stereotypes". Explain the quotation. Identify the stereotype assigned to each student.
4. Give your opinion about stereotypical portrayal of cliques at school.

M 2   Conducting a crime investigation – Creating a plan

Tasks

1. Read the manual below on how to investigate a crime. Highlight procedures that you deem essential for an investigation in the case of Simon Kelleher's death.

The stages of a crime investigation

The investigation of a crime is usually carried out in three different stages: 1) on the crime scene, 2) in the lab / at the police station and 3) in the court room. This manual will concentrate on the investigation at the crime scene and the police work after having collected the evidence at the crime scene.

Stage 1: What do police officers do on the crime scene?
If a crime has already happened, police officers try to find out and piece together exactly what happened at the crime scene. They collect as much evidence as possible.
Possible jobs include: apprehending suspects, locating and questioning witnesses, securing and preserving the scene, collecting and preserving physical evidence, taking photographs for later reference.

Stage 2: What do police officers do after they have left the crime scene?
After the evidence is collected at the scene, forensic specialists, ballistic technicians, latent evidence technicians and digital analysts help the police with their investigation.
Possible jobs include: analysing DNA, inspecting weapons, identifying the murder weapon based on crime scene evidence, collecting and identifying fingerprints, analysing latent evidence, analysing digital data (e.g. profiles, accounts, messages etc.)

---

2. Pretend you are a team of investigators dealing with the case of Simon Kelleher:
    a) Make a precise plan for your investigation process. Use the stages suggested in the manual above.
    b) Identify witnesses and suspects and develop a short questionnaire for each of them.
    c) Develop a working hypothesis regarding the cause of Simon Kelleher's death.
    d) Present your plan, suspects and questions in a poster presentation. The presentation will be directed at other investigators involved in the case. You find suggestions for structuring your presentation in the box below.
3. Based on your knowledge from the first two chapters of *One of Us Is Lying*, make a list of information that a good investigator might already have about the case.

Skill file: the structure of your presentation
a) welcome your audience – b) introduce yourself and your topic – c) give a roadmap for the presentation – d) introduce your poster and present your ideas in a logical order – e) present your conclusion / hypothesis

Phrases you can use for your presentation
a) Good morning / afternoon / evening everyone … – b) As you all know, we are going to be talking about …; By the end of the meeting, we will all be informed about the latest … – c) We'll keep things brief. This talk will concentrate on / be divided into …; Feel free to interrupt, if you have any questions / additions – d) This poster shows our latest findings … – e) To draw a conclusion … / All that result in the hypothesis, that …

Who tells the story? – The matter of narrative perspectives

M 3

Tasks

1. Look at the comic of the fairy tale *Little Red Riding Hood*. Briefly tell the story starting with *"Once upon a time there was a little girl. Everybody called her Little Red Riding Hood …"*
2. Now, change the narrative perspective: write the story from either the wolf's *or* the hunter's perspective. Before you start, define the parameters of your perspective.

- Beginning and ending of your story: consider what happens to your character before he/she/it enters the story.
- Define the emotions, opinions and thoughts that your character might have throughout the phases of the plot.
- Think about the background information your character might (not) have about the other characters in the story.
- Style, tone and register: consider how to portray your character on a language level.

3. Explain the importance that the choice of perspective has for a story.
   - Consider the advantages and disadvantages of e.g. first-person and omniscient narrators.
   - Identify the narrative perspective employed in *One of Us Is Lying*. Explain the intended effect, the advantages and drawbacks connected to the choice of perspective.
   - Assess the impact of the choice of perspective on the stereotypical perception of the four students.
4. Imagine part of the third chapter of *One of Us Is Lying* was written from the leading detective's perspective. Write the beginning of the third chapter (p. 26) in style of a first-person narrator. The heading of your chapter will – as customary for the novel – be your name, the date and time. Collect ideas for your chapter in the table below. The aspects from the graphic above will help you.

Ideas for the starting point, climax and ending	Emotions, opinions and thoughts
Background information	Style, tone and register

M 4

Writing a mediation about PTSD – Skill file and practice

Mediating is a technique used to make communication between two people who do not share a common language possible. More specifically, it means summarising (either orally or in writing) a spoken or written text in another language.

> **Skill file: how to write a mediation**
>
> **STEP ❶: How to prepare the mediation**
> Make sure that you read the task and your source carefully. You need to be able to define
> a) the addressee (the person you talk/write to)
> b) the purpose of writing and the context/situation
> c) the type of text you are expected to write
> d) the focus of your task (what ideas of the original text do you have to focus on?)
>
> **STEP ❷: How to outline the relevant information from a German text**
> 1. Procedure that applies to all mediations in general:
>   a) State your source of information.
>   b) Only sum up the information that is relevant to your addressee(s).
>   c) Include short explanations or background information that are necessary for the reader (e.g., when a certain cultural concept might not be known to them).
>   d) Structure the content logically and link the ideas.
>   e) Adapt your language, style and register to your addressee.
>
> 2. Criteria that apply to writing a mediation in form of an email:
>   a) Header: include the addressee's and the sender's email addresses. Include a subject line.
>   b) Greeting: greet your addressee.
>   c) Introduction: state your reason for writing and connect it to why you are outlining the information.
>   d) Conclusion: end your email by highlighting the main idea of your summary. If appropriate, reflect upon the context of your email and finally say goodbye in a manner that fits the addressee.

Task

The guidance counsellor at Bayview High is concerned that one of the students who witnessed Simon's death might be traumatised. She contacts a German colleague who is more experienced in the field of PTSD. Her German colleague comes across a recent article about how to cope best with the situation. Write an email from the German colleague to Bayview High's guidance counsellor, in which she/he – building on the information provided in the article – gives the guidance counsellor advice on how to support the four students.

Posttraumatische Belastungsstörung: Mit dem Leid leben lernen
von Adelheid Müller-Lissner

Flucht, Krieg, sexuelle Gewalt: Nicht jeder wird nach einem traumatischen Erlebnis psychisch krank. Doch Betroffene brauchen schnelle Hilfe.

Was mich nicht umbringt, macht mich stärker. Der Spruch klingt hart, ganz falsch ist er nicht: Menschen können ihren Lebensmut und sogar ihre Fröhlichkeit zurückgewinnen, nachdem sie einen Unfall oder eine lebensbedrohliche Krankheit überstanden haben, sie können als psychisch stabile Erwachsene aus einer schweren Kindheit hervorgehen. Schlimme Erlebnisse können ihre seelische Widerstandsfähigkeit, die Resilienz, stärken. Es kann sogar vorkommen, dass Soldaten aus einem Kampfeinsatz zurückkommen und ein seelisches Problem los sind, das vor dem Einsatz bestand.

Doch Vorsicht. Studien zeigen, dass es ein großer Unterschied ist, ob ein solches Ereignis die Ausnahme bleibt oder ob es sich wiederholt, wie der sexuelle Missbrauch eines Kindes in der Familie. Und dass es eine wichtige Rolle spielt, ob es sich um einen Schicksalsschlag handelt oder um eine Verletzung, die Mitmenschen uns zufügen. Nur einer von zehn Opfern eines schweren Verkehrsunfalls, aber die Hälfte der Vergewaltigungsopfer leidet danach unter einer Posttraumatischen Belastungsstörung (PTBS), sagt der Epidemiologe Frank Jacobi von der TU Dresden.

Der Begriff ist in den Medien schnell bei der Hand, wenn es um die psychischen Folgen von Krieg, Folter, Flucht und sexueller Gewalt geht. In der Medizin ist er jedoch klar definiert und im Diagnose-Handbuch ICD-10 festgehalten. „Es ist eine der wenigen psychischen Störungen, bei denen man die Ursache genau festlegen kann", sagt Iris Hauth, Präsidentin der Deutschen Gesellschaft für Psychiatrie, Psychotherapie, Psychosomatik und Nervenheilkunde (DGPPN) und Ärztliche Direktorin am Alexianer St.-Joseph-Krankenhaus in Berlin-Weißensee. Das muss immer eine konkrete seelische Verletzung sein, die so groß ist, dass sie viele andere Menschen ebenfalls aus der Bahn werfen würde. Tage bis Wochen, vielleicht Monate oder Jahre danach kommt es zu den Symptomen, die typisch sind für eine PTBS. Erinnerungen drängen sich immer wieder auf, tagsüber oder nachts in Albträumen. Der Betroffene wird schreckhaft, versucht bestimmten Schlüsselreizen aus dem Weg zu gehen. Er zieht sich zurück, wird eventuell von Scham- und Schuldgefühlen geplagt, weil er sich eine Mitschuld einredet. […]

Wie kann […] geholfen werden? Eine israelische Studie von 2012 zeigte, dass Psychotherapie besser wirkt als Medikamente. Dabei geht es nicht um ellenlange Therapien: „Schon fünf Stunden bringen etwas", sagt Ulrich Frommberger, Psychiater in der MediClin Klinik an der Lindenhöhe in Offenburg. Bewährt habe sich die traumafokussierte Psychotherapie, in der Therapeut und Patient immer wieder über das Erlebnis reden – auch wenn das für beide sehr belastend ist. So kann es gelingen, den Vorfällen ihren Platz in der Biografie zuzuweisen. In einem Leben, das ein unbeschwertes „Davor" beinhaltet und zusätzlich die Perspektive für ein erträgliches, vielleicht erfülltes „Danach" bieten muss. […] Nicht jeder braucht nach einem traumatischen Erlebnis psychologische Hilfe. Und beileibe nicht immer handelt es sich um PTBS, wenn die Seele infolge eines Traumas krank wird. Psychiater und Psychologen sprechen deshalb allgemeiner von „Traumafolgestörungen". Dazu können Depressionen oder Angsterkrankungen gehören. Und körperliche Beschwerden, etwa Kopfschmerzen, die ein Folteropfer chronisch plagen. […]

Andere greifen zum Alkohol. Eine kurzfristig wirksame, auf Dauer aber ungünstige Bewältigungsstrategie. Sie kann zudem dazu führen, dass die PTBS unbehandelt bleibt. […]

Adelheid Müller-Lissner: Posttraumatische Belastungsstörung: Mit dem Leid leben lernen, in: Tagesspiegel 29.04.2015, zu finden unter https://www.tagesspiegel.de/wissen/mit-dem-leid-leben-lernen-5453560.html [letzter Abruf: 04.01.2023]

M 5 — The impact of social media – Discussing pros and cons

> "A sex tape. A pregnancy scare. Two cheating scandals. And that's just this week's update. If all you knew of Bayview High was Simon Kelleher's gossip app, you'd wonder how anyone found time to go to class. 'Old news, Bronwyn,' says a voice over my shoulder. 'Wait till you see tomorrow's post.'"
>
> Karen McManus: One of us is lying, Delacorte Press/Penguin Random House: New York 2017, p. 3.

Tasks

1. Read the first few lines of the novel.
   a) Explain the picture it creates of social media use at Bayview High.
   b) Compare and contrast the use of social media at Bayview High to your own use of social media / the use of social media at your school / in your class.
2. Use the three quotations below as a starting point to write a short comment on whether *About That* is an unacceptable means to terrorise the students at Bayview High or whether Simon was justified to publish people's secrets.

Cooper: "[…] I hate that thing. Almost all my friends have been on it at one point or another, and sometimes it causes real problems. […] And if I'm being honest, I'm pretty freaked at what Simon could write about me if he put his mind to it. […]"

Bronwyn: "[…] The thing with About That was … you could pretty much guarantee every word was true."
Addy: "[…] Jake usually defended Simon, though, when our friends got down on him for About That. It's not like he's lying, he'd point out. Stop doing sneaky shit and it won't be a problem. […]"

Karen McManus: One of us is lying, Delacorte Press/Penguin Random House: New York 2017, p. 12, p. 28, p. 44.

3. Watch the video clip on the advantages and disadvantages of social media: https://www.youtube.com/watch?v=kaSET4_NNsQ [last access: 04/01/2023]
   a) While watching make a list of pros and cons in bullet points.
   b) Based on the pros and cons, create arguments for a discussion about what responsible and positive social media use might look like.
4. Bearing in mind what has been said in the classroom discussion "post" a Tweet about the situation at Bayview High.
   Tip: If you have never posted a Tweet before, watch the instructions in the video link https://edu.gcfglobal.org/en/twitter/how-to-tweet/1/ [last access: 04/01/2023]. Start at 0:39.

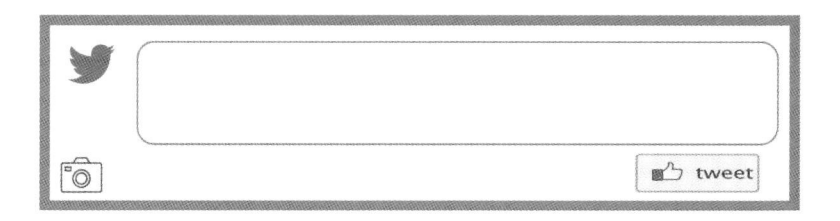

Witnesses and motives – Creating an on-site TV report

M 6

As you can imagine, the tragic death of Simon Kelleher has got the attention of all local news stations in the Bayview area, especially after the two anonymous Tumblr posts.

Tasks

1. Step into the role of a member of a reporter team of a TV station and prepare a report about the incident.

   Elements that should be featured in your TV report are
   - an introduction by the news anchor
   - the on-site report by a reporter
   - interviews with e.g., paramedics, witnesses, school staff etc.

   How to prepare and create your on-site TV report
   Before you start …
   a) collect ideas on how to organise a good TV news report and share them in class.
   b) watch the (not entirely serious) clip on the elements of good news reporting: https://www.youtube.com/watch?v=29elOIr7I4s. [last access: 04/01/2023] Write down the most important tips and add them to your list of ideas.

   © LightFieldStudios/iStock/Getty Images Plus

2. Now that you have heard about the latest developments in the case of Simon Kelleher's death, look into the motives that each of the students might have had for killing Simon.

   a) Copy the grid below onto a sheet of paper. Write down what secrets might have motivated the individual students to act against Simon. The following passages might give you some ideas:
   - **Addy:** chapter 4, pages 44/45, lines 25–1; chapter 5, page 64, lines 11–13
   - **Bronwyn:** chapter 3, page 28, lines 12–14; chapter 3, page 33, lines 3–5; chapter 5, page 53, lines 18/19
   - **Cooper:** chapter 1, page 12, lines 8/9; chapter 3, page 40, lines 7–13; chapter 6, page 68, lines 15–22
   - **Nate:** chapter 3, page 39, lines 16–18; chapter 4, page 47, lines 1–8
   - **All students:** chapter 4, pages 50/51 (first Tumblr post)

	Addy	Bronwyn	Cooper	Nate
Possible motives				

   b) In addition, make a list of people who might also serve as suspects and why.

Extra: Using your knowledge on the responsible use of social media, create a statement that your news station could publish on its online site. Bear in mind that a news update should be short, precise and factual. It should also answer the usual W-questions: Who? Where? What? When? Why? and if possible: How?

M 7 Stereotypes: harmful or harmless? – An essay

How do high school stereotypes influence students? Do some research and write an essay.

Tasks

1. Watch the video *What Highschool Stereotype Are You?* and do the test:
   https://www.youtube.com/watch?v=bGlQSSZR1js [last access: 04/01/2023]
   In order to evaluate your result, you need a pen, a piece of paper and maybe a calculator.
2. First reactions: what do you think about your type casting? Why does it (not) fit you? Explain.
3. Write a comment on having been type-casted. How did you feel when being stereotyped as the typical jock / nerd / …? How would you feel if you were constantly treated as that kind of person?
4. Read the article in the box. Use it as a starting point for an essay on the question "High school stereotypes – harmless or harmful?" You may research further arguments and examples online. The following websites might help you:
   - https://www.betterhelp.com/advice/stereotypes/how-high-school-stereotypes-hurt-teens/
   - https://theparentingco.com/decoding-high-school-stereotypes/
   - https://college.taylors.edu.my/en/life-at-taylors/news-events/news/the-good-the-bad-and-the-what-of-stereotypes.html
   [last access: 04/01/2023]

Tips: Use the essay organiser (ZM 1) to structure your thoughts and to develop your line of argument. Use the linking words (ZM 2) to connect your ideas logically and to form a coherent line of argumentation.

High school stereotypes are harmful

Stereotypes are a problem in high schools. Students that are the ones being stereotyped can be harmed by these comments.

Some of the stereotypes include the overachiever, the nice guy, nerd, geek and much more. They can be harmful to students by putting them in social classes. Social classes are groups that people view themselves and others in such as jocks or the gamers.

A study by Valerie Taylor Ph.D. and Gregory Walton shows that a threat of being a certain stereotype can negatively affect learning. Students become less focused on the material at hand and do more poorly than normal.

People can be hurt by these stereotypical social classes and may feel down or even sad that they are in a lower group and think lowly of themselves because of it.

Students like to use these stereotypes as sort of a self-esteem boost, or as a way to bully a kid to make them feel bad about themselves.

Stereotypes are not true. A person should only be able to judge him- or herself based on how only that person feels, not how others feel about them.

Stereotypes are around our school and can be defied.

Source: https://glhsreflection.org/2017/10/09/high-school-stereotypes-are-harmful/ [last access: 15/09/2021]

Defying stereotypes – Creating a yearbook entry

M 8

What is a yearbook? Find out and create your own yearbook entry.

© CSA-Archive / DigitalVision Vectors

Tasks

1. Watch the video *A Yearbook is …*:
   https://www.youtube.com/watch?v=tLqjMHVjd68 [last access: 04/01/2023]
   After having watched the video, write a short definition of what a yearbook is into the box.

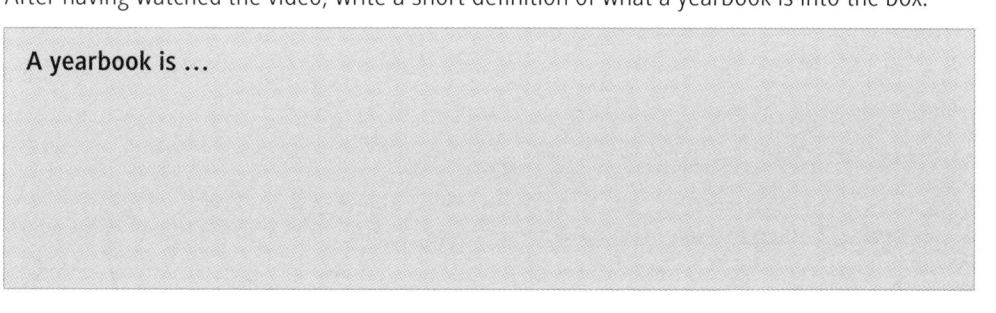

   A yearbook is …

2. Choose one of the four students (Addy, Bronwyn, Cooper *or* Nate). Write two different yearbook texts for the student you chose:
   a) The first text is published by the yearbook team. It reflects how the student is seen by the rest of the students. Start your text like this:

   "To us, you were always the stereotypical ...".

   b) The second text is a handwritten tribute to the student added by a close friend on the last day of school. Start your text like this:

   "To me, you were never the stereotypical ..."

3. Another challenge for each yearbook team is to take the students' photos.
   a) In pairs: discuss what the photos of each of the four students should look like to
      - reflect their character and personality and
      - reflect their high school stereotype.
   b) Make a list of props that you need to dress up as the four characters.
   c) Take the photos.
   d) Present your photos in class. Explain why you chose to portray the characters the way you did.
      Discuss your portrayal of the characters:
      - What are the similarities / differences between the photos?
      - Why do they fit / not fit the characters?
      - What could have been improved?

© Gregor Hofbauer

M 9 — Who are you? – Writing a characterisation

Tasks

1. *Conversational speed dating*: Arrange tables and chairs in a long row. Place the chairs on opposite sides of the tables (all students must have a seat). Once everybody is seated, every student should have a partner across from him/her (see sketch below). Your teacher will now name one topic per speed dating round. Per round, each pair has two minutes to discuss the topic.

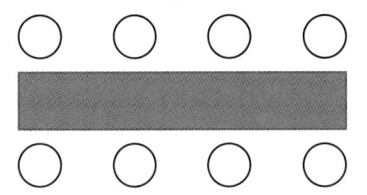

2. Clarify the meaning of the words and expressions a)–l) from the box below. Explain how they relate to the suspects.

a) spotless record	b) scapegoat
c) reputation	d) (to) hook up
e) (to) be a suspect	f) (to) conspire to do something
g) (to) cheat	h) overachiever
i) probation violation	j) juicing
k) enhanced performance	l) beauty pageant

3. Prepare a characterisation of either Addy, Bronwyn, Cooper *or* Nate. Therefore, recap what you know about them from the previous chapters. Create a grid in which you collect information about the following aspects:
   a) basic information about the character
   b) the character's outward appearance
   c) the character's character traits
   d) observable behaviour shown by the character
   e) the character's relationships/friendships/family
   f) the character's opinions and beliefs
   g) other people's opinion about the character

4. Use the skill file below to write a characterisation about your chosen character.

Skill file: characterisation

Introduction	• Briefly introduce the character (name, basic information, outward appearance). • State the character's function in the novel and mention the most significant relationship(s) in his/her life. The narrative perspective needs to be reflected upon.
Body	• Describe the character's traits and behaviour, relationships that are crucial for his/her development and behaviour and other people's opinion about him/her. • Make sure to provide examples and quotations to support your statements.
Conclusion	• Sum up your opinion about the character. • Briefly outline the character's development.

Hot seat – The characters in interview

M 10

Here, you will be introduced to a method called the "hot seat".

© klyaksun / iStock / Getty Images Plus

> **Method: Hot seat**
> The hot seats will be chairs in the front of the classroom, ready for students to sit on.
> Once you sit down, you will step into the role of a character from the novel *One of Us Is Lying*. Then, the class will ask you – as that character – questions, for example, about your feelings, your actions, your motives, your relationships etc. in the story.
> The situation is similar to a press conference: the interviewees are in the hot seats and the others sit in a half-circle (or a similar arrangement) around them.
> Today, five characters from the novel (Addy, Cooper, Bronwyn, Nate and officer Budapest) will sit in the hot seats. They will be interviewed regarding their involvement in the death of Simon Kelleher, their potential motives, and the impact the incident had on their lives. They will also have to present their theories as to who might be the murderer.

Tasks

Pre-hot-seat activity

Prepare *both* roles: the one of a character and the one of an interviewer:

1. As *one* of the five **characters**: prepare your role by writing down the most important aspects about your character. Also think of questions that the interviewers might ask you and answer them.
2. As one of the **interviewers**: collect questions for the five characters. Write down at least four questions per character. The questions should be a mixture of easy and tricky ones.

M 11 The state of the investigation – Creating an investigation board

Tasks

1. Collect all the information you already have about the incidents/occurrences/situation surrounding Simon Kelleher's death.
2. Write down everything that you know about Simon Kelleher. The aspects below can get you started.
3. Collect information about the suspects. Also define who is a suspect for you.
4. Collect all the hints provided by the anonymous creator of the Tumblr posts.

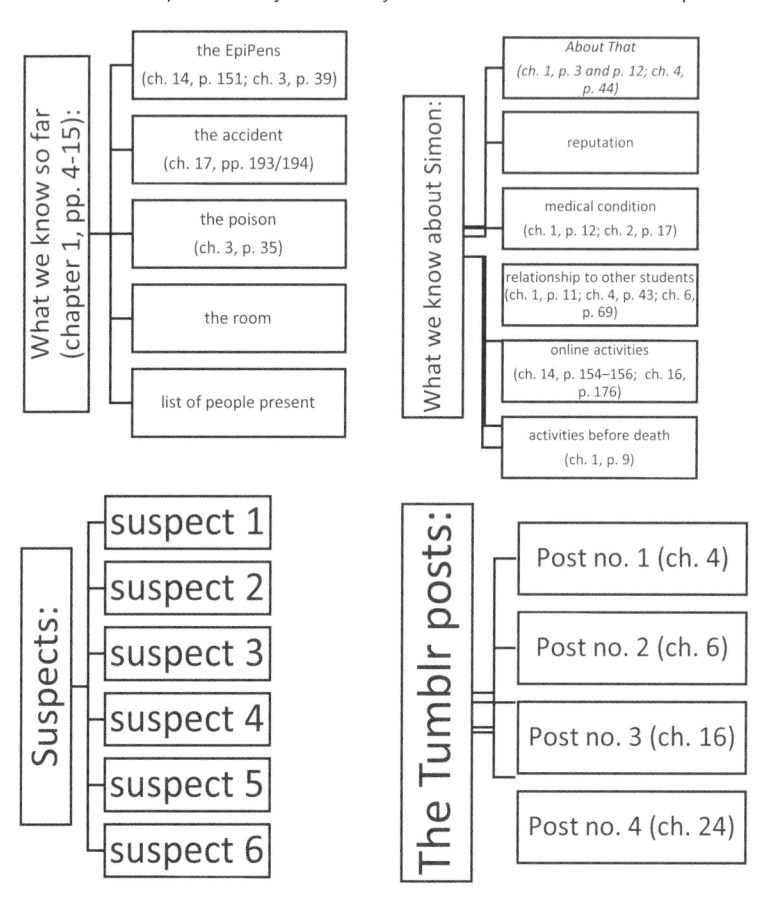

What we know so far (chapter 1, pp. 4-15):
- the EpiPens (ch. 14, p. 151; ch. 3, p. 39)
- the accident (ch. 17, pp. 193/194)
- the poison (ch. 3, p. 35)
- the room
- list of people present

What we know about Simon:
- About That (ch. 1, p. 3 and p. 12; ch. 4, p. 44)
- reputation
- medical condition (ch. 1, p. 12; ch. 2, p. 17)
- relationship to other students (ch. 1, p. 11; ch. 4, p. 43; ch. 6, p. 69)
- online activities (ch. 14, p. 154–156; ch. 16, p. 176)
- activities before death (ch. 1, p. 9)

Suspects:
- suspect 1
- suspect 2
- suspect 3
- suspect 4
- suspect 5
- suspect 6

The Tumblr posts:
- Post no. 1 (ch. 4)
- Post no. 2 (ch. 6)
- Post no. 3 (ch. 16)
- Post no. 4 (ch. 24)

5. Get together in small groups of police investigators (3 to 4 students):
   a) Share the information you have collected.
   b) Develop a working hypothesis on who committed the murder.

6. Present your facts and conclusions to the rest of the police department:
   a) Create an investigation board to present your theories, finding and conclusion.
   b) Think of a logical way to show all the connections.
   c) The oral part of the presentation should be three to five minutes.

© Tetiana Lazunova / iStock / Getty Images Plus

Investigative journalism – Writing an article

M 12

What is investigative journalism? Find out and try yourself.

© Nora Carol Photography

© RonBailey / iStock / Getty Images Plus

Tasks

1. Watch the video clip *What Is Investigative Journalism?* by David E. Kaplan that explains investigative journalism:
   https://www.youtube.com/watch?v=TCVU52T6Cbs [last access: 04/01/2023]
   Answer the following questions:
   a) How can investigative journalism be defined?
   b) What topics do investigative journalists cover?
   c) What methods are used by investigative journalists?

2. Re-read the second Tumblr post (pages 70/71). Imagine you were an investigative journalist commissioned to write an original piece on the murder of Simon Kelleher.
   a) Based on the starting point (Tumblr post) form a thesis/hypothesis for the start of your investigations.
   b) Write down a set of eight to ten questions that you would like to answer during your time undercover at Bayview High.

3. Based on your hypothesis as well as the systematic inquiry which you conducted at Bayview High, write an article about the murder of Simon Kelleher.

LEK

Writing a newspaper article and a mediation

Tasks

I. Writing (75%)	
1. Read the extract from chapter 28 of *One of Us Is Lying*. Outline the methods used by "the murder club" to find out more about Simon's death and their results.	**30%**
2. Analyse the means used by the author to show the growing bond between the members of the "murder club" and how it helps them to solve the murder case.	**35%**
3. Write an article for Bayview High's student paper. After having discovered the whole truth about Simon's death, Bronwyn, Nate, Addy and Cooper decide to publish an article on their experiences during their time as suspected murderers. Use your knowledge about the four students' situations during the investigation to write an article for the student newspaper.	**35%**

II. Mediation (25%)
One of your English-speaking friends is looking for a recommendation for a new series that does not meet all the usual teen comedy clichés. Per chance, you come across the article *"'Noch nie in meinem Leben' bricht Teenie Klischees"*. Write an email to your friend in which you summarise the article's view on the series.

I. Writing: Summary, analysis and newspaper article

Chapter 28
Cooper, Wednesday, November 7, 7:40 p.m.

These murder club meetings are becoming a regular thing. We need a new name, though. This time we're at a coffee shop in downtown San Diego, crammed into the back table because our numbers keep expanding. Kris came with me, and Ashton with Addy. Bronwyn's got all her Post-it notes on a bunch of manila folders, including the newest one:

5 *Simon paid two kids to stage a car accident.* She says Sam Barron promised to call Eli and let him know. How that'll help Nate, I have no idea. […]

Bronwyn clears her throat and makes a big production of rearranging her Post-it notes. "No reasons. So anyway." She shoots a businesslike look around the table. "Thanks for coming. Maeve and I keep going over this stuff and it never makes any sense. We thought

10 a meeting of the minds might help."

Maeve and Ashton return from the counter, balancing our orders on a couple of recylble trays. They hand drinks around, and I watch Kris methodically open five packets of sugar and dump them into his latte. "What?" he asks, catching my expression. […] "You like sugar, huh?" It's a dumb thing to say. What I mean is, *I have no idea how you take your*

15 *coffee because this is the first time we've been out in public together.* Kris presses his lips together, which shouldn't be attractive but is. I feel awkward and jittery and accidentally bump his knee under the table.

"Nothing wrong with that," Addy says, tipping her cup against Kris's. The liquid inside hers is so pale it barely resembles coffee. […]

Bronwyn has some kind of steaming tea that looks too hot to drink. She pushes it aside and props one of the manila folders against the wall. "Here's all the stuff we know about Simon: He was going to post rumors about us. He paid two kids to stage a car accident. He was depressed. He had a creepy online persona. He and Janae seemed on the outs. He had a thing for Keely. He used to be friends with Jake. Am I missing anything?"

"He deleted my original About That entry," I say.

"Not necessarily," Bronwyn corrects. "Your entry was deleted. We don't know by whom."

Fair enough, I guess.

"And here's what we know about Jake," Bronwyn continues. "He wrote at least one of the Tumblr posts, or helped somebody else write it. He wasn't in the school building when Simon died, according to Luis. He –"

"Is a complete control freak," Ashton interrupts. Addy opens her mouth in protest, but Ashton cuts her off. "He *is,* Addy. He ran every part of your life for three years. Then as soon as you did something he didn't like, he blew up." Bronwyn scribbles *Jake is a control freak* on a Post-it with an apologetic lance at Addy.

"It's a data point," Bronwyn says. "Now, what if –"

The front door bangs and she goes bright red. "What a coincidence." I follow her gaze and see a young guy with wild hair and a scruffy beard enter the coffee shop. He looks familiar, but I can't place him. He spots Bronwyn with an exasperated expression that turns alarmed when he takes in Addy and me.

[…] "This is Eli Kleinfelter," Bronwyn says. "He's with Until Proven. Their offices are upstairs. He's, um, Nate's lawyer."

"*Who cannot talk to you,*" Eli says, like he just remembered. He gives Ashton a lingering look, but turns away and heads for the counter. Ashton shrugs and blows on her coffee. I'm sure she's used to having that effect on guys.

Addy's eyes are round as she watches Eli's retreating back. "God, Bronwyn. I can't believe you stalked Nate's lawyer."

Bronwyn looks almost as embarrassed as she should be, taking the envelope I'd given her out of her backpack. "I wanted to see if Sam Baron ever got in touch, and pass along his information if he hadn't. I thought if I ran into Eli casually, he might talk to me. Guess not."

She darts a hopeful look at Ashton. "I bet he'd talk to *you,* though."

Addy locks her hands on her hips and juts her chin in outrage. "You can't pimp out my sister!"

Ashton smiles wryly and holds out her hand for the envelope. "As long as it's for a good cause. […]"

Ashton heads for the counter, and we all sip our drinks in silence. When she returns a minute later, […] [Maeve says] "Simon and Jake, […] they're connected. But how?"

"Excuse me," Kris says mildly, and everyone looks at him like they'd forgotten he was at the table. Which they probably had. He's been quiet since we got here. Maeve tries to make up for it by giving him an encouraging smile. "Yeah?"

"I wonder," Kris says, […] "There has always been so much focus on who was in the room. That's why the police originally targeted the four of you. Because it would be almost impossible for anyone who wasn't in the room to kill Simon. Right?"

"Right," I say.

"So." Kris removes two Post-its from one of the folders. "If the killer wasn't Cooper, or

65 Bronwyn, or Addy, or Nate – and nobody thinks the teacher who was there could have had anything to do with it – who does that leave?" He layers one Post-it on top of the other on the wall next to the booth, then sits back and looks at us with polite attentiveness.

Simon was poisoned during detention. Simon was depressed.

We're silent for a long minute, until Bronwyn exhales a small gasp. "I'm the omniscient
70 narrator," she says.

"What?" Addy asks.

"That's what Simon said before he died. I said there wasn't any such thing in teen movies, and he said there was in life. Then he drained his drink in one gulp." […]

"So you're saying …" Ashton stares around the table until her eyes land on Kris. "You
75 think Simon committed suicide?"

Kris nods. "But why? Why like that?"

Karen McManus: One of us is lying, Delacorte Press/Penguin Random House: New York 2017, chapter 28.

II. Mediation: Email

***Noch nie in meinem Leben* bricht mit Teenie-Klischees, aber einen Fehler darf Staffel 3 jetzt nicht machen**

Netflix' *Noch nie in meinem Leben* scheint vor Klischees nur so zu strotzen. Doch der genaue Blick zeigt, wie Staffel 2 sie unterwandert – was Staffel 3 beibehalten muss.

Noch nie in meinem Leben ist auch in Staffel 2 eine der genialsten Teenie-Serien, die Netflix aktuell zu bieten hat. Das liegt zu großen Teilen daran, dass sie die Klischees von High-
5 school-Romanzen erst bedient und dann über den Haufen wirft. […]

Wer mehr als eine Highschool-RomCom gesehen hat, wird schnell feststellen, dass viele Themen ständig wiederkehren und dadurch schnell zu Klischees im Genre Romantischer Komödien verkommen. *Noch nie in meinem Leben* greift in Staffel 1 und 2 bei Netflix vor allem drei dieser Erzähl-Motive auf:

10 • Klischee 1: Der Jock / beliebte Schüler verliebt sich in das nerdige Mauerblümchen
• Klischee 2: Die Dreiecks-Beziehung konfrontiert eine Schülerin mit zwei Love Interests
• Klischee 3: Das Mädchen erkennt, dass echte Zuneigung und Intelligenz dem Aussehen eines Partners überlegen ist

Oberflächlich betrachtet schlägt *Noch nie in meinem Leben* sauber in die Kerben dieser
15 drei Teenie-Schablonen: Die unerfahrene Devi begehrt erst den sportlich-heißen Paxton und erkennt zugleich ihre Gefühle für den anfangs von ihr verachteten klugen Ben. Am Ende von Staffel 1 liegen ihr plötzlich beide Herren zu Füßen.

Doch wer in Staffel 2 von Noch nie in meinem Leben eine schnelle Aufklärung des Dilemmas erwartete, irrt: Weil Devi sich nicht entscheiden kann, entscheidet sie sich eben nicht.
20 Zweigleisig mit mehreren festen Freunden zu fahren, geht aber auch nicht lange gut. So steht sie schnell wieder allein da und muss sich den Respekt und die Freundschaft ihrer zwei Ex erneut verdienen.

Auch wenn die Netflix-Serie Devi in die klassische Teenie-Rolle des Mädchens steckt, das sich nach ihrem ersten Freund sehnt, denkt die Schülerin gar nicht daran, sich brav an
25 diesen vorgeschriebenen Part zu halten. Der Spieß wird umgedreht: Indem die Hauptfigur ihre zwei Partner verletzt, katapultiert sie alle drei Figuren aus dem Klischee-Gefängnis. […]

Weil *Noch nie in meinem Leben* die eingangs genannten Stereotypen gleichzeitig aufgreift und gegeneinander ausspielt, geht etwas Neues daraus hervor. Die Dreiecksbeziehung endet, der Jock ist plötzlich kein Jock mehr und Aussehen und Klugheit werden relativiert. Kurzum: Das Bekannte wird zugunsten des Unerwarteten über Bord geworfen:

Paxton muss sich in Staffel 2 neu definieren: Als ein vom Nerd gedemütigter Schwimmer mit gebrochenem Arm (und Herzen) beginnt er, seine schulischen Leistungen jenseits des Sportunterrichts zu überdenken.

Ben muss seine Gefühle zu der Person hinterfragen, mit der er auf einer Intelligenz-Wellenlänge schwimmend ursprünglich so perfekt zusammengepasst hat.

Und Devi, die mit ihrem Egoismus von Anfang an unsere Sympathien auf den Prüfstand stellte, steht nun endgültig als Arschloch *und* Geek da – eine Rollen-Kombination, die wir im Teenie-RomCom-Genre noch nicht häufig zu Gesicht bekommen haben. […]

Mit neu gemischten Karten schreitet Noch nie in meinem Leben in Staffel 2 frisch zur Tat, unsere Erwartungen zu unterwandern: Während Devi die blauen Flecke von Paxtons Ego mit Nachhilfe behandeln kann, hat sie ihr Auge in dieser Season eindeutig stärker auf Ben geworfen, der nun aber mit Aneesa zusammenkommt.

Interessanterweise verschiebt sich während ihrer Bemühungen um Ben der Fokus der Zuschauenden von Team Ben zu Team Paxton: Wer zuvor noch Devi und Ben shippte, kann sich am Ende von Staffel 2 über die eigene Erleichterung wundern, dass die Schülerin mit Paxton auf der Tanzfläche steht. Trotz aller Fehltritte haben beide sich nämlich zum Besseren verändert und geben ein unerwartet gutes Paar ab.

Offiziell wurde von Netflix noch keine 3. Staffel zu Noch nie in meinem Leben bestellt. Doch mit dem Ende der 2. Staffel ist es offensichtlich, dass Pläne für Staffel 3 vorhanden sind. […] vielleicht hat die Netflix-Serie in Staffel 3 noch eine weitere unvorhersehbare Wendung in petto, die alles zunichte macht, was wir über Teenie-Highschool-RomComs zu wissen glaubten. Nach dem, was Noch nie in meinem Leben bisher vorgelegt hat, ist das nicht mal unwahrscheinlich.

Source: Esther Stroh: Noch nie in meinem Leben bricht mit Teenie-Klischees aber einen Fehler darf Staffel 3 jetzt nicht machen, Moviepilot 24.07.2021, zu finden unter https://www.moviepilot.de/news/noch-nie-in-meinem-leben-bricht-mit-teenie-klischees-aber-einen-fehler-darf-staffel-3-jetzt-nicht-machen-1132747 [letzter Abruf 04.01.2023]

Hinweise und Erwartungshorizonte

Als Hausaufgabe zur ersten Unterrichtsstunde haben die Schülerinnen und Schüler das erste Kapitel des Romans „One of Us Is Lying" gelesen und lesebegleitend das erste *reading quiz* (ZM 1) bearbeitet.

1. Stunde

Hinweise (M 1)

Ziel: Die Schülerinnen und Schüler sind mit dem Fall Simon Kelleher vertraut und kennen das Genre sowie die Hauptfiguren des Romans.

Didaktisch-methodischer Hinweis

Die Lehrkraft erstellt gemeinsam mit den Lernenden im Unterrichtsgespräch zur **Sicherung** eine Tabelle der auf „One of Us Is Lying" (nicht) zutreffenden Elemente des Genres „*closed circle mystery*" *(task 1 a)*.

Hausaufgabe

Die Schülerinnen und Schüler lesen das zweite Kapitel und lösen *reading quiz 2* (ZM 1). Alle *reading quizzes* finden Sie als Download.

Erwartungshorizont (M 1)

1.
a) Pro the genre:
   – The crime committed is a murder. (chapter 1, page 15, lines 19–23 and page 12, line 25)
   – Simon died in a classroom and all suspects were in the same room and close-by. (chapter 1, page 4, line 21–page 5, line 16)
   – There is a quickly established circle of suspects (the other four students that were in the room at the time (plus Mr Avery).
   – Everybody has a motive because of the app Simon has created. (chapter 1, page 3, line 9; chapter 1, page 11, lines 1–9; chapter 1, page 12, lines 1–9)
   – The teacher does not like the app and is against the new types of technology in general. (chapter 1, page 7, line 3–page 8, line 13)
   – All four students had the opportunity to kill Simon.

   Con the genre:
   – The students are not part of the upper class.
   – The scene of the crime is untraditional: a school instead of a country house. (chapter 1, page 3, line 2; chapter 1, page 4, line 21)
   – Potentially not sure whether the circle of suspects could be extended to the entire school.
   – There is no detective (yet).

b)

Addy Prentiss	Bronwyn Rojas	Cooper Clay	Nate Macauley
• princess • very pretty • cries after incident • boyfriend is Cooper's best friend	• brain • Mathlete • part of the student council • never breaks the rules	• jock • same clique as Addy • überpopular, voted homecoming king • Captain America face • baseball player • pressured by dad • writes with his right hand to protect his left hand • Cooperstown	• criminal • been in trouble since fifth grade • on probation for DUI or drug dealing • notorious supplier of drugs • messy dark hair, leather jacket

2. Individual results that should reflect some of the information from the table above.

3.
   – Simon thinks the others are clichés (Addy = princess; Cooper = jock; Bronwyn = brain; Nate = criminal).
   – He says that they rather belong in a teen film than in reality.
   – Simon calls himself the omniscient narrator of their story; thus, sets himself apart from them; possible reference to his gossip app
4. possible opinions about stereotypes: unrealistic; superficial; unfair to people; might harm students that are e.g., called geek, loner etc.; funny; harmless; part of life at school; might lead to bullying; in the murder case they might lead to stigmatisation/prejudices/suspicion etc.

Hinweise (M 2)

2. Stunde

Ziel: Die Lernenden verschaffen sich einen Überblick über den Fall Simon Kelleher, fügen die Informationen, die sie bisher aus den Perspektiven der Verdächtigen gewonnen haben, zusammen und gewinnen durch den Perspektivwechsel, sowie die Ableitung auf der Metaebene praktische und theoretische Kenntnisse über die Funktion und Effekte von Erzählperspektiven.

Didaktisch-methodischer Hinweis

Indem die Lernenden zu Ermittlerinnen und Ermittlern im Fall Simon Kelleher werden, übernehmen sie eine Perspektive, die im multiperspektivischen Roman, der aus der Sicht der vier verdächtigen Jugendlichen erzählt wird, nicht angeboten wird. Der **Perspektivwechsel** leitet somit bereits zu M 3 über, das die Schülerinnen und Schüler in der folgenden Unterrichtsstunde bearbeiten und in dem sie einen Ermittlungsplan erstellen.

Hausaufgabe

Die Schülerinnen und Schüler erstellen eine Liste der bereits bekannten Fakten zum Fall Simon Kelleher (*task 3*).

Erwartungshorizont (M 2)

1./2.
- a) The plan might include a number of the following ideas:

  secure the detention room; collect evidence, e.g., Simon's cup and other items from Simon's bag; take photos of the crime scene; determine Simon's location in the room as well as the other students' positions; analyse the liquid in the cup; analyse what Simon wanted to publish next; read previous *About That* posts to identify suspects; interview the four students and Mr Avery; interview the nurse about the EpiPen.

- b) A selection of possible questions for suspects and witnesses:

For all students	• Did Simon know any dark secrets about you? • Why were you at detention and do you think the prank on you was connected to Simon's death? • What can you tell us about the cup that Simon drank from?
Addy	• Why did you react more emotionally than all the others?
Bronwyn	• What did Simon and you talk about when you entered detention?
Cooper	• Did you play dumb when you handed Nate a regular pen?
Nate	• How did you know about Simon's allergy? • Given your criminal record – why shouldn't you be our prime suspect?
Mr Avery	• Why weren't you in the room when Simon collapsed?
Nurse	• How do you explain the absence of the EpiPens?

- c) Examples for possible working hypotheses:

  One of the students at detention killed Simon. – The car accident was connected to the murder. – The murderer took the EpiPens from the nurse's office. – The murder must be connected to Simon's *About That* activities. – Nate Macauley is highly suspicious because of his criminal record. – Simon was poisoned on purpose; his death was not an accident.

3./4. Stunde

Hinweise (M 3)

Ziel: Die Schülerinnen und Schülern kennen die Bedeutung der Perspektive in Erzählungen und können den Blick auf (dieselben) Ereignisse ändern. Sie erhalten einen ersten Eindruck, warum die Autorin einen multiperspektivischen Erzählansatz wählt (auch bezüglich des Aufbrechens von Stereotypen).

Didaktisch-methodischer Hinweis

Dadurch, dass die Lernenden anhand des Märchens *Rotkäppchen* im **Einstieg** einen ersten **Perspektivwechsel** (*task 1*) vornehmen, fällt ihnen das Hineinversetzen in die Figuren leichter und die folgenden Aufgaben werden vorentlastet. Die Lehrkraft zeigt den Schülerinnen und Schülern hierzu zu Beginn der Doppelstunde eine Bildergeschichte von Rotkäppchen. Es gibt zahlreiche Versionen im Internet (zum Beispiel unter: https://www.pinterest.de/nathalieelsen/m%C3%A4r-chen-routk%C3%A4ppchen/).

Sicherung

Die Lernenden stellen ein bis zwei Geschichten (*task 2*) pro Perspektive im Plenum vor. Im Anschluss an die Präsentation erklären sie, welchen Einfluss der Perspektivwechsel auf das Märchen hat und warum man als Leserin oder Leser die Perspektive bei der Deutung des Textes berücksichtigen sollte.

Hinweis zur Differenzierung

Schülerinnen und Schülern, denen das freie Schreiben (*task 3*) schwerfällt, können auch die Passage aus Kapitel 3 *„Cooper, Thursday, September 27, 12:45 p.m."* umschreiben, in der Officer Hank Budapest die Schülerinnen und Schüler befragt.

Hausaufgabe

Die Lernenden lesen das dritte Kapitel von *„One of Us Is Lying"* und bearbeiten das *reading quiz 3* (ZM 1).

Erwartungshorizont (M 3)

1. Aspects of the plot of *Red Riding Hood* that should be mentioned in the re-telling:
   Little Red Riding Hood sent out by mother to bring a basket with food to her sick grandma; girl not supposed to stray off the path; once in the woods, she meets the wolf who pretends to be friendly; wolf tricks the girl into telling him that she is on her way to her grandma, she also includes directions in her account; wolf decides to pay the grandmother a visit and to devour her; after having devoured the old lady, he disguises himself as the grandmother and places himself in her bed to trick Little Red Riding Hood; the girl enters the house but is suspicious of her "grandmother's" appearance; she asks the wolf, "Why do you have such a big nose … such big eyes … such a big mouth?"; the wolf answers the respective questions with, "So that I can smell you better … see you better … eat you better!"; the wolf tries to eat the girl; the hunter hears the screams and comes to investigate; the hunter kills the wolf, he frees the grandmother from the wolf's stomach.

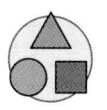

2. Exemplary beginning for the story written from the wolf's perspective:
   "I'm sitting here pondering my fate as the most misunderstood creature in the entire forest. I have no clue how I have acquired such a bad reputation! It is true: I eat other animals but I am a carnivore so I can hardly go vegetarian, it's just not in my nature. But honestly, I am not malicious about it, I only kill animals when I am hungry, and it is not as if I am the only predator in the woods. However, nobody ever complains about the owls, the foxes or the snakes. I am so upset that during the last five days I have not eaten anything and don't know how much longer I will be able to put up with it …"

Exemplary beginning for the story written from the hunter's perspective:
"Today was not like any other day. Let me tell you what happened: Just as every other day, I set out for a stroll through the woods early in the morning. The sun was shining amiably, the birds were singing, and it seemed like the perfect day for counting the local wildlife. After two hours of walking, I decided to take a little break and sat down for a brief picnic. From afar, I could see a little girl, whom I immediately recognised as Little Red Riding Hood, strolling down the path. I assumed that she was headed to her grandmother's house because I knew that the old lady had taken ill. Since the girl seemed to know her way and clearly had instructions not to stray off the path, I was happy to not disturb her …"

3. The narrator is the person/voice who tells the story; thus, the reader is strongly influenced by the choice of the narrative point of view from which the plot is told. Especially the choice of establishing a first-person narrator has the tendency to make the reader identify with the character from whose perspective the story is told since the readers know everything about the character's feelings, opinions, experiences etc. Because this point of view is limited, it is also subjective and not necessarily a reliable source of information (other than for example a third-person omniscient narrator). The author of *One of Us Is Lying* chose to tell the story from multiple perspectives. The reader learns about the events from the point of view of the four suspects in the case which helps to break with the stereotypical perception of the students as the reader gets more inside into their private lives and thoughts.

4. Aspects that should be mentioned in the students' version of chapter three:
   - Officer Hank Budapest, Tuesday, September 25, 6 a.m.
   - Simon died last night; apparent cause of death: allergic reaction caused by water in the cup; the victim's allergy was known; the victim was the creator of a notorious gossip app; motive for murder linked to app?
   - witnesses/suspects: four students at detention (and the teacher); one student – Nate – has a criminal record; star athlete and girl with stellar academic record seem unlikely suspects; pretty girl reacted oddly emotional after the incident; officer's impression of the kids / expectations given their stereotypes
   - curious disappearance of the EpiPens from the nurse's office; weird accident in parking lot happened simultaneously which made the teacher leave; students seem to have been pranked into detention (hidden phones)

5. Stunde

Hinweise (M 4)

Ziel: Die Schülerinnen und Schüler greifen den Aspekt der Multiperspektivität auf. Die vier verdächtigen Romanfiguren werden aus einem anderen Blickwinkel betrachtet: nicht als Verdächtige, sondern als Opfer einer potenziell traumatischen Erfahrung. Die Lernenden üben die Arbeitsform „Mediation".

Hinweis zur Erweiterung

Ergänzend zur Mediation können in einer Vertiefungsphase die in der E-Mail zusammengefassten Ratschläge handlungsorientiert umgesetzt werden, indem die Lernenden eine Sitzung zwischen einem der vier Schülerinnen und Schüler und dem *guidance councellor* in Form eines Dialogs ausarbeiten.

Hausaufgabe

Die Schülerinnen und Schüler lesen Kapitel vier bis sechs von „*One of Us Is Lying*" und lösen das *reading quiz 4* (ZM 1).

Erwartungshorizont (M 4)

Exemplary solution for a mediation:

from: GermanColleague@University.com
to: O'Farrell@guidancecouncellor.com
subject: Advice on trauma prevention

Dear Mr O'Farrell,

I was shocked to learn about the tragic incident at your school. From a professional perspective, it is a highly interesting case as the four witnesses will need your support and guidance over the next couple of weeks. In our last exchange, you asked me for advice on how to best support students who have experienced a potentially traumatising situation. I rummaged through some old research of mine and found an article called *PTSD: How to learn to live with the suffering* that provides some suggestions on the matter that might get you started in your sessions with the four students.

The article says that it is important to realise that not everybody that has experienced a traumatising situation will suffer from PTSD afterwards. However, it is important that help and support are offered immediately after one such situation to determine the extent of the trauma. You are at an advantage in your sessions because PTSD is the only psychological disorder whose cause/trigger can be clearly determined, and with your four students, you can pinpoint the event.

You might be happy to learn that in the case of your students, it is rather unlikely that one will develop PTSD since singular traumatising events offer more chances for recovery, and sometimes, patients can even build more resilience when not lacking support. Even though it must have been a great shock to your students to witness the death of a classmate, they are lucky in the sense that they have not been through an event in which harm was done to them by friends or family as that would significantly lower their chances for recovery.

During your sessions with the four, you should look for the following symptoms – they can show immediately or even weeks or years later: nightmares, flashbacks, anxiety, social withdrawal, guilt, depression and avoidance of situations that remind them of the incident.

The article also stresses that therapy and counselling are much more effective than medication. In your session, you should guide your students into a happy "after".

I hope my advice can help you. If you have any further questions, don't hesitate to contact me.

Kind regards,
Tina Jörissen

6. Stunde	**Hinweise (M 5)**

Ziel: Die Schülerinnen und Schüler reflektieren die Rolle und den Einfluss sozialer Medien in ihrem Leben und an der Bayview High.

Hausaufgabe
Die Lernenden sammeln in Vorbereitung auf die nächste Unterrichtsstunde Inhalte, über die sie in einer Fernsehreportage über die Vorkommnisse an der Bayview High berichten würden.

Erwartungshorizont (M 5)

1.
   a) portrays Bayview High as gossip-driven / controlled by gossip; seems as if there is an update almost every day; scandals that are published are of a rather harmful nature / embarrassing; the gossip app is created by one student / a member of the student body; the creator seems to confront / pressure the people around him with the fact of regular updates

   b) comparison: use of social media to communicate with friends, to post photos and comments, to get updates on events and topics that one is interested in; regularity of use: e.g., every day, several hours per day; relevance of gossip can be commented on; types of social media platforms and their respective functions can be mentioned

2. Introduction / inclusion of quotations:
   Quotations on the left: people are afraid of what might be published on the app next; the fear of the next publication puts a lot of pressure on students and their behaviour; the consequences of the publication appear to be drastic / to destroy students' lives (which makes them unacceptable); nobody seems to be safe from having secrets published about them (pressure, depression, fear of making mistakes)

   Quotations on the right: Simon's publications are not lies; they seem to accurately reflect people's bad behaviour/lies/secrets; possible that misbehaviour is the problem not its publication; students seem to be divided over the question of Simon's app

   The personal comment might include: the app makes people susceptible for blackmail/ pressure; constant control/surveillance; Simon as an individual has a lot of power over the rest of students; Simon as a teenager cannot always calculate the consequences a publication might have for another student/their family/friends etc.; open for abuse; some secrets are not about misbehaviour or lies; thus, are not the student's "fault"; hence, the publication loses its "justification"; the publication of certain secrets might lead to stigmatisation.

3.
   a)

Pros	Cons
• greater connectivity: easily and quickly allows people to communicate and connect with others • mostly for free • access to a lot of information: staying updated • self-representation on social media profiles etc. • creation of inspiration for others (e.g. movements, political participation, funding of projects)	• lack of face-to-face communication (detrimental effects on social skills / mental health) • idealised self-representation can make people more self-conscious about own imperfections • online bullying • distraction, waste of time, addiction • solidification of existing divides in society due use of algorithms • fake news • data and privacy issues

   b)
   <u>Examples</u>: build new relationships and stay connected with old friends across the globe; offer comments that support and motivate; spread facts/news that deserve attention of a wide range of people; find your own voice / make your opinion heard and help those less privileged to do so as well; foster learning and education by posting helpful videos/links; support creativity and art you like

Hinweise (M 6)

7./8. Stunde

Ziel: Die Schülerinnen und Schüler versetzen sich in die Rolle eines Nachrichtenteams, das in Bayview High einen Bericht der Ereignisse produziert.

Didaktisch-methodischer Hinweis
Im Plenum sammeln die Lernenden zunächst in einem Brainstorming Kriterien für einen guten Nachrichtenbeitrag (*task 1*). Die Lehrkraft zeigt daraufhin das Video *„How to make a great news report"*: https://www.youtube.com/watch?v=29eIOIr7I4s und die Schülerinnen und Schüler ergänzen die noch fehlenden Kriterien in ihren Aufzeichnungen.

Alternative
Die Reportagen können als Rollenspiel oder als tatsächliche Videoaufnahme präsentiert werden, wobei die Lehrkraft für die letzte Variante mehr Zeit einplanen muss.

Hausaufgabe
Die Lernenden lesen Kapitel sieben bis zehn von *„One of Us Is Lying"* und lösen das *reading quiz 5* (ZM 1).

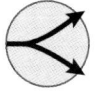

Erwartungshorizont (M 6)

1.
   a) be short and precise; use formal language; mention the important information first; speak clearly; structure your story logically; use body language; narrate your story; use examples to clarify

   b) do your research properly / know what needs to be known about your topic; identify a strong story; bring your story to life (images, statistics etc.); find a great interviewee; summarise at the end

2.
   a)

	Addy	Bronwyn	Cooper	Nate
Possible **motives / scandals** that Simon might have wanted to publish	• cheating on Jake with TJ Forrester (ch. 5, p. 64)	• something about her improvement in chemistry (ch. 3, p. 33) • something that might look bad on her application to Yale (ch. 5, p. 53)	• doping at baseball to improve his performance (ch. 6, p. 68) • friendship/relationship he is keeping secret from Keely (ch. 3, p. 40)	• continued dealing of pain killers even though he is on probation (ch. 6, p. 73)

   b) Mr Avery because he hates modern technology; Leah because Simon's post about her resulted in her suicide attempt.

9./10. Stunde — Hinweise (M 7)

Ziel: Die Lernenden sammeln praktische Erfahrungen mit der Zuweisung bestimmter Stereotypen und wenden ihre eigenen Erfahrungen, ihr Wissen aus dem Roman und aus weiterer Recherche an, um sich ein Urteil darüber zu bilden, ob Stereotypen eher harmlos oder schädlich sind.

Didaktisch-methodischer Hinweis

Der **Einstieg** in die Doppelstunde über Stereotypen erfolgt in Form eines **Selbsttests** (*task 1*), wie er auch häufig in Jugendmagazinen zu finden ist. Hierzu sehen sich die Lernenden das Video „*What High School Stereotype Are You?*" des YouTube-Kanals BuzzMoy, einer sozialen Plattform, die unterschiedliche Arten von Persönlichkeitstests anbietet: https://www.youtube.com/watch?v=bGlQSSZR1js Die Laufzeit des Videos beträgt 06:25 Minuten. Die Schülerinnen und Schüler schreiben sich die Punktwerte für die von ihnen gewählten Antworten auf.

Hinweis zur Differenzierung

Lernschwächere Schülerinnen und Schülern stehen als Hilfestellung ein *essay organiser* (ZM 2) und *linking words* (ZM 3) für das Verfassen ihres *essays* als Download zur Verfügung.

Hausaufgabe

Die Lernenden lesen Kapitel elf bis 13 von *„One of Us Is Lying"* und lösen das *reading quiz 6* (ZM 1).

Erwartungshorizont (M 7)

1. Individual test results.

2. First reactions could include:
   the result shows only one aspect of my character; the test is too superficial; nobody is only one thing; the stereotype fits my personality but does not show all my facets; I would not describe myself as

3. The comments for the different stereotypes might include the following elements:
   - Loner: disappointed; afraid of other people's opinions about oneself; afraid of social life; sad
   - Clown: afraid of never being taken seriously; underestimated; glad to be able to entertain others; anxious because of being the focus of attention
   - Nerd: pressured; afraid of failing / doing not so well academically; awkward; socially underappreciated; anxious about reputation at school
   - Jock: flattered; pressured because of expectations; reduced to one aspect of personality
   - Average: overlooked; feeling of fitting in; afraid of standing out; feeling of being normal
   - Emo: stigmatised; judged; afraid of being bullied; feeling of empathy being underappreciated

4. The line of argumentation could include a selection of the following arguments:

harmful	harmless
- problematic because they can lead to harmful comments/bullying (ch. 3, p. 31) - they might distract students - they could negatively affect one's self-image; self-fulfilling prophecy (ch. 2, p. 20; ch. 8, pp. 94 and 96; ch. 7, p. 84) - they can put e.g. jocks or nerds under a lot of pressure to perform (ch. 3, p. 32; ch. 5, p. 53; ch. 6, p. 68; ch. 8, p. 92; ch. 10, pp. 116/117) - if based on fear and prejudice they can lead to violence, racism etc.	- might boost one's self-confidence if positive - are simply entertaining - it is obvious that they are unrealistic - part of everyday life, cannot be avoided - usually, they only state a first impression, they do not stick once you know the person (ch. 2, pp. 20–25; ch. 4, pp. 46–49; ch. 10, pp. 111/112; ch. 5, p. 58) - there is such a thing as healthy stereotyping (e.g. identifying people by uniform)

	Examples from the novel
<ul><li>Bronwyn feels the need to cheat in chemistry.</li><li>Addy is very self-conscious about her looks; she immediately identifies herself as useless after the incident.</li><li>Nate is being stigmatised by his peers and the police.</li><li>Cooper is afraid that he cannot be successful if he goes public with his relationship.</li></ul>	<ul><li>Bronwyn is socially active even though she is classified a nerd.</li><li>Bronwyn and Nate come to like and appreciate each other despite their contradicting stereotypes.</li></ul>

11. Stunde

Hinweise (M 8)

Ziel: Die Lernenden wenden ihr in der vorherigen Unterrichtsstunde gewonnenes theoretisches Wissen über die Vor- und Nachteile von Stereotypen in Form zweier Jahrbucheintragsvarianten an.

Hinweis zur Differenzierung
Vor die Beschreibung einer der vier Figuren für das Jahrbuch aus stereotypischer und aus persönlicher Sicht kann eine Partnerarbeit gestellt werden, in der Aspekte für die Texte zunächst stichpunktartig gesammelt werden.

Hausaufgabe
Die Schülerinnen und Schüler lesen Kapitel 14 bis 17 von „One of Us Is Lying" und lösen das *reading quiz 7* (ZM 1).

Erwartungshorizont (M 8)

1. <u>Possible definition</u>:
   A yearbook is the story of one school year in pictures and short texts. It tells the story of all events, occasions, achievements and competitions throughout a year. It is a love letter a school writes to itself: it pays homage to all the staff members and students that shaped the school during a specific year, e.g., students council members, athletes, band members and also people who would never expect to be shown. In retrospective, it shows who you once were and who you might still become in the future.

2. Aspects that could be mentioned for each of the students:

Student	Stereotype	Personal homage
Addy	- beauty queen (ch. 1, pp. 6/7; ch. 2, p. 19) - princess (ch. 1, p. 11) - has the perfect boyfriend - homecoming court (ch. 1, p. 11) - belongs to everything without even trying (ch. 11, p. 126)	- insecure (ch. 2, pp. 16–20; ch. 11, p. 125) - loving sister (ch. 7, p. 84; ch. 9, pp. 97 ff.) - fan of the Food Network - likes her coffee with lots of cream and sugar (ch. 9, p. 97) - cute freckles if she does not wear make-up (ch. 12, p. 133)
Bronwyn	- spotless record (behaviour and academic) (ch. 1, pp. 4/5) - the brain (ch. 1, p. 11) - ivy-league bound student Mathlete (ch. 3, p. 32)	- reckless at times (motorbike, alcohol) (ch. 2, pp. 20/21) - watches *Buffy the Vampire Slayer* but hates horror films (ch. 5, p. 52; ch. 12, pp. 137 and 139; ch. 13, pp. 145–147 - caring sibling for sick sister (ch. 5, pp. 53/54) - bad at chemistry (ch. 8, p. 90)
Cooper	- Captain America face (ch. 1, p. 6) - star athlete/jock (ch. 1, p. 11) - bound for baseball scholarship - überpopular (ch. 10, pp. 116/117)	- loyal friend (ch. 10, p. 114) - gay (ch. 10, pp. 115/116) - southern accent (ch. 12, p. 133; ch. 13, p. 143) - fond of his grandmother (ch. 13, pp. 140–143)
Nate	- messy dark hair, ratty leather jacket (ch. 1, p. 6) - criminal/dealer (ch. 1, p. 11) - man whore (ch. 3, p. 31) - spotty attendance record (ch. 3, p. 31) - scapegoat (ch. 8, pp. 94 and 96)	- helpful/supportive when push comes to shove (ch. 1, p. 12; ch. 12, p. 137) - fond of his lizard (ch. 4, p. 47) - took care of his mother when he was younger; father's dying (ch. 11, p. 123; ch. 13, pp. 144/145) - not one for small talk / pleasantries

12. Stunde

Hinweise (M 9)

Ziel: Die Schülerinnen und Schüler verschriftlichen und vertiefen ihr Wissen über die Hauptfiguren, indem sie eine Charakterisierung schreiben.

Einstieg

In einem *conversational speed dating* **(task 1)** tauschen sich die Lernenden über ihr **Vorwissen** zu den **Romanfiguren** aus.

Die Lehrkraft sagt pro Runde die Themen an:
- *First round: What are the four students' stereotypes and why?*
- *Second round: What are the students' supposed motives for having killed Simon?*
- *Third round: How do the characters not meet their stereotypes?*
- *Fourth round: What can be said about the characters' relationships towards each other?*
- *Fifth round: What do you know about the four students' families?*

Hinweis zur Differenzierung

Vor Beginn der Lektüre hat die Lehrkraft lernschwächere Schülerinnen und Schüler auf die vier verdächtigen Romanfiguren aufgeteilt, sodass diese bereits lesebegleitend alle wesentlichen Informationen zu der oder den ihnen zugeteilten *suspects* notiert haben. Sie müssen die Informationen an dieser Stelle nicht mehr zusammentragen, sondern konzentrieren sich auf das Verfassen ihrer Charakterisierung (**task 4**).

Hausaufgabe

Die Schülerinnen und Schüler lesen Kapitel 18 und 19 von „One of Us Is Lying" und lösen das *reading quiz 8* (ZM 1).

Erwartungshorizont (M 9)

1. <u>Aspects that can be mentioned during the speed dating round</u>:

   <u>First round</u>:
   Nate: criminal (deals with drugs, shabby look, man whore, does not socialise much)
   Addy: princess (participated in beauty pageants, popular, has the perfect boyfriend, part of homecoming court)
   Cooper: jock (baseball ace, Captain America face, scouted by university teams, liked by everybody)
   Bronwyn: brain (ivy-league bound, perfect academic record, never breaks the rules, Mathlete)

   <u>Second round</u>:
   Addy: afraid of her affair becoming public
   Bronwyn: afraid that colleges find out about her cheating on chemistry or/and angry that Simon targeted her sister Maeve
   Cooper: use of steroids and/or his homosexuality
   Nate: probation violation and/or Simon having found out about his mother

Third round:
Addy: realises the shallowness of her friendships; discovers her freedom e.g., riding a bike and cutting off her hair
Bronwyn: establishes a relationship with Nate; does not tell on Maeve's hacking
Cooper: gay, supports Addy even though his friends do not, cute relationship to his grandmother
Nate: likes piano music, has to support his father

Fourth round:
Bronwyn and Nate seem to fall in love with each other; Bronwyn invites Addy to have lunch at their table; Cooper is still supportive of Addy

Fifth round:
Bronwyn and her sister Maeve are close; Maeve looks into Simon's *About That* admin panel; Nate's father is close to death; mysterious re-appearance of his mother; Addy is never good enough for her mother, but re-connects with her sister Ash who helps her re-discover who she really is; Cooper is under a lot of pressure from his dad, has a loving relationship to his Nonny who even gives him relationship advice.

2. Examples for connections that can be made:
   a) Bronwyn and Cooper have a spotless record; they have not been to detention before
   b) Nate's reputation is that of a criminal and a man whore
   c) all students are suspected of having committed murder
   d) Addy cheated on Jake while he was on vacation; Bronwyn cheated on her chemistry test; Cooper may have cheated by enhancing his performance
   e) Nate has committed a probation violation by distributing painkillers
   f) and k) Cooper is suspected of having enhanced his performance by juicing
   g) Nate is the obvious scapegoat because he already has a criminal record
   h) Addy hooked up with TJ at his beach house
   i) according to the police, the four may have conspired to get rid of Simon
   j) Bronwyn is an overachiever
   k) Addy has taken part in beauty pageant when younger, but only ever came in second

3./4. Example of characterisation about Nate:
   a) basic information about the character:
      reputation as drug dealer; drives a motorcycle; has been in trouble since fifth grade; is on probation; bad reputation; owns a bearded dragon

   b) character's outward appearance:
      often wears a leather jacket and a Guiness t-shirt; messy / dishevelled dark hair; tall, rangy build; angular cheekbones

   c) character's character traits:
      tough, reckless, defensive

   d) observable behaviour shown by the character:
      keeps cool / a straight face under pressure (e.g. interrogation); reacts fast when push comes to shove (EpiPens during Simon's allergic reaction); sketchy attendance record at

school; likes to watch horror films; has liked to tease Bronwyn ever since they were in fourth grade (Nativity Play); is the one to instigate the relationship to Bronwyn (drops by unannounced, supplies the phones)

e) character's relationships/friendships/family:
has to take care of himself because his father is a drunk whose liver is failing and his mother is "dead" / has left the family years ago; develops a close friendship with Bronwyn, seems to fall in love with her; the probation officer as a steadying influence, he respects her but also finds her annoying

f) character's opinions and beliefs:
believes that you cannot trust anybody; ashamed of their house; partly despises himself for selling drugs because they ruined his mother

g) other people's opinion about the character:
the children at school believe in his bad-boy image (criminal, man whore, walking STD); Bronwyn's friends behave towards him like he is an unpredictable zoo animal in a flimsy cage; everybody thinks he's the obvious outlier and scapegoat; Bronwyn's dad sees him as a bad influence

13. Stunde

Hinweise (M 10)

Ziel: Die Lernenden wenden ihr Wissen über die Romanfiguren in der *hot seat*-Methode handlungsorientiert an, indem sie sich in die Rolle der Figuren einfinden und aus deren Perspektive Fragen beantworten.

Didaktisch-methodischer Hinweis
Es werden nicht alle Schülerinnen und Schüler im *hot seat* sitzen. Pro Figur wird entweder auf freiwilliger Basis oder per Losverfahren eine Person für den *hot seat* ausgewählt.

Hinweis zur Differenzierung
Je nach Lernstärke der Lerngruppe entscheidet die Lehrkraft, ob die Lernenden ihre Rollen per Zufallsprinzip zugeteilt bekommen oder ob jeder die Rolle vorbereitet, die er auch in der Charakterisierung eingenommen hat.

Hausaufgabe
Die Schülerinnen und Schüler lesen Kapitel 20 bis 23 von „*One of Us Is Lying*" und lösen das *reading quiz 9* (ZM 1).

Erwartungshorizont (M 10)

Questions that could be asked:
a) for Addy:
– How has your separation from Jake impacted your life?
– What is the significance of your new haircut?
– How do the new kids you hang out with differ from your former friends?
– Why have you started to include Janae in your circle of friends?

b) for Bronwyn:
- Do you expect that ivy-league colleges will still accept you?
- Why did Simon's post about your sister Maeve upset you so much?
- Why do you take the risk to be in a relationship with Nate?
- If you had to make an educated guess: who is the murderer?

c) for Cooper:
- How do you explain that Simon apparently got your dark secret wrong?
- Do you think that your baseball career has been destroyed by the Tumblr posts?
- Why did you not follow suit in shunning Addy?
- If your relationship with Kris became public knowledge, what do you think would happen?

d) for Nate:
- Do you consider yourself the obvious outlier and scapegoat? Why (not)?
- What upsets you more at the moment: the fact that you are a suspect in a murder case or your mother's return?
- Why do you not like Bronwyn's idea to get help from Until Proven?
- Does your reputation bother you?

e) for Officer Budapest:
- Which of the four students seems the most likely suspect to you?
- Does the police consider anybody else as a suspect? If yes, who and why?
- What is the police's evaluation of the anonymous Tumblr posts?
- What is your working hypothesis on murderer and motive?

Hinweise (M 11)

14./15. Stunde

Ziel: Die Lernenden knüpfen an die Rolle des Officer Budapest aus dem *hot seat* an und versetzen sich in die Rolle des Ermittlerteams. Sie tragen alle Informationen zusammen und führen diese sowie ihre Thesen in einem *investigation board* zusammen.

Didaktisch-methodischer Hinweis
Die Schülerinnen und Schüler bringen als Hausaufgabe Bastelmaterialien für das *investigation board* mit (zum Beispiel bunte Fäden, Post-its, alte Zeitschriften, Filzstifte, Kleber, Schere, Klebeband, Plakate, buntes Papier etc.).

Hausaufgabe
Die Schülerinnen und Schüler lesen Kapitel 24 bis 27 von „*One of Us Is Lying*" und lösen das *reading quiz 10* (ZM 1).

Erwartungshorizont (M 11)

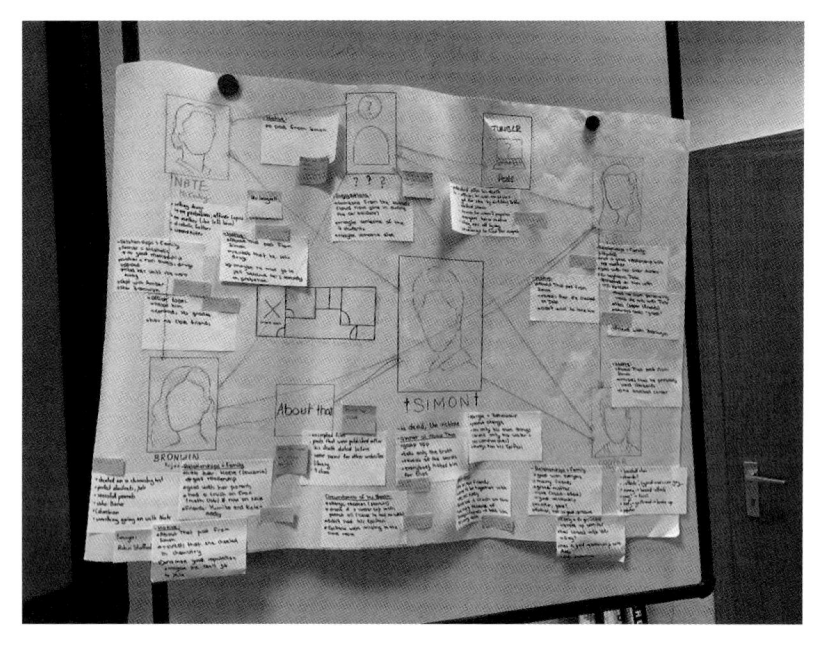

© Anne-Kathrin Weisbrod

16. Stunde

Hinweise (M 12)

Ziel: Die Schülerinnen und Schüler rekapitulieren und bewerten abschließend die Inhalte des Kriminalromans, indem sie einen investigativen Zeitungsartikel verfassen.

Hausaufgabe
Die Lernenden lesen „One of Us Is Lying" zu Ende.

Hinweise (LEK)

Für die Klausur plant die Lehrkraft 135 Minuten (ohne Mediation) ein. Die Klausur richtet sich sowohl an Leistungs- als auch an Grundkurse. Wird die Klausur in einem Grundkurs eingesetzt, wählt die Lehrkraft die Aufgaben entsprechend aus. Klausurwörterbücher dienen den Schülerinnen und Schülern als Hilfsmittel.

Erwartungshorizont (LEK)

I. Writing

1. <u>Outline</u>:

    Formal aspects
    - author
    - title
    - genre
    - date of publication
    - place of publication

- summarising sentence that states the key element

Content
- methods
    - meetings because Maeve and Bronwyn ended up with no results when going over the notes again and again
    - expanding numbers, new members added to the club
    - collection of results on Post-it notes and in manila folder (Bronwyn)
    - stalking Nate's lawyer (Bronwyn) to pass on information
- results
    - what they know about Simon:
        - wanted to publish gossip about each of them
        - paid two boys to fake the car accident
        - he was depressed
        - Simon was poisoned during detention
        - he published creepy content online under a pseudonym
        - the relationship between him and Janae seemed less close lately
        - he and Jake were friends back in the day
    - Cooper's entry was deleted, but it remains unclear by whom
    - what they know about Jake:
        - wrote one Tumblr post (or helped somebody do it)
        - was not in the school building when Simon died
        - is a very controlling person
        - he and Simon are somehow connected
    - → final result: Simon committed suicide

2. <u>Analysis</u>:
    - The author creates a group identity for the group gathered at the café.
        - "murder club" (l. 1) – neologism/choice of words (linking it to an extracurricular activity)/irony
    - The author creates a relaxed atmosphere between the members of the "murder club" to show that they support each other.
        - use of humour, e.g. l. 1: "We need a new name, though."
        - detailed description of body language and facial expressions, e.g. l. 7; ll, 12 ff; ll. 53/54
        - use of colloquial language/slang, e.g. l. 31: "control freak"; l. 51/52: "You can't pimp out my sister!"
        - use of repetition/repeated use of the characters' beverages in context (e.g.: ll. 11–15; ll. 18/19; l. 43
    - The author highlights the characters' interdependence and shows that they cannot solve the case alone.
        - use of metaphor "meeting of the minds" (l. 10)
        - use of repetition/parataxis when quoting the Post-it notes, e.g. l. 6; ll. 21–24
    - The author chooses to portray the situation from Cooper's perspective to highlight the relevance and acceptance of the new members of the group.
        - choice of perspective (ll. 2 f.)
        - use of dialogue (ll. 55–76) and constant interchange between parataxis and hypertaxes to show everybody's contribution to the process

3. Newspaper article:
   Individual results.

II. Mediation

Genre and context
- email head
- greeting
- first sentence states reason for writing
- ending formula
- recommendation provided
- formal language, some colloquial elements

Content
- *Never Have I Ever* does not comply with teen film clichés
- at first glance the series meets all the usual stereotypes but only to break with them at a later point
- three typical clichés used in series: popular guy falls in love with nerdy girl; nerdy girl has to choose between two guys; girl realises that looks aren't everything
- however, teenage girl does not meet the expectations linked to her role; she does not decide on one of the two boys but rather has a relationship with them both and hurts both along the way; at the end of the first season, she is alone again and contrary to the usual cliché not everybody's darling
- jock was humiliated by nerdy girl and has to redefine his role (since a swim star with a broken arm does not meet the stereotypical description either)
- series also plays with the audience's loyalties towards the two love interests by portraying different facets of the two boys and making them develop throughout the seasons
- bonus: several unexpected turns of events (maybe even in a potentially upcoming season 3)

Unterrichtsmagazin

Realistic simulations to improve communicative skills – 6 Simulationen für den flexiblen Einsatz im Unterricht (Klassen 8–11)

Ekkehard Sprenger

„Handlungsbezogen", „lernendenorientiert", „kommunikativ" – Dies sind nur einige der Anforderungen an Lernmaterialien sowie an Unterrichtsstil der Lehrkräfte und Lernverhalten der Schülerinnen und Schüler, die als Qualifikationskriterien angewendet werden. Die Materialien der hier angebotenen sechs Simulationen erfüllen diese Kriterien in besonderem Maße und fördern so die kommunikative Kompetenz Ihrer Lernenden in realitätsnahen Unterrichtssituationen.

KOMPETENZPROFIL

Klassenstufe:	8–11
Dauer:	1–2 Unterrichtsstunden
Kompetenzen:	1. Sprechkompetenz: an Gesprächen funktional-kommunikativ teilnehmen; 2. Lesekompetenz: ausgewählten Textsorten relevante Informationen entnehmen; 3. Sozialkompetenz: Kooperationsbereitschaft, Kompromiss- und Konfliktfähigkeit demonstrieren; 4. Selbstkompetenz: Selbstdisziplin, emotionale Intelligenz und Selbstreflexion demonstrieren
Thematische Bereiche:	Radioprogramm, Abend in der Stadt, Familienausflug, Planung einer Straße, Entscheidung im Einzelhandel, Flughafenansiedlung

Fachliche Hinweise

Was sind Simulationen?

Simulationen sind keine Unterrichtsverfahren, sondern **Lernereignisse**. Eine ihrer wesentlichen Funktionen ist es, den **Schülerinnen und Schülern Verantwortung für ihr Lernen** zu geben.

In Simulationen gibt es keinen Platz für Lehrkräfte. Die Lehrkräfte werden zu **Moderierenden** (*facilitators*), die für den Ablauf des Lernereignisses verantwortlich sind, die jedoch nicht versuchen, die Teilnehmenden (*participants*) zu Entscheidungen oder zur Suche nach den „richtigen" Antworten zu bewegen. Eine Simulation, bei der die Teilnehmenden Fehler machen oder etwas falsch einschätzen, ist kein misslungenes, sondern wahrscheinlich ein sehr erfolgreiches Lernereignis, bei dem man aus Erfahrungen lernen kann.

Die Simulation wird zur Realität, in der die Lernenden **sprachlich und argumentativ handeln**. Sie produzieren Sprache, die in diesem speziellen realistischen Kontext relevant ist. Zu den Vorteilen von Simulationen gehören, dass ...

- sie das **Bedürfnis der Lernenden nach Realismus** befriedigen – den Wunsch, eine Beziehung zum realen Leben außerhalb des Klassenzimmers herzustellen.
- sie die normale Lehrer-Lernenden-Beziehung auflösen, sodass die Lernenden **die Kontrolle über ihr eigenes Lernen** im Rahmen der Simulation übernehmen.

Drei definierende Elemente von Simulationen unterstützen diese Wirkung:

1. **Realitätsnähe der Funktion (*reality of function*)** – Den Teilnehmenden werden Rollen zugewiesen, die sie intellektuell und verhaltensmäßig so akzeptieren müssen, als wären sie tatsächlich diese Personen.
2. **Simulierte Umgebung (*simulated environment*)** – Es gibt ein quasi-realistisches Umfeld, das die Rollenakzeptanz durch die Verwendung quasi-authentischer Materialien fördert.
3. **Struktur (*structure*)** – Die gesamte Aktion ist um Probleme oder Aufgaben herum aufgebaut und folgt damit dem aufgabenbasierten Unterrichtsmodell (*task-based learning*).

Didaktisch-methodische Hinweise

Zur Lerngruppe und den curricularen Vorgaben

Der Erwerb von funktionalen kommunikativen Kompetenzen ist Bestandteil jedes Lehrplans der Bundesländer. Zu den wichtigsten Aufgaben von Englischlehrkräften gehört es daher, Methoden einzusetzen, die diese Kompetenzen der Lernenden fördern. Simulationen leisten das. Sie können das Klassenzimmer in **eine quasi-authentische Umgebung** verwandeln, in der Sprache unter realistischeren Bedingungen als normal angewendet werden kann.

Lernenden wird eine Simulationsaufgabe gestellt, bei der sie ein Problem **sprach-handelnd** lösen. Dabei aktivieren sie ihre lexikalische und grammatikalische Kompetenz, während sie gleichzeitig ihre kommunikativen Kompetenzen einsetzen und ausbauen (*expressing an opinion, defending a point of view, agreeing and disagreeing, negotiating, concluding* etc.).

Insbesondere die **Anwendung von Redemitteln** sollte im Vorweg gründlich vorbereitet werden. Ein entsprechendes Material für leistungsschwächere Lerngruppen finden Sie im Zusatzmaterial (**ZM 1**) zum **Download**.

Grundsätzliches zum methodischen Ablauf

Eine Simulation folgt prinzipiell den folgenden drei Phasen.

Das *briefing*

Die Lehrkraft fertigt für das *briefing* **eine Checkliste an mit den Aspekten**, die vor dem Beginn der Simulation gesagt werden müssen. Sie fasst sich dabei kurz und gibt keine Tipps für die Durchführung. Die Teilnehmenden sind für die Aktion verantwortlich, und wenn sie etwas falsch machen, ist das eine Gelegenheit zum **Erfahrungslernen**. Lehrkräfte beschränken sich darauf, die Mechanismen des Lernereignisses zu erklären – etwa den Zeitplan, die Rollenverteilung und die Ressourcen. Sie sollten das Ereignis nicht mit technischen Hilfsmitteln – Aufnahmegeräten (z. B. Smartphones), Videokameras und dergleichen – überfrachten; es sei denn, diese sind im Rahmen des Szenarios plausibel (wie bei dem Radioprogramm). Es bestünde die Gefahr, dass solche Geräte nicht reibungslos funktionieren und dadurch die Aufmerksamkeit der Teilnehmenden ablenken.

Die Durchführung

Zum pädagogischen Konzept von Simulationen gehört, dass die **Verantwortung bei den Teilnehmenden** liegt. Während der Aktion besteht die Aufgabe der Lehrkraft als *facilitator* lediglich darin, die Vorbereitung (*briefing*) zu moderieren, nicht zu unterrichten oder zu helfen. Eine der Stärken der Methode ist, dass sie den Teilnehmenden Autorität verleiht. Damit wird ihre persönliche Verantwortung für den Lernprozess bekräftigt.

Die entscheidende Voraussetzung ist, dass **die Teilnehmenden sich an die Rollen und Regeln halten**. In einem Spiel müssen Spieler und Spielerinnen gewinnen wollen, denn das ist das übliche Anliegen. Auch die Teilnehmenden an einer Simulation müssen ihre Rollen akzeptieren. Sie dürfen nicht zu Spielverderbern werden und nicht den Clown spielen. Ein solches Verhalten würde die Simulation sabotieren.

Das Ziel der Methode ist das Erfahrungslernen mit Sprache. Die Teilnehmenden müssen die Möglichkeit haben Fehler zu machen. Der Versuch der Moderierenden zu lehren, zu instruieren oder zu helfen, würde das Grundkonzept der Methode missverstehen. Die Lehrkraft ist bei der Durchführung der Simulation gleichsam unsichtbar. Sie beantwortet Fragen zum organisatorischen Ablauf („*Can we use another room?*"), aber keine Frage zum inhaltlichen Geschehen („*Should we elect a chairperson?*"). Sie gibt dann vor, nicht anwesend zu sein. Diese Unsichtbarkeit versetzt die Lehrkraft in die Position, das Geschehen beobachten zu können. Sie interveniert nur bei **grobem Fehlverhalten** oder einem **grundsätzlichen Missverständnis**, das so erheblich ist, dass es das Lernereignis zu gefährden droht.

Das *debriefing*

Obwohl Emotionen wahrscheinlich im Mittelpunkt der Nachbesprechung stehen werden, muss die Lehrkraft keine Expertise in Psychologie haben. Das Ziel der Nachbesprechung ist **die Sensibilisierung der Teilnehmenden** für ihr persönliches Lernverhalten. Die Lehrkräfte sollten diese Phase nicht zu einem inhaltlichen Unterrichtsgespräch machen.

Ein *debriefing* wird zunächst in Kleingruppen oder in Partnerarbeit durchgeführt. Fragen und Impulse könnten von der Lehrkraft zur Verfügung gestellt werden. Diese befinden sich im Zusatzmaterial (**ZM 2**) zum **Download**. Die Ergebnisse dieser **ersten Sondierung** werden dann dem Plenum zur Kommentierung, Erläuterung und Diskussion vorgestellt.

Es ist üblich, wenn auch nicht zwingend, dass die Lehrkraft (jetzt wieder in der Funktion ‚Lehrkraft') die Nachbesprechung leitet. Es ist auch denkbar, dass **ein oder zwei Lernende diese Aufgabe übernehmen**. Das sollte jedoch ein oder zwei Tage vor dem Ereignis mit ihnen besprochen werden, um ihnen Zeit zur Vorbereitung zu geben.

Vielleicht gibt es bei der Nachbesprechung keine eindeutigen Ergebnisse. Die Teilnehmenden werden in den Stunden und Tagen nach dem Ereignis selbst eine Nachbesprechung durchführen. Diese

Art des **rückblickenden Lernens und Bewusstwerdens** ist besonders wertvoll, weil sie in kleinem Rahmen und ohne Druck erfolgt.

Lehrwerksbezug

Die Simulationen lassen sich an *Units* der aktuellen Lehrwerke anknüpfen, in denen der Erwerb von kommunikativen Kompetenzen im Vordergrund steht. Thematisch passen die Simulationen u.a. zu:

- **Green Line 4** (Klett-Verlag), Unit 4, *London, a world city*
- **Green Line 4** (Klett-Verlag), Unit 1, *Kids in America*
- **Access 8** (Cornelsen), Unit 1, *London Changing*
- **Context** (Cornelsen), Chapter 6, *The World of Work – Just a Job to Do?*
- **Context** (Cornelsen), Chapter 7, *The Media – Tool, Drug, Manipulator, Friend?*

Auf einen Blick

1. Simulation

Thema:	What is todays' news? – Producing and recording of a radio show
M 1	***News and views at 7* – Producing a radio show** / *notes for the participants* sowie die Rahmenbedingungen lesen, um eine Radio-Show zu produzieren (GA)
M 2	**What are todays' events? – News items** / Bilder für das Schreiben der Nachrichten verwenden (GA)
Benötigt:	☐ Kopien von M 1 in Klassenstärke; M 2 je drei Mal für jede Gruppe
	☐ Aufnahmegeräte (z. B. Smartphones oder Tablets)

2. Simulation

Thema:	A night on the town – A discussion
M 3	**A night on the town – Making a plan** / *notes for the participants* sowie Rollenkarten verwenden, um den gemeinsamen Abend zu planen (GA)
M 4	**Where to go? – Entertainment guide and eating-out guide** / Unterhaltungs- und Essensempfehlungen für die Diskussion verwenden (GA)
Benötigt:	☐ Kopien von M 3 in Klassenstärke; M 4 zweimal für jede Gruppe

3. Simulation

Thema:	A family trip to a country fair – A discussion
M 5	**A family trip to a country fair – Making a plan** / *notes for the participants* sowie Rollenkarten nutzen, um den Familienausflug zu planen (GA)
M 6	**Who are you? – Participant cards** / Rollenkarten
Benötigt:	☐ Kopien von M 5 in Klassenstärke; M 6 zerschnitten je einmal für jede Gruppe

4. Simulation

Thema:	Freeway planning – Work together to find an appropriate solution
M 7	**Freeway planning – Finding an appropriate solution** / mithilfe der *notes for participants* sowie dem Punktesystem und einer Straßenkarte eine angemessene Lösung für alle Beteiligten finden (EA, GA)

M 8	**A new freeway – Road map /** die Straßenkarte nutzen um die neue Autobahn zu planen (EA, GA)
Benötigt:	☐ Kopien von M 7 und M 8 in Klassenstärke

5. Simulation

Thema:	Shoplifting – Discuss a solution with the help of expert's opinions
M 9	**Shoplifting – Subliminal messages as solution? /** mithilfe der *notes for participants* sowie Rollenkarten und zugrundeliegenden Dokumenten eine Lösung finden (GA)
M 10	**Who are you? – Participant cards /** Rollenkarten
M 11	**A collection of documents – Expert's opinions /** Dokumente als Entscheidungsgrundlage verwenden
Benötigt:	☐ Kopien von M 9 und M 11 in Klassenstärke; M 10 zerschnitten jeweils in halber Klassenstärke

6. Simulation

Thema:	A new airport for Yakima – Discuss a controversial topic and find a solution
M 12	**A new airport for Yakima – A controversial topic /** *notes for participants* und Rollen *guidelines* sowie Berichte verwenden, um ein kontroverses Thema zu diskutieren (GA)
M 13	**Investigation of possible solutions – Two reports /** Berichte durch Beauftragung der Regierung (A) sowie der *Regional Development Board representatives* (B)
M 14	**Views of your group /** Einstellungen der Rollen auf einem Übersichtsblatt festhalten (GA)
Benötigt:	☐ Kopien von M 12 in Klassenstärke; M 13 zerschnitten je 4-mal für die entsprechende Gruppe, M 14 2-mal für jede Gruppe

Zusatzmaterialien im Online-Archiv bzw. in der ZIP-Datei

ZM 1_Expressions_Negotiations	Nützliche Redemittel für Verhandlungen, relevant für alle Simulationen und leistungsschwächere Lerngruppen
ZM 2_Debriefing	Fragen und Impulse der Lehrkraft für das *debriefing* bei allen Simulationen

News and views at 7 – Producing a radio show

M 1

Notes for participants

Work in groups of 6. Your group is an American radio news team. Your task is to produce a news broadcast. The news items will be presented to you on another worksheet.
Here are your tasks:
Task 1: Work out the stories that are presented in the **news items**. Then write down each news item in about 50 words. Write each item on a separate piece of paper. Make sure to consider the **memo** of the station manager.
Task 2: Prepare to make your broadcast. Each member of the team must read at least one news item. Practise reading these items aloud. When you are ready, record your broadcast live. Begin with the words, "This is Radio Olympia FM with the news and views at 7."

Memo of the station manager

Radio Olympia FM
To: Production staff of *News and views at 7*
From: Station manager, Radio Olympia FM
News and views at 7 is a 5-minute show. That does not mean 5 minutes and 20 seconds, or 5 minutes and 2 seconds. Please be very careful with the time.
Please practise and check the time before you record your show. It might be a good idea to have one or two extra bits at hand in case you underrun the time a bit or have a minute or two to fill. An announcement or maybe even a short commercial?
Points to keep in mind:
- Listeners remember best what they hear first and last. So, discuss and decide which news item to place there.
- Always include the weather forecast.
- Before you begin the production, remember that our listeners love interviews. So, choose any one of the stories of the day and work out a short interview with one (or more) of the people in the story. The interview should take about one minute.
- Avoid asking questions which can be answered by yes or no. Begin the questions with letter 'H' or 'W': how? why? what? And follow up interesting answers. Listen to what the person is saying.
- **Again, try to make a show of exactly 5 minutes. But aim to come out somewhere within the last ten seconds before the national network comes in.**

Now produce your show. Here are some tips for the newcomers on your team:
- Write the text for each news story on a separate sheet of paper.
- Each member of the team must read at least one item of your show.
- When you are ready, record your broadcast. Begin with the words, "This is Radio Olympia FM with the news and views at 7".

We have received great feedback last week. So, keep up the good work.
Myra

M 2 What are todays' events? – News items

virus	the President, no mask	ambulance	injection	bad infection

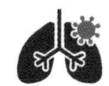

Champions League Final last night

Real 3 – Man City 2	Junior 3 goals	14th time

Yesterday

mountain hike	bear encounter	talk loudly	bear retreated

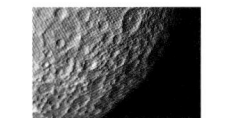

rock from the moon	team of scientists	research	extraterrestrial life

5th Avenue Theater	ABBA – avatars	their greatest hits	crowd – crazy

city planning	urban gardening	healthy vegetables	subscribe to veggie boxes

Today		Tomorrow	
a.m.	p.m.	a.m.	p.m.

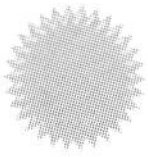

Traffic — heavy traffic on Interstate 5 and 405 – use Highway 16 to downtown

A night on the town – Making a plan

M 3

Notes for participants

You are a group of four tourists who are visiting London. From your hotel you can reach London's West End (an area with many theatres, clubs and restaurants). The journey takes 30 minutes by Underground or by car and 45 minutes by bus.

Task

You decide to have a night out together, starting any time after 6 p.m. Read your **role card** carefully. Use the **entertainment guide** and **eating-out guide**. Work out with your group:
- how you want to travel to the West End and back
- what you want to do during the evening
- where you want to eat and at what time

Discuss these questions until everyone agrees to do the same thing at the same time.

Role cards

	Transport	Entertainment	Food	Other points
Card A	You've got a car, but you don't like driving in London. Also, it is extremely hard and expensive to park in the West End.	You like musicals and comedies. You quite like opera but hate loud discos and jazz clubs.	You love excellent meals and drinks in a first-class restaurant.	You have an important meeting tomorrow. That's why you do not want to be back at the hotel very late.
Card B	You like driving your sports car. It's small. Four get in, but it is not comfortable.	You hate sitting still and just listening or watching. You like pubs and discos.	Your favorite type of food is Asian. The next best is Mexican food.	It is your birthday, and you want to have a good time. You are not working tomorrow.
Card C	In your view, it is best and easiest to go by Underground. The last train back leaves at 12.30 a.m.	You love thrillers and comedies and quite like opera.	You are a vegetarian.	You are strongly against smoking and alcohol. You want to see some of the sights of London by night.
Card D	You think going by bus is best. The last bus back leaves at midnight.	Films are your favourite but you quite like anything to do with music.	You want to eat something quick and cheap.	You have heard a lot about London pubs. You would like to visit several.

M 4 Where to go? – Entertainment guide & eating-out guide

Entertainment guide

© uchar/E+
The Royal Ballet at Covent Garden:
Swan Lake

© dwphotos/iStock/ Getty Images Plus
Billy Bragg in concert at The Rock Hall

© Terry Vine/The Image Bank
Royal Festival Hall
Dvorak 9th Symphony

© Colourbox
ABC Cinema "Leave no trace"

© Mike Powell/The Image Bank
Welsh Opera presents "La Traviata"

© Busà Photography/Moment
A Magical Musical: *Les Misérables*

© Flashpop/DigitalVision
Annie's Club – disco with excellent house music

© track5/E+
At the Garrick Theatre:
Jim Carsons and his Brass Band

© mechichi/iStock/Getty Images Plus
St. Martin's Theatre
The Day of the Dead

Eating-out guide

© Hugo Abad/Moment
"El Tacoria" – best Mexican food

© Cris Cantón/Moment
Papa Murphy "The Pasta House"

© Juj Winn/Moment
Piccadilly "The Onion" –
American snack bar

© Sellwell/Moment
"La Table" – superb cuisine – romantic atmosphere

© Willie B. Thomas/DigitalVision
"Soup 'n' Cheese" – quick snacks

© Alexander Spatari/Moment
"The Salad Bowl" – fresh vegetarian all night

© Richard T. Nowitz/The Image Bank
"Chopsticks" – best Sushi in town

© Witthaya Prasongsin/Moment
"The Coach" – pub and jazz

© VICUSCHKA/Moment
"Been Fishing" – delicious fish'n chips

A family trip to a country fair – Making a plan

M 5

Notes for participants

You are a family of five planning a trip to a country fair.

Country fairs are family events that include entertainment and competitions. Common to county fairs are contests. Contests at fairs award the smartest animals, the most beautiful flowers, the best paintings etc. Entertainment is also important. There are fair rides for all ages, music bands and lots of delicious food.

Fairs have a bandstand, animal barns and exhibition halls to display farm equipment, prize-winning crafts, fruits and vegetables etc. Sometimes, there is a track for car races and the demolition show, in which cars crash into each other until only one is still running.

Fairs are loud events full of energy. They give families a chance to be together and have a good time.

Tasks:
1. Form groups of five. You are going to represent one of five family members.
   - Amanda (wife and mother)
   - Dave (husband and father)
   - Jordan (son and brother – 16 years old)
   - Maria (daughter and sister – 12 years old)
   - Grandad George
2. Each group gets a set of **participant cards** face down. Each member of the group takes a card. It is important that you read only your own card. Do not share your information with other members of your group.
3. You have 20 minutes to discuss and decide how the family will spend the day at the fair. Family members should each try to accomplish the things they want to do. **Compromises will often be necessary.**
4. One family member takes notes on what the family has decided to do.
5. Write down the schedule your group (family) will follow when you go to the fair.

© Achim Thomae/Moment

M 6 — Who are you? – Participant cards

Card 1: Amanda (wife and mother)
- You're worried about your daughter getting into trouble. That's why you would like her to stay with you.
- You have entered a watercolour painting arts contest. The winners will be announced in the exhibition hall at 2:00 p.m. and you want to be there.
- You want everyone to have lunch together in the food court at 12:00 p.m.
- You do not like country fair rides.
- It is your wedding anniversary the day after tomorrow. You would like to surprise your husband with a present.

Card 2: Dave (husband and father)
- Your father has an aching back and cannot walk much. Someone must stay with him at all times.
- You want the family to watch the opening of the old farm equipment show at 2:30 p.m.
- You are worried that your son will get into trouble. It has happened before.
- You definitely want to see the modern farm equipment display at the exhibition hall.
- It's your wedding anniversary soon. You want to buy a present for your wife.

Card 3: Jordan (son and brother – 16 years old)
- You want to see the demolition show at the racetrack very much! It runs all day, but the best part starts at 2:30 p.m.
- You do not want your friends to see you with your family. You would rather walk alone.
- Your little sister annoys you.
- You really want to see the modern farm equipment display at the exhibition hall.
- You want to bring your dog to the "Smartest Dog" contest at the bandstand at 11:30 a.m.

Card 4: Maria (daughter and sister – 12 years old)
- You adore your grandad and love to spend much time with him.
- Your science club has an experiment in the science contest. You want your family there with you. The winners will be announced in the exhibition hall at 2:00 p.m.
- You hate the smell of animals.
- You love country fair rides.
- You have lots of energy. You like to be very active all the time.

Card 5: Grandad George
- Your roses are being judged in the exhibition hall at 10:30 a.m. The prizes for "the most beautiful roses" will be awarded.
- Walking is sometimes difficult for you, and you need to rest often.
- You want to see the "Smartest Dog" contest at the bandstand at 11:30 a.m.
- You would like to buy presents for the family.
- You would be happy to sit and listen to music at the bandstand.

Freeway planning – Finding an appropriate solution

M 7

Notes for participants

You are taking part in a City Council meeting. The task is to select a new freeway route which goes from any one of the bottom-most hexagons to any one of the six top-most hexagons. Participants are assigned to one of the following groups:
- **City Council:** If at all possible, you want to avoid the route touching the resident and business area.
- **Taxpayers' Association:** You want to keep costs low by avoiding hills and business areas.
- **University Archeologists:** If possible, no route through historic and digging sites.
- **Residents' Association:** You would hate traffic noise and polluted air near your homes.
- **Merchants' Association:** A route construction through business areas would affect your business negatively.
- **City Engineers:** To construct a route through hills would be very complicated and expensive. So better go around hills.

Participants try to plan the freeway on the **road map** so it will cost the group they are working in the fewest **points** (i.e., money).
- Each group receives a penalty for length – 5 points for each hexagon used.
- Each group receives a penalty for going through hexagons with symbols. Each group is penalised according to the chart.
  (Note: Penalty is for EACH symbol, so a hexagon with 2 hills costs the engineer 19 points – 5 for the hexagon and 7 for each hill.)

Tasks:

Here are the steps to do this:
1. Individual work. Select a route with your assigned role.
2. Form groups with all others of same role (i.e., all engineers, all City Council members etc.).
3. Agree on the best route for your group.
4. Form new groups made up of one member from each group (i.e., 1 engineer, 1 archeologist, 1 City Council member etc.).
5. Select a route which all members of this new group can agree with. The group must "pay" for …
- using a hexagon (5 points)
- the sum of what the participants have to pay as representatives of their group (see chart). Altogether, the group wants to "pay" as little as possible. Negotiating and finding compromises are a must.

	🏠	❘	▲	🔔	🦴
City Council	5	3	1	1	1
Archeologists	1	1	1	3	5
Taxpayers' Association	1	3	5	1	1
Taxpayers' Association	7	1	1	1	1
Taxpayers' Association	1	7	1	1	1
City Engineer	1	1	7	1	1

© Ekkehard Sprenger

M 8   A new freeway – Road map

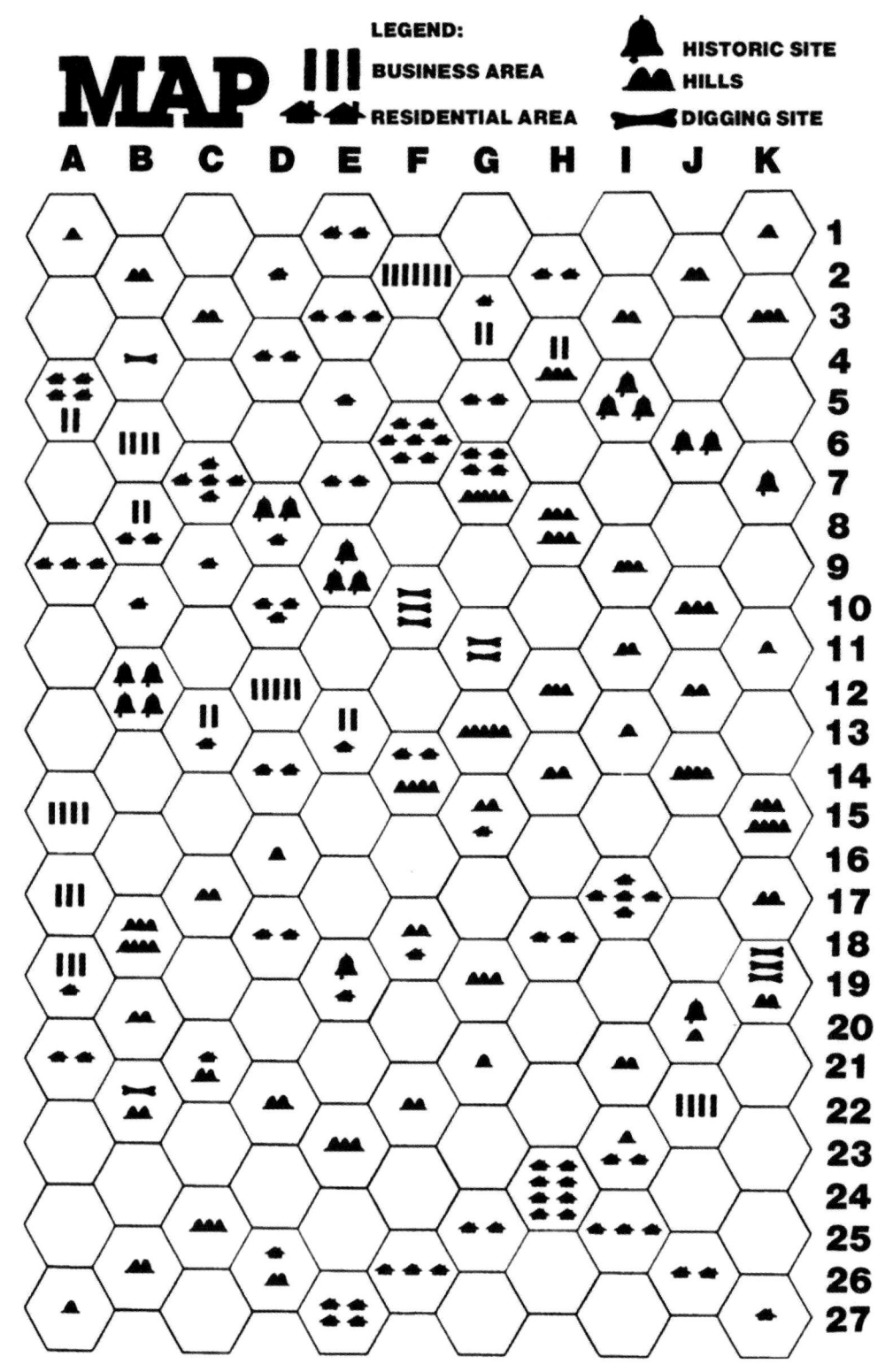

Shoplifting – Subliminal messages as solution?

M 9

Notes for participants

You are about to take part in a meeting at which a decision will be taken on whether or not to introduce subliminal messages onto streamed background supermarket music to discourage people from shoplifting. These people are taking part in the meeting:
- **Mr/Ms Perry**, managing director of the Budget Supermarkets
- **Mr/Ms Joling**, manager of the Blaine branch of Budget Supermarkets
- **Mr/Ms Freeman**, assistant manager of the Blaine branch of Budget Supermarkets
- **Mr/Ms Carlson**, representative of Cloud Cover Music Ltd (company which sells streamed background music to supermarkets)
- **Mr/Ms Anderson**, president, National Consumer Association
- **Mr/Ms Peters**, managing director of Security Risks Ltd
- **Mr/Ms Cross**, a regular customer at the Blaine Budget store

You will find all the information you need on your **participant card** and in the **documents** that you may consult freely.

Note: The managing director starts the meeting, acts as chairperson and makes sure that a decision is reached. Only Mr/Ms Perry, Mr/Ms Joling, and Mr/Ms Freeman take part in the decision-making. It is up to the other participants to influence this decision in their own interest. Mr/Ms Carlson, Mr/Ms Anderson, Mr/Ms Peters, and Mr/Ms Cross may be played by one or two people according to the number of people taking part in the simulation.

Who are you? – Participant cards

M 10

Participant card A: Mr/Ms Perry, managing director of the Budget Supermarkets

You are very worried about a proposal by one of your managers to introduce subliminal messages onto the streamed background music played in your supermarkets. Your chief worry is that the press could make a scandal out of this by considering it to be manipulative. Journalists would suggest that it is open to all sorts of abuses, such as selling products that people do not really need and influencing their behaviour generally. This would not only do damage to the image of your supermarkets, which you consider as respectable, fair-dealing, family-orientated places but also to yourself as you have played a prominent role in many liberal political campaigns. You have the reputation of being a moral and straight person. However, your supermarkets are not doing too well at the moment, and your policy is to encourage managers to keep up a good profit margin.

You have asked the manager in question, Mr/Ms Joling, to arrange a meeting at which you may inform yourself better on the following aspects of the problem:
- What are subliminal messages, and how do they work?
- What are customer reactions likely to be?
- What is the Consumer Association's reaction likely to be?

When you have heard all the points of view, you should reach a decision with your manager, Mr/Ms Joling and his/her assistant, Mr/Ms Freeman.

Participant card B: Mr/Ms Joling, supermarket manager, Blaine branch; Mr/Ms Freeman, assistant manager, Blaine branch

You are very much interested in introducing this new system of subliminal messages. Your supermarket has not been doing very well lately. This is not good for your promotion prospects, and your bonuses have been small. One of the problems is shoplifting, which has reached the alarming proportions of 11.5 per cent of your total sales far above the national average. You have tried other methods of discouraging shoplifters over the past few years, but do not like any of them, such as:

- Random or systematic searches of customers create a bad image and influence business negatively.
- More security guards are very expensive and eat up profits.
- Complicated electronic surveillance equipment is expensive and probably not very effective anyway.

Streamed background music carrying subliminal messages are obviously the cheapest and most effective way of getting rid of this problem, but recent newspaper articles have been suggesting that there is something immoral in using what they call "manipulative techniques". Your role is to protect the consumer, and so the questions you must ask yourself are:

- Is the consumer being manipulated?
- What are the alternative means available for controlling shoplifting?
- Are these just as effective and morally more acceptable?

In the absence of any legislation, you can refer to the document on shoplifting issued by the Chamber of Commerce.

Participant card C: Mr/Ms Carlson, representative of Cloud Cover Music Ltd

You work for a firm that sells streamed background music to supermarkets, restaurants and offices etc. Your most recent product are subliminal messages to discourage shoplifting in supermarkets.

You have been invited to attend a meeting of the Budget Supermarkets to present the product to the managing director, and the manager and assistant manager of the supermarket in which the use of a test run is being envisaged. Your product is the one described in the article in *The Daily Gazette*.

You are not very interested in the moral aspects of subliminal messages. You are simply marketing a product that works. Your arguments are:

- There is convincing evidence in the United States that subliminal messages lessen the number of shopliftings.
- The music you put out is already designed to influence customers and make them buy more. Including subliminal messages is not more manipulative than this.
- You explain that nobody is aware of the message unless it is amplified, so the public need not even be told about the technique.

To be sure of gaining an opportunity to market this new product, you must listen carefully to any objections and answer them as best you can.

Participant card D: Mr/Ms Peters, managing director of Security Risks Ltd
You have been advising Budget Supermarkets on all aspects of security for several years. Your company provides store detectives to watch customers, a policy that has been used periodically by Budget Supermarkets. Now you are invited to attend a meeting at Budget Supermarkets to advise on the effectiveness of subliminal messages on the supermarket's streamed background music.
You are there in an advisory capacity and take no part in the decision-making process. Your own interests are at stake, for if the supermarket chain adopted the solution of subliminal messages and it worked, it would have far less use for your services. You should refer to the alternative means of reducing shoplifting described recently in an issue of *Supermarket Management*. It is in your interest to defend the solution which will involve the most sales of security equipment or which will use the most manpower.

Participant card E: Mr/Ms Anderson, president of the National Consumer Association
You have been invited to a meeting organised by the Budget Supermarkets to consider whether they should introduce subliminal messages onto the streamed background music played in the supermarket. You are there to advise on the moral aspect of the problem as, at the moment, there is no legislation concerning subliminal messages, but you do not take part in the decision-making.
Your role is to protect the consumer, and so the questions you must ask yourself are:
- Is the consumer being manipulated?
- What are the alternative means available for controlling shoplifting?
- Are these just as effective and morally more acceptable?

In the absence of any legislation, you can refer to the document on shoplifting issued by the Chamber of Commerce.

Participant card F: Mr/Ms Cross, customer
You are a regular customer at the Budget Supermarket. The manager has asked you to come to a meeting to discuss the introduction of subliminal messages onto the streamed background music that is played in the supermarket. You are simply asked to give your opinion as a regular shopper and not to participate in the decision-making.
First, you must find out more about subliminal messages by reading a recent article in the press (*The Daily Gazette*). You know several people who have been involved in shoplifting cases, a middle-aged friend and one of your children's schoolfriends. A short while ago, you witnessed an incident when a customer, suspected of shoplifting, was searched at the check-out. His bag was full of goods, but the manager let him go. The incident created quite a scene.
You must make up your mind whether subliminal messages amount to manipulation on the part of the supermarket. You have heard a lot of rumors about subliminal messages in pop music and how these affect young people. Some people even believe that this is the main reason that sects have such a strong influence on young people. Decide whether you think there is any danger in subliminal messages and convince the supermarket management of your point of view.

M 11

A collection of documents – Expert's opinions

- Extract from Chamber of Commerce report on shoplifting
- An article on *How to keep shoplifters at bay* from *Supermarket Management*
- An article from *The Daily Gazette* on subliminal messages in supermarkets in the USA
- An article on shoplifting from *The Evening Post*

Chamber of Commerce Report
Extracts on shoplifting

1. The reduction in stock between delivery and sale (including breakages) is known as shrinkage and estimated at a total of $460 million per year in the USA.
2. Shoplifting and thefts by staff normally average between 1 to 3 per cent of sales. Anything less than 2 per cent should be considered acceptable and inevitable.
3. Shoplifting is lowest in January and August and greatest in November and April.
4. Shoplifting is increasing – in 2006 there were 218,288 cases in the USA. In 2016 there were 280,993 and in 2020 there were 378,345.

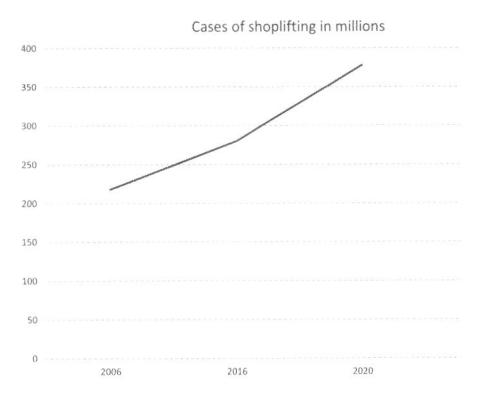

Cases of shoplifting in millions (graph showing increase from 2006 to 2016 to 2020, values approximately 220, 280, 380)

5. Shopkeepers cannot continue to blame the customer for shoplifting if they carry on designing supermarket layouts that do not take shoplifting into account. Placing expensive, but unnecessary items on open display and placing sweets where children can help themselves are two examples of such strategies.
6. About 27 per cent of all shoplifters caught are under the age of sixteen.

How to keep shoplifters at bay

Still a favorite method against shoplifting is the closed-circuit TV camera. Although the initial expense of buying the equipment is high, the supermarket manager will soon recover the investment by being able to spot regular offenders and identify them as soon as they enter the shop.

TV screens placed strategically around the supermarket can also discourage small-time or would-be shoplifters, at least for the first six months after installation. Unfortunately, beyond this period, shoppers get wise to the screens or simply forget them, and employees watching the screens become less observant, so that the long-term effects of such devices are not always significant.

Many shops are beginning to mark all their goods with a special ink which will trigger an alarm when removed from the shop, unless cancelled at the check-out. This is obviously the solution for the future, as the equipment is inexpensive and the surveillance technique inoffensive for the shopper. However, marking the products uses up considerable store labour and the problem of in-house theft remains.

It does not look as if the traditional store detective is out of a job yet, though. This is obviously an expensive solution in terms of manpower but, as Dan Freeman who has been in the store detective business for 30 years says, "You just can't miss them. When they start watching you, you watch them. I can tell a shoplifter the moment he steps into the shop, just by the way he walks."

Extract from Supermarket Management; Author: Ekkehard Sprenger

Good-bye to shoplifting

Great anxiety is being expressed by consumer associations about recent trends in supermarket management. In an attempt to discourage shoplifting, two major chains of supermarkets have already introduced subliminal messages onto their streamed background music that are an inevitable accompaniment to any shopping experience nowadays. It is thought that many other supermarkets will shortly follow suit.

Widely used in the USA, these messages are claimed to produce spectacular results. Drops in shoplifting losses of up to 40 per cent have been reported. The shopper cannot consciously hear the message, as to be audible to a human ear, it must be amplified considerably.

Cloud Cover Music Ltd, one of the firms that makes these messages recently allowed me to listen to an amplified version. Beneath a soft voice of singer, the message came over only too clearly. A low and gentle voice was saying at regular intervals, "Do not shoplift. Shoplifting is wrong. Do not shoplift. Shoplifting is wrong."

"Where's the harm?" says Bill Fasano, Cloud Cover Music Ltd top executive. "The supermarket is happy – there is less shoplifting. Potential shoplifters are happy – they are protected from their own vice. And the ordinary shopper just never knows anything is going on."

However, consumer associations fear that unscrupulous supermarkets could use advertising messages in the same way. In any case, they claim that this type of procedure is manipulative and therefore immoral. As such it contravenes the Fair-Trading Act (1985). "Supermarkets are not the place for music", says Consumer Association Chairperson, Rachel Sanders.

Extract from The Daily Gazette; Author: Ekkehard Sprenger

Never again

Thirteen-year-old Amy was lucky this time. Caught by a store detective with a bottle of hair conditioner, eye-lash dye, and a copy of *Young Teens Today* hidden in her bag, she found herself in a car being driven to the police station. Even more upset than Amy was her Mum. She was as white as a ghost when she went to collect Amy from the police station and burst into tears.

Amy says, "I was lucky. Police officers came to my home, which is very middle class and respectable. I think that's why they let me off. They even asked to see my schoolbooks."

Amy has decided to stop shoplifting after two years. The reason she did this, she says, was boredom and not to impress her friends, as many young people do. However, she has grown out of it after getting frightened and has decided to pursue other interests.

Extract from The Evening Post; Author: Ekkehard Sprenger

M 12 — A new airport for Yakima – A controversial topic

Notes for participants

The situation

Distances
Yelm to Maryville – 190 min.
Yelm to Studebaker Airport – 12 min.
Yelm to Pullman – 35 min.

Owing to the projected increase in the number of passengers using Yakima's airports and the present congestion of the capital's airport, Studebaker, an **investigation of possible solutions** was requested by the **government**. A summary of this **report (A)** is given. The report was prepared by an impartial and **independent body** and dismissed the proposal to develop Maryville Airport as unrealistic. Maryville is Yakima's second largest city. In reply, **the Regional Development Board**, which consists of members of parliament and representatives of Maryville's business community, has published its **own report (B)** on airport policy. Their views have a large following in parliament as it is felt that the north of Yakima has too often been disadvantaged as far as development is concerned. A **meeting** has been arranged to **discuss the recommendations made in the two reports** and **prepare a preliminary decision**.

Form groups of 9 students: 1 student in each group acts as chairperson. Group 1 (4 students) represents the government. Group 2 (4 students) represents the Regional Development Board.

Guidelines for representatives

Government representatives

As far as you are concerned, the report's (A) recommendations are conclusive. Any further development at Maryville would be unlikely to solve the problem of congestion in the south-west. You do, however, have sympathy for the economic problems of the north. The Regional Development Board also has a lot of support in parliament, and you may have to make concessions in order to ensure that the government is not defeated in parliament. **Study the two reports and the map. Use the table to write down your views.**

Regional Development Board representatives

For you, the government report (A) is another example of the south-west being favoured over the north. You see the development of Maryville Airport as the key to the economic recovery of the north. You believe that you may be able to find enough support to block the government in parliament if they ignore your arguments. **Study both reports and the map. Use the table to write down your views.**

Investigation of possible solutions – Two reports

M 13

Investigation report (A)

The number of people seeking to use Yelm's airport is projected to rise from 25 million next year to 39 million by the end of the decade. For the regional airport at Maryville, the figure will rise from 9 million to 15 million. This approaches 100 per cent of capacity in both cases. This report was commissioned to determine Yakima's airport policy for the future. The following proposals were considered:

- The expansion of Studebaker Airport near Yelm
- The construction of a new airport at Pullman
- The expansion of Maryville Airport

The expansion of Studebaker Airport

This is inevitable as no other short-term solution exists. At the moment, Studebaker handles 22 million passengers, which means it is already being used to full capacity with planes landing or taking off every two minutes during peak times. There are thousands of passengers jamming the terminals and the trains and roads that serve the airport.

A new terminal would expand Studebaker's capacity to almost 40 million within 10 years. This would also involve the provision of better road and rail links including the extension of the Underground system. The aircraft noise around Studebaker (1.2 million people affected) is a problem, but there will be substantial improvements in the future.

The construction of a new airport at Pullman

The envisaged large-scale airport at Pullman is aimed at establishing a balanced airports system for Yakima well into the 21st century. Only Pullman can provide the additional capacity to meet demand in the next decade. The necessary planning permission to enable Pullman Airport to be built to carry a capacity of 10 million passengers per annum should be granted as expeditiously as possible. The ultimate capacity should not exceed 15 million.

The number of people likely to be affected by the noise at Pullman would be small (51,000 people). There are, therefore, no grounds for the noise consideration to prevent the construction of Pullman. There is little difference between 5 million passengers a year and 15 million as far as noise is concerned.

However, there should be a government undertaking that there will be no further expansion of Pullman above the 15 million mark. To develop the airport further would lead to an unprecedented and wholly unacceptable major environmental disaster.

The economy around Pullman would benefit from the airport. At first, an additional 6,500 houses will be needed rising to, at the most, 8,000. The loss of agricultural land should not stand in the way of Pullman's construction.

The expansion of Maryville Airport

Maryville is currently being expanded to cope with 14 million passengers by the end of the decade. There is no evidence that the growing congestion in the south-west could be relieved by the further development at Maryville Airport. The overriding fact is that 80 percent of the passengers who use Studebaker Airport are beginning or ending their journeys in Yelm or the south-west. However congested Studebaker is, to these passengers, it is preferable to flying into or from the regional airport at Maryville.

The only solution to the problem of congestion in the south-west lies in the south-west itself.

Conclusion

The necessary additional capacity cannot be provided other than at Studebaker or Pullman, or both. The complementary capacity contributions to be made by development at Studebaker and construction at Pullman will provide a flexible and well-balanced capability in the country's airports system well into the 21st century.

The Regional Development Board's report on airport policy (B)

Maryville Airport is big and successful. Last year, 9 million people used it. Its single runway can take jumbo jets and could easily handle up to 20 million passengers a year. Expansion at Maryville would be a boost to the economy and would relieve to a large extent the economic problems of the country's north-east.

The expansion of Maryville would create 25,000 jobs. It would help to create hi-tech industries and would be of enormous benefit to the business community. The airport currently employs 8,000 and generates an estimated 25,000 more jobs in related firms. The airport is one of the few growth areas in a region where unemployment stands at around 15 percent against a national average of 13.4 percent, an average of 9.95 percent in the south-west and an average of only 8 percent in the Pullman area.

The cost of increasing the number of passengers at Maryville by 12 million a year could be achieved at a third of the cost of building Pullman and extending Studebaker. The money should be spent on improving the north-east's infrastructure rather than in the rural south-west on a plan that most of the locals oppose on environmental grounds. The Studebaker area residents resent the threat of even more air traffic and the Pullman residents are appalled at the prospect of the pollution of their countryside.

We are concerned to achieve a balanced economic growth throughout the country; we feel that a national airports policy is needed, not just one for the south-west.

Views of your group

M 14

Supporting arguments	Evidence

Anticipated objections

Counter-arguments	Evidence

Possible compromises

Hinweise und Erwartungshorizonte

Hinweise (gültig für alle sechs Simulationen)

Die **primären Ziele** aller sechs Simulationen sind die **Festigung und Automatisierung** der kommunikativen Kompetenzen.

Methodische Hinweise

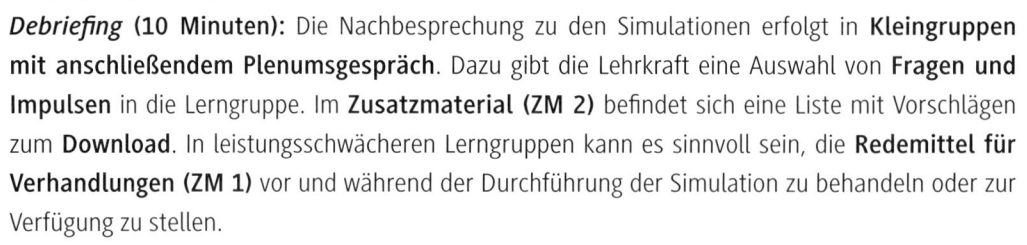

Debriefing (10 Minuten): Die Nachbesprechung zu den Simulationen erfolgt in **Kleingruppen mit anschließendem Plenumsgespräch**. Dazu gibt die Lehrkraft eine Auswahl von **Fragen und Impulsen** in die Lerngruppe. Im **Zusatzmaterial (ZM 2)** befindet sich eine Liste mit Vorschlägen zum **Download**. In leistungsschwächeren Lerngruppen kann es sinnvoll sein, die **Redemittel für Verhandlungen (ZM 1)** vor und während der Durchführung der Simulation zu behandeln oder zur Verfügung zu stellen.

1. Simulation

Hinweise (M 1 und M 2)

Sekundäre Ziele von **M 1** und **M 2** sind es, sprachlich **wohlgeformte Kurztexte** zu formulieren, zu entscheiden, welche Nachricht an erster und welche an letzter Stelle positioniert werden soll, ein Interview zu führen und eine simulierte Nachrichtensendung von 5 Minuten aufzunehmen.

Methodische Hinweise

Briefing (5 Minuten): Die Lehrkraft verteilt und erläutert ausschließlich die Hinweise für die Teilnehmenden (M 1). Dabei wird betont, dass die Schülerinnen und Schüler ihre Rolle und Aufgabe als *news team* **konsequent akzeptieren** müssen. Es wird sichergestellt, dass die Lernenden die **Rahmenbedingungen genau verstehen** und ein **Smartphone** für die Aufnahme zur Verfügung haben. Die Lehrkraft gibt vor Beginn der Simulation präzise an, um **welche Uhrzeit die Nachrichten** gesendet werden sollen.

Durchführung (25 Minuten): Nachdem M 2 ebenfalls an die Gruppen ausgegeben wurden, wird die Simulation wie in den Materialien vorgegeben durchgeführt. Bezüglich des Aufnahmezeitpunkts übernimmt die Lehrkraft oder ein instruierter Schüler bzw. eine instruierte Schülerin die Aufgabe der Regie im Hintergrund. Mindestens eine Aufnahme wird im Plenum präsentiert.

Hinweise zur Differenzierung

Für **leistungsstarke Gruppen** kann die Regie kurz vor der Aufnahme der Nachrichtensendung eine *breaking news* auf einem Zettel in die Redaktionssitzung geben. Diese Nachricht muss unbedingt aufgenommen werden. Beispiel:

> **Breaking news:** car bomb explodes – city hall of the capital – presumed to be the work of radical political group – many casualties

Diese Intervention erhöht **den Druck** auf das *news team* zu **entscheiden**, wie der Nachrichtenplan noch einmal kurzfristig geändert werden muss.

Erwartungshorizont (M 1 und M 2)

<u>Examples for selected news items</u>: "This is Radio Olympia FM with the news and views at 7". Early this morning, the president was diagnosed with a COVID infection. He had been present at a meeting

last week without a mask. He was taken to hospital by ambulance, where he immediately received an injection. Both his lungs are affected by the virus. He is doing well under the circumstances. – While hiking in the Olympic Mountains, Bob Woofter of Tacoma had a dangerous encounter. He was surprised by a black bear. Mr. Woofter remained calm, stopped and spoke loudly to the bear. Fortunately, the bear turned around and disappeared into the forest.

Excerpt from an interview: Radio Olympia: "Thank you for coming, Bob. Please tell our listeners about your bear encounter." – Bob: "Well, I was on a hike in the Olympic Mountains. I did not realise that I was in bear country, so I was not bear aware. Suddenly, I heard a noise in the bushes in front of me and saw a black bear coming towards me." – Radio Olympia: "So, what did you do? Where you scared?" – Bob: "Oh yes, I was very scared. But I tried to stay calm, did not run away. I stood up very straight, made myself tall and spoke in a loud, deep voice, 'Bear, go away, bear.' And miraculously, the bear turned around and retreated into the forest. I was so relieved." …

The weather report: And here is Radio Olympia's weather. Well, we're starting the day with some rain, but the afternoon will be dry with heavy clouds. Tomorrow will be partly sunny in the morning, with sunshine later in the day.

The traffic report: This is the Radio Olympia traffic report at 7. The traffic on Interstates 5 and 405 is very heavy everywhere. Use Highway 16 to Downtown.

Hinweise (M 3 und M 4)

2. Simulation

Sekundäres Ziel von **M 3** und **M 4** ist es, in einer **Gruppendiskussion zu entscheiden**, wie ein Abend in London gemeinsam verbracht werden soll.

Methodische Hinweise

Briefing **(5 Minuten):** Die Lehrkraft verteilt und erläutert ausschließlich die Hinweise für die Teilnehmenden (M 3). Es ist entscheidend, dass die Schülerinnen und Schüler **ihre Rollen und Aufgaben in einer Touristengruppe konsequent akzeptieren**.

Durchführung (25 Minuten): Nachdem M 4 an die Gruppen ausgegeben wurde, wird die Simulation wie in den Materialien vorgegeben durchgeführt. Es ist sinnvoll, wenn die Gruppen ihren **Plan schriftlich fixieren**.

Hinweise (M 5 und M 6)

3. Simulation

Sekundäres Ziel von **M 5** und **M 6** ist es, in einer **Gruppendiskussion (Familie) zu entscheiden**, wie ein Tag auf einem *country fair* gemeinsam verbracht werden soll.

Methodische Hinweise

Briefing **(5 Minuten):** Die Lehrkraft verteilt und erläutert ausschließlich die Hinweise für die Teilnehmenden (M 5). Es ist entscheidend, dass die Schülerinnen und Schüler **ihre Rollen und Aufgaben in einer Familie konsequent akzeptieren**. Es ist hilfreich, wenn die Lernenden sich **Namensschilder** anfertigen und vor sich aufstellen.

Durchführung (25 Minuten): Nachdem M 6 an die Gruppen ausgegeben wurde, wird die Simulation wie in den Materialien vorgegeben durchgeführt. Es ist sinnvoll, wenn die Gruppen ihren **Tagesplan schriftlich fixieren**.

4. Simulation

Hinweise (M 7 und M 8)

Sekundäre Ziele von **M 7** und **M 8** sind es, in einer **simulierten Stadtratssitzung (Gruppendiskussion)** den Verlauf einer neuen Straße **zu diskutieren und zu entscheiden**.

Methodische Hinweise

Briefing **(5 Minuten):** Die Lehrkraft verteilt und erläutert ausschließlich die Hinweise für die Teilnehmenden (M 7). Es ist entscheidend, dass die Schülerinnen und Schüler **ihre Rollen und Interessen konsequent akzeptieren**. Es ist hilfreich, wenn die Lernenden sich **Schilder mit ihrer Funktion anfertigen** und vor sich aufstellen.

Durchführung (40 Minuten): Nachdem M 8 an die Gruppen ausgegeben wurde, wird die Simulation wie in den Materialien vorgegeben durchgeführt. Es ist sinnvoll, wenn die Gruppen ihren Straßenverlauf in den Plan eintragen.

5. Simulation

Hinweise (M 9–M 11)

Sekundäres Ziel von **M 9–M 11** ist es, in einer **simulierten Geschäftssitzung (Gruppendiskussion)** zu entscheiden, ob **unterschwellige Botschaften** hinzugefügt werden sollen.

Methodische Hinweise

Briefing **(5 Minuten):** Die Lehrkraft verteilt und erläutert ausschließlich die Hinweise für die Teilnehmenden (M 9). Es ist entscheidend, dass die Schülerinnen und Schüler **ihre Rollen konsequent akzeptieren**. Es ist hilfreich, wenn die Lernenden sich Schilder mit ihrem **Namen und Funktion anfertigen** und vor sich aufstellen.

Durchführung (40 Minuten): Nachdem M 10 und M 11 an die Gruppen ausgegeben wurde, wird die Simulation wie in den Materialien vorgegeben durchgeführt.

6. Simulation

Hinweise (M 12–M 14)

Sekundäres Ziel von **M 12–M 14** ist es, in einer **simulierten Komiteesitzung (Gruppendiskussion) vorläufig zu entscheiden**, wie die Situation der Flughäfen eines Landes (Yakima) verbessert und zukunftsfähig gemacht werden kann.

Methodische Hinweise

Briefing **(5 Minuten):** Die Lehrkraft verteilt und erläutert ausschließlich die Hinweise für die Teilnehmenden (M 12). Es ist entscheidend, dass die Schülerinnen und Schüler **ihre Rollen konsequent akzeptieren**. Es ist hilfreich, wenn die Lernenden sich **Schilder mit ihrer Funktion** (*representative of …*) anfertigen und vor sich aufstellen.

Durchführung (40 Minuten): Nachdem M 13 und M 14 an die Gruppen ausgegeben wurde, wird die Simulation wie in den Materialien vorgegeben durchgeführt.

Erwartungshorizonte gültig für Simulationen 2–6

Individuelle Gruppenlösungen.

V.278

Unterrichtsmagazin

Ketanji Brown Jackson: The first Black female U.S. Supreme Court justice – Orientierungswissen zum historischen Ereignis erwerben (Klassen 10–13)

Anne-Kathrin Wölfel

© Adam Schultz/White House Photo/public domain

"It has taken 232 years and 115 prior appointments for a Black woman to be selected to serve on the Supreme Court of the United States." – Im April 2022 wurde Ketanji Brown Jackson als erste schwarze Richterin am *U.S. Supreme Court* bestätigt und am 30.06.2022 vereidigt. In der vorliegenden Kurzeinheit erwerben die Lernenden Orientierungswissen zu diesem historischen Ereignis und reflektieren seine Bedeutung vor dem Hintergrund gesellschaftspolitischer Entwicklungen in den USA.

KOMPETENZPROFIL

Klassenstufe:	10–12 (G8), 11–13 (G9)
Dauer:	ca. 5 Unterrichtsstunden
Kompetenzen:	1. Leseverstehenskompetenz: Texten relevante Informationen entnehmen; 2. Hör-Seh-Verstehenskompetenz: Audios, Videos und Cartoons relevante Informationen entnehmen; 3. Interkulturelle Kompetenz: verstehen, wie Richterinnen und Richter in den USA ernannt werden
Thematische Bereiche:	*Politics, culture, society in the USA – between tradition and change; ethnic identity; U.S. political system*

Fachliche Hinweise

Der **Oberste Gerichtshof** der USA wurde im Jahr 1789 gegründet. Unter den **115 *Supreme Court justices***, die bis 2021 ernannt wurden, waren nur fünf Frauen (Sandra Day O'Connor, Ruth Bader Ginsburg, Sonia Sotomayor, Elena Kagan und Amy Coney Barrett) und drei *people of colour* (Thurgood Marshall, Clarence Thomas und Sonia Sotomayor). Als der 83-jährige liberale Richter Stephen Breyer Anfang 2022 seinen Rückzug zum Sommer ankündigte, löste Präsident Joe Biden sein Wahlversprechen ein, die **erste schwarze Frau** für den *Supreme Court* zu nominieren. Nach erfolgreicher Bestätigung durch den Senat im April 2022 wurde **Ketanji Brown Jackson** am 30.06.2022 als **116. Richterin am *U.S. Supreme Court*** vereidigt. Auch wenn sich die Mehrheitsverhältnisse im *Supreme Court* dadurch nicht verändern (6:3 konservativ zu liberal) – die Ernennung Jacksons ist ein bedeutender Schritt hin zu mehr **Diversität** und ein **Meilenstein in der Geschichte der USA.**

Didaktisch-methodische Hinweise

Die Kurzeinheit richtet sich an Lernende der Einführungs- und Qualifikationsphase (gA und eA). Sie kann lehrwerksunabhängig im Rahmen der Beschäftigung mit unterschiedlichen **gesellschaftspolitischen Themen der USA** eingesetzt werden, zum Beispiel *politics, culture, society in the USA – between tradition and change; ethnic identity; U.S. political system*. Gerade in Anbetracht aktueller Entscheidungen des durch seine konservative Mehrheit geprägten *Supreme Courts* (beispielsweise das Kippen von *„Roe vs Wade"* [Recht auf Abtreibung]) sowie der Präsidentschaftswahlen 2024 bietet die Kurzeinheit zu Ketanji Brown Jackson eine interessante Ergänzung für den Oberstufenunterricht. Für die Arbeit mit den Materialien sollten die Lernenden Grundkenntnisse über das politische System der USA (Zweiparteiensystem, Gewaltenteilung, Institutionen) sowie über die Geschichte der *African Americans* haben (*slavery, Civil War, segregation, Civil Rights Movement* etc.).

Lehrwerksbezug

Für die **Einführungsphase** lässt sich die Einheit an *Topic 3 **„Bridging the gap"*** von Green Line Transition (Klett 2018) und für die **Qualifikationsphase** an Kapitel 6 ***„The US – A diverse nation"*** von Green Line Oberstufe (Klett 2021) anknüpfen.

Mediathek

- https://edition.cnn.com/2022/03/24/politics/supreme-court-justices-minorities-cec/index.html
  Ein Artikel über die Demographie des *Supreme Court* seit dessen Gründung (Hintergrundinfos für Lehrkräfte und Lernende).
- https://www.spiegel.de/ausland/ketanji-brown-jackson-erste-schwarze-richterin-am-supreme-court-bestaetigt-a-95bea162-417c-43fe-9eb9-4965c308631b
  Ein deutschsprachiger Artikel über die Bestätigung von Ketanji Brown Jackson als erste schwarze Richterin am *Supreme Court*. (Hintergrundinfos für Lehrkräfte; Mediationsaufgabe)
- https://www.washingtonpost.com/investigations/2022/06/10/ginni-thomas-election-arizona-lawmakers/
  Ein Artikel über Ginni Thomas' Versuch Joe Bidens Sieg zu verhindern (Zusatzinfos für Lehrkräfte zu dem Richter Clarence Thomas).

[letzter Abruf: 05.12.2022]

Auf einen Blick

1./2. Stunde

Thema:	Members of the U.S. Supreme Court – An introduction
M 1	**How do U.S. Supreme Court justices get appointed? – Working with a video** / anhand eines Videoclips Orientierungswissen erarbeiten (EA)
M 2	**Members of the U.S. Supreme Court – A group puzzle** / Internetrecherche und Gruppenpuzzle zu den Supreme Court Richtern durchführen; einen Cartoon analysieren (EA/GA)
Benötigt:	☐ PC-Raum und Beamer bzw. digitale Endgeräte und Kopfhörer

3. Stunde

Thema:	Getting to know Ketanji Brown Jackson
M 3	**The Federal Court System – Studying an infographic** / eine Grafik erarbeiten (EA)
M 4	**Who is Ketanji Brown Jackson? – Creating a profile** / Orientierungswissen über die *Supreme Court* Richterin mithilfe eines Podcast erarbeiten (EA)
Homework:	*Finish your acrostic about Ketanji Brown Jackson using information from the podcast. Prepare to justify your choices at the beginning of the following lesson.*
Benötigt:	☐ digitale Endgeräte und Kopfhörer

4./5. Stunde

Thema:	Ketanji Brown Jackson's Supreme Court confirmation – A historic "first"
M 5	**Ketanji Brown Jackson's historic confirmation (I) – Reading the speech** / Aufgaben zum Leseverstehen erarbeiten (EA)
M 6	**Ketanji Brown Jackson's historic confirmation (II) – Creating a visualisation** / den Inhalt eines Redeauszugs mithilfe von Schlüsselbegriffen visualisieren (EA; PA/GA)
M 7	**Ketanji Brown Jackson's historic confirmation (III) – Describing cartoons** / zwei Karikaturen beschreiben und erklären (PA)
M 8	**"More than just representation" – Understanding and discussing a podcast** / von einem Audiobeitrag ausgehend mit *„firsts"* und *„representation"* auseinandersetzen (EA/PL)
Benötigt:	☐ PC und Lautsprecher bzw. digitale Endgeräte und Kopfhörer ☐ Schere, Kleber, DIN-A3-Papier; alternativ: Tablet (M 6)

M 1

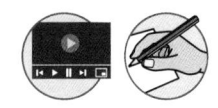

How do U.S. Supreme Court justices get appointed? – Working with a video

Task

Watch the video "How do U.S. Supreme Court justices get appointed?" by Peter Paccone on TED Ed (4:30 min.). While viewing, fill in the information in the table below.
https://raabe.click/JusticesAppointment [last access: 05/12/2022]

a) What three things have to happen if an individual wants to become a justice on the Supreme Court?	
b) What qualifications for a Supreme Court justice does the Constitution specify?	
c) How many Supreme Court justices were foreign-born?	
d) Most presidents nominate individuals who …	
e) What other factors come up for consideration? Name three factors.	
f) What is the nominee asked during the hearings by the Senate Judiciary Committee? Name two aspects.	
g) At the end of the hearings, the Judiciary Committee …	
h) In what cases has a nominee been rejected by the Senate?	
i) Supreme Court justices are appointed for life (i.e., until they die), unless … Name three aspects.	
j) In the words of Irving R. Kaufman, a U.S. Supreme Court justice is expected to be … Name three aspects.	

Members of the U.S. Supreme Court – A group puzzle

M 2

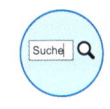

Tasks

1. A group puzzle
   a) Get into groups of four. This is your home group. Decide who researches which Supreme Court justices on the Internet. Therefore, decide who is person A, B, C and D. Fill in the table. The justices in the table were the members of the U.S. Supreme Court before Ketanji Brown Jackson took her seat on 30 June 2022.

   A: J. Roberts; S. Sotomayor; A. Coney Barrett
   B: C. Thomas; E. Kagan
   C: S. Breyer; N. Gorsuch
   D: S. Alito; B. Kavanaugh

   b) Form expert groups (A-A-A-A, B-B-B-B, …). Compare and add to your notes.
   c) Get together in your home groups. Present your Supreme Court justices to your group members. Listen and complete your table.
2. On the basis of your findings, analyse the cartoon below using expressions from the box.

© JD Crowe, Alabama Medi Group/AL.com

MAGA = Make America Great Again – **SCOTUS** = Supreme Court of the United States – **QAnon** = conspiracy theory and political movement in the USA

> **Useful expressions to talk about cartoons**
> The cartoon was published on (date) in response to (event) – In the foreground / background / centre there is / are … – On the left-hand side / right-hand side you can see … – There is a caption / speech bubble / thought bubble under / next to / above … – The cartoonist makes fun of /satirises / criticises / draws attention to … – (the cross) represents / symbolises … – The cartoon's message is accentuated / reinforced by …

	John G. Roberts, Jr (Chief Justice)	Clarence Thomas	Stephen G. Breyer	Samuel A. Alito, Jr.	Sonia Sotomayor	Elena Kagan	Neil M. Gorsuch	Brett M. Kavanaugh	Amy Coney Barrett
date/place of birth									
university education									
member of the Supreme Court since									
appointed by President									
Ideological/ political leanings									
additional information									

Photos: Public Domain

The Federal Court System – Studying an infographic   M 3

Tasks

1. Study the infographic about the U.S. Federal Courts on the right.
2. Match the words and their translation/definition in the table below. Use a dictionary or the Internet if necessary. You can also do this task as a *LearningApp*: https://learningapps.org/watch?v=pm8rxp9pc22

Graphic: United States District Court

1. the Bar (AE)	A. a person who is guilty of a crime
2. (to) be admitted to the Bar	B. official protection from legal action, for example, not being judged in a court or punished for a crime
3. public defender	C. President Donald Trump and his government (2016–2020)
4. law school	D. (to) gain a qualification as a lawyer
5. The Harvard Law Review	E. an independent scholarly journal published by students at Harvard Law School
6. (to) rise up the legal ranks	F. (to) work as a law clerk, i.e. work with a judge and help the judge make decisions
7. detainee	G. all lawyers thought of as a group
8. prestigious	H. *der/die stellvertretende/r Vorsitzende/r*
9. lenient	I. *die juristische Fakultät (an der Universität)*
10. offender	J. the quality of being honest and having strong moral principles that you refuse to change
11. diligence	K. *als Jurist/Juristin beruflich aufsteigen*
12. immunity	L. the quality of working carefully and with a lot of effort
13. the Trump administration	M. very much respected and admired, usually because of being important or of high quality
14. (to) clerk	N. a lawyer paid for by the government to represent an accused person who cannot pay for a private lawyer (*der Pflichtverteidiger, die Pflichtverteidigerin*)
15. integrity	O. not as severe in punishment as one would expect
16. Vice Chair	P. a person kept in prison, especially for political reasons

M 4 Who is Ketanji Brown Jackson? – Creating a profile

Tasks

1. First, read the *Task sheet*. Then listen to the podcast *Judge Ketanji Brown Jackson*: https://raabe.click/PodcastJudgeJackson [last access: 05/12/2022]
2. If necessary, listen again. Respond to the tasks on the sheet.
3. Work with a partner. Share and complete your notes.
4. Create an acrostic about KETANJI BROWN JACKSON using information from the podcast. Prepare to justify your choices at the beginning of the following lesson.

> **What is an acrostic?**
> An acrostic consists of a group of phrases or words; the first letters of which – when taken consecutively – form a word, name, phrase or other predetermined entity.

Task sheet

1. The Supreme Court is approximately _____ years old.
2. The National Bar Association is the nation's oldest network of _____
3. Who was Charlotte E. Ray?
4. Take notes about the following aspects of Ketanji Brown Jackson's life:
   a) early years / childhood
   b) parents/family
   c) school years at Miami Palmetto Senior High School
5. What did Jackson's teachers tell her when she said she wanted to go to Harvard and become a lawyer?
6. At Harvard Law School, a group of students hung a Confederate flag from their window. What did Jackson do?
7. Apart from being a member of the Black Student Association, what hobby did Jackson have at Harvard?
8. What is said about Jackson's husband, Patrick Jackson?
9. What did Jackson do after her graduation in 1992?
10. When did she marry Patrick Jackson?
11. Ketanji Brown Jackson's legal career:
    a) What did she do at the start of her legal career?
    b) For whom did she work in 1999?
    c) She juggled _____ with _____, served as a _____ for a while, went into _____, at one point representing a number of prisoners detained at _____ .
    d) From _____ , she was Vice Chair of the U.S. Sentencing Commission. Republicans accuse her of being _____ because:
       • _____
       • _____

e) In 2013, Ketanji Brown Jackson became a judge on the

   _____ .

   Thomas B. Griffith says Ketanji Brown Jackson was widely admired around the courthouse for

   - _____
   - _____
   - _____

f) When Supreme Court Justice Antonin Scalia died in 2016, what did her 11-years-old daughter Thalia do?

g) Ketanji Brown Jackson's nine years on the District Court proved highly eventful. What example(s) does the podcast give?

h) In _____ , Ketanji Brown Jackson was promoted to the position of Judge on the U.S. Court of Appeals for the D.C. Circuit.

12. What was Joe Biden's election promise?
13. What does Kim Keanan, former President of the National Bar Association, say about Ketanji Brown Jackson towards the end of the podcast?

Photo: Adam Schultz/White House Photo/public domain

M 5

Ketanji Brown Jackson's historic confirmation (I) – Reading the speech

The following excerpt is the final part of Ketanji Brown Jackson's speech at the White House after her Supreme Court confirmation on 8 April 2022.

Task
1. Read the excerpt from Ketanji Brown Jackson's speech. Determine important ideas and information. Highlight keywords.

> **READ: Ketanji Brown Jackson's remarks at the White House after her Supreme Court confirmation**
>
> […] It has taken 232 years and 115 prior appointments for a Black woman to be selected to serve on the Supreme Court of the United States. (Applause.)
>
> But we've made it. (Applause.) We've made it, all of us. All of us.
>
> And – and our children are telling me that they see now, more than ever, that, here in America, anything is possible. (Applause.)
>
> They also tell me that I'm a role model, which I take both as an opportunity and as a huge responsibility. I am feeling up to the task, primarily because I know that I am not alone.
>
> I am standing on the shoulders of my own role models, generations of Americans who never had anything close to this kind of opportunity but who got up every day and went to work believing in the promise of America, showing others through their determination and, yes, their perseverance[1] that good – good things can be done in this great country – from my grandparents on both sides who had only a grade-school education but instilled in my parents the importance of learning, to my parents who went to racially segregated schools growing up and were the first in their families to have the chance to go to college. I am also ever buoyed[2] by the leadership of generations past who helped to light the way: Dr. Martin Luther King Jr., Justice Thurgood Marshall[3], and my personal heroine, Judge Constance Baker Motley[4]. (Applause.)
>
> They, and so many others, did the heavy lifting that made this day possible. And for all of the talk of this historic nomination and now confirmation, I think of them as the true pathbreakers. I am just the very lucky first inheritor of the dream of liberty and justice for all. (Applause.)
>
> To be sure, I have worked hard to get to this point in my career, and I have now achieved something far beyond anything my grandparents could've possibly ever imagined. But no one does this on their own. The path was cleared for me so that I might rise to this occasion.
>
> And in the poetic words of Dr. Maya Angelo[5], I do so now, while "bringing the gifts … my ancestors gave." (Applause.) I – "I am the dream and the hope of the slave." (Applause.)
>
> So as I take on this new role, I strongly believe that this is a moment in which all Americans can take great pride.
>
> We have come a long way toward perfecting our union.
>
> In my family, it took just one generation to go from segregation to the Supreme Court of the United States. (Applause.)

35 And it is an honor – the honor of a lifetime – for me to have this chance to join the Court, to promote the rule of law at the highest level, and to do my part to carry our shared project of democracy and equal justice under law forward, into the future.

Thank you, again, Mr. President and members of the Senate for this incredible honor.

Source: CNN https://edition.cnn.com/2022/04/08/politics/ketanji-brown-jackson-confirmation-speech/index.html [last access 05/12/2022]

1 **perseverance:** continued effort to do or achieve sth., even when this is difficult or takes a long time – 2 **buoyed:** *here:* encouraged – 3 **Justice Thurgood Marshall** (1908–1993)**:** the first Black U.S. Supreme Court Justice – 4 **Constance Baker Motley** (1921–2005)**:** the first Black woman to serve as a federal judge in the USA – 5 **Dr. Maya Angelou** (1928–2014)**:** U.S. American poet and Civil Rights activist

2. Are the statements true or false? Tick the right option and give the line(s). Then correct the wrong statements.

		true	false	line(s)
a)	Ketanji Brown Jackson does not want to be seen as a role model.			
b)	Jackson's role models are hard-working people from past generations aspiring to create something better for themselves and their families.			
c)	Education was very important to Ketanji Brown Jackson's grandparents.			
d)	Ketanji Brown Jackson was the first person in her family to go to college.			
e)	She says that her professional success is only due to the achievements of past generations.			
f)	Jackson is convinced that the confirmation of the first Black female Supreme Court Justice is something that white Americans should be proud of, too.			

_____
_____
_____
_____
_____
_____
_____
_____
_____
_____

M 6

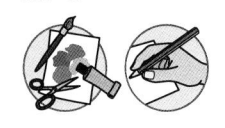

Ketanji Brown Jackson's historic confirmation (II) – Creating a visualisation

Tasks

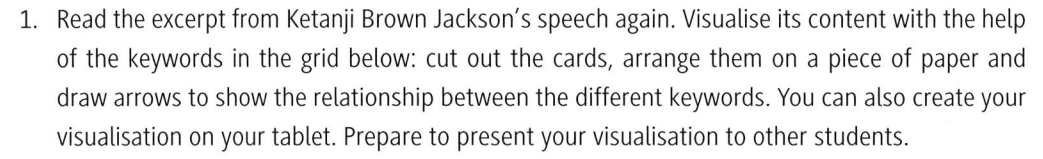

1. Read the excerpt from Ketanji Brown Jackson's speech again. Visualise its content with the help of the keywords in the grid below: cut out the cards, arrange them on a piece of paper and draw arrows to show the relationship between the different keywords. You can also create your visualisation on your tablet. Prepare to present your visualisation to other students.
2. *Extra:* Write a summary of the excerpt in no more than four to five sentences.

Ketanji Brown Jackson	pathbreakers	determination	all Americans
pride	hard work	responsibility	role model
opportunity	perseverance	opportunity	honour
historic confirmation as Supreme Court Justice	the shared project of democracy and equal justice under law	past generations of Americans including her parents and grandparents	leaders of past generations

Ketanji Brown Jackson's historic confirmation (III) – Describing cartoons

M 7

Task

Describe and explain your cartoon to a partner and relate it to the excerpt from Ketanji Brown Jackson's speech.

Partner A:

© Adam Zyglis

Partner B:

© Joe Heller/Hellertoons

M 8

"More than just representation" – Understanding and discussing a podcast

Tasks

1. Listen to the podcast *A Black woman on the High Court is a good start. But representation has limits* by Sandhia Dirks from 9 February 2022 (4 min.):
   https://raabe.click/PodcastRepresentationLimits
   While listening, fill in the information. You do not need to write complete sentences.

a) What was LaDoris Cordell asked when she was appointed the first Black woman judge in Northern California in 1982?	
b) What is Cordell's response?	
c) Out of the 115 justices appointed to the Supreme Court, how many of them were … • women? • people of colour?	
d) To whom did the founding principles of the USA not apply? Name three aspects.	
e) According to Cordell, why does it matter that there be a Black woman justice?	
f) According to Margaret Russell, we should not underestimate the power of …	
g) Why does Russell not have illusions about the impact of Ketanji Brown Jackson on the decisions coming up in the Supreme Court?	
h) What is Tomiko Brown-Nagin hoping for?	
i) She warns against summing up a nominee by just their race and gender because … Name two aspects.	
j) What was Ruth Bader-Ginsburg's answer to the question of how many women justices would be enough?	

2. "Diversity alone will not change a system." – Discuss this statement from the podcast.
3. Harvard Professor Tomiko Brown-Nagin is glad about Jackson's nomination but also has the dream that one day society will have moved beyond these "firsts". In your opinion, what must be done in society to reach this dream? Write your opinion down.

Hinweise und Erwartungshorizonte

Hinweise (M 1 und M 2)

1./2. Stunde

Ziel von **M 1** und **M 2** ist es, für das Stundenthema zu sensibilisieren und Orientierungswissen zum *Supreme Court* zu erarbeiten.

Methodische Hinweise

Zum **Einstieg** präsentiert die Lehrkraft den folgenden Satzanfang: *"It has taken 232 years and 115 prior appointments for …"*. Die Schülerinnen und Schüler bilden Hypothesen über das Stundenthema, indem sie den Satz mit ihren Ideen vervollständigen. Anschließend wird ihnen das richtige Ende präsentiert (*"… a Black woman to be selected to serve on the Supreme Court of the United States"*; Zitat von Ketanji Brown Jackson aus ihrer Rede nach der Bestätigung als *Supreme Court* Richterin).

Erwartungshorizont (M 1)

a) You have to be nominated by the president of the United States; your nomination needs to be approved by the Senate; the president must formally appoint you to the court
b) none; the Constitution does not specify any qualifications
c) six
d) broadly share their ideological view
e) three of the following: experience; personal loyalties; ethnicity; gender
f) their law record (if applicable); where they stand on key issues (to discern how they might vote)
g) votes to send the nomination to the full Senate with a positive or negative recommendation
h) when the Senate majority has been a different political party than the president
i) they resign; they retire; they are removed from the court by impeachment
j) a paragon of virtue; an intellectual titan; an administrative wizard

Erwartungshorizont (M 2)

1. a)–c)
   <u>John G. Roberts:</u> born in 1955 (Buffalo, New York) ▪ Harvard College; Harvard Law School ▪ since 2005 ▪ by George W. Bush ▪ conservative ▪ additional information: Chief Justice; has sometimes tried to find a middle ground / has sometimes sided with liberal arguments
   <u>Clarence Thomas:</u> born in 1948 (in the Pinpoint community near Savannah, Georgia) ▪ College of the Holy Cross; Yale Law School ▪ since 1991 ▪ by George H. W. Bush ▪ very conservative ▪ additional information: the second African American U.S. Supreme Court Justice
   <u>Stephen G. Breyer:</u> born in 1938 (in San Francisco, California) ▪ Stanford University, Magdalen College Oxford (UK); Harvard Law School ▪ since 1994 ▪ by Bill Clinton ▪ liberal ▪ additional information: retired from the Supreme Court on 30 June 2022
   <u>Samuel A. Alito, Jr.:</u> born in 1950 (in Trenton, New Jersey) ▪ Princeton University; Yale Law School ▪ since 2006 ▪ by George W. Bush ▪ conservative ▪ additional information: has opposed stricter gun regulations; wrote the majority opinion to overturn "Roe v Wade" (right to abortion) in 2022
   <u>Sonia Sotomayor:</u> born in 1954 (in Bronx, New York) ▪ Princeton University; Yale Law School ▪ since 2009 ▪ by Barack Obama ▪ liberal ▪ additional information: the third woman, first woman of colour, and the first Hispanic and Latina to serve on the Supreme Court

Elena Kagan: born in 1960 (in New York, New York) ▪ Princeton University; Oxford University (UK); Harvard Law School ▪ since 2010 ▪ by Barack Obama ▪ liberal ▪ additional information: the fourth woman to serve on the Supreme Court

Neil M. Gorsuch: born in 1967 (in Denver, Colorado) ▪ Columbia University; Harvard Law School; Oxford University (UK) ▪ since 2017 ▪ by Donald Trump ▪ conservative ▪ additional information: was the first Supreme Court Justice to serve together with a justice for whom he clerked in the past (Anthony Kennedy)

Brett M. Kavanaugh: born in 1965 (in Washington, D.C.) ▪ Yale College; Yale Law School ▪ since 2018 ▪ by Donald Trump ▪ conservative ▪ additional information: when asked about the accusations of sexual assault against him during his Supreme Court confirmation hearings he denied and talked about drinking habits in his youth

Amy Coney Barrett: born in 1972 (in New Orleans, Louisiana) ▪ Rhodes College; Notre Dame Law School ▪ since 2020 ▪ by Donald Trump ▪ conservative ▪ additional information: a practising Catholic; mother of seven children; was nominated by Trump only 38 days before the 2020 presidential election (after the death of liberal Justice Ruth Bader Ginsburg)

2. The cartoon "KBJ in SCOTUS MAGA Cave" was published by J.D. Crowe on 30 June 2022 in response to Ketanji Brown Jackson taking her seat on the U.S. Supreme Court that same day. It shows the nine current members of the Supreme Court sitting and standing in two rows as if posing for an official photograph. Front row, left to right: Sonia Sotomayor, Ketanji Brown Jackson, John Roberts, Clarence Thomas, Samuel Alito. Second row, left to right: Elena Kagan, Neil Gorsuch, Amy Coney Barrett, Brett Kavanaugh.

- On the left: the three liberal justices (Sotomayor, Kagan, Jackson) dressed in black robes → suggests they perform their task as Supreme Court justices in a professional way / with the necessary respect for the position
- On the right: five conservative justices (Gorsuch, Coney Barrett, Kavanaugh, Thomas, Alito), having dressed down, i.e., wearing a white undershirt (Brett Kavanaugh even wearing only a white sheet instead of an undershirt) and a red Trump base cap → The cartoonist suggests that these justices are not fulfilling their task with the respect one would expect of Supreme Court justices (especially not Kavanaugh) and are supporting Donald Trump's ideologies.
- Symbols: Barrett: wooden cross → staunch Catholic ▪ Alito: firearm → pro guns ▪ Kavanaugh: beer helmet → relating to his statements during his confirmation hearings: when asked about the accusations of sexual assault against him he denied and talked about drinking habits in his youth and mentioned several times that he liked beer
- Thomas: QAnon → reference to his wife Ginni Thomas, a conservative activist involved in conspiracy theories about voter fraud after the 2020 presidential elections
- In the centre: Chief Justice Roberts half wearing his robe, half showing his undershirt; no base cap → suggests that despite being a conservative, he also often tries to find a middle ground
- The cartoonist is caricaturing the prevailing situation in the once honourable Supreme Court that is now characterised by a majority of conservative justices and by controversies surrounding individual justices. Under these circumstances, it will not be easy for Jackson to do effective work at the Supreme Court.

Hinweise (M 3 und M 4)

3. Stunde

Ziel von **M 3** und **M 4** ist der Erwerb von Orientierungswissen über das System der Bundesgerichte in den USA und über Ketanji Brown Jackson anhand eines BBC-Podcast.

Methodische Hinweise

M 3 dient der inhaltlichen und sprachlichen Vorentlastung des Podcast (*Federal Court System* der USA; Wortschatz zum Themenfeld „Jura/Recht"). **M 4** dient der Erarbeitung des Podcasts, den die Lernenden auf ihren digitalen Endgeräten (wie zum Beispiel auf Ihren Smartphones) hören. Wenn möglich mit Kopfhörern, da dies ihnen ermöglicht, Teile des Podcasts in individuellem Tempo mehrfach anzuhören. In Partnerarbeit vergleichen und ergänzen die Lernenden ihre Erträge. M 4 eignet sich auch gut für das häusliche Arbeiten. Die Lösungen sollten anschließend im Unterricht bereitgestellt/besprochen werden

Digitalhinweis (M 3)

Task 2 liegt auch digital in *LearningApps* vor und ist mit Konto bearbeitbar („ähnliche App erstellen" anklicken):

https://learningapps.org/display?v=pm8rxp9pc22

Hausaufgabe

Falls während der Stunde noch nicht geschehen, stellen die Lernenden in Vorbereitung auf die Folgestunde ihr Akrostichon zu „KETANJI BROWN JACKSON" fertig, welches sie zu Beginn der nächsten Stunde vorstellen.

Erwartungshorizont (M 3)

1. 1G, 2D, 3N, 4I, 5E, 6K, 7P. 8M, 9O. 10A, 11L, 12B, 13C, 14F, 15J, 16H

Erwartungshorizont (M 4)

1.–3. **1)** 233 ▪ **2)** predominantly African American attorneys and judges. ▪ **3)** the first Black woman to be admitted to the bar in America ▪ **4a)** Jackson was born in Washington, D.C. in December 1970; was raised in Miami; the eldest of two children ▪ **4b)** her parents came of age in times of segregation; her mother was an administrator at a school; her father was a history teacher, he went to law school at night and became a lawyer; young Jackson watched him study as a child, and he became her first professional role model; two of her uncles and her brother were/are police officers ▪ **4c)** Jackson excelled at school; she was elected class president; she became a debating champion; her childhood friend Stephen Rosenthal recalls meeting Jackson for the first time when they were both 12 (in 1982): she had a big smile, was incredibly friendly, very smart, a living legend, she won tournaments at state level and national level ▪ **5)** not to set her dreams so high ▪ **6)** she participated in the protest but then said to her friends that the best way to protest is to go to the library and study ▪ **7)** she was a member of a comedy group ▪ **8)** he is white and from an elite Boston family ▪ **9)** she took a year off, worked for the Time Magazine, enrolled at Harvard Law School, became an editor of the prestigious Harvard Law Review ▪ **10)** in 1996 ▪ **11a)** She clerked for two judges; ▪ **11b)** Supreme Court justice Stephen Breyer; ▪ **11c)** She juggled <u>raising her family / two daughters</u> with <u>legal work</u>, served as a <u>public defender</u> for a while, went into <u>private practice</u>, at one point representing a number of prisoners detained at Guantanamo Bay. ▪ **11d)** From 2010–2014, she was Vice Chair of the U.S. Sentencing Commission. Republicans accuse her of being soft on crime because: she cut sentences for 30,000 prisoners in jail for drug crimes; she was too lenient with child pornography offenders. ▪ **11e)** In 2013, Ketanji Brown Jackson became a judge on the U.S. District Court. Thomas B. Griffith says Ketanji Brown Jackson was widely admired around the courthouse for her diligence, care, attention to detail. ▪ **11f)** she wrote a letter to President Obama asking him to add her mother to the list ▪ **11g)** she delivered several high-profile rulings against the Trump administration, including one in 2019 about immunity from testifying into alleged Russian election interference; she famously declared: "Presidents are not kings" ▪ **11h)** 2021 ▪ **12)** to nominate a Black woman for the Supreme Court ▪ **13)** Jackson is opening a door that did not exist for Black women lawyers before this time; Keanan is hopeful that Jackson will be judged not by what she looks like but by the content of her characters, on her integrity and her ability to fulfil the duties of a Supreme Court justice.

1. Individual results. For example:

"Presidents are not **K** ings"	Stephen **B** reyer	**J** oe Biden
excell **E** nt	Pat **R** ick	d **A** ughters
deba **T** ing	c **O** medy	**C** lass president
Harv **A** rd	la **W** yer	Blac **K** student association
hard-worki **N** g	public defe **N** der	fir **S** t
J ustice		district c **O** urt
Miam **I**		intellige **N** t

....

4./5. Stunde

Hinweise (M 5–M 8)

Ziel von **M 5**–**M 8** ist die Erarbeitung von Wissen zur Ernennung von Ketanji Brown Jackson als Richterin am *Supreme Court*.

Methodische Hinweise
Zu Beginn der Stunde stellen die Lernenden ihre zu Hause verfassten Akrosticha über Ketanji Brown Jackson vor. **M 5** und **M 6** dienen der Verständnissicherung. Als Zusatzaufgabe ist in *task 2* eine schriftliche Inhaltsangabe des Auszugs zu verfassen.
In der Vertiefungsphase folgt ausgehend von einem im Rahmen des *Black History Month* erschienenen Audiobeitrags eine Auseinandersetzung der Lernenden mit „*representation*" und „*firsts*" (**M 8**).

Erwartungshorizont (M 5)

1. Individual results.
2.

		true	false	line(s)
a)	Ketanji Brown Jackson does not want to be seen as a role model.		X	ll. 8/9
b)	Jackson's role models are hard-working people from past generations aspiring to create something better for themselves and their families.	X		ll. 9–16
c)	Education was very important to Ketanji Brown Jackson's grandparents.	X		ll. 13–16
d)	Ketanji Brown Jackson was the first person in her family to go to college.		X	ll. 14–16
e)	She says that her professional success is only due to the achievements of past generations.		X	ll. 23–25
f)	Jackson is convinced that the confirmation of the first Black female Supreme Court Justice is something that white Americans should be proud of, too.	X		ll. 28–29

Corrections:
a) Ketanji Brown Jackson sees it as both opportunity and responsibility, and she feels up to the task.
d) Her parents were the first in their families to go to college.
e) She says that past generations cleared the way for her and "did the heavy lifting" (l. 20) that made that day possible. → "The path was cleared for me so I might rise to this occasion" (l. 25). But to get to this point of her career, she also had to work very hard.

Erwartungshorizont (M 6)

1. Individual results. For example:

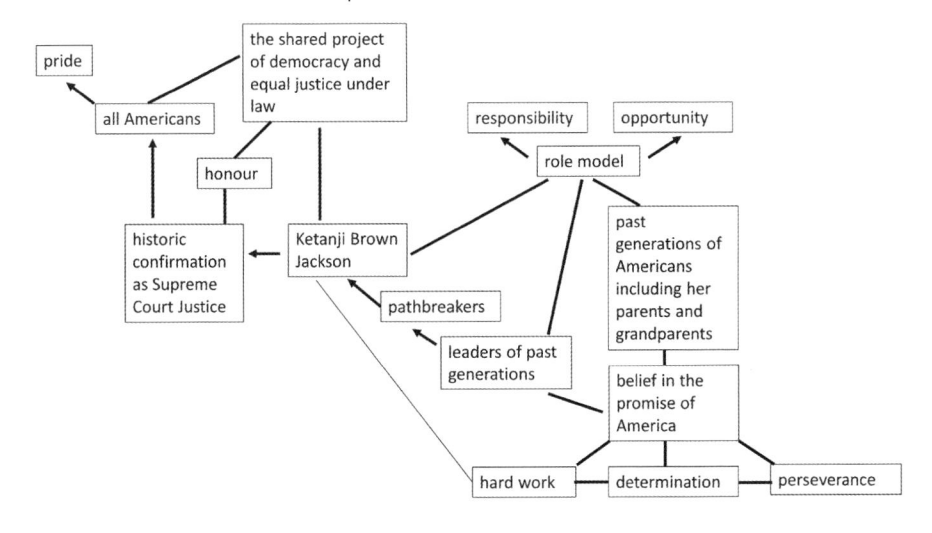

2. In the final part of her speech delivered on 8 April 2022, Ketanji Brown Jackson states that the confirmation of the first Black female Supreme Court justice is of historic importance for the country because it shows that anything is possible in America.

She is ready to be a role model to others because she feels encouraged and supported by her own role models.

Though making clear that she worked hard to get to this point of her career, Jackson points out that she owes this historic moment to the pathbreaking African American leaders of past generations without whose work and efforts she would never have achieved this.

She makes clear that the confirmation of the first Black female U.S. Supreme Court justice should be a moment of pride for all Americans and concludes by saying that she takes on her new role as Supreme Court Justice with great honour.

Erwartungshorizont (M 7)

Partner A: The cartoon "A new Justice" was published by Adam Zyglis on 9 April 2022 in response to Ketanji Brown Jackson's Supreme Court confirmation on 8 April. It shows the arm and hand of a white man wearing a white long-sleeve shirt underneath a stars-and-stripes jacket holding a newspaper with the headline, "Today, Supreme Court looks a little more like America", featuring a photograph of Ketanji Brown Jackson. In the top left-hand corner of the cartoon, a sign is showing the word "Confirmed".

The cartoonist criticises the fact that the Supreme Court does not reflect the population of the USA. (Of the 115 Supreme Court justices who have served since 1789, only seven have not been white men). He celebrates Ketanji Brown Jackson's confirmation as the first Black female U.S. Supreme Court Justice as a step towards more diversity and representation.

Partner B: The cartoon "Ketanji Brown Jackson" was published by Joe Heller on 8 April 2022 in response to Ketanji Brown Jackson's Supreme Court confirmation that same day. It shows a little Black girl taking a selfie with her phone in front of a big TV screen showing Jackson and the headline "Ketanji Brown Jackson makes history". On the right-hand side, a Black man and woman (supposedly the girl's parents) are sitting on a couch watching the girl and smiling. Above the scene there is a sign with the word "Confirmation".

The cartoon highlights Ketanji Brown Jackson's function as a role model and the fact that her historic confirmation will have a positive impact on young girls / women of colour: By seeing another woman of colour in a position of power, they gain confidence in their own abilities.

Erwartungshorizont (M 8)

1. **a)** "Maybe you just got appointed because you're Black?" ▪ **b)** "I would rather be appointed because I'm Black than not be appointed because I'm Black." ▪ **c)** five; three ▪ **d)** women; poor people; people of colour ▪ **e)** It moves the nation a little closer to fulfilling its promise. ▪ **f)** envisioning yourself in power ▪ **g)** because there is a conservative supermajority that seems intent on overturning major civil rights rulings ▪ **h)** that one day an appointment like this (of Ketanji Brown Jackson) is not considered history-making / that we get to the point that it is not so significant that a Black woman is appointed to some prestigious position ▪ **i)** it diminishes their remarkable accomplishments; it creates this false impression that somebody will rule a certain way just because they are Black ▪ **j)** nine
2. Individual results. Students might mention the following aspects:
   Arguments from the podcast: it is important not to sum up a person by their race and

gender because it (1) diminishes their individual accomplishments and (2) creates the false impression that somebody will rule a certain way because of their race. Diversity is important to change the system in the long run because we have not yet reached the point Brown-Nagin mentions in the podcast, "where it's not so significant that a Black woman is appointed to some prestigious position"

Arguments by Cordell: a representational democracy must reflect its people; it is important that people of different backgrounds are in positions of power → exchange of ideas; different perspectives on issues → enriching and more effective

Argument by Russell: "firsts" open up what future generations believe is possible: "When you see someone [in power], after an entire life of never seeing anyone who looks like you, it transforms your idea of the possibilities of what that institution could be and in what you as a person can be"; …

3. Individual results. Students might mention the following aspects:
promote diversity and representation → they are hugely meaningful; try to reduce the causes of inequities in the USA (which are, however, very complex and ingrained in history and society) → a lot needs to be done to bring about positive change in the system and move towards a more equal society (e.g. regarding health care, education, immigration, the economy, criminal justice system, voting rights); try to unite the divided country

RAAbits

**Impulse und Materialien
für die kreative Unterrichtsgestaltung**

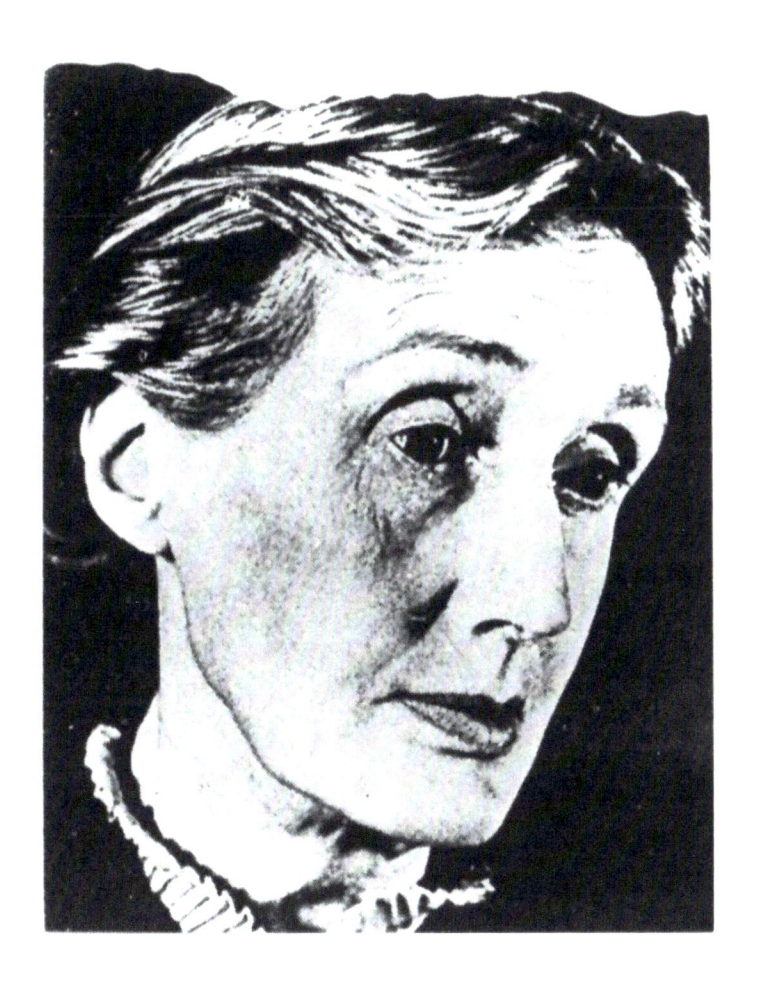

ENGLISCH

S II

RAABE
NACHSCHLAGEN – FINDEN
Ein Unternehmen der Klett Gruppe

RAAbits
Impulse und Materialien für die kreative Unterrichtsgestaltung

Englisch

Sekundarstufe II

Dr. Josef Raabe Verlags-GmbH
Ein Unternehmen der Klett Gruppe

Dr. Josef Raabe Verlags-GmbH
Rotebühlstraße 77, 70178 Stuttgart
Postfach 10 39 22, 70034 Stuttgart
Telefon (0711) 6 29 00-0, Telefax: (0711) 6 29 00-10

Die Deutsche Bibliothek – CIP-Einheitsaufnahme
RAAbits: Impulse und Materialien für die kreative
Unterrichtsgestaltung. – Stuttgart: Raabe. – Losebl.-Ausg.

Englisch, Sekundarstufe II
Grundwerk
ISBN 978-3-8183-0091-3

© 1994 Dr. Josef Raabe Verlags-GmbH, Stuttgart

Das Werk einschließlich aller seiner Teile ist urheberrechtlich geschützt. Jede Verwertung außerhalb der engen Grenzen des Urheberrechtsgesetzes ist ohne Zustimmung des Verlages unzulässig und strafbar. Dies gilt insbesondere für Vervielfältigungen, Übersetzungen, Mikroverfilmungen und die Einspeicherung und Verarbeitung in elektronischen Systemen.

Redaktionsleitung:	Dagmar Storck
Redaktion:	Dagmar Storck, Juliane Thon, Stefanie Schultze
Redaktionelle Mitarbeit:	Ellen Black, Chris Smeeton, Johanna Stotz, Glyn Thomas
Beraterin:	Ilona Königsfeld
Umschlaggestaltung:	MDM Mungenast Direktmarketing GmbH
	Hintergrundphotographie: Skyline New York. © Bavaria Bildagentur
	Einklinker: Virginia Woolf. © AKG Berlin
Satz:	Textdruck Michaela Rother, Altlußheim

Printed in Germany
ISSN 0946-5294
ISBN 978-3-8183-0091-3

Für jedes Material wurden Rechte nachgefragt. Sollten dennoch an einzelnen Materialien weitere Rechte bestehen, bitten wir um Benachrichtigung.

Gedruckt auf chlorfrei gebleichtem Papier.

RAABE
Stuttgart
Bratislava · Budapest · Prag · Sofia

Inhaltsübersicht

Vorwort

Hinweise zur Benutzung

Verzeichnis der Ergänzungslieferungen

Teil II: Sekundarstufe II

Literatur

B. 2	Novels
B. 2.15	*Suzanne Collins' „The Hunger Games" – Anhand eines dystopischen Romans auf mündliche Prüfungen vorbereiten*
B. 2.17	*T. C. Boyles „The Tortilla Curtain" – Die Konflikte zwischen illegalen mexikanischen Einwanderern und Amerikanern nachvollziehen*
B. 3	Plays and Radio Plays
B. 3.7	*Introducing Shakespeare – Den literarischen Superstar für Schüler heute erfahrbar machen*

Landeskunde

C. 4	Political Life in Great Britain
C. 4.3	*British Monarchy and Modern Democracy: Reality Meets Fiction – Auszüge aus Alan Bennetts „The Uncommon Reader" mit landeskundlichem Wissen erschließen*
C. 5	Political Life in the USA
C. 5.6	*From Rags to Riches? – The American Dream Revisited – Eine Landeskundereihe für die Oberstufe*
C. 7	Divisions and Groupings in Society
C. 7.3	*East is East – Interkulturelle Erfahrungen im Spiegel eines Films*

Teil V: Unterrichtsmagazin

195.	*How to Improve Your Writing Style – Methodentraining für die Klassen 10–13*
203.	*„Where's the boy for me?" – Die handlungsorientierte Erarbeitung einer Short Story unter Einführung abiturrelevanter Aufgabenformate*
211.	*Our Blue Planet – Our Changing World: Materialien zur Durchführung einer mündlichen Prüfung in der Einführungsphase*
215.	*Let's talk! – Mit speaking cards die Sprechfertigkeit fördern*

Inhaltsübersicht

Vorwort

Liebe Lehrerinnen, liebe Lehrer,

die stetig wachsenden Anforderungen unserer Kommunikations- und Informationsgesellschaft stellen auch den Fremdsprachenunterricht vor ständig neue Herausforderungen: Aus einer Fülle von Informationen müssen Sie tagtäglich neue Themen sowie schülergerechte und motivierende Materialien auswählen und für Ihren Unterricht aufbereiten. Zwangsläufig gestaltet sich die Unterrichtsvorbereitung immer anspruchsvoller und damit auch zeitraubender.

RAAbits Englisch bietet Ihnen für diese Problematik eine unkomplizierte und vielfach erprobte Lösung.

Welche Vorteile bietet Ihnen RAAbits Englisch?

Da ist zunächst einmal die **Form**. RAAbits verbindet die Vorteile einer **Loseblattsammlung** mit den Möglichkeiten bewährter Lehrerhandreichungen: Themenvielfalt, Aktualität, Ergänzbarkeit und Systematik. Somit finden Sie alle unverzichtbaren Voraussetzungen für eine effektive Unterrichtsvorbereitung in einem Werk vereint.

Da ist aber auch der **Aufbau**. Anhand zahlreicher Gespräche mit Lehrerinnen und Lehrern aus verschiedenen Bundesländern wurden Anregungen und Wünsche ermittelt, die von uns in Zusammenarbeit mit Muttersprachlern in ein Gesamtkonzept umgesetzt wurden, das folgende Bereiche umfasst:

- **Unterrichtsreihen** zu lehrplanrelevanten Themen, deren Schwerpunkt auf einem umfangreichen Materialteil liegt;
- Vorschläge zum **projektorientierten Unterricht** in der Form fächerübergreifender Unterrichtsreihen oder „reiner" Projekte, wie sie die neuen Richtlinien in zunehmendem Maße fordern;
- aktuelle und flexibel einsetzbare **Einzelmaterialien** für maximal drei Unterrichtsstunden, die Sie zur Auflockerung bzw. Vertiefung der Lehrbucharbeit, zur „Überbrückung" zwischen zwei thematischen Schwerpunkten oder einfach mal zwischendurch einsetzen können;

Alle Materialien sind mit Arbeitsaufträgen, Hinweisen zur methodischen Umsetzung und einem Erwartungshorizont in der Fremdsprache versehen. An welchen Stellen sich die jeweiligen Materialien in das Unterrichtskonzept einfügen, können Sie der schematischen Verlaufsübersicht entnehmen. Selbstverständlich haben Sie aber auch die Möglichkeit, hier individuell und mit Blick auf Ihre Lerngruppe zu variieren und eigene Schwerpunkte zu setzen. Das Ergebnis ist ein moderner und kreativer Englischunterricht – verbunden mit optimaler und effektiver Vorbereitung.

Vorwort

Als weiteren Service bieten wir Ihnen Vorschläge für **Klassenarbeiten** und **Klausuren**, stellen in der Rubrik *„Kontext"* Anregungen für eine Erweiterung des Unterrichtsgegenstandes bereit und geben in der *„Mediothek"* hilfreiche Tipps für weiterführende Literatur, Internetadressen und andere Medien.

Ob Sie gerade Ihr Referendariat absolvieren, erst seit kurzer Zeit unterrichten oder aber einfach auf der Suche nach neuen Impulsen für Ihren Unterricht sind:

RAAbits – Impulse und Materialien für die kreative Unterrichtsgestaltung hilft Ihnen Ihre Zeit effektiver zu nutzen, hält Sie auf dem aktuellen Stand der Dinge und unterstützt Ihre Kreativität.

Zu guter Letzt noch zwei grundsätzliche Dinge, auf die wir Sie hinweisen möchten:

Auch wenn wir bemüht sind, den Beiträgen eine möglichst einheitliche Gestaltung zu verleihen, so hat doch jeder Gegenstand seine spezifischen Bedürfnisse und muss entsprechend vorgestellt werden. Unterschiedliche Präsentationsformen beruhen also auf „Sachzwängen."

Und: Jede Lehrerin bzw. jeder Lehrer favorisiert einen oder mehrere didaktische Ansätze. RAAbits Englisch bietet in dieser Hinsicht Vielfalt und Ausgewogenheit, so dass Sie sowohl kognitiv ausgerichtete Unterrichtsentwürfe vorfinden als auch solche, die stärker handlungs- und produktionsorientiert ausgerichtet sind. Denn unser Ziel ist es, Abwechslung in Ihren Unterrichtsalltag zu bringen und Sie dabei zugleich in Ihrer täglichen Arbeit zu unterstützen.

Der Verlag

Hinweise zur Benutzung

1. Wie ist *RAAbits Englisch* aufgebaut?

RAAbits Englisch ist eine Loseblattsammlung, die regelmäßig ergänzt und aktualisiert wird. Sobald ein Ordner gefüllt ist, können Sie mit der folgenden Ergänzungslieferung einen neuen Ordner bestellen.

Der Aufbau von RAAbits Englisch gewährleistet eine schnelle und mühelose Handhabung, wenn folgendes beachtet wird:

1.1. Die erste Gliederungsebene: Teil I bis Teil VI

RAAbits Englisch ist in sechs Teile gegliedert, die durch römische Ziffern gekennzeichnet sind:

– Teil I
 Sekundarstufe I
– Teil II
 Sekundarstufe II
– Teil III
 Projektorientierter Unterricht
– Teil IV
 Bilingualer Unterricht
– Teil V
 Unterrichtsmagazin

1.2. Die zweite Gliederungsebene: Themenbereiche

Die Teile I bis III sind in einzelne Themenbereiche untergliedert. Die Gliederungspunkte sind jeweils durch einen Großbuchstaben gekennzeichnet.

Eine Übersicht über diese Bereiche finden Sie links auf der inneren Umschlagseite des Ordners.

Teil I (S I) und Teil II (S II) sind in die gängigen Großthemen des Fachbereichs Englisch gegliedert.

Die beiden Gliederungspunkte von Teil III entsprechen den Organisationsformen des projektorientierten Arbeitens an der Schule.

Teil IV ist im aktuellen Grundwerk nicht abgedeckt. Für das Fach Geschichte gibt es ein gesondertes Produkt, RAAbits Bilingual Geschichte.

Teil V, das Unterrichtsmagazin, umfasst kompakte, flexibel einsetzbare Einzelmaterialien für maximal drei Unterrichtsstunden, die zur Auflockerung bzw. Vertiefung der Lehrbucharbeit oder einfach zwischendurch eingesetzt werden können.

RAAbits Englisch

Hinweise zur Benutzung

Beispiel:

I/E I = Teil I = Sekundarstufe I / E = Landeskunde

III/B III = Teil III = Projektorientierter Unterricht / B = Projekte

1.3. Dritte Gliederungsebene: Kapitel innerhalb der Themen

Die meisten Themenbereiche sind aus inhaltlichen Gründen und im Interesse einer größeren Systematik in fortlaufend nummerierte Kapitel untergliedert.

Beispiel:

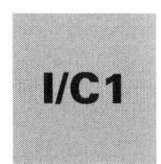

I/C1 I = Teil I / C = Lektüren, Lieder und Sachtexte / 1 = Novels and Stories

1.4. Kennzeichnung und Aufbau der Beiträge

Jedes Kapitel bzw. jeder Themenbereich umfasst mehrere Beiträge. Die Beiträge sind fortlaufend nummeriert.

Jeder Beitrag und jede Seite in RAAbits Englisch hat eine Signatur, die deren Platz in der Loseblattsammlung kennzeichnet. Diese Signatur besteht aus einem so genannten Tab (graues Rechteck am äußeren Rand jeder Seite) und dem so genannten Balken (grau, am oberen Rand jeder Seite).

Die Informationen im Tab betreffen die ersten drei Gliederungsebenen:

Beispiel:

II/B II = Teil II / B = Literatur

Hinweise zur Benutzung

Die Informationen im Balken betreffen den Aufbau eines jeden Beitrages. Die Beiträge der Teile I, II und III/A werden als Reihen bezeichnet. Alle Reihen für die S I und S II sind weitgehend identisch aufgebaut.

Beispiel für eine Reihe aus Teil I oder II:

Introducing Shakespeare					
Reihe 7	**Verlauf** S 1	**Material**	**LEK**	**Kontext**	**Mediothek**

Erläuterung des Balkens:

Im durchgehenden Balken wird der Kurztitel der Reihe auf jeder Seite genannt. Die Beschriftung im ersten Kästchen des Balkens bedeutet in unserem Beispiel, dass diese Reihe die zweite Reihe zu dem Themenbereich ist, der im Tab ausgewiesen ist.

Das zweite Kästchen des Balkens („Verlauf") signalisiert, dass hier die Verlaufsübersicht zur Reihe sowie zu den einzelnen Unterrichtsstunden gegeben wird.

Die einzelnen Teile einer Reihe sind jeweils mit einer Seitenzählung versehen. Als visuelle Orientierungshilfe sind immer jene Teile im Balken dunkel hinterlegt, in denen Sie sich befinden.

Beispiel:

Introducing Shakespeare					
Reihe 7	**Verlauf**	**Material** S 1	**LEK**	**Kontext**	**Mediothek**

Erläuterung:

Sie befinden sich auf Seite 1 des Materialteils der Reihe 7.

Die schematische Verlaufsübersicht und die Stundenübersichten schließen an das didaktisch-methodische Konzept an.

Dem Materialteil ist eine Materialübersicht vorangestellt, der eine mit Arbeitsaufträgen versehene Zusammenstellung des Materials folgt.

Den Stundenübersichten können Sie die Zuordnung der Materialien zu den einzelnen Phasen entnehmen.

Vorschläge zu Lernerfolgskontrollen, zusätzliche Informationen zum Unterrichtsgegenstand („Kontext") und eine Mediothek komplettieren die Reihe.

Hinweise zur Benutzung

2. Wie finden Sie, was Sie suchen?

Wenn Sie eine Reihe zu einem bestimmten Thema suchen, sollten Sie die **Inhaltsübersicht** aufschlagen. Dort werden alle Themenbereiche und Kapitel mit den bereits erschienenen Reihen genannt.

ABKÜRZUNGEN

Die Abkürzungen beziehen sich ausschließlich auf den Materialteil.

M	Material
Ab	Arbeitsblatt
Bd	Bildliche Darstellung
Co	Überprüfung des Hör- bzw. Leseverstehens *(comprehension)*
Gd	Graphische Darstellung
Ha	Hausaufgabenstellung
Hö	Hörbeispiel
Im	Gesprächs- bzw. Handlungsimpuls
Ka	Karte
Sch	Schülerbeispiel
Tb	Tafelbild
Tx	Text
Üb	Übung zu Wortschatz oder Grammatik
Vi	Film und Video
Wo	Wortschatzliste

Verzeichnis der Ergänzungslieferungen

Bitte sortieren Sie die Ergänzungslieferungen regelmäßig ein. Nur so wird der systematische Aufbau gewährleistet.

Zur besseren Übersicht empfehlen wir Ihnen, jede neue Nachlieferung auf diesem Kontrollblatt zu vermerken. Legen Sie die Blätter entsprechend der jeweiligen Einordnungsanleitung im Ordner ein.

Kontrollblatt				
Ergänzungs-lieferungen	Monat/ Jahr	Bemerkungen	Erledigungsvermerk	
			eingeordnet am:	Hand-zeichen

RAAbits Englisch

Verzeichnis der Ergänzungslieferungen

Kontrollblatt				
Ergänzungs-lieferungen	Monat/Jahr	Bemerkungen	Erledigungsvermerk	
			eingeordnet am:	Hand-zeichen

RAAbits Englisch

Suzanne Collins' „The Hunger Games" (S II)

Reihe 15 S 1 | Verlauf | Material | LEK | Kontext | Mediothek

Suzanne Collins' „*The Hunger Games*" – Anhand eines dystopischen Romans auf mündliche Prüfungen vorbereiten (S II)

Verena Enajite, Köln

II/B2

Auf CD:
- ✓ Word-Datei
- ✓ Kopiervorlage für reading log
- ✓ Fragebogen zum Vergleich Buch/Film
- ✓ zusätzliches Bildmaterial in Farbe

Werden Katniss und Peeta die *Hunger Games* gewinnen?

"The rules [...] are simple. [E]ach of the twelve districts must provide one girl and one boy, called tributes, to participate. Over a period of several weeks, the competitors must fight to the death. The last tribute standing wins." Finden Sie gemeinsam mit Ihren Schülern heraus, in welcher Gesellschaft ein solches Spiel veranstaltet wird und was dessen Hintergründe sind.

Nutzen Sie den unter Jugendlichen äußerst populären Roman aber nicht nur zur klassischen Textanalyse, sondern auch dazu, lebensweltnahe Themen wie „Familie", „Liebe", „Armut" und „Reality-TV" zu behandeln. Die Verfilmung bietet zudem die Möglichkeit des Vergleichs mit der Romanvorlage. Nebenbei werden Ihre Schüler durch zahlreiche Sprechanlässe und in konkreten Übungen auf die neuen mündlichen Prüfungsformate vorbereitet.

Klassenstufe: 10–12

Dauer: ca. 13 Unterrichtsstunden

Bereich: Roman, *Young Adult Literature*, *Visions of the Future – Exploring Alternative Worlds, Utopia–Dystopia*, Themen „*Social Classes*", „*Poverty*", „*Media*", „*Love*", „*Friendship*"

Kompetenzen:
1. Kommunikative Kompetenz: klares und detailliertes Darstellen themenbezogener Sachverhalte im mündlichen Sprachgebrauch; 2. Lesekompetenz: Verstehen eines längeren und komplexen literarischen Texts; 3. Hör-Seh-Verstehen: Verstehen umfangreicher audiovisueller Medien

Suzanne Collins' „The Hunger Games" (S II)

Sachanalyse

Zur Autorin und ihrem Werk

Suzanne Collins wurde 1962 im US-Bundestaat Connecticut geboren. Ihr Roman *„The Hunger Games"* erschien 2008. Die Idee hierfür kam der Autorin, als sie im Fernsehen eine **Reality-TV-Show** und die Besetzung des Iraks durch das US-amerikanische Militär sah. Beides verknüpfte sich in ihrer Fantasie zum Thema für ihren Roman – der medialen Darstellung von Kämpfen auf Leben und Tod. Als weitere Einflüsse auf ihr Werk nennt sie die Legende des griechischen **Sagenhelden Theseus** und die **Gladiatorenkämpfe** im antiken Rom.

„The Hunger Games" ist der erste Teil einer **Trilogie**. Das zweite Buch *„Catching Fire"* erschien ein Jahr darauf und der letzte Roman der Serie 2010 unter dem Titel *„Mockingjay"*. Alle drei Bücher wurden zu einem großen kommerziellen Erfolg. So war *„The Hunger Games"* 60 Wochen am Stück auf Platz eins der ***„New-York-Times"*-Bestsellerliste**.

Zum Inhalt des Romans

Die 16-jährige **Katniss Everdeen, die Heldin des Romans,** lebt im **armen Distrikt 12 in Panem**, einem fiktiven Land, das in Nordamerika liegt. Panem, das nach einer **Apokalypse** entstanden ist, wird durch die Hauptstadt **Capitol** beherrscht und kontrolliert. Als Erinnerung an die sogenannten *Dark Days*, in denen sich ein Distrikt gegen das Regime der Metropole auflehnte, werden jedes Jahr die **Hunger Games** veranstaltet. Das Capitol stellt so seine uneingeschränkte Macht zur Schau und wirkt Aufständen aus der Bevölkerung entgegen. Bei den Spielen müssen aus jedem Distrikt Panems ein Junge und ein Mädchen im Alter von 12 bis 18 Jahren antreten. Diese sogenannten *tributes* sind dazu gezwungen, in einer kameraüberwachten Arena gegeneinander **auf Leben und Tod zu** kämpfen. Nur einer kann die Arena als Sieger verlassen. Der Rest der Nation verfolgt dieses Ereignis als **Unterhaltungsshow** an den Fernsehgeräten.

Für die 74. *Hunger Games* treten Katniss Everdeen und **Peeta Mellark** für Distrikt 12 an. Noch bevor Katniss und Peeta in die Arena ziehen, gesteht Peeta in einer TV-Show seine **Liebe zu Katniss**. Das Geständnis macht diese wütend, da sie dahinter eine Taktik vermutet, durch die Peeta versucht, **Sponsoren** für die Spiele zu gewinnen. Die Sponsoren versorgen favorisierte Tribute mit Lebensmitteln, Medikamenten und Werkzeugen, die in der Wildnis der Arena überlebenswichtig sein können.

Katniss und Peeta schaffen es, bis zum Finale zu überleben. Eine **Regeländerung** erlaubt zunächst, dass beide als Sieger aus den Spielen hervorgehen können. Diese wird jedoch im letzten Moment widerrufen, um die beiden in einem dramatischen Finale gegeneinander aufzubringen. Indem Katniss und Peeta beschließen, gemeinsam Selbstmord zu begehen, bringen sie das Capitol schließlich dazu, doch beide zu **Siegern** zu erklären. Obwohl ihnen ein gebührender Empfang bereitet wird, gilt Katniss aufgrund des geplanten Suizids fortan als Staatsfeindin.

Zu den zentralen Themen des Romans

Unterdrückung und Machtmissbrauch sind zentrale Themen des Romans. Die totalitäre Regierung der dystopischen Gesellschaft Panems übt mit der jährlichen Veranstaltung der *Hunger Games* Druck auf die Bevölkerung aus. Unter allen Umständen gilt es, Überlegenheit zu demonstrieren und Aufstände im Keim zu ersticken. Damit diese Botschaft auch bei allen Bewohnern ankommt, werden die Spiele in Form eines brutalen und geschmacklosen **Reality-TV-Events** live übertragen.

Suzanne Collins' „The Hunger Games" (S II)

Reihe 15 S 3

Aufstände wären eine nachvollziehbare Reaktion auf die Spiele und das **soziale Ungleichgewicht**, das zwischen den verschiedenen Distrikten herrscht, in die sich Panem gliedert. In **Armut** aufgewachsen, schlägt sich die Protagonistin Katniss tapfer durch ihren Alltag und die *Hunger Games*. Dabei werden auch für Teenager relevante Themen wie die widersprüchlichen Gefühle, die Katniss für Gale und Peeta empfindet, oder die **Liebe** zu ihrer jüngeren Schwester Prim aufgegriffen.

Textausgabe: Collins, Suzanne: The Hunger Games. Stuttgart: Ernst Klett Sprachen 2013. Annotierte Ausgabe mit Zusatztexten. Preis: 8,99 €.

Zur Verfilmung des Romans

Der auf der Romanvorlage basierende **Science-Fiction-Film** wurde von Mai bis September 2011 in den USA gedreht. **Regie** führte dabei der Drehbuchautor und Regisseur **Gary Ross** (*„Pleasantville"*). Suzanne Collins arbeitete am **Drehbuch** mit. So wurde gewährleistet, dass viele Elemente ihrer Geschichte umgesetzt wurden. Dennoch wurden auch Änderungen und einige Kürzungen vorgenommen (vgl. M 14).

Die Verfilmung hatte im Mai **2012** sowohl in den USA als auch in Deutschland Premiere und spielte bereits bis September 2012 über 686 Millionen US-Dollar ein. In den Vereinigten Staaten ist *„The Hunger Games"* auf Platz 13 der erfolgreichsten Filme. Die Fortsetzungen werden jeweils im Herbst 2013 bis 2015 erscheinen.

Film (deutsche Filmausgabe mit Originalversion und Untertiteln): „Die Tribute von Panem – The Hunger Games" (USA 2012), Regie: Gary Ross.

Verfilmung des Romans mit Jennifer Lawrence (Oscar-Gewinnerin für ihre Rolle in *„Silver Linings Playbook"*) und Josh Hutcherson (*„Little Manhattan"*) in den Hauptrollen. Erhältlich z. B. bei www.amazon.de für ca. 7,97 €.

II/B2

Didaktisch-methodisches Konzept

Zur Lerngruppe

Diese Unterrichtsreihe eignet sich vor allem für die **Einführungsphase** in die Oberstufe oder für **Grundkurse**. Hier wurde sie bereits erfolgreich eingesetzt.

Es wird vorausgesetzt, dass die Schülerinnen und Schüler mit englischsprachigen Ganzschriften vertraut sind und diese eigenständig in Hausarbeit lesen können.

Zum Aufbau und den Methoden

Im Zentrum der Einheit steht sowohl die Förderung der sprachlichen Kompetenz anhand **kommunikativer Aufgabentypen** als auch die Auseinandersetzung mit den Figuren des Romans in klassischen **Analyseaufgaben**. Beides bereitet die Lernenden schrittweise auf die mündlichen Prüfungen am Ende der Reihe vor. So diskutieren sie gleich zu Beginn der Einheit in einer *pyramid discussion* **(M 2)**, was zum Überleben in der Wildnis notwendig ist, oder bereiten die **Präsentation einzelner Charaktere** unter Prüfungsbedingungen vor (7. Stunde).

Zuvor verschaffen sie sich jedoch durch das Erstellen einer *character map* **(M 8)** einen Überblick über die Personenkonstellationen und erarbeiten anhand einer *concept map* **(M 6)** wesentliche Zusammenhänge des Romans.

Durch die Methode *„good angel – bad angel"* **(M 12)** machen sie sich den Konflikt bewusst, in dem sich besonders Katniss am Ende der *Hunger Games* befindet.

Suzanne Collins' „The Hunger Games" (S II)

| Reihe 15 S 4 | Verlauf | Material | LEK | Kontext | Mediothek |

Die Reihe endet mit einer Vorbereitungsstunde für die mündlichen Prüfungen, in der ein **mock exam (M 15)** durchgeführt wird.

Zum Leseprozess

Das Lesen der Lektüre wird vorab als **Hausaufgabe** aufgegeben. Als Zeitrahmen hierfür eignen sich ca. **zwei Wochen** (z. B. Oster-, Herbst- oder Weihnachtsferien). Die erste Stunde dieser Reihe sollte allerdings **am letzten Tag vor den Ferien** durchgeführt werden, da in dieser auf den Roman neugierig gemacht wird. Das Gelesene wird durch das Führen eines **Lesetagebuches (M 3)** zusammengefasst und durch einen **Textkenntnistest (M 4)** überprüft.

Ein **mögliches Problem** könnte sein, dass einige Schülerinnen und Schüler das Buch bzw. den Film bereits kennen. Es ist daher wichtig zu vermitteln, dass es Unterschiede zwischen Roman und Filmversion gibt und dass es nötig ist, die englische Originalversion zu lesen, um im Unterricht mitmachen und sich auf die mündlichen Prüfungen vorbereiten zu können.

Zum Einsatz des Films

Der Film wird am Ende der Unterrichtsreihe gezeigt, die bewusst keinen filmanalytischen Schwerpunkt aufweist. Die Filmpräsentation ermöglicht eine **vergleichende Gegenüberstellung** von Romaninhalt und filmischer Umsetzung.

Zur LEK

Am Ende der Reihe steht eine mündliche Prüfung, da in NRW ab 2014 „in einem der ersten drei Halbjahre der Qualifikationsphase **eine Klausur in den modernen Fremdsprachen durch eine mündliche Prüfung ersetzt** [wird]" (http://www.standardsicherung.schulministerium.nrw.de/cms/muendliche-kompetenzen-entwickeln-und-pruefen/angebot-home). Es ist daher sinnvoll, die Lernenden bereits in der Einführungsphase mit dieser Art von Prüfung vertraut zu machen.

Die mündliche Prüfung besteht aus **zwei Teilen**. Im ersten Teil stellen die Schülerinnen und Schüler in einer **90-sekündigen Präsentation** eine der Figuren aus dem Roman vor. Der zweite Teil besteht aus einer **Partnerdiskussion** eines Romanthemas, für die drei Minuten anzusetzen ist. Insgesamt sollten für jede Prüfung mindestens 15 Minuten eingeplant werden.

Tipps: Besonders wichtig ist es, ausreichend Pausen zwischen den Prüfungen einzulegen, da die Abnahme und das Protokollführen Konzentration und Sorgfalt erfordern.

Die Prüfungen sollten zudem von **zwei Lehrkräften** durchgeführt werden. Dies hat den Vorteil, dass beide sich über ihre Einschätzung der Lernenden austauschen und die Notenfindung gemeinsam besprechen können.

Suzanne Collins' „The Hunger Games" (S II)

| Reihe 15 S 5 | Verlauf | Material | LEK | Kontext | Mediothek |

Schematische Verlaufsübersicht

Suzanne Collins' „The Hunger Games" – Anhand eines dystopischen Romans auf mündliche Prüfungen vorbereiten (S II)

1. Stunde:	Introducing *The Hunger Games* – an extract
2. Stunde:	Reviewing *The Hunger Games* – test and reading log
3. Stunde:	Important elements of *The Hunger Games* – concept mapping
4. Stunde:	Who's who in *The Hunger Games*? – A character map
5./6. Stunde:	*The Hunger Games* – background knowledge
7. Stunde:	Characterisation of the people from Panem
8. Stunde:	External and internal conflicts – good angel vs bad angel
9. Stunde:	*The Hunger Games* movie – raising expectations
10.–12. Stunde:	Comparing the novel and the movie – what are the differences?
13. Stunde:	Preparing for the oral exams

Minimalplan: Sollte weniger Zeit zur Verfügung stehen, können die **Stunden 9–12 entfallen**, sodass in der Einheit ausschließlich der Roman behandelt wird.

1. Stunde

Diese Stunde findet ca. zwei Wochen vor der zweiten Stunde statt.

Thema
Introducing The Hunger Games *– an extract*

Material	Verlauf
M 1	**An extract from the novel** / Lesen eines Romanauszugs; Beantworten von Fragen und Aufstellen von Hypothesen zum Inhalt
M 2	**Pyramid discussion** / Diskutieren über Gegenstände, die man in der Wildnis benötigt, um zu überleben
M 3	**Homework:** *Read the novel. While reading, fill in the reading log.*
CD GW	**Reading log** / Kopiervorlage für ein veränderbares Lesetagebuch
Zusätzlich benötigtes Material: Klassensatz der Lektüre; Folien und Folienstifte	

2. Stunde

Thema
Reviewing The Hunger Games *– test and reading log*

Material	Verlauf
M 4	**Test: What do you remember about *The Hunger Games*?** / Bearbeiten eines Textkenntnistests zur Überprüfung des Gelesenen
M 3	**Talking about your impressions of the novel** / Austausch von Leseeindrücken und Klären von Fragen zum Roman anhand des Lesetagebuchs; Vergleich der Ergebnisse des Lesetagebuchs
M 5	**What's your opinion?** / Stellungnahme zu wesentlichen Romanthemen; Formulierung von Katniss' Meinung zu diesen

3. Stunde

Thema
Important elements of The Hunger Games – concept mapping

Material	Verlauf
	What are the important elements of the novel? / Sammeln von Elementen, die von hoher inhaltlicher Relevanz sind
M 6	**Creating a concept map** / Anlegen einer Übersicht zu wichtigen Begriffen und Inhalten mithilfe der Struktur-Lege-Technik
M 7	**Homework:** *Re-read chapter one of the novel and make notes on the categories from the first person perspective of either Katniss or Gale. Write a short role biography from their point of view.*
Zusätzlich benötigtes Material: ggf. M 6 auf Folie kopiert und zerschnitten	

4. Stunde

Thema
Who's who in The Hunger Games? – A character map

Material	Verlauf
M 7	**Evaluation of homework** / Besprechung der Rollenbiografie anhand der *Hot-Seat*-Methode
M 8	**Creating a character map** / Anfertigung einer Übersicht zu wichtigen Charakteren und deren Beziehungen untereinander
	Homework: *Brainstorm sources of inspiration for authors.*
Zusätzlich benötigtes Material: leere Folie, Folienstifte	

5./6. Stunde

Thema
The Hunger Games – background knowledge

Material	Verlauf
CD GW	**Pictures stimulus – the Roman Colosseum** / Beschreiben erster Unterschiede und Gemeinsamkeiten zwischen Gladiatorenkämpfen und den *Hunger Games* anhand einer Folienkopie
M 9	**Collins' sources of inspiration: Gladiators and Theseus** / Internetrecherche zu Inspirationsquellen der Autorin
	Giving feedback / Evaluation der Ergebnispräsentationen anhand eines Feedbackbogens
M 10	**Picture stimulus** / Herstellen einer Verbindung zur eigenen Lebenswelt anhand eines Bildimpulses, der als Folie oder über den Beamer gezeigt wird; Diskutieren der Rolle von Reality-TV in der Gesellschaft
	Homework: *Lately there has been a growth of competitive shows and survival shows. Discuss this phenomenon with respect to The Hunger Games.*

Suzanne Collins' „The Hunger Games" (S II)

7. Stunde

Thema
Characterisation of the people from Panem

Material	Verlauf
M 11	**Direct vs indirect characterisation** / Zuordnen von Definitionen und Beispielen; Erklären der Beispiele
	Writing a short characterisation / Charakterisierung wichtiger Figuren
	Homework: Prepare a 90-second presentation on each character in this lesson as well as on Katniss.
Zusätzlich benötigtes Material: 5 leere Folien, mindestens 5 Folienstifte, Gefäß für Zettel	

8. Stunde

Thema
External and internal conflicts – good angel vs bad angel

Material	Verlauf
	Evaluation of homework / Präsentation einer der Figuren unter Prüfungsbedingungen
M 12	**What are Katniss' external and internal conflicts?** / Benennen von Katniss' Konflikten; Vergleichen mit eigenen Konflikten
	Good angel vs bad angel – acting it out / Analysieren und Darstellen der Notlage von Katniss und Peeta am Ende der Spiele
	Homework: Write a diary entry from Katniss' or Peeta's perspective including their feelings and thoughts about the results of the Games and what is going to happen afterwards.

9. Stunde

Thema
The Hunger Games movie – raising expectations

Material	Verlauf
	Evaluation of homework / Vorlesen einzelner Tagebucheinträge; Wahl der gelungensten Hausaufgabe
M 13	**Having a look at the movie poster** / Beschreiben und Analysieren des Filmplakats
M 14	**What could be difficult to film?** / Antizipation der Möglichkeiten und Grenzen einer filmischen Umsetzung des Romans
	Film: Watching the first part of the movie (DVD 00:00:00–00:27:47) / Anschauen des ersten Filmausschnitts; Notieren von Unterschieden zwischen Romanvorlage und Verfilmung

	CD GW	**Comparing the novel and the movie** / Bearbeitung des Fragebogens während der Filmpräsentation
		Homework: *Complete the list with the differences between novel and movie/the questionnaire with everything you can say up to this point.*

Zusätzlich benötigtes Material: DVD-Player; DVD „*The Hunger Games*"

10.–12. Stunde

Thema
Comparing the novel and the movie – what are the differences?

Material	Verlauf
M 14	**Film: Watching the second part of the movie (DVD 00:27:47–01:22:00)** / Anschauen des zweiten Filmausschnitts; Notieren von Unterschieden zwischen Romanvorlage und Verfilmung
CD GW	**Comparing the novel and the movie** / Bearbeitung des Fragebogens während der Filmpräsentation
	Evaluating the novel and the movie / Evaluieren des Romans und der Verfilmung mithilfe des Fragebogens
	Homework: *Explain to what extent the film fulfilled your expectations and whether you'd recommend reading the novel or watching the film.*

Zusätzlich benötigtes Material: DVD-Player; DVD „*The Hunger Games*"

13. Stunde

Thema
Preparing for the oral exams

Material	Verlauf
M 15	**Exam preparation** / Vorbereitung des dialogischen Teils der Prüfung anhand von Diskussionsfragen zum Roman
CD GW	**Useful phrases for a discussion** / Liste mit zusätzlichen Redemitteln für Diskussionen

Zusatzmaterial auf der **CD Grundwerk (CD GW)**

Suzanne Collins' „The Hunger Games" (S II)

| Reihe 15 | Verlauf | **Material S 1** | LEK | Kontext | Mediothek |

Materialübersicht

1. Stunde: **Intoducing *The Hunger Games* – an extract**
M 1 (Ab) Rules of the game – an extract from a novel
M 2 (Ab) Surviving in the woods – how would you manage?
M 3 (Ab/Ha) *The Hunger Games* – keeping a reading log
CD GW (Ab) What happens in *The Hunger Games*? – A reading log

2. Stunde: **Reviewing *The Hunger Games* – test and reading log**
M 4 (Ab) *The Hunger Games* – a test
M 5 (Ab) Issues from *The Hunger Games* – what's your opinion?

3. Stunde: **Important elements of *The Hunger Games* – concept mapping**
M 6 (Ab) *The Hunger Games* – creating a concept map
M 7 (Ab/Ha) *The Hunger Games* – Katniss and Gale

4. Stunde: **Who's who in *The Hunger Games*? – A character map**
M 8 (Ab) *The Hunger Games* – creating a character map

5./6. Stunde: ***The Hunger Games* – background knowledge**
CD GW (Bd) Picture stimulus – the Roman Colosseum
M 9 (Ab) *The Hunger Games* – exploring cultural references
M 10 (Bd) Picture stimulus – reality TV

7. Stunde: **Characterisation of the people from Panem**
M 11 (Ab) Defining characterisation – direct vs indirect

8. Stunde: **External and internal conflicts – good angel vs bad angel**
M 12 (Ab) Katniss and Peeta's conflict – good angel vs bad angel

9. Stunde: ***The Hunger Games* movie – raising expectations**
M 13 (Bd) Movie poster: *The Hunger Games*
M 14 (Ab) *The Hunger Games* – comparing the novel and the movie

10.–12. Stunde: **Comparing the novel and the movie – what are the differences?**
M 14 (Ab) *The Hunger Games* – comparing the novel and the movie
CD GW (Ab) Comparing the novel and the movie – a questionnaire

13. Stunde: **Preparing for the oral exams**
M 15 (Ab) Preparing for the oral exams
CD GW (Ab) Useful phrases for a discussion

Für den Einsatz dieser Materialien wird ein **DVD-Player** benötigt.

Zusatzmaterial auf **CD Grundwerk (GW)**.

RAAbits Englisch

M 1 Rules of the game – an extract from a novel

Read an extract taken from a novel you are going to read. What could it be about?

Tasks

1. Work on your own:

Read the extract from the novel. While reading, take notes on the content.

2. Work with a partner:

a) Talk about the extract:

- What did you understand?
- What was in the extract that you didn't understand?

b) Take notes:

- Explain what you think about a game with these rules.
- Outline the nature of a society in which a game like this is part of the culture.
- Would you watch the game on TV? Justify your answer.
- Explain what your strategy would be if you had to participate.

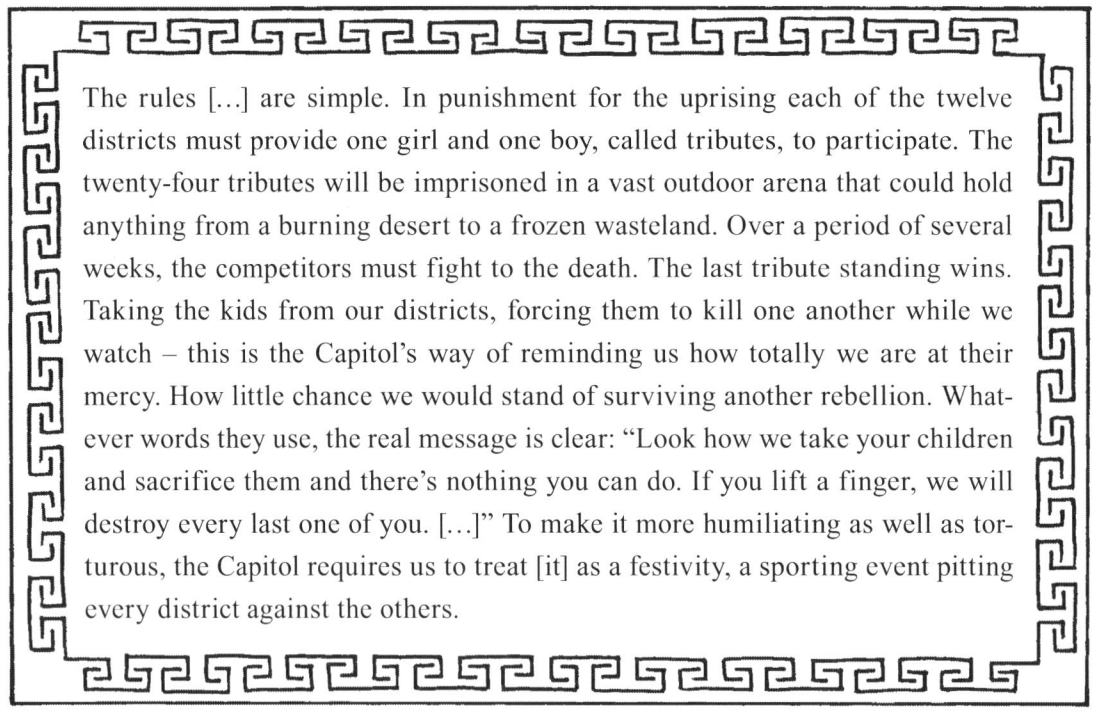

The rules [...] are simple. In punishment for the uprising each of the twelve districts must provide one girl and one boy, called tributes, to participate. The twenty-four tributes will be imprisoned in a vast outdoor arena that could hold anything from a burning desert to a frozen wasteland. Over a period of several
5   weeks, the competitors must fight to the death. The last tribute standing wins. Taking the kids from our districts, forcing them to kill one another while we watch – this is the Capitol's way of reminding us how totally we are at their mercy. How little chance we would stand of surviving another rebellion. Whatever words they use, the real message is clear: "Look how we take your children
10 and sacrifice them and there's nothing you can do. If you lift a finger, we will destroy every last one of you. [...]" To make it more humiliating as well as torturous, the Capitol requires us to treat [it] as a festivity, a sporting event pitting every district against the others.

THE HUNGER GAMES by Suzanne Collins. Copyright © 2008 by Suzanne Collins. Reprinted by permission of Scholastic Inc.

Vocabulary Aids

1 **uprising:** der Aufstand – 3 **vast:** riesig, gewaltig – 4 **wasteland:** das Ödland – 10 **to sacrifice:** opfern – 11 **humiliating:** demütigend, erniedrigend – 11 **torturous:** qualvoll – 12 **to pit sb. against sb.:** jmndn. gegen jmndn. antreten lassen

Suzanne Collins' „The Hunger Games" (S II)

M 2 Surviving in the woods – how would you manage?

The protagonists of the novel are "imprisoned in a vast outdoor arena". How would you survive in such hostile surroundings? Discuss this question with your classmates.

Tasks

1. Imagine you had to survive alone in the woods for a couple of weeks. You could take 10 items with you. What would you take?

   On your own: Make a list of 10 items you would take along to survive in the woods.

   With a partner: Compare your lists, agree on 10 items and put them into order by starting with the most important item and ending the list with the least important item.

   With another pair of students: Compare your lists and again agree on 10 items and put them in order of importance. Write the list on a transparency and present it to the class. You have to mention why you need those items and justify your ranking.

2. Which character traits do you have that would help you survive in the wilderness? Discuss.

Language support

In my opinion …

I agree with you.

You're right up to a point.

By and large I would accept your ideas, but …

I am firmly/entirely/fully in agreement with you.

That's right.

That's a good/great/brilliant idea.

Why do you think … is more important than …?

This issue cannot simply be ignored.

I think … is more important to survive in the woods because …

I must admit that your arguments have convinced me.

Suzanne Collins' „The Hunger Games" (S II)

M 3 *The Hunger Games* – keeping a reading log

What happens in the novel? The reading log will help you to keep track of the events.

Tasks

1. Draw a table in your exercise book. Draw one column for the three books (*The Tributes*, *The Game*, *The Victor*) in the novel, one for the chapters and one for the content. *The Hunger Games* has 27 chapters so you'll need the same number of lines. After having finished a chapter, summarise its content in a few sentences.

	Chapter	Content
The Tributes	1	
	2	
	3	
	4	
	5	
	...	

2. Choose one of the following tasks.

a) Draw either District 12, the Capitol or the arena while reading *The Hunger Games*.

b) Copy the chart below onto an extra sheet and complete it with the names of the tributes from each district, their cause of death and the district's industry. Some tributes' names are not mentioned in the novel, mark them with a * and only write down their cause of death. On some districts' industry you only get information in the second and third part of the trilogy, *Catching Fire* and *Mockingjay*. Mark them with a #.

District	Tributes and their cause of death	Industry
1		
2		
...		

c) Search for a **map of North America** on the Internet. Print it out, locate the districts of Panem and draw them on the map. The novel gives you several clues as to where the Capitol and District 12 are located. It also mentions how the districts are arranged around the Capitol. There is no official map of Panem – there are several possibilities for the location of some districts.

Suzanne Collins' „The Hunger Games" (S II)

| Reihe 15 | Verlauf | Material S 5 | LEK | Kontext | Mediothek |

II/B2

Hinweise (M 1–M 3; 1. Stunde)

In der Einstiegsstunde, die **vor dem Lesen des Romans** stattfindet, wird das Interesse der Lerngruppe durch einen Ausschnitt aus *„The Hunger Games"* geweckt. Dieser regt zur Diskussion des möglichen Romaninhalts an. Die Textpassage wurde dem ersten Kapitel entnommen. Hier werden **Ursprung und Sinn der Spiele** erklärt.

Als Einstieg dient der **Romanauszug (M 1)**. Das Arbeitsblatt wird den Schülerinnen und Schülern ohne den Materialtitel und die Quellenangabe kopiert. Der Aufgabenapparat ist an die *Think-Pair-Share*-**Methode** angelehnt. Die Lernenden fertigen zunächst in Einzelarbeit Notizen zum Inhalt an (*task 1*), bevor sie sich mit einem Partner über ihre Eindrücke austauschen und schriftlich Fragen zum Inhalt beantworten (*task 2*). Die Ergebnisse werden im Plenum diskutiert und der Titel des Romans bekanntgegeben.

In **M 2** versetzen sie sich in die Situation der *tributes*, die mitten im Ödland um ihr Überleben kämpfen müssen. In einer **Pyramidendiskussion** verteidigen die Gruppenmitglieder Gegenstände, die sie als überlebensnotwendig erachten, und finden **Kompromisse**, indem sie sich mehrfach neu einigen (*task 1*). Ein bis zwei Gruppen stellen ihre Ergebnisse auf Folie vor. Abschließend überlegen die Schülerinnen und Schüler zunächst in Partnerarbeit und dann im Plenum, welche Charaktereigenschaften notwendig sind, um in der Wildnis überleben zu können (*task 2*).

Differenzierung: Der *language support* (**M 2**) ist für lernschwächere Schüler oder Kurse gedacht und kann je nach Bedarf mit kopiert oder abgetrennt werden.

Am Ende der Stunde erhalten die Lernenden den **Roman**. Sie lesen ihn innerhalb von ca. zwei Wochen zu Hause. Parallel führen sie ein **Lesetagebuch (M 3)**. Dieses dient als Übersicht und Orientierung während des weiteren Unterrichtsverlaufs. Hier fassen die Schülerinnen und Schüler den Inhalt eines jeden Kapitels in wenigen Sätzen zusammen (*task 1*). In *task 2* wählen sie, ob sie eine Zeichnung eines der wichtigen Schauplätze anfertigen *(a)*, eine tabellarische Übersicht aller *tributes* samt ihrer Distrikte und Todesarten zusammenstellen *(b)* oder einer Karte von Panem anfertigen *(c)*. Durch die Bearbeitung dieser Aufgaben verschaffen sie sich einen Überblick über die fiktive Welt Panems. Außerdem verfolgt insbesondere die Tabelle die Absicht, die Lernenden neugierig auf den zweiten und dritten Teil der Trilogie zu machen und sie so zum Lesen der beiden Romane anzuregen.

Auf der **CD Grundwerk** findet sich eine **veränderbare Kopiervorlage des** *reading log*. So kann man u. a. die Spalten bei Bedarf um die Kategorien *Day/Time, Place, People, Important quote, Suspense* etc. erweitern.

Erwartungshorizont (M 1)

1. Individual answers

2. a) <u>What did you understand?</u>: The extract is about rules for a game; in this game 12 districts must provide one girl and one boy each; the tributes will be imprisoned in an arena for several weeks to fight to the death; "we" (somebody) watch(es); there was a rebellion before; the Capitol requires it to be treated like an event.

   <u>What didn't you understand?</u>: Who/what is the Capitol?; Why does the passage mention "another rebellion"?; Was there a rebellion before? If yes, what happened?

   b) <u>What you think about a game with these rules</u>: Very brutal, cruel, especially since children are taking part in it; hard to imagine how people can watch it on TV.

   <u>The nature of a society in which such a game is part of the culture</u>: An oppressed, brutal, inhuman, perverted, cruel society dominated by a totalitarian government or a dictator.

Would you watch the game on TV?: **No** because it is too brutal; those shows should not be rewarded with a high number of viewers; **Yes** because even though it is brutal, a lot of people will be talking about it: I want to have first-hand information; I would because the extract of the novel says that it is obligatory.

What would your strategy be if you had to participate?: Individual answers

Erwartungshorizont (M 2)

1. <u>Useful items for surviving in the woods</u>: Matches, weapons, compass, tent, mosquito net, mobile phone, map, water, food …

2. <u>Useful character traits</u>: Having a strong will, being positive, confident, brave …

Erwartungshorizont (M 3)

1.

	Chapter	Content
The Tributes	1	Katniss hunts in the woods where she meets Gale; Madge gives Katniss a mockingjay pin; at the town square they attend the reaping where Prim is chosen as tribute for the 74th Hunger Games.
	2	Katniss volunteers for her sister Prim; the other tribute from District 12 is Peeta.
	3	Katniss and Peeta say goodbye to their families; Katniss tells Gale to take care of her family; a train takes them to the Capitol; they get to know Effie, Trinket and Haymitch Abernathy.
	4	Katniss, Peeta and Haymitch make a deal: If they don't interfere with his drinking, Haymitch will help them; they arrive at the Capitol.
	5	Katniss meets her stylist Cinna, who creates costumes for them which resemble District 12's industry of coal mining; as Katniss and Peeta ride through the main plaza, their costumes light up with synthetic flames, and the two of them are the most memorable tributes.
	6	Katniss mentions that she knows one of the servants; Effie tells her that she cannot know an Avox because Avoxes are people who committed a crime and therefore had their tongue cut out; Katniss pretends that it must be a mistake; Katniss and Peeta meet at the roof; Katniss explains to him where she knows the Avox from (She saw her in the wood where the girl was captured).
	7	All tributes train at the training centre; they have private sessions with the Gamemakers; Katniss shoots with a bow and arrow but most of the Gamemakers pay no attention; Katniss surprises them by shooting an arrow at an apple; then she walks off.
	8	Katniss is nervous about the result of her performance because a low score can make it difficult for her to get sponsors, which are crucial for her survival; the scores are announced; Peeta gets eight and Katniss eleven out of twelve points; Katniss misses Gale; Peeta asks to train separately.
	9	Katniss prepares for a TV interview; she apologises to the Avox girl for not helping her in the woods; Katniss is anxious about the upcoming interview; Cinna tells her to be herself; she comes over as very charming, the crowd loves her; when it's Peeta's turn for the interview, he admits that he has a crush on Katniss.

	10	The crowd goes crazy over Peeta's confession; Katniss is angry at him; Haymitch explains to her that Peeta did her a favour by making her look desirable; she apologises; both of them say goodbye to the others; Haymitch's advice for them is to run and find water; the tributes board a hovercraft and are injected with a tracker; Cinna gives Katniss the mockingjay pin and encourages her; the Games begin.
	11	Katniss runs off into the woods; there is a huge bloodbath and eleven tributes die; Katniss prepares to sleep in a tree; she notices someone making a fire nearby; the girl who made it is killed by the Career Tributes; Peeta is among them.
	12	Katniss is shocked that Peeta is hunting with the Careers; she is severely dehydrated; she curses Haymitch for not sending her water but he intentionally does so to indicate to her that water is near; she finally finds it; in the middle of the night she is woken by a fire.
	13	The fire was made by the Gamemakers to get the tributes closer together; Katniss runs from it and is severely injured; she hears voices and climbs up a tree; the Careers and Peeta approach her but are unable to climb the tree; they decide to wait until she comes down; Katniss sees a girl from District 11 in a tree nearby.
The Game	14	The girl (Rue) points to a nest of tracker jackers; Katniss tries to saw the branch but it's too loud; she decides to wait until the morning; Haymitch sends her a gift which relieves the pain and helps her wounds heal; she finally saws the branch; the nest breaks on the ground and the other tributes are attacked by the bees; Katniss collects a bow and arrow from dead Glimmer; meets Peeta who protects her from Cato; she runs off and collapses.
	15	Katniss wakes days later; she has a feeling that she could win the Games now that she has a bow and arrow; Katniss and Rue form an alliance; Rue tells Katniss about the Careers' camp where they have plenty supplies.
	16	Katniss and Rue work out a plan to destroy the Careers' food supply; Katniss goes to their camp while Rue makes a fire to attract them and lead them away from their camp; Katniss finds out that the supply is booby-trapped; she shoots arrows at apples; the dropping apples set off an explosion which destroys all the food and Katniss' sense of hearing in her left ear.
	17	The Careers return; Cato kills a boy from District 3; Katniss heads back to the woods to meet Rue; Katniss hears Rue scream but only comes to find her entangled in a net, stabbed by a boy (Marvel) from District 1.
	18	Katniss shoots Marvel and frees Rue; Rue is dying; Katniss sings for her, covers her body in flowers and holds out her fingers in a gesture of respect; Katniss receives bread from District 11; there is an announcement of a change of rules: Two tributes can be declared winners if they are both from the same district; Katniss calls out for Peeta.

	19	Katniss finds Peeta near a stream; he is injured; Katniss carries Peeta to a cave where she kisses him; Haymitch sends hot broth: He wants her to keep up the romance.
	20	Peeta's infection is spreading; the Gamemakers announce a feast, where there will be a backpack for everyone containing something they need; Katniss wants to go but Peeta holds her back; Haymitch sends sleep syrup; she gives it to Peeta and goes to the feast.
	21	When she arrives, Foxface runs to grab her backpack before anyone can react; as Katniss runs to get it, she is attacked by Glove who tries to kill her; Thresh hinders Glove and saves Katniss because she was an ally to Rue but says that now they're even; Katniss runs back to the cave.
	22	Katniss talks to Peeta; she is sad and does not want anybody else to die, she wants to go home; Katniss realises that she truly cares for Peeta; they kiss; Katniss feels safe with him; the next day Haymitch sends them a basket of food.
	23	Thresh dies and only Foxface and Cato remain as competitors; Katniss and Peeta try to hunt but Peeta scares away all game; they split up; Peeta collects roots and berries while Katniss hunts; when Katniss does not hear Peeta anymore she panics; when they meet again the cannon sounds and Foxface is portrayed; they think Cato is near but Foxface secretly ate something Peeta collected: deadly berries.
The Victor	24	They keep the rest of the berries; the Gamemakers have dried the streams; the remaining tributes are forced to go to the lake near the Cornucopia; suddenly Cato comes out of the woods and runs towards them; Katniss' arrows can do no harm; as they prepare for an attack by Cato, he runs past them; he is followed by mutts who chase him.
	25	They run towards the Cornucopia; Cato is already there, takes Peeta in a headlock and threatens Katniss that if she shoots at him, both will go down; Katniss shoots Cato in the hand; Cato lets go and Peeta throws him down; the mutts attack Cato but do not kill him to prolong the spectacle; out of pity, as well as out of fear of losing Peeta, Katniss kills Cato; the cannon sounds and they think they have won; Templesmith states that the previous rule change has been revoked and there can only be one winner; Katniss cannot kill Peeta even if he tells her to do so; she wants them to both eat the remaining berries; just as they are about to eat the berries, Templesmith declares them both winners.
	26	Katniss gains her hearing ability back and Peeta gets a new leg; Haymitch tells Katniss that she is in danger because the Capitol is angry at her attempt to fool them with the berries; her only justification can be that she is madly in love with Peeta; so she has to keep up the romance.
	27	They are interviewed about their love and the berries; Katniss is careful and explains that she did it because she couldn't bear the thought of losing Peeta; Peeta finds out that Haymitch has been coaching Katniss; Peeta questions Katniss' feelings for him; Katniss becomes confused about her feelings towards Peeta; when they arrive in District 12 a crowd awaits them; Peeta holds Katniss hand; she is scared of the moment she finally has to let go.

Suzanne Collins' „The Hunger Games" (S II)

2.

a) Individual results

b) Industries marked with a # are only named in the second and third part of the trilogy. Unnamed tributes are marked with a *.

Tributes and their cause of death sorted by their district's number: 1. Marvel (killed by Katniss with an arrow); Glimmer (killed by Katniss with the tracker jacker nest); 2. Cato (killed by mutts and Katniss who shot him); Clove (killed by Thresh with a rock); 3. * Boy who was killed by Cato (who snapped his neck); girl who was killed in the bloodbath at the Cornucopia; 4. * Boy was killed in the bloodbath at the Cornucopia; girl was killed by Katniss (tracker jacker nest); 5. Foxface (ate the poisonous berries); * Boy was killed in the bloodbath at the Cornucopia; 6.* Boy and girl killed in the bloodbath at the Cornucopia; 7. * Boy and girl killed in the bloodbath at the Cornucopia; 8. * Boy was killed in the bloodbath at the Cornucopia; girl built a fire which attracted the Careers, Peeta killed her; 9. * Boy was killed by Clove who threw a knife in his back; girl was killed in the bloodbath at the Cornucopia; 10 * Boy (crippled foot kid) was killed by the Careers; girl was killed in the bloodbath at the Cornucopia; 11. Thresh (probably killed by Cato); Rue (killed by Marvel with a spear); 12. Peeta; Katniss; Industry sorted by district's number: 1. Luxury items; 2. # *Masonry and weaponry*; 3. # *Electronics*; 4. # *Fishing*; 5. # *Electricity*; 6 # *Transportation*; 7. # *Lumber and paper*; 8. # *Textiles including uniforms*; 9. Grain, many factories; 10. # *Livestock*; 11. Agriculture; 12. Coal (mining)

c) The Capitol lies in the Rocky Mountains; District 12 in the Appalachian Mountains; the single districts are arranged around the Capitol; District 11 has a border to District 12, because it's an agricultural district with many fruit trees it might lie in the South; District 13 has been destroyed.

Schülerbeispiel:

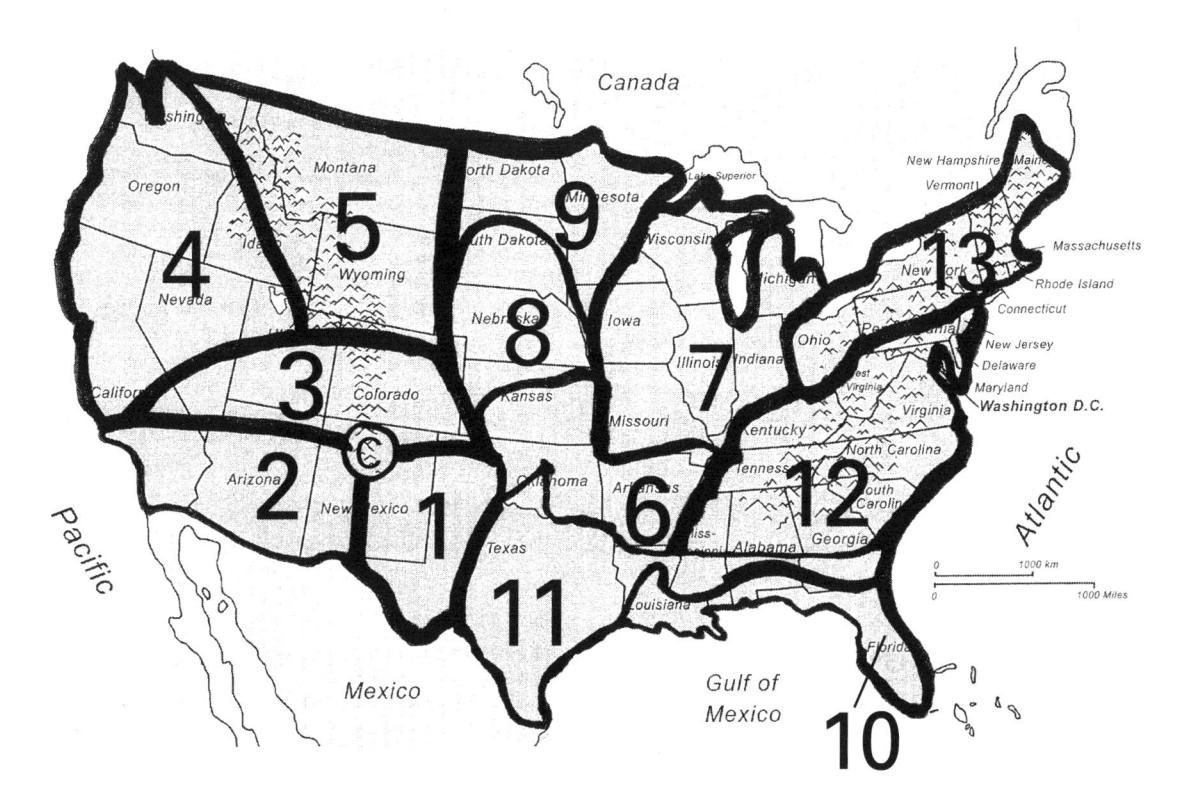

M 4 *The Hunger Games* – a test

1. What does Peeta do that surprises Katniss on their first night in the arena?

   _____

2. Gale is better than Katniss at what skill?

   _____

3. When Katniss is severely dehydrated, how does Haymitch indicate to her that she's near water?

   _____

4. Who gives Katniss the mockingjay pin?

   _____

5. Why does the Capitol hold the Hunger Games?

   _____

6. Under which circumstances did Katniss first meet Peeta?

   _____

7. What are tesserae?

   _____

8. What does Peeta tell Katniss he wants to do in the Games?
   - [ ] Kill as many Career Tributes as possible
   - [ ] Hide
   - [ ] Find a way to escape the arena
   - [ ] Show the Capitol he's not just a piece in their game

9. What item does Katniss manage to grab at the Cornucopia when the Games begin?
   - [ ] A bow
   - [ ] A knife
   - [ ] A backpack
   - [ ] A helmet

10. Why does Thresh spare Katniss' life when he has the chance to kill her?

    _____

M 5 Issues from *The Hunger Games* – what's your opinion?

Tasks: 1. Read the statements and tick whether you agree or disagree. Give reasons.
2. Discuss your answers with a partner and determine what Katniss would think about these statements. Give reasons.

---

1. Older siblings are responsible for their younger siblings!

☐ Agree ☐ Disagree

Reason: _____

How Katniss would respond to that statement:

---

2. Hunting is wrong!

☐ Agree ☐ Disagree

Reason: _____

How Katniss would respond to that statement:

---

3. Cosmetic surgery should be used to express yourself!

☐ Agree ☐ Disagree

Reason: _____

How Katniss would respond to that statement:

---

4. Citizens should speak up when their government does something wrong!

☐ Agree ☐ Disagree

Reason: _____

How Katniss would respond to that statement:

---

5. It is never right to kill another human being!

☐ Agree ☐ Disagree

Reason: _____

How Katniss would respond to that statement:

---

6. You should always be yourself!

☐ Agree ☐ Disagree

Reason: _____

How Katniss would respond to that statement:

Hinweise (M 4 und M 5; 2. Stunde)

In dieser Stunde wird das **Leseverständnis** der Schülerinnen und Schüler überprüft und erste **Eindrücke und Meinungen** zum Roman werden besprochen.

Zu Stundenbeginn wird ein **Textkenntnistest (M 4)** ausgeteilt, den die Lerngruppe in ca. 10 Minuten bearbeitet. Die Fragen sind so gestellt, dass man sie nur richtig beantworten kann, wenn man lediglich den Film gesehen hat. Der Test wird eingesammelt und benotet.

Im zweiten Teil der Stunde besprechen die Lernenden in Partnerarbeit mithilfe ihres **Lesetagebuchs** Fragen, die während des Leseprozesses aufgekommen sind, und tauschen ihre **Eindrücke** aus. Anschließend finden sich immer vier Schülerinnen und Schüler zusammen, die die gleiche Aufgabe (M 3, *task 2 a–c*) bearbeitet haben. In den Vierergruppen einigen sie sich begründet auf die Arbeit eines Schülers und finden sich dann mit einer zweiten Gruppe zusammen, deren Mitglieder ebenfalls diese Aufgabe bearbeitet haben. Auch hier einigen sie sich auf die gelungenere der beiden Darstellungen, die dann im Plenum präsentiert wird. Die Zeichnungen bzw. die Tabelle werden entweder im Klassenzimmer aufgehängt oder von der Lehrkraft für alle kopiert.

Auf den freien Austausch folgt eine **persönliche Stellungnahme (M 5)** zu Aussagen, die sich inhaltlich auf den Roman beziehen. Die Lernenden begründen in Einzelarbeit, warum sie den Aussagen (nicht) zustimmen (*task 1*). Die Ergebnisse werden zuerst mit einem Partner diskutiert, bevor sie im Plenum besprochen werden. Ein Rückbezug auf den Roman findet statt, indem die Lernenden zu zweit überlegen, welche **Position Katniss** einnehmen würde (*task 2*), und so die eigene Lebenswelt mit der Welt der Heldin vergleichen.

Sollte in der Stunde nicht mehr genügend Zeit zur Verfügung stehen, ist *task 2* **Hausaufgabe**.

Erwartungshorizont (M 4)

1. He teams up with the Career Tributes; 2. Gale is better than Katniss at setting snares; 3. Haymitch shows Katniss that water must be nearby by not sending her anything; 4. Madge (the mayor's daughter) gives Katniss the mockingjay pin; 5. The Capitol holds the Hunger Games annually to remind the people of Panem of the Dark Days/to show its power/to entertain its citizens; 6. Peeta gave Katniss (burnt) bread when she was starving (He threw it into her direction); 7. A tesserae is a token worth a year's supply of grain and oil for one person; 8. Show the Capitol he's not just a piece in their game; 9. A backpack; 10. He spares her life (only once) because Katniss helped Rue in the arena (Thresh and Rue are both from District 11).

Erwartungshorizont (M 5)

1. Individual answers

2. Katniss' response: 1. I feel responsible for the well-being of my little sister; am willing to risk my life for her; 2. Hunting is illegal in Panem but it saves my family from starvation; 3. Cosmetic surgery stands for abundance; only rich people can afford to think about shallow things like looks; 4. The Capitol is the enemy; I suffer from restrictions and starvation; rebel against the government by sneaking out over the fence; speak against the government with Gale; considering eating the berries at the end of the Games can be seen as an act of rebellion; 5. Killing is not right but under special circumstances it happens (e.g. to help a friend (Marvel), out of self-defence (Glimmer), out of pity and to help Peeta (Cato); 6. Sometimes it is necessary to cover up true feelings to stay alive; I constantly struggle whether I should keep up appearances or stay true to myself.

Suzanne Collins' „The Hunger Games" (S II)

| Reihe 15 | Verlauf | Material S 13 | LEK | Kontext | Mediothek |

M 6 *The Hunger Games* – creating a concept map

Task: Cut out all the cards with terms from the novel. Rearrange them in a way you think makes sense. This is called concept mapping. There are multiple ways of doing this and there is no right or wrong arrangement. However, you have to be able to explain and justify your layout.

TV	Seam	North America	trespassing	Capitol
fire	to kill	to love	to suffer	victor
Careers	defiance	to reap	Peacekeeper	competitor
food	mockingjay	to recognise	rich	arena
entertainment	to volunteer	to hunt	Panem	poor

II/B2

RAAbits Englisch

Suzanne Collins' „The Hunger Games" (S II)

| Reihe 15 | Verlauf | Material S 14 | LEK | Kontext | Mediothek |

M 7 *The Hunger Games* – Katniss and Gale

Katniss and Gale are important protagonists in the trilogy. Have a closer look at them.

Task

Re-read chapter one of the novel (pp. 13–27) and make notes on the categories listed below from the first person perspective of either Katniss or Gale. Write a short role biography from their point of view.

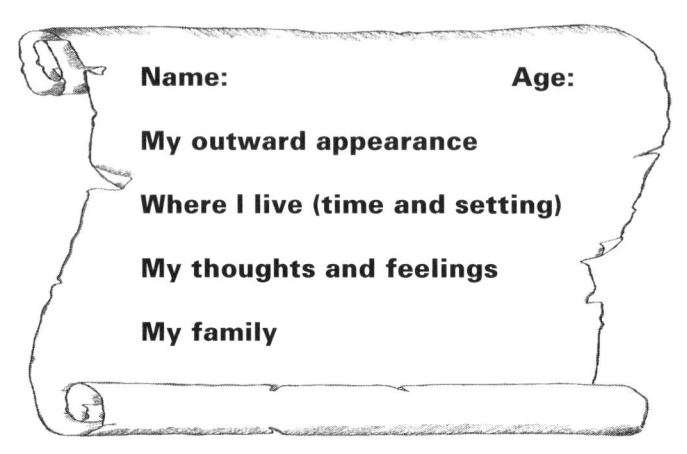

> Name: Age:
>
> **My outward appearance**
>
> **Where I live (time and setting)**
>
> **My thoughts and feelings**
>
> **My family**

Hinweise (M 6 und M 7; 3. Stunde)

In dieser Stunde verschaffen sich die Schülerinnen und Schüler einen Überblick über **wesentliche Elemente** der *Hunger Games*.

Als **Einstieg** überlegen sie sich **drei Begriffe** bzw. Elemente, die ihrer Meinung nach wesentlich für den Roman und die darin dargestellte Gesellschaft sind. In Partnerarbeit stellen sie sich diese vor und begründen ihre Wahl. Sie einigen sich gemeinsam auf einen Begriff. Alle Begriffe werden dann im Plenum gesammelt und können später der *concept map* hinzugefügt werden, indem die Lernenden sie auf leeren Zetteln notieren.

In der *concept map* **(M 6)** sind die Begriffe nicht systematisch geordnet. Ziel ist es, dass die Lernenden sich einen Zugang zu den verschiedenen Begriffen und Elementen erarbeiten, indem sie diese in einen **logischen Zusammenhang** bringen. Bei der **Struktur-Lege-Technik** gibt es keine richtigen und falschen Lösungen. Die *concept map* wird in Einzelarbeit erstellt. Die Auswertung findet in Partnerarbeit statt, sodass alle Schülerinnen und Schüler sprechen und ihre Anordnung präsentieren.

Sollte die Struktur-Lege-Technik dem Kurs noch nicht bekannt sein, kann sie durch folgendes Tafelbild eingeführt werden:

> **Creating a concept map**
>
> **What?**
> – Cards with terms on them
> – Blank cards for additional terms and general terms
>
> **How?**
> – Put the cards in a logical order
> – Use blank cards to categorise the terms
>
> **Why?**
> – To see connections between concepts and elements

Suzanne Collins' „The Hunger Games" (S II)

| Reihe 15 | Verlauf | Material S 15 | LEK | Kontext | Mediothek |

Unbekannte **Vokabeln** werden vorher im Plenum geklärt (*trespassing:* übertreten, unerlaubtes Betreten; *defiance:* der Trotz, die Missachtung; *to reap:* hier: das Auslosen der Tribute).

Tipp: Zusätzlich kann die Lehrkraft die **concept map auf Folie** kopieren, die Karten ausschneiden und die Anordnung auf dem OHP von einzelnen Schülern vornehmen und erläutern lassen.

Hausaufgabe dieser Stunde ist es, mithilfe des ersten Kapitels entweder Katniss oder Gale in Form einer **Rollenbiografie (M 7)** zu charakterisieren. Auf diese Weise werden Informationen über den Hintergrund der Figuren und zu Zeit und Ort der Handlung gesammelt.

Erwartungshorizont (M 6)

Individual answers

Erwartungshorizont (M 7)

Name: Katniss Everdeen, **Age:** 16 years old (p. 15, l. 4/5)

Where I live: District 12, the Seam in Panem; the district is surrounded by an electric fence (p. 14, ll. 16–21) and its people are poor and starving.

Time in which I live: The post-apocalyptic future (no precise time given).

Outward appearance: Straight black hair, olive skin, grey eyes (p. 17, l. 13/14); I usually wear hunting boots, trousers, and a shirt and tuck my hair into a cap (p. 13 f.).

My family: My father died in a mine explosion when I was 11; I still have nightmares about it (p. 15, l. 5); I live together with my mother, my younger sister Prim, a cat named Buttercup and a goat called Lady (p. 13, l. 15; p. 23, l. 31); I have an ambivalent relationship with my mother; I'm the provider for my family, I go hunting to feed my family; I volunteer for the 74th Hunger Games to save my sister.

My thoughts and feelings: Usually I hide my feelings about District 12 and the Capitol (p. 15, l. 28–31); I never want to have kids (p. 18, l. 25); my best friend and hunting partner is Gale (p. 16, l. 6/7); I'm a survivor.

Name: Gale Hawthorne, **Age:** 18

Where I live: District 12, the Seam in Panem; the district is surrounded by an electric fence (p. 14, ll. 16–21) and its people are poor and starving.

Time in which I live: The post-apocalyptic future (no precise time given).

Outward appearance: Straight black hair, olive skin, grey eyes (could be Katniss' brother, but we are not related) (p. 17, ll. 13–15); tall, good-looking, strong enough to handle the work in the mines.

My family: I have three younger siblings; am very devoted to my family; my father died in a mining accident; I provide for my family.

My thoughts and feelings: I want to run off and live in the woods (p. 18, l. 13); I despise the government; am very angry at the circumstances; devoted to Katniss; I want to have kids one day.

M 8 *The Hunger Games* – creating a character map

Let's find out how the protagonists are linked and what their relationships are like.

Task

Work together in groups of three and create a character map of all relevant characters of *The Hunger Games*.

Your map must include:

- Katniss Everdeen
- Peeta Mellark
- Gale Hawthorne
- Haymitch Abernathy
- Effie Trinket
- Prim Everdeen
- Rue
- Cinna

Other characters are optional.

Show connections between the characters by using arrows and symbols (e.g. a heart, a crown, an animal …) you associate with the character or with his or her relationship to another character.

Hinweise (M 8; 4. Stunde)

In dieser Stunde verschaffen sich die Lernenden mithilfe einer *character map* einen Überblick über **alle wichtigen Figuren**.

Den **Einstieg** in die Stunde bildet die Besprechung der **Hausaufgabe (M 7)** anhand der *Hot-Seat*-**Methode**. Die Schülerinnen und Schüler notieren in Partnerarbeit Fragen, die sie an den von ihnen nicht bearbeiteten Protagonisten haben. Dann übernimmt jeweils ein Schüler die Rolle Katniss' oder Gales. Beide nehmen vorne im Klassenzimmer Platz und beantworten die Fragen der Mitschüler mithilfe ihrer Rollenbiografie.

In **M 8** erstellen die Lernenden in Dreiergruppen eine **character map**. Diese dient dazu, die wichtigen Romanfiguren übersichtlich darzustellen und in Verbindung zueinander zu setzen. Alle Schülerinnen und Schüler notieren die Ergebnisse der Gruppenarbeit. Eine Gruppe erhält zusätzlich eine Folie, auf der sie ihre *character map* festhält. Die anschließende Präsentation dieser *map* im Plenum wird durch die anderen Gruppen ergänzt.

Als **Hausaufgabe** notieren die Lernenden, wo Autoren Inspirationen für ihre Werke finden.

Erwartungshorizont (M 8)

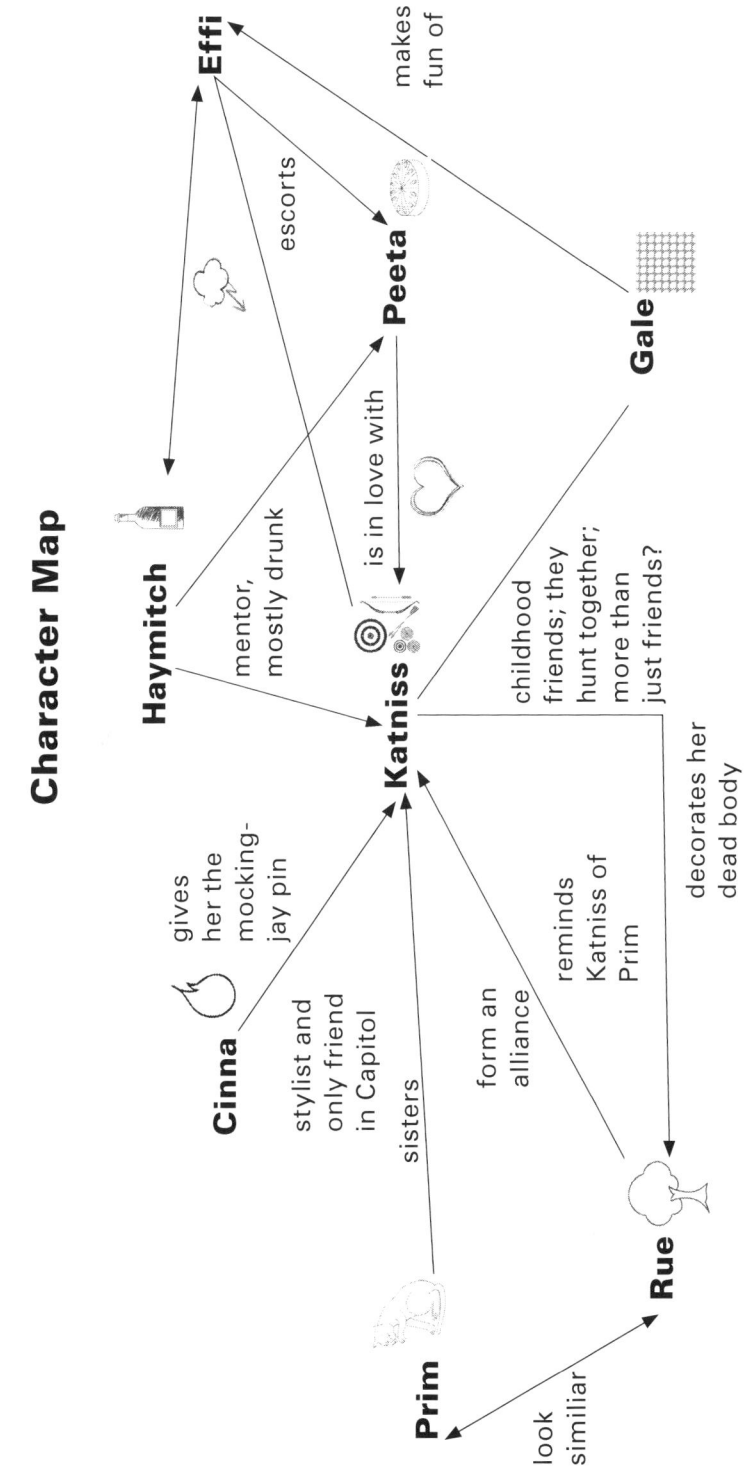

Character Map

- **Cinna** → **Katniss**: gives her the mockingjay pin; stylist and only friend in Capitol
- **Prim** ↔ **Katniss**: sisters
- **Haymitch** ↔ **Katniss**: mentor, mostly drunk
- **Haymitch** ↔ **Effi**
- **Effi** → **Peeta**: escorts
- **Effi** — makes fun of — **Katniss**
- **Peeta** → **Katniss**: is in love with
- **Katniss** ↔ **Gale**: childhood friends; they hunt together; more than just friends?
- **Katniss** ↔ **Rue**: form an alliance; reminds Katniss of Prim; decorates her dead body
- **Rue** ↔ **Prim**: look similiar

Possible symbols:

Katniss: Bow and arrow (She hunts to support her family), mockingjay pin (It's her lucky charm in the Games); **Rue:** Tree (She climbs well, helped Katniss to climb onto the tree and worked on an orchard in District 11); **Prim:** Cat (Buttercup) or goat (Lady), little girl with braids; **Cinna:** Flames (He puts Katniss and Peeta in the limelight with them); **Haymitch:** Bottle (He is always drinking); **Effie:** Make-up (She is always concerned with her looks), watch (She is always on time); **Peeta:** Cake with nice decoration (Peeta learned how to decorate cakes in his parents' bakery, this put him at an advantage in the arena); **Gale:** Snare (He went hunting with Katniss and is better with snares than she is); **Peeta and Katniss:** Heart (Peeta is in love with Katniss and they are pretending to be in a romantic relationship); **Haymitch and Effie:** Lightning (There are tensions between them and they argue a lot).

M 9 *The Hunger Games* – exploring cultural references

While writing the novel, Suzanne Collins was inspired by different sources. Find out more about them.

Task 1: Work in pairs and visit the websites to gather information on Collins' sources of inspiration. Be prepared to give a 5-minute presentation of your results to the class. Also add your classmates' findings to your notes.

Research Group A: Gladiator games in the Roman Empire

– Explain the background and the course of events of the gladiator games.

– Compare the Hunger Games to the Roman gladiator games.

Useful Websites:

www.ushistory.org/civ/6e.asp

http://ancienthistory.about.com/od/romeslavery/p/Gladiators.htm

Keywords "Gladiator Games" on youtube.de

Research Group B: The Greek Legend of Theseus

– Summarise the myth of Theseus and the Minotaur.

– Compare the Hunger Games to the legend of Theseus.

Useful Websites:

www.mythencyclopedia.com/Sp-Tl/Theseus.html

http://ancienthistory.about.com/od/theseus/tp/Theseus.-0jY.htm

http://www.youtube.com/watch?v=YzG3-vA_DCA

Task 2: While following the presentations, tick the appropriate smiley and give the groups feedback.

	☺	😐	☹
Your presentation was well-structured.			
The information was conveyed clearly.			
You were well-prepared.			
Your presentation was interesting.			
You had eye contact with your audience.			
You spoke with confidence and enthusiasm.			
Your transparency contains all necessary information.			

Suzanne Collins' „The Hunger Games" (S II)

M 10 Picture stimulus – reality TV

Tasks

1. Describe the picture.

2. Relate the picture to *The Hunger Games*.

3. Which reality shows have you watched? Describe what effect they had on you.

4. Lately there has been a growth of competitive shows and survival shows. Discuss this phenomenon.

M 13 Movie poster: *The Hunger Games*

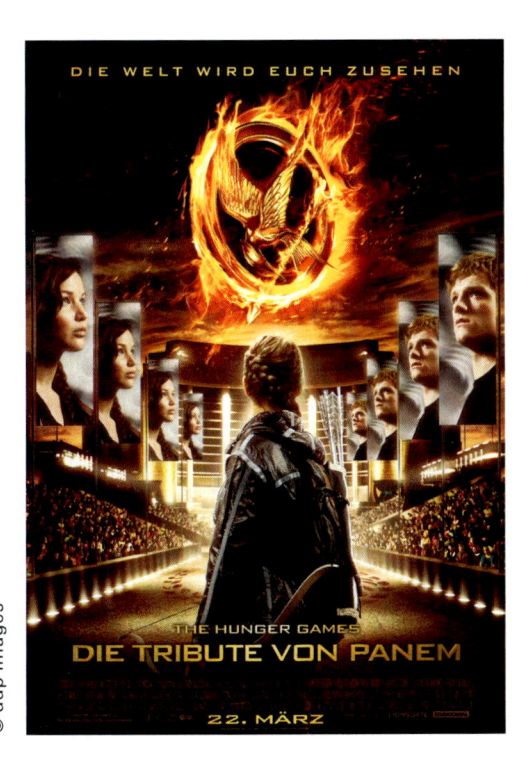

Tasks

1. Describe the movie poster.

2. Explain which aspects of the novel the movie poster emphasises.

3. Explain how far the movie poster matches your expectations. If you could re-create the movie poster, what would you do differently?

Hinweise (M 9 und M 10; 5./6. Stunde)

Ziel dieser Doppelstunde ist es, die Schülerinnen und Schüler **Hintergrundwissen** zu **kulturellen Bezügen** erarbeiten zu lassen, die die Autorin beim Schreiben des Romans beeinflusst haben (vgl. Sachanalyse „Zur Autorin und ihrem Werk").

Zu Beginn der Stunde werden die **Hausaufgaben** besprochen: *Brainstorm sources of inspiration for authors (music/lyrics; literature; nature; films; stories from friends and family ...)*.

Differenzierung: Schwächeren Kursen kann anschließend ein **Bild des römischen Kolosseums** als Folie aufgelegt und die dazugehörigen Impulsfragen gestellt werden. Auf diese Weise wird die anschließende Rechercheaufgabe vorentlastet.

Die nähere Auseinandersetzung mit den Inspirationsquellen Suzanne Collins' geschieht über eine **Internetrecherche (M 9)**, für die hilfreiche Links bereits vorgegeben sind. Hierzu werden Schülerpaare jeweils den Gruppen A oder B zugeteilt. Für die Recherche sollten in etwa 25 Minuten eingeplant werden.

Die **Präsentation** der Ergebnisse durch jeweils ein Paar der zwei Gruppen findet im Plenum statt. Die gesammelten Informationen werden auf Folie vorgestellt. Hierzu sollte einem Schülerpaar einer jeden Gruppe zuvor eine leere Folie ausgeteilt worden sein. Die zuhörenden Schülerinnen und Schüler ergänzen ihre Aufschriebe und bewerten die Präsentation ihrer Mitschüler anhand des **Feedbackbogens (*task 2*)**.

Am Ende der Stunde stellen die Lernenden anhand eines **Screenshots (M 10)** der Reality-TV-Show „Ich bin ein Star – Holt mich hier raus!", der als Folie kopiert aufgelegt oder über Beamer gezeigt werden kann, einen **Bezug zu ihrer Lebenswelt** her, indem die *Hunger Games* mit real existierenden Reality-Shows verglichen werden.

Die schriftliche Bearbeitung von *task 4* ist **Hausaufgabe**.

Erwartungshorizont (M 9)

Research Group A:

Gladiators are men who fight to the death in an arena to entertain the audience; the fight isn't supposed to be short, the audience would be disappointed otherwise; the crowd is allowed to order a gladiator to be killed if they are dissatisfied with his fighting; background: the Roman Empire held the games to distract and entertain the poor masses to keep them from revolting; some people volunteered to be gladiators, they risked death for the chance to gain fame; there were special schools that trained them how to fight.

<u>Similarities between the Hunger Games and the gladiator games</u>: Both for means of entertainment and control; mainly unwilling participants; the citizens follow the games as a spectacle; fights take place in an artificial environment; winners can become heroes; both are fights to the death.

<u>Differences</u>: Gladiator fights took place more often; gladiators also fought against convicted criminals.

Research Group B:

Theseus is a hero of Greek mythology; according to the myth he was the illegitimate son of the Athenian king Aegeus; his father hid a sword and sandals underneath a rock so that, when his son was old and strong enough, he would find them and come to find his father in Athens; on his way to the throne in Athens Theseus lives through many adventures; one of them is defeating the Minotaur to rescue an oppressed society:

Minos, king of Crete, captured Athens and wanted to destroy it unless its citizens would send seven boys and girls as tributes to confront the Minotaur (half-bull, half-human) who is trapped in a labyrinth; Theseus volunteers; falls in love with Mino's daughter at a parade before the game; Mino's daughter gives him a ball of yarn; with the help of the yarn he finds his way out of the labyrinth after having killed the Minotaur.

Similarities: Theseus volunteers as a tribute just like Katniss although he doesn't volunteer to save a relative but to free Athens from the king of Crete; Katniss and Theseus share the awareness of the injustice in their societies and are both strong; they both succeed through love; both games are very cruel and a public spectacle.

Differences: Theseus actually manages to rescue an oppressed society, despite Katniss' rebellious act of planning to eat the berries together with Peeta, she doesn't free Panem; Katniss is helped several times by Peeta as Theseus is helped by Ariadne but Katniss isn't in love with Peeta; the people of Athens are horrified about the game whereas the people of Panem are mainly distracted by them.

Erwartungshorizont (M 10)

1. Description of the picture: In the picture you can see two women in bathing costumes sitting in a boat on the water; they are surrounded by a lot of trees that look tropical; hanging above their heads are boxes made out of glass or transparent plastic; one of them is opening just as the picture is shot; what seem to be insects fall out of the box and onto the women; they look disgusted but nevertheless are stretching out their arms and hands; it seems as if they need to catch the insects.

2. Relation to *The Hunger Games*: The picture also shows a reality show; its name is *"Ich bin ein Star – holt mich hier raus!"* and you can watch it on German television; like in *The Hunger Games* people are sent to an artificial camp which is in the Australian jungle; the show's goal is for someone to become the winner of the game by making the audience like you; on their way to the throne of the jungle they don't have to fight their competitors to death but they also have to pass tests in order to win food; they are not allowed to take more than one personal item with them; there isn't a lot of food and people start fighting each other while the viewers watch and vote for them.

3. Reality Shows: *Big Brother, Biggest Loser; Germany's next Topmodel; "Ich bin ein Star – Holt mich hier raus!"*.

4. The shows have good ratings; many people seem to enjoy watching them; reasons for this could be easy distraction from one's own problems; following a star or person you like; supporting this person (like supporting a sports team); funny presenters; but it also seems that people like to see other people suffer to a certain degree; the TV concept can be argued to be disgusting and degrading; it could also be seen as evidence for the incapacity of a society which enjoys and tolerates programmes like that; questions it raises are e.g. what is next and how can this be managed for an audience that soon will be bored and wants to see even more pain and scandals; where is this going to lead?

M 11 Defining characterisation – direct vs indirect

Characterisation is the process by which the writer reveals the personality of a literary character. The personality can be revealed through direct characterisation and indirect characterisation.

Tasks

1. Together with a partner match the definitions 1. and 2. with the correct examples a) or b).

> **1. Direct characterisation** tells the reader what the personality of a character is like. This can be through:
>
> – **The narrator** who describes another character or comments on him/her.
>
> – **Another character** who describes a character or comments on him/her in thoughts or verbally.
>
> – **The character** who describes him-/herself in thoughts or verbally.

> **2. Indirect characterisation** is more complex. It hints at things which reveal the character of a protagonist. This can be by interpreting things that a character reveals about him-/herself or by interpreting what the narrator or other characters say about the character. This can be through:
>
> – **Speech:** Does he or she have an accent, a low or a high-pitched voice. Does he or she whisper, scream, cry etc.?
>
> – **Thoughts:** What does the character think? Does he or she act accordingly or differently?
>
> – **Effect on others:** How do his or her actions and words influence other people?
>
> – **Looks:** What does he or she look like? Is he or she comfortable with his or her appearance? What kind of clothes does he or she wear?
>
> – **Action:** How does the character behave?

> **a)** When Prim is chosen at the reaping, Katniss volunteers for her:
>
> "'Prim!' A strangled cry comes out of my throat, and my muscles begin to move again. 'Prim!' I don't need to shove through the crowd. The other kids make way immediately allowing me a straight path to the stage. I reach her just as she is about to mount the steps. With one sweep of my arm, I push her behind me. 'I volunteer!' I gasp. 'I volunteer as tribute!'" (p. 28, ll. 26–31)

> **b)** When Katniss and Gale hunt together in the woods, Katniss describes him as follows:
>
> "Gale won't have any trouble finding a wife. He's good-looking, he's strong enough to handle the work in the mines, and he can hunt. You can tell by the way the girls whisper about him when he walks by in a school that they want him." (p. 19, ll. 6–10)

2. Explain how the quotations fit the definition of direct and indirect characterisation.

3. Explain which of the above quotations would be stronger evidence when used in a character analysis.

4. With a partner characterise your protagonist by taking notes in bullet point form.

Suzanne Collins' „The Hunger Games" (S II)

| Reihe 15 | Verlauf | Material S 23 | LEK | Kontext | Mediothek |

II/B2

Hinweise (M 11; 7. Stunde)

Diese Stunde dient der direkten **Vorbereitung auf die mündlichen Prüfungen** am Ende der Einheit, indem die Lernenden wie in Teil 1 des *oral exam* eine der **Figuren charakterisieren**.

In **M 11** setzen sich die Schülerinnen und Schüler zunächst mit den Unterschieden zwischen **direkter und indirekter Charakterisierung** auseinander. Sie ordnen in Partnerarbeit die Beispiele den richtigen Definitionen zu (**task 1**).

Im Plenum werden die Ergebnisse besprochen und die Lernenden erklären, inwiefern die Beispiele den Definitionen entsprechen (**task 2**) und welche Art der Charakterisierung als Beleg aussagekräftiger ist (**task 3**).

Anschließend schreiben sie in Partnerarbeit eine stichpunktartige **Charakterisierung** für jeweils eine Figur (**task 4**). Die Zuordnung der Figuren erfolgt über ein „**reaping**". Jeder Schüler schreibt hierzu seinen Namen auf einen Zettel. Diese werden dann in einem Gefäß gesammelt. Die Figuren stehen an der Tafel (Peeta Mellark, Haymitch Abernathy, Effie Trinket, Cinna und Rue). Je nach Kursstärke werden die Schülerinnen und Schüler nun einer Figur zugelost. In Partnerarbeit charakterisieren sie diese stichpunktartig. Einem Schülerpaar einer jeden Figur wird eine Folie ausgeteilt, auf der die Ergebnisse festgehalten werden.

Die **Präsentation** der Charakterisierung findet im Plenum statt. Die Lernenden machen sich zu jeder nicht von ihnen bearbeiteten Figur Notizen.

Als **Hausaufgabe** bereiten sie eine **Kurzpräsentation** für jede der oben aufgeführten Figuren und Katniss vor, da in der darauffolgenden Stunde der erste Teil der Prüfung simuliert wird.

Erwartungshorizont (M 11)

1. Match the definitions 1. and 2. with the correct examples a) or b):

1. b); 2. a)

2. Explain how the quotations fit the definitions:

a) It is indicated indirectly that Katniss is brave: She saves Prim and risks her own life; although she is nervous (voice), she does something outstanding (the others give way) and is determined (she repeats "I volunteer").

b) Katniss is directly telling the reader about Gale: He is handsome, strong and desired.

3. Which of the quotations would be stronger evidence?:

An indirect characterisation is a stronger proof for a person's character. Actions speak louder than words: It is important that a person does not only claim to do certain things, but actually does them.

4.

Peeta Mellark:

16 years old, medium height, stocky build, ashy blond hair, blue eyes, strong; has two older brothers, a strict mother, a kind father (baker); his family does not believe in him, they think Katniss will win the Hunger Games; wants to stay himself during the Hunger Games and wants to sacrifice himself for Katniss; has a conflict with Haymitch; uses his decorating skills to hide/survive; clever, underestimated, soft, sensitive, funny, generous, brave, honest, can manipulate the audience, helpful; desperately in love with Katniss since he was five years old.

Haymitch Abernathy:

Katniss and Peeta's mentor; only survivor of the Hunger Games from District 12 (won them 24 years ago); clever, but drunk most of the time; finds good sponsors; sends all necessary gifts, gives them hints by sending or not sending gifts; his strategy which helped Katniss and Peeta to survive: a romance; he is worried about Katniss and Peeta after they have won the Hunger Games because the Capitol is furious and might take revenge.

Effie Trinket:

Escort for District 12's tributes; usually wears colourful wigs, costumes and lots of make-up; strives for perfection; loyal towards the Capitol; thinks it's an honour to participate in the Hunger Games; would like to be transferred to a richer and better district; punctual, emotional, ignorant, naïve, ambitious, arrogant but supportive; has a love-hate relationship with Haymitch.

Cinna:

Katniss' stylist and her only friend in the Capitol; his first time as a stylist for the Hunger Games; asked to be responsible for the poorest district (12); helps Peeta and Katniss to an unforgettable performance by putting them on fire; green eyes, brown hair; unlikely for people from the Capitol, he wears no make-up apart from golden eyeliner; he cares about Katniss and encourages her to be herself; understands the situation Katniss is in and how she feels; gives her helpful advice for her TV interviews.

Rue:

Girl tribute from District 11; tiny; 12-year-old; her name is an archaic term for *regret*; reminds Katniss of her sister Prim; they become allies; they share food, supply and stories about life; after her death Katniss covers her body in flowers.

M 12 Katniss and Peeta's conflict – good angel vs bad angel

As readers you learn a lot about the conflicts of the first person narrator Katniss. Let's have a closer look at them.

> Internal and external conflicts drive a plot forward and make a story interesting.
>
> **External conflict:** Struggle between a literary character and an outside force such as nature or another character, which drives the dramatic action of the plot.
>
> **Internal conflict:** Psychological struggle within the mind of a literary character, the resolution of which creates the plot's suspense.

Tasks

1. a) Read trough the the definitions above. Together with your partner point out external and internal conflicts Katniss goes through in *The Hunger Games*.

    b) Juxtapose Katniss' everyday conflicts with the conflicts you have/had to deal with in your life. Do they differ or are there similarities?

2. Put yourself in the position of Katniss or Peeta at the end of the Hunger Games:

    You have survived all obstacles, you have fought against all other tributes, you have killed, you have seen people dying and you are the last one(s). You are happy and relieved to be the winner of the 74th Hunger Games. Then you hear Templesmith's announcement that the rule change has been revoked and there can be only one winner. Peeta/Katniss stands opposite you and looks at you in astonishment:

    What should you do?

> **Girls:** Get together in groups of three and put yourself in Katniss' position. Discuss her options and think of more examples other than eating the berries. Imagine there are little angels on her shoulders advising her on what to do. Formulate advice the two angels might give Katniss.

> **Boys:** Get together in groups of three and put yourself in Peeta's position. Discuss his options and think of more examples other than eating the berries. Imagine there are little angels on his shoulders advising him on what to do. Formulate advice the two angels might give Peeta.

Role play: Be prepared to act out the scene in front of the class with one of you being the character and the others being the good and the bad angel. It is not obligatory to take their decision but if some angels are particularly convincing, Katniss/Peeta can follow their advice.

3. Together with your partner discuss what is worth dying for.

Hinweise (M 12; 8. Stunde)

In dieser Stunde setzen sich die Lernenden mit dem **Dilemma** auseinander, in dem sich Katniss und Peeta am **Ende des Romans** befinden: Sollen sie nach der erneuten Regeländerung den anderen töten und als Gewinner aus den Spielen hervorgehen oder gemeinsam sterben?

Den **Einstieg** in die Stunde bilden die **90-Sekunden-Präsentationen** der Figuren. Hierbei werden die **Prüfungsbedingungen simuliert** (vgl. M 15 und „Zur LEK"), indem die Lehrkraft genau auf die Einhaltung der Zeit achtet. So ist es auch möglich, dass jeder Protagonist einmal vorgestellt wird.

In einem zweiten Schritt sammeln die Schülerinnen und Schüler in Partnerarbeit wesentliche **externe und interne Konflikte**, in denen Katniss sich in „The Hunger Games" befindet (*task 1 a*). Die Begriffe *external* und *internal conflict* werden zuvor anhand der Infobox (M 12) im Plenum geklärt. In *task 1 b)* vergleichen sie Katniss' Konflikte in Partnerarbeit mit solchen, vor denen sie selbst in ihrem alltäglichen Leben stehen.

In Dreiergruppen erarbeiten die Lernenden anschließend anhand der Methode *„Good Angel – Bad Angel"* den schwierigen **Konflikt**, in dem sich Katniss und Peeta am Ende der Spiele befinden (*task 2*). Die Ergebnissicherung findet im Plenum statt, indem mindestens zwei Gruppen ihre Argumente in einem **Rollenspiel** vortragen.

Im Rahmen der Auswertung ist darauf einzugehen, wie **realistisch** die dargestellten **Ratschläge im Kontext des Werks** erscheinen. Festzuhalten ist hier, dass Peeta Katniss gegenüber sehr loyal ist. Daher ist es unwahrscheinlich, dass er lange darüber nachdenkt, ihr etwas anzutun. Im Plenum sollte thematisiert werden, dass er zwar negative Gedanken haben könnte, er diesen jedoch nicht nachgeben würde, da ihm Katniss' Leben mehr Wert ist als das eigene. Impulse hierfür könnten sein:

– *Comment on Katniss and Peeta's relationship: Is it balanced?*
– *Do you think Katniss is in love with Peeta too?*
– *What would you have done if you were Peeta or Katniss?*

Abschließend diskutiert der Kurs in Partnerarbeit, welche Personen, Ziele oder Ansichten so wichtig sind, dass sie für diese sterben würden (*task 3*).

Hausaufgabe dieser Stunde ist das Verfassen eines **Tagebucheintrags** Katniss' oder Peetas, in dem Gedanken und Gefühle zum Ausgang der Spiele festgehalten werden.

Erwartungshorizont (M 12)

1.

a) **External conflicts:** The other tributes; Haymitch and Effie in order to get and maintain sponsors; the rule change.

   Internal conflicts: Asks herself constantly if she should give up or kill other people but promised Prim to stay alive; has feelings for Gale and Peeta and can't always say of which nature they are; appearance vs reality.

b) Individual answers

2. **Katniss' good angel:**

– Pretend to eat poisonous berries and play a trick on the Capitol, they'd rather have two victors than no victor at all.

– Just sit it out: If the Capitol is not entertained and it sees that you are not willing to fight anymore, it will terminate the Hunger Games.

- Team up with Peeta and try to find a way out of the Arena; look for the most deadly weapons and kill yourselves simultaneously, you will have peace in death (where you will be reunited).
- If you kill Peeta, you will always regret it, he is ready to sacrifice everything for you – you cannot be so selfish.

Katniss' bad angel:

- Just kill him, then it's finally over and you can go home to your family.
- Don't try to fool the Capitol, they are stronger than you and might take revenge on you; make sure only he eats the berries.
- Do not eat the berries, he might play a trick and hide them under his tongue so that only you die and he will be the victor.
- Just run off, you are much better at surviving in the woods and he will die anyway because of his injured leg; this way you don't have to kill him but you can still be the victor.

Peeta's good angel:

- Don't kill the person you love the most – even if you survive, without her your life will be meaningless.
- Trust her and eat the berries.
- Kill each other simultaneously and then you will be united in death.
- Run off and let destiny decide who will win.
- Just sit it out: if the Capitol is not entertained and sees that you are not willing to fight anymore, it will terminate the Hunger Games.
- Try to find a way out of the arena.

Peeta's bad angel:

- Kill Katniss, be the victor and go home to your family, you will live a prosperous life in the Victors' village.
- Make sure only Katniss eats the berries.

3. Possible answers:

Family; friends; girlfriend/boyfriend; freedom; home country; own children; risking your life in order to help a stranger who is in danger; an opinion; a belief; an ideology.

Suzanne Collins' „The Hunger Games" (S II)

| Reihe 15 | Verlauf | Material S 28 | LEK | Kontext | Mediothek |

II/B2

M 14 The Hunger Games – comparing the novel and the movie

Suzanne Collins' novel The Hunger Games *was made into a film by director Gary Ross. It was released in 2012.*

Tasks

1. Which aspects of the novel do you think are difficult to realise in the movie?
2. Describe how you, as a director, would deal with such passages.
3. While watching the film take notes on the differences between the novel and the movie.

© ddp images

Hinweise (M 13 und M 14; 9. Stunde)

In dieser Stunde analysieren die Schülerinnen und Schüler das **Filmposter** und schauen die ersten knapp 28 Minuten der **Verfilmung**. In diesen wird der Zuschauer in die Welt des Distrikt 12 eingeführt und es wird gezeigt, wie Katniss sich nach dem *reaping* zusammen mit Peeta und Haymitch auf den Weg in die Capitol macht. Dabei dreht sich alles um eine Frage: Kann sie die Spiele gewinnen und wenn ja, wie?

Den **Einstieg** in die Stunde bildet die Besprechung der **Hausaufgabe** (Tagebucheintrag Katniss' oder Peetas). Einzelne Arbeiten werden im Plenum vorgetragen, während der Rest des Kurses darauf achtet, ob die Darstellung der Gefühle und Gedanken im Kontext des Romans realistisch erscheint.

Nach dem Hausaufgabenvortrag werden folgende weiterführende **Impulsfragen** gestellt:

– *How does the victory tour affect Katniss and Peeta's relationship?*
– *How does it affect their view on the future?*
– *Which message does* The Hunger Games *have for any society and you personally?*
– *What do you think is going to happen in the second book of the trilogy?*

Im Plenum beschreiben die Schülerinnen und Schüler das deutsche Filmplakat **(Seite 19, M 13, *task 1*)**, das auf Folie kopiert auf dem Overhead-Projektor präsentiert werden kann. Sie vergleichen die Inhalte des Buches mit deren Darstellung auf dem Filmposter **(*task 2*)** und gleichen ihre Erwartungshaltung an das Filmposter mit dem tatsächlichen Poster ab **(*task 3*)**.

In **M 14** überlegen sie anschließend in Partnerarbeit, welche Romanstellen filmisch schwer umzusetzen sind **(*task 1*)** und wie sie als Regisseur mit diesen Herausforderungen umgehen würden **(*task 2*)**. Die Ergebnisse werden im Plenum gesammelt.

Nach der Antizipation der Probleme einer filmischen Umsetzung zeigt die Lehrkraft den **Film bis Minute 00:27:47** (Haymitch rät Katniss, sich Peeta als Beispiel zu nehmen). Während der Filmpräsentation notieren sich die Lernenden Unterschiede zwischen Roman und Verfilmung **(*task 3*)**.

> Falls die Verfilmung detaillierter besprochen werden soll, kann statt M 14, *task 3* ein **Fragebogen** mit zusätzlichen *while-viewing tasks* eingesetzt werden (vgl. **CD Grundwerk**). Hier liegt der Schwerpunkt des Vergleichs auf den **Figuren** und dem *setting*.

Abschließend wird im Plenum besprochen, wie die in M 14 (*task 1*) antizipierten Probleme der filmischen Umsetzung bis zu dieser Stelle des Films vom Regisseur gelöst wurden.

RAAbits Englisch

Suzanne Collins' „The Hunger Games" (S II)

Als **Hausaufgabe** vervollständigen die Schülerinnen und Schüler ihre **Notizen zum Film.**

Erwartungshorizont (M 13)

1. Description of the movie poster:

   In the picture you can see an arena with a huge audience sitting on both sides. Above them, on the left and right of the arena, there are screens showing the picture of a girl and a boy. In the middle of the arena there is a girl turning her back towards the viewer. She is dressed in dark colours and is wearing a backpack. Above the arena there is a burning symbol showing, the mockingjay pin.

2. Aspects of the novel emphasised:

   It becomes clear that the Games are a public media spectacle (big audience and screens); Katniss and Peeta, as main protagonists taking part in the Games, are depicted although Katniss is, of course, in the centre of the picture (first-person narrator); on top of the picture there is the mockingjay pin as a lucky charm which shows that you need all your luck to win the Games; the dark colours together with the masses create an atmosphere of pressure and fear.

3. Individual answers

Erwartungshorizont (M 14)

1. Aspects difficult to realise:

   It's difficult to depict the thoughts of a first person narrator (Katniss) when turning a piece of literature into a movie; what might be a challenge for the actress playing Katniss is to depict her inner conflicts; a flashback into the Dark Days could also be difficult and expensive; hunting scenes might bore the audience as there is a lot of waiting.

2. Possible answers:

   A solution for depicting the thoughts of a first person narrator are inner monologues or strong facial expressions which show the mood of the characters or their feelings; shorten passages of the novel which are not interesting to watch in cinemas.

3. Differences between the novel and the movie:

   - The first person narrator (novel) changed to a third person narrator in the movie, so the viewer can e.g. watch Gale back at home as he watches Katniss and her romance on screen.

   - The fence which Katniss has to pass to go into the woods is less spectacular in the movie; she does not even stop to listen to a hum indicating electricity.

   - The mockingjay pin is given to Katniss by Madge, the mayor's daughter in the novel; in the movie she gets it from Greasy Sae at the Hob; Madge does not even appear in the movie.

   - Katniss is not visited by Peeta's father before they take off to the Capitol, the viewers do not get to know that Peeta's father was once in love with Katniss' mother.

   - Avoxes do not appear in the movie, there are merely servants.

   - The girl making the bonfire and Cato's deaths are shortened (probably not to show the brutality in detail).

   - In the book Katniss goes several days without water and is severely dehydrated; in the movie she finds water relatively quickly.

- The audience does not find out that Katniss is especially protective towards Rue because she reminds her of her sister Prim.
- In the book, Haymitch's gifts have no notes on them; Katniss has to find out their function and meaning herself.
- In the novel Katniss is deaf in her left ear after causing the explosion at where the food was supplied, in the movie she only momentarily loses her hearing.
- The mutations chasing the remaining three tributes have no similarities with the dead tributes in the movie; in the novel they have Glimmer and Co's eyes.
- The revolution shown breaking out in District 11 after Rue's death is not mentioned in the novel (Katniss would not have known about it).
- Seneca Crane, the Gamemaker, has a more prominent role in the movie (due to the third person narrator).

Hinweise (M 14; 10.–12. Stunde)

Der **Film** wird in dieser Stunde von Minute 00:27:47 bis zum Ende (Minute 01:22:00) angeschaut. Dabei untersuchen die Schülerinnen und Schüler die **Unterschiede zwischen Roman und filmischer Umsetzung**.

Den Lernenden wird der letzte Teil des Films vorgespielt. Währenddessen machen sie sich in Einzelarbeit Notizen zu den Unterschieden zwischen Roman und Verfilmung **(M 14, *task 3*)** bzw. füllen den **Fragebogen** aus.

Nach Beendigung der Filmpräsentation werden die Ergebnisse von *task 3* bzw. die des Fragebogens in Partnerarbeit verglichen, vervollständigt und anschließend im Plenum diskutiert. Hierbei wird auch auf die möglichen Gründe für die Änderungen in der filmischen Umsetzung eingegangen.

In der **Hausaufgabe** fassen die Schülerinnen und Schüler schriftlich zusammen, inwiefern der Film ihren Erwartungen entsprochen hat und begründen, ob sie eher empfehlen würden das Buch zu lesen oder den Film zu schauen.

M 15 Preparing for the oral exams

Tasks

1. Together with a partner, choose one topic and prepare a discussion. Write down as many arguments as possible and conduct the discussion for at least three minutes.

Possible topics for the oral exam
a) How does the fact that the tributes are constantly being filmed affect their behaviour? Does being filmed make it easier or harder for them? Discuss.
b) Is Haymitch a good mentor for Katniss and Peeta? Discuss.
c) In what way does Katniss' background (being from District 12, being able to hunt etc.) affect her chances in the Hunger Games? Discuss.

2. Change your partner and choose another topic. Again, write down as many arguments as possible. This time use the following means of expression to structure your discussion.

Useful phrases for your discussion
You're right, but …
That's true, but you also have to consider that …
You've got a point there, but what about …
I agree with you./I am afraid I have to disagree with you.
I (don't) share your opinion.
That's not what I was trying to say.
On the one hand … on the other hand …

3. Change your partner to discuss the last question. Make sure you use the phrases above. Watch your time: You have only one minute to prepare for your three-minute-discussion.

Structure of the oral exam
I. 90-second presentation on one of the following topics (chosen at random)
– Katniss Everdeen   – Peeta Mellark
– Effie Trinket   – Haymitch Abernathy
– Cinna   – Rue
– The history of Panem
II. Three-minute discussion: You should ensure you:
– mention as many different arguments as possible.
– do not repeat yourself.
– connect to what the other person says.
– you come to a conclusion, which must not necessarily be a consensus but can be a compromise.
You have **one-minute preparation** time of the chosen discussion question, you can talk to your partner and take notes.

Suzanne Collins' „The Hunger Games" (S II)

| Reihe 15 | Verlauf | Material S 32 | LEK | Kontext | Mediothek |

Hinweise (M 15; 13. Stunde)

Diese Stunde dient der **Vorbereitung** des zweiten Teils der **mündlichen Prüfungen** am Ende der Unterrichtseinheit.

Durch einen **informierenden Einstieg** wird der Kurs über den genauen **Ablauf der Prüfung** in Kenntnis gesetzt (vgl. „Zur LEK") und bestehende Fragen werden geklärt. Der **Bewertungsbogen für mündliche Prüfungen** in der Sekundarstufe II in Nordrhein-Westfalen wird ebenfalls gemeinsam besprochen. Er findet sich unter:

http://www.standardsicherung.schulministerium.nrw.de/cms/upload/muendl_kompe-tenzen/2013_Muendliche_Pruefung_SII_Bewertungsraster.pdf.

In **M 15** werden die Schülerinnen und Schüler schrittweise an die Anforderungen der mündlichen Prüfungen herangeführt. Sie erhalten drei verschiedene Themen, die sie vorbereiten und anschließend paarweise diskutieren. Bei jedem Durchgang beachten die Lernenden dabei einen neuen Aspekt, der wesentlich für die Prüfung ist. So verwenden sie in *task 2* **Redemittel** und sind in *task 3* angehalten, die angegebene **Vorbereitungszeit** nicht zu überschreiten.

Eine Liste mit **zusätzlichen *discussion phrases*** findet sich auf der **CD Grundwerk**.

Die Lernenden arbeiten nicht nur mit einem Partner zusammen, sondern wechseln diesen bei jeder Aufgabe. Diese Vorgehensweise ermöglicht ihnen, auf mehrere Personen einzugehen und unterschiedliche Strategien (z. B. aktives Zuhören, Hinhaltestrategien, Widersprechen, Zustimmen) einzuüben, mit denen sie auf spontane Äußerungen reagieren können.

Zwei bis drei Partnerdiskussionen werden abschließend exemplarisch im Plenum vorgetragen. Diese werden anhand des Bewertungsbogens besprochen und evaluiert.

Erwartungshorizont (M 15)

a) How does the fact that the tributes are constantly being filmed affect their behaviour? Does being filmed make it easier or harder for them?:

- The tributes are conscious of being filmed.
- They know that it is obligatory for Panem's population to watch the Hunger Games.
- Their families and friends are watching them as well.
- It is difficult for the tributes to be constantly watched, this means that the people they care about watch them as they kill.
- It also means that their families and friends have to watch as they die.
- For Katniss it is twice as hard to play the romance with Peeta because her family and especially Gale watch her as she kisses Peeta and tells him "you don't have much competition anywhere.
- It also encourages the tributes to be or to act strongly because they don't want their families and friends to watch them suffering.

b) Is Haymitch a good mentor for Katniss and Peeta?:

- Haymitch is District 12's only winner of the Hunger Games; he lives alone in the Victors' Village, without family or friends; he drinks a lot of alcohol and is drunk most of the time.
- When Katniss and Peeta first meet Haymitch he is drunk and falls off the stage; at their second encounter he is drunk again and vomits all over himself.

- Haymitch does not believe in Katniss and Peeta; he has mentored so many tributes from District 12 during the last 24 years and watched all of them die.
- He is very dismissive and does not want to build up a relationship to someone who has no chance of survival.
- Haymitch realises that both Katniss and Peeta have their special qualities (Peeta is very charming and popular and Katniss can be impulsive, demanding and determined), he makes a deal with them: He helps them as long as they don't interfere with his drinking.
- He finds sponsors and supports Katniss with gifts.
- He advises them to play the romance in order to gain more sponsors.
- With his gifts he also sends messages to Katniss (hot broth, for example, to reinforce the romance), by not sending Katniss water when she is severely dehydrated, he indicates that water is near.
- He does not just mentor Katniss and Peeta during the Games, after the Games are over, he warns Katniss about the Capitol.

c) In what way does Katniss' background affect her chances in the Hunger Games?:

- To be from District 12 has several advantages as well as disadvantages for her.
- District 12 is one of the poorest districts of Panem where starvation is common and a frequent cause of death.
- She is used to small rations of food, she knows how to hunt and how to live self-sufficiently.
- It is very advantageous for Katniss that her father taught her how to use a bow and arrow.
- Another advantage is that she is used to the forest and she can climb trees.
- Being used to the woods, she is also familiar with its inhabitants, e.g. rabbits, and its plants, e.g. katniss (the plant with edible roots) and nightlock.
- But Katniss is also not as well trained as the Career Tributes are; she never had a chance to learn how to handle other weapons; there are no training centres in District 12 and there are no former victors but Haymitch to give advice.

The Hunger Games – oral exam

Task 1: Choose a character and prepare a 90-second presentation.

Haymitch Abernathy

Effie Trinket

Rue

Cinna

Task 2: Choose one question and discuss it with your partner.

Before the Games start, Peeta tells Katniss, "I want to die as myself ... I don't want them to change me in there. Turn me into some kind of monster that I'm not."

Is he able to stay true to himself during the Games? Discuss.

Are Katniss and Peeta actually in love? Discuss.

Discuss why the tributes form alliances in the arena and whether this is advantageous for them or not.

What do you think is the cruelest part of the Hunger Games? Discuss.

Discuss who has contributed the most to Katniss and Peeta's survival.

Are the Hunger Games an adequate punishment for the population of Panem? Discuss.

What effect do genetically modified animals have on the Games? Discuss.

Suzanne Collins' „The Hunger Games" (S II)

| Reihe 15 | Verlauf | Material | **LEK** **S 2** | Kontext | Mediothek |

II/B2

Hinweise (LEK)

Für **eine Prüfung** sind jeweils **15 Minuten** anzusetzen.

Der **erste Teil der Prüfung** besteht aus einem **monologischen Sprechakt** über eine der Figuren des Romans (***task 1***). In ***task 2*** stellen die Prüflinge ihre Kompetenzen im Bereich des **dialogischen Sprechens** unter Beweis. Die Themen für die beiden Aufgaben können ausgedruckt, auf stabile Pappe geklebt oder laminiert werden. Sie werden den Lernenden **verdeckt** als Auswahlmöglichkeit dargeboten.

Nach den mündlichen Prüfungen bietet es sich an, diese mit den Schülerinnen und Schülern zu besprechen. Dies geschieht anhand des **Evaluationsbogens** der Standardsicherung NRW: www.standardsicherung.schulministerium.nrw.de/cms/upload/ muendl_kompetenzen/Evaluationsbogen_Muendliche_Pruefungen_SII.pdf.

Erwartungshorizont (LEK)

1. See *"Erwartungshorizont"* M 11.

2. Before the Games start, Peeta tells Katniss, "I want to die myself ... I don't want them to change me in there. Turn me into some kind of monster I'm not." Is he able to stay true to himself during the Games?:

   On the one hand: able to stay himself; has been in love with Katniss for many years and stays in love with her; does everything to protect her; he would sacrifice his life to save her; he teams up with the Career Tributes only to protect Katniss and to hinder them from finding her; he trusts her at the end of the Games and eats the berries; on the other hand he commits murder; he is the one who finally kills the girl at the bonfire after the Careers have injured her; so he played his role in the Games and acted the way the Capitol expected of him.

   Are Katniss and Peeta actually in love?:

   Peeta has had a crush on Katniss since he was little; he admits his love in an interview on TV; he never really had a chance to talk to Katniss or spend time with her; he eventually falls in love with her when they are in the arena; her life means more to him than his own; he does not know about Haymitch's advice for Katniss about acting out a romance with Peeta; everything Katniss does (kissing him, telling him that there's no competition for him, neither inside nor outside the arena) is real to Peeta; **Katniss** is not in love with him; she is even furious when Peeta admits his love for her; she acts as if she was in love with him to get more sponsors; the reader gets the impression that she actually has feelings for Gale, her childhood friend; but she states that "there's never been anything romantic" between her and Gale; by pretending to be in love with Peeta, she actually cares for him; she does not let him die but risks her own life for him; she also saves him from Cato; when she has the chance to kill him and be the only victor, she plays the trick with the berries so that both of them can win; after the Games she misses Peeta (p. 316, l. 5; p. 316, l. 16).

   Discuss why the tributes form alliances in the arena and whether this is advantageous for them or not:

   To attack other tributes and to defend themselves as a team; it is a tradition that the **Career Tributes** form a team, consisting of the strongest tributes which usually come from the wealthier districts where it is an honour to fight in the Hunger Games; by forming an alliance they can more easily get hold of weapons and secure their food supply; they can always have someone to be on guard; but once the other tributes are all dead, they turn against each other without any liabilities; **Katniss and Rue** also form an alliance because they have similar skills and Rue reminds Katniss of her little sister Prim; they share food, shelter and stories and they can learn from each other (e.g. to communicate via mockingjays); **Disadvantages of alliances:** The Career Tributes never really know when someone will turn against them; when Katniss loses Rue it throws her off track: questions the Hunger Games, does not protect herself anymore, she covers Rues corpse with flowers to show the Capitol that Rue was a friend rather than an enemy, Rue's death also induced Katniss first killing (she shot Marvel who killed Rue).

What do you think is the cruelest part of the Hunger Games?:

The reaping, sending innocent children to the Games; advantages tributes from wealthier districts have over others; the TV coverage, that it is shown as entertainment and even compulsory to watch; conducted for 74 years without any rebellion against it; the Games destroy families; two tributes from the same district, who might have known each other for years, have to kill each other; the victor has to live alone in the Victors' Village; so a lot of money is spent on creating the arena, paying the prep team, camera teams, the host etc. which would have been better used for supporting the poorer districts and preventing people from starving.

Who has contributed the most to Katniss' and Peeta's survival?:

Haymitch gives them tips on how to act in the arena; he finds sponsors for them and sends Katniss gifts for her survival; he was also the one to advise Katniss on pretending to have a romance with Peeta, which made them very popular as a couple; Cinna helps them by creating their outfits and made Katniss *the girl on fire* for which she became so popular; Cinna is also her only friend in the Capitol and he encourages her to be herself and to believe in herself; Rue forms an alliance with Katniss and helps her out of the dangerous situation with the Careers; her friendship to Rue also makes Thresh spare her life; Claudius Templesmith contributed to their survival by announcing a rule change (twice) for which he even paid with his own life.

Are the Hunger Games an adequate punishment for the population of Panem?:

The Capitol reminds the population about the Dark Days, when a formerly existing 13th district rebelled against the Capitol and was destroyed; by annually holding the Hunger Games and making it obligatory to watch them the Capitol demonstrates its power and shows Panem's population that there is nothing they can do against it; the Games are held to keep the districts in order so they will not rebel again; the Capitol even directs the people to see the Hunger Games as a festivity and it encourages Career Tributes to volunteer to take part in the Games and to see it as an honour; it is not an adequate punishment; the people who started the rebellion are not punished but rather innocent children are instead; this stands in no relation to the rebellion and is part of the dictatorship and reign of violence and terror the Capitol holds.

What effect do genetically modified animals have on the Games?:

Mockingjays are advantageous for Katniss, they help her to communicate with Rue; **tracker jackers** are life-threatening to the tributes since their venom is deadly; Katniss is stung by them several times and falls unconscious; she makes use of them by making them attack the other tributes; again she turns the mutations to an advantage; the **mutts** resemble huge wolves but can balance on their hind legs and have the eyes of the dead tributes; they charge the remaining three tributes and put their lives in danger, Katniss, Peeta and Cato can fight them off and make their way to the top of the Cornucopia, Cato gets hold of Peeta and threatens Katniss that both of them will be torn apart by the mutts, Katniss and Peeta outsmart Cato, who falls down and is attacked by the mutts, they do not kill Cato, but prolong his death, Katniss finally shoots Cato.

T. C. Boyles „The Tortilla Curtain" (S II)

Reihe 17 S 1 | Verlauf | Material | LEK | Kontext | Mediothek

T. C. Boyles *„The Tortilla Curtain"* – Die Konflikte zwischen illegalen mexikanischen Einwanderern und Amerikanern nachvollziehen (S II)

Dr. Diana Tappen-Scheuermann, Oberursel

II/B2

Auf CD:
✓ Word-Datei
✓ language support
✓ alternative Klausur

Die mexikanisch-amerikanische Grenze haben Cándido und América bereits illegal überquert. Welche Hindernisse werden sie noch überwinden müssen?

Der Anglo-Amerikaner Delaney hält sich für einen liberalen Humanisten. Nachdem er einen illegalen Einwanderer angefahren hat, wird sein Selbstbild jedoch genauso erschüttert wie der amerikanische Traum des Unfallopfers …

In dieser Reihe beschäftigen sich Ihre Schüler mit der Situation illegaler Einwanderer in den USA und dem *American Dream*. Dabei werden Themen wie „Rassismus" und „Vorurteile" aufgegriffen. Neben analytisch-interpretatorischen Aufgaben setzen sich Ihre Lerner auf kreative Weise in einem Rollenspiel mit dem Thema *„gated communities"* auseinander und werden auf dem Hot Seat befragt. Einen aktuellen Bezug bietet der Fall Trayvon Martin, der 2012 vermutlich aufgrund seiner Hautfarbe in einer *„gated community"* erschossen wurde.

Klassenstufe: 11/12 (G8); 12/13 (G9)

Dauer: ca. 13 Unterrichtsstunden

Bereich: Literatur, Landeskunde USA, Themen: *„American Dream"*, *„Illegal immigration"*, *„Hispanics in the USA"*, *„Racism"*, *„Poverty"*

Kompetenzen:

1. Lesekompetenz: Lesen und Verstehen eines komplexen literarischen Texts;
2. Schreibkompetenz: Interpretieren eines literarischen Texts; 3. Kommunikative Kompetenz: klares und detailliertes Darstellen themenbezogener Sachverhalte

T. C. Boyles „*The Tortilla Curtain*" (S II)

| Reihe 17 S 2 | Verlauf | Material | LEK | Kontext | Mediothek |

II/B2

Sachanalyse: T. C. Boyles „*The Tortilla Curtain*"

Zum Autor und seinem Werk

Der US-Amerikaner **Thomas Coraghessan Boyle** (*1948) begann während seines Geschichtsstudiums zu schreiben. Nach einer kurzen Tätigkeit als Lehrer promovierte er in englischer Literatur. Boyle ist inzwischen Autor von 14 Romanen und mehr als 60 Kurzgeschichten. Literaturkritisch am meisten Beachtung fand bislang sein dritter Roman „*World's End*". Für den Generationenroman, der die Geschichte einer amerikanischen Familie über mehrere Jahrhunderte hinweg erzählt, erhielt er 1988 den PEN/Faulkner Award.

Sein sechster und bisher erfolgreichster Roman **„*The Tortilla Curtain*" erschien 1995**. Der Roman, in dem es um illegale Einwanderung in Kalifornien geht, wurde aufgrund der sozialpolitischen Thematik zunächst kritisch rezipiert. So wurde dem Autor vorgeworfen, dass er die Immigranten als isoliert und entfremdet darstellt, obwohl diese häufig in engen Gemeinschaften leben. Positiv aufgenommen wurde hingegen, dass Boyle in seinem Roman keine Patentlösung für die dargestellten Probleme anbietet und viele Fragen offen lässt. Mittlerweile gilt „*The Tortilla Curtain*" als **moderner Klassiker**, der häufig auch in Schulen und an Universitäten gelesen wird.

Zum Inhalt des Romans

„*The Tortilla Curtain*" thematisiert die Spannungen zwischen der **anglo-amerikanischen Mittelschicht** und den **illegalen mexikanischen Einwanderern** in Südkalifornien. Der Roman wird parallel aus der Sicht zweier Paare dieser beiden Gesellschaftsgruppen erzählt.

Cándido Rincón und seine schwangere Frau **América** halten sich illegal in den USA auf. Sie kampieren am Topanga Canyon und finanzieren sich durch Gelegenheitsjobs Cándidos. Die beiden haben ihre Heimat Mexiko verlassen, um ihren amerikanischen Traum von einem besseren Leben zu verwirklichen.

Das zweite Paar, der Anglo-Amerikaner **Delaney Mossbacher** und seine Frau **Kyra**, sind vor kurzem in eine *gated community* auf dem Topanga Canyon gezogen. Kyra arbeitet erfolgreich als Immobilienmaklerin, während Delaney den Haushalt führt, sich um Kyras Sohn aus erster Ehe kümmert und eine Kolumne für ein Naturmagazin schreibt.

Die Geschichte beginnt mit einem **Autounfall**, durch den sich die Wege **Delaneys** und **Cándidos** zum ersten Mal kreuzen. Obwohl Cándido verletzt ist, möchte er keine medizinische Hilfe in Anspruch nehmen, da er fürchtet, des Landes verwiesen zu werden. Delaney billigt dies und verrät so zum ersten Mal seine humanistische Einstellung, über die er sich eigentlich identifiziert. Von diesem Moment an werden die Leben der beiden immer wieder voneinander beeinflusst.

Für Cándido und seine siebzehnjährige Frau América bedeutet der Unfall den Beginn einer **Pechsträhne**, die sich über die folgenden sechs Monate, die erzählte Zeit des Romans, erstreckt: Kurz nachdem América zum ersten Mal bezahlt gearbeitet und dadurch ihr Selbstbewusstsein gestärkt hat, wird sie vergewaltigt. Kaum ist Cándido nach dem Unfall wieder physisch in der Lage, Arbeit anzunehmen, wird das Paar ausgeraubt. Und knapp dem Buschfeuer entkommen, das Cándido versehentlich verursacht hat, bringt América ein blindes Kind zur Welt.

Für Delaney markiert der Unfall den Beginn einer Entwicklung **vom toleranten Linksliberalen zum Rassisten**. Die negativen Ereignisse nach dem Unfall bringt er mit den illegalen Einwanderern und im Besonderen mit Cándido in Verbindung. So wird zum Beispiel der **Kojote**, der trotz eines Zauns die Hunde seiner Frau reißt, für Delaney zum Symbol für die Bedrohung, die von den *Hispanics* ausgeht. Die meisten seiner Nachbarn fühlen sich ebenfalls durch die Einwanderer bedroht und beschließen, eine **Mauer** um die Wohnanlage errichten zu lassen.

Im letzten Teil des Romans macht Delaney keinen Hehl mehr aus seiner Xenophobie. Er begibt sich auf eine obsessive **Verfolgungsjagd** auf Mexikaner. Als das versehentlich durch Cándido verursachte Buschfeuer auch Delaneys Nachbarschaft bedroht, sucht er bewaffnet nach diesem. Er findet Cándido als die Hütte des mexikanischen Paares durch einen überfluteten Fluss davongeschwemmt wird. Der Roman endet damit, dass Cándido seinem Verfolger Delaney die Hand reicht, um ihm das Leben zu retten.

Illegale Einwanderung von Mexiko in die USA

52 % der in den USA lebenden illegalen Immigranten sind Mexikaner[1]. Der Hauptgrund für die illegale Überschreitung der nahe liegenden Grenze liegt im Unterschied der Lebensqualität in den beiden Ländern. Viele illegale Einwanderer kommen aus von **Armut** geplagten Teilen Mexikos und hoffen, in den Vereinigten Staaten ihren **American Dream** von einem besseren Leben verwirklichen zu können. Das Arbeiten für einen Niedriglohn in den USA bedeutet für sie bereits eine Verbesserung ihres Lebensstandards, denn der Durchschnittslohn in Mexiko beträgt $ 4,15 und die Anzahl derer, die arbeitslos bzw. unterbeschäftigt sind, ist hoch[2].

Die illegale Einwanderung wird durch die Arbeit der **U.S. Border Patrol** erheblich erschwert, die die 3144 Kilometer lange Grenze überwacht und dabei von der Nationalgarde unterstützt wird. Viele der illegalen Einwanderer nehmen daher die Dienste eines sogenannten *„coyote"* in Anspruch. Sie bezahlen diese Schmuggler, damit sie ihnen über die Grenze helfen. Diejenigen, die es in die USA schaffen, werden dort nicht selten von Verwandten oder Freunden aufgenommen oder führen zunächst ein Leben im Verborgenen, das sie sich häufig durch Schwarzarbeit finanzieren. Auf lange Sicht hoffen sie, eine *green card* zu erhalten.

Zu den zentralen Themen des Romans

Ein zentrales Thema des Romans ist die Frage, inwiefern die USA ein Einwanderungsland sind, in dem jeder dieselben **Aufstiegschancen** hat. Die Antwort, die der Roman gibt, kann als **Kritik** am *American Dream* gelesen werden: Die **illegalen Einwanderer** Cándido und América haben in den USA mit **Rassismus** und **Armut** zu kämpfen. Dies wird auch durch die Darstellung der Wohnsiedlung Arroyo Blanco Estates verdeutlicht: Die wohlhabenden anglo-amerikanischen Bewohner der **geschlossenen Wohnanlage** versuchen, sich von den illegalen Einwanderern abzuschotten, denen gegenüber sie zahlreiche **Vorurteile** haben. Wie aktuell diese soziale Problematik ist, zeigt in der Realität das Beispiel des 2012 in einer vergleichbar geschlossenen Wohnanlage getöteten Afroamerikaners Trayvon Martin (s. M 11).

Ein weiteres aktuelles Thema ist die Situation der **hispanischen Einwanderer**, die die am **schnellsten wachsende Minderheit** der USA bilden[3] und politisch einen hohen Einfluss haben. Das Beispiel der Wiederwahl Obamas, die insbesondere mithilfe dieser gesellschaftlichen Gruppe gewonnen wurde, macht dies deutlich. Wie wichtig die *Hispanics* für die US-amerikanische Politik und Gesellschaft geworden sind, zeigt ebenfalls das Beispiel Julián Castros. Dem mexikanischstämmigen Bürgermeister San Antonios wird vorausgesagt, zukünftig eine große Rolle in der amerikanischen Politik zu spielen (s. LEK).

---

[1] New York Times: "Number of Illegal Immigrants in U.S. Maybe on Rise Again, Estimates Say". www.nytimes.com/2013/09/24/us/immigrant-population-shows-signs-of-growth-estimates-show.html?_r=0 (abgerufen am 11.10.2014).

[2] US Immigration Support: "Illegal Immigration from Mexico". www.usimmigrationsupport.org/illegal-immigration-from-mexico.html (abgerufen am 11.10.2014).

[3] Bloomberg: „Hispanics Are Fastest-Growing Minority Group, U.S. Census Says". www.bloomberg.com/apps/news?pid=newsarchive&sid=aQxcsvmWDhpE (abgerufen am 11.10.14)

T. C. Boyles „The Tortilla Curtain" (S II)

| Reihe 17 S 4 | Verlauf | Material | LEK | Kontext | Mediothek |

Didaktisch-methodisches Konzept

„The Tortilla Curtain" schildert auf bewegende Weise das **Aufeinanderprallen bitterer Armut** aufseiten der illegalen Einwanderer mit dem **Wohlstand** der anglo-amerikanischen Mittelschicht. Die Fragen, die der Roman dabei aufwirft, sind in einer globalisierten Welt omnipräsent und für die Schülerinnen und Schüler[1] somit hochaktuell: Darf sich der reiche Westen von ärmeren Ländern abgrenzen? Wer bestimmt, wo Grenzen verlaufen? Und welche Vorurteile prägen unser Miteinander? Durch die anschauliche Darstellung der beiden Mikrokosmen Topanga Canyon, wo das mexikanische Paar kampiert, und der Villensiedlung Arroyo Blanco Estates, in der Delaney und Kyra wohnen, werden diese **sozialpolitischen Themen** für die jugendlichen Leser lebendig. Die personale Erzählweise aus den vier Perspektiven der Protagonisten erleichtert die **Identifikation mit den Figuren**. Insbesondere die charakterlich detaillierte Darstellung des mexikanischen Migrantenpaares ermöglicht dem westlich geprägten Leser das Einfühlen in dessen Lebensverhältnisse.

1 Im weiteren Verlauf wird aus Gründen der besseren Lesbarkeit nur „Schüler" verwendet.

Zur Lerngruppe

Die Unterrichtsreihe eignet sich für den Einsatz in **Leistungskursen** und **leistungsstarken Grundkursen**. Für die in dieser Reihe vorgesehenen Leseabschnitte sollte in einem Grundkurs etwas mehr Zeit eingeplant werden.

Zum Leseprozess

Der Roman wird **zu Hause** gelesen und sollte den Schülern gegen Ende der 1. Stunde dieser Einheit ausgeteilt werden. Mögliche Leseabschnitte für eine **sukzessive Lektüre** in Abstimmung auf die Unterrichtsstunden der Reihe sind:

1. Stunde: Diese stimmt die Schüler auf das Lesen des Romans ein.

2./3. Stunde: In dieser Doppelstunde haben die Schüler Teil I, Kapitel 1 und 2 gelesen.

4. Stunde: In dieser Stunde haben die Lerner Teil I, Kapitel 3 und 4 gelesen.

5. Stunde: In dieser Stunde haben die Schüler Teil I, Kapitel 5 bis Teil II, Kapitel 4 gelesen.

6. Stunde: In dieser Stunde haben die Lernenden bis zum Ende von Teil II gelesen.

9. Stunde: In dieser Stunde haben die Schüler Teil III gelesen.

Zu den Methoden

Der Unterrichtsreihe liegen verschiedene handlungsorientierte Methoden zugrunde. So analysieren die Lernenden die Protagonisten Delaney und Kyra durch das Anfertigen einer **Personenkonstellation (M 5)** und die Befragung der beiden auf dem **Hot Seat (M 6)**. Anhand einer **Internetrecherche (M 10)** erschließen sie sich eigenständig die Bedeutung des Motivs des Kojoten. In einem **Rollenspiel (M 12)** diskutieren sie die Vor- und Nachteile von *gated communities* und interpretieren die Bildsprache des dritten Romanteils mithilfe von **Standbildern (M 15)**. Die schüler- und handlungsorientierten Phasen werden mit einer **kognitiven Sicherungsphase** abgeschlossen. Die einzige Ausnahme bildet die letzte Stunde, in der eine individuelle Reflexion über den Roman in Form einer **E-Mail an den Autor (M 17)** stattfindet.

T. C. Boyles „The Tortilla Curtain" (S II)

| Reihe 17 S 5 | Verlauf | Material | LEK | Kontext | Mediothek |

Schematische Verlaufsübersicht

> **T. C. Boyles „The Tortilla Curtain"** – Die Konflikte zwischen illegalen mexikanischen Einwanderern und Amerikanern nachvollziehen (S II)

1. Stunde:	*The Tortilla Curtain* – *getting into the text*
2./3. Stunde:	The crash – two worlds clashing
4. Stunde:	Meeting the Mossbachers – analysing Delaney and Kyra
5. Stunde:	Sense or sensibility? – Analysing Cándido and América
6. Stunde:	The coyote – analysing a major theme of *The Tortilla Curtain*
7./8. Stunde:	On gated communities – a panel discussion
9. Stunde:	The book of Job – having a closer look at Cándido
10. Stunde:	Who is América? – A character analysis
11. Stunde:	Imagery in Part Three of the novel – what does it stand for?
12./13. Stunde:	*The Tortilla Curtain* – a final evaluation

Minimalplan: Im Zentrum der Einheit steht die Behandlung des Primärtextes. Sollte weniger Zeit zur Verfügung stehen, kann die Einheit daher um die 1. Stunde (*pre-reading*) sowie um die 12./13. Stunde (*post-reading*) gekürzt werden.

1. Stunde

Thema
The Tortilla Curtain – *getting into the text*

Material	Verlauf
M 1, OHP	**Picture stimulus: Iron vs Tortilla Curtain** / Vergleichen des Eisernen Vorhangs mit dem Tortilla Curtain anhand eines Bildimpulses; Reaktivieren von Vorwissen zu mexikanischen Einwanderern
M 2	**Reading the blurb** / Lesen des Klappentextes; Formulieren von Fragen und Hypothesen zum Inhalt
	Homework: *Read Part One, Chapters 1 and 2 of* The Tortilla Curtain *and take notes on the reactions of the two protagonists to the crash.*
Zusätzlich benötigtes Material: M 1 auf Folie kopiert; Klassensatz der Lektüre	

2./3. Doppelstunde

Thema
The crash – *two worlds clashing*

Material	Verlauf
M 3	**Quotation from the movie *Crash*** / Interpretieren eines Zitats; Herstellen eines Bezuges zu dem Unfall in „The Tortilla Curtain"

T. C. Boyles „The Tortilla Curtain" (S II)

Reihe 17 S 6 | Verlauf | Material | LEK | Kontext | Mediothek

II/B2

	How does a crash change a life? / Beschreiben der Ursachen, Folgen und Konsequenzen eines Unfalls; Übertragen der Ergebnisse auf den Roman
M 4	**Two different perspectives** / Vergleichen der Reaktionen Cándidos und Delaneys auf den Unfall; Benennen der Erzählperspektive
M 5	**Homework:** *While reading Part One, Chapters 3 and 4 of* The Tortilla Curtain, *collect information about Delaney and Kyra. Take notes on the categories given.*
Zusätzlich benötigtes Material: ggf. Internetzugang oder DVD „Crash"; Abspielgerät	

4. Stunde

Thema
Meeting the Mossbachers – analysing Delaney and Kyra

Material	Verlauf
	How do you like the Mossbachers? / Notieren persönlicher Eindrücke zu dem Paar auf DIN-A3-Karten
M 5	**Evaluation of homework** / Vorstellen der Personenkonstellationen in einem *double circle*
M 6	**Hot seat** / Vorbereiten von Fragen und möglichen Antworten für Delaney und Kyra; Befragen der Figuren zu dem Unfall und dem Tod ihres Hundes
	Homework: *Read Part One, Chapter 5 to Part Two, Chapter 4 of* The Tortilla Curtain. *Note down information on Cándido and América's relationship.*
Zusätzlich benötigtes Material: DIN-A3-Karten; Magnete o. Ä.	

5. Stunde

Thema
Sense or sensibility? – Analysing Cándido and América

Material	Verlauf
	Elements of a well-functioning relationship / Nennen und Diskutieren der wichtigsten Elemente einer gut funktionierenden Beziehung in einer Murmelphase
M 7	**Cándido and América's relationship** / Analysieren der Beziehung Cándidos und Américas; Diskutieren über die Grundlage ihrer Beziehung
M 8	**Homework:** *Read Part Two, Chapter 5 to the end of Part Two of* The Tortilla Curtain. *Read the statements and decide whether they are true or false. Correct the false statements.*

T. C. Boyles „*The Tortilla Curtain*" (S II)

6. Stunde

Thema
The coyote – analysing a major theme of The Tortilla Curtain

Material	Verlauf
M 8	**Evaluation of homework** / Besprechen der True-/False-Aussagen
M 9, OHP	**Beware of the coyote!** / Vergleichen der Darstellung des Kojoten auf einer Warntafel mit dessen Darstellung im Roman; Herstellen eines Bezugs zu Delaneys Kolumne für das Naturmagazin
M 10	**The coyote and the Mexican** / Analysieren des Schlüsselmotives „Kojote" anhand einer Internetrecherche
	Delaney and Darwinism / Analysieren der Einstellung Delaneys zu den mexikanischen Immigranten anhand der Theorie von Darwin
M 11	**Homework:** 1. Read the article and summarise the arguments for and against gated communities. 2. a) Do some Internet research in order to find out more about the Trayvon Martin case. Be prepared to give a 5-minute presentation. or b) Imagine your school has done an exchange with Sanford High, the school Trayvon Martin went to. Write an announcement for your school's website, commemorating Trayvon's death.
Zusätzlich benötigtes Material: M 9 auf Folie kopiert; Internetzugang	

7./8. Stunde

Thema
On gated communities – a panel discussion

Material	Verlauf
M 11	**Evaluation of homework** / Kurzpräsentation zum Fall Trayvon Martin; Vortragen eines Trauertexts zum Tod von Martin; Nennen der im Text genannten Argumente für und gegen *gated communities*
M 12	**Role play** / Vorbereiten und Durchführen einer Podiumsdiskussion zum Bau einer Mauer um die Arroyo Blanco Estates
ZIP	**How to take part in a panel discussion** / Folienvorlage für eine Anleitung zur Vorbereitung und Durchführung einer Podiumsdiskussion
ZIP	**Language support – discussion phrases** / thematische Wortschatzliste
	Forms of racism / Herausarbeiten der verschiedenen Formen von Rassismus der Figuren
	Homework: Read Part Three of The Tortilla Curtain. Jot down the main events from Cándido's point of view.

T. C. Boyles „The Tortilla Curtain" (S II)

| Reihe 17 S 8 | Verlauf | Material | LEK | Kontext | Mediothek |

9. Stunde

Thema
The book of Job – having a closer look at Cándido

Material	Verlauf
	Evaluation of homework / Nennen der wesentlichen Vorkommnisse in Teil III aus Cándidos Sicht
M 13	**Job's story** / Lesen der Hiobsgeschichte; Äußern von spontanen Eindrücken
	Job and Cándido / Vergleichen der Ereignisse in den beiden Geschichten und der Reaktionen der beiden Figuren auf diese
	Think tank / Sammeln von Ideen zu der Botschaft der beiden Geschichten; Diskutieren der Ideen
	Homework: *Have a closer look at América (Part One, Chapters 4, 6 and 8; Part Two, Chapter 7 and Part Three, Chapters 2, 4, 6 and 8.). Outline her high and low points.*

10. Stunde

Thema
Who is América? – A character analysis

Material	Verlauf
	"I like to be in America because ..." / Vervollständigen des Satzes in einer Blitzlichtrunde
M 14	**Listening to the song *America*** / Anhören des Songs und Zusammenfassen des Inhalts
	América and *America* / Beziehen des Songs auf die Figur América; Erstellen einer Mindmap zur Figur América
	A German title / Formulieren eines deutschen Titels für den Roman; Kommentieren und Evaluieren der Titel; Vergleichen mit dem deutschen Originaltitel
	Homework: *Write an Internet review commenting on the German title of the novel* The Tortilla Curtain.
	How to write a comment / Anleitung zum Schreiben einer Erörterung
Zusätzlich benötigtes Material: Internetzugang für Lied „America"; leere Folie; DIN-A3-Karten; Magnete o. Ä.	

T. C. Boyles „The Tortilla Curtain" (S II)

| Reihe 17 S 9 | Verlauf | Material | LEK | Kontext | Mediothek |

II/B2

11. Stunde

Thema
Imagery in Part Three of the novel – what does it stand for?

Material	Verlauf
	Evaluation of homework / Präsentieren und Bewerten der *Internet reviews*
M 15	**What is imagery?** / Definieren des Begriffs „*imagery*"; Vergleichen der Ergebnisse mit der Definition auf dem Arbeitsblatt
	Freeze-frames / Interpretieren der sprachlichen Bilder des Romans mithilfe von Standbildern; Präsentation der Standbilder
	The ending / Formulieren der Botschaft des Romans an den Leser
M 16, task 1	**Homework:** Outline the impact of illegal immigration on the US economy.
Zusätzlich benötigtes Material: Symbole entsprechend der Kursgröße mehrfach auf Zetteln notiert	

12./13. Stunde

Thema
The Tortilla Curtain – *a final evaluation*

Material	Verlauf
M 16, task 2	**Evaluation of homework** / Umschreiben eines Dialogs zwischen Delaney und Jack Jardine mithilfe der Notizen aus der Hausaufgabe
M 17	**Milling around** / Diskutieren von Fragen, die der Autor in seinem Roman aufwirft; Evaluieren der Methode „*milling around*"; Vorstellen der interessantesten Ergebnisse
	An email to the author / Schreiben einer E-Mail an T. C. Boyle

(ZIP) Zusatzmaterial auf der **CD Grundwerk (CD GW)**.

T. C. Boyles „*The Tortilla Curtain*" (S II)

| Reihe 17 | Verlauf | Material S 1 | LEK | Kontext | Mediothek |

Materialübersicht

1. Stunde: *The Tortilla Curtain* – getting into the text
M 1 (Im) Picture stimulus – the Iron Curtain and the Tortilla Curtain
M 2 (Ab) What could *The Tortilla Curtain* be about? – Talking about the blurb

2./3 Stunde: The crash – two worlds clashing
M 3 (Ab) A crash – causes, effects and consequences
M 4 (Ab) The crash – Delaney and Cándido's points of view
M 5 (Ab, Ha) Delaney and Kyra – creating a character constellation

4. Stunde: Meeting the Mossbachers – analysing Delaney and Kyra
M 6 (Ab) Delaney and Kyra – an interview on the hot seat

5. Stunde: Sense or sensibility? – Analysing Cándido and América
M 7 (Ab) Cándido and América – a well-functioning relationship?
M 8 (Ab) Comprehension tasks on Part Two Chapter 5 to the end of Part Two

6. Stunde: The coyote – analysing a major theme of *The Tortilla Curtain*
M 9 (Im) Picture stimulus – beware of the coyote!
M 10 (Ab) The coyote and the Mexican immigrant – what do they have in common?
M 11 (Tx, Ha) *The Threat of Gated Communities* – reading an article

7./8. Stunde: On gated communities – a panel discussion
M 12 (Ab) A wall around the Arroyo Blanco Estates? – Role cards
CD GW (Ab) How to take part in a panel discussion
CD GW (Ab) Language support – discussion phrases

9. Stunde: The book of Job – having a closer look at Cándido
M 13 (Ab) The Book of Job – comparing Job and Cándido

10. Stunde: Who is América? – A character analysis
M 14 (Ab) "I like to be in America!" – Having a closer look at América
CD GW (Ab) How to write a comment

11. Stunde: Imagery in Part Three of the novel – what does it stand for?
M 15 (Ab) Imagery in Part Three – interpreting symbols and metaphors

12./13. Stunde: *The Tortilla Curtain* – a final evaluation
M 16 (Tx) Illegal immigration – what is its impact on the American economy?
M 17 (Ab) Discussing questions the novel raises – answering T. C. Boyle

CD GW (LEK) Cándido and América – their relationship and the American Dream

Zusatzmaterial finden Sie auf der **CD Grundwerk (CD GW).**

T. C. Boyles „The Tortilla Curtain" (S II)

| Reihe 17 | Verlauf | Material S 2 | LEK | Kontext | Mediothek |

M 1 Picture stimulus – the Iron Curtain and the Tortilla Curtain

①

②

Tasks

1. Describe the pictures. **2.** Compare the two borders. **3.** Talk to your partner: What do you know about illegal Mexican immigrants in the USA?

M 9 Picture stimulus – beware of the coyote!

WARNING!
Coyotes in the Area

Coyotes are wild animals and can be dangerous. Do not encourage them to approach. They are smart, fast, and will take what they can get.

All pets <u>must</u> be kept under direct control. For your safety and the safety of the animals …

KEEP THEM AT A DISTANCE!

NEVER FEED COYOTES!

Tasks

1. Compare the depiction of the coyote on the warning sign with the one in *The Tortilla Curtain*.

2. Relate the sign to Delaney's column in „Pilgrim in Topanga Creek".

RAAbits Englisch

M 2 What could *The Tortilla Curtain* be about? – Talking about the blurb

Have a look at the blurb[1] of the novel you are going to read. What could the novel be about?

Tasks

1. Work on your own:

Read the blurb of *The Tortilla Curtain*. While reading take notes on the following questions:

- What do you expect from the content of the novel?
- What makes you curious?
- What would you like to find out?

2. Work with a partner:

Talk about the blurb: Compare your answers and speculate about the content of the novel.

1 **blurb:** der Klappentext

Hinweise (M 1 und M 2; 1. Stunde)

Die Schüler verfügen in dieser Stunde noch über keine Romankenntnisse. Die Stunde dient der **thematischen Einführung** durch die Interpretation des Titels „The Tortilla Curtain". Außerdem bauen die Lernenden durch das Lesen des Klappentextes eine **Erwartungshaltung** an den Roman auf.

Einstieg: Die beiden **Bildimpulse (M 1)** werden als **Folie** kopiert aufgelegt oder über den Beamer gezeigt (s. Beitrag im Word-Format). Das erste Bild zeigt die Berliner Mauer. Auf dem zweiten Foto ist ein Stacheldrahtzaun zu sehen, der die mexikanisch-amerikanische Grenze markiert. Hinter dem Zaun schaut von links ein Kojote ins Bild. Die Lernenden beschreiben die Bilder **(task 1)**.

Die Lehrkraft schreibt die Begriffe **Iron Curtain** und **Tortilla Curtain** an die Tafel. Die Lernenden interpretieren die beiden Grenzbezeichnungen und vergleichen die Grenzen im Plenum miteinander **(task 2)**. Die Schülerantworten werden von der Lehrkraft gegenüberstellend an der Tafel gesammelt (s. u.).

Das **Vorwissen** der Lernenden wird reaktiviert, indem sie in einer **Murmelphase** zu zweit sammeln, was sie bereits über illegale mexikanische Einwanderer wissen **(task 3)**. Die Ergebnisse werden im Plenum zusammengetragen.

Anschließend erhalten die Schüler die Lektüre. Sie lesen den **Klappentext** und beantworten in Einzelarbeit Fragen zum möglichen **Inhalt** und ihren **Erwartungen** an den Roman **(M 2, task 1)**. Darauf vergleichen sie ihre Ergebnisse mit einem Partner und spekulieren über den Romaninhalt **(task 2)**. Die Vermutungen über den Inhalt werden im Plenum geteilt.

Hausaufgabe: Die Lernenden lesen Teil I, Kapitel 1 und 2 von „The Tortilla Curtain" und machen sich Notizen zu den Reaktionen der beiden Protagonisten auf den Autounfall.

T. C. Boyles „The Tortilla Curtain" (S II)

Erwartungshorizont (M 1)

1. Description of the pictures:

Picture 1: The picture is divided into two parts: The upper part shows a cloudless sky. Underneath, in the bottom half, there is dry grass, perhaps prairie. The prairie is divided by a barbed wire fence. From behind the barbed wire fence a wolf, dog or coyote is looking out of the picture.

Picture 2: In the picture you can see a massive stone wall. In front of it there is a sign saying "You are leaving the American sector" in English, Russian, French and German.

2. Tafelbild „Comparison of the borders"

Iron Curtain (term by Winston Churchill, 1945)	Tortilla Curtain (term by T. C. Boyle, 1995)
Metal → hard, invincible	Traditional Mexican food → cultural differences
- Border between East and West; symbol of the Cold War	- Border between Mexico and the USA
- Dismantled, historic	- Recently strengthened
- Almost impenetrable	- Only impenetrable in parts
- Effective	- Ineffective (The number of illegal immigrants has hardly been reduced.)
- Separated socialism and capitalism	- Separates the rich (Anglo-Americans) and the poor (Mexicans)
→ Kept people in	→ Keeps illegal immigrants out

Similarities
Strict border controls
No trespassing
Separate two worlds

3. Illegal Mexican immigrants (possible answers): They come to the US for economic reasons, their country is poor and they strive to enhance their living conditions; some of them try to sneak through the border themselves, others are smuggled into the country; they risk their lives by crossing the border (dehydration, wild animals, bad weather, border controls); some of them find jobs as unskilled illegal workers in the USA e.g. in agriculture.

T. C. Boyles „The Tortilla Curtain" (S II)

| Reihe 17 | Verlauf | Material S 5 | LEK | Kontext | Mediothek |

M 3 A crash – causes, effects and consequences

How does a crash change the life of a person? And what role does it play in the novel? Let's have a closer look at the impacts of crashes in general and the impact it has on the protagonists in the novel.

Tasks

1. Together with your partner interpret the quotation and relate it to the crash in *The Tortilla Curtain*.

> "It's the sense of touch. In any real city, you walk, you know? You brush past people; people bump into you. In L.A., nobody touches you. We're always behind this metal and glass. It's the sense of touch. I think we miss that touch so much that we crash into each other, just so we can feel something."

2. Describe the causes of crashes and the effects and consequences a crash can have on people's lives. Fill in the chart below.

3. Examine the actual as well as the metaphorical meaning of the crash for the course of events in the novel. Add your findings to the chart.

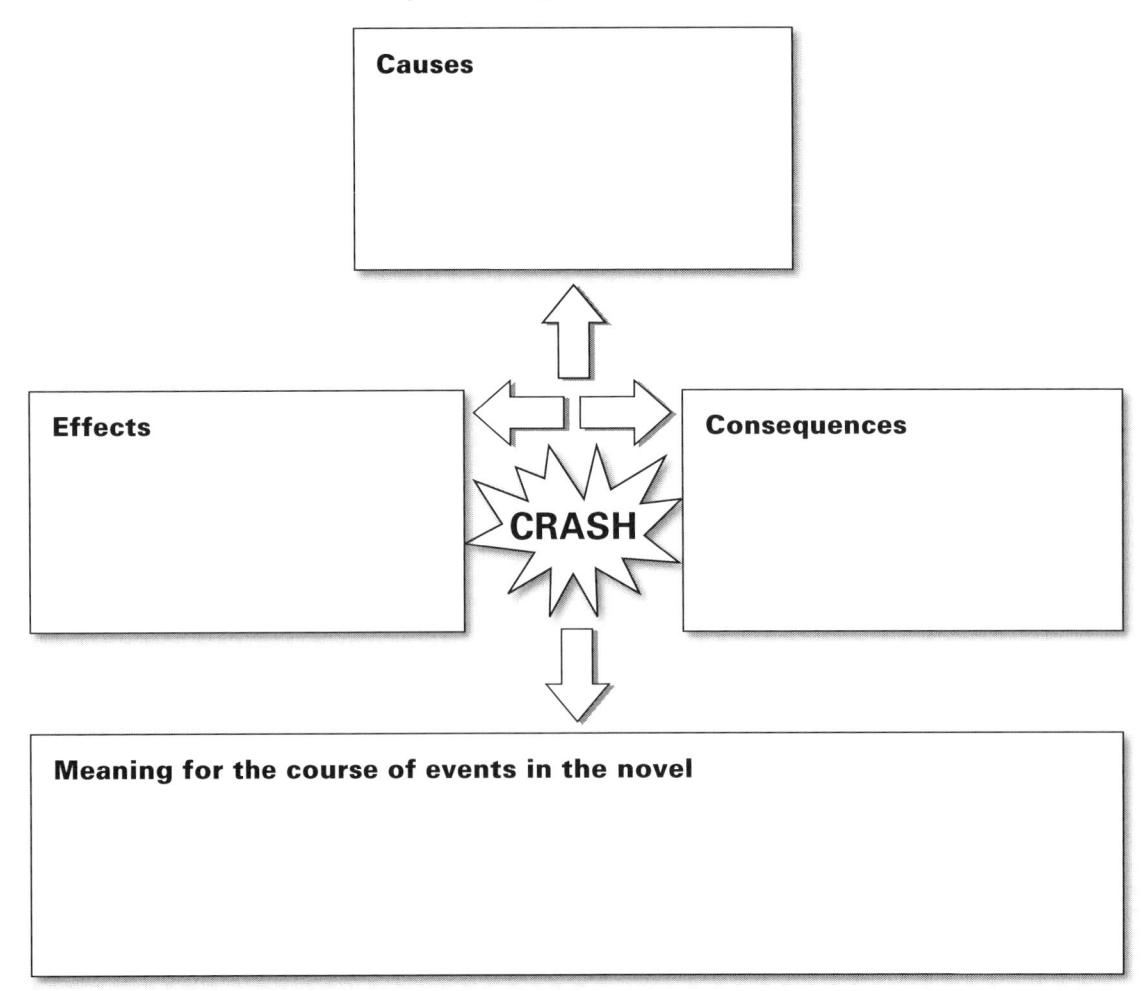

Causes

Effects

CRASH

Consequences

Meaning for the course of events in the novel

T. C. Boyles „The Tortilla Curtain" (S II)

Reihe 17 | Verlauf | Material S 6 | LEK | Kontext | Mediothek

M 4 The crash – Delaney and Cándido's points of view

Find out how Delaney and Cándido react to the car crash.

Task

1. Together with your partner compare Delaney and Cándido's views on the crash. Scan Chapter 1 and Chapter 2 for information on the aspects in the table.
2. Compare your results with another pair and add your findings.

An accident triggers various emotions.

II/B2

	Delaney	**Cándido**
Immediate physical reaction		
Immediate thoughts		
Thoughts about the other person involved		
Emotions		
⇨ **Consequences**		
The crash reveals …		
Narration technique		

M 5 Delaney and Kyra – creating a character constellation

Who are the Mossbachers? Have a closer look at their relationship and their attitudes towards life.

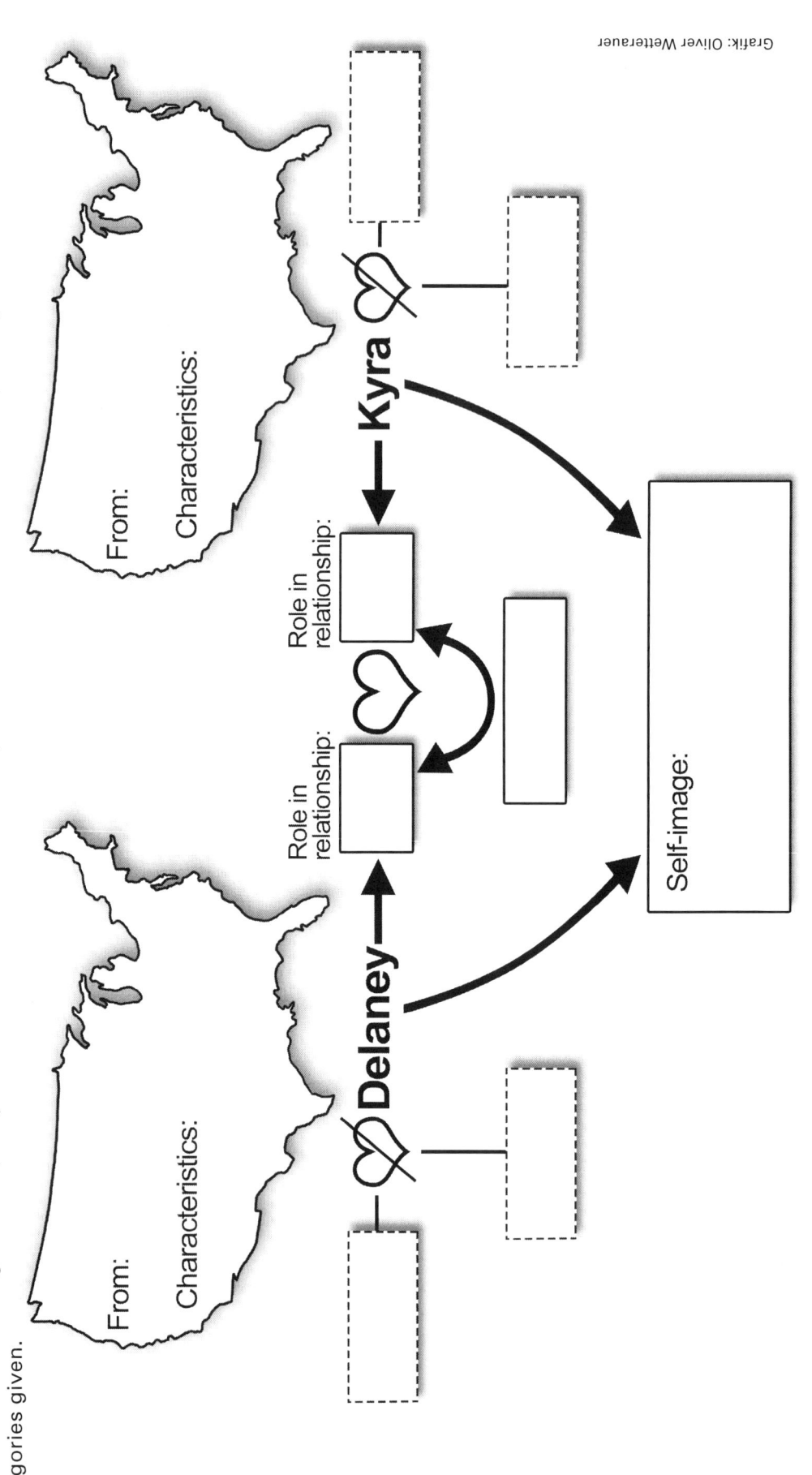

Task: While reading Part One, Chapters 3 and 4 of *The Tortilla Curtain*, collect information about Delaney and Kyra. Take notes on the categories given.

Delaney
From:
Characteristics:

Kyra
From:
Characteristics:

Role in relationship:
Role in relationship:

Self-image:

Grafik: Oliver Wetterauer

T. C. Boyles „*The Tortilla Curtain*" (S II)

| Reihe 17 | Verlauf | Material S 8 | LEK | Kontext | Mediothek |

II/B2

Hinweise (M 3–M 5; 2./3. Stunde)

Im Mittelpunkt der Doppelstunde steht der **Autounfall**, bei dem Delaney Cándido anfährt und verletzt. Die Lernenden arbeiten die **tatsächliche** und die **metaphorische Bedeutung** des Unfalls sowie die besondere Bedeutung der Schlüsselszene für Delaney und Cándido heraus. Indem sie Delaneys Reaktion auf den Unfall der Cándidos gegenüberstellen, werden ihnen auch die zentralen **erzählerischen Eigenschaften** des Romans bewusst.

Einstieg: Die Lehrkraft führt den **Trailer** des Films „*Crash*" vor, der circa 2:28 Minuten dauert. Dieser kann zum Beispiel über YouTube abgespielt werden (www.youtube.com/watch?v=durNwe9pL0E). Das Episodenfilm-Drama „*Crash*" zeigt, wie in Los Angeles die Leben von circa zwölf Menschen zufällig kollidieren und sich deren Wege daraufhin immer wieder kreuzen. Dabei thematisiert der Film den Rassismus und die Vorurteile, mit denen sich Personen unterschiedlicher ethnischer Herkunft begegnen. Die Schüler interpretieren in Partnerarbeit das *voice over* des Filmtrailers und setzen es in Zusammenhang mit dem Unfall im Roman (**M 3, task 1**). Wie im Roman wird der Unfall im Trailer als schicksalbeeinflussendes Motiv beschrieben, das zwei unterschiedliche Welten miteinander zusammenprallen lässt.

Alternative: Die Lehrkraft liest das Zitat aus „*Crash*" (M 3) vor und die Lernenden bearbeiten darauf *task 1*.

In einer **Grafik** (*task 2*) notieren die Schüler in Einzelarbeit Ursachen, Folgen und Konsequenzen eines Unfalls und halten dessen Bedeutung im Roman für den Handlungsverlauf fest (*task 3*). Die Ergebnisse werden im Plenum besprochen.

In **M 4** analysieren sie zu zweit anhand einer Tabelle die **Reaktionen** von **Delaney** und **Cándido** auf den Unfall (*task 1*). Dabei können die Schüler auch auf die Notizen der **Hausaufgabe** zurückgreifen. Die beiden letzten Zeilen der Tabelle werden später zusammen im Plenum ausgefüllt und zunächst freigelassen.

Es finden sich immer zwei Paare zusammen, die sich gegenseitig ihre Ergebnisse präsentieren. Das zuhörende Paar ergänzt jeweils seine Notizen (*task 2*). Die Präsentation der Ergebnisse durch ein Paar im Plenum kann entweder mündlich oder anhand des ausgefüllten Arbeitsblattes auf Folie kopiert erfolgen. Die letzten beiden Spalten der Tabelle werden gemeinsam im Plenum ausgefüllt.

Hausaufgabe: Die Lernenden lesen Teil I, Kapitel 3 und 4 von „*The Tortilla Curtain*" und bearbeiten lesebegleitend **M 5**.

Differenzierung: Lernstärkere Schüler können die grafische Darstellung der Beziehung Delaneys und Kyras eigenständig vornehmen.

Erwartungshorizont (M 3)

1. <u>Interpretation of the quotation and relation to the crash in the novel:</u>

   In the quote the speaker says the cause of accidents in L.A. is that people there miss human contact. As they don't walk and only move from one place to another in their cars, they are usually protected from the outside world behind the metal and glass of their cars. To get in touch with other people, they subconsciously cause crashes. Delaney's car in *The Tortilla Curtain* is also depicted as a shelter protecting him from interaction with other social groups until he accidently runs over Cándido with his car.

2. **Causes:** Loss of control of the car (cannot be undone; people can't prepare for it to happen).

Effects: Interruption of daily life, requires further interactions with the other person ("In L.A., nobody touches you.").

Consequences: Materialistic: cost/damages; physical: injuries; psychological: post-traumatic syndrome.

3. **Meaning for the course of events in the novel:** Life-changing event for Cándido and Delaney; metaphor for the clash of cultures and the problems emerging when two different cultural groups have to interact ("the collision of opposing forces", p. 9).

Erwartungshorizont (M 4)

	Delaney	**Cándido**
Immediate physical reaction	– State of shock: tension, dizziness, shaking, sweating (p. 10).	– Headache ("It felt as if a bomb had gone off [...]", p. 23), suffers from concussion; becomes aware of his wounds; finally has a breakdown.
Immediate thoughts	– First, worries about the damage to his material possessions (p. 10). – Second, worries about his image as a responsible driver (p. 10).	– Struggles to grasp the situation ("What had happened to him?", p. 23). – Thinks about his injuries. – Thinks of América. → Shows his need for help.
Thoughts about the other person involved	– Considers the victim as his third thought. – Is torn between his moral obligation to help and his emotional urge to see himself as the victim of the accident ("Why did this have to happen to him?", p. 12). – Compares Cándido to animals. → Use of similes ("like some feral thing", p. 9; "like an insect pinned to a mounting board", p. 14).	– Biased expressions ("pink-faced gabacho", p. 24). → Reveals his prejudiced attitude towards Anglo-Americans. – Thinks about the contrast of the two worlds due to the threatening materialism of Delaney's appearance ("All that steel, that glass, that chrome [...] – it was like a tank coming at him, and his only armor was a cotton shirt and pants and a pair of worn-out *huaraches*.", p. 24).

	Delaney	**Cándido**
Emotions	– Anger on imagining the victim as a homeless person roaming and littering the canyon. → Stops himself from feeling guilty and gives himself the opportunity to be in denial.	– Confusion, pain, fear. – Becomes unconscious: Dreams about his childhood/mother's death. → Feels the same helpless neglect he felt as a child.
Consequences	– Wants to believe that Cándido is responsible for his predicament ("It was crazy to refuse treatment like that [...]. But he had. And that meant he was illegal.", p. 16). – Delaney justifies his failure to give assistance to Cándido once he realises Cándido is an illegal immigrant ("I told you – he was *Mex*ican.", p. 22). → Reveals his prejudiced attitude towards Mexican immigrants although he is a self-declared liberal.	– Incapable of working. – América has to earn their keep. → Loss of typical gender role model; increases insecurity and self-consciousness. – Questions his typical view on gender roles and sees his dominant part in the relationship threatened ("And then the thing happened that he didn't want to happen, the thing he'd been dreading [...]", p. 31; "Nobody can tell me I cannot feed my own wife.").
The crash reveals ...	... that prejudices run deep: Cándido as well as Delaney reveal their stereotypical way of looking at the other person, seeing the different ethnic background and social groups they belong to rather than treating each other as humans.	
Narration technique	The novel is told from four alternating points of view; third-person narrator, limited.	

T. C. Boyle's *The Tortilla Curtain* (S II)

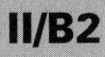

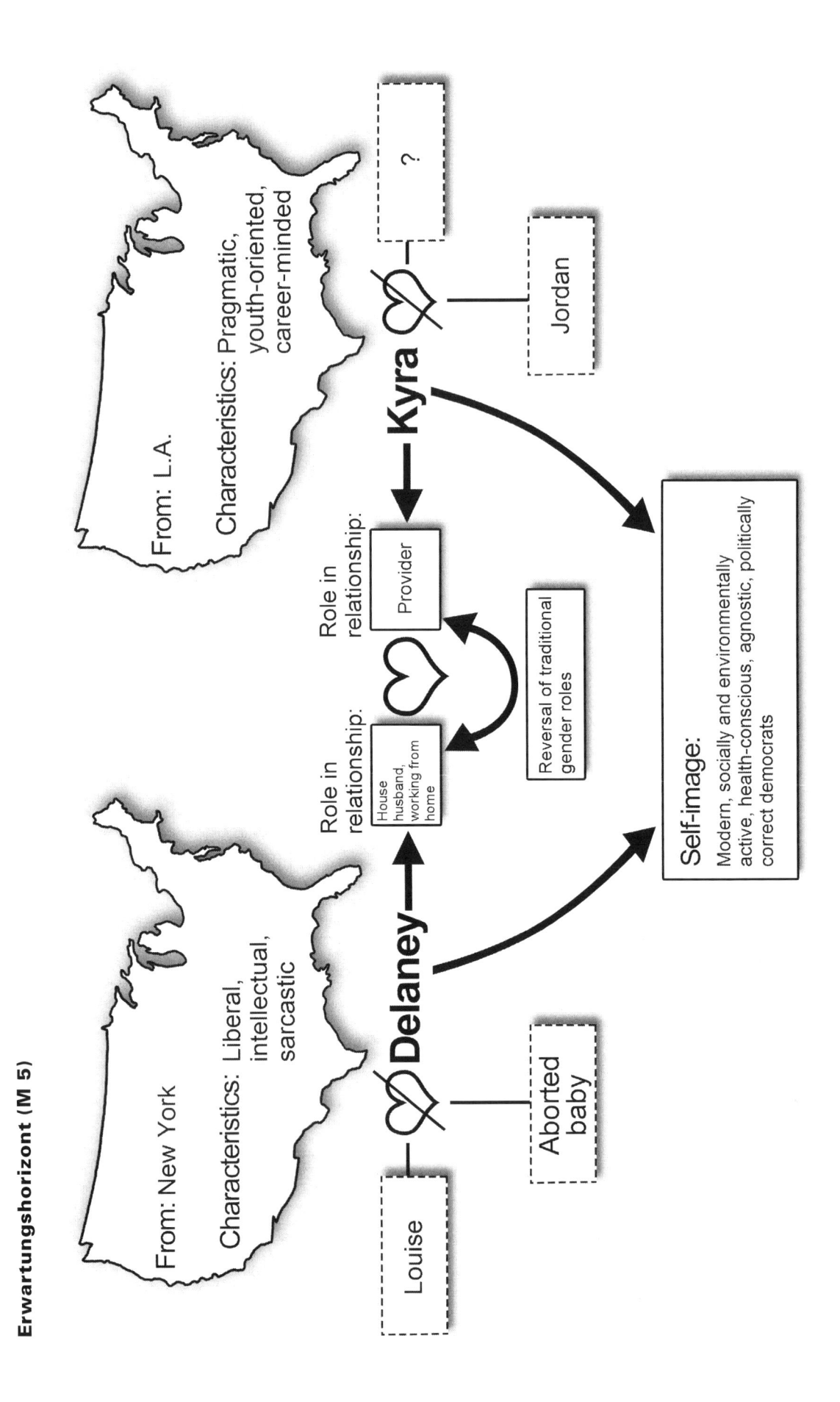

Erwartungshorizont (M 5)

Kyra
- From: L.A.
- Characteristics: Pragmatic, youth-oriented, career-minded
- Role in relationship: Provider
- Jordan
- ?

Delaney
- From: New York
- Characteristics: Liberal, intellectual, sarcastic
- Role in relationship: House husband, working from home
- Louise
- Aborted baby

Reversal of traditional gender roles

Self-image: Modern, socially and environmentally active, health-conscious, agnostic, politically correct democrats

M 6 Delaney and Kyra – an interview on the hot seat

The Mossbachers, especially Delaney, are people of high principles. Let's have a closer look at them by analysing their reactions to two situations we find them in at the beginning of the novel.

The hot seat method

The hot seat is a method to discuss a characters' attitudes, feelings, thoughts, motives etc.

Some of you will step into the shoes of Delaney and others into the shoes of Kyra. You will sit in front of the class and answer any questions about your actions and reactions about the accident with Cándido and the intrusion of the coyote.

Tasks

Form three groups:

1. One group (three people) will prepare Delaney for the hot seat. A second group (three people) will prepare Kyra for the hot seat.

2. The others will be the questioners. Split into groups of three to four and prepare questions for both characters.

3. In order to prepare the characters as well as the questions, re-read the following chapters: the accident with Cándido (Part One, Chapter 1) and the intrusion of the coyote (Part Two, Chapter 3).

Delaney: The students who will answer as Delaney should prepare themselves: Anticipate the questions you might be asked by your classmates and think of possible answers. Consider the important passages in the text. Think about how Delaney must have felt in the given situations and what it tells us about him. Work together and answer the questions by taking turns or adding points.

Kyra: The students who will answer as Kyra should prepare themselves: Anticipate the questions you might be asked by your classmates and think of possible answers. Consider the important passages in the text. Think about how Kyra must have felt in the given situations and what it tells us about her. Work together and answer the questions by taking turns or adding points.

Questioners: Prepare questions to find out what Delaney's and Kyra's real attitude is, and whether they really live according to their claimed principles and values. Consider the important passages in the text.

T. C. Boyles „The Tortilla Curtain" (S II)

| Reihe 17 | Verlauf | Material S 13 | LEK | Kontext | Mediothek |

Hinweise (M 6; 4. Stunde)

In dieser Stunde analysieren die Schüler **Delaney** und **Kyra Mossbacher**. Das Selbstbild des Paares wird anhand ihrer Reaktionen auf den Unfall mit Cándido und die Tötung ihres Hundes durch einen Kojoten untersucht.

Einstieg: Die Lernenden notieren spontan ihre **Eindrücke** zu den **Mossbachers** auf DIN-A3-Karten. Zu zweit einigen sie sich auf die zutreffendste Aussage über das Paar und befestigen diese an der Tafel (mögliche Antwort: *I don't really like them; they seem a bit cold*). Am Ende der Stunde kann so auf die gesammelten Eindrücke zurückgegriffen werden.

Die Präsentation der **Hausaufgabe (M 5)** findet in einem ***double circle*** statt. Die Lerngruppe steht sich hierzu in einem Außen- und einem Innenkreis gegenüber, sodass sich immer ein Schülerpaar seine **Personenkonstellation** vorstellen kann. Nach circa zwei Minuten gibt die Lehrkraft ein akustisches Signal und die Schüler wechseln den Partner im Uhrzeigersinn. Nach zwei bis drei Runden werden im Plenum offene Fragen geklärt und besonders interessante Ergebnisse besprochen.

Delaney und Kyra beantworten auf dem **Hot Seat (M 6)** Fragen zu dem **Unfall** und dem **Angriff** des **Kojoten** auf Kyras Hund. Hierzu wird die Klasse in **drei Gruppen** eingeteilt: Drei Schüler versetzen sich in die Rolle Delaneys und eine zweite Dreiergruppe bereitet Kyra vor. Der Rest der Lerngruppe formuliert Fragen an die beiden Figuren. Durch die Mehrfachbesetzung der Rollen ist der Ideenpool größer, sodass verschiedene Facetten der Protagonisten beleuchtet werden.

Die drei Delaneys und Kyras nehmen auf Stühlen vor der Lerngruppe Platz und beantworten die vorbereiteten Fragen. Auf diese Weise wird das **Selbstbild des Paares** hinterfragt und in Zweifel gezogen. Die Ergebnisse werden als **Tafelbild** (s. u.) stichpunktartig gesichert und die Reaktionen auf die beiden Ereignisse werden im Unterrichtsgespräch kontrastiert.

Am Ende der Stunde werden die **Eindrücke**, die im Einstieg gesammelt wurden, wieder aufgegriffen. Es ist davon auszugehen, dass die Schüler die Mossbachers instinktiv als „*bigots*" erkannt haben. Sie erklären deren Verhalten und finden Beispiele für dieses in ihrem eigenen Umfeld:

- *You felt that the Mossbachers are bigots judging by what they believe in and how they act. Explain their behaviour.*

- *Think of examples from your own experiences in life which resemble that of the Mossbachers.*

Hausaufgabe: Die Lerner lesen Teil I, Kapitel 5 bis Teil II, Kapitel 4 des Romans. Während des Lesens machen sie sich Notizen zu Cándidos und Américas Beziehung.

T. C. Boyles „The Tortilla Curtain" (S II)

Reihe 17 | Verlauf | **Material S 14** | LEK | Kontext | Mediothek

Erwartungshorizont (M 6)

Tafelbild Hot Seat

Crash	*Delaney*	*Kyra*
Initial reaction?	– Mixed feelings: guilt and concern.	– Concern as she fears for her son; fears material and judicial consequences.
Lasting influence?	– Mixed feelings turn into anger.	– None since she doesn't feel any empathy for the victim.
Handling?	In secret: Only five people in the community know.	
Triggers?	– Xenophobic feelings as a way to justify his action.	– No further action or thoughts.
Intrusion of the coyote	*Delaney*	*Kyra*
Initial reaction?	– Frantic action, reduced to instincts.	– Very emotional, in "a state" (p. 47).
Lasting influence?	– In shock about the incident (more than about the loss of the pet); can't really determine his feelings; flips out at the community meeting.	– Depressed.
Handling?	Openly: Revealed at the community meeting.	
Triggers?	A feeling of insecurity, threat and fear and the need for protection. à Separation, isolation.	
⇒ *The contrast shows …*	… that their human-liberal position stops at the unknown, at the "other".	

II/B2

M 7 Cándido and América – a well-functioning relationship?

	Equality	p.	Respect	p.	Independence	p.	Attraction	p.	Honesty and Trust	p.
América										
Cándido										

The basis for Cándido and América's relationship:
⇧

Tasks: 1. Together with your partner discuss what elements form the foundation of a well-functioning relationship. Agree on the three most important elements. **2.** Together with your partner examine how far the elements apply to Cándido and América's relationship. Find examples in the text and note them down in the table. **3.** What is the basis of Cándido and América's relationship? Discuss.

T. C. Boyles „*The Tortilla Curtain*" (S II)

M 8 Comprehension tasks on Part Two Chapter 5 to the end of Part Two

Task

Read Part Two Chapter 5 to the end of Part Two of *The Tortilla Curtain*. Read the statements and decide whether they are true or false. Correct the false statements.

II/B2

Statment	T/F	Correction
1. Delaney and Kyra support Jack Jardine in his endeavour to build a wall.		
2. Delaney catches Navidad selling insurance to the community.		
3. Cándido loses all of his savings through gambling.		
4. América is depressed but Cándido continues to look for work despite their misfortune.		
5. Cándido steals a turkey for Thanksgiving.		

Hinweise (M 7 und M 8; 5. Stunde)

Die Stunde dient der Analyse der **Beziehung Cándidos** und **Américas**. Dabei wird die starke Orientierung an traditionellen Geschlechterrollen und die damit verbundene Ungleichheit der beiden innerhalb ihrer Beziehung deutlich.

Einstieg: In einer **Murmelphase** tragen die Schüler zu zweit die ihrer Meinung nach wichtigsten **Elemente** einer **funktionierenden Beziehung** zusammen und einigen sich auf die drei wesentlichsten (**M 7, task 1**). Die Ergebnisse werden im Plenum diskutiert.

Tipp: Die Aufgabe sollte separat kopiert, an der Tafel notiert oder mündlich gestellt werden, damit die Ergebnisse durch die Tabelle auf dem Arbeitsblatt nicht vorweggenommen werden. Die Elemente einer funktionierenden Beziehung sind dort vorgegeben, werden aber mit hoher Wahrscheinlichkeit von den Schülern im Einstieg genannt.

Im Anschluss analysieren die Schüler die Beziehung des mexikanischen Paares auf die Elemente hin, indem sie die **Tabelle** in Partnerarbeit ausfüllen (**task 2**). Die letzte Zeile wird dabei zunächst freigelassen.

Tipp: Sollte wenig Zeit zur Verfügung stehen, kann die Tabelle arbeitsteilig ausgefüllt werden. Hierzu bearbeitet jedes Schülerpaar zwei Elemente.

Die Ergebnisse werden im Plenum gesammelt und ergänzt. Dabei wird deutlich, dass die Grundlagen einer funktionierenden Partnerschaft bei América und Cándido kaum gegeben sind. Die Schüler diskutieren, was die Beziehung der beiden ihrer Meinung nach zusammenhält (**task 3**), sodass abschließend festgehalten wird, dass die Grundlage ihrer Beziehung der gemeinsame **amerikanische Traum** ist.

Hausaufgabe: Die Schüler lesen Teil II zu Ende. Lesebegleitend beantworten sie die True-/False-Aufgaben (**M 8**) und korrigieren die falschen Aussagen.

T. C. Boyles "The Tortilla Curtain" (S II)

Erwartungshorizont (M 7)

	Equality	p.	Respect	p.	Independence	p.	Attraction	p.	Honesty and Trust	p.
América	Young and inexperienced.	171	Respects his guidance first, but gradually learns to doubt his competence and despises him for his willingness to endure humiliation.	206	Has never worked for money before, but embraces it when she has the chance.	129	Sees in Cándido the possibility to live a better life.	145	Doesn't tell him about her being raped.	185 f.
Cándido	Doesn't consider her an equal in terms of having a fair say in their decisions due to América's gender and age.	60	Attacks her physically and hurts her on purpose.	60	Opposes her developing independence, as it makes him feel belittled. → Wants to hold on to his traditional gender concept.	186	Finds her attractive.	171	Doesn't tell her that he suspects her of being sexually assaulted.	186

The basis for Cándido and América's relationship:

Their common American Dream seems to be the only foundation for their relationship.

Erwartungshorizont (M 8)

1. False: Only Kyra is in favour of the wall. Delaney is against it and only accepts her point of view to keep the peace in their marriage. **2.** False: Navidad distributes fliers. **3.** False: He is knocked unconscious and robbed. **4.** True. **5.** False: He is given a free turkey by two young men.

T. C. Boyles „The Tortilla Curtain" (S II)

Reihe 17 | Verlauf | Material S 18 | LEK | Kontext | Mediothek

M 10 The coyote and the Mexican immigrant – what do they have in common?

Tasks

1. Work in pairs: Visit the websites and read the text passages to gather information on either the coyote or the Mexican immigrant. Be prepared to give a 5-minute presentation of your results. Also add your classmates' findings to your notes.

Research Group A: The coyote

Collect information on the coyote:
- Historical background (e.g. Where does he come from? Where does his name derive from?)
- Living conditions (e.g. What is he threatened by? How does he adapt to the changes?)

Useful websites:

http://en.wikipedia.org/wiki/Coyote

www.coyoteyipps.com

Useful passages in the novel: Part Two, Chapter 5

Research Group B: The Mexican immigrant

Collect information on the Mexican immigrant:
- Historical background (e.g. What are the historical connections between Mexico and the USA? Why did he come to the USA in the first place?)
- Living conditions (e.g. What is he threatened by? How does he adapt to the changes?)

Useful websites:

http://people.howstuffworks.com/immigration5.htm

www.loc.gov/teachers/classroommaterials/presentationsandactivities/presentations/immigration/mexican8.html

Useful passages in the novel: Part Two, Chapter 7

2. Read the info box about Darwinism and Social Darwinism. Relate the two theories to Delaney's perspective on Mexican immigrants in general and Cándido in particular.

Darwinism

Charles Darwin's contribution to the theory of biological evolution states that all species of organisms are subject to natural selection, a process where an individual's ability to compete, survive, and reproduce is influenced by inherited variations.

Social Darwinism

Social Darwinism is the competition between strong and weak individuals or groups within society. Members of society seek to increase their wealth and power and this struggle may be between individuals in capitalism or be between national or racial groups.

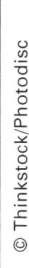

M 11   *The Threat of Gated Communities* – reading an article

> Trayvon Martin, a 17-year-old African American was shot and killed in 2012, in Florida, United States by George Zimmerman, the neighbourhood watch coordinator of a gated community. Martin was shot after an argument.
> Zimmerman was taken into custody but released again by the police, who said there was no evidence to refute[1] Zimmerman's claim of having acted in self-defense. On hearing the news thousands of people started protesting across the country. Zimmermann was later arrested and charged with murder.
>
> 1 **to refute:** to say or prove that a person, statement is wrong

The Threat of Gated Communities by Sarah Goodyear

[...] The shooting death of Trayvon Martin has caused an epidemic of soul-searching in the United States. In the weeks since George Zimmerman pulled the trigger in that Florida gated community, it feels as though the entire nation has been busy trying to explain to
5 ourselves what happened and why. [...]

The Retreat at Twin Lakes, where Martin died, is the kind of place where people choose to live when they want to be safe – from crime, from outsiders, from economic uncertainty. Of course, it doesn't always work that way. By fostering suspicion and societal
10 divisions, the argument goes, gated communities can paradoxically compromise safety rather than increasing it. And because they cut residents off from the larger community, writes Edward Blakely, author of *Fortress America*, they can "shrink the notion of civic engagement and allow residents to retreat from civic responsibility." [...]

I called Richard Schneider, a professor of urban and regional planning at the University of Florida and
15 a specialist in place-based crime prevention, to find out what he thought of the discussion surrounding Martin's death. The answer is, according to Schneider, that there are no easy answers. "It's hard to make a generalization," he tells me, pointing out that there are many different types of gated communities catering to all parts of the economic and social spectrum. Some of them are walkable; some are not. Some are racially mixed (as is the Retreat at Twin Lakes), and some are not. Some are relatively
20 affordable – you can find gated trailer parks – and some are filled with McMansions. Many of them are indistinguishable from any other suburban neighborhood. Did the built environment play a role in Martin's death? Add it to the list of things we can never really know for sure about this terrible case.

As for whether gated communities deliver on one of their main selling points – protection from crime – Schneider says that research to date has been inconclusive. "It's not a panacea," he says about
25 erecting gates. "You're just as likely to be burgled by your next-door neighbor, especially if there are teenagers." Criminals from outside are also quick to figure out how to get in. "They learn the code from the pizza guy," says Schneider. "The effects of gating decay over time." [...]

If the case of Trayvon Martin has shown us anything, it's that a society's problems — inequity, racism, and fear among them — have no problem getting through the gates.

© 2014 The Atlantic Media Co., as first published in CityLab.com. All rights reserved. Distributed by Tribune Content Agency

A gated community

2 **soul-searching:** die Selbstanalyse – 3 **to pull the trigger:** to fire a gun – 9 **to foster sth.:** to encourage the development or growth of ideas – 12 **civic:** bürgerlich – 20 **McMansion:** (coll.) a large and pretentious house – 24 **inconclusive:** without a result – 24 **panacea:** sth. that will solve all problems

Tasks: 1. Read the article and summarise the arguments for and against gated communities.
2. Choose one of the following tasks: **a)** Do some Internet research to find out more about the Trayvon Martin case. Be prepared to give a 5-minute presentation. **b)** Imagine your school has done an exchange with Dr. Michael M. Krop High School, the school Trayvon Martin went to. Write an announcement for your school's website, commemorating Trayvon's death.

T. C. Boyles „The Tortilla Curtain" (S II)

Reihe 17 | Verlauf | **Material** S 20 | LEK | Kontext | Mediothek

II/B2

Hinweise (M 9–M 11; 6. Stunde)

In dieser Stunde wird der **Kojote** als eines der **zentralen Motive** des Romans analysiert. Die ambivalente Haltung der Protagonisten gegenüber den Kojoten spiegelt sich in deren Einstellung gegenüber den illegalen Einwanderern wider: Sowohl die Kojoten als auch die mexikanischen Einwanderer überschreiten Grenzen und werden daher für ihren Mut bewundert sowie für die Überschreitung gefürchtet und gehasst.

Die **Hausaufgaben** (M 8) werden gemeinsam im Plenum besprochen.

Einstieg: Als Einstieg dient die **Warntafel (M 9**, Seite 2), die auf die Problematik des *urban coyotes* verweist. Anhand des Bildes vergleichen die Schüler die Darstellung des Kojoten auf der Warntafel mit der im Roman *(task 1)* und stellen einen Bezug zu Delaneys Kolumne *„Pilgrim in Topanga Creek"* her *(task 2)*.

Die Auseinandersetzung mit dem Motiv des Kojoten geschieht über eine **Internetrecherche (M 10, *task 1*)**, für die hilfreiche Links und Textpassagen vorgegeben sind. Schülerpaare werden jeweils den **Gruppen A** (*The coyote*) oder **B** (*The Mexican immigrant*) zugeteilt. Für die Recherche sollten in etwa 25 Minuten eingeplant werden.

Die **Präsentation** der Ergebnisse durch jeweils ein Schülerpaar der beiden Gruppen findet im Plenum statt. Die zuhörenden Lernenden ergänzen ihre Aufschriebe.

Die Lehrkraft hält während der Präsentationen die Information zu dem *coyote* und dem *Mexican immigrant* fest (s. u.). Dabei wird der Zusammenhang zwischen der nicht-metaphorischen Ebene, dem Kojoten als Tier, und der metaphorischen Ebene, dem Kojoten als Metapher für den mexikanischen Immigranten, deutlich und das Leitmotiv des Romans aufgeschlüsselt.

Abschließend wird Delaneys Sichtweise auf den *urban coyote* mittels des **Darwinismus** interpretiert *(task 2)*. Delaneys darwinistische Perspektive ist ein Grund, warum es zu keiner gelingenden Kommunikation zwischen ihm und Cándido kommt.

Hausaufgabe: Die Schüler lesen einen **Onlineartikel (M 11)** und notieren die in dem Text genannten Argumente für und gegen *gated communities (task 1)*. Sie wählen zwischen der Aufgabe, eine Kurzpräsentation zum Fall Trayvon Martin vorzubereiten *(task 2 a)* oder einen Trauertext zum Tod des Jungen zu verfassen *(task 2 b)*.

Erwartungshorizont (M 9)

1. <u>Comparison of the depiction of the coyote on the warning sign and in the novel</u>: As described on the warning sign, the coyotes in the novel are wild and dangerous and people must secure the safety of their pets. The coyotes come over the Mossbacher's fence and kill their two dogs. They keep on coming to the Arroyo Blanco Estates because some of the inhabitants feed them which, according to the sign, should not be done.

2. <u>Relation of the warning sign to the column</u>: Delaney also warns his readers about feeding the coyotes and letting them come too close. Convinced that they are dangerous, he thinks it is best to leave them alone and not to meddle with their habitat. His statements could also be applied to the illegal Mexican immigrants in general and Cándido in particular.

T. C. Boyles „The Tortilla Curtain" (S II)

Erwartungshorizont (M 10)

Tafelbild

1.

The coyote		The Mexican immigrant
The name derives from Mexican Spanish; the coyote has been on the continent for ages; its territories span from Mexico to Canada.	The historical and cultural background shows ⇒ a close connection ⇐ between the USA and Mexico.	1821: Mexico gained independence from Spain; California became one of the provinces until 1847.
Urbanisation which is reducing the coyote's territories.	Threatened by	Unemployment and difficult living conditions.
New conditions, e.g. drinks water from pools, eats kitchen leftovers, preys on small pets.	Adapts to	A new environment, e.g. takes on and endures any work, eats litter, gets by with little, endures physical pain.
More formidable, mischievous, evasive and dangerous than before; fit for survival.	Develops and embraces new qualities.	Inventive to find niches in US society.
	Cause insecurity and fear.	

2. Delaney sees both the struggle between man and coyote and white Anglo-American and Mexican immigrant from a Darwinian perspective: Both species fight alike to assure their survival. → Communication between Delaney and Cándido fails as they regard each other in terms of Social Darwinism.

Erwartungshorizont (M 11)

1. **Pros of gated communities:** They offer safety from crime, outsiders and economic uncertainty. **Cons of gated communities:** They foster suspicion and societal division; therefore they might even reduce safety; they isolate their inhabitants from the rest of the community; they make residents retreat from their civic responsibility; inhabitants can also be burgled by their neighbours; criminals from outside will find out how to get in.

2.
a) George Zimmerman called the police after he saw Martin unarmed and walking from a convenience store to the place of his father's girlfriend who lived in the gated community. Zimmerman thought Martin looked suspicious and called the police again after Martin started running and said he was following him; the police told him he didn't have to. Meanwhile, Martin complained on the phone to his girlfriend that he was being followed by a scary white guy; soon afterwards, he was shot dead by Zimmerman. Zimmerman, who was taken into custody but released soon after, told the police that he had followed Martin but lost track of him and was then attacked by him from behind; he shot Martin in self-defence. Eye-witnesses say that before the two men started attacking each other, they had a loud argument. The police let Zimmerman go but officers didn't share the same opinion on whether Martin was guilty or not. The case triggered a nationwide discussion about the law on guns, self-defence and racism. Zimmerman was accused of murder but a jury found him not guilty.

T. C. Boyles „The Tortilla Curtain" (S II)

Reihe 17 | Verlauf | Material S 22 | LEK | Kontext | Mediothek

M 12 A wall around the Arroyo Blanco Estates? – Role cards

First it is a fence, now the inhabitants are discussing if a wall should be erected around the Arroyo Blanco Estates ...

Tasks

1. Work together in groups of three. Prepare arguments for your role by reading the text passage(s) on your role card. The host group prepares questions for the participants of the panel discussion.

2. Choose one representative who will take part in the panel discussion.

II/B2

Jack Jardine Sr.

You are the chairman[1] of the Arroyo Blanco Home Owners' Association and head of the campaign for the wall.

You are a nativist[2], opposed to mass immigration, believing that immigrants undermine[3] American culture, as they are unwilling to adapt to American society.

Text passage: p. 107 f.

1 **chairman:** a person in charge of a meeting –
2 **nativist:** a person who thinks that people born in a country are better than immigrants –
3 **to undermine sth.:** to make sth. less powerful

Jack Jardine Jr.

You are Jack Jardine Jr., an adolescent racist, harassing Mexican immigrants out of sheer aggression and boredom.

Text passages: p. 54 f. and p. 226

to harass sb.: to continue to annoy sb. over a period of time

---

Kyra Mossbacher

You are Kyra and you are not opposed to immigration on principle. However, recent events regarding your private and business life have made the idea of living in a gated community seem attractive to you.

Text passage: p. 220–223

Delaney Mossbacher

You are Delaney and you find – as a self-declared liberal and environmentally aware person – the idea of living in a confined place appalling[1]. Nonetheless, some recent experiences have had a certain impact on you. Additionally, opposing the wall might trigger an enormous marital crisis[2] ...

Text passages: p. 119, p. 126 and p. 230

1 **appalling:** shocking and very bad –
2 **marital crisis:** die Ehekrise

Todd Sweet

You are Todd Sweet, somebody who is rooted in the liberal 1960s student movement. You are a steadfast opponent of the wall trying to convince Delaney to join your point of view.

Text passage: p. 228 f.

steadfast: staying the same for a long time

Host

You are the host of the panel discussion. You start, moderate and end the discussion. Think of questions to ask the participants of the discussion. Make sure that every participant will make his point. At the end, sum up the main arguments briefly.

Hinweise (M 12; 7./8. Stunde)

Die Schüler diskutieren die Vor- und Nachteile von **gated communities** in einem **Rollenspiel**. Dabei setzen sie sich auch mit den unterschiedlichen Formen von **Rassismus** auseinander, die im Roman durch die Bewohner der Arroyo Blanco Estates repräsentiert werden.

Einstieg: Zwei bis drei Schüler präsentieren ihre **Hausaufgabe** (Kurzpräsentation zum Fall Trayvon Martin oder Trauertext, M 11, *task 2*). Die Lerner haben anschließend Gelegenheit, sich im Plenum über den Fall auszutauschen: Welchen Standpunkt nehmen sie ein? Spielt ihrer Meinung nach die *gated community* eine Rolle? Kennen sie aus den Medien ähnliche Fälle?

Der erste Teil der **Hausaufgabe** (M 11, *task 1*) wird gesichert, indem die Argumente für und gegen *gated comunities* gesammelt werden. Die Schüler vergleichen im Plenum den im Artikel dargestellten Sachverhalt mit der Situation in den **Arroyo Blanco Estates**.

Die Vorbereitung des Rollenspiels findet in Dreiergruppen statt. Hierzu erhält jede Gruppe eine **Rollenkarte (M 12)**. Die Lernenden sammeln Argumente sowie Antworten auf mögliche Fragen für ihre Rolle. Abschließend bestimmen sie ein Gruppenmitglied, das an der Podiumsdiskussion teilnimmt. Die **Präsentation** des Rollenspiels findet im Plenum statt. Die Zuschauer notieren sich die vorgebrachten Argumente.

Differenzierung: Die Rolle des Moderators sollte von **sprachlich sicheren** Schülern gespielt werden. Sollte die Lerngruppe unerfahren in dieser Art der Diskussion sein, kann zuvor anhand des Zusatzmaterials *„How to take part in a panel discussion"* der Ablauf der Diskussion erläutert werden. Zudem stehen für lernschwächere Schüler *discussion phrases* bereit.

Ausgehend von den im Rollenspiel präsentierten Argumenten, werden im Plenum deren unterschiedliche **Formen von Rassismus** herausgearbeitet. Die Ergebnisse werden als Tafelbild (s. u.) festgehalten.

Am Ende der Stunde äußern die Schüler ihre Meinung zu *gated communities*: *Can you imagine living in a gated community? Why (not)?*

Hausaufgabe: Die Schüler lesen Teil III des Romans und notieren sich die Ereignisse aus Cándidos Sicht.

Erwartungshorizont (M 12)

Tafelbild

Character	Form of racism	Explanation	Represents
Jack Jardine Sr.	Overt, cunning	Intellectual nativist.	Academic right-wing
Jack Jardine Jr.	Overt, aggressive	Influenced by his upbringing (name: "like father, like son").	Narrow-mindedness, violence
Kyra	Covert, pragmatic	Is indifferent towards immigration as long as she's not affected.	Material aspect of the American Dream
Delaney	Covert (beginning) Overt (ending)	Hypocritical behaviour. Racism triggered by several events (e.g. pollution of the canyon, car theft). → Projects his anger and anxiety against Cándido.	Hypocrisy of Western civilisation

→ *The xenophobia is intensified by the growing anxiety.*

M 13 The Book of Job – comparing Job and Cándido

The Book of Job (Old Testament)

Job is a wealthy man living with his family and extensive flocks. He is an upright citizen always careful to avoid doing anything wrong. When one day Satan appears before God, God boasts to Satan about Job's goodness but Satan argues that Job is only good because he has been blessed with many things. Satan challenges God that, if given permission to punish the man, Job will turn and curse God. God accepts the challenge allowing Satan to torment Job.

Job with skin sores

Job receives four messages, each bearing separate news that his livestock, servants, and ten children have all died. Job demonstrates his mourning by tearing his clothes and shaving his head but he still prays to God. Satan appears again before God, being granted another opportunity to test Job. This time, Job is tormented with terrible skin sores. His wife encourages him to curse God and to give up and die but Job refuses.

	Job	Cándido
Events		
Reactions		
Message		

Tasks

1. Compare Job and Cándido regarding the events in their lives and their reactions to them by filling in the table together with your partner.

2. Form think tanks of four people and discuss the following questions:
   - What is the message of the biblical story?
   - What is the message behind Cándido's actions and sufferings?

> A **think tank** is a group to generate and discuss ideas. This method suggests that you collect your ideas first, then discuss them and come to an agreement. If you cannot find an agreement, it is all right to outline the discussed ideas when asked to present your results. Other classmates may then pick up on your suggestions and elaborate.

T. C. Boyles „The Tortilla Curtain" (S II)

Reihe 17 | Verlauf | **Material S 25** | LEK | Kontext | Mediothek

II/B2

Hinweise (M 13; 9. Stunde)

Die **biblische Geschichte Hiobs** wird als Interpretationsfolie für **Cándido** verwendet. Ähnlich der alttestamentarischen Figur scheint Cándido vom Pech verfolgt und erfährt, ohne den Glauben an seinen Traum zu verlieren, beim Versuch, gute Lebensbedingungen für seine Familie zu schaffen, nur Unglück und Demütigung.

Einstieg: Die Ergebnisse der **Hausaufgabe** (Ereignisse aus der Sicht Cándidos) werden im Plenum besprochen: *Name events which are relevant for Cándido's development in Part Three of the novel (The fire, the flood, the birth of the blind child, the encounter with the raging Delaney, the loss of his daughter).*

Die Lerner lesen die Geschichte Hiobs **(M 13)**. Sie äußern spontan ihre Eindrücke: *What do you think about/associate with the story? (It's very brutal: Job has to bear a constant burden of bad luck; It reminds me of Cándido who also seems to be unlucky).*

Im Anschluss vergleichen sie die Ereignisse in Hiobs und Cándidos Leben und die Reaktionen der Figuren darauf in Partnerarbeit (***task 1***, Zeile 1 und 2 der Tabelle). Die Ergebnisse werden im Plenum besprochen.

In ***think tanks*** diskutieren sie die jeweilige Botschaft der beiden Geschichten (***task 2***, Zeile 3 der Tabelle). Hierzu sammeln sie zunächst Ideen, die sie dann in Vierergruppen diskutieren. Die Diskussion wird abschließend ins Plenum verlegt. Mit dem zusätzlichen Impuls *Compare the protagonists Cándido and Delaney against the backdrop of their conviction and their actions.* wird Delaneys theoriegeleiteter Ansatz, seine Umwelt einzuordnen hinterfragt und Cándidos Menschlichkeit, die eher instinktiv als rational begründet ist, betont.

Die Schüler werden nach ihrer persönlichen Meinung gefragt:

- *Is there anything Cándido could have done to change his situation?*
- *To what extent is the story more about an unjust system than about one individual's bad luck?*
- *Is the ending of the novel optimistic?*
- *Would you hold out your hand to a person who was chasing after you in such a situation?*

Hausaufgabe: Die Schüler notieren Américas Hoch- und Tiefpunkte.

Erwartungshorizont (M 13)

	Job	Cándido
Events	– Death of his children. – Loses his livestock. – Destruction of his environment by natural disasters. – Skin disease. – His wife tries to influence him.	– His daughter dies. – Robbed of all his money; Jack Jr. destroys his camp. – Threatened by fire and flood. – Injuries caused by the accident. – América tries to persuade him.
Reactions	– Remains faithful to God. – Remains an upright and blameless person. – Endures the challenges forced upon him by Satan.	– Remains faithful to the idea that he can make it in America (American Dream). – Remains good and human when faced with the decision to rescue Delaney. – Endures the challenges caused by bad luck and partially by himself.
Message	– Keep up your faith in God no matter the challenges – as he/she works in mysterious ways. Forgive your enemies and remain a good person.	– No matter the atrocities done to you stay human and forgive your enemies.

→ Delaney becomes the victim of his own conviction (Social Darwinism) whereas Cándido, who is a non-academic neither following any self-ordained principles nor theories, manages to stay truly human in times of crisis.

T. C. Boyles „The Tortilla Curtain" (S II)

M 14 "I like to be in America!" – Having a closer look at América

The song America *from the musical* West Side Story *deals with two opposing views on the American Dream from the perspective of the Puerto Rican immigrant couple Anita and Bernardo.*

Tasks

1. Listen to the song. While listening summarise the two attitudes towards America. Fill in the speech bubbles with the dialogue between Anita and Bernardo.

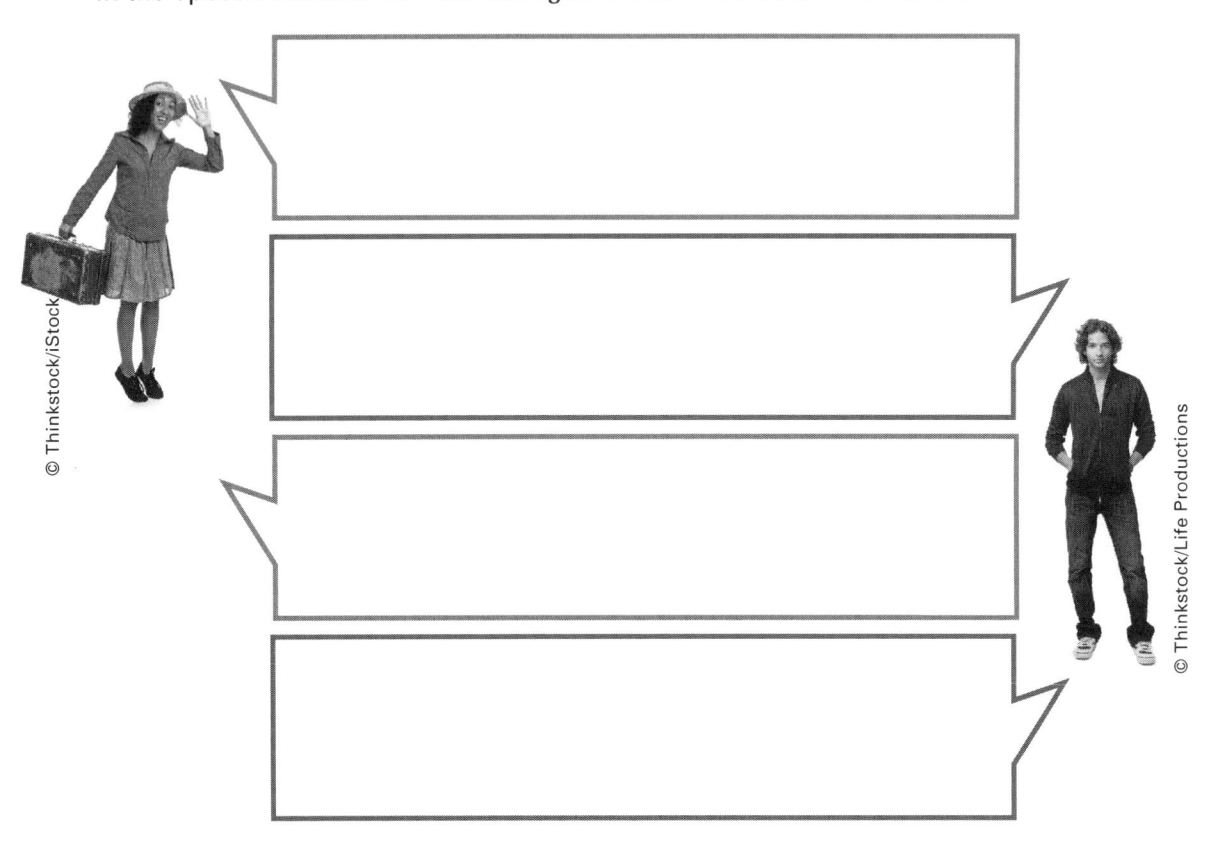

2. Relate the song *America* to the character América. Examine her development accordingly.

3. Work with a partner: Copy the mind map into your exercise books and fill it in with ideas from task 2 and your homework.

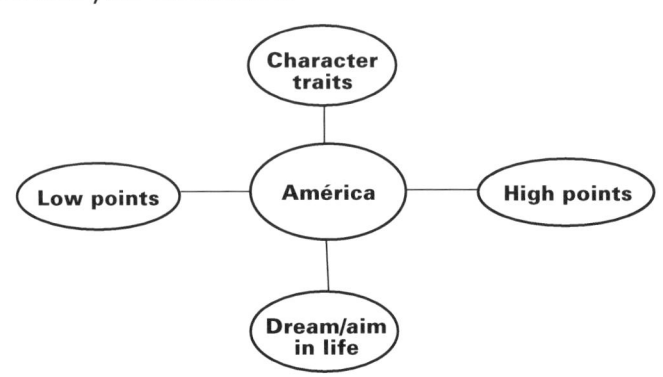

- Character traits
- Low points
- América
- High points
- Dream/aim in life

4. Exchange your results with another pair. Add more ideas to your mind map and present your results in class.

T. C. Boyles „*The Tortilla Curtain*" (S II)

| Reihe 17 | Verlauf | Material S 28 | LEK | Kontext | Mediothek |

II/B2

Hinweise (M 14; 10. Stunde)

In dieser Stunde wird die **Figur América** und deren *American Dream* analysiert.

Einstieg: Die Schüler vervollständigen den Satz *I like to be in America because ...* spontan in einer **Blitzlichtrunde**. Auf diese Weise wird das Lied inhaltlich und sprachlich vorentlastet.

Das **Lied „*America*"** wird vorgespielt. Es findet sich zum Beispiel bei YouTube: www.youtube.com/watch?v=YhSKk-cvblc9. Der Clip wird bis Minute 3:07 angehört. Es sollte nach Möglichkeit die Version der Verfilmung vorgespielt werden, da manche Musicalinszenierungen von der Rollenverteilung abweichen.

Als *while-listening task* notieren die Schüler in Einzelarbeit den **Inhalt** des **Dialogs** zwischen Anita und Bernardo (**M 14, task 1**). In dem Song lobpreist Anita die Vorzüge eines Lebens in den USA, während Bernardo die USA kritisiert und als fremdenfeindlich beschreibt. Aufgrund des spanischen Akzents sollte der Song mindestens zweimal vorgespielt werden. Die Ergebnisse werden in einer *buddy correction* verglichen und ergänzt. Während der Korrektur kann das Lied erneut vorgespielt werden. Die Ergebnisse werden darauf im Plenum besprochen.

Anschließend stellen die Lernenden in Einzelarbeit einen Bezug zwischen dem Inhalt des Liedes und der Figur América her (***task 2***).

Die Sicherung von *task 2* und der **Hausaufgabe** (Américas Höhen und Tiefen) erfolgt zu zweit in Form einer **Mindmap**, die sowohl die **Charaktereigenschaften** und die **Entwicklung Américas** abbildet als auch ihren persönlichen **amerikanischen Traum** zeigt (***task 3***). Die Ergebnisse werden einem weiteren Schülerpaar vorgestellt und ergänzt (***task 4***). Ein Schülerpaar, das die Mindmap auf **Folie** angelegt hat, präsentiert sein Ergebnis. Die Mitschüler ergänzen die Mindmap gegebenenfalls.

Zum Schluss formulieren die Schüler einen möglichen **Titel** für die **deutsche Ausgabe** des „*Tortilla Curtain*". Die Lehrkraft schreibt den Originaltitel mittig an die Tafel. Die Vorschläge werden von den Lernenden auf DIN-A3-Karten notiert und um den Originaltitel herum an die Tafel geheftet. Im Plenum werden die Titel sortiert (zum Beispiel nach Themen) und von den Lernern kommentiert.

Tipp: Vorab kann gemeinsam gesammelt werden, was eine gute Übersetzung eines Romantitels ausmacht (*What should an appropriate translation of a book title entail? A good translation should ... be in idiomatic German; ... sum up the spirit and core of the novel; ... sound catchy and be memorable; ... be original; ... contribute to the interpretation of the text*).

Die Lehrkraft konfrontiert die Schüler mit dem deutschen Romantitel *América*, den sie an die Tafel schreibt. Die Lerner kommentieren den deutschen Titel und vergleichen die beiden Titel im Plenum.

Hausaufgabe: Die Lernenden schreiben einen Kommentar zum Titel der deutschen Ausgabe des Romans.

Differenzierung: Auf der **CD Grundwerk** steht das Arbeitsblatt „*How to write a comment*", das den Schülern bei Bedarf ausgeteilt werden kann.

Erwartungshorizont (M 14)

1. The two attitudes towards America from the song: **Anita:** I will have my own washing machine, a terraced apartment; life in America is full of abundance ("skyscrapers", "cadillacs", "industry boom"); I will be free to be anything I want ("free", "pride").
   Bernardo: You will not own anything (everything is expensive, bad jobs for foreigners) and not be treated equally ("charge twice", "doors slamming in our face",

T. C. Boyles *"The Tortilla Curtain"* (S II)

„accent") nor have the same opportunities as the Anglo-Americans have ("only for whites", "stay on your own side").

2. <u>Relation of the song to América</u>: In comparison to Anita's American Dream, América's American Dream is more modest. But, as with Anita, she is determined to fulfil it and overcomes many obstacles on her way. América has to experience the negative sides of living in the USA as an immigrant Bernardo mentions in the song. From being naïve and dependent on her husband Cándido in making her wish come true, she slowly develops into an independent and free young woman.

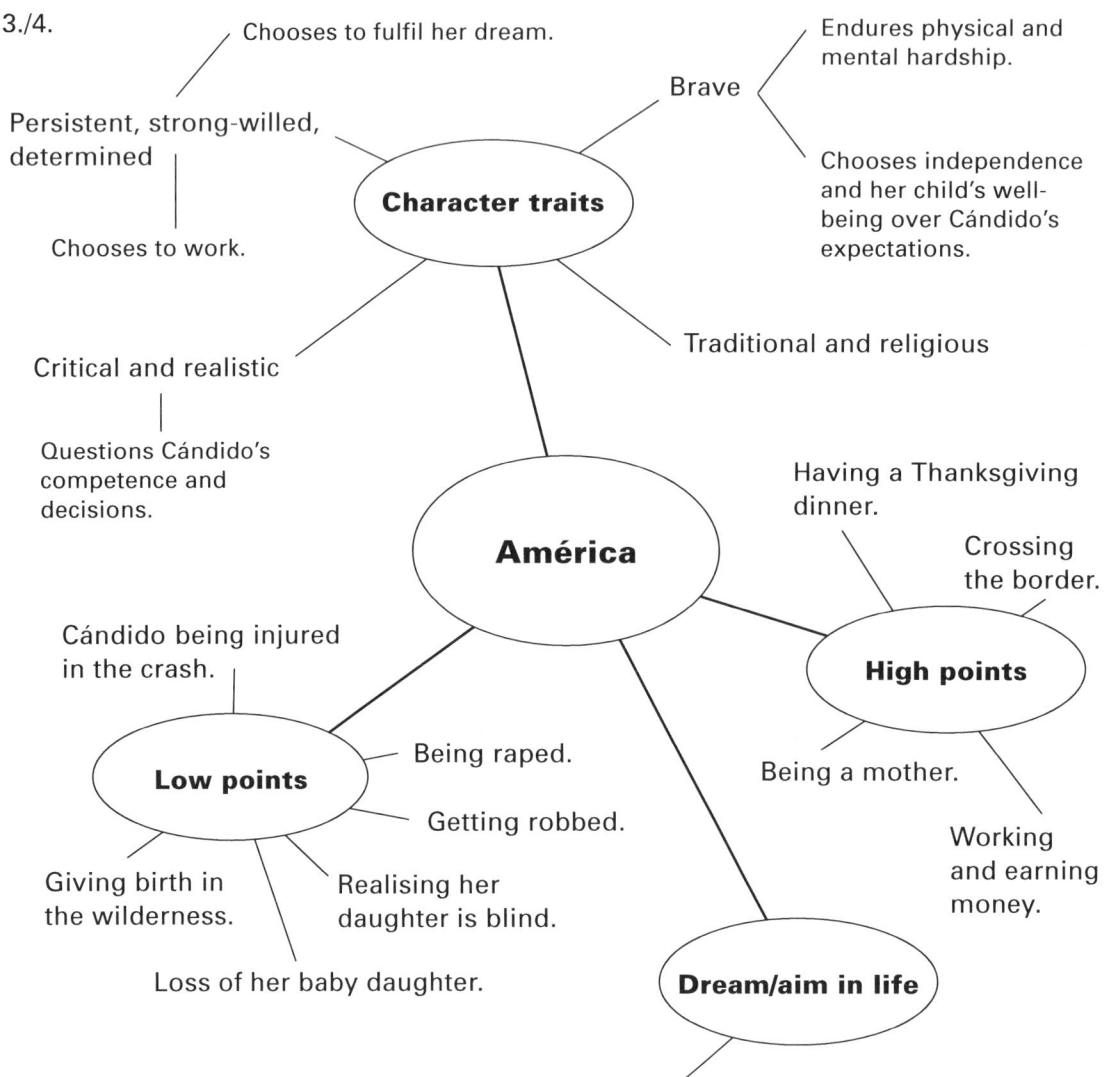

3./4.

Character traits
- Chooses to fulfil her dream.
- Persistent, strong-willed, determined
- Chooses to work.
- Brave
  - Endures physical and mental hardship.
  - Chooses independence and her child's well-being over Cándido's expectations.
- Traditional and religious
- Critical and realistic
- Questions Cándido's competence and decisions.

América

Low points
- Cándido being injured in the crash.
- Being raped.
- Getting robbed.
- Giving birth in the wilderness.
- Realising her daughter is blind.
- Loss of her baby daughter.

High points
- Having a Thanksgiving dinner.
- Crossing the border.
- Being a mother.
- Working and earning money.

Dream/aim in life
- A modest American Dream: Starting from the bottom of society lacking human necessities and striving towards a life in the midst of society. → Basic material possessions to provide adequate living conditions for her family

Erwartungshorizont (Internet review)

Form: Comment (introduction, transition, arguments supporting the given opinion, conclusion). **Content:** Individual answers, e.g. (+) The title … entails the symbolic contents of the character América; … is a catchy play-on-words; (–) The title … only focuses on one aspect of the novel; … can only be understood in its ambiguity when somebody is familiar with the novel; … neither contains the clash of cultures nor the actual and metaphorical meaning of borders and boundaries.

T. C. Boyles „The Tortilla Curtain" (S II)

| Reihe 17 | Verlauf | Material S 30 | LEK | Kontext | Mediothek |

M 15 Imagery in Part Three – interpreting symbols and metaphors

What is imagery and what does the imagery in Part Three of the novel stand for?

Definition of imagery

Imagery is a figurative, evocative language meaning something beyond the literal level. Imagery is used by the author to create vivid images in the mind of his readers. It attempts to engage the readers' senses. Imagery embraces all types of rhetorical figures. In Part Three of *The Tortilla Curtain* the following means of imagery are used:

Metaphor – A metaphor compares two different things in a figurative sense. "Like" is not used in a metaphor (e.g. the curtain of the night).

Symbol – A word, place, character, or object representing an abstract idea. In literature symbols can be cultural or contextual (e.g. flowers as symbols: roses stand for love).

Source: Ansgar Nünning, Carola Surkamp: Englische Literatur unterrichten. Grundlagen und Methoden. Kallmeyer 2006, S. 323.

Tasks

1. In groups of three, interpret the imagery given to you. Fill in the corresponding line in the table below.
2. Build a freeze-frame that shows your interpretation of the imagery. Be careful: Don't show the imagery on a literal level but show what it stands for.
3. Present your freeze-frame. The audience tries to explain what it is showing and gives the presenting group feedback on their freeze-frame.

Imagery in Part Three of *The Tortilla Curtain*			
Cultural symbols	Chapter	Taken from …	Stands for …
Fire and flood	1–3 7–8		
Birth	4		
Metaphor	Chapter	Stands for …	
The blind child	6, 8		
Contextual symbol	Chapter	Stands for …	
The saving hand	8		
Message of the novel:			

T. C. Boyles „*The Tortilla Curtain*" (S II)

Reihe 17 — Verlauf — **Material S 31** — LEK — Kontext — Mediothek

II/B2

Hinweise (M 15, 11. Stunde)

Teil III des Romans, der sich durch seine reichhaltige Bildersprache von den ersten beiden Teilen abhebt, wird anhand seiner Symbole und Metaphern interpretiert.

Einstieg: Zwei bis drei Schüler tragen ihre **Hausaufgabe** (Schreiben einer *Internet review*) im Plenum vor. Die Zuhörer achten dabei besonders auf die Einhaltung der formalen Struktur eines *comment*, die vorher noch einmal im Plenum abgefragt werden kann (*Introduction: getting the reader's attention, introducing the problem; main body: presenting one's own opinion with all the arguments, examples and evidence; conclusion: summary of the main points*).

Die Lehrkraft notiert den Begriff **„*imagery*"** an der Tafel. Es wird an das Vorwissen der Lernenden angeknüpft, indem diese den Begriff zu zweit in ein bis zwei Sätzen **definieren**. Die Ergebnisse werden im Plenum zusammengetragen und mit dem Infokasten auf **M 15** verglichen.

Anschließend werden Dreiergruppen gebildet. Jede Gruppe erhält ein von der Lehrkraft auf einen Zettel notiertes Symbol bzw. eine Metapher, die im dritten Teil des Romans eine maßgebliche Rolle spielen („*fire*", „*flood*", „*birth*", „*the blind child*", „*the saving hand*"). Während Feuer und Flut sowie die Geburt Soccoros als christlich-kulturelle Symbole zu interpretieren sind, handelt es sich bei dem „blinden Säugling" um eine Metapher und bei der „rettenden Hand" um ein kontextuelles Symbol, deren Bedeutung sich insbesondere aus dem Text heraus erklären lassen. Jede Gruppe interpretiert ihr Bild, indem sie die entsprechende Zeile der **Tabelle** ausfüllt (*task 1*) und die **Interpretation** in einem **Standbild** darstellt (*task 2*).

Tipp: Da die ersten beiden Symbole aus dem biblischen Kontext stammen, sollte die Lehrkraft bei der Verteilung darauf achten, dass sie von Schülern mit einem entsprechenden kulturellen Hintergrund bearbeitet werden. Gegebenenfalls kann die Lehrkraft diesen Gruppen auch erläuternd Hilfestellung geben.

Differenzierung: Das Bild des verlorenen Säuglings kombiniert mit der rettenden Hand kann für lernstärkere Schüler eine reizvolle Interpretationsaufgabe sein (Stands for: *Anglo-Americans live at the expense of (illegal) Mexican immigrants, exploiting them in order to secure their living standard*). Zudem kann eine lernstärkere Gruppe zunächst selbst überlegen, ob es sich bei den Bildern um eine Metapher oder ein Symbol handelt.

Die Gruppen präsentieren im Plenum nacheinander ihre Standbilder, die von den zuschauenden Schülern beschrieben und bewertet werden. Die Ergebnisse werden auf **M 15** als **Folie** kopiert festgehalten.

Abschließend wird im Unterrichtsgespräch ausgehend von Teil III eine Gesamtdeutung des Romans vorgenommen: *Taking Part Three into account, what is the message of the novel?* Die Tabelle wird entsprechend ergänzt (letzte Zeile).

Hausaufgabe: Die Schüler bearbeiten *task 1* auf **M 16**.

Erwartungshorizont (M 15)

Imagery in Part Three of *The Tortilla Curtain*			
Cultural symbols	Chapter	Taken from …	Stands for …
Fire and Flood	1–3 7–8	Noah (Gen 6–8, Old Testament) Psalm 66: 12 2. Peter 3: 7	– Testing Cándido's ability to believe in his dream (fire) and his humanity (flood). – A new start (Kyra reflects on the meaning of her work; América reconsiders her decision to live in the US; all appear equal in the light of a natural disaster).
Birth	4	The Nativity (New Testament): Birth of Jesus Christ	– New hope (Socorro born on American soil automatically holds US citizenship). – Gives the Rincóns a new sense of purpose.
Metaphors	Chapter	Stands for …	
The blind child	6, 8	– … the deprivation the baby was born into. – … Cándido and América's bad luck. – … the exclusion and isolation from American society.	
Contextual symbol	Chapter	Stands for …	
The saving hand	8	… the questioning of Delaney's approach of Social Darwinism responding to his warlike, frantic actions with a gesture of humanity and forgiveness.	

Message of the novel:

Part Three can be regarded a parable as it gives instruction to the reader on how to behave: On a general level the ending suggests that it is possible to overcome prejudice and racism by going beyond theories and models such as environmental or Darwinian models.

M 16 Illegal immigration – what is its impact on the American economy?

Adam Davidson, international business and economics correspondent at National Public Radio (NPR) is the author of the article "Q&A: Illegal Immigrants and the U.S. Economy".

Tasks

1. Outline the impact of illegal immigration on the US economy.

2. Read pp. 107/108, l. 24. Together with your partner re-write the dialogue between Delaney and Jack Jardine. Use your notes from task 1 to help Delaney in the discussion. You can also come up with further arguments. Be prepared to act out the dialogue in class.

Illegal Immigrants and the U.S. Economy by Adam Davidson

[M]any economists say the effect of an estimated 11 million undocumented workers is minimal. While illegal immigrants have a negative impact on unskilled workers – many of whom lack technical training or a high school diploma – economists believe
5 that overall, the American economy benefits a small amount from illegal immigration – a little bit less than 1 percent [...]. That finding [...] suggests that neither side of the immigration issue has a strong economic argument to make [...].

Illegal immigration has both negative and positive impacts on different parts of the economy.
10 As noted above, wages for low-skilled workers go down. But that means the rest of America benefits by paying lower prices for things like restaurant meals, agricultural produce and construction. Another negative impact is on government expenditures. Since undocumented workers generally don't pay income taxes but do use schools and other government services, they are seen as a drain on government spending.

15 There are places in the United States where illegal immigration has big effects (both positive and negative). But economists generally believe that when averaged over the whole economy, the effect is a small net positive. Harvard's George Borjas says the average American's wealth is increased by less than 1 percent because of illegal immigration.

The economic impact of illegal immigration is far smaller than other trends in the economy,
20 such as the increasing use of automation in manufacturing or the growth in global trade. Those two factors have a much bigger impact on wages, prices and the health of the U.S. economy.

© Adam Davidson

Vocabulary Aids

1 **estimated:** to guess the cost or value of sth. – 11 **agricultural produce:** products from farming – 12 **construction:** building – 12 **expenditure:** the total amount of money spent – 14 **drain:** hier: die Belastung – 16 **to average over:** to result in an average figure – 17 **net:** here: on balance after taking all positive and all negative things into account – 17 **George Borjas:** US economist – 20 **manufacturing:** the business of producing goods in large numbers

T. C. Boyles „The Tortilla Curtain" (S II)

Reihe 17 | Verlauf | Material S 34 | LEK | Kontext | Mediothek

M 17 Discussing questions the novel raises – answering T. C. Boyle

According to T. C. Boyle his novel raises and deals with the questions in the box. What is your opinion on these questions?

Tasks

1. Mill around[1] the classroom and discuss the questions with your classmates. You can form groups with up to three members.

   - Do you really own your own property?
   - Do you have a right to fence people out?
   - Do we have an obligation to assist people who come over that border, that wall, that gate?
   - How is it that Americans are allowed to have this incredible standard of living while others do not?

   Source: www.tcboyle.com/books/book_10rg.html

3. Write an email to T. C. Boyle evaluating how much *The Tortilla Curtain* deals with these questions. In the email, also give your opinion on the novel.

1 **to mill around:** If a group of people mill around, they move about in no fixed direction

---

Hinweise (M 16 und M 17; 12./13. Stunde)

In der letzten Doppelstunde geht es um den Einfluss der illegalen Einwanderung auf die US-amerikanische Wirtschaft. Eine **Gesamtbewertung des Romans** anhand von Fragen, mit denen sich der Roman beschäftigt, und einer E-Mail an den Autor wird im zweiten Teil der Stunde vorgenommen.

Einstieg: Die **Hausaufgabe (M 16, *task 1*)** wird überprüft, indem die Schüler ihre Notizen nutzen, um in Partnerarbeit den **Dialog** zwischen **Jack Jardine** und **Delaney** umzuschreiben und einzuüben (*task 2*). Hierzu lesen sie erneut das Gespräch zwischen den beiden Männern. Während Jack die illegalen Einwanderer als eine Last für den Sozialstaat sieht, versucht Delaney die Immigration zu verteidigen. Dies gelingt ihm jedoch nicht, da er sich Jack argumentativ unterlegen fühlt und sich verunsichern lässt. Während zwei Paare ihr Rollenspiel präsentieren, achten die Zuhörer darauf, dass die Argumente aus M 16 genannt werden. Nach der Präsentation werden diese an der Tafel festgehalten (s. u.).

Im zweiten Teil der Doppelstunde **diskutieren** die Schüler **Fragen**, die laut T. C. Boyle in „*The Tortilla Curtain*" aufgeworfen werden (**M 17, *task 1***). In einem ***milling around*** gehen die Lernenden durch den Klassenraum und diskutieren die Fragen in variierenden Kleingruppen zu zweit oder dritt.

Tipp: Eine **Feedbackrunde** zur **Methode** kann im Plenum erfolgen. Dabei reflektieren die Lernenden die Effektivität der Methode. Auch die Ergebnisse werden an dieser Stelle noch einmal zusammengefasst:

- *How effective did you find the milling around?*
- *Report the results you found most interesting.*

Abschließend schreiben die Schüler eine **E-Mail** an **T. C. Boyle (M 17, *task 2*)**, in der sie evaluieren, inwiefern er sich in seinem Roman tatsächlich mit den Fragen auseinandersetzt, und ihre persönliche Meinung zu dem Roman festhalten. Sollte nicht genügend Zeit zur Verfügung stehen, kann dies auch **Hausaufgabe** sein.

Erwartungshorizont (M 16)

Tafelbild

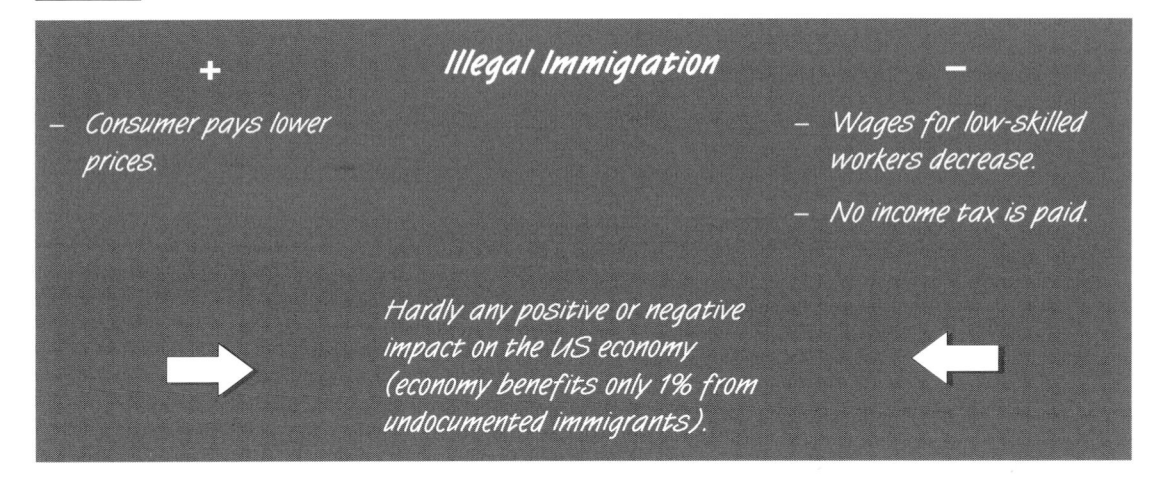

```
               +         Illegal Immigration         −

   − Consumer pays lower                    − Wages for low-skilled
     prices.                                  workers decrease.
                                            − No income tax is paid.


           →    Hardly any positive or negative    ←
                impact on the US economy
                (economy benefits only 1% from
                undocumented immigrants).
```

Erwartungshorizont (M 17)

1. Example for an opinion on the questions: I agree with the message of the American Dream that, when you worked for what you own, you can claim what you own as your own property. However, everybody should have the same starting conditions. Since this is not the case, the Americans – who are better off than most people in the world – have the obligation to help others.

2. Example for the content of an email to Boyle:
   - The novel implies that fear – especially fear of the unknown (other cultures) – can lead to racism and discrimination.
   - However, the text deals more with the question of integration rather than with criticism of abundance and consumption. Only when Kyra accepts the bonus turkey even though they already have one, materialism and greed is criticised.
   - The issues of who owns what and why is only indirectly depicted as the white Anglo-Saxons are not as elaborately shown as the Mexican immigrants.
   - The novel depicts problems arising from the conflict of the distribution of wealth, especially illegal immigration.
   - All in all, the novel rather asks questions than gives actual answers. This seems to be the obligation of the reader.

T. C. Boyles „The Tortilla Curtain" (S II)

Reihe 17 | Verlauf | Material | **LEK S 1** | Kontext | Mediothek

II/B2

The role of Hispanics in US society and politics

Julián Castro, grandson of a Mexican immigrant and mayor of San Antonio is expected to collect votes from the Hispanics for the democrats.

Julián Castro: Ist er der nächste Obama? Von Martin Klingst, 20. April 2014

[...] Schmal und schüchtern steht der 39-jährige Bürgermeister der texanischen Stadt San Antonio in seinem Büro. Er wirkt noch jungenhafter als Barack Obama am Anfang seiner politischen Karriere. Die Demokraten hoffen, dass Castro ihm eines Tages als Präsident nachfolgen wird – als erster Latino in diesem Amt. Seine Großmutter stammt aus Mexiko. [...]

5 Im vergangenen Mai haben die Bürger von San Antonio Castro zum dritten Mal zu ihrem Stadtoberhaupt gewählt, mit über 60 Prozent der Stimmen. Eine Sensation. [...]

[...] Erfolgreiche Latino-Politiker werden derzeit von beiden Parteien dringend gesucht: [...] Keine andere Bevölkerungsgruppe wächst so rasant. [...] Es ist nur eine Frage der Zeit, wann der erste Latino ins Weiße Haus einziehen wird. Die Demokraten glauben, mit Julián Castro ihren Kandidaten
10 gefunden zu haben.

Die Latinos gehören besonders oft zu den armen Familien von San Antonio. Weil viele von ihnen nicht richtig Englisch können und im Lesen und Schreiben hinterherhinken, bekommen sie später nur schlecht bezahlte Jobs. „Das muss sich ändern", sagt Castro, „da müssen wir als Staat helfen, das ist unsere Pflicht." Seine Mutter Rosie habe immer gepredigt: „Wir Latinos werden erst wirklich
15 dazugehören und erfolgreich sein, wenn wir genauso gut ausgebildet sind wie die weißen Anglos."

[...] Seine Familiengeschichte hat ihn tief geprägt. Seine Großmutter kam als 14-jähriges Waisenkind über den Rio Grande in die USA und brachte sich selbst Lesen und Schreiben bei. „Lernen zu dürfen", predigte sie, „ist ein Geschenk." Jahrelang schlug sie sich als Haushaltshilfe durch, damit ihre Tochter zur Schule und aufs College gehen konnte. [...]

20 In einem Land, in dem die Minderheiten bald die Mehrheit stellen werden und ein Schwarzer nach über 200 Jahren Präsident werden konnte, sind Identität und Herkunft wieder wichtig geworden. Nicht um andere auszugrenzen, sondern um zu zeigen, dass man es auch als Nicht-Weißer nach ganz oben schaffen kann.

Die meisten Einwanderer aus Lateinamerika kamen erst in den vergangenen Jahrzehnten als billige
25 Arbeitskräfte in die USA und lassen sich am ehesten mit den Türken in Deutschland vergleichen. Sie reisen zwischen ihrer alten und neuen Heimat hin und her, reden im Alltag Spanisch und schauen spanisches Fernsehen. Wer in Amerika eine Bank oder ein Telefonunternehmen anruft, kann das Gespräch auf Spanisch führen. Als Pendler zwischen den Welten verändern die Latinos ihre neue Heimat ebenso, wie die neue Heimat sie verändert. [...]

© Martin Klingst „Julián Castro: Ist er der nächste Obama? In: DIE ZEIT Nr. 16/2014 vom 20. April 2014.

Tasks

1. As an exchange student in San Antonio you are asked your impression of the German perspective on Latinos in the US. You have just read an article about this subject. Summarise in English (app. 250 words) the most important information from the article taken from the German newspaper *"Die Zeit"*.

2. Compare the situation of Hispanic immigrants depicted in the article to the one shown in *The Tortilla Curtain*.

3. The Rincóns' failure can be seen as criticism of the American Dream. Discuss.

T. C. Boyles „*The Tortilla Curtain*" (S II)

| Reihe 17 | Verlauf | Material | **LEK** S 2 | Kontext | Mediothek |

II/B2

Hinweise (LEK)

Der Klausurvorschlag ist für **Leistungskurse** konzipiert und setzt zur Bearbeitung eine **Doppelstunde** voraus. Bei weniger detaillierten Erwartungen kann die Klausur auch in **Grundkursen** eingesetzt werden. Für den zweiten Teil der Klausur kann die Lektüre verwendet werden.

In dem **Zeitungsartikel** der deutschen Wochenzeitung *Die Zeit* geht es um den Bürgermeister San Antonios, **Julián Castro**, der als erfolgreicher Politiker mit mexikanischen Wurzeln die große Hoffnung einer immer stärker wachsenden US-amerikanischen Bevölkerungsgruppe ist. Der Artikel beschäftigt sich mit Castros Familiengeschichte und seinen politischen Zielen sowie der Situation der Latinos in den USA.

Da die Sprachmittlung in dieser Einheit nicht explizit geübt wurde, steht ein **alternativer Klausurvorschlag** mit rein analytisch-interpretatorischen Aufgaben auf der **CD Grundwerk** zur Verfügung. Dieser wurde ebenfalls für eine Doppelstunde konzipiert und kann sowohl im Grund- als auch im Leistungskurs eingesetzt werden. Die Lektüre darf für die Textarbeit verwendet werden.

Erwartungshorizont (LEK)

1.

- Julián Castro, mayor of San Antonio, Texas with Mexican roots, was re-elected by more than 60% of the voters.

- Being the fastest-growing minority group, it only seems to be a matter of time until a Latino will have finally moved into the White House. That is why Hispanic politicians are popular amongst both parties in the US.

- As Latinos tend to be poorly educated, in particular regarding their language skills, they often belong to the poorest group of society. Castro, sharing his grandmother's conviction that education is the key to success, sees the improvement of opportunity for Latinos as a political duty.

- His grandmother's history, immigrating to the US as a 14-year-old orphan and working hard as a maid to support her daughter's college education, has made a deep impact on Castro.

- The election of Obama as president indicates that origin and race has become important again – simply to show that still everybody can make it in America.

- Hispanic immigrants have predominantly only arrived in the US during the last decades, working as cheap labourers. Their situation is comparable to that of Turkish immigrants in Germany: Latinos tend to live in-between old and new habits, for instance they tend to speak Spanish at home. That is how they gradually change the US, just as much as they have themselves changed since immigrating to their new home country.

2.

- In the article as well as in *The Tortilla Curtain* Latinos are depicted as a low social group due to their poor education. For example, América is said to be a good student, yet has never worked or considered further education. Instead she is completely dependent on Cándido and accepts his guidance in the first part of the novel without any doubts.

- Since Cándido and América are willing to work hard and show a great capacity for suffering and endurance, they might have been able to supply their daughter with the opportunity to advance to a higher social class. Their ability to make sacrifices and their poor background as well as their attitude is comparable to the depiction of Castro's grandmother.

- In *The Tortilla Curtain* Hispanic immigrants are solely depicted as being discriminated against due to prejudice, and are therefore not able to work their way up in American society – unlike Julián Castro. The only assimilated American-Mexican in the novel is Al Lopez, who hires and exploits illegal immigrants and is not in any way politically or socially involved in the matter of improving living conditions for Hispanic immigrants.

- The article emphasises the role of Spanish as a language in American society, suggesting that its bilingual use could promote cultural intermixtures. Whereas in the novel Spanish is perceived as the language of underdogs and even threatening ("dark language", p. 111). However, the Mexican's attitude towards the English language is also negative (p. 62).

3.

Individual results

Form:

Introduction, main body with pro/contra arguments: topic sentence, explanation, example; conclusion

Content:

True:

- Due to prejudice and discrimination they are not treated fairly in the USA by Anglo-Americans which questions the US status as a country of immigration and the foundation of the American Dream that everyone should be equal.

- Although they are willing to work hard, fate seems to let them down. This suggests luck as a key factor in being successful.

- New immigrants are not welcome and not able to pursue happiness, nor (modest) wealth.

False:

- Cándido is partly responsible for the situation they are in.

- The Rincóns may have made it in the US if it weren't for their enormous amount of bad luck.

Mediothek

Primärtext

Boyle, T. C.: The Tortilla Curtain. Berlin: Cornelsen 2012.

Auf diese annotierte Textausgabe beziehen sich die Seitenangaben der vorliegenden Unterrichtsreihe. Der Roman umfasst 351 Seiten. Im Anhang findet sich ein Glossar der spanischen Begriffe, die im Roman verwendet werden.

Erhältlich u. a. bei www.amazon.de für 9,95 € (ISBN-13 978-3464310717).

Sekundärliteratur

Schuhmacher, Karl Erhard: T. C. Boyle: The Tortilla Curtain. Stuttgart: Klett 2013.

Die Lektürehilfe beinhaltet ausführliche Informationen zu den Figuren des Romans, zu Hintergründen und literarischen Motiven sowie dem sozio-politischen Hintergrund. Die Lektürehilfe ist in Englisch verfasst.

Erhältlich bei Ernst Klett Sprachen für 9,95 € (ISBN 978-3-12-923001-59).

Internetseiten

www.tcboyle.com

T. C. Boyles offizielle Webseite, mit Informationen über den Autor, Bildern, einer Liste aller veröffentlichten Romane und Erzählungen sowie Neuigkeiten rund um den Autor und seine Werke.

www.tcboyle.net

Die Seite bietet Informationen über den Autor T. C. Boyle und seine Werke. Sie beinhaltet zum Beispiel Interviews mit Boyle und Analysen einiger seiner Romane und Kurzgeschichten.

www.gradesaver.com/the-tortilla-curtain/study-guide

Diese Seite bietet u. a. eine ausführliche Inhaltsangabe des Romans, eine Liste aller wichtigen Figuren und ein Quiz zum Roman, in dem die Schüler ihr Wissen zum Inhalt überprüfen können.

www.nytimes.com/books/98/02/08/home/boyle-tortilla.html?_r=2

Eine interessante Buchkritik der „New York Times" über *„The Tortilla Curtain"* ist hier zu finden.

www.youtube.com/watch?v=YhSKk-cvblc9

Unter diesem Link finden Sie das Lied *„America"* aus der *„West Side Story"*, das in der 10. Stunde zum Einsatz kommt.

Introducing Shakespeare (S II)

| Reihe 7 S 1 | Verlauf | Material | LEK | Kontext | Mediothek |

Introducing Shakespeare – Den literarischen Superstar für Schüler heute erfahrbar machen (S II)

Marcus Michels, Brühl

II/B3

Auf CD:
✓ PDF-Datei der Einheit

William Shakespeare superstar – zeitlos und modern

„Shakespeare Superstar" – wie nähert man sich heute einem literarischen Genie, dessen Ruhm mehr als 400 Jahre nach seinem Tod ungebrochen ist? Wie kann man einen Autor begreifen, über den meterlange Regale an Sekundärtexten, eine Vielzahl an berühmten Theater- und Filmproduktionen und mehr als 97 Millionen Einträge im Internet allein bei Google existieren? Wie bekommt man Zugang zu Texten, die nicht aus unserer Zeit stammen, deren Botschaften aber dennoch zeitlos und modern sind?

Klassenstufe: 11/12 (G8); 12/13 (G9)

Dauer: Ca. 14 Unterrichtsstunden + Klausur

Bereich: Drama, *Shakespeare and his time and language, analysis of character, active approach to literary texts*

Die folgende Reihe bietet eine Einführung in die Welt Shakespeares, die unabhängig von der Erarbeitung eines bestimmten Stückes einsetzbar ist. Im Zentrum stehen dabei motivierende Zugänge: Einerseits veranschaulichen aktuelle Texte aus dem Internet die ungebrochene Aktualität Shakespeares. Andererseits bietet das Konzept ganz praktische Tipps für einen kreativen und aktiven Umgang mit der Sprache und Gedankenwelt des Genies. Curtains up!

Introducing Shakespeare (S II)

| Reihe 7 S 2 | Verlauf | Material | LEK | Kontext | Mediothek |

Sachanalyse

Warum Shakespeare heute?

Die Frage der Bedeutung und Aktualität Shakespeares erübrigt sich angesichts der unbestrittenen Reputation von Autor und Werk. Shakespeare ist fraglos ein Meilenstein der Weltliteratur, ein globales Phänomen und demzufolge auch aus dem Curriculum für das Fach Englisch nicht wegzudenken.

Für die Bedeutung des britischen Barden im Kontext Schule gibt es viele gute Gründe. Die Stücke beschäftigen sich mit Themen, die für das **Wesen des Menschen** und zwischenmenschliche Beziehungen zentral sind und damit nicht veralten können. Zu nennen sind hier Gefühle wie etwa Liebe und Eifersucht, aber auch Hass und Verrat. Dies lässt sich beispielsweise anhand der Komödie *„Much Ado About Nothing"* illustrieren. Die Figur des Schurken ist die Personifizierung eines ganz und gar schlechten Charakters. Auch sie beruht auf typisch menschlichen Eigenschaften. Beispiele hierfür finden sich u.a. in *„King Lear"* und *„Macbeth"*.

Gleichzeitig steht Shakespeare aber auch für die Faszination des gesprochenen Wortes und eine **lebendige Theaterkultur**, die damals anders war als unsere heute: das *Elizabethan theatre*. Hier gilt es, die Schülerinnen und Schüler mit den Besonderheiten der Shakespearebühne vertraut zu machen. Das *Globe* in London vermag diese Erfahrung heute authentisch zu vermitteln, was beispielsweise das Zeugnis eines Schauspielers aus unserer Zeit belegt (vgl. M 15).

Doch auch die Theaterlandschaft bei uns ist maßgeblich geprägt durch **Neuinszenierungen** der „Klassiker" Shakespeares. Und ebenfalls die Anzahl genialer filmischer Adaptationen scheint bis zum heutigen Tag kein Ende zu nehmen. Zu erinnern sei an *„Shakespeare in Love"* oder die moderne Verfilmung von *„Romeo & Juliet"* durch Baz Luhrmann. Auch der bekannte Schauspieler Ralph Fiennes hat beim diesjährigen Berliner Filmfestival seine erste Regiearbeit, die Verfilmung von *„Coriolanus"*, vorgestellt.

Trotz dieser aktuellen Bezüge darf aber nicht vergessen werden, dass uns heute mehr als 400 Jahre von der Entstehungszeit der Werke trennen. In die Besonderheiten der Sprache und der Gedankenwelt – wie beispielsweise das Weltbild der damaligen Zeit – müssen die Lernenden deshalb eingeführt werden. Hierbei sind didaktische Überlegungen entscheidend, die der Motivation und der Schwierigkeit des Ausgangsmaterials Rechnung tragen.

Didaktisch-methodisches Konzept

Lerngruppe und Einsatz der Reihe

Die Reihe eignet sich gleichermaßen für den Einsatz in **Grund- und Leistungskurs**.

Zwei zentrale Ziele wurden in der Planung verfolgt: **Erstens** soll eine kompakte Einführung zu Autor und Werk geboten werden, die **unabhängig** von der Behandlung eines Einzelwerks **einsetzbar** ist. Die Reihe kann der Beschäftigung mit einem speziellen Stück vorangestellt oder gemäß dem **Bausteinprinzip** auch ausschließlich in Auswahl eingesetzt werden (vgl. Minimalplan). Dieser Ansatz bedingt eine Vorgehensweise, die konsequent exemplarisch ist und mit den für das Verständnis von Shakespeares Stücken zentralen Aspekten vertraut macht. In dieser Reihe sind das: Besonderheiten der Sprache, zentrale Themen wie etwa Liebe und Eifersucht, typische Figuren wie der Schurke, das elisabethanische Weltbild und Besonderheiten der Bühne der Zeit.

Zweitens stehen bei der inhaltlichen Erarbeitung solche Verfahren im Mittelpunkt, die einen motivierenden Zugang ermöglichen (vgl. Methode: *active approach*). Eine zentrale Leitlinie hierbei muss sein, dass die Stücke Shakespeares als Skript für die

Introducing Shakespeare (S II)

lebendige Aufführung im Theater und nicht als Lesetexte für eine monologisierende Beschäftigung im Einzelstudium geschrieben wurden.

Die Vorgehensweise ist bewusst anders als die in den gängigen Einführungen und Biografien. Denn bereits zu Beginn der Reihe erfolgt die Legitimierung des Themas über die Auseinandersetzung mit dem Erfolg und der Aktualität Shakespeares. Diese zentrale Frage der Aktualität wird am Anfang und am Schluss stehen: zunächst als Motivierung der Schülerinnen und Schüler und abschließend als Abrundung und Wissensüberprüfung.

Textauswahl

Für diese Reihe wurden Texte ausgewählt, an denen sich ganz zentrale Aspekte aufzeigen lassen. Gleichzeitig bestehen bei ihnen auch deutliche Parallelen in Bezug auf Figuren und Motive, sodass zentrale Zusammenhänge erkannt werden können. Als Auftakt wurde ein Auszug aus der Komödie *„Much Ado About Nothing"* ausgewählt, um für die Lerngruppe einen unterhaltenden Einstieg zu wählen. Auch das **Thema „Liebe"** dürfte motivierend sein. Weil der Text inhaltlich nicht schwer ist, eignet er sich auch für die exemplarische Thematisierung von **Besonderheiten der Sprache**.

Die **Figur des Schurken** wird am Beispiel von Edmond in *„King Lear"* illustriert (optional kann eine Ergänzung durch Don John in *„Much Ado About Nothing"* erfolgen; vgl. Hinweise M 9 und M 10). Anhand der Tragödie *„Macbeth"* wird schließlich das **elisabethanische Weltbild** mit *The Great Chain of Being*, d.h. die Konsequenzen der Zerstörung von Ordnung, veranschaulicht.

Um die Welt des **Theaters der Shakespearezeit** erfahrbar zu machen, wurde der Kommentar eines heute lebenden Schauspielers über das *Globe* in London ausgewählt (M 15). Diese zeitgenössische Erfahrung ist leicht zugänglich und bildet doch die damalige Wirklichkeit ab. Der Text spricht alle Sinne der Schülerinnen und Schüler an und lässt die Bühne vor ihrem geistigen Auge lebendig werden.

Ebenfalls wird in der Reihe das Verständnis des **Begriffes der Tragödie** veranschaulicht. Hierzu wird auf Beispiele der aktuellen Presse zurückgegriffen – Schreckensmeldungen unserer Tage, die allen in bleibender Erinnerung sein dürften; diese illustrieren ein umgangssprachliches Begriffsverständnis von Tragödie, das sich von dem literarischen unterscheidet.

Methode: active approach

Aus Gründen der Motivation und wegen der Schwierigkeit der Ausgangstexte kommt in dieser Reihe verstärkt der *active approach* zum Einsatz. Hiermit ist die **spielerische, kreative** und eben **aktive Aneignung** eines Textes gemeint. Sie ermöglicht jedem Lernenden einen persönlichen Zugang zur Sprache, den Gedanken und dem Stück insgesamt. Gleichzeitig spielt aber auch der Aspekt des gemeinsamen Lernens eine wichtige Rolle.

Ein solches Vorgehen ist vergleichbar mit Elementen einer Theaterproduktion, in die jeder Einzelne eingebunden ist. Durch die Übernahme eigener Verantwortung beim Lernprozess – Stichwort: autonomer Lerner – entstehen sowohl Motivation, die Freisetzung eigener Kräfte als auch die Stärkung des Selbstbewusstseins (vgl. hierzu: Stredder, 2009, S. 6). Bei einer solchen Vorgehensweise ist es der Lernende selbst, der **aktiv die Textbedeutung kreiert**, anstatt nur passiv auf den Text zu reagieren.

Dieses gemeinsame, einführende und praktische Arbeiten wird zur wichtigen Voraussetzung, ja zur **Motivationsgrundlage** für das sich anschließende, intensivere Interpretieren des Textes durch jeden Einzelnen. Dieser Ansatz erscheint allein schon deshalb sinnvoll, weil die Texte Shakespeares nicht für die Lektüre, sondern die Aufführung im Theater geschrieben wurden. Die vorliegende Reihe trägt diesem Ansatz

Introducing Shakespeare (S II)

Rechnung durch Arbeitsaufträge, bei denen die Schülerinnen und Schüler selbst aktiv werden:

- etwa durch den spielerischen Umgang mit der Sprache beim **betonten Lesen** (Rekonstruktion des *plots* in *„Much Ado About Nothing"*; M 6),
- dem **szenischen Spiel** (Liebeszene in *„Much Ado About Nothing"*; M 7),
- dem **Spekulieren** über das **Aussehen** von Figuren (Hexen in *„Macbeth"*; M 11) oder
- dem **Planen einer Inszenierung** einer bekannten Textstelle (M 15).

Schematische Verlaufsübersicht

Introducing Shakespeare – Den literarischen Superstar für Schüler heute erfahrbar machen (S II)

1. Stunde:	Addressing the question: Is Shakespeare still relevant today?
2./3. Stunde:	Shakespeare alive and kicking – Examples of current interest in Shakespeare
4./5. Stunde:	Plot in action – A spoken summary of *Much Ado About Nothing* (active approach)
6. Stunde:	Shakespeare talk / Famous characters ... and what they are after I: lovers (active approach)
7./8. Stunde:	Famous characters ... and what they are after II: villains
9./10. Stunde:	Famous characters ... and what they are after III: the Elizabethan view of the world in *Macbeth* (active approach)
11. Stunde:	Hands on drama: What is a tragedy? – Understanding the term's double meaning
12./13. Stunde:	'All the world's a stage' – The Elizabethan theatre (active approach)
14. Stunde:	Back to the beginning – The question of relevance again

Minimalplan:

Die Einstiegsstunden 1–3 bilden Bausteine einer verkürzten Reihe, die eine sinnvolle Vorbereitung auf das Abiturthema „Shakespeare" einleiten. Die **sprachlichen Besonderheiten** können auch allein aufgrund des Materials M 8 der 6. Stunde und ohne den ausführlichen Exkurs zu *„Much Ado About Nothing"* thematisiert werden.

Ähnliches gilt für die Beschäftigung mit dem **Weltbild der Elisabethanischen Zeit** in der 9. und 10. Stunde. Auch dieses kann losgelöst vom dramatischen Werk *„Macbeth"* lediglich anhand des Sachtextes M 13 *„The Great Chain of Being"* besprochen werden. Um die **damalige Theaterwelt** erfahrbar zu machen, bildet das Zeugnis des Schauspielers zur Bühne des *Globe* (M 15) einen weiteren Baustein.

Introducing Shakespeare (S II)

| Reihe 7 S 5 | Verlauf | Material | LEK | Kontext | Mediothek |

II/B3

1. Stunde

Thema
Addressing the question: Is Shakespeare still relevant today?

Material	Verlauf
M 1	**Shakespeare the superstar** / Beschreiben und Vergleichen eines modernen Porträts Shakespeares mit dem Bildnis aus der *First Folio*-Ausgabe
	Shakespeare today? / Reflektieren über die Aktualität Shakespeares *(Think-Pair-Share)*; Ordnen der Gedanken in einer *Mind Map*
	Results / Sichern der Ergebnisse und Ergänzen der *Mind Map*
M 2	**Homework:** 1. Read the three texts carefully. For each text choose keywords / short phrases which summarize the most important arguments. 2. Add these keywords to the mind map you started in class.

2./3. Stunde

Thema
Shakespeare alive and kicking – Examples of current interest in Shakespeare

Material	Verlauf
	Evaluation of homework / Zusammentragen und Ergänzen der Argumente für die Aktualität Shakespeares in der *Mind Map*
M 3–M 5	**Shakespeare's presence on the Internet** / Veranschaulichen der Aktualität Shakespeares anhand eines Gruppenpuzzles
	Feedback / Zusammenfassen der Ergebnisse in der *Mind Map* und Rückblick auf eigene vorherige Position
M 3–M 5	**Homework:** Read the texts you haven't looked at yet. On the basis of what you have found out in class, comment on the question of whether Shakespeare is still relevant today. Your keywords in your mind map may help you.

4./5. Stunde

Thema
Plot in action – A spoken summary of Much Ado About Nothing *(active approach)*

Material	Verlauf
	Evaluation of homework / Zusammentragen der Gedanken zu Shakespeares Aktualität in einem kurzen Rückblick
M 6	**Plot in action** / Zuordnen von Zitaten zu Passagen der Inhaltszusammenfassung von „Much Ado About Nothing"
	Active approach: Enacting quotations / Arbeiten mit Zitaten durch Interpretation und Kontextualisierung
	Plot retold with student participation / Anwenden der eingeübten Sprechweisen

RAAbits Englisch

Introducing Shakespeare (S II)

| Reihe 7 S 6 | Verlauf | Material | LEK | Kontext | Mediothek |

II/B3

M 7	**Homework:** *1. Read the extract from* Much Ado About Nothing *first to understand what it is about. In your own words explain what their conversation is about.*
	2. Practise reading the passage several times so that in your performance the particular situation and the emotions of the characters become obvious. You can concentrate on one character you would like to perform when reading out the dialogue in class.

6. Stunde

Thema

Shakespeare talk / Famous characters ... and what they are after I: lovers *(active approach)*

Material	Verlauf
M 7	**Active approach: Reading out loud** / Einüben und Vortragen des Dialogs der Liebenden in Partnerarbeit
M 7, M 8	**Shakespeare talk** / Beschreiben der sprachlichen Besonderheiten von *thou* vs *you;* Spekulieren über und Erarbeiten der Bedeutung der unterschiedlichen Verwendung innerhalb des Kontextes: Dialog der Liebenden
M 9	**Homework:** *1. Read the plot outline of* King Lear *carefully. 2. Create a visualization (keywords and arrows) which shows the relationships and conflicts between the characters. You can also look online for more information on the plot and the characters of the play.*

7./8. Stunde

Thema

Famous characters ... and what they are after II: villains

Material	Verlauf
M 10	**Pre-reading activity: What is a villain?** / Sensibilisierung für das Thema des Schurken Edmond aus *„King Lear"* – Arbeit mit Textauszügen
	Conclusion / Zusammenfassen typischer Eigenschaften und Motive von *villains*
	Transfer / Übertragen der Figur des Schurken auf die heutige Zeit
M 10	**Homework:** *Analyse the character of the villain, Edmond. What do we learn about him? Analyse the language with which he describes himself.*

9./10. Stunde

Thema

Famous characters ... and what they are after III: the Elizabethan view of the world in Macbeth *(active approach)*

Material	Verlauf
	Evaluation of homework / Besprechen der Schüleranalysen
M 11	**Pre-reading activity and extract from the tragedy** / Beschäftigen mit dem Setting und den Figuren der Hexen mittels *active approach*

RAAbits Englisch

Introducing Shakespeare (S II)

| Reihe 7 S 7 | Verlauf | Material | LEK | Kontext | Mediothek |

M 12	**Extract from *Macbeth*** / Spekulieren über die Bedeutung von *„disorder"* in einem Gruppenpuzzle
M 13	**Concept of the Great Chain of Being** / Erarbeiten des philosophischen Konzepts von Ordnung in einem Gruppenpuzzle
M 12, M 13	**Sharing results** / Austauschen der Ergebnisse zum elisabethanischen Weltbild und Anwenden auf das gesamte Drama
	Following plot / Hinweis auf weitere Dramenhandlung

II/B3

11. Stunde

Thema
Hands on drama: What is a tragedy? – Understanding the term's double meaning

Material	Verlauf
M 14	**Hands on drama: What is a tragedy?** / Versuch einer Begriffsbestimmung
M 14	**Some uses of the word "tragedy"** / Zuordnen von Überschriften und Definitionen zum literarischen und umgangssprachlichen Begriff der Tragödie; Bennenen der Gemeinsamkeiten und Unterschiede
	Homework: 3. What Lear experiences in the play is regarded to be a tragedy. Explain why on the basis of what we discussed in previous lessons. Also make use of Aristotle's definition of tragedy.

12./13. Stunde

Thema
'All the world's a stage' – The Elizabethan theatre (active approach)

Material	Verlauf
	Evaluation of homework / Besprechen der Schüleranalysen zur Begründung warum *„King Lear"* eine Tragödie ist
M 15	**Experiencing the Shakespeare stage today** / Einführen in die Besonderheiten des elisabethanischen Theaters
	Active approach: Bringing a scene to the stage / Sammeln von Ideen für eine mögliche Inszenierung einer bekannten Szene unter Berücksichtigung der gewonnenen Informationen zum elisabethanischen Theater

14. Stunde

Thema
Back to the beginning – The question of relevance again

Material	Verlauf
M 16	**Back to the beginning** / Rückanbindung an die Eingangsfrage nach der Aktualität Shakespeares; Erstellen eines Clusters zu den Themen der Reihe

Introducing Shakespeare (S II)

| Reihe 7 | Verlauf | Material S 1 | LEK | Kontext | Mediothek |

Materialübersicht

1. Stunde: **Addressing the question: Is Shakespeare still relevant today?**
M 1   (Bd)   Shakespeare superstar – two portraits

2./3. Stunde: **Shakespeare alive and kicking – Examples of current interest in Shakespeare**
M 2   (Tx/Ab)   Is Shakespeare still relevant today?
M 3   (Tx/Ab)   Shakespeare fans in the 21st century
M 4   (Tx/Ab)   2b or not 2b – Shakespeare goes mobile
M 5   (Tx/Ab)   Shakespeare and the 2012 London Olympics

4./5. Stunde: **Plot in action – A spoken summary of *Much Ado About Nothing* (active approach)**
M 6   (Tx/Ab)   Getting started with a comedy: *Much Ado About Nothing*

6. Stunde: **Shakespeare talk / Famous characters ... and what they are after I: lovers (active approach)**
M 7   (Tx/Ab)   Famous characters ... and what they are after – lovers
M 8   (Tx)   Shakespeare talk

7./8. Stunde: **Famous characters ... and what they are after II: villains**
M 9   (Ab/Tx)   *The Tragedy of King Lear* – an outline of the plot
M 10   (Tx/Ab)   *The Tragedy of King Lear* – extracts

9./10. Stunde: **Famous characters ... and what they are after III: the Elizabethan view of the world in *Macbeth* (active approach)**
M 11   (Ab/Tx)   An encounter with the witches from *Macbeth*
M 12   (Tx/Ab)   Disorder or what happens if you kill the king
M 13   (Tx/Ab)   The Elizabethan view of the world: The Great Chain of Being

11. Stunde: **Hands on drama: What is a tragedy? – Understanding the term's double meaning**
M 14   (Tx/Ab)   Hands on drama: What is a tragedy?

12./13. Stunde: **'All the world's a stage' – The Elizabethan theatre (active approach)**
M 15   (Tx/Ab)   'All the world's a stage': The Elizabethan Theatre

14. Stunde: **Back to the beginning – The question of relevance again**
M 16   (Ab)   Cluster: Is Shakespeare still relevant today?

Introducing Shakespeare (S II)

Reihe 7 | Verlauf | **Material S 2** | LEK | Kontext | Mediothek

II/B3

M 1 Shakespeare superstar – two portraits

Shakespeare by Mirco Ilic

Shakespeare, copperplate engraving of the
First Folio Edition by Martin Droeshout, 1623

Tasks

1. Describe what you can see in the first picture (foreground and background). Mention as many details as possible.

2. What can we guess about the man judging from what we see?

3. What do you think the artist's intention might be?

4. Is Shakespeare still of interest today?

RAAbits Englisch

Introducing Shakespeare (S II)

| Reihe 7 | Verlauf | Material S 3 | LEK | Kontext | Mediothek |

Hinweise (M 1; 1. Stunde)

Zu Beginn der Reihe steht die Frage nach der Aktualität Shakespeares im Vordergrund.

Ein Überraschungsmoment stellt das **moderne Porträt Shakespeares** (**M 1**) dar, das die Lernenden im Unterrichtsgespräch kommentieren. Dazu deckt die Lehrkraft zunächst das untere Bild ab. Schülerinnen und Schüler, die schon einmal eine traditionelle Shakespeare-Abbildung gesehen haben, werden ein Wiedererkennungserlebnis haben. Es dürfte nicht schwerfallen, das verfremdete Bildnis dieses Mannes zu beschreiben, da er aus unserer Zeit zu stammen scheint, steht er doch vor der Kulisse des *Times Square* in *New York*.

Bei der **Bildbeschreibung** muss die Lehrkraft wahrscheinlich Vokabelhilfen geben (siehe Erwartungshorizont M 1). Die Lernenden sollten sowohl auf Details der Person – Kleidung, Gesicht – sowie auf den Hintergrund – Reklametafeln, Straßenszene – eingehen. Danach werden Rückschlüsse zur Person selbst angestellt; diese sind frei und spekulativ (*Task 2*).

An dieser Stelle kann bereits auf das weltbekannte Porträt Shakespeares aus der *First Folio*-Ausgabe hingewiesen werden. Es existiert kein zeitgenössisches, authentisches Porträt – das Titelbild der *First Folio*-Ausgabe stammt aus dem Jahr 1623; Shakespeare war schon sieben Jahre tot –, sodass über sein wirkliches Aussehen nur Vermutungen angestellt werden können.

In der anschließenden **Kontrastierung beider Porträts** fällt es besonders leicht, die vom Künstler intendierten Verfremdungen herauszuarbeiten. Der Vergleich beider Bilder führt notwendigerweise zur Frage nach der Aussage des modernen Shakespeare-Porträts (*Task 3*) und der Klärung, warum der Künstler seine Verfremdungen vorgenommen hat. An dieser Stelle erfolgt die Fokussierung auf den zentralen Aspekt zu Beginn der Reihe, der **Frage nach der Aktualität Shakespeares**.

Vertieft wird sie in der folgenden Unterrichtsphase mittels **Think-Pair-Share**. Die Lernenden erstellen allein eine **Mind Map** zu der Frage, warum man sich heute noch mit Shakespeare beschäftigen sollte (*Think*), vergleichen ihre Ergebnisse mit einem Partner und ergänzen ggf. ihre eigene *Mind Map* (*Pair*), zuletzt erfolgt ein Vergleich der Ergebnisse im Plenum (*Share*). Hierfür ist es hilfreich, wenn vorher exemplarisch eine *Mind Map* zusätzlich auf **Folie** angefertigt wurde und diese nun als Vergleichsgrundlage dienen kann. Wiederum erfolgt eine Ergänzung der eigenen *Mind Map*. Diese wird auch in der **Hausaufgabe** und der folgenden Stunde den Arbeitsprozess begleiten. Am Ende der Reihe wird sie noch einmal eine Kontrollfunktion haben.

Erwartungshorizont (M 1)

1. Possible aspects: – **foreground:** picture of middle-aged man in a black leather jacket (medium shot); he is wearing a white T-shirt with print of green leaves (hashish plant?); egg shaped face with receding hairline (Stirnglatze); hair: medium-length, silver/grey black; blue eyes; frowning/looks serious/sad/concentrated; piercing in left eyebrow; earring in left ear; unshaven/moustache – **background:** billboards (neon signs)/advertisements (Burger King, Sony, Coca Cola, JVC etc.); street with yellow cabs (behind man)

2. Might be living in New York or visiting the city (background: Times Square and yellow cabs); might be a rock star on tour (leather jacket and earring); might be fond of drugs/addicted to drugs (T-shirt with hashish plant); modern/fashionable because of leather jacket and piercing; might have trouble/problems because he looks sad and perhaps is worried

3. Shows Shakespeare as being very modern, timeless; addition (by the teacher): The artist Mirko Ilic in his painting expresses what a contemporary poet of Shakespeare, Ben Jonson, put in words after the death of the genius: "He was not of an age, but for all time!"; he is one of us; he could be walking down the street today; allusion to our knowledge of the First Folio picture (reminds one of the Andy Warhol version of Marylin Monroe)

4. Compare *Erwartungshorizont* M 1–M 5 (Mind Map)

M 2   Is Shakespeare still relevant today?

The following extracts are answers to the question of whether Shakespeare is still of interest today. Being on the Internet they are intended to be read by anyone who might be interested and not just experts on literature. If you wish, you can of course check the link under each text for the complete information.

Answer 1

[...] In Shakespeare's time, great books were thought of as mirrors. When you read a great book, the idea is, you are looking into a mirror – a pretty special mirror, one that reflects the world in a way that allows us to see its true nature. What is more, as we hold the volume of Shakespeare in front of us, we see that it reflects not only the world around us, but also ourselves. What is it that we find in Shakespeare? Nothing less than ourselves and the world – certainly worthy subjects to study in college.

[...] Literature teaches you about life, and the better you understand literature, the better you understand life. It also is true, though, that the more you know about life, the better equipped you are to understand what you find in literature. This two-way mirroring means that learning about literature and learning about life go hand in hand. And it means that finding beauty and meaning in Shakespeare is a sort of proving ground for finding beauty and meaning in life.

As you learn to read Shakespeare, you are learning to read the world. As you interpret Shakespeare's characters, you are practicing [AE] figuring out life's characters. Struggling with the complexities involved in interpreting Shakespeare is a superb preparation for struggling with the complexities of life. Shakespeare offers a world of vicarious experience – a virtual reality, a sort of flight simulator – that gives you a great advantage when [the time] comes [...] to venture out into the real world.

Source: answers.yahoo.com/question/index?qid=20090107184926AA0AoKv, abridged, slightly adapted

© Michael E. Doyle. AKA: Dr. Mick. Vice President. Trinidad State Junior College. Colorado, USA

10 **to be equipped:** to be prepared for an activity or task – 17 **superb:** excellent – 18 **vicarious:** felt or experienced by watching or reading about sb. else doing sth. rather than by doing it yourself – 20 **to venture:** to go somewhere even though you know that it might be dangerous or unpleasant

Answer 2

I can imagine that as a high school student, you must have wondered why you still have to read Shakespeare in your English or literature class. What could Shakespeare possibly have to add to your life in the 21st century, in which almost nothing is the same as in his time? What could his texts, four centuries old, have to offer you?

Although we are separated from Shakespeare by 400 years, some things have not changed. We are still human beings, we are born and we die and in the time in between we try to enjoy our lives and look for ways to give meaning and sense to it. This essence of human life has not changed; it has existed as long as human beings have existed. The value of Shakespeare lies in the fact that his plays and poetry can add something to your life in many different ways. In his work, Shakespeare deals with many different human emotions such as: joy, sorrow, fear, anger, desire, hate and love. His plays also deal with ethical dilemmas. [...] The plays confront you with complex issues such as racism, the differences

Introducing Shakespeare (S II)

between man and woman, display of power and the abuse of power and colonialism. The plays may challenge you to look at these issues in a new and different way. This is why it is worthwhile to read and study Shakespeare. His works have meaning and value even when the world around them, the context of the 16th century, has changed enormously.

Another reason to read Shakespeare is because he has a very deep influence on the English language and on western culture. Although you may not appreciate everything, he is partly responsible for the world that you grew up in and for the ideas, words and expressions that, perhaps unconsciously, shaped you and the culture you live in.

Source: www.rennyekhart.nl/cat/24-, slightly adapted and abridged

8 **essence (of sth.):** the most important quality of sth. that makes it what it is – 13 **sorrow:** feeling of great sadness – 14 **ethical dilemmas (pl.):** situation in which you have to make a very difficult choice between things of equal importance, here: a choice concerning the beliefs about what is right or wrong – 17 **to challenge sb. (to sth.):** to invite sb. to enter a competition, fight, etc. – 18 **worthwhile (to do sth.):** important – 21 **to appreciate sth.:** to recognize the good qualities of sth. – 23 **to shape sth.:** to give sth. a certain form

Answer 3

[...] When young people watch or read Shakespeare today, they are pulled into a world that is both alien and familiar to them. In one scene, his treatment of love, jealousy, racism, mourning or power can seem strikingly relevant; in the next moment, the audience or reader might have to engage with concepts of religion, or family, or fashion completely different from their own. Shakespeare constantly challenges and confounds us: we might be asked to laugh in a painful scene or engage with profound philosophical questions in a comic one.

Watching, performing and reading the work of this extraordinary poet and playwright asks us both to challenge and celebrate our social and personal lives. Shakespeare can open up brave new worlds to young people and offer them fresh ways of dealing with familiar ones. His work can challenge our language skills and introduce us to new realms of poetic playfulness. He can extend our concepts of what fiction can do, and of what stories a drama can tell. Working with Shakespeare can be challenging but is eminently rewarding, rich and fulfilling. [...]

"Shakespeare for all ages and stages" (https://www.education.gov.uk/publications/eOrderingDownload/ShakespearesBooklet.pdf). © Crown copyright 2008. Contains public sector information licensed under the Open Government Licence v1.0. (http://www.nationalarchives.gov.uk/doc/open-government-licence/), abridged

2 **alien (to sb./sth.):** strange and frightening – 3 **treatment:** a way of dealing with a person or thing – 3 **mourning:** sadness that you show and feel because sb. has died – 4 **strikingly:** auffällig – 5 **to engage with sth./sb.:** to become involved and try to understand sb./sth. – 7 **to confound:** to confuse or surprise sb. – 11 **playwright:** person who writes plays for the theatre – 12/13 **brave new worlds:** Shakespeare's play *The Tempest* is set on a remote island. It resembles an idealized new world. Miranda says, referring to this strange world: O, wonder! / How many goodly creatures are there here! / How beauteous mankind is! O brave new world / That has such people in't; here: schöne neue Welten – 14 **realm:** here: an area of activity, interest or knowledge – 16 **rewarding:** worth doing; it makes you happy because you think it is useful or important

Tasks

1. Read the three extracts carefully. For each text choose some keywords or short phrases which summarize the most important arguments concerning the importance of Shakespeare today.
2. Add these keywords to the mind map you started in class.

M 3 Shakespeare fans in the 21st century

Discover which popularity the Renaissance's most famous dramatist has even in the IT world of today. There must be something to his ingenuity, after all, mustn't there? Otherwise he would have been forgotten. Try to think what this might be. Why is Shakespeare still of interest?

Shakespeare has more friends than J.K. Rowling

Relaxnews

Saturday, 13 November 2010

Based on overwhelming popularity on Facebook, the top author on the social networking site is Stephen King with 1.3 million fans. Perhaps more surprisingly is George Orwell's ranking at number three, followed by *Twilight Saga* author Stephenie Meyer in sixth.

With a combination of contemporary and classic writers, the eclectic group listed has been compiled according to the number of Facebook fans, gathered with statistical tools from the website AllFaceBook.com.

These were the top 10 authors, as of November 11:

1. Stephen King (1,302,973 fans), 2. Nicholas Sparks (506,300), 3. George Orwell (399,403), 4. Shakespeare (356,920), 5. Nora Roberts (290,836), 6. Stephenie Meyer (261,176), 7. Jane Austen (230,814), 8. Anne Rice (229,192), 9. Jodi Picoult (209,637), 10. Sidney Sheldon (207,727)

Others in the top 20 include the venerable Agatha Christie with 191,972 fans, at 11, J.K. Rowling with 186,942, at 13, Edgar Allen Poe, at 14, suspense author Tom Clancy, at 17, Khalil Gibran, at 18, Paulo Coelho, at 19, and J.R.R. Tolkien at 20.

RC

Shakespeare, copperplate engraving of the First Folio Edition by Martin Droeshout, 1623

Source: http://www.independent.co.uk/arts-entertainment/books/shakespeare-has-more-friends-than-jk-rowling-2133227.html © AFP

9 **eclectic:** bunte Mischung – 10 **to compile sth.:** to collect sth.

Tasks

1. Read the text carefully and underline the most important information.
2. Take notes which will help you to explain to your classmates why Shakespeare is still of interest today.
3. Add the keywords you have decided on in your group to your own mind map.

M 4 2b or not 2b – Shakespeare goes mobile

This article refers to services connected to Shakespeare. Find out more about it.

Shakespeare makes inroads into hitech world

Monday 12 December 2011

How many times a day do you receive a text message? Are you tired of reading the same advertising blurb on your mobile or Smart-phone? As a welcome
5 and creative alternative how about receiving

"A horse, a horse! My kingdom for a horse!"

Shakespeare appears to have made
10 inroads into the world of modern communication. After being successful with their poem.me service which allows customers to receive a poem every day by email, an innovative British company has
15 recently launched its shake.me service where you are offered the chance to see the Bard in a fresh light.

Quote or sonnet?

This messaging service enables people to
20 subscribe to a short quote from a play, poem or sonnet. Subscribers can choose a daily, weekly or monthly service for a small fee.

"Thou art a very ragged wart."

During your hectic day take a few seconds to sit back and enjoy a literary 25 break. If you want a change from Shakespeare try other services like love poems or try to solve a daily riddle.

Educationalists believe that this is an attractive way to learn more about Shake- 30 speare and hope that young people will be encouraged to read and appreciate Shakespeare more in the future.

After all it was a Shakespearean quote that inspired Huxley to entitle his book 35 *Brave New World*.

Shake-me: a good business idea or not – that is the question.

Text: Christopher Smeeton

3 **blurb:** a short description of a book, film, or other product written for promotional purposes, Klappentext – 10 **to make inroads into sth.:** in etw. vorstoßen – 15 **to launch:** etw. auf den Markt bringen – 20 **to subscribe to sth.:** etw. abonnieren – **ragged:** lacking finish, smoothness, or uniformity, (of cloth or clothes) old and torn – **wart:** (informal) an obnoxious or objectionable person

Tasks

1. Read the text carefully and underline the most important information.
2. Take notes which will help you to explain to your classmates why Shakespeare is still of interest today.
3. Add the keywords you have decided on in your group to your own mind map.

M 5 Shakespeare and the 2012 London Olympics

This article gives an account of the importance of Shakespeare's plays not only in the English speaking world but also internationally.

Shakespeare plays in 38 languages for 2012 Olympics

AFP   Sunday, 23 January 2011

Each of William Shakespeare's 38 plays will be performed in a different language, including Arabic, Spanish and Urdu, during a theatre season in Britain to mark the London 2012 Olympic Games.

Shakespeare's Globe theatre in the British capital said Thursday it would host the special season over six weeks, beginning next year on April 23, the playwright's birthday.

Shows will include "The Taming of the Shrew" in Urdu, starring Pakistani television star Nadia Jamil as Katherine, and "King Lear" in Australian Aboriginal languages.

Other performances include "Julius Caesar" in Italian, "Troilus and Cressida" in Maori, "The Tempest" in Arabic and "Love's Labour's Lost" in British sign language.

Photo: Marcus Michels

"The Globe will create an international Shakespeare community in the heart of London, as a prelude to the internationalism which will fill the capital later in the year with the Olympics," said the Globe's artistic director Dominic Dromgoole.

The project is part of the London 2012 Cultural Olympiad which was set up in 2008 to celebrate the Olympics. The Globe is a reconstruction of a theatre where many of Shakespeare's plays were performed before it burnt down in 1613.

Source: http://www.independent.co.uk/sport/shakespeare-plays-in-38-languages-for-2012-olympics- 2192140.html © AFP slightly adapted

Tasks

1. Read the text carefully and underline the most important information.
2. Take notes which will help you to explain to your classmates why Shakespeare is still of interest today.
3. Add the keywords you have decided on in your group to your own mind map.

Hinweise (M 2–M 5; 2. und 3. Stunde)

Auch in dieser Doppelstunde befassen sich die Lernenden mit der Beliebtheit Shakespeares in der heutigen Zeit.

Die Stunde beginnt mit der Besprechung der **Hausaufgabe**, in der die zentralen Aspekte aus den **Internetkommentaren (M 2)** benannt und erläutert werden. Bei der Besprechung sollte ein Rückbezug zu ihren in der Mind Map festgehaltenen Ideen hergestellt werden, da in dieser Stunde eine Vertiefung erfolgt.

Die **Internet- und Verfassertexte (M 3–M 5)** illustrieren in anschaulicher Weise das ungebrochene Interesse, das an Shakespeare gerade in unserer Zeit besteht. Für die Erarbeitung der Materialien in der Doppelstunde wird das Verfahren des **Gruppenpuzzles** gewählt. Diese Methode gewährleistet Eigenverantwortung der Lernenden für ihren Lernprozess. Es ermöglicht vor allem aber auch, dass eine Vielzahl an Materialien umgewälzt und mündlich kommuniziert wird.

Zum Verfahren: Zunächst wird der Kurs in gleichgroße Arbeitsgruppen aufgeteilt. In Abhängigkeit von der Kursgröße bearbeitet eine Gruppe arbeitsteilig einen oder mehrere Texte (M 3–M 5). Um das Vorgehen in der zweiten Phase zu erleichtern, werden die Kopien einer Gruppe jeweils mit einem Großbuchstaben versehen und durchnummeriert. Die Schülerinnen und Schüler der ersten Gruppe haben den Buchstaben A und jeder von ihnen eine Zahl von 1 bis x, die zweite Gruppe ist durch B und ebenfalls die Zahlen 1 bis x gekennzeichnet usw.

Die **Arbeitsanweisungen** in diesen Gruppen sind identisch. Zunächst erfolgt eine Beschäftigung mit dem Material und *Task* 1 in Einzelarbeit. Anschließend tauschen sich die Lernenden in der Gruppe aus. Die Gruppe einigt sich auf Stichwörter zu den zentralen Informationen aus ihrem Material (*Task 2*). Wiederum wird die bereits vorhandene eigene Mind Map um diese Stichworte ergänzt (*Task 3*).

In der zweiten Phase des Gruppenpuzzles erfolgt der Austausch über die jeweils erarbeiteten Informationen in neuen Gruppen, d.h. die Puzzleteile der unterschiedlichen Texte werden zusammengesetzt. Hierzu gehen die Lernenden mit der gleichen Nummer zusammen. In der neuen Zusammensetzung erfolgt wiederum ein Austausch der Ergebnisse mit anschließender Ergänzung der Mind Map.

Auswertung: Als Ergebnissicherung im Plenum wird exemplarisch wieder die Mind Map auf Folie vorgestellt. Dabei handelt es sich um die Folie mit den Ergebnissen der ersten Stunde, die nun nach und nach ergänzt wird. Hierbei fungieren jeweils diejenigen Schülerinnen und Schüler als Experten, die den Text ursprünglich bearbeitet haben. Sie nehmen auch zu neuen Erkenntnissen hinsichtlich der Aktualität Shakespeares Stellung.

Zum Schluss bekommen alle die ihnen noch fehlenden Texte für die häusliche Lektüre. Die **Hausaufgabe** stellt eine Vertiefung und schriftliche Sicherung dar.

Introducing Shakespeare (S II)

Erwartungshorizont (M 1–M 5)

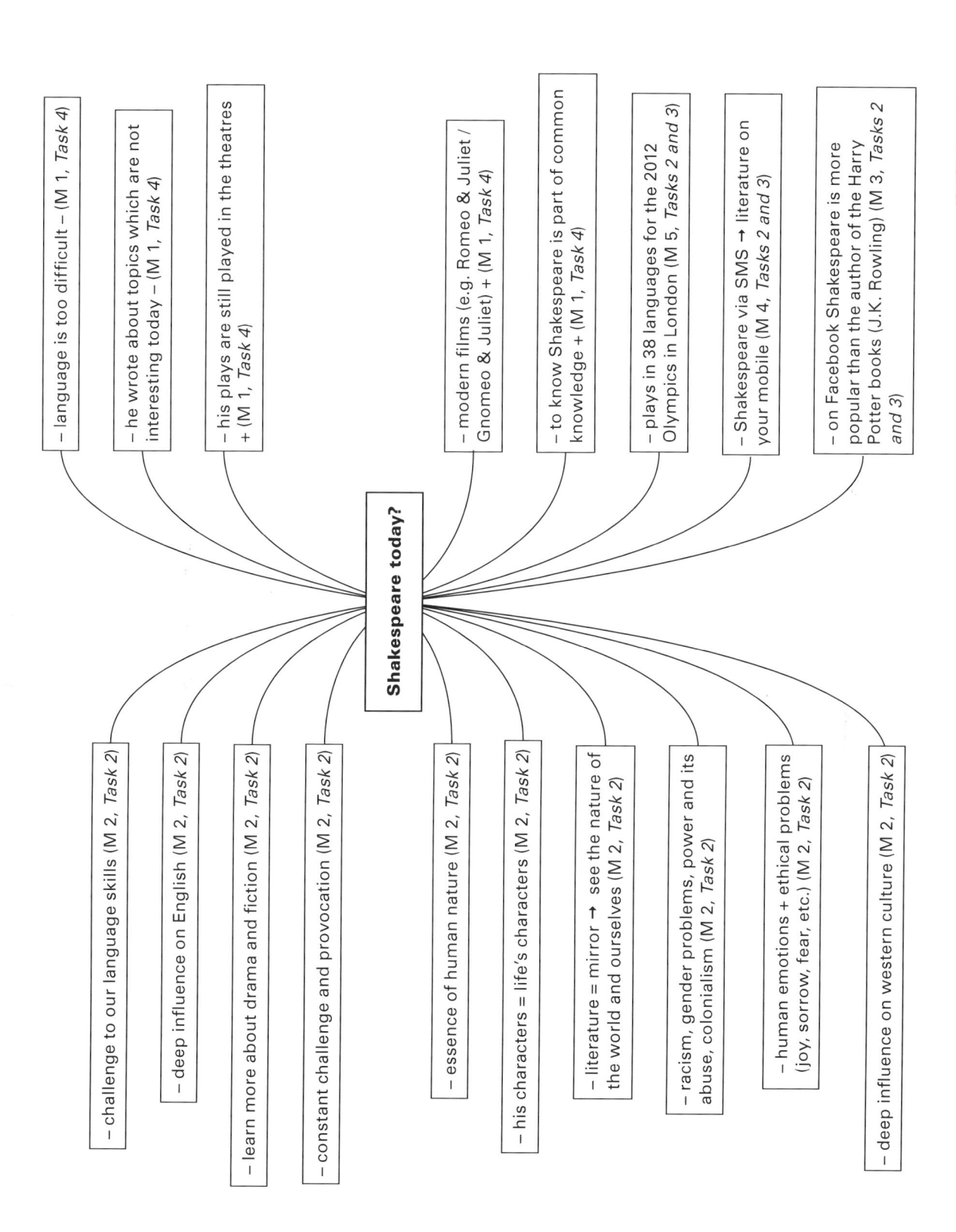

Shakespeare today?

- language is too difficult – (M 1, Task 4)
- he wrote about topics which are not interesting today – (M 1, Task 4)
- his plays are still played in the theatres + (M 1, Task 4)
- modern films (e.g. Romeo & Juliet / Gnomeo & Juliet) + (M 1, Task 4)
- to know Shakespeare is part of common knowledge + (M 1, Task 4)
- plays in 38 languages for the 2012 Olympics in London (M 5, Tasks 2 and 3)
- Shakespeare via SMS → literature on your mobile (M 4, Tasks 2 and 3)
- on Facebook Shakespeare is more popular than the author of the Harry Potter books (J.K. Rowling) (M 3, Tasks 2 and 3)
- challenge to our language skills (M 2, Task 2)
- deep influence on English (M 2, Task 2)
- learn more about drama and fiction (M 2, Task 2)
- constant challenge and provocation (M 2, Task 2)
- essence of human nature (M 2, Task 2)
- his characters = life's characters (M 2, Task 2)
- literature = mirror → see the nature of the world and ourselves (M 2, Task 2)
- racism, gender problems, power and its abuse, colonialism (M 2, Task 2)
- human emotions + ethical problems (joy, sorrow, fear, etc.) (M 2, Task 2)
- deep influence on western culture (M 2, Task 2)

M 6 Getting started with a comedy: *Much Ado About Nothing*

Discover who falls in love with whom in Shakespeare's play Much Ado About Nothing, *who doesn't want to marry – ever – and why all's well that ends well.*

Tasks

1. Read the following plot summary carefully. Decide which parts of the plot the quotations relate to and write the correct quotation on the line.

2. Together with a partner now work with one quotation intensively. Try out different ways of speaking; use a pause, make use of gestures or build a freeze frame on the basis of the quote.

I) Quotations from the play

A) Give me your hand before this holy friar. I am your husband, if you like of me.

B) Let me bid you welcome, my lord. Being reconciled to the prince your brother, I owe you all duty.

C) I do love nothing in the world so well as you.

D) I will live a bachelor.

E) What was it you told me of today, that your nice Beatrice was in love with Signor Benedick?

F) I had rather hear my dog bark at a crow than a man swear he loves me.

G) That I love her, I feel.

H) That young start-up hath all the glory of my overthrow. If I can cross him any way, I bless myself every day.

I) There, Leonato, take her back again.

J) Let's have a dance ere we are married, that we may lighten our own hearts and our wives' heels.

II) Plot of *Much Ado About Nothing*

Let's all travel to the island of Sicily in Italy. All the action takes place in the house and gardens of the Governor of Messina. His name is Leonato. At the beginning of the play Don Pedro, the Prince of Arragon returns home from a military conflict with his half-brother Don John. Both have made peace now. Together with these two comes Claudio: He was a true hero in the fighting. The fourth man to return is Benedick. In order to welcome them all Leonato addresses Don Pedro. He says the following to him:

1. quote: Let me bid you welcome, my lord. Being reconciled to the prince your brother, I owe you all duty. (B)

Together with Leonato are his beautiful daughter Hero and his niece Beatrice. Even before he has arrived, Beatrice makes critical remarks about Benedick whom she knows from former times. Beatrice has a very strong negative opinion about the opposite sex. At the beginning of the play a battle of words begins between her and Benedick. It goes on for quite a while. Beatrice clearly says that she does not want to get involved with a man:

2. quote: _____

Introducing Shakespeare (S II)

| Reihe 7 | Verlauf | Material S 12 | LEK | Kontext | Mediothek |

The same is true for Benedick. He also clearly shows his dislike of Beatrice and his conviction that he will never marry a woman and live his life as an unmarried man:

3. quote: _____

Exactly the opposite is true for Claudio who falls in love instantly with Hero when he sees her for the first time:

4. quote: _____

II/B3

[more dramatically] But there is a big problem. Different from the others, Don John is not happy at all on returning home. He is the nasty character in the play. He lost in the conflict with his half-brother Don Pedro, but most of all he is jealous of Claudio who was so heroic in the fight and now is in a better position than Don John himself. This is the reason why Don John tries to prevent Claudio from getting an even better position in society by marrying the Governor's daughter Hero. He wants to plot against this and explains his attitude:

5. quote: _____

Meanwhile, Don Pedro has also worked out a plot but his ambitions are honourable. He wants to make Benedick and Beatrice fall in love with each other. To achieve this he arranges a meeting together with Claudio and Leonato in the garden and he makes sure that their conversation is overheard by Benedick. He is hiding behind some bushes and hears what the others have invented about Beatrice's affection for him. Don Pedro pretends to be curious about hearing what Leonato heard in his house:

6. quote: _____

Hero and her maid are part of Don Pedro's plans, too. At the same time, when Benedick is tricked into loving Beatrice, they do the same with her. Both women make Beatrice overhear their invented conversation about Benedick's praise of Beatrice. The plan works out for both Beatrice and Benedick, who, after what they have heard, have no doubts about the other's affection.

For Claudio and Hero, however, it is a completely different story. Another nasty character in the play is Borachio who organises the plan to disinherit Hero. Don John uses his services and both of them make Claudio believe that Hero is unfaithful to him and that she has already had an affair. So the very day when the marriage ceremony is about to begin, Claudio refuses to marry Hero and dishonours her in public which of course is a big scandal:

7. quote: _____

Shortly after this nightmare for one couple in the play, a happier meeting of another couple takes place. Benedick confesses his love to Beatrice in the chapel:

8. quote: _____

Beatrice also confirms her love to Benedick. Luckily, not much later the evil plotting of Don John, who has run away, comes to light. Don John is arrested and has to face his punishment. Now there is nothing that can hinder the love and marriage of Claudio and Hero. This time Claudio is ready to accept her as his wife:

9. quote: _____

And finally, the play ends happily with a double marriage: Claudio marries Hero and Benedick marries Beatrice. After all the trouble before, Benedick invites them all to be cheerful and dance:

10. quote: _____

RAAbits Englisch

Introducing Shakespeare (S II)

Reihe 7 | **Verlauf** | **Material S 13** | **LEK** | **Kontext** | **Mediothek**

II/B3

Hinweise (M 6; 4. und 5. Stunde)

In dieser Doppelstunde wird an ein erstes **konkretes Werk** und damit auch an die **Sprache Shakespeares** herangeführt. Nach der umfassenderen Einführungsphase nähern sich die Schülerinnen und Schüler dem Stück *„Much Ado about Nothing"* deduktiv.

In einer ersten Arbeitsphase erfolgt der Zugang zum *plot* des Stückes über das richtige **Zuordnen ausgewählter Zitate** (Task 1) in **Partnerarbeit**. Durch dieses vorangestellte Sicherstellen des Textverständnisses wird zugleich die anschließende kreative Spracharbeit entlastet. Die Sicherung findet im Plenum statt (Vortrag der vollständigen Inhaltsangabe).

In der zweiten Phase erfolgt ebenfalls in Partnerarbeit (arbeitsteilig) die **Auseinandersetzung mit jeweils einem Zitat**. Die Einteilung nimmt die Lehrkraft vor. Nun erarbeiten sich die Schülerinnen und Schüler ihren Textbaustein, indem sie verschiedene Vortragsweisen einüben (Task 2) mit beispielsweise betontem Lesen, Gebrauch von Pausen, Einsatz von Mimik und Gestik, Darstellen der Situation in einem Standbild etc. Ein Schüler übernimmt später im Plenum beim wiederholten Vortrag die Sprecherrolle.

Diese Phase des Experimentierens führt die Gruppe behutsam an sprachliche Auffälligkeiten heran, ohne dass ein kompliziertes Regelwerk und eine Theorieeinheit vorangestellt werden müssen. Der Eigenart der Texte als Skript für das Theater wird Rechnung getragen und dies hat den wichtigen motivierenden Effekt, dass die Lernenden Shakespeare verstehen können – eine für sie wichtige Erfahrung.

Nach dieser ausführlicheren Einübungsphase wird der *plot* nun noch einmal entweder durch die Lehrkraft oder einen Kursteilnehmer gesprochen. An den entsprechenden Stellen bringen die Schüler ihre eingeübten Zitate ein.

Erwartungshorizont (M 6)

1–B; 2–F; 3–D; 4–G; 5–H; 6–E; 7–I; 8–C; 9–A; 10–J

M 7 Famous characters ... and what they are after – lovers

Now that you know the plot of Much Ado About Nothing *immerse yourself in the following scene and make yourself familiar with the way the protagonists talk to each other. Enjoy their spicy puns.*

W. Shakespeare, Much Ado About Nothing, Act 4, Scene 1, vv. 254–292

At the beginning of the play we see that Benedick and Beatrice have always had a war of words with each other. Both of them swear never to get married. In the following extract, however, which follows the marriage ceremony which was called off because of Claudio's rejection of Hero, we get a completely different impression of the two of them. Both are in the chapel:

Benedick: Lady Beatrice, have you wept all this while?

Beatrice: Yea, and I will weep a while longer.

Benedick: I will not desire that.

Beatrice: You have no reason, I do it freely.

5 Benedick: Surely I do believe your fair cousin is wronged.

Beatrice: Ah, how much might the man deserve of me that would right her!

Benedick: Is there any way to show such friendship?

Beatrice: A very even way, but no such friend.

10 Benedick: May a man do it?

Beatrice: It's a man's office, but not yours.

Benedick: I do love nothing in the world so well as you, is not that strange?

Beatrice: As strange as the thing I know not: it were as possible
15 for me to say, I loved nothing so well as you, but believe me not, and yet I lie not, I confess nothing, nor I deny nothing: I am sorry for my cousin.

Benedick: By my sword, Beatrice, thou lovest me.

Beatrice: Do not swear and eat it.

Benedick: I will swear by it that you love me, and I will make him eat it that says I love not you.

20 Beatrice: Will you not eat your word?

Benedick: With no sauce that can be devised to it. I protest I love thee.

Beatrice: Why then God forgive me.

Benedick: What offence, sweet Beatrice?

Beatrice: You have stayed me in a happy hour, I was about to protest I loved you.

25 Benedick: And do it with all thy heart.

Beatrice: I love you with so much of my heart, that none is left to protest.

Benedick: Come bid me do anything for thee.

Beatrice: Kill Claudio.

Benedick: Ha, not for the wide world.

30 Beatrice: You kill me to deny it, farewell.

Benedick (Barring her way): Tarry, sweet Beatrice.

Beatrice: I am gone, though I am here, there is no love in you, – nay, I pray you, let me go.

Benedick: Beatrice.

Tasks

1. Read the extract from *Much Ado about Nothing* first to understand what it is about.

2. Practise reading the passage several times so that in your performance both the particular situation and the characters become obvious.

3. Is there anything unusual in the way both address each other? Examine this.

Introducing Shakespeare (S II)

Beatrice: In faith I will go.

35 Benedick: We'll be friends first.

Beatrice: You dare easier be friends with me than fight with mine enemy.

Benedick: Is Claudio thine enemy?

Beatrice: Is a not approved in the height a villain, that hath slandered, scorned, dishonoured my kinswoman? Oh that I were a man! What, bear her in hand, and until they come to take hands, and then
40 with public accusation, uncovered slander, unmitigated rancour? Oh God that I were a man! I would eat his heart in the market place.

Benedick: Hear me, Beatrice.

Beatrice: Talk with a man out at a window, a proper saying.

Benedick: Nay, but Beatrice.

45 Beatrice: Sweet Hero, she is wronged, she is slandered, she is undone.

Benedick: Beat –

Beatrice: Princes and counties! Surely a princely testimony, a goodly count, Count Comfect, a sweet gallant, surely, oh that I were a man for my sake! Or that I had any friend would be a man for my sake! But manhood is melted into curtsies, valour into compliment, and men are only turned into tongue, and
50 trim ones too: he is now as valiant as Hercules, that only tells a lie, and swears it: I cannot be a man with wishing; therefore I will die a woman with grieving.

Benedick: Tarry, good Beatrice, by this hand I love thee.

Beatrice: Use it for my love some other way than swearing by it.

Benedick: Think you in your soul the Count Claudio hath wronged Hero?

55 Beatrice: Yea, as sure as I have a thought, or a soul.

Benedick: Enough, I am engaged, I will challenge him, I will kiss your hand, and so I leave you: by this hand, Claudio shall render me a dear account: as you hear of me, so think of me: go comfort your cousin, I must say she is dead, and so, farewell. [*Exeunt*]

Source text: William Shakespeare, *Much Ado About Nothing*, The New Cambridge Shakespeare, Cambridge: CUP, 2005² (Text first published 1988), pp. 115,117,119.

Vocabulary Aids

5 **is wronged:** Claudio does her wrong when he suspects her to be unfaithful – 9 **even:** direct, frank – 11 **office:** task, responsibility – 12 **you:** second personal pronoun singular: Höflichkeitsform: Sie – 14 **the thing I know not:** I don't know what – 17 **By my sword:** An oath sworn on the cross by a Christian gentleman, using the hilt of his sword; a gentleman's last opportunity to defend sb's honour – 17 **thou:** second personal pronoun singular: du – 18 **eat it:** to eat his own words – 21 **to protest:** to state, to swear – 21 **thee:** personal pronoun: dich – 22 **God forgive me:** for ignoring normal convention and be the first to declare her love – 24 **stayed:** stopped – 24 **in a happy hour:** at an opportune or appropriate moment – 24 **protest:** object – 31 **Tarry:** please stay, don't leave me – 32 **I am gone ... here:** 'Although I am physically held here against my will my spirit has already gone.' – 38 **Is a not:** isn't he ... ? – 39 **bear her in hand:** lead her on in a deceptive way, conceal his real aims – 39 **take hands:** give each other their hand in marriage – 40 **uncovered:** open, obvious, bare-faced, blatant – 40 **unmitigated rancour:** uncontrolled anger/resentment – 43 **proper saying:** likely story – 45 **undone:** ruined – 47 **counties:** counts – 47 **a goodly count:** a fine allegation, Beatrice makes a triple pun on the word 'count' (meaning Claudio, an account/narrative, and a legal indictment) – 47 **Count Comfect:** Count Candy – 49 **curtsies (pl.):** courtesies, ceremonies, formal and polite gestures such as those that would be used in court – 49 **compliment:** flattery – 49 **only ... tongue:** can do nothing but talk – 50 **trim:** superficial, false – 50 **Hercules:** the hero of superhuman strength of classical mythology – 51 **with wishing:** even if I wish it – 57 **render ... account:** pay dearly for his actions

M 8 Shakespeare talk

In contrast to the Modern English we use today, the English of the era when Shakespeare wrote his plays is called Early Modern English or Elizabethan English. It was a time of great changes in the language. Shakespeare was a genius with words. He invented about 1,500 new words by making use of influences from Latin, French and Italian and coined expressions which are still in use today.

By my sword, … thou lovest me.

I) In his book *Shakespeare on Toast* the actor and author Ben Crystal gives an explanation for the difference between thou and you. He compares it to the French convention:

"Ask someone to 'speak Shakespearean' and they'll probably throw in a couple of phrases like *thou art a blaggard* or *thou art an arse*, without knowing why they're saying thou instead of you. An awful lot of people coming to Shakespeare don't know why both these second-person pronouns (to give them their official title) are there, and often want to change all the *thous* to *yous* to make everything look neat and tidy.

Why can't we – or shouldn't we – ignore them? Ever learnt French? If you have, you'll know that there are two ways of saying you. A polite and a formal way (*vous*), which can be used to address one person or a group of people; and a more sociable and informal way (*tu*), which is used only when speaking to one person.

There used to be a similar option in the English language: in Old English, *thou* was used to address one person and *you* was used to address more than one. But from the 13th century onwards, in Middle English, *you* started to develop and add connotations of politeness, probably because people wanted to copy the respected French way of speaking; and they began to use *you* in one-on-one conversations. The assumption was that if you spoke French, you must therefore be rich and intelligent; and those who couldn't afford to learn French simply changed their own language to sound more learned.

So by the time Shakespeare was writing – when our language was known as Early Modern English – there was a choice:

Opener	Used when …	Normal reply
you	upper classes are talking to each other, even when they're closely related	you
thou	lower classes are talking to each other	thou
thou	superiors are talking to inferiors, for instance: – parents to children – masters to servants	– you – you
thou	for special intimacy, for instance: – talking to a lover – addressing God or a god (e.g. Jupiter)	thou
thou	a character talks to someone absent	–
thou	a character talks to someone near to them on stage	thou
you	a character talks to someone far away from them on stage	you

When going through a play, you'll find *thou* and *you* in various different forms, depending on how they're being used:

The *thou* forms are *thou, thee, thy, thine,* and *thyself.*

You-forms are *you, your, yours,* and *yourself/yourselves.*

In a scene, when someone changes from using *thou* to using *you*, or the other way round, *it always means something* – Shakespeare consciously chose when to switch them – and it usually implies a change of attitude, or a new emotion or mood.

It could be anything: a sign of extra affection or of anger; an insult or a compliment; a piece of playfulness or an indication that the speaker is adopting a more businesslike or professional attitude, distancing themselves socially or physically; or trying to become more formal or informal." [...]

Source: Hintergründe zu Shakespeares Sprache in: Ben Crystal, *Shakespeare on Toast*, London: Icon Books, 2008, pp. 99–101 and also his analysis of Shakespeare's use of the iambic pentameter pp. 118–138. © Icon Books

2 **blaggard:** 'black-hearted' person; person of ill intent; villain – 2 **arse (slang):** part of the body you sit on – 5 **neat and tidy:** tidy and in order; carefully done or arranged – 12 **connotation:** an idea suggested by a word in addition to its main meaning – 18 **opener:** beginning of a conversation – 36 **consciously (adv.):** being aware of doing sth. – 38 **affection (for sb./sth.):** the feeling of liking or loving sb./sth. very much and caring about them – 38 **insult:** remark that is said in order to offend sb.

Task

Read the text above. Why is there a difference in the use of the forms "you" and "thou"? Explain.

II) Prose vs verse

In Shakespeare plays, two different types of speech have to be distinguished: free flowing texts in prose, and texts with a certain pattern in the verse. A broad distinction would be that verse is restricted to Kings and upper class speakers whereas prose is left to everyone else but in most Shakespeare plays there are variations to this rule of thumb. With Shakespeare there is always a reason why a character chooses one particular style of speaking or switches between the two options.

Having texts in verse means that more attention of the audience is given to a single thought in one verse and also attention is built up for the thought that follows. Line after line creates a certain rhythm. There is another very practical reason for using this sort of text in a drama: single lines of verse are easier for the actors to memorize.

Metre: Iambic pentameter

The verse pattern that Shakespeare uses both in his sonnets and his plays is called blank verse, which consists of non-rhyming lines which each have five stressed syllables. Iambus is the metre that has got one unstressed syllable followed by a stressed one (Didum x 5) and it most resembles the rhythm of how English is spoken. A more refined way of speech other than blank verse would be the rhyming equivalent in form of a sonnet (e.g. the prologue of *Romeo & Juliet* and the speech of some characters when it is very important). Being the genius he was however, Shakespeare experimented with his use of the iambic pentameter and did not always follow the convention. He thereby added much drama and effect to the way his characters speak on stage.

Introducing Shakespeare (S II)

| Reihe 7 | Verlauf | Material S 18 | LEK | Kontext | Mediothek |

II/B3

Hinweise (M 7 und M 8; 6. Stunde)

Nachdem in der letzten Stunde eine erste Annäherung an die Sprache Shakespeares erfolgt ist, wird dieser Aspekt in dieser Stunde vertieft.

Eine Vorbereitung stellt die **Hausaufgabe** dar, bei der die Lernenden die **Liebeserklärung** von Benedick und Beatrice in „Much Ado About Nothing" erarbeiten (**M 7**). Aus dem Kontext der Handlung ist die Besonderheit der Situation – das Liebesbekenntnis beider Sprecher – nachzuempfinden. In **Partnerarbeit** werden zunächst beide Rollen noch einmal eingeübt, worauf die Präsentation im Plenum durch wechselseitiges **intoniertes Lesen** erfolgt (*Task* 2). Anschließend werden die Schülervorträge gemeinsam ausgewertet. Dabei findet gleichzeitig Berücksichtigung, inwieweit die Szene inhaltlich erfasst wurde (*Task* 1).

In der Sprechweise der Akteure sollte zum Ausdruck kommen, dass Benedick von seiner Liebe zu Beatrice tief ergriffen ist. Beatrice erwidert dieses Liebesbekenntnis, ist zugleich aber voller Sorge und Zorn wegen der Anschuldigungen gegen ihre Cousine Hero. Gegen Ende des Auszugs sollte ihre Stimme diesen Zorn mit Nachdruck zum Ausdruck bringen, verlangt sie hier doch von Benedick, dass er Claudio zur Wiedergutmachung der entstandenen Entehrung töten soll – was dieser jedoch entschieden ablehnt.

Tipp: Zur Illustration dieses Auszugs bietet es sich an, den entsprechenden Ausschnitt aus der BBC-**Verfilmung** von Kenneth Branagh zu zeigen und mit den Schülervorträgen zu vergleichen (zu beziehen über amazon.de; timecode: 1:06:26–1:10:33).

In *Task* 3 lenken die Lernenden nun ihre Aufmerksamkeit auf die **Besonderheit** der **Sprache** und erkennen, wie stark diese und der Inhalt ineinandergreifen. Bei der Lektüre des Auszugs sollte bereits der unterschiedliche Gebrauch des zweiten Personalpronomen Singular *thou / you* aufgefallen sein. Weil diese Formen sowie die Objekt- und Possessivpronomen eine grundlegende Besonderheit für die Sprache in den Shakespeare-Dramen sind, werden sie an der **Tafel** gesammelt: *you*: Sie; *thou*: du; *thee*: dich; *thy*: dein; *thine*: dein.

Anschließend stellen die Lernenden Vermutungen über mögliche Gründe für diese unterschiedlichen Formen des zweiten Personalpronomens an: *Can you think of reasons why there is a change in the use of the forms* **you** *and* **thou**? Der **Wechsel** drückt hier besonders eindrucksvoll unterschiedliche Formen der Nähe und Distanz zwischen beiden aus.

Zunächst dominiert das höflichere und **distanzierendere „you"**. Dies gilt selbst noch für das Liebesbekenntnis Benedicks: „*I do love nothing in the world so well as you. Is not that strange?*". Schließlich ist es Benedick, der einen Schritt weiter geht und die **Nähe**, die er zu Beatrice verspürt, auch in seiner Sprache durch das vertrautere **„thou"** zum Ausdruck bringt: „*By my sword, Beatrice, thou lovest me*". Später verwendet er das entsprechende Objektpronomen *thee* und das Possessivpronomen *thy*: *I protest I love thee. [...] And do it with all thy heart.*

Beatrice bleibt kontrolliert und auf Distanz. Sie benutzt das vertrauliche „*thou*" nicht ein einziges Mal; ihre Sorge gilt in diesem Moment weniger dem eigenen Glück als dem von Hero. Wie aufgebracht sie wegen des geschehenen Unrechts ist, verdeutlicht ihr auffallend höherer Redeanteil. Benedick befindet sich zwischen den Fronten des befreundeten Claudio und der geliebten Beatrice. Seine wachsende Unruhe und Unsicherheit zeigen sich darin, dass seine Sätze wiederholt fragmentarisch bleiben und schließlich immer kürzer werden, nachdem Beatrice ihn aufgefordert hat, Claudio zu töten: „*Beatrice –; Hear me, Beatrice –; Nay, but Beatrice –; Beat–.*"

Am Ende des Dialogs scheint er sich wieder gefasst zu haben. Hier wechselt er wieder in die *you*-Form: „*Think you in your soul the Count Claudio hath wronged Hero?*" An dieser Stelle nimmt Benedick eine offizielle Haltung ein, weil er sich als Gentleman für Hero bei Claudio einsetzen will. Natürlich verfolgt er dabei auch sehr private Interessen. Er möchte Beatrice gefallen und ihre Liebe nicht verlieren.

Falls möglich, werden weitere sprachliche Besonderheiten des Textauszugs genannt: etwa die konjugierte Verbform „*lovest*" für „*you love*" (Z. 17); „*hath*" für „*has*" (Z. 38). Abschließend lässt die Lehrkraft den **Textauszug** (**M 8**) aus dem Buch von Ben Crystal laut vorlesen, der den Schülerinnen und Schülern den Unterschied der beiden Personalformen *you / thou* auf einfache Art und Weise verdeutlicht. Dies gelingt, weil der Autor die Analogie zum Französischen benutzt. Die Aufgabe, die der Sicherung dient, wird im Unterrichtsgespräch bearbeitet.

Als **Hausaufgabe** lesen die Lernenden zur inhaltlichen Vorbereitung auf die nächste Stunde den Plot von „*King Lear*".

M 9 *The Tragedy of King Lear* – an outline of the plot

The range of characters in a play or novel is very important for the creation of meaning. Read the abridged outline of the plot of The Tragedy of King Lear *and don't forget that visualization is a useful technique for future reading tasks. Learn more about a King who wants to test his daughters to find out how much they love him and in doing so loses everything.*

Since he wants to live his remaining years in tranquillity the king of Britain, King Lear, wants to divide up his country between his three daughters, Gonerill, Regan and Cordelia. He thinks the best way to do this is to measure how much to give each daughter by the amount of love the daughters confess to having for their father. Both
5 Gonerill and Regan boast of their strong and deep feelings and receive their promised parts (a third of the kingdom each).

The youngest daughter, Cordelia, however, is the only one to honestly say what she feels; she does not want to put on an act as her sisters did. She says that she loves her father according to her duty as a child. Lear takes this as a clear insult; he cannot distinguish the truth from flattery. In an act of madness he
10 therefore disinherits Cordelia and even banishes her from his country. The Earl of Kent defends Cordelia in front of Lear but for saying this unwanted truth he also is banished.

The kingdom is equally divided between the other two daughters who become rulers over these parts. But it does not take long for the King to find out the true nature of his two daughters' love. Agreements that were made about living alternately with one or other of them are quickly disregarded. They let
15 him feel that he is a burden to them and that they were only interested in the inheritance. Both of them together turn nasty against him which finally really drives Lear mad. Cordelia is the one who truly loves her father and finally saves him. Both are reconciled.

The action to do with a villain called Edmond can be regarded as a sub-plot to all of this. He is the bastard son of the Duke of Gloucester. His half-brother is Edgar. Right from the start of the play Edmond thinks
20 up an evil plot to disinherit Edgar, become the Earl himself, and to betray the King to put himself in his place. With a fake letter he makes Gloucester, his father, believe that his brother Edgar wants to betray the father. But not Edgar but Edmond is the villain. It does not take long for him to become the Earl of Gloucester.

At one stage in the play he becomes the focus of attention when both of Cordelia's sisters, though they
25 are both married, set their eyes on him. Edmond has kept both his options open because he had declared his love to both of them. After her husband dies Regan declares her intention to marry Edmond. This leads to the jealousy of her sister Goneril, who then poisons her own sister but when her husband finds out about this, she kills herself.

Cordelia together with her father Lear have become prisoners in a conflict between the two kingdoms,
30 of Britain and France. Edmond has clear intentions of having both of them be killed but it turns out that there is no need for that: in her grief Cordelia has killed herself and Lear cannot bear to see the daughter who really loved him dead and dies himself, too.

After all his evil doings and treasons have been discovered, Edmond is finally killed and reported dead by a messenger. It is finally Goneril's husband, the Duke of Albany, who follows Lear on the throne and
35 becomes king of Britain.

9 **flattery**: excessive and insincere praise – 10 **to disinherit so.**: to prevent so. from inheriting one's property – 33 **treason**: the action/crime of betraying so. or one's country

Tasks

1. Read the plot outline of *King Lear* carefully.
2. Create a visualization (keywords and arrows) which shows the relationships and conflicts between the characters. You can also look online for more information on the plot and the characters of the play.

Introducing Shakespeare (S II)

| Reihe 7 | Verlauf | Material S 20 | LEK | Kontext | Mediothek |

M 10 *The Tragedy of King Lear* – extracts

The character of the villain does not only appear in King Lear, *but in other plays too. Find out more about them as they are of considerable importance to Shakespeare's plays.*

> **Pre-reading activity:**
>
> *A villain is a bad character in a story or play; a person who is morally bad or responsible for causing trouble or harm. (Oxford English Dictionary)*
>
> Work together with a partner. Answer the following questions:
>
> – Give some possible motives for a person to behave as a villain.
>
> – What can a villain do in a play in order to cause trouble or harm?
>
> – Why does a villain play an important role in a play?

II/B3

Getting to know a typical Shakespearean villain

The following extracts are monologues in which Edmond speaks about his situation and his intentions.

W. Shakespeare, *The Tragedy of King Lear* (extracts)

Act 1, Scene 2, vv. 1–22

Edmond: Thou, Nature, art my goddess; to thy law / My services are bound. Wherefore should I / Stand in the plague of custom and permit / The curiosity of nations to deprive me? / For that I am some twelve or fourteen moonshines / Lag of a brother? Why 'bastard'? Wherefore 'base'? / When my dimensions are as well compact, / My mind as generous, and my shape as true / As honest madam's
5 issue? Why brand they us / With 'base'? with 'baseness?' 'bastardy'? 'base, base'? / Who in the lusty stealth of nature take / More composition and fierce quality / Than doth within a dull, stale, tired bed / Go to th'creating a whole tribe of fops / Got 'tween a sleep and wake? / Well then, / Legitimate Edgar, I must have your land. / Our father's love is to the bastard, Edmond, / As to th'legitimate. Fine word, 'legitimate'. / Well, my legitimate [*Takes out a letter*] if this letter speed / And my invention thrive,
10 Edmond the base / Shall to th'legitimate. I grow; I prosper; / Now gods, stand up for bastards! […]

Vocabulary Aids

1 **Thou … bastards:** Edmond's soliloquy is similar to the one by Richard III. Both share the Elizabethan belief that the trusting nature of other people can be taken advantage of and used for their own ends → origin is the Italian Nicolo Machiavelli – 1 **law:** natural laws as opposed to laws of religion and society – 2 **custom:** what is normally accepted, used with the force of law – 2 **For that:** because – 3 **moonshines:** months – 3 **Lag of:** Coming after or later than – 3 **Why … 'base'?:** Being illegitimate troubles him considerably. He also questions the inference that being base-born means that he is base in other respects – 4 **dimensions:** the proportions of his body – 4 **compact:** composed, formed – 4 **generous:** noble, worthy of a gentleman – 4 **true:** proper, correct – 4 **honest:** pure – 5/6 **lusty nature:** secret pleasure in one's natural sexual appetite – 6 **take … quality:** Either (1) acquire more physical and mental elements as well as more energy, or (2) require a stronger and more robust physical and mental constitution. Both may be meant here. – 6 **a dull … bed:** what could happen after being married for a long time – 7 **fops:** fools – 9 **speed:** is a success – 9 **invention:** plan, strategy, device – 10 **Shall to th'legitimate:** my plan shall come to fruition so that I can advance and replace the legitimate

RAAbits Englisch

Introducing Shakespeare (S II)

Act 1, Scene 2, vv. 104–116

Edmond: This is the excellent foppery of the world, that when we are sick in fortune, often the surfeits of our own behaviour, we make guilty of our disasters the sun, the moon, and stars; as if we were villains on necessity, fools by heavenly compulsion, knaves, thieves, and treachers by spherical predominance, drunkards, liars, and adulterers by an enforced obedience of planetary influence; and all what
5 we are evil in, by a divine thrusting on. An admirable evasion of whoremaster man, to lay his goatish disposition on the charge of a star! My father compounded with my mother under the Dragon's tail, and my nativity was under Ursa major, so that it follows, I am rough and lecherous. I should have been that I am had the maidenliest star in the firmament twinkled on my bastardising. [...]

Vocabulary Aids

1 **excellent:** (1) highest (2) superb – 1 **sick in fortune:** i.e. to have bad luck – 1 **surfeits:** overindulgences, excesses – 3 **on:** by – 3/4 **spherical predominance:** in astrology the belief that at the time of one's birth, if the influence of a heavenly body was especially strong – because of its ascendant position – this would accordingly have a great influence on that person's destiny or on their character. This concept is known as 'planetary influence'. – 4 **of:** to – 5 **divine thrusting:** supernatural force – 5/6 **lay ... charge of:** to attribute his lascivious or 'goaty' tendencies to ...; For Elizabethans goats symbolised excessive sexual desire – 6 **compounded:** made love to – 6 **Dragon's tail:** The constellation Draco; as astrological sign it is often regarded as evil – 7 **nativity:** birth – 7 **Ursa major:** The constellation Great Bear, or Big Dipper. Astrologically speaking Mars is predominant but Venus is also influential, too. Mars imparts attributes like being daring and impulsive and Venus produces people with lascivious tendencies – these attributes are known as temperaments.

Act 1, Scene 2, vv. 151–156

Edmond: A credulous father and a brother noble, / Whose nature is so far from doing harms / That he suspects none; on whose foolish honesty / My practices ride easy. I see the business. / Let me, if not by birth, have lands by wit. / All with me's meet that I can fashion fit.

Vocabulary Aids

2 **practices ride easy:** my plans develop easily – 3 **All ... fit:** Everything is fine with me that I can change to meet my own purposes

Tasks

Work together in a group. Write down keywords relating to the following questions:

1. What do we learn about the situation of the villain? What are the character's reasons or motives for planning mischief later in the play?

2. What are the villain's reflections on his own deeds – in the second extract?

3. Think of people who have behaved like villains, nowadays or in the past. Name some examples.

Homework

4. Analyse how the villain Edmond describes himself by identifying the stylistic devices.

Introducing Shakespeare (S II)

Hinweise (M 9 und M 10; 7. und 8. Stunde)

Die Bedeutung des *villain* für Shakespeares Stücke ist Gegenstand dieser Doppelstunde. Exemplarisch untersuchen die Schülerinnen und Schüler den Schurken Edmond aus „King Lear" und verorten den Charakter in der Renaissance.

In einer hinführenden Partnerarbeit bereiten sich die Lernenden zunächst auf den inhaltlichen Schwerpunkt durch eine *pre-reading activity* vor (**M 10**). Dazu setzen sie sich mit dem Begriff des Schurken, mit seinen Motiven und seiner Funktion auseinander. Hierdurch soll eine erste Sensibilisierung für die Thematik erreicht werden. Die Ergebnisse dieser Arbeitsphase werden in einem **Cluster** an der Tafel gesammelt, weil sie am Ende der Stunde noch einmal gebraucht werden (vgl. Erwartungshorizont M 10).

Die Visualisierung zum **Beziehungsgefüge bei King Lear** aus der Hausaufgabe (**M 9**) kann der Besprechung des villain Edmond vorangestellt werden. Ausführlicher muss die Konstellation aber nicht thematisiert werden, weil der *plot* bereits in der Hausaufgabe erarbeitet wurde. Es reicht an dieser Stelle, die zentralen Figuren sowie die Handlung in groben Zügen zu nennen.

Anschließend wird arbeitsteilig in **Gruppen** gearbeitet, um den Lernenden den Zugang zu den **Monologen** Edmonds zu erleichtern (**M 10**). Die Ergebnisse zu Edmonds Situation und seinen Motiven werden im Plenum zusammengetragen. Es sollte deutlich werden, dass Schurken typische Eigenschaften haben (vgl. *features of a villain*, Erwartungshorizont M 10). Sie fühlen sich benachteiligt und wagen es, gegen ihre Position aufzubegehren. Die Ergebnisse werden mit den Vorüberlegungen zu Beginn der Stunde verglichen.

Abschließend sollte auch mit der Gruppe reflektiert werden, warum die Schurken sich in den Stücken ausnahmslos ganz deutlich zu erkennen geben, und warum sie schon zu Beginn ihre Motive so klar benennen. Besonders interessant sind die Reflexionen von Edmond, weil dieser im Sinne der **Renaissance** sehr modern denkt und sich seiner **Eigenverantwortung im Bezug auf sein Handeln** völlig bewusst ist (vgl. *Act 1, Scene 2, vv. 104–116*). Wichtig erscheint der Hinweis, dass es in den Stücken weniger auf komplexe Charakterstudien – wie beispielsweise in einem Roman – als auf das Nachvollziehen der Handlung ankommt. Dafür ist das klare Verständnis des gesprochenen Wortes ganz entscheidend. An dieser Stelle kann auch bereits auf eine Unterscheidung zwischen **Komödie und Tragödie** verwiesen werden (z. B. im Bezug auf den Schurken, vgl. Erwartungshorizont M 10).

Tipp: Eine sinnvolle Erweiterungsoption stellt die Thematisierung des Schurken, Don John, in „Much Ado About Nothing" dar, weil die Lerngruppe mit dem Stück bereits vertraut ist. Hier bietet sich die Erarbeitung der dritten Szene, Akt 1, Vers 1–61 an. Reicht die Zeit nicht aus, sollte auf Don John sowie weitere klassische Beispiele verwiesen werden: z.B. Iago (*Othello*) und Richard III (*Richard III*), verdeutlicht am Beispiel der Klausur.

Als **Transfer** stellen sich die Lernenden am Ende die Frage nach der Aktualität der Thematik. Sie überlegen, wen sie im realen Leben – in unserer Zeit oder in der Vergangenheit – als Schurken bezeichnen würden (*Task* 3). Die **Hausaufgabe** der Stunde ist bewusst analytisch, weil sie bereits einen Baustein zur Vorbereitung der Klausur darstellt.

Introducing Shakespeare (S II)

Erwartungshorizont (M 10)

Tafelbild *pre-reading activity*, 1. und 2.

Features of villains (Pre-reading activity)	The villain Edmond in King Lear (Task 1)
– hatred	
– jealousy	– is jealous of his half-brother who is legitimate and entitled to have the inheritance and the title
– bad experience	
– dissatisfaction	– not happy with his situation which he finds unfair
– …	– illegitimate child (bastard)
– play tricks on people, tell lies, kill people, find people who help them	– plots against his half-brother and his father (with a false letter), against Goneril and Regan (promises his love to both of them) – wants to kill Lear and Cordelia – he is fully aware of the fact that it is his own free will that is the cause of what he is doing; he does not blame it on the stars (precondition / fate) (*Task 2*)

Some typical features of villains in Shakespeare plays:
- driven by e.g. hatred, jealousy, etc.
- tell lies; people believe them (manipulation)
- might use others for their evil actions
- make their intentions clear right from the start; have a clear awareness of what they are doing themselves
- make evil plots which cause harm to others → if no one dies / they are brought to justice = comedy
  → if other good characters (heroes) die / they might die, too = tragedy

Why does a villain play an important role in a play? *(pre-reading activity)*
villain and evil plots = reason for conflicts in a play; make the plot dramatic; danger/threat for the good characters which leads to a rise in tension (dramatic action) because the audience wants to find out who wins

3. **Think of people who behave like villains in our time or the past. Name examples.**
   - terrorists like Osama Bin Laden; dictators like Adolf Hitler or Saddam Hussein, etc..

4. **Analysis of how the villain Edmond describes himself (Homework)**
   - **apostrophe:** "Thou, Nature […]"; "Now gods, stand up for bastards!" → emotional appeal to mother nature and the gods; he mourns the injustice that he was born a bastard and does not want to accept his fate; he challenges the gods who he blames for his illegitimacy
   - **metaphor:** "plague of custom" → being a bastard is like a disease because it makes him an outcast in society – "I grow" → he does not accept his position in society and foresees his social advancement
   - **use of many questions / playing around with forms of the words 'bastard' and 'base':** "Lag of a brother? Why 'bastard'? Wherefore 'base'?" etc. → these questions express the feeling of injustice he has; he reproaches nature and society for treating him badly
   - **enumeration:** "we make guilty the sun, the moon, and the stars; as if we were villains on necessity, fools by heavenly compulsion, knaves, thieves and treachers by spherical predominance, drunkards, liars, and adulterers" → by giving examples he clearly illustrates his rational understanding that everyone is free to live the life she/he wants and fate cannot be blamed

M 11 An encounter with the witches from *Macbeth*

Discover more about the Elizabethan age by finding out which topics and underlying principles concerned not only Shakespeare but other writers as well. Get started by reading an excerpt from Macbeth.

Pre-reading activity

Work together with a partner.

Imagine you put on a production of Shakespeare's *Macbeth*. At the beginning of the play the Thane of Glamis (a thane is a nobleman), named Macbeth, meets three witches who make predictions about his future. What kind of a setting would you choose for this encounter? What do the witches look like (costumes, makeup, etc.)?

An encounter with the witches from Macbeth

After a victorious battle Macbeth, a Scottish nobleman, returns home. This is when he and Banquo meet three witches who make prophecies about both their futures.

W. Shakespeare, Macbeth, Act 1, Scene 3, vv. 1– 65, A heath

Thunder. Enter the three Witches

First Witch: Where hast thou been, sister?

Second Witch: Killing swine.

Third Witch: Sister, where thou?

5 First Witch: A sailor's wife had chestnuts in her lap / And munched, and munched, and munched. 'Give me', quoth I. / 'Aroint thee, witch', the rump-fed ronyon cries. / Her husband's to Aleppo gone, master o'th'Tiger: / But in a sieve I'll thither sail, / And like a rat without a tail, / I'll do, I'll do, and I'll do.

Second Witch: I'll give thee a wind.

10 First Witch: Thou'rt kind.

Third Witch: And I another.

First Witch: I myself have all the other, / And the very ports they blow, / All the quarters that they know / I'th'shipmans's card. / I'll drain him dry as hay: / Sleep shall neither night nor day / Hang upon his penthouse lid; / He shall live a man forbid. / Weary sennights nine times nine, / Shall he dwindle,
15 peak, and pine. / Though his bark cannot be lost, / Yet it shall be tempest-tossed. / Look what I have.

Second Witch: Show me, show me.

First Witch: Here I have a pilot's thumb, / Wrecked as homward he did come.

Drum within

Third Witch: A drum, a drum; / Macbeth doth come.

20 All: The weïrd sisters, hand in hand, / Posters of the sea and land, / Thus do go, about, about, / Thrice to thine, and thrice to mine, / And thrice again, to make up nine. / Peace, the charm's wound up.

Enter Macbeth *and* Banquo

Macbeth: So foul and fair a day I have not seen.

Banquo: How far is't called to Forres? What are these, / So withered and so wild in their attire, / That
25 look not like th'inhabitants o'th'earth, / And yet are on't? – Live you, or are you aught / That man may question? You seem to understand me, / By each at once her choppy finger laying / Upon her skinny lips; you should be women / And yet your beards forbid me to interpret / That you are so.

Macbeth: Speak if you can: what are you?

First Witch: All hail Macbeth, hail to thee, Thane of Glamis.

30 Second Witch: All hail Macbeth, hail to thee, Thane of Cawdor.

Third Witch: All hail Macbeth, that shalt be king hereafter.

Banquo: Good sir, why do you start and seem to fear / Things that do sound so fair? – I'th'name of truth / Are ye fantastical, or that indeed / Which outwardly ye show? My noble partner / You greet with present grace and great prediction / Of noble having and of royal hope / That he seems rapt withal. To 35 me you speak not. / If you can look into the seeds of time / And say which grain will grow and which will not, / Speak then to me, who neither beg nor fear / Your favours nor your hate.

First Witch: Hail.

Second Witch: Hail.

Third Witch: Hail.

40 First Witch: Lesser than Macbeth, and greater.

Second Witch: Not so happy, yet much happier.

Third Witch: Thou shalt get kings, though thou be none. / So all hail Macbeth and Banquo. […]

Vocabulary Aids

6 **Aroint thee:** get lost! – 6 **rump-fed ronyon:** spoilt slut: verwöhnte Schlampe – 12 **quarters:** directions – 13 **card:** compass – 14 **penthouse lid:** eyelid – 14 **forbid:** damned, ill-fated – 14 **sennights:** seven nights, a week – 17 **pilot:** sb. who navigates ships to harbour – 20 **weïrd sisters:** mythological goddesses of fate who prophesy the future in Anglo-Saxon mythology – 20 **Posters:** those who travel at great speed – 21 **charm:** spell – 25 **aught:** anything, nothing – 29 **Glamis:** pronounced 'Glahms', a village in Angus, Scotland – 30 **Cawdor:** The Thane of Cawdor is the title of a nobleman who is next in line to the throne. The witches tell Macbeth that he will become the next thane. Shortly after meeting the witches Macbeth finds out that the current Thane of Cawdor has been sentenced to death for committing treason. He then receives the title and the witches prediction comes true. – 33 **fantastical:** imaginary – 34 **noble having:** new titles of nobility, his future title of thane – 34 **rapt:** entranced, hypnotisiert – 42 **get:** be father of

Tasks

Work together in groups. Get a feeling for the characters. You do not have to understand each word.

1. Imagine how the witches speak in this scene. Practise reading the above extract. When you read aloud the first time, take it in turns. Each one of you reads one line. When you practise reading a second time, try out different things: some of you can speak the parts of one witch together; use stress, pauses, a high-pitched voice and a low-pitched voice when reading; try to act out (gestures, body language) while you read, etc.

2. Compare your description of the witches from the beginning of the lesson to the one we get from Banquo in this extract.

3. What does Macbeth learn from the witches about his own future? How will he react to this news? What do you think will happen when human beings get involved with dark powers – here: the witches?

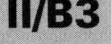

Introducing Shakespeare (S II)

| Reihe 7 | Verlauf | **Material** S 26 | LEK | Kontext | Mediothek |

II/B3

M 12 Disorder or what happens if you kill the king

Both ambition and the influence of his wife make Macbeth change from being a successful war hero to a tyrannical murderer. So first he kills King Duncan and his guards. Later in the play he will follow Duncan to the throne and be the new King of Scotland. But only the audience and no one on stage knows that Macbeth is the murderer. The King's two sons, Malcolm and Donalbain, are under suspicion because they have fled. In the following scene Ross, also a thane, and an old man talk about strange changes which they have both witnessed since the death of the King. Later, the Thane of Fife, Macduff, joins them.

Act 2, Scene 4, vv. 1–32, Outside Macbeth's castle

Enter Ross, with an Old man

Old Man: Threescore and ten I can remember well; / Within the volume of which time, I have seen / Hours dreadful and things strange, but this sore night / Hath trifled former knowings.

Ross: Ha, good father, / Thou seest the heavens, as troubled with man's act, / Threatens his bloody
5 stage. By th'clock 'tis day / And yet dark night strangles the travelling lamp. / Is't night's predominance, or the days's shame, / That darkness does the face of earth entomb / When living light should kiss it?

Old Man: 'Tis unnatural, / Even like the deed that's done. On Tuesday last, / A falcon tow'ring in her pride of place / Was by a mousing owl hawked at and killed.

Ross: And Duncan's horses, a thing most strange and certain, / Beauteous and swift, the minions of
10 their race, / Turned wild in nature, broke their stalls, flung out, / Contending 'gainst obedience as they would / Make war with mankind.

Old Man: 'Tis said, they eat each other.

Ross: They did so, to th'amazement of mine eyes / That looked upon't.

Enter Macduff

15 Here comes the good Macduff. / How goes the world, sir, now?

Macduff: Why, see you not?

Ross: Is't known who did this more than bloody deed?

Macduff: Those that Macbeth has slain.

Ross: Alas the day, / What good could they pretend?

20 Macduff: They were suborned. / Malcolm and Donalbain, the king's two sons, / Are stol'n away and fled, which puts upon them / Suspicion of the deed.

Ross: 'Gainst nature still. / Thriftless ambition that will ravin up / Thine own life's means. Then 'tis most like / The sovereignty will fall upon Macbeth.

Macduff: He is already named and gone to Scone / To be invested. [...]

2 **Threescore and ten:** a score is twenty, so the old man means seventy years – 3 **Hath trifled former knowings:** the events of this night make other unpleasant events in the past pale into insignificance/make them seem trivial – 4/5 **heavens/act/stage:** theatrical metaphors – 5 **travelling lamp:** metaphor for the sun – 6 **the day's shame:** Duncan's murder – 6 **entomb:** cover as if buried – 10 **stalls:** stables – 20 **suborned:** bribed (to murder Duncan) – 22 **Thriftless:** greedy – 22 **ravin up:** consume – 24 **named:** the thanes have already elected him king – 24 **Scone:** a place near Perth, where Scottish monarchs were crowned

Tasks: 1. On the basis of the above conversation find out what strange happenings and consequences the murder of King Duncan has led to. Write down keywords so that you can tell your classmates about what you have found out. 2. Imagine what the description above means with regard to the plot of the whole play.

RAAbits Englisch

M 13 The Elizabethan view of the world: The Great Chain of Being

If you want to understand what Shakespeare's plays are all about, you will have to read the following text. Just think what happens if a villain or other character challenges "The Chain of Being". Which motives – apart from ambition – might lead to such foolishness or vanity? And what are the underlying causes for characters being driven by exaggerations of any kind whatsoever? Find out everything about order and disorder.

The Great Chain of Being

Among the most important of the continuities with the Classical Period was the concept of the Great Chain of Being. Its major premise was that every existing thing in the universe had its "place" in a divinely planned hierarchical order, which was pictured as a chain vertically extended. ("Hierarchical" refers to an order based on a series of higher and lower, strictly ranked gradations.)

An object's "place" depended on the relative proportion of "spirit" and "matter" it contained – the less "spirit" and the more "matter," the lower down it stood. At the bottom, for example, stood various types of inanimate objects, such as metals, stones, and the four elements (earth, water, air, fire). Higher up were various members of the vegetative class, like trees and flowers. Then came animals; then humans; and then angels. At the very top was God.

Then within each of these large groups, there were other hierarchies. For example, among metals, gold was the noblest and stood highest; lead had less "spirit" and more matter and so stood lower. (Alchemy was based on the belief that lead could be changed to gold through an infusion of "spirit.") The various species of plants, animals, humans, and angels were similarly ranked from low to high within their respective segments.

Finally, it was believed that between the segments themselves, there was continuity (shellfish were lowest among animals and shaded into the vegetative class, for example, because without locomotion, they most resembled plants).

Besides universal orderliness, there was universal interdependence. This was implicit in the doctrine of "correspondences," which held that different segments of the chain reflected other segments.

For example, Renaissance thinkers viewed a human being as a microcosm (literally, a "little world") that reflected the structure of the world as a whole, the macrocosm; just as the world was composed of four "elements" (earth, water, air, fire), so too was the human body composed of four substances called "humours," with characteristics corresponding to the four elements. (Illness occurred when there was an imbalance or "disorder" among the humours, that is, when they did not exist in proper proportion to each other.)

"Correspondences" existed everywhere, on many levels. Thus the hierarchical organization of the mental faculties was also thought of as reflecting the hierarchical order within the family, the state, and the forces of nature. When things were properly ordered, reason ruled the emotions, just as a king ruled his subjects, the parent ruled the child, and the sun governed the planets.

But when disorder was present in one realm, it was correspondingly reflected in other realms. For example, in Shakespeare's *King Lear*, the simultaneous disorder in family relationships and in the state (child ruling parent, subject ruling king) is reflected in the disorder of Lear's mind (the loss of reason) as well as in the disorder of nature (the raging storm). Lear even equates his loss of reason to "a tempest in my mind."

40 Though Renaissance writers seemed to be quite on the side of "order," the theme of "disorder" is much in evidence, suggesting that the age may have been experiencing some growing discomfort with traditional hierarchies. According to the chain of being concept, all existing things have their precise place and function in the universe, and to depart from one's proper place was to betray one's nature.

45 Human beings, for example, were pictured as placed between the beasts and the angels. To act against human nature by not allowing reason to rule the emotions – was to descend to the level of the beasts. In the other direction, to attempt to go above one's proper place, as Eve did when she was tempted by Satan, was to court disaster. [...]

Political Implications of the Chain of Being

50 The fear of "disorder" was not merely philosophical – it had significant political ramifications. The proscription against trying to rise beyond one's place was of course useful to political rulers, for it helped to reinforce their authority. The implication was that civil rebellion caused the chain to be broken, and according to the doctrine of correspondences, this would have dire consequences in other realms. It was a sin against
55 God, at least wherever rulers claimed to rule by "Divine Right." (And in England, the king was also the head of the Anglican Church.)

In Shakespeare, it was suggested that the sin was of cosmic proportions: civil disorders were often accompanied by meteoric disturbances in the heavens. (Before Halley's theory about periodic orbits, comets, as well as meteors, were thought to be disorderly
60 heavenly bodies.) [...]

Source: http://academic.brooklyn.cuny.edu/english/melani/cs6/ren.html, abridged and slightly adapted

© English Department, Brooklyn College, City University of New York

Vocabulary Aids

1 **continuities:** a connection or line of development with no sharp breaks – 1 **Classical Period:** associated with classical culture in ancient Greece – 2 **premise:** a statement or an idea that forms the basis for a reasonable line of arguments – 3 **hierarchical:** hierarchy: a system, especially in a society or an organization, in which people are organized into different levels of importance from highest to lowest – 5 **ranked gradations:** position of so. on a scale – 6 **spirit:** Geist – 6 **matter:** Materie – 8 **inanimate:** not alive in the way that people, animals and plants are – 13 **lead:** Blei – 14 **Alchemy:** Alchemie – 19 **locomotion:** movement or the ability to move – 20 **interdependence:** depending on each other – 20 **implicit (in sth.):** forming part of sth. – 23 **microcosm:** a thing, a place or a group that has all the features and qualities of sth. much larger – 35 **realm:** kingdom – 44 **betray (sb./sth. to so.):** to give information about sb./sth. to an enemy or here not to be true to one's own nature – 48 **court:** to try to please sb. in order to get sth. you want, especially the support of a person, an organization, etc. – 50/51 **ramifications (pl.):** number of complicated and unexpected results that follow an action or a decision – 51 **proscription:** saying officially that sth. is banned – 54 **dire:** very serious

Tasks

Work together in small groups. One group works on task 1 and the other on task 2:

1. Find out in which respect the above text deals with disorder. Write down keywords so that you can tell your classmates about what you have found out.

2. Draw a visualization of the most important elements of the concept of the Great Chain of Being.

Introducing Shakespeare (S II)

| Reihe 7 | Verlauf | Material S 29 | LEK | Kontext | Mediothek |

II/B3

Hinweise (M 11–M 13; 9. und 10. Stunde)

Anhand der Tragödie „Macbeth" wird in dieser Doppelstunde das Weltbild der Elisabethanischen Zeit mit der wichtigen philosophischen Grundlage, der „Great Chain of Being", illustriert.

Um ein Gefühl für die dunkle und schaurige Atmosphäre im Drama „Macbeth" zu bekommen und einen Kontrast zu der analytischen Vorgehensweise der letzten Stunde zu erreichen, setzen sich die Lernenden zunächst kreativ mit dem **Auftritt der Hexen** auseinander. Sie stellen in einer Pre-reading activity Überlegungen zum Setting für diese Begegnung und zu dem Aussehen der drei Hexen an (**M 11**).

Anschließend steht die aktive Spracharbeit im Sinne des **active approach** im Vordergrund. Dies bedeutet: performance geht vor understanding. Dazu experimentieren die Schülerinnen und Schüler in Gruppenarbeit mit verschiedenen Formen des **betonten Lesens (Task 1)**. Nach mehreren Präsentationen im Plenum wird im Unterrichtsgespräch an die Vorüberlegungen zu den Hexen zu Beginn der Stunde angeknüpft und Banquos Beschreibung mit denen der Schülerinnen und Schüler verglichen (Task 2).

Nun erfolgt eine Annäherung an das zentrale Thema der Doppelstunde: das zeitweise Außerkrafttreten der elisabethanischen Weltordnung. In Aufgabe 3 stellen die Lernenden mithilfe ihres Vorwissens Vermutungen dazu an, welche Folgen es haben könnte, wenn sich eine Figur auf die Weissagungen dunkler Mächte einlässt. Ihre **Hypothesen** überprüfen die Schülerinnen und Schüler in der nun folgenden arbeitsteiligen Gruppenarbeit.

Hierfür erarbeiten sie mit der **Think-Pair-Share-Methode** zwei unterschiedliche **Texte** (**M 12 und M 13**). Der **Sachtext (M 13)** erläutert die philosophische Grundlage, das Konzept der **„Great Chain of Being"**, während **M 12** eine **exemplarische Szene aus dem Drama** ist, welche die literarische Umsetzung dieses Konzeptes anschaulich illustriert. Jeweils die Hälfte der Klasse erhält einen der beiden Texte. Beide Gruppen beschäftigen sich mit dem Aspekt „disorder" und fassen die zentralen Aussagen in Stichwörtern zusammen (Think). Die Gruppen, die sich mit dem Sachtext beschäftigen, bearbeiten arbeitsteilig Task 1 oder 2, weil die Aufgaben sonst zu umfangreich sind.

Nach dem Austausch in der eigenen Gruppe werden die Informationen aus beiden Texten zusammengebracht, indem sich jeder einen Partner aus der Gruppe mit dem anderen Text aussucht (Pair). Die Paare fassen ihr Wissen zusammen. In der abschließenden Runde im Plenum übertragen die Lernenden die Thematik der disorder beziehungsweise der Chain of Being auf das gesamte Drama: What function does the description of disorder in nature have in the context of the tragedy Macbeth? (Share) Dieser **Transfer** sollte von einer Arbeitsgruppe bereits vorbereitet worden sein (Text M 12, Task 2).

Zuletzt **spekulieren** die Schülerinnen und Schüler über die **weitere Handlung** beziehungsweise das Ende der Tragödie. Die Lehrkraft fasst die wichtigsten Ereignisse anhand folgender Stichwörter zusammen:

> **Keywords for the following plot:**
>
> – in order to secure his position on the throne Macbeth hires murderers to get Banquo and his son killed (It was predicted by the witches that Banquo's sons would be future kings and this, Macbeth fears, could endanger his own ambitions); – Banquo's son manages to escape but Banquo is killed and later at a banquet appears before Macbeth as a ghost; – Macbeth again seeks advice from the three witches; – Macbeth has Macduff's family murdered since Macduff has fallen into disgrace and fled to England; – Macduff swears revenge; a war between England and Scotland breaks out; – Lady Macbeth kills herself (sleepwalking scene); – the final showdown is the fight between Macbeth and Macduff in which Macbeth is finally killed by Macduff; in the end it turns out that Macbeth, blind with ambition, has misunderstood all the prophecies of the witches and thus sealed his own fate; – order is finally restored when Duncan's oldest son, Malcolm, becomes the new King of Scotland

Introducing Shakespeare (S II)

| Reihe 7 | Verlauf | Material S 30 | LEK | Kontext | Mediothek |

Erwartungshorizont (M 11)

Pre-reading und 1. Individual answers.

2. Outer appearance of the witches (according to Banquo):
   – withered and wild; – look as if they are no creatures of the earth; – choppy fingers; – skinny lips; – have got beards

3. The witches greet him as Thane of Glamis, which means that he will follow the Thane of Glamis and be the future king of Scotland. There can be two possible reactions to this: astonishment and pride but also greed and the want for the fulfilment of the prophecies.

   Getting involved with dark forces normally does not lead to anything good (cf. In Goethe's Faust his getting involved with the devil causes harm, even death)

Erwartungshorizont (M 12)

Tafelbild 1. und 2.

> **Disorder according to the extract from *Macbeth***
>
> There is total chaos in nature / everything is unnatural like the killing of the king was ("the deed that's done"):
>
> – it is dark during the day (personification: "darkness does the face of earth entomb"),
>
> – an owl kills a falcon,
>
> – Duncan's tame horses have turned wild ("war with mankind"); they even eat each other

Erwartungshorizont (M 13)

1. Disorder according to the concept of the Great Chain of Being

Every existing thing has got its rightful place in a divine hierarchical order. The position of human beings is due to their ability to use their reason to rule over their emotions. Disorder is created by acting against this human nature or by leaving your natural position in the hierarchical system. With regard to the tragedy of Macbeth this means that by killing the king Macbeth has destroyed the natural order and put nature and society into a state of chaos. He was led by ambition and not reason. Only at the end of the play the rightful order is re-established when the murderer Macbeth himself is killed and a rightful king is crowned again.

2. Visualization

The picture may be copied on a transparency.

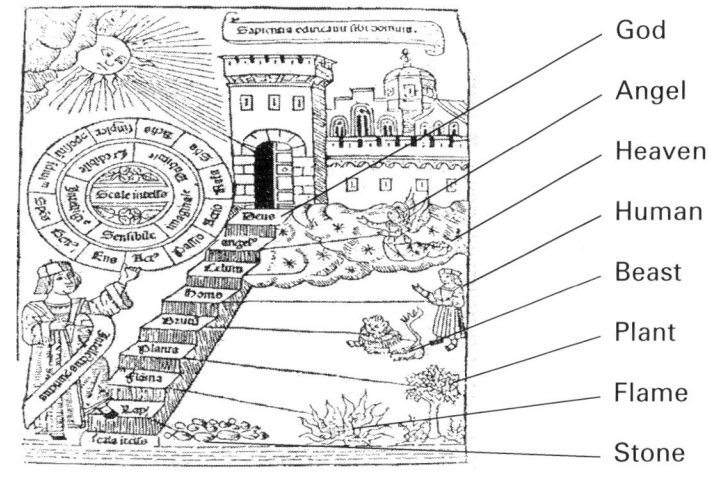

Labels: God, Angel, Heaven, Human, Beast, Plant, Flame, Stone

Source: wikipedia

M 14 Hands on drama: What is a tragedy?

Today Shakespeare's plays are still very popular worldwide. But why, you may ask, is drama or literature in general of any use today and of which use was it in Elizabethan times? Start by thinking why you watch the news.

Pre-reading-activity

Explain what a tragedy is. Write a short definition for a dictionary.

Some uses of the word "tragedy"

Text 1

The Norwegian Prime Minister Jens Stoltenberg paid tribute to those that died in the recent tragedy in Oslo, which included two people he knew personally, with a moving speech. [...]

'Each and every one of those who've left us is a tragedy – together, it's a national tragedy.' He wept as he recalled two of the dead he knew personally, including one named Monica who had worked at the island youth camp for 20 years.

'She has died, shot and killed while she tried to create safety and happiness for young people,' he said. [...]

Annotations

The 32-year-old Norwegian Anders Behring Breivik killed 76 people when he planted a bomb in the country's capital, Oslo, and later carried out the youth camp massacre on Utoeya island on Friday, 22nd July 2011.

Source: http://www.metro.co.uk/news/870288-norwegian-pm-pays-tribute-to-oslo-dead-in-national-tragedy

Text 2

The 2010 Love Parade in the German city of Duisburg [...] ended in tragedy after 19 people died and hundreds were injured in a stampede. Panic broke out in a tunnel after the festival site was closed due to overcrowding. [...]

Annotations

Hundreds of people were seriously injured in the panic and the final death toll was 21.

"Nineteen Dead after Panic Breaks Out at Love Parade". Source: SPIEGEL ONLINE – 24. Juli 2010. URL: http://www.spiegel.de/international/germany/0,1518,708347,00.html

Text 3

"A tragedy, then, is the imitation of an action that is serious and also, as having magnitude, complete in itself; in language with pleasurable accessories, each kind brought in separately in the parts of the work; in a dramatic, not in a narrative form; with incidents arousing pity and fear, wherewith to accomplish its catharsis of such emotions."

Clifford Leech: Tragedy. London and New York: Routledge 1969. P.1.

Text 4

1. a dramatic composition, often in verse, dealing with a serious or sombre theme, typically that of a great person destined through a flaw of character or conflict with some overpowering force, as fate or society, to downfall or destruction.
2. the branch of the drama that is concerned with this form of composition.
3. the art and theory of writing and producing tragedies. [...]

Related words for: **tragedy**

calamity, cataclysm, catastrophe, disaster

Source: http://dictionary.reference.com/browse/tragedy

Introducing Shakespeare (S II)

Reihe 7 | Verlauf | Material S 32 | LEK | Kontext | Mediothek

Headlines / sources

A) Dictionary entry (Internet)

trag·e·dy /ˈtrædɪdi/ –**noun, plural** -dies.

Source: http://dictionary.reference.com/browse/tragedy

B) Definition from a book on tragedy

The Greek philosopher Aristotle wrote a book on the different types of literature: Aristotle, *The Poetics*, translated by Ingram Bywater, Chapter VI Oxford, 1909

Clifford Leech: Tragedy. London and New York: Routledge 1969. P.1.

C) Newspaper article on the Internet

METRO NEWS REPORTER – 25th July, 2011

Norwegian PM pays tribute to Oslo dead in 'national tragedy'

Source: http://www.metro.co.uk/news/870288-norwegian-pm-pays-tribute-to-oslo-dead-in-national-tragedy

D) Magazine article on the Internet

SPIEGEL ONLINE

07/24/2010

Tragedy at German Techno Festival

Nineteen Dead after Panic Breaks Out at Love Parade

"Nineteen Dead after Panic Breaks Out at Love Parade". Source: SPIEGEL ONLINE – 24. Juli 2010. URL: http://www.spiegel.de/international/germany/0,1518,708347,00.html

Tasks

Work together with a partner on tasks 1 and 2.

1. The above texts (1–4) lack their headlines and their information about the sources they were taken from. Match the four texts with the right corresponding information (letters A–D)

2. What do the texts have in common and what is different?

3. What Lear experiences in the play is regarded to be tragedy. Explain why on the basis of what we discussed in previous lessons. Also make use of Aristotle's definition of tragedy.

Introducing Shakespeare (S II)

| Reihe 7 | Verlauf | Material S 33 | LEK | Kontext | Mediothek |

II/B3

Hinweise (M 14; 11. Stunde)

In dieser Stunde unternimmt die Gruppe einen kurzen Ausflug in den Bereich Dramentheorie. Eine Hinführung ist bereits in der 7./8. Stunde durch die grobe Unterscheidung zwischen Komödie und Tragödie erfolgt.

Zunächst definieren die Schülerinnen und Schüler kurz den **Begriff „tragedy"** in einer *pre-reading activity*, beispielsweise in Form eines kurzen Lexikoneintrags von ein bis zwei Sätzen. Darauf tauschen sie ihre Definitionen aus.

Die folgende Arbeitsphase vermittelt ein Bewusstsein dafür, dass zwei verschiedene Definitionen des Begriffes „tragisch/Tragödie" zu unterscheiden sind: eine **umgangssprachliche** und eine **literaturwissenschaftliche**. Das Material, das hierzu gewählt wurde, umfasst Pressetexte aus dem Internet, einen Lexikoneintrag sowie die klassische Definition aus der Poetik von Aristoteles.

Durch den einfachen Arbeitsauftrag – die **Zuordnung von Überschriften zu den jeweiligen Quellen** – setzen sich die Lernenden in Partnerarbeit mit unterschiedlichen Verwendungsweisen des Begriffes auseinander (*Task 1*). Im zweiten Arbeitsschritt **reflektieren** sie diesen Bedeutungswandel (*Task 2*).

In der Auswertung wird auf die einzelnen Beispiele genauer eingegangen, beispielsweise durch die Erläuterung der Aspekte *pity / fear* und **catharsis** bei **Aristoteles**. Abschließend erfolgt ein Rückbezug zu den zu Beginn der Stunde genannten Vorüberlegungen. Dabei sollte deutlich werden, dass ein „Fehler" gemäß des literarischen Verständnisses zu einem tragischen Ende führt und meist keine Chance besteht, dieses abzuwenden.

In der **Hausaufgabe** (*Task 3*) leisten die Lernenden einen Transfer durch praktische Anwendung, denn sie vertiefen das erworbene Wissen durch eine Übertragung auf das Beispiel Lear in *„King Lear"*.

Erwartungshorizont (M 14)

1. Individual answers.

2. 1 – C; 2 – D; 3 – B; 4 – A

3. **The tragedy of King Lear**

What Lear goes through in the play is a tragedy. He is a good character and only has the best intentions for all of his daughters. His flaw, however, is that he is vain or perhaps also naive because he wants them all to express how much they love him. Most importantly, however, is he blind because he does not see that two of his daughters have deceived him and that only Cordelia is honest with him. He also does not want to take any advice from Kent who also is honest and clearly tells him that he is doing the wrong thing. That means that he has chances to decide differently and thus avert his fate but he does not take them. That makes the situation tragic because a bad outcome could have been prevented. In the end he dies because he cannot bear what his mean daughters have done to him but most importantly because with Cordelia he has lost the daughter who really loved him.

> Information added by the teacher:
>
> Another important tragic element is that most of the time the audience know more than the characters on stage, e.g. details about the evil plots of Edmond. It is this different level of information and the obvious mistakes Lear makes that help to create tension and lets the audience feel and suffer (Aristotle: **pity** and **fear**) with a character on stage. Since the viewers do not have to make this experience themselves and just watch they are purged from the emotions of pity and fear (**catharsis**).

Introducing Shakespeare (S II)

| Reihe 7 | Verlauf | Material S 34 | LEK | Kontext | Mediothek |

M 15 'All the world's a stage': The Elizabethan Theatre

Of course Shakespeare's plays weren't meant to be read but to be live acts that were spoken much more quickly than what we are used to when watching modern adaptations. Find out more about that exciting atmosphere.

Experiencing the Shakespeare stage today

The Globe Theatre which you can see in London today is an exact copy of the theatre Shakespeare himself had invested money in and where his theatre company performed. He wrote many of his plays for this unique stage.

Ché Walker is an actor who has got much experience acting on the Globe's stage. In the following text he talks about what makes it special.

Photo: Marcus Michels

The Globe

'The first night was the strangest experience I have ever had on stage. The audience were so unruly – they moved around, they chat, they talk about you, they go out and get a drink, they come back. They hissed Iago at certain points and went woooo when Othello and Desdemona kissed. It was so much fun! I don't think I have ever had as much fun on stage. It was brilliant! It was very exciting because you could see
5 them.

I am used to modern theatres where they shine a light on you and the audience are in the dark. You can kind of perceive shapes and you sort of notice glinting glasses sometimes, but at the Globe they are just there! There is nothing between you. It is so democratic. The effect it had on me was that it was so easy to be distracted, that I had to really lock on to the other actors twice as hard – focus on what they are saying
10 and really make sure I am in the moment. It was very adrenalizing. It was incredibly warm and just really exciting. I learnt a lot about Shakespeare.

When I teach Shakespeare, the kids' previous experience has been negative, that they aren't clever enough to understand it. But here it is clear that the audience understand everything that happens on that stage and the fact that they are so visceral and vocal in their responses to the play proves it! This experience
15 has been very inspiring.'

Paul Shuter, Discovering Shakespeare's Globe. London: *Shakespeare's Globe*, 2009, p. 49. © Shakespeare's Globe Trust, 2009.

1 **unruly:** difficult to control or manage – 2 **hiss:** to make a sound like a long 's' expressing displeasure – 3 **Iago:** villain in Shakespeare's tragedy "Othello" – 3 **Othello and Desdemona:** characters from "Othello"; Othello is tricked by Iago into mistrusting his wife Desdemona and therefore finally kills her – 7 **to perceive:** to notice – 7 **glinting:** to glint: produce a small flash of light – 10 **adrenalizing:** feeling excitement in your body – 14 **visceral:** emotional – 14 **vocal:** telling people your opinions or protesting about sth. loudly

Tasks

Work together with a partner.

1. What makes performing on the stage of the Globe so special for Ché Walker? Write down some keywords.
2. What do you think a stage has to look like to have these effects? Think about the special shape of a stage that allows all the audience to watch the actors performing. Draw a sketch of the theatre.

RAAbits Englisch

Introducing Shakespeare (S II)

| Reihe 7 | Verlauf | Material S 35 | LEK | Kontext | Mediothek |

II/B3

3. On the basis of what you have found out about the stage, imagine you were the director of a theatre production in the Globe today. Think of the plays we studied in our lessons. What would be important for putting a particular scene of a certain play on a stage today?

You can also invent a new scene that matches what you already know about the plot of the play. Think of how you can present your ideas to your classmates (sketch of the stage, freeze frame of one part of the scene, etc.) Consider the following aspects:

- cast: who would be a good actor for which role (people you know; they do not necessarily have to be professional actors)?
- stage: how would you make use of this special stage?
- costumes: what would people wear in order to show who they are?
- props /effects: what would be helpful to illustrate the action? In Shakespeare's time they did not use many props on stage.
- ...

4. Find out more about the Elizabethan theatre. Use the Internet for your research.

Introducing Shakespeare (S II)

| Reihe 7 | Verlauf | Material S 36 | LEK | Kontext | Mediothek |

M 16 Cluster: Is Shakespeare still relevant today?

This task is about rounding off the course work: After finding out more about Shakespeare in the past lessons, think again about the question we started with: Is Shakespeare still relevant today?

Task

Reconsider what you have learnt in this course and name some examples, topics and aspects that show that Shakespeare is still relevant today.

II/B3

Shakespeare today?

Photo: Marcus Michels

Hinweise (M 15; 12. und 13. Stunde)

Um einen Eindruck davon zu vermitteln, was die **Eigenart der Bühne und des Theaters** der **Shakespearezeit** ausmacht, wurde ein prägnanter und leicht zugänglicher Text ausgewählt. Es handelt sich um einen Erfahrungsbericht von einem Schauspieler unserer Zeit, der aber gleichzeitig einen authentischen Eindruck der Situation der Shakespearezeit vermittelt, da er im besonderen Bau des **Globe Theatre** auftritt. Die Lernenden erschließen sich die Informationen bei einer kreativen Umsetzung (*Task* 2).

Um dem Themenaspekt des Theaters von damals gerecht zu werden, sind natürlich weitere Hintergrundinformationen notwendig, die hier nicht alle angeführt werden können. Dafür bietet der online Text der *Cambridge University Press* einen prägnanten Überblick (*Task* 4). Die Lektüre stellt wahlweise eine vertiefende Hausaufgabe dar oder aber die Lernenden erschließen sich die Zusatzinformationen in einer **arbeitsteiligen Gruppenarbeit**.

Ein wichtiges Augenmerk der Stunde sollte aber auch auf die **kreative Aufgabe** (*Task* 3) gerichtet werden, weil hier die Möglichkeit besteht, das erworbene Wissen im Sinne des *active approach* spielerisch auszuprobieren und noch einmal zu reflektieren. Den Abschluss bilden **Präsentationen der Arbeitsgruppen**, die ganz unterschiedlicher Art sein können: *freeze frame; sketch of the stage, necessary props* and position of the actors; spoken presentation, etc.

Hinweise (M 16; 14. Stunde)

Zum Schluss der Reihe gibt es eine Anknüpfung an die anfangs gestellte Frage zur Aktualität Shakespeares, die die Schülerinnen und Schüler jetzt mit Blick auf das erworbene Wissen fundierter beantworten können. Hierdurch werden gleichzeitig noch einmal die wichtigsten **Themen und Motive** vor der Klausur wiederholt und die Reihe abgerundet (*Cluster*).

Erwartungshorizont (M 16)

Cluster: Is Shakespeare still of interest today?

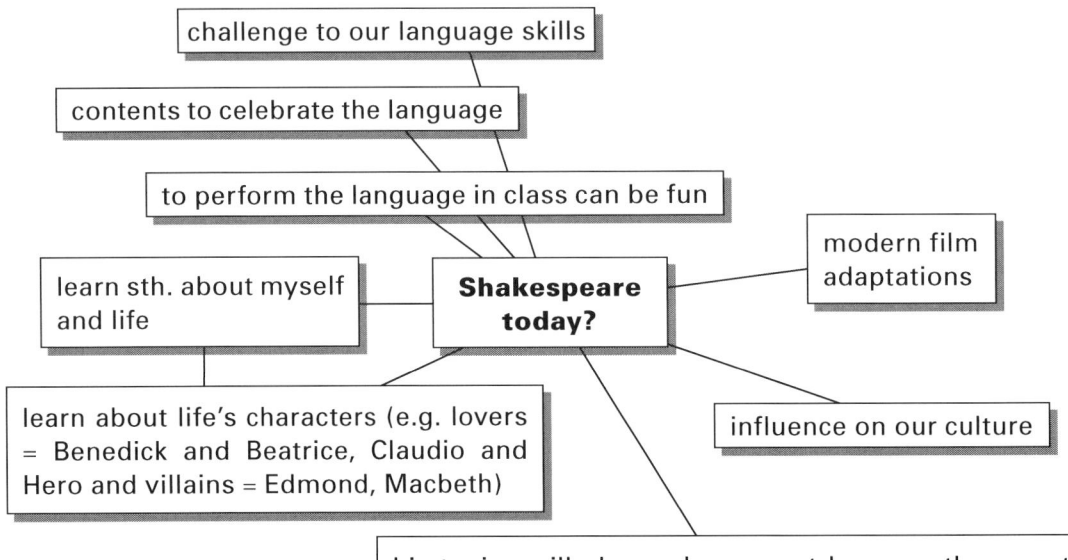

- challenge to our language skills
- contents to celebrate the language
- to perform the language in class can be fun
- learn sth. about myself and life
- modern film adaptations
- **Shakespeare today?**
- learn about life's characters (e.g. lovers = Benedick and Beatrice, Claudio and Hero and villains = Edmond, Macbeth)
- influence on our culture
- his topics will always be current because they are to do with human nature, emotions and ethical problems: e.g. love, revenge, hatred, joy, sorrow, etc.

Introducing Shakespeare (S II)

Examination

William Shakespeare, Richard III (1592–93)

The following text is an extract from the beginning of Shakespeare's historical play Richard III. Together with the original there is a modern version which is easier to understand.

The play centres around Richard, the Duke of Gloucester, who without any scruples ensures that people who hinder his plans are killed. He becomes King Richard III in 1483. His reign lasts for just two years. In the end he is killed.

At the beginning of the play Richard has strong ambitions to get on to the throne. To achieve this, he has deceived his brother, Edward IV, into arresting their brother, George, the Duke of Clarence. Richard reflects on the situation of his family and himself:

Original Text	Modern Text
Enter **RICHARD**, Duke of Gloucester, solus	**RICHARD**, Duke of Gloucester, enters alone.
RICHARD Now is the winter of our discontent Made glorious summer by this son of York, And all the clouds that loured upon our house In the deep bosom of the ocean buried. 5 Now are our brows bound with victorious wreaths, Our bruisèd arms hung up for monuments, Our stern alarums changed to merry meetings, Our dreadful marches to delightful measures. 10 Grim-visaged war hath smoothed his wrinkled front; And now, instead of mounting barbèd steeds To fright the souls of fearful adversaries, He capers nimbly in a lady's chamber 15 To the lascivious pleasing of a lute. But I, that am not shaped for sportive tricks, Nor made to court an amorous looking glass; I, that am rudely stamped and want love's majesty 20 To strut before a wanton ambling nymph; I, that am curtailed of this fair proportion, Cheated of feature by dissembling nature, Deformed, unfinished, sent before my time Into this breathing world, scarce half made up, 25 And that so lamely and unfashionable That dogs bark at me as I halt by them – Why, I, in this weak piping time of peace, Have no delight to pass away the time, Unless to see my shadow in the sun 30 And descant on mine own deformity.	**RICHARD** Now all of my family's troubles have come to a glorious end, thanks to my brother, King Edward IV. All the clouds that threatened the York family have vanished and turned to sunshine. Now we wear the wreaths of victory on our heads. We've taken off our armor [AE] and weapons and hung them up as decorations. Instead of hearing trumpets call us to battle, we dance at parties. We get to wear easy smiles on our faces rather than the grim expressions of war. Instead of charging toward our enemies on armored [AE] horses, we dance for our ladies in their chambers, accompanied by sexy songs on the lute. But I'm not made to be a seducer, or to make faces at myself in the mirror. I was badly made and don't have the looks to strut my stuff in front of pretty sluts. I've been cheated of a nice body and face, or even normal proportions. I am deformed, spit out from my mother's womb prematurely and so badly formed that dogs bark at me as I limp by them. I'm left with nothing to do in this weak, idle peacetime, unless I want to look at my lumpy shadow in the sun and sing about that.

And therefore, since I cannot prove a lover To entertain these fair well-spoken days, I am determinèd to prove a villain And hate the idle pleasures of these days. 35 Plots have I laid, inductions dangerous, By drunken prophecies, libels and dreams, To set my brother Clarence and the king In deadly hate, the one against the other; And if King Edward be as true and just 40 As I am subtle, false, and treacherous, This day should Clarence closely be mewed up About a prophecy which says that "G" Of Edward's heirs the murderer shall be. Dive, thoughts, down to my soul. Here Clarence 45 comes!	Since I can't amuse myself by being a lover, I've decided to become a villain. I've set dangerous plans in motion, using lies, drunken prophecies, and stories about dreams to set my brother 35 Clarence and the king against each other. If King Edward is as honest and fair-minded as I am deceitful and cruel, then Clarence is going to be locked away in prison today because 40 of a prophecy that "G" will murder Edward's children. Oh, time to hide what I'm thinking—here comes Clarence.

http://nfs.sparknotes.com/richardiii/page_2.html. © 2011 SparkNotes LLC, All Rights Reserved.

Vocabulary Aids

2 **sun:** (1) the badge of the Yorkists, emblem; (2) **son:** King Edward is the son of the Duke of York – 3 **loured:** (hanging) dark and menacing – 7 **monuments:** reminders, trophies – 8 **alarums:** 'Alar(u)m' can mean either (1) call to arms or (2) sudden attack – 9 **measures:** elegant dances at court – 10/11 **wrinkled front:** a grim, frowning face – 12 **barbèd:** bearing armour on flanks and breast – 14 **He:** the warrior, or war → personified; perhaps alluding to King Edward – 15 **lascivious pleasing:** pleasant music awakening sexual desires – 18 **rudely stamped:** not having a fine appearance, coarse or ugly – 20 **ambling:** walking in a way to impress sb. – 20 **nymph:** a beautiful young woman – 21 **curtailed:** reduce or deprive sb. of sth.; being made a 'curtal': an animal that has lost its tale – 22 **feature:** denoting the form or proportions of a body or a physical feature, here: a body of normal shape – 22 **dissembling:** concealing; his deformity conceals what lies beneath: his real qualities – 24 **breathing:** lively, living, energetic – 24 **made up:** completed – 25 **lamely:** flawed – 26 **to halt:** to walk with a limp – 27 **piping:** (1) the music of pastoral pipe instruments; (2) piping sound of the high-pitched voices of women and children – 30 **descant:** remark – 32 **entertain:** find sth. to do – 32 **well-spoken:** expressive, praised – 33 **am determined:** have chosen – 34 **idle:** without purpose or effect, spend time doing nothing; light-hearted – 35 **inductions:** preparations – 41 **mewed:** imprisoned – 42 **G:** the Duke of Clarence's name, George, begins with a 'G'

Tasks

1. Outline what we learn about the situation after the war as well as Richard's own mood at the beginning of the play. (Comprehension)

2. Analyse the language Richard III uses in his soliloquy. Pay attention to the imagery used to describe the situation at the beginning and his own description of himself. (Analysis)

3. You have got a choice here:

    A) Compare the character of Richard and the way he describes himself to the description of a villain you have come across in class (Edmond in *King Lear* or Macbeth in *Macbeth)*. What is similar and what is different? (Evaluation)

    or

    B) Imagine Richard III and Edmond from Shakespeare's *King Lear* meet to exchange their evil thoughts. Both of them let go of their frustration and talk openly about the motivation for their deeds. The meeting is set in the present. Write their conversation. (Re-creation of text)

Erwartungshorizont (Examination)

1. Richard celebrates a victory his brother, King Edward IV, has achieved. This means a total change concerning their lives. All their family's troubles have ended and have been replaced by merriment. Their weapons and armour are no longer used and instead of the trumpet announcing war it now invites the characters to dance and have a party. The serious looks on their faces because of the war have been replaced by smiles.

2. Richard's powerful, articulate and very strong language is very poetic and full of metaphors. He uses images of nature and the seasons to illustrate his family's situation and everyone's mood as a consequence of his brother's victory. Using many rhetorical devices he describes himself as a villain.

Language that illustrates the situation after the war:

– **metaphors and antithesis:** "the winter of our discontent (is) / Made glorious summer" → the time of winter which is a time when nature is not alive has been replaced by summer which is a time of energy and life; "winter" and "summer" and "discontent" and "glorious" are opposing terms – **personification:** "clouds that loured upon our house / In the deep bosom of the ocean buried." → the clouds stand for the threatening situation of the war which put the family into danger; the danger is now resting in the deep sea; the bosom guards it there and makes it stay there; "Grim-visaged war hath smoothed his wrinkled front" → war has got human features: before it had an ugly and menacing face which now has lost its wrinkles of menace and worries

– **anaphora, parallelism, enumeration:** "Now ... Now"; "Our ... Our ... Our": → intensification – **antithesis:** "bruisèd arms hung up for monuments"; "stern alarums changed to merry meetings"; "dreadful marchest to delightful measures" → everything negative and associated with war and grief has been changed into something positive and cheerful – **alliteration:** "merry meetings" → sounds positive and cheerful – **pars pro toto:** "the souls of fearful adversaries" → the soul stands for the whole soldier

Language with which he describes himself as being a villain:

– **metaphor:** "sportive tricks" → amorous adventures; "court an amorous looking glass" → he is not handsome enough to fall in love with his own reflection in the mirror – **words and phrases with negative connotations, enumeration:** "curtailed"; "Cheated"; "Deformed"; "unfinished"; "sent before my time"; "scarce half made up"; "lamely"; "unfashionable"; "no delight"; "deformity" → all of this expresses his disdain for his own appearance – **antithesis:** "I cannot prove a lover [...] / I am determined to prove a villain" → he is an outcast of his merry surrounding; the displeasing outer appearance goes together with a nasty character; "true and just [...] subtle, false and treacherous" → opposing character traits

– **enumeration:** "Plots have I laid, inductions dangerous, / By drunken prophecies, libels and dreams"; "subtle, false and treacherous" → his evil plans appear menacing

– **personification:** "deadly hate" = his hate causes death for everyone interfering with his ambitious plan to become king; "Dive, thoughts, down to my soul" → wants to hide his evil thoughts from others; they should fill his soul and thus be the motivation for all his actions

3. A) **Richard and Edmond** (*King Lear*): – **similarities:** both have got the impression that nature was unfair to them: Edmond was born a bastard and Richard a cripple; both plot against a brother; both trick someone else into getting a wrong impression of someone who is innocent (George, Duke of Clarence in *Richard III* and Edgar in *King Lear*); both want to become a king (similarity to Macbeth); both do not hesitate to have others killed to achieve their goals (similarity to Macbeth); both make their plans clear right from the start – **differences:** Richard's outer appearance also makes him look evil; this is not the case with Edmond

Richard and Macbeth (*Macbeth*): – **similarities:** both have got the ambition to become a king; both kill people in order to achieve their aims – **differences:** Macbeth is a war hero to start with and then changes; Richard seems to be mean right from the start

B) Compare to *Richard and Edmond*, but dialogue

Mediothek

Shakespeare allgemein

Crystal, Ben: *Shakespeare on Toast.* London: Icon Books 2008.

Auch für den Experten noch ein *must read*, weil hier der gelernte Sprachwissenschaftler und Schauspieler unverstellte Einblicke in die Sprachkunst des Genies gibt. Schlankes Taschenbuch, das sich zugleich fesselnd und unterhaltend liest und dabei sehr aufschlussreich ist.

Dunton-Downer, Leslie und Riding, Alan: *Essential Shakespeare Handbook.* London u.a.: Dorling Kindersley 2004.

Generelle Einführung zu Autor und Werk, die einen schnellen Überblick ermöglicht; mit vielen Illustrationen sehr ansprechend und unterhaltend gemacht.

Schabert, Ina (Hrsg.): Shakespeare-Handbuch, Die Zeit, Der Mensch, Das Werk, Die Nachwelt. Stuttgart: Kröner 2009.

Nach wie vor die „Bibel" zu Shakespeare, weil sehr kenntnis- und umfangreich angelegt. Übersichtlich durch klare Strukturierung und Einzelkapitel.

Shakespeare Didaktik

Der Fremdsprachliche Unterricht. *Sammelband Unterricht Englisch. Shakespeare.* Seelze: Friedrich Verlag 2007.

Vereint die wichtigsten, praxiserprobten Didaktik-Konzepte der letzten Jahre; diese werden gewohnt anschaulich dokumentiert.

Gibson, Rex: *Teaching Shakespeare.* Cambridge: CUP 1998.

Mittlerweiler bereits der Klassiker, der den überzeugenden *active approach* konsequent vertritt und Ideen vorstellt, die auf die verschiedensten Texte übertragbar sind.

Stredder, James: *The North Face of Shakespeare, activities for teaching the plays.* Cambridge: CUP 2009.

Führt die Linie des *active approach* konsequent weiter.

Internet

Bei YouTube lassen sich eine Vielzahl von Videos zur Person und Werk (z. B. Gedicht-Lesungen) nutzen. Eine wahre Fülle von Einträgen ist komfortabel und schnell über eine Suchmaschine, beispielsweise über Google auffindbar, deshalb sollen nur die wichtigsten Entdeckungen genannt werden:

http://nfs.sparknotes.com/

Die Sparknotes liefern eine Gegenüberstellung der Texte (Original vs. moderne Fassung) und stellen eine enorme Verständnishilfe dar.

http://absoluteshakespeare.com/glossary/a.htm

Diese Seite bietet sprachliche Unterstützung. Sie enthält ein Wörterbuch und Glossar.

http://www.elizabethan-era.org.uk/elizabethan-theatre.htm

Auf dieser Seite finden Sie einen Überblick zu Theater und Zeit.

British Monarchy and Modern Democracy (S II)

| Reihe 3 S 1 | Verlauf | Material | LEK | Kontext | Mediothek |

British Monarchy and Modern Democracy: Reality Meets Fiction – Auszüge aus Alan Bennetts „The Uncommon Reader" mit landeskundlichem Wissen erschließen (S II)

Manuela Olde Daalhuis, Düsseldorf

II/C4

Auf CD:
✓ Word-Datei
✓ language support
✓ thematischer Wortschatz „British Monarchy"

Was passiert, wenn die Queen ihren Verpflichtungen nicht mehr nachkommen möchte?

© Thinkstock/iStock Editorial

Worin liegen die Aufgaben der Queen im modernen demokratischen Großbritannien? Welche Rolle kommt dem Prime Minister zu? Und wie werden die beiden als literarische Figuren in einem aktuellen britischen Kurzroman dargestellt? Ihre Schüler erarbeiten anhand von Sachtexten und einem Internetclip Wissen zu britischen Werten, der Monarchie und dem Parlament. Parallel untersuchen sie, wie Alan Bennett die Queen in seiner Novelle „The Uncommon Reader" darstellt. Halboffene Aufgabenformate unterstützen Ihre Lerner, exemplarische Auszüge aus dem Kurzroman zu verstehen und zu deuten. Abschließend beschäftigen sie sich anhand eines Zeitungsartikels mit der Frage, ob die britische Monarchie noch zeitgemäß ist. Nebenbei üben sie, die abiturrelevanten Zieltextformate „Interview" und „Leserbrief" zu verfassen.

Klassenstufe: 11/12 (G8); 12/13 (G9)

Dauer: ca. 5 Doppelstunden

Bereich: Literatur, Landeskunde Großbritannien, *Tradition and changes in politics: monarchy and modern democracy*

Kompetenzen:

1. Interkulturelle Kompetenz: die Rolle und Bedeutung der britischen Monarchie heute anhand unterschiedlicher Texte nachvollziehen;
2. Lesekompetenz: authentische Texte vor dem Hintergrund ihres kommunikativen und kulturellen Kontextes verstehen und deuten;
3. Schreibkompetenz: Formen des kreativen Schreibens üben (Interview, Leserbrief)

RAAbits Englisch

British Monarchy and Modern Democracy (S II)

Reihe 3 S 2 | Verlauf | Material | LEK | Kontext | Mediothek

II/C4

Sachanalyse

Zum Autor und seinem Werk

Der britische Schriftsteller, Dramatiker und Regisseur **Alan Bennett** wurde 1934 in Leeds, England geboren. Bekannt wurde er vor allem durch seine zahlreichen **Theaterstücke** und **Drehbücher**. Seine Komödie „The Madness of George III" (1991) wurde 1994 mit namhaften Schauspielern wie Helen Mirren und Rupert Everett verfilmt. Bennetts **2007** erschienener Kurzroman *„The Uncommon Reader"* erhielt durchweg positive Kritiken und wurde als „amüsant", „geistreich" und „typisch britisch" bezeichnet.

Zum Inhalt des Kurzromans

„The Uncommon Reader" stellt die Wandlung der britischen Königin von einer pflichtbewussten Monarchin zu einer passionierten Leserin dar. Bei einem Gang in den Schlossgarten geraten die Hunde der **Queen** außer Rand und Band, denn ein **Bibliotheksbus** steht im Park. Sie betritt die Bibliothek, um sich für das Verhalten ihrer Hunde zu entschuldigen. Dabei lernt sie den Bibliothekar Mr. Hutchings sowie den Küchenjungen **Norman Seakins**, einen begeisterten Leser, kennen. Aus Höflichkeit entleiht die Queen ein Buch. Nach kurzer Zeit entwickelt sie eine Leidenschaft für das **Lesen** und folgt den Lesetipps von Norman, den sie kurzerhand zu ihrem Leseberater befördert. Wegen ihres Drangs zu lesen stellt sie einige öffentliche Pflichten hintan, sodass sie zum Beispiel eine Unpässlichkeit vortäuscht, um ihr Buch zu Ende lesen zu können. Die königliche Familie und vor allem ihr Privatsekretär **Sir Kevin Scatchard** sind angesichts der **Pflichtvernachlässigungen** besorgt. Als Erinnerungen an ihre Pflichten nicht helfen, spinnt Sir Kevin Intrigen, um das Hobby der Königin einzuschränken. So verschwindet zum Beispiel ein Buch, weil der Sicherheitsdienst es als explosiven Fremdkörper entsorgt hat. Die Auswirkungen, die das Lesen auf die Queen hat, machen sich auch bei öffentlichen Veranstaltungen bemerkbar. Sie hält nicht mehr den üblichen Smalltalk, sondern fragt ihre Gesprächspartner nach ihren Lieblingsbüchern. Dem **Premierminister** ergeht es in den wöchentlichen Audienzen mit der Queen ähnlich. Infolge ihrer **Leseerfahrungen** entwickelt sie mehr Feinfühligkeit gegenüber ihren Mitmenschen und entdeckt, dass sie bisher wegen ihrer gesellschaftlichen Sonderstellung keinem persönlichen Interesse jemals intensiv gefolgt ist. Zu ihrem 80. Geburtstag lädt die Queen alle Mitglieder des Geheimen Rats ein, um ihnen zu verkünden, dass sie beabsichtigt, ihre **Memoiren** zu schreiben. Bennett lässt die Novelle mit einem Knall enden: Die Queen kündigt an, dass sie wegen des Vorhabens zu schreiben abdanken wird, um sich ganz ihrem Projekt zu widmen.

Zu den zentralen Themen des Kurzromans

Die Novelle konzentriert sich auf die Aufgaben und den Alltag der britischen **Monarchin**. Im **modernen demokratischen Großbritannien** ist sie zwar nicht mehr alleinige Herrscherin des Landes, dennoch hält sie sowohl konstitutionelle als auch repräsentative Funktionen inne und ihr Privatleben wird von ihrer gesellschaftlichen Stellung dominiert. Pflichtbewusstsein, ein strenger Zeitplan und höfische Etikette treffen auf eigene Bedürfnisse, die sie bisher hintangestellt hat. Der Kontrast verdeutlicht dem Leser, wie stark die literarische Königin ihr Leben in den Dienst des Volkes gestellt hat. Parallelen zu den realen Verpflichtungen von Königin Elizabeth II. sind vorhanden. Ein weiteres Thema ist die **Kraft** und die **Inspiration**, die Lesenden durch die **Literatur** zuteilwerden können, und die Veränderungen, die Lesen und Schreiben bewirken können.

Didaktisch-methodisches Konzept

Zur Lerngruppe

Die Reihe eignet sich aufgrund der inhaltlichen und sprachlichen Anforderungen insbesondere für den Einsatz in einem **Grundkurs**. Da die Novelle nur in Auszügen gelesen wird, lässt sich der Text auch von leistungsschwächeren Schülerinnen und Schülern[1] gut in kurzer Zeit bewältigen. Auch die unterstützenden, zumeist halboffenen Aufgabenformate tragen zum Textverständnis bei.

Zum Leseprozess

Der Kurzroman „The Uncommon Reader" wird in der Reihe in **exemplarischen Auszügen** im Unterricht gelesen. Alle relevanten Textauszüge sind auf den Materialblättern abgedruckt. Im Leistungskurs ist es auch möglich, die Gesamtlektüre zu behandeln (s. Mediothek) und die vorliegenden Materialien als Ergänzung zu verstehen.

Zum Aufbau und den Methoden

Die Einheit ermöglicht es, die grundlegenden Elemente eines Prosatextes (*setting, conflict, character*) anhand von Auszügen zu **analysieren**. Des Weiteren werden Impulse angeboten, um das **kreative Schreiben** gängiger Zieltextformate wie **„Leserbrief"** (M 15) und **„Interview"** (M 5) zu trainieren. Die Schüler erweitern außerdem ihre interkulturelle Kompetenz, indem sie Sachinformationen über das Königshaus und das britische Parlament in Form eines **Quiz** (M 2) und eines **Infotextes** (M 3) beziehungsweise einer **Internetrecherche** (M 10) sammeln. Das Hintergrundwissen hilft ihnen, die subtilen Anspielungen auf die Realität in den Auszügen der Novelle zu verstehen. Sie lesen geeignete Ausschnitte und erkennen Leerstellen in der Erzählung, die es dem Autor erlauben, humorvoll die fiktionale Figur der Queen mit Gefühlen und Handlungen auszubauen. Die Schüler **analysieren** die literarische **Figur der Queen** (M 8) und deren Verhältnis zum **Prime Minister** (M 11). Nach der Auseinandersetzung mit *„The Uncommon Reader"* arbeiten die Schüler Vor- und Nachteile der britischen Monarchie aus einem Kommentar (M 13) heraus, um sie in einem Leserbrief zu ergänzen und zu diskutieren.

Zur Klausur

Beim Klausurtext handelt sich um einen Textauszug aus der Novelle, anhand dessen die Schüler die literarische **Figur** der **Queen charakterisieren**. Als kreative Schreibaufgabe verfassen sie als Zieltextformat ein **Interview** über die Vor- und Nachteile der britischen Monarchie.

---

[1] Im weiteren Verlauf wird aus Gründen der besseren Lesbarkeit nur „Schüler" verwendet.

British Monarchy and Modern Democracy (S II)

Schematische Verlaufsübersicht

British Monarchy and Modern Democracy: Reality Meets Fiction
– Auszüge aus Alan Bennetts *„The Uncommon Reader"* mit landeskundlichem Wissen erschließen (S II)

1. Doppelstunde: What is British? – The monarchy as part of Britishness
2. Doppelstunde: The Queen's duties – in reality and in fiction
3. Doppelstunde: The fictional Queen – analysing a character
4. Doppelstunde: The audiences with the Prime Minister – comparing facts and fiction
5. Doppelstunde: *Do We Really Need the Monarchy?* – Discussing the necessity of British monarchy

1. Doppelstunde

Thema
What is British? – The monarchy as part of Britishness

Material	Verlauf
M 1	**Opinions on Britishness** / Durchführen eines Brainstormings zum Thema *„Typically British"*; Lesen von Meinungen zum Thema, Zusammenfassen der Meinungen in einem *word cluster*; Vergleichen mit den eigenen Vorstellungen von *Britishness*
M 2	**Quiz** / Beantworten von Multiple-Choice-Fragen zur britischen Monarchie in einem Quiz
M 3	**The Queen's working day** / Lesen eines Sachtexts über die Aufgaben der Queen, Herausarbeiten von konstitutionellen und repräsentativen Aufgaben; Zuordnen von Verben und Begriffen zum Thema *„The Queen's duties"*
Zusätzlich benötigtes Material: Folie, Folienstifte, OHP	

2. Doppelstunde

Thema
The Queen's duties – in reality and in fiction

Material	Verlauf
M 4	**What are the Queen's duties?** / Wiederholen der konstitutionellen und repräsentativen Aufgaben der Queen anhand eines Bildimpulses
M 5	**An interview** / Erstellen eines Terminplans für die Queen; Verfassen eines Interviews über die Aufgaben der Queen
ZIP	**Useful expressions for writing an interview** / Wortschatzhilfe
ZIP	**Topic vocabulary** / Wortschatzliste als Lernhilfe
M 6	**The Queen in the library** / Lesen des Beginns von *„The Uncommon Reader"*, Beantworten von Verständnisfragen zum Text
M 7	**Setting and conflict** / Analysieren der Exposition des Kurzromans
Zusätzlich benötigtes Material: M 4 auf Folie kopiert, OHP	

3. Doppelstunde

Thema
The fictional Queen – analysing a character

Material	Verlauf
M 8	**Summing it up** / Zusammenfassen des ersten Textauszugs
	What is the literary Queen like? / Untersuchen der Darstellung der fiktionalen Queen
M 9	**The Queen's schedule in fiction** / Analysieren der Erzählperspektive

4. Doppelstunde

Thema
The audiences with the Prime Minister – comparing facts and fiction

Material	Verlauf
M 10	**Introduction to Parliament** / Sammeln von Informationen über das britische Parlament und über die Funktionen seiner Mitglieder anhand eines Internetclips
	Who am I ? / Erraten der Identitäten von Parlamentsmitgliedern anhand von Definitionen ihrer Funktion
M 11	**Meeting the Prime Minister** / Lesen des zweiten Textausschnitts aus „The Uncommon Reader", Beantworten von Verständnisfragen zum Text
M 12	**The audiences** / Analysieren der fiktionalen Darstellung der wöchentlichen Audienzen der Queen und des Premierministers
Zusätzlich benötigtes Material: ausreichend Internetzugänge, sodass immer zwei bis drei Schüler an einem Computer arbeiten können	

5. Doppelstunde

Thema
Do We Really Need the Monarchy? – *Discussing the necessity of British monarchy*

Material	Verlauf
M 4	**Prince George** / Spekulieren über die offizielle Rolle von Prince George in der Zukunft anhand eines Bildimpulses
M 13	**An article** / Lesen eines Zeitungsartikels, Unterstreichen der Pro- und Kontraargumente
M 14	**Reading comprehension** / Bearbeiten von Multiple-Choice-Fragen und True-/False-Statements zum Artikel; Gegenüberstellen der Argumente aus dem Artikel
M 15	**A letter to the editor** / Sammeln eigener Argumente; Verfassen eines Leserbriefes
	Useful phrases to express an opinion / Wortschatzhilfe
M 4 auf Folie kopiert, OHP	

British Monarchy and Modern Democracy (S II)

| Reihe 3 | Verlauf | **Material S 1** | LEK | Kontext | Mediothek |

Materialübersicht

1. Doppelstunde: What is British? – The monarchy as part of Britishness

M 1	(Ab)	What does Britishness mean? – An opinion survey
M 2	(Ab)	What do you know about the royal family? – Do a quiz!
M 3	(Ab)	What does the Queen do? – A typical working day of the monarch

2. Doppelstunde: The Queen's duties – in reality and in fiction

M 4	(Bd)	Picture stimulus for the unit
M 5	(Ab)	The Queen is busy, isn't she? – Writing an interview
	(Ab)	Topic vocabulary – British monarchy and democracy 🗜
	(Ab)	Language support – useful expressions for writing your own interview 🗜
M 6	(Tx)	*The Uncommon Reader* – the beginning of the novella
M 7	(Ab)	It was the dogs' fault ... – analysing the setting and the conflict

3. Doppelstunde: The ficitional Queen – analysing a character

| M 8 | (Ab) | How is the Queen depicted? – Analysing a character |
| M 9 | (Ab) | The Queen's schedule – analysing the narrative perspective |

4. Doppelstunde: The audiences with the Prime Minister – comparing facts and fiction

M 10	(Ab)	Who runs Britain? – The British Parliament
M 11	(Tx)	*The Uncommon Reader* – audiences with the Prime Minister
M 12	(Ab)	The Queen and the Prime Minister – analysing thoughts and feelings

5. Doppelstunde: *Do We Really Need the Monarchy?* – Discussing the necessity of British monarchy

M 13	(Tx)	*Do We Really Need the Monarchy?* – Reading an article
M 14	(Ab)	*Do We Really Need the Monarchy?* – Understanding the article
M 15	(Ab)	*Do We Really Need the Monarchy?* – Writing a letter to the editor
	(Ab)	Language support – useful phrases to express an opinion 🗜

| LEK | | *The Uncommon Reader* – the appeal of reading |
| | (LEK) | Rhetorical devices 🗜 |

🗜 Diese Materialien finden Sie auf der **CD Grundwerk**.

M 1 What does Britishness mean? – An opinion survey

Tasks

1. Brainstorm: What is typically British for you?
2. Read the speech bubbles. Sum up each persons' main ideas of Britishness in 2–5 keywords.
3. Together with a partner, create a word cluster in which you categorise the main ideas presented in the speech bubbles.
4. Compare the findings with your own ideas about Britishness.

① I was born in Wales, but have lived in England for half of my life. I have never lost my Welsh identity, but feel British. For me, Britishness means the royal family and tradition. One of the major highlights is the jubilee. This event is important because we can celebrate the Queen and think about how important she is for our country. Nowadays although she is a figurehead, she still may use her power to veto any new laws. She defends our country and its values against anyone who becomes too powerful like a dictator. I also associate Britishness with rather bizarre events like the cheese rolling race.

Daniel Bernard-Crowe, 68, retired chef from Birmingham

② I'm originally from Bath, but am now living in Bristol. I feel British and not English and I want England, Scotland and Wales to stay united. I don't relate much to the monarchy. For me Britishness means freedom of choice and being able to give your opinion. Britain is a democratic country and Parliament – not the Queen – exemplifies what is British, though to an outsider a parliamentary debate must sometimes seem rather strange. I think we are more critical and more secular than the Americans. I must say that I am concerned about our economy and how capitalism seems to serve the privileged few at the expense of the other poorer areas of society. I feel that my generation should be more optimistic and not to think that Britain's best days are a thing of the past. We should not be involved in so many wars but should rather concentrate on becoming a leading nation in research so that we can be a centre of innovation for the whole world.

Max Richards, 23, student from Bristol

③ I live in a Hastings which is a nice but peculiar town. It's a place where people come to get away from things. I suppose we have our own form of chaos here like pram races, boat races on the sea and a unique and traditional festival called Jack in the Green. This is all rather British but that's what Britishness is; being eccentric and accepting others for what they are and involving them in our strange little lives.

Maggie King, 45, organic food shop owner from Hastings

3 **jubilee:** here: celebration of the day the Queen was crowned – 5 **figurehead:** a person who is officially a leader but who has little power – 5 **to veto:** to refuse to accept a new law or a formal decision – 13 **to exemplify:** to give a typical example of something – 15 **secular:** not religious – 17 **to serve:** to be of use for – 17 **at the expense of:** here: costing or harming another group – 23 **peculiar:** not usual, strange – 25 **pram:** vehicle for moving a baby around – 25/26 **Jack in the Green:** traditional figure in an English May Day parade

M 2 What do you know about the royal family? – Do a quiz!

Princess Catherine recently gave birth to her second child. What else do you know about the British royal family?

Task

Check what you already know about the royal family. Tick ☑ the correct answer.

1. What is the recent Queen's name?
   a) ☐ Queen Victoria IV
   b) ☐ Queen Elizabeth II
   c) ☐ Queen Mary I

2. Where does the Changing of the Guard take place?
   a) ☐ 10, Downing Street
   b) ☐ Buckingham Palace
   c) ☐ Palace of Westminster

3. The monarch …
   a) ☐ rules but does not reign the country.
   b) ☐ governs but does not rule the country.
   c) ☐ reigns but does not rule the country.

The British Queen

4. HRH stands for …
   a) ☐ Her/His Royal Highness.
   b) ☐ Harry, Ron and Hermione.
   c) ☐ historic royal houses.

5. Who was killed in a car crash in Paris in the year 1997?
   a) ☐ Princess Anne
   b) ☐ Princess Sarah
   c) ☐ Princess Diana

The Changing of the Guard

6. What are the names of Prince William's and Prince Catherine's children?
   a) ☐ Prince Alexander and Princess Louise
   b) ☐ Prince George and Princess Charlotte
   c) ☐ Prince Henry and Princess Beatrice

7. After Queen Elizabeth's death, Prince Charles will become the monarch. Who is third in line to the throne?
   a) ☐ Prince William
   b) ☐ Prince Harry
   c) ☐ Prince George

Princess Catherine and Prince William with their baby son

M 3 What does the Queen do? – A typical working day of the monarch

Queen Elizabeth II is not only the representative of the British nation. For many people, she personifies values like duty and service to the country. Since her coronation in 1953, she has spent her working days with various representational and constitutional duties. The British monarch starts her working day by reading letters and the daily newspapers. Afterwards, a private secretary works with her on official papers such as information from government ministers and from representatives in the Commonwealth.

The Queen reads, approves and signs the papers. The private secretary carries them to the monarch in red boxes. The monarch has to deal with every document in the box. This is part of the constitutional duties.

Queen Elizabeth II (on the right) greets the audience in Frankfurt, on June 25, 2015.

Afterwards, the monarch officially holds meetings or audiences of 10 to 20 minutes with important persons like ambassadors or prize winners. Sometimes, the Queen presents honours and decorations in a one-hour ceremony called "investiture".

In the afternoon, her majesty often carries out representational duties in the public. She meets people, opens buildings or holds speeches. This also means travelling by air if the place is outside London. The Prime Minister and the monarch have a regular meeting that is absolutely confidential every week.

In the evening, the monarch receives a daily report of Parliament's work to read. Occasionally, the Queen is present at a concert, a film premiere or a reception; she may also give a reception herself.

Another constitutional task is to open Parliament once a year and after a change of government. As regards the representational tasks, the sovereign's garden parties have become famous for being rather relaxed and informal royal events to honour people.

Source: www.royal.gov.uk

4 **coronation:** a ceremony at which a person is made king or queen – 6 **representational:** here: doing sth. to represent the country symbolically – 6 **constitutional:** regulated by the political principles of a country – 11 **Commonwealth:** an organisation of independent countries that in the past belonged to the British Empire – 19 **decoration:** a medal given to so. as an honour – 23 **confidential:** secret

Tasks: 1. Read the text and underline the Queen's representational and constitutional duties. Use two different colours. **2.** Match the verbs in the table with the correct expressions from the box.

Parliament duty honours meeting report audience ~~the country~~ values	
a) to serve	the country
b) to perform a	
c) to hold an	
d) to have a regular	
e) to receive a	
f) to personify	
g) to present	
h) to open	

British Monarchy and Modern Democracy (S II)

Reihe 3 | Verlauf | **Material S 5** | LEK | Kontext | Mediothek

II/C4

Hinweise (M 1–M 3; 1. Doppelstunde)

In der ersten Doppelstunde aktivieren die Schüler ihr **Vorwissen** zu Großbritannien und der *royal family*. Sie vertiefen ihr Wissen anhand eines Sachtextes.

Der **Einstieg** erfolgt mit einem **Brainstorming** zum Thema *„Britishness"*, in dem die Lernenden ihre Assoziationen zu Großbritannien schriftlich in Einzelarbeit sammeln (**M 1, task 1**). In einer „Blitzlicht"-Runde präsentieren sie zügig ihre Ideen im Plenum.

Alternative: Sie können auch typisch britische Gegenstände in einer „Wundertüte" mitbringen (zum Beispiel einen U-Bahn-Fahrplan, Tee, englisches Weingummi, eine Tasse mit Bild vom englischen Königshaus, eine DVD von Mr. Bean etc.). Als Impuls können Sie folgende Frage stellen: *Why are these things typically British? Explain.*

Die Schüler lesen in Einzelarbeit drei **Aussagen** von Briten zur Frage, was sie als **britisch** betrachten, und fassen die Aussagen mit **Schlüsselwörtern** zusammen (*task 2*). In Partnerarbeit erstellen sie ein *word cluster*, in dem die Aussagen übersichtlich dargestellt und kategorisiert werden (*task 3*). Ein Schülerpaar präsentiert im Plenum sein Cluster auf Folie. Die Lernenden **vergleichen** ihre eigenen Ideen aus dem Brainstorming mit den Ergebnissen und vervollständigen gegebenenfalls das Cluster (*task 4*).

In der zweiten Hälfte der Doppelstunde greift die Lehrkraft einen genannten Aspekt von *Britishness*, die **Monarchie**, auf. Die Schüler testen ihr Allgemeinwissen über die **royal family** und die Monarchie, indem sie das **Quiz (M 2)** in Einzelarbeit beantworten und mit der Lehrkraft im Plenum vergleichen.

Eingestimmt auf das Thema „Britische Monarchie" lesen die Schüler einen **Sachtext** über einen **typischen Arbeitstag** der **Queen (M 3)**, der repräsentative und konstitutionelle Verpflichtungen beinhaltet. Als *while-reading task* unterstreichen sie die beiden unterschiedlichen Aufgabenbereiche in zwei Farben (*task 1*). Die Lehrkraft sammelt mit den Schülern Beispiele für die Arten der Aufgaben an der Tafel. Es folgt eine **Wortschatzaufgabe (*task 2*)**, in der die Lernenden in Einzelarbeit Ausdrücke aus dem Bereich „Aufgaben der Königin" zuordnen. Die Ergebnisse werden im Plenum verglichen.

Erwartungshorizont (M 1)

1. <u>Possible answers:</u>

    Pub, beer, football, black cab, double-decker bus, red letter box, fish and chips, the Queen, tea, English breakfast, hooligans, the rainy weather, cricket, driving on the left

2. <u>Keywords from the speech bubbles:</u>

    ① The royal family, tradition, the Queen, bizarre

    ② Democracy, freedom (of speech), Parliament, Parliamentary debate, secular

    ③ Peculiar, chaos, tradition, eccentric, accepting others

3./4. Example of a word cluster:

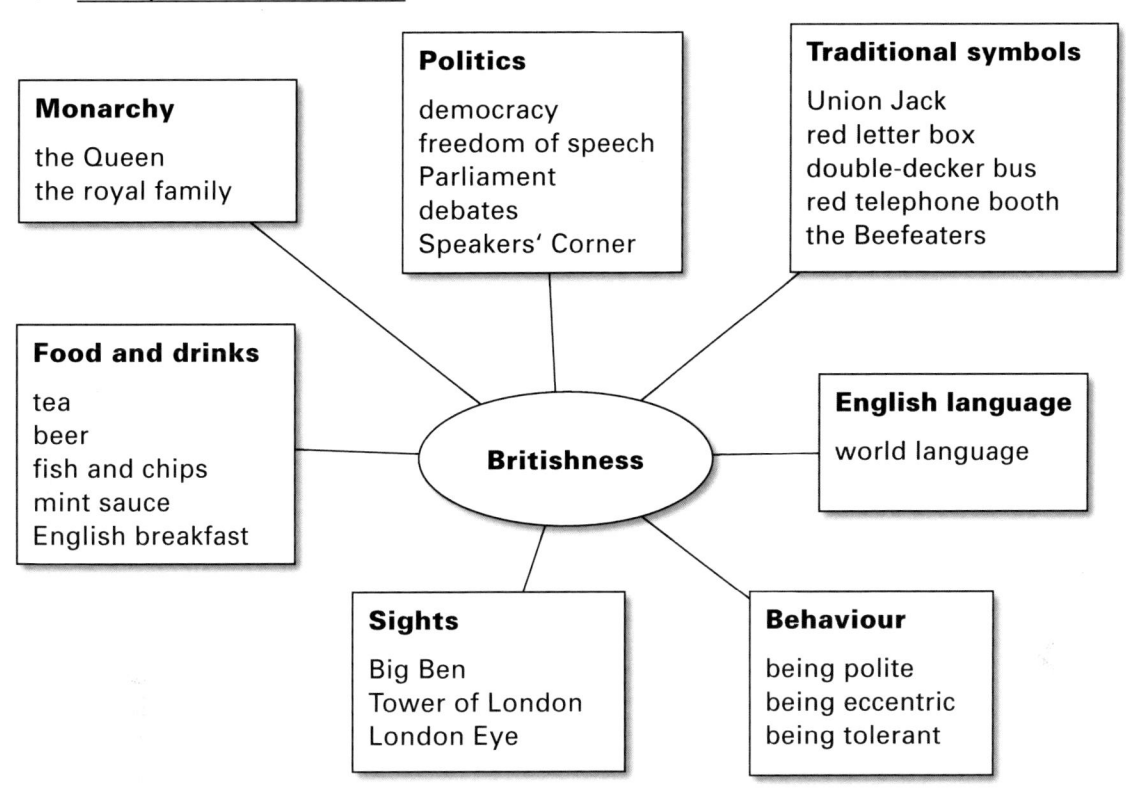

Monarchy
the Queen
the royal family

Politics
democracy
freedom of speech
Parliament
debates
Speakers' Corner

Traditional symbols
Union Jack
red letter box
double-decker bus
red telephone booth
the Beefeaters

Food and drinks
tea
beer
fish and chips
mint sauce
English breakfast

Britishness

English language
world language

Sights
Big Ben
Tower of London
London Eye

Behaviour
being polite
being eccentric
being tolerant

Erwartungshorizont (M 2)

1. b); 2. b); 3. c); 4. a); 5. c); 6. b); 7. c)

Erwartungshorizont (M 3)

1. Representational duties: Being a national symbol of duty and service; holding meetings and audiences with important people; presenting honours; meeting people; opening buildings; holding speeches; travelling; attending concerts/film premieres/receptions; giving receptions and parties

   Constitutional duties: Reading and working on official papers from the government and the Commonwealth; meetings with the Prime Minister on a weekly basis; reading Parliament's daily report; opening Parliament once a year

2.
   a) to serve the country
   b) to perform a duty
   c) to hold an audience
   d) to have a regular meeting
   e) to receive a report
   f) to personify values
   g) to present honours
   h) to open Parliament

British Monarchy and Modern Democracy (S II)

| Reihe 3 | Verlauf | Material S 7 | LEK | Kontext | Mediothek |

M 4 Picture stimulus for the unit

M 4 Queen Elizabeth II opening a station

M 13 Prince George with his father Prince William

British Monarchy and Modern Democracy (S II)

| Reihe 3 | Verlauf | Material S 8 | LEK | Kontext | Mediothek |

M 5 The Queen is busy, isn't she? – Writing an interview

Practise writing an interview based on your knowledge about the Queen's duties.

Tasks

1. Choose duties to fill in a typical daily schedule for the Queen that contains representational duties as well as constitutional duties together with a partner.

Tuesday, 15th May

Time	Representational duties	Constitutional duties	Activities
10:00	☐	☑	deal with official papers
11:00	☐	☐	
11:20	☐	☐	
14:00	☐	☐	
17:00	☐	☐	
18:00	☐	☐	
20:30	☐	☐	

How to write an interview	
The interviewer (the person who asks)	**The interviewee** (the person who answers)
– Prepare questions carefully. They should be clear and easy to understand. – Ask direct, open questions (Why/how/when/what?). – Be polite and stay neutral. – Round off the interview by thanking your partner.	– Be ready to give your opinion by preparing important arguments. – Use some expressions to correct misunderstandings or to ask for clarification. – Make sure you know some phrases to gain time or to change the topic.

2. Some members of the public criticise the Queen for doing nothing but spending tax money. As a journalist from the conservative newspaper *Daily Telegraph*, you interview the Queen's private secretary. You would like to show what range of duties the Queen fulfils during a day and ask the secretary to give examples. Read the advice on how to write an interview and write the interview together with a partner.

3. Practise the interview.

4. Present the interview to the class.

M 6 *The Uncommon Reader* – the beginning of the novella

Queen Elizabeth II is fond of dogs and owns Welsh Corgis herself. Find out how the author Alan Bennett uses this fact to set off the action of his novella The Uncommon Reader *written in 2007.*

It was the dogs' fault. They were snobs and ordinarily, having been in the garden, would have gone up the front steps, where a footman generally opened them the door. Today, though, for some reason they careered along the terrace, barking their heads off, and scampered down the steps again and round the end along the side of the house, where she could hear them yapping at something in one of the yards.

A Welsh Corgi

It was the City of Westminster travelling library, a large removal-like van parked next to the bins outside one of the kitchen doors. This wasn't a part of the palace she saw much of, and she had certainly never seen the library there before, nor presumably had the dogs, hence the din, so having failed in her attempt to calm them down she went up the little steps of the van in order to apologise. The driver was sitting with his back to her, sticking a label on a book, the only seeming borrower a thin ginger-haired boy in white overalls crouched in the aisle reading. Neither of them took any notice of the new arrival, so she coughed and said, "I'm sorry about this awful racket," whereupon the driver got up so suddenly he banged his head on the Reference section and the boy in the aisle scrambled to his feet and upset Photography & Fashion.

She put her head out of the door. "Shut up this minute, you silly creatures" – which, as had been the move's intention, gave the driver/librarian time to compose himself and the boy to pick up the books.

"One has never seen you here before, Mr ..."

"Hutchings, Your Majesty. Every Wednesday, ma'am."

"Really? I never knew that. Have you come far?"

"Only from Westminster, ma'am."

"And you are ...?"

"Norman, ma'am. Seakins."

"And where do you work?"

"In the kitchen, ma'am."

"Oh. Do you have much time for reading?"

"Not really, ma'am."

"I'm the same. Though now that one is here I suppose one ought to borrow a book."

Mr Hutchings smiled helpfully.

"Is there anything you would recommend?"

"What does Your Majesty like?"

The Queen hesitated, because to tell the truth she wasn't sure. She'd never taken much interest in reading. She read, of course, as one did, but liking books was something she left to other people. It was a hobby and it was in the nature of her job that she didn't have hobbies. Jogging, growing roses, chess or rock-climbing, cake decoration, model aeroplanes. No. Hobbies involved preferences and preferences had to be avoided; preferences excluded people. One had no preferences. Her job was to take an interest, not to be interested herself.

And besides, reading wasn't doing. She was a doer. So she gazed round the book-lined van and played for time. "Is one allowed to borrow a book? One doesn't have a ticket?"

"No problem," said Mr Hutchings.

"One is a pensioner," said the Queen, not that she was sure that made any difference.

"Ma'am can borrow up to six books."

"Six? Heavens!"

Alan Bennett: The Uncommon Reader. Profile Books London 2008, pp. 5–10.

Vocabulary Aids

4 **to career:** to move fast and wildly – 4 **to bark one's head off:** to produce loud, rough sounds as a dog – 4/5 **to scamper:** to run with small, quick steps – 6 **to yap at sth.:** to make short, high sounds as a dog – 8 **City of Westminster:** central part of London where the Parliament buildings are – 8 **removal-like van:** a vehicle used to transport furniture – 10 **presumably:** probably – 10 **hence:** because of that – 11 **din:** loud noise – 13 **ginger-haired:** hair of red, orange-brown colour – 13 **to crouch:** to bend your knees and lower yourself – 13 **aisle:** the long, narrow space between two rows of shelves – 15 **racket:** noise – 15 **to bang one's head on sth.:** to hit one's head against sth. – 16 **Reference section:** shelf with books containing facts (e.g. dictionary, encyclopedia) – 16 **to scramble to one's feet:** to get up quickly with the help of your hands – 16 **to upset:** to push sth. out of its usual position by accident – 19 **move:** here: step – 19 **to compose o.s.:** to make yourself calm again after being upset – 38 **chess:** a board game for two players moving 16 pieces each across the board – 43 **doer:** so. who gets actively involved in sth. instead of just talking about it – 43 **to gaze round sth.:** to look around in surprise or admiration

Task: Understanding the text:

Tick ☑ the correct finishing of the sentence. Correct the false statement(s) in your exercise books.

Statements	True	False
a) The dogs bark because they enjoy running around in the park.	☐	☐
b) In the van, the driver and a boy are having a snack.	☐	☐
c) When the Queen enters, both get nervous.	☐	☐
d) The Queen enters because she wants to borrow a book.	☐	☐

M 7 It was the dogs' fault ... – analysing the setting and the conflict

The worksheet helps you to examine how the author Alan Bennett creates the setting and starts the story of his novella The Uncommon Reader.

Tasks

> The term **setting** describes the place and/or time in which an action in a literary text takes place.

1. What is the setting like at the beginning of Alan Bennett's novella?

___

> The term **suspense** describes a feeling of tension or expectation aroused in the reader about the further development of the plot (= the set of events connected by cause and effect). Usually, the action is centred around a **conflict**.

2. How does the author create suspense in the beginning of the novella? What is the conflict?

British Monarchy and Modern Democracy (S II)

| Reihe 3 | Verlauf | Material S 12 | LEK | Kontext | Mediothek |

II/C4

Hinweise (M 4–M 7, 2. Doppelstunde)

In der zweiten Doppelstunde verfassen die Schüler ein **Interview** über die Verpflichtungen der Queen. Damit bereiten sie sich auf das Lesen und Deuten des Beginns von „The Uncommon Reader" vor, in dem sie die fiktionale Figur der Queen kennenlernen.

Einstieg: Die Lehrkraft zeigt das **Foto** von **Queen Elizabeth II (M 4)** auf Folie kopiert oder über den Beamer. Es zeigt die Monarchin 2014 bei der Eröffnung des Bahnhofs Reading Station. Die Lernenden beschreiben das Bild und ordnen die Aufgabe der Queen als **repräsentativ** oder **konstitutionell** ein. Sie nennen weitere Beispiele für repräsentative und konstitutionelle Aufgaben der Monarchin, um an das erworbene Wissen aus der ersten Doppelstunde anzuknüpfen (zum Beispiel *representative functions*: *opening a building, meeting a famous person*; *constitutional functions*: *reading official papers, signing a law*).

Die **landeskundlichen Informationen** aus dem Sachtext **(M 3)** wenden die Lernenden in **M 5** kreativ an. Zur Vorbereitung eines schriftlichen Interviews einigen sie sich in Partnerarbeit auf einen **Tagesablauf** der Queen, der sowohl repräsentative als auch konstitutionelle Aufgaben enthält (*task 1*). Anschließend verfassen sie zu zweit ein **Interview**, in dem der Privatsekretär der Queen einem Journalisten erläutert, was die Monarchin üblicherweise an einem Tag macht (*task 2*). Als Hilfestellung dienen Tipps, wie man Interviews verfasst. Nach dieser Erarbeitung üben die Lernenden, ihr Interview mündlich vorzutragen (*task 3*). Zwei bis drei Paare **präsentieren** es abschließend im Plenum (*task 4*). Die Lehrkraft und die Mitschüler geben ihnen Rückmeldung. Vor der Präsentation legt die Lehrkraft daher mit den Schülern drei Beobachtungskriterien für die Zuhörer fest, anhand derer diese den Vortrag bewerten und gegebenenfalls Tipps zur Verbesserung geben:

– *Identify three expressions the interviewer uses to introduce a new question/topic.*
– *Identify three expressions the interviewee uses to gain time and/or change the topic.*
– *Identify three expressions the interviewee uses to express his/her opinion.*

Die **CD Grundwerk** enthält eine **thematische Wortschatzliste** (Zusatz_Topic vocabulary_British monarchy and democracy.doc). Sie dient den Schülern als sprachliche Unterstützung während der Einheit und kann ihnen als Hilfe zum Schreiben des Interviews ausgeteilt werden. Die Vokabeln können am Ende der Stunde als Hausaufgabe aufgegeben werden. Die Lernenden formulieren pro Wort jeweils einen Beispielsatz.

Differenzierung: Ebenfalls auf der **CD Grundwerk** finden Sie eine Tabelle mit hilfreichen Formulierungen für das Verfassen von Interviews für lernschwächere Kurse (Zusatz_Language support_useful expressions for writing an interview.doc).

In der zweiten Hälfte der Doppelstunde lesen die Schüler in Einzelarbeit den **ersten Textausschnitt** aus *„The Uncommon Reader"* **(M 6)**. Ihre Aufgabe ist es, herauszufinden, wie die Hunde der Queen ihren üblichen Tagesablauf durcheinanderbringen. In Einzelarbeit überprüfen sie ihr **Textverständnis** durch True-/False-Statements. Die Ergebnisse werden im Plenum gesichert, bevor die Schüler in Partnerarbeit mithilfe von **M 7** zentrale Elemente der **Exposition** untersuchen (*setting, conflict*). **Erzählerische Mittel** (*setting, suspense, plot, conflict*) werden in M 7 anhand kurzer Definitionen in Infokästen wiederholt. Die Ergebnisse werden im Plenum gesichert.

Abschließend spekulieren die Schüler anhand ihres Allgemeinwissens über bekannte Persönlichkeiten, ob sie es für realistisch halten, dass ein Mitglied der königlichen Familie oder die Queen solch ein Gespräch in einer mobilen Bücherei führen würde. Gehört dies zum Smalltalk von Berühmtheiten, oder ist dies eine eher unglaubwürdige Situation?

British Monarchy and Modern Democracy (S II)

| Reihe 3 | Verlauf | Material S 13 | LEK | Kontext | Mediothek |

Erwartungshorizont (M 5)

1. Example of the Queen's time schedule:

Tuesday, 15th May			
Time	Representational duties	Constitutional duties	Activities
10:00	☐	☑	*Deal with official papers*
11:00	☑	☐	Present honours to the winner of a national music contest
11:20	☑	☐	Meet an ambassador
14:00	☑	☐	Travel to Leeds
17:00	☑	☐	Hold a speech at a charity organisation
18:00	☐	☑	Hold an audience with the Prime Minister
20:30	☑	☐	Visit the first night of the latest James Bond film

2. Example of an interview about the Queen's duties:

A: Mr Swan, welcome to this interview and thank you for coming.

B: Thank you for inviting me today.

A: Many people say that the Queen spends our tax money but does not do anything useful. How do you feel about that?

B: Oh, this is just a fairy tale. Her Majesty is always busy and has an extremely tight time schedule. There are many representational and some constitutional duties she performs every day. They fill up most of her working day.

A: Can you give us some examples, please?

B: In the morning, the Queen first deals with official papers. Afterwards, she holds audiences. Today at 11.20 a.m., for example, she is holding an audience with a new ambassador. Then she is going to honour a person for his services to the community. At 2 p.m. she has to catch a plane to travel to Leeds.

A: Really? What is she going to do in Leeds?

B: She will be holding a speech. Afterwards, she will return to London and meet the PM, as it is always the case on Tuesdays.

A: Let's get back to my original question. Do you think that her tasks are useful?

B: I must admit I wonder about the question. People all over Britain and also worldwide expect the Queen to honour them or their work, or represent the country in style. This sends a wonderful message to the nation and also to other countries. Who could replace her? She personifies our pride in our traditions.

A: I see. So do you think the money the Queen spends opening a building or giving a reception is well spent?

B: As regards people's motivation, I would agree. It is our country's way of honouring service and showing our strength and continuity.

A: Thank you very much for your time.

B: Thank you for having me.

Erwartungshorizont (M 6)

a) False: The dogs bark because there is a van parked close to the kitchen doors.

b) False: There are Mr Hutchings, the librarian who is labelling a book, and Norman Seakins, a thin ginger-haired boy who normally works in the kitchen and is reading a book in the van.

c) True

d) False: She wants to apologise for the dogs' noise and feels obliged to borrow a book.

Erwartungshorizont (M 7)

1. Setting of the beginning of *The Uncommon Reader*:

   The text excerpt does not give any specific information as regards time except that it should be during daytime. The scene takes place in the garden of Buckingham Palace. To be precise, it is set in the garden where a mobile library van is parked. The Queen enters and the action develops.

2. Suspense and conflict in the beginning of *The Uncommon Reader*:

   The reader would like to find out why the dogs are barking and expects an explanation. Next, the reader is intrigued by the Queen meeting two persons unknown to her in a situation she has not yet faced: the visit of the mobile library. She feels uncomfortable because she does not know which book to choose and is playing for time.

M 8 How is the Queen depicted? – Analysing a character

Let's analyse the Queen's character as presented in Alan Bennett's exposition of the novella The Uncommon Reader.

> **Implicit vs explicit characterisation**
>
> A character in a fictional text is a person developed through action, description, and language. If the narrator or another character tells the reader something about the character **explicitly**, this is a **direct** characterisation.
>
> If the reader has to read between the lines to interpret the character's actions, thoughts, words, feelings, and interaction with others, the characterisation is **implicit (indirect)**.

Tasks

1. Work on your own: Partner A concentrates on action and interaction, partner B on language and description.
2. Work with your partner: Compare your findings. Add to your partner's ideas. Are there any interpretations where you disagree?

Partner A

Action: what the Queen does (implicit characterisation)		
Lines	Actions	What does it reveal about the Queen's character?

Interaction: how other people react to the Queen (implicit characterisation)		
Lines	Interactions	What does it reveal about the Queen's character?

Partner B

	Language: what the Queen says and how she uses words (implicit characterisation)	
Lines	Language use	What does it reveal about the Queen's character?
	Word choice:	
	Syntax:	
	Other:	

	Description: what the narrator says about the Queen (explicit characterisation)	
Lines	Descriptions	What does it reveal about the Queen's character?

3. Imagine the Queen asks you for a good read: What kind of reading would you suggest to the Queen? Discuss.
4. Can you think of any novels/thrillers/comics/stories/children's books you think anyone should know? Discuss.

M 9 The Queen's schedule – analysing the narrative perspective

Find out how Alan Bennett presents the monarch's daily duties in this novella excerpt.

> Still, though reading absorbed her, what the Queen had not expected was the degree to which it drained her of enthusiasm for anything else. It's true that at the prospect of opening yet another swimming-bath her heart didn't exactly leap up, but even so, she had never actually resented having to do it. However tedious her obligations had been – visiting this,
> 5 conferring that – boredom had never come into it. This was her duty and when she opened her engagement book every morning it had never been without interest or expectation.
>
> No more. Now she surveyed the unrelenting progression of tours, travels and undertakings stretching years into the future only with dread. There was scarcely a day she could call her own and never two. Suddenly it had all become a drag. "Ma'am is tired," said her
> 10 maid, hearing her groan at her desk. "It's time ma'am put her feet up occasionally."
>
> But it wasn't that. It was reading, and love it though she did, there were times when she wished she had never opened a book and entered into other lives. It had spoiled her. Or spoiled her for this, anyway.

Alan Bennett: The Uncommon Reader. Profile Books London 2008, pp. 81/82.

1 **to absorb so.:** to take up so.'s attention completely – 2 **to drain so. of enthusiasm:** to reduce so.'s interest in sth. – 2 **prospect (fig.):** possibility – 3 **to leap up:** to beat quickly because of excitement – 4 **to resent doing sth.:** to feel angry because you have been forced to accept sth. you do not like – 5 **to confer:** to give (a title, honour) to so. – 6 **engagement book:** appointment calendar – 7 **to survey sth.:** to consider, look at sth. – 7 **unrelenting:** not slowing down, full of force – 7 **progression:** a continuous series of events – 7/8 **undertaking:** job, business – 8 **dread:** fear, terror – 9 **drag:** burden – 10 **to groan:** to sigh – 12 **to spoil so. for sth.:** to reduce so.'s pleasure in sth.

Tasks
1. Name the typical duties of the Queen mentioned in the excerpt.
2. Examine how reading influences the Queen's thoughts about her daily duties by looking at the narrative perspective. Read the info box and continue the sentence beginnings below. Provide proof of your findings from the text.
   a) As the story is told by a ... narrator, the reader ...
   b) The fictional character of the Queen is portrayed as ...
   c) The dialogue with her maid shows that ...
   d) The enumeration of typical duties underlines ...
   e) The author compares the past and the present in order to ...

Narrative perspective

Differentiate: The author **writes** a text. (= Alan Bennett) vs

The narrator **tells** a story. (= the narrator in the text)

A **first-person** narrator tells the story from his/her own perspective and is also a character in the story. The reader gets to know this character's view only. (= I)

A **third-person** narrator tells the story from the outside. (= he/she/they)

A third-person narrator with a **limited view** only describes feelings and thoughts from the point of view of one character. A third-person narrator with an **omniscient view** can tell the reader about all characters' thoughts and feelings and can also foreshadow action.

British Monarchy and Modern Democracy (S II)

Hinweise (M 8 und M 9; 3. Doppelstunde)

In der dritten Doppelstunde untersuchen die Lernenden die **literarische Figur der Queen**.

Einstieg: Zur Wiederholung fasst ein Schüler den Textauszug **(M 6)** im Plenum zusammen, anhand dessen die Lernenden in dieser Stunde die Queen analysieren.

Arbeitsteilig machen sich die Schüler in Partnerarbeit Notizen zur **direkten** und **indirekten Charakterisierung** der **Queen (M 8)**. Als Hilfestellung werden im Infokasten auf dem Arbeitsblatt kurz die wesentlichen Elemente der **direkten** und **indirekten Charakterisierung** (action, interaction, language, description) definiert. In Einzelarbeit füllen die Lernenden zunächst Teil A oder B aus **(task 1)**, um sich dann von ihrem Partner den nicht selbst untersuchten Teil in der zweiten Phase erläutern zu lassen und ihre Ergebnisse zu vergleichen und zu ergänzen **(task 2)**. Zwei Paare schreiben ihre Ergebnisse auf Folie, sodass sie anschließend im Plenum präsentiert und ergänzt werden können.

Tipp: Sie können die schriftliche Ausformulierung der Charakterisierung als Hausaufgabe aufgeben.

Mit dem Wissen um die Eigenarten der fiktionalen Figur der Queen können die Schüler in **task 3** im Plenum diskutieren, welche **Leseempfehlung** sie der Figur geben würden. Zugleich haben sie Raum, ihre **eigenen Leseerfahrungen** zu reflektieren: Was hat ihnen Leselust bereitet? Welcher Text hat sie geprägt? Sie nennen ein Buch, das ihrer Meinung nach jeder gelesen haben sollte **(task 4)**.

Tipp: Sollte der Kurs zügig arbeiten, können Sie *task 3* auch als kleines **Rollenspiel** in Partnerarbeit darstellen lassen. Ein Schüler spielt die Queen im Bibliotheksbus, ein anderer ist ein weiterer Besucher der Bibliothek und gibt Lesetipps.

Hinweis zur Weiterführung: Arbeitet die Lerngruppe interessiert, kann die Lehrkraft die Schüler zu Hause vorbereitend auf der Website www.royal.gov.uk folgendes Hintergrundwissen recherchieren lassen:

a) Was hat die reale Queen für Interessen? (Hunde, Pferderennen, Tanz)

   http://www.royal.gov.uk/HMTheQueen/Interests/Overview.aspx

b) Wie spricht man die Queen korrekt an?

   http://www.royal.gov.uk/HMTheQueen/GreetingtheQueen/Overview.aspx

Dieses Faktenwissen können die Lernenden dann in die Leseempfehlungen bzw. das Rollenspiel einbinden.

Abschließend **wiederholen** die Schüler ihr Wissen zur **Erzählperspektive** und wenden dies an einem weiteren kurzen **Textausschnitt (M 9)** an. Der Auszug zeigt, wie die Queen aufgrund ihrer Leselust ihre Verpflichtungen immer stärker als Last empfindet. Indem die Schüler in Einzelarbeit vorgegebene **Sätze vervollständigen**, untersuchen sie die Wirkung der Erzählperspektive.

Erwartungshorizont (M 8)

Partner A

Action: what the Queen does (implicit characterisation)		
Lines	**Actions**	**What does it reveal about the Queen's character?**
"Neither of them [...] racket" (ll. 14/15)	She coughs to get attention and speaks.	She knows how to make people listen to her.
"She put her head [...] to pick up the books." (ll. 18–20)	She allows time for others to overcome their surprise about facing her.	She is polite, she is aware of her effect/influence on other people.
"She was a doer [...] ticket?" (ll. 43–45)	She asks a question to gain more time for thinking.	She can bridge gaps in a conversation.

Interaction: how other people react to the Queen (implicit characterisation)		
Lines	**Interactions**	**What does it reveal about the Queen's character?**
"Neither of them [...] Fashion." (ll. 14–17)	The librarian bangs his head, the boy upsets a bookshelf.	Ordinary people do not expect to meet the Queen, they are surprised, maybe anxious and nervous.
"One has never seen [...] Wednesday, ma'am." (ll. 21/22)	Mr Hutchings addresses the Queen with the right expression.	Mr Hutchings shows respect towards her.

Partner B

Language: what the Queen says and how she uses words (implicit characterisation)		
Lines	**Language use**	**What does it reveal about the Queen's character?**
"One has never seen you here before, Mr ...." (l. 21)	**Word choice:** She often uses the pronoun "one" to speak about herself.	She is distanced, formal and reserved.
"Really? [...] far." (l. 23)	**Syntax:** She asks a lot of questions, talks about trivia, and speaks in short sentences.	She keeps a polite conversation going, shows interest and keeps the topic simple.
"Oh. Do you have much time for reading?" (l. 29)	**Other:** She uses exclamations like "Really?", "Oh", "Heavens!"	She tries to keep the dialogue going and shows she is listening.

British Monarchy and Modern Democracy (S II)

| Reihe 3 | Verlauf | Material S 20 | LEK | Kontext | Mediothek |

Description: what the narrator says about the Queen (explicit characterisation)		
Lines	Descriptions	What does it reveal about the Queen's character?
"The Queen hesitated [...] interested herself." (ll. 35–42)	The narrator explains that the Queen has no hobbies because of her position.	She follows her duties as a Queen. She does not follow personal interests. She tries to take no sides in order to avoid offence. She does not really know what she likes herself.
"And besides [...] doer." (l. 43)	The narrator calls her a "doer".	She is an active person who makes things happen.

II/C4

Erwartungshorizont (M 9)

1. Duties mentioned in the excerpt:
   – (Swimming-bath) openings
   – Visits
   – Travels
   – Honours

2. Finishing of the sentence beginnings:

   a) As the story is told by a third-person limited narrator, the reader gets to know the Queen's inner feelings in detail as for example in ll. 1–2 ("Still, though ... else.")

   b) The fictional character of the Queen is portrayed as attracted by reading but tired of representational duties. Proof can be found in ll. 7/8 ("Now she ... dread.").

   c) The dialogue with her maid shows that her surroundings interpret her lack of enthusiasm as a sign of becoming old (l. 9 ("Ma'am is tired.")).

   d) The enumeration of typical duties underlines how tight and busy every day is and that it does not offer much room for private interests (ll. 3/4 ("yet another swimming-bath come into it")).

   e) The author compares the past and the present in order to highlight the change reading has caused in the Queen's willingness to perform her duties. While she did not question her duties in the past, she now disapproves of the endless number of tasks and the time being consumed by them. This is resumed with the colloquial expression "drag" ("Suddenly it had all become a drag.", l. 9).

British Monarchy and Modern Democracy (S II)

| Reihe 3 | Verlauf | Material S 21 | LEK | Kontext | Mediothek |

M 10 Who runs Britain? – The British Parliament

Revise and check your knowledge about the British Parliament.

Tasks

1. Watch the following video clip to inform yourself about the British Parliament:

   www.parliament.uk/education/teaching-resources-lesson-plans/an-introduction-to-parliament-ks3-5-video

   Take notes about the function of the
   - Prime Minister
   - Monarch
   - House of Lords
   - House of Commons
   - The speaker

   Houses of Parliament

2. Each pupil draws a card with the description of a function in the Parliament. The pupil reads out the description and the class guesses who he/she is: the monarch, the Prime Minister, the Speaker, a Member of Parliament …?

Descriptions	Functions
The monarch asked me to form a government.	Prime Minister
I choose MPs to join the government.	Prime Minister
I lead the party with the most MPs in the House of Commons.	Prime Minister
I ask the leader of the winning party to form a government after a general election.	Monarch
I sign all new laws passed by Parliament.	Monarch
I hold a speech to open Parliament officially.	Monarch
I represent the public of my constituency.	Member of Parliament, House of Commons

British Monarchy and Modern Democracy (S II)

I approve laws or vote against them.	Member of Parliament, House of Commons
I have been elected to the house.	Member of Parliament, House of Commons
The house I work in can delay bills.	Member of Parliament, House of Lords
I have been asked to join the house because of my expertise.	Member of Parliament, House of Lords
I have been appointed to the house.	Member of Parliament, House of Lords
I question and challenge the government.	Member of Parliament, House of Lords, and/or opposition in the House of Commons
I keep order during the debates.	Speaker
I must remain neutral at all times during debates.	Speaker
I decide who can speak next.	Speaker
I have been elected by MPs from all parties.	Speaker
I can ask MPs to be quiet and stop using bad language and behaviour.	Speaker

M 11 *The Uncommon Reader* – audiences with the Prime Minister

In The Uncommon Reader *the Queen has become someone who enjoys spending a lot of time on reading. As a consequence, she takes less care of her official duties and her looks. This excerpt from the novella focuses on the Queen's weekly audiences with the Prime Minister. The Queen tries to make them more interesting for herself by sharing her interest in books. Find out what happens.*

Still, though he saw her every week, the occasional want of variation in the Queen's attire and the sameness of her earrings went unnoticed by the prime minister.

It had not always been so, and at the start of his term of office he had frequently complimented the Queen on what Her Majesty was wearing and her always discreet jewellery. He was younger then, of course, and thought of it as flirting, though it was also a form of nerves. She was younger, too, but she was not nervous and had been long enough at the game to know that this was just a phase that most prime ministers went through (the exceptions being Mr Heath and Mrs Thatcher) and that as the novelty of their weekly interviews diminished so, too, did the flirting.

It was another aspect of the myth of the Queen and her prime minister, the decline of the prime minister's attention to her personal appearance coinciding with his dwindling concern with what Her Majesty had to say, how the Queen looked and how the Queen thought, both of diminishing importance, so that, earrings or no earrings, making to her occasional comments she felt not unlike an air hostess going through the safety procedures, the look on the prime minister's face that of benevolent and minimal attention from a passenger who has heard it all before.

The British Prime Minister David Cameron greets Queen Elizabeth II at Number 10 Downing Street.

The inattention, though, and the boredom were not all his, and as she had begun to read more, she resented the time these meetings took up and so thought to enliven the process by relating them to her studies and what she was learning about history. This was not a good idea. The prime minister did not wholly believe in the past or in any lessons that might be drawn from it. One evening he was addressing her on the subject of the Middle East when she ventured to say, "It is the cradle of civilisation, you know."

"And shall be again, ma'am," said the prime minister, "provided we are allowed to persist," and then bolted off down a side alley about the mileage of new sewage pipes that had been laid and the provision of electricity substations.

She interrupted again. "One hopes this isn't to the detriment of the archaeological remains. Do you know about Ur?"

He didn't. So as he was going she found him a couple of books that might help. The following week she asked him if he had read them (which he hadn't).

"They were most interesting, ma'am."

"Well, in that case we must find you some more. I find it fascinating."

This time Iran came up and she asked him if he knew of the history of Persia, or Iran (he had scarcely even connected the two), and gave him a book on that besides, and generally began to take such an interest that after two or three sessions like this, Tuesday evenings, which he had hitherto looked forward to as a restful oasis in his week, now became fraught with apprehension. She even questioned him about the books as if they were homework. Finding he hadn't read them she smiled tolerantly.

"My experience of prime ministers, Prime Minister, is that, with Mr Macmillan the exception, they prefer to have their reading done for them."

British Monarchy and Modern Democracy (S II)

| Reihe 3 | Verlauf | Material S 24 | LEK | Kontext | Mediothek |

"One is busy, ma'am," said the prime minister.
45 "One is busy," she agreed and reached for her book. "We will see you next week."
Eventually Sir Kevin got a call from the special adviser.
"Your employer has been giving my employer a hard time."
"Yes?"
"Yes. Lending him books to read. That's out of order."
50 "Her Majesty likes reading."
"I like having my dick sucked. I don't make the prime minister do it. Any thoughts, Kevin?"
"I will speak to Her Majesty."
"You do that, Kev. And tell her to knock it off."

II/C4

Alan Bennett: The Uncommon Reader. Profile Books London 2008, pp. 115–119.

Vocabulary Aids

1 **want:** lack – 2 **attire:** clothes – 2/3 **to go unnoticed by so.:** to be overlooked by so. – 4 **term of office:** time period in which so. has an official responsibility in government – 7/8 **a form of nerves:** a sign of being nervous – 8/9 **to be long enough at the game (coll.):** to be experienced in the job – 10 **Mr Heath:** British Prime Minister, Conservative Party (1970–1974) – 11 **novelty:** sth. new – 12 **to diminish:** to decrease, become less – 15 **to coincide with sth.:** to happen at the same time – 15 **to dwindle:** to become less – 19 **air hostess:** a woman who serves passengers on a plane – 20 **benevolent:** kind, helpful – 22 **to resent sth.:** to be very angry about sth. – 22 **to relate:** to find a connection between two or more things – 25 **cradle (fig.):** origin, beginning – 27 **to persist:** to try to continue doing sth. even if it is unreasonable – 28 **to bolt off down a side alley (fig.):** to change the topic – 28 **mileage:** distance in miles – 28 **sewage pipe:** a tube that contains waste water, e.g. toilet water – 29 **provision:** supply – 29 **electricity substation:** *das Stromumspannwerk* – 30 **detriment:** disadvantage – 30 **remains:** rest – 31 **Ur:** an ancient city in Mesopotamia, a famous archaeological site – 39 **restful:** relaxing – 39 **fraught with apprehension:** causing fear – 42 **Mr Macmillan:** British politician, Prime Minister (1957–1963), Conservative Party – 49 **That's out of order:** You can't do it this way. – 51 **dick (vulg.):** penis – 53 **to knock sth. off (coll.):** to stop doing sth.

Task: Understanding the text

Tick ☑ the correct answers. Provide proof by naming the line(s).

1. The Queen has the impression the Prime Minister is less attentive than before ...
   a) ☐ because he does not pay her any compliments.
   b) ☐ because he checks his mobile every minute.
   c) ☐ because she has to repeat her questions for him.

   Line(s): _____

2. The Queen starts talking about ...
   a) ☐ the present debate in Parliament about tax cuts.
   b) ☐ the history of the Middle East.
   c) ☐ former Prime Ministers and their polite behaviour.

   Line(s): _____

3. When the Queen recommends books to the Prime Minister, he ...
   a) ☐ thanks her and enjoys reading.
   b) ☐ thanks her and declines the offer because he is too busy.
   c) ☐ makes his adviser call Sir Kevin.

   Line(s): _____

British Monarchy and Modern Democracy (S II)

| Reihe 3 | Verlauf | Material S 25 | LEK | Kontext | Mediothek |

M 12 The Queen and the Prime Minister – analysing thoughts and feelings

Analyse the relationship between the Prime Minister and the Queen.

Tasks

1. Fill in the chart with information from the text and indicate the respective lines.

	At the start of the PM's term of office	Lines
What the Queen feels		
What she does		
What the PM feels		
What he does		

	Once the PM is used to meeting the Queen	Lines
What the Queen feels		
What she does		
What the PM feels		
What he does		

	When the Queen starts talking about books	Lines
What the PM feels		
What he does		
What he says		

2. Describe where you can detect a discrepancy between a character's thoughts and his/her words. What is the effect?

3. The Queen tells her husband Prince Philip what she really thinks about the Prime Minister and their meetings. Write the dialogue in informal English. Be prepared to act it out in class.

RAAbits Englisch

British Monarchy and Modern Democracy (S II)

Hinweise (M 10–M 12; 4. Doppelstunde)

In der vierten Doppelstunde erarbeiten die Schüler Grundkenntnisse über das **britische Parlament**, um einzelne Funktionen und die Stellung des Premierministers sowie der Monarchin zu erkennen. Anschließend lesen sie in einem Auszug aus *„The Uncommon Reader"*, wie Bennett die **Audienz** des **Premierministers bei der Queen** literarisch darstellt.

Einstieg: Die Lernenden schauen einen circa 8-minütigen **Videoclip** über das Ober- und das Unterhaus des Parlaments im Internet an:

www.parliament.uk/education/teaching-resources-lesson-plans/an-introduction-to-parliament-ks3-5-video.

Als *while reading task* machen sie sich Notizen zu den Funktionen der vorgestellten Parlamentsmitglieder (**M 10, task 1**).

Alternative: Sollten in der Stunde keine Computerarbeitsplätze zur Verfügung stehen, schauen die Schüler den Clip vorbereitend zu Hause. Steigen Sie dann mit einem Bildimpuls auf Folie kopiert (zum Beispiel ein Bild vom Palace of Westminster von außen oder ein Bild vom House of Commons von innen) in die Stunde ein. Fragen Sie, was die Lernenden darüber in dem Clip erfahren haben.

Ihr Wissen überprüfen die Schüler in einem **Ratespiel** im Plenum (*task 2*). Dazu hält die Lehrkraft die **Karten** ausgeschnitten bereit. Jede Karte beschreibt aus der Ich-Perspektive eine **Funktion** im **Parlament**. Die Lehrkraft geht umher, jeder Schüler zieht eine *description card* und liest sie vor. Die Mitschüler wenden ihr Wissen aus dem Clip an und erraten, in welcher Funktion der Mitschüler spricht. Dann liest der nächste Schüler seine Karte vor.

Hinweis zur Differenzierung: In einem lernschwächeren Kurs können Sie die rechte Lösungsspalte neben der Definition stehen lassen.

Als Überleitung weist die Lehrkraft auf die wöchentlichen Audienzen der Queen mit dem Premierminister hin, in denen die Monarchin den Premierminister beraten soll. Wie Alan Bennett diesen realen Fakt in seinen Kurzroman einbindet, wird im nächsten **Textausschnitt** aus *„The Uncommon Reader"* (**M 11**) deutlich: Die fiktionale Queen langweilt sich während der wöchentlichen Audienzen mit dem Premierminister. Sie versucht daher, zum Widerwillen des Premierministers, ihr Interesse für Geschichte und ihre neue Leidenschaft für Bücher einzubringen. Ihr **Textverständnis** überprüfen die Lernenden in Einzelarbeit anhand von Multiple-Choice-Fragen, die im Plenum verglichen werden. In **M 12**, *task 1* **analysieren** die Schüler in Einzelarbeit die **Äußerungen** und **Gefühle** der beiden Figuren. Die Ergebnisse werden im Plenum besprochen und ergänzt. *Task 2* macht deutlich, wie Bennett durch Ungesagtes **Humor** schafft: Die Gedanken der beiden Figuren unterscheiden sich deutlich von dem, was sie denken und fühlen. Dank des allwissenden Erzählers ist der Leser jedoch über diese Diskrepanz informiert. In *task 3* füllen die Schüler die Leerstelle im Text mit einem **Rollenspiel** kreativ aus. Die Queen macht ihrem Ärger über die Treffen mit dem Premierminister im Gespräch mit ihrem Ehemann Luft.

Erwartungshorizont (M 10)

Die Funktionen und Beschreibungen sind auf dem Material in der richtigen Reihenfolge abgedruckt.

Erwartungshorizont (M 11)

1. a) Line(s) 13–20: „It was another aspect [...] all before."

2. b) Line(s) 24–31: „One evening he was addressing [...] Do you know about Ur?"

3. c) Line(s) 46–53: „Eventually Sir Kevin got a call from [...] knock it off."

Erwartungshorizont (M 12)

1.

	At the start of the PM's term of office	Lines
What the Queen feels	She understands that the PM has to overcome his nervousness.	"She was younger [...] flirting." (ll. 8–12)
What she does	She keeps calm and is unimpressed.	"She was younger [...] flirting." (ll. 8–12)
What the PM feels	He is nervous but thinks he is flirting.	"He was younger [...] nerves." (ll. 6–8)
What he does	He flatters her and comments on her dress and style.	"at the start [...] jewellery." (ll. 4–6)

	Once the PM is used to meeting the Queen	Lines
What the Queen feels	She is bored by the meetings. She is annoyed that they keep her from reading.	"The inattention [...] took up" (ll. 21/22)
What she does	She discusses history and books with the PM. She checks his knowledge.	"she resented [...] history." (ll. 21–23)
What the PM feels	He seems to be bored. He behaves as if he does not have any use for the meetings. He is no longer intimidated by the monarch.	"It was another aspect of the myth [...] all before." (ll. 13–20)
What he does	He pays less attention to her words and looks. He forgets to pay compliments. He does not notice her boredom.	"It was another aspect of the myth [...] all before." (ll. 13–20)

British Monarchy and Modern Democracy (S II)

	When the Queen starts to talk about books	**Lines**
What the PM feels	He fears the next meeting. He can no longer relax, he feels like a schoolboy.	"Tuesday [...] apprehension." (ll. 38/39)
What he does	He makes his adviser call Sir Kevin to make him stop the Queen.	"Eventually [...] hard time." (ll. 46/47)
What he says	He states his interest in her book recommendations but also admits that he is too busy.	"They were most interesting, ma'am." (l. 34), "One is busy, ma'am" (l. 44)

2. There is a discrepancy between the PM's words towards the Queen and his real thoughts as the third-person narrator presents them. In addition, the dialogue between Sir Kevin and the PM's adviser underlines the contrast between words and action. This creates humour.

M 13 *Do We Really Need the Monarchy?* – Reading an article

Cambridge University student George Danker assesses the advantages and disadvantages of the British Monarchy and questions whether its existence is ideologically acceptable in a modern democratic society.

Task

While reading, underline the advantages and disadvantages of the British Monarchy mentioned in the article in two different colours.

Most people seem to be in favour of the UK remaining as a constitutional monarchy. Earlier this month, 1.2 million people defied the pouring rain to watch the Diamond Jubilee Pageant from
5 the banks of the River Thames – that's around 15% of the population of London. A further 10 million watched the Pageant on television, and the Diamond Jubilee Concert garnered the biggest television audience of the year so far.
10 This is firmly in line with recent polls, which suggest that public support for the monarchy has never been higher; 80% of people want to keep the status quo, with only 13% saying they would rather abolish the Royal Family (Ipsos MORI).

People waving flags and taking photos of the Queen Elizabeth II Diamond Jubilee Pageant in London, 2012.

15 Yet there are uncomfortable questions that remain. Why exactly are the vast majority in favour of the monarchy in this age of democracy? Has the Queen brainwashed the entire nation? Economically, there seems to be no need for a monarch. The Sovereign Grant, which will replace the Civil List from 2013, is expected to be in the region of £34 million per year, although the campaign group Republic claims that the total cost to the taxpayer is closer to £200 million.
20 Many argue that this is merely an investment that reaps rewards for the tourism industry, but according to Visit England, none of the royal residences are in the list of England's top 20 tourist attractions. Indeed, England's most visited historic residence is the Tower of London, which is no longer run by the Crown. If the monarchy were abolished tomorrow, the economy would likely receive a boost from having Buckingham Palace and other residences fully open to fee-
25 paying tourists.

If there is one word that the Diamond Jubilee commentators were keen to ram into the minds of the British public, then it is 'duty'. Of course, it is true that the Queen has rarely, if ever, taken a day off during her 60-year reign, and the same can be said of most of the other senior royals. Perhaps even the staunchest republicans would not deny her this accolade. Yet it is hard
30 to understand why so many, especially those in the media, see this as a sufficient condition for holding the position of Head of State. Is the Queen the most hard-working British citizen? Unlikely. She does incredibly well for an 86-year-old with vast resources, but if Heads of State were appointed based on a sense of 'duty', my vote would go to the single mother of three who works 15 hours a day, every day, to give her children the best possible start in life without
35 relying on government handouts. […]

A more subtle reason for arguing in favour of the status quo is that the alternative, becoming a republic nation, has few concrete advantages. We are already in an age of political apathy, with the most recent local election turnout percentages languishing in the low-30s. […] The fact that the Queen is largely "irrelevant to the political process", as Republic points out, actually seems to be more of a positive than a negative – our Head of State represents the UK, not the ephemeral, often unpopular politics of the UK. She is, quite literally, the face of the nation.

However, the most common arguments for abolishing the monarchy are not economic or political – they are ideological. With an unelected Head of State, our democracy is incomplete, a notion that republicans simply cannot bear, and it is easy to understand why. It doesn't feel particularly fair that one family has privilege and millions of taxpayers' pounds thrust upon them, whilst being totally unaccountable to the outside world. [...]

Perhaps the most important factor in the debate is actually the simplest one; the public feels good about the monarchy. It may well be the case that the Queen has brainwashed the entire nation – the Royal Family probably spends a lot of money on PR – but she is certainly a more revered leader than any of the current political elite. Following the lives of the royals offers a unique brand of escapism that cannot easily be replicated – it is akin to watching a real-life fairytale, or perhaps a very posh version of EastEnders. So do we really need the monarchy? Not really, but that's probably the wrong question. Whatever the reasons may be, we do like the monarchy, and that should be enough for now.

George Danker: Do we really need the monarchy?, © Cambridge Union Society 2012

Vocabulary Aids

2 **constitutional monarchy:** a system in which the monarch's power is very limited because he/she acts on the advice of the politicians who form the government – 3/4 **to defy the pouring rain:** here: to ignore the hard rain – 4 **Diamond Jubilee Pageant:** a ceremony performed outside in honour of the Queen being 60 years on the throne in 2012 – 10 **poll:** a study in which people are asked for their opinions – 12/13 **to keep the status quo:** to change nothing – 14 **to abolish:** to get rid of sth. – 14 **Ipsos MORI:** the name of a market research company – 17/18 **the Sovereign Grant/the Civil List:** the amount of money given by the government to the royal household to support the monarch's official duties – 19 **Republic:** an organisation that criticises monarchy – 21 **Visit England:** the official tourist organisation for England – 24 **boost:** improvement, increase – 26/27 **to ram sth. into the minds of so.:** to repeat constantly so that the listeners will not forget – 29 **staunch:** always loyal – 29 **accolade:** praise – 33 **to appoint so.:** to select so. for an office – 35 **handout:** sth. given to so. who is poor – 37 **apathy:** the feeling of not having much emotion or interest – 38 **election turnout percentages languishing in the low-30s:** the numbers of given votes being unpleasantly around 30 percent for a while – 41 **ephemeral:** lasting only for a short time – 45 **to thrust sth. on so.:** to force so. to accept sth. – 46 **unaccountable:** no one expects you to explain your actions – 50 **revered:** very much respected – 51 **escapism:** an activity that lets you forget about the real problems of life – 51 **to be replicated:** to be made again – 51 **to be akin to:** to be close to – 52 **posh:** typical of people who have a high social status, expensive, high-quality – 52 **EastEnders:** a British soap opera concentrating on the private and professional lives of people in a London neighbourhood

British Monarchy and Modern Democracy (S II)

| Reihe 3 | Verlauf | Material S 31 | LEK | Kontext | Mediothek |

M 14 *Do We Really Need the Monarchy?* – Understanding the article

This worksheet helps you to understand the article better.

Task 1

Tick ☑ the correct finishing of the sentences. Provide proof from the text by naming the line(s).

a) Most British people …
   ☐ consider the monarchy as an outdated system.
   ☐ want to abolish the British monarchy.
   ☐ are happy with the monarchy as it is.

   Line(s): _____

b) The monarch …
   ☐ is the most hard-working person in the UK.
   ☐ owns England's top ten tourist attractions.
   ☐ costs the taxpayer £200 million per year.

   Line(s): _____

c) The most convincing argument for the author against the monarchy is …
   ☐ an economic reason: it saves money.
   ☐ a political reason: people might concentrate more on the politicians than the royal family.
   ☐ an ideological reason: it is undemocratic to give someone power without an election.

   Line(s): _____

Task 2

Are the paraphrased statements from the article true or false? Tick ☑ the correct box and correct the false statement(s) in your exercise books.

Statements	True	False
a) The public watched the Diamond Jubilee festivities outdoors and on TV.	☐	☐
b) The monarch is a symbol of the nation.	☐	☐
c) The royal family watches fairy tales on TV to escape from reality.	☐	☐

Task 3

What are the pros and cons the author of the article mentions as regards monarchy? Complete the chart in your exercise books. Provide proof from the text by naming the line(s).

Pros	Cons
– The royal festivities attract a lot of attention in the media and in the public. (ll. 2–9)	– Republic criticises the fact that the monarch costs about £200 million. (l. 19)
– …	– …

RAAbits Englisch

M 15 *Do We Really Need the Monarchy?* – Writing a letter to the editor

Readers can react to articles from newspapers and magazines by writing a letter to the editor in the form of an actual letter or an email. In the letter to the editor you agree or disagree with the author and express your own opinion in formal language.

Task

You comment on the effect the royal family has on you as a foreigner and tourist. Do you think a monarch is outdated in today's Europe? Or are you fascinated by the British royal traditions? Write a letter to the editor in the form of an actual letter and give reasons for your position.

Step 1: Together with a partner, collect own arguments for and against the British monarchy and write them in a table in your exercise books. You can also add arguments you collected from the article.

Pros	Cons
– British tradition	– Too much pomp
– Unusual and spectacular	– Outdated in modern Europe
– …	– …

Step 2: Read the advice before writing your letter to the editor.

How to write a letter to the editor	
Formal letter	**Formal email**
Write your **address** without your name in the top right corner. Write the address you are writing to on the left. Write the **date** on the right.	Not necessary
Write a **heading** to explain what your letter is about.	Fill in the **subject line** to explain what you are writing about.
Start the main part with: Dear Sir or Madam **Start** the next line with a capital letter like in any sentence.	Start the main body with: Dear Sir or Madam **Start** the next line with a capital letter like in any sentence.
Use formal English. Use long forms (I am, this does not, it will not) instead of short forms (I'm, this doesn't, it won't).	Use formal English. Use long forms (I am, this does not, it will not) instead of short forms (I'm, this doesn't, it won't).
Close by *signing* your letter and typing your name.	**Close** by giving your name, address and phone number.

Step 3: Write your letter to the editor. Afterwards, reread it to check if you have used at least five phrases to express an opinion.

Hinweise (M 13–M 15; 5. Doppelstunde)

In der fünften Doppelstunde geht es um die öffentlich häufig diskutierte **Frage**, ob die **britische Monarchie** noch **zeitgemäß** ist oder abgeschafft werden sollte.

Einstieg: Die Lehrkraft zeigt ein **Foto** vom Kleinkind **Prince George (M 4)** über den Overheadprojektor oder Beamer. Als Impuls stellt sie folgende Fragen: *Do you think Prince George will really be the future king of the UK? Will the UK still be a monarchy when he has grown up?*

Mit dem **Kommentar** aus der Huffington Post **(M 13)** erarbeiten die Schüler einige **Vor-** und **Nachteile** der **britischen Monarchie**, die der Autor George Danker in seinem Artikel anführt. Das Vokabular des Textes und seine Länge sind anspruchsvoll. Deshalb wenden die Schüler ihre **Lesekompetenz** schrittweise mithilfe von **M 14** an, indem sie **geschlossene** und **halboffene Aufgabenformate** zum Textverständnis in Partnerarbeit lösen. Die Ergebnisse werden im Plenum gesichert.

In der zweiten Hälfte der Doppelstunde ergänzen die Schüler die Ergebnisse aus M 14, *task 3* um ihre Sichtweise **(M 15)**. Dies hat zum Ziel, dass sie später einen kommentierenden Leserbrief schreiben. Die Lernenden sammeln in Partnerarbeit eigene **Argumente** für beziehungsweise gegen die Monarchie (*step 1*), lesen zur Wiederholung, welche **Elemente** ein Leserbrief enthält (*step 2*) und wenden das Wissen beim Schreiben eines *letter to the editor* in Einzelarbeit an (*step 3*). Am Ende der Stunde lesen mindestens zwei Schüler ihre Briefe im Plenum vor. Die Briefe werden gemeinsam im Unterrichtsgespräch auf Format, inhaltliche Argumente und Redemittel zur Meinungsäußerung geprüft.

Differenzierung: Für lernschwächere Schüler steht auf der **CD Grundwerk** ein *language support* mit Redemitteln für die Meinungsäußerung bereit (Language support_useful phrases to express an opinion.doc).

Tipp: Je nach Lernstärke des Kurses bietet es sich an, nach dem Sammeln der Argumente in Partnerarbeit (*step 1*) eine kurze mündliche Diskussion im Plenum durchzuführen. Dies unterstützt die schwächeren Schüler, genügend Argumente zu sammeln.

Erwartungshorizont (M 14)

1. Correct finishing of the sentences:
   a) Most British people are happy with the monarchy as it is.
      "Most people [...] monarchy." (ll. 1/2)
   b) The monarch costs the taxpayer £200 million per year.
      "The Sovereign Grant [...] million per year" (ll. 17/18)
   c) The most convincing argument for the author against the monarchy is an ideological reason: it is undemocratic to give someone power without an election.
      "With an unelected [...] incomplete" (l. 43)

2. Correct answers:
   a) True
   b) True
   c) False: For many people, the royal family's life is like a fairy tale.

3. Arguments for and against British monarchy from the article:

Pros	Cons
– The royal festivities attract a lot of attention in the media and in the public: "Earlier this month [...] television audience of the year so far." (ll. 2–9)	– Republic criticises the fact that the monarch costs about £200 million: "although the campaign group [...] £200 million." (ll. 18/19)
– It is good value for money as it attracts tourists: "Many argue [...] tourism industry" (l. 20)	– The royal residences are not among England's top 20 tourist attractions: "but according to [...] top 20 tourist attractions." (ll. 20–22)
– The Queen is hard-working: "Of course, it is true that [...] senior royals." (ll. 27–29)	– The economy would benefit if the royal residences were fully opened to tourists: "If the monarchy were [...] fee-paying tourists." (ll. 23–25)
– There are no advantages in a republic in an age of political apathy: "A more subtle [...] the face of the nation." (ll. 36–41)	– There are other hard-working people: "Is the Queen the most hard-working [...] handouts." (ll. 31–35)
– The public feels good about the monarchy; the Queen is a revered leader: "the public feels [...] we do like the monarchy" (ll. 47–54)	– The Head of State is not elected; an unfair process, a privilege: "With an unelected [...] outside world." (ll. 43–46)
– The royal family life is like a fairy tale: "It may well be [...] EastEnders." (ll. 48–52)	

Erwartungshorizont (M 15)

Step 1: Examples of own arguments for and against the British monarchy:

Pros	Cons
– It's a symbol of the British identity. – The monarch creates income from the royal buildings, farmlands etc. → Earns money, is a tourist attraction – The monarchy sets the UK apart from some other European countries. It is like a trademark. – The members of the royal family are like stars, leading a life of glamour and style; many people are interested in their private lives. → Good for people's interest in the UK, too.	– It is unfair that you can only be born into the position of the monarch (hereditary principle). – The monarch does not exercise any real political power. – It does not make sense that the Head of State is chosen because of birthright instead of competence. – The UK could earn much more money if the royal places were accessible to the public all year round like in France. – The private scandals of the members of the royal family damage the UK's reputation. – The British nation could still celebrate its traditions without a monarch as many other European countries do.

Step 3: Example of a letter to the editor:

An der Kalwei 16
40325 Düsseldorf
00 49 2 11 24 35 53 29

Huffington Post

24th July 2012

Article *Do We Really Need the Monarchy*, 2nd July 2012 by George Danker

Dear Sir or Madam

With reference to your article of 2nd July 2012, *Do We Really Need the Monarchy*, I would like to add my ideas to the topic. The author George Danker has my full support when he argues that the Queen represents the face of the nation. As far as I see it as a German pupil, the Queen is well-known by everyone. Many people are interested in visiting the UK because they want to see Buckingham Palace, the Tower of London and the Changing of the Guards. In my opinion, only a few pupils my age know the British Prime Minister's name, for example.

However, the reason that the British people love the monarchy is not convincing. I find it hard to believe that you are happy to pay a lot of money for the royal family's garden parties, palaces etc. in times of economic crisis.

Nowadays, it seems very old-fashioned to have a country with a monarchy in Europe. Admittedly, there are several examples like the Netherlands and Sweden. Still, I believe that European countries should overcome outdated principles where you gain a high position just by being born into it. Representative roles should be played by people that have shown their competence in the first place, such as with ambassadors, not to mention the German Chancellor who is also well-known all over Europe.
Finally, I would like to mention France, a former monarchy, where people still celebrate traditions and respect royal residences without the need of a monarch.

Yours faithfully

Anne Reinhold

Anne Reinhold

The Uncommon Reader – the appeal of reading

In The Uncommon Reader *the Queen develops a passion for reading. Her family and her advisers do not like her new hobby because the Queen has started to neglect her duties. In the extract, her equerry Sir Kevin, who is from New Zealand, advises the Queen to concentrate on her priorities.*

"It's important", said Sir Kevin, "that Your Majesty should stay focused. [...] I can understand", he said, "Your Majesty's need to pass the time."

"Pass the time?" said the Queen. "Books are not about passing the time. They're about other lives. Other worlds. Far from wanting time to pass, Sir Kevin, one just wishes one had more of it. If one wanted to pass
5 the time one could go to New Zealand."

With two mentions of his name and one of New Zealand Sir Kevin retired hurt. Still, he had made a point and he would have been gratified to know that it left the Queen troubled, and wondering why it was that at this particular time in her life she had suddenly felt the pull of books. Where had this appetite come from? Few people, after all, had seen more of the world than she had. There was scarcely a country she had not
10 visited, a notability she had not met. Herself part of the panoply of the world, why now was she intrigued by books which, whatever else they might be, were just a reflection of the world or a version of it? Books? She had seen the real thing.

"I read, I think," she said to Norman, "because one has a duty to find out what people are like," a trite enough remark of which Norman took not much notice, feeling himself under no such obligation and reading purely
15 for pleasure, not enlightenment, though part of the pleasure was the enlightenment, he could see that. But duty did not come into it.

To someone with the background of the Queen, though, pleasure had always taken second place to duty. If she could feel she had a duty to read then she could set about it with a clear conscience, with the pleasure, if pleasure there was, incidental. But why did it take possession of her now? This she did not discuss with
20 Norman, as she felt it had to do with who she was and the position she occupied.

The appeal of reading, she thought, lay in its indifference: there was something lofty about literature. Books did not care who was reading them or whether one read them or not. All readers were equal, herself included. Literature, she thought, is a commonwealth; letters a republic. Actually she had heard this phrase, the republic of letters, used before, at graduation ceremonies, honorary degrees and the like, though without knowing
25 quite what it meant. At that time talk of a republic of any sort she had thought mildly insulting and in her actual presence tactless to say the least. It was only now she understood what it meant. Books did not defer. [...]. It [reading] was anonymous; it was shared; it was common. And she who had led a life apart now found that she craved it. Here in these pages and between these covers she could go unrecognised.

Alan Bennett: The Uncommon Reader. Profile Books London 2008, pp. 38–41.

6 **to make a point:** to express one's opinion clearly – 7 **to be gratified:** to be very happy – 8 **to feel the pull of sth.:** to feel attracted by sth. – 10 **notability:** well-known person – 10 **panoply:** impressive group of people – 13 **trite:** *abgedroschen, banal* – 14 **obligation:** duty – 15 **enlightenment:** understanding – 18 **to set about sth.:** to start doing sth. – 19 **incidental:** secondary, accidental – 21 **lofty:** arrogant – 23 **commonwealth:** here: pun with the term „common wealth", sth. that belongs to everyone – 23 **letters (pl.):** world of literature, all literary works – 23/24 **republic of letters:** a country of academics without a king/queen – 24 **honorary degree:** event when an academic title is given as an honour – 26 **to say the least:** to put it mildly – 26 **to defer:** to give in, to adapt – 28 **to crave sth.:** to long for sth., to have a strong feeling of wanting sth.

Tasks

1. Briefly sum up what the Queen thinks and feels about reading and her life.
2. Analyse the way in which the Queen is portrayed in this excerpt by examining the language and the narrative techniques.
3. In March 2015, Natalie Bennett, the Green Party leader, stated she would support a referendum on the abolition of the monarchy. Imagine you are a press reporter from *The Guardian* and question Mrs Bennett on her position. Write the interview. Make sure your interviewee explains what she thinks about typical counter-arguments by the supporters of the monarchy as well.

British Monarchy and Modern Democracy (S II)

| Reihe 3 | Verlauf | Material | **LEK** S 2 | Kontext | Mediothek |

II/C4

Hinweise (LEK)

Der Klausurvorschlag ist für den Grundkurs konzipiert und setzt zur Bearbeitung zwei bis drei Stunden voraus. In dem **Textausschnitt** aus *„The Uncommon Reader"* überlegt die Queen, warum sie vom Lesen so in den Bann gezogen wird, und kontrastiert das Lesen mit ihren königlichen Verpflichtungen und Werten. Die Textlänge mit circa 490 Wörtern ist angemessen. Vokabelhilfen entlasten das Verständnis. Die Schüler erarbeiten den Inhalt (*comprehension: summary*), deuten den Text (*analysis*) und nehmen Stellung, indem sie ein Interview zur Frage verfassen, ob die Monarchie abgeschafft werden sollte (*evaluation: recreation of the text*). Als Hilfsmittel stehen ein ein- sowie ein zweisprachiges Wörterbuch zur Verfügung.

Differenzierung: Ist Ihre Lerngruppe in der Analyse rhetorischer Mittel geübt, so kann in *task 2* der Erwartungshorizont um diesen Aspekt erweitert werden. Eine entsprechende Ergänzung des Erwartungshorizonts finden Sie auf der **CD Grundwerk** (Zusatz_Erwartungshorizont LEK_Rhetorical devices. doc).

Erwartungshorizont (LEK)

1. Summary
   – She does not read to pass the time.
   – She wonders why she has developed such a passion for reading at her age.
   – She has travelled the world and met lots of famous people.
   – She wants to find out what people are like and sees reading as a duty.
   – She has always followed her duties first.
   – She feels attracted by books because it makes her become common like any other reader.

2. Analysis
   – Omniscient third-person narrator who informs the reader about the Queen's, Sir Kevin's and Norman's feelings.
   – Interior monologue: rhetorical questions, ellipsis typical of spoken English → To see something through the eyes of the character.
   – The Queen repeats Sir Kevin's question (l. 3 "Pass the time?"). → To contradict Sir Kevin, to show her surprise.
   – Neutral, standard English
   – Ironic, offending tone towards Sir Kevin (ll. 4/5 "If one wanted [...] New Zealand.").
   – The narrator tells the reader explicitly that Sir Kevin would be pleased to know that he had worried the Queen (ll. 6–8 "Still, he had made a point [...] books."). → The Queen and Sir Kevin have a tense relationship but are rather neutral on the surface.
   – A passage of direct speech towards Norman (ll. 13–16 "I read, I think [...] come into it.") "→ To render the Queen's thoughts and feelings more vividly for the reader; to initiate her reflections on her reading passion and her look back on her unique life.
   – The narrator comments on Norman's and Sir Kevin's attitudes towards reading (ll. 1/2, "I can understand [...] pass the time."; ll. 13–16, "I read, I think [...] he could see that. But duty did not come into it."). → To contrast the characters' attitudes towards reading with the Queen's attitude, to raise the question for the reader whether reading is for distraction, pleasure or information.

- The Queen shares some thoughts with Norman, but not all her thoughts (ll. 17–20: "To someone with […] position she occupied."). → Her action underlines her special social position apart from her subjects; in general, she trusts Norman but prefers to keep delicate thoughts to herself. → Trustful and cautious behaviour; she also emphasises her obligation towards duty.
- In the Queen's interior monologue in the last two paragraphs, she ponders about the importance of literature and why it affects her so much (ll. 17–28: "To someone with […] unrecognised"). → Her reflections show that she tries to understand her fascination for literature and thus herself better; she is clever; she discovers that she truly longs to be like anyone else without being discovered.
- She refers back to her experiences in life by using words like commonwealth, country visits, ceremonies and degrees. → The word choice refers to her typical tasks.
- The indirect monologue reveals that she dislikes being reminded of a republic (ll. 23–25: "Literature, she thought […] what it meant."). → She does not like criticism of the monarchy.

3. Evaluation: example of an interview

   A: Welcome, Mrs Bennett, thank you for coming and taking part in this interview.

   B: Thank you for the opportunity to tell your readers more about our plans for the political future in the UK.

   A: To start off, tell us something about yourself and your plans for the future.

   B: I am Natalie Bennett, the Green Party leader. I firmly believe we need a new political system without a royal family.

   A: Why do you think so?

   B: To my mind the royal system is undemocratic. You don't get elected into the royal family, you get born into it and instantly have more power than any normal citizen. This is undemocratic. I favour an elected president.

   A: Oh, that is very radical. The royal family offers the nation also a lot of advantages such as money from tourism. What do you think about that?

   B: In my opinion, tourists don't come to Britain to see the royal family. They want to see the royal buildings which are maintained by our taxes. Let me explain in detail. If we abolish monarchy, we will not destroy the buildings, the tourists will still come. And if there are no mugs with the Queen's face, people will buy mugs with Sherlock Holmes's or Wayne Rooney's face. So I don't think we'll lose any income.

   A: That sounds logical, but don't you think that the Queen is a British symbol known worldwide?

   B: Fish and chips are also typically British.

   A: Well, what makes you criticise our best-known symbol, famous worldwide?

   B: I am glad you asked the question. Personally, I quite like the Queen's service and duty. I appreciate her because she symbolises British continuity. But who will be the next in line to the throne? We need to stop monarchy before it is too late and there will be a tyrant working against the government one day. We have to act now! And we want the people to decide on the question, not one privileged family.

   A: Thank you for sharing your opinion and ideas concerning the future of the British constitution.

   B: You're welcome. Thank you for the chance to speak to you.

Mediothek

Primärtext

Bennett, Alan: The Uncommon Reader. Ernst Kemmner (Hrsg.). Stuttgart: Reclam 2009.

Annotierte, ungekürzte und unveränderte Ausgabe. Das Nachwort bietet einen hervorragenden Überblick über die Novelle.

Erhältlich u. a. bei www.amazon.de für ca. 5 € (ISBN 978-3150197622).

Sekundärliteratur

O'Driscoll, James: Britain for learners of English. Oxford: Oxford University ELT (2. Auflage) 2009.

Das Lehrbuch auf Englisch bietet klar gegliedert informatives Kulturwissen über Großbritannien.

Erhältlich u. a. bei www.amazon.de für ca. 26,99 € (ISBN 978-0194306447).

Petermeier, Andreas: Britain's Past and Present. From Empire to Commonwealth. Stuttgart: Klett 2014.

Ein Lehrerhandbuch zum Thema „Großbritannien" mit vielen Unterrichtsanregungen.

Erhältlich bei Ernst Klett Sprachen für ca. 19,99 € (ISBN 978-3-12-513581-9).

Schoeneberg, Victoria und Sprunkel, Marc: The Uncommon Reader. Teacher's Manual. Berlin: Cornelsen 2014.

Lehrkräfte die sich entscheiden, den Kurzroman vollständig im Unterricht zu bearbeiten, finden hier lektüreübergreifende Unterrichtsmaterialien.

Erhältlich bei Cornelsen für ca. 16,25 € (ISBN 978-3-06-033471-1).

Hörbuch

Bennett, Alan: The Uncommon Reader. Audio CD. London: BBC Audio 2007.

Eine verlängerte Version von Alan Bennetts BBC 4 Lesung.

Erhältlich u. a. bei www.amazon.de für ca. 28,40 € (ISBN 978-1405687478).

Internetseite

www.royal.gov.uk

Die offizielle Seite des Königshauses bietet unter anderem zahlreiche Informationen über die Monarchie, die Aufgaben der Monarchin, Reden und Videos.

From Rags to Riches? – The American Dream Revisited –
Eine Landeskundereihe für die Oberstufe (S II)

Ekkehard Sprenger, Preetz

Der *American Dream* in Gefahr? Straßenprotest in Washington

Worin besteht der *American Dream*? Was bedeutet er für den einzelnen Amerikaner? Und gibt es ihn heute überhaupt noch?

Die Reihe ermöglicht den Schülern in literarischen und expositorischen Texten eine Auseinandersetzung mit den unterschiedlichsten Perspektiven auf den *American Dream*. Auch ein vergleichender Blick nach Europa wird gewagt: Träumen wir Europäer etwa den besseren Traum?

Die Lernenden erhalten vielfach die Gelegenheit, ihr Selbst- und Fremdbild zu hinterfragen, und sich sowohl mit Klischees als auch mit der amerikanischen Realität auseinanderzusetzen.

Klassenstufe: 11/12 (G8); 12/13 (G9)

Dauer: ca. 8 Doppelstunden

Bereich: Landeskunde USA, *American Dream*, Lebensentwürfe von Immigranten

Kompetenzen:

1. Umgang mit Texten: analytische Auseinandersetzung mit unterschiedlichen Textsorten
2. Methodenkompetenz: kooperatives Lernen
3. Interkulturelle Kompetenz: den Entwurf und die Bedeutung des amerikanischen Traums anhand ausgewählter literarischer Beispiele nachvollziehen und mit den eigenen Lebensentwürfen vergleichen

Sachanalyse

The American Dream – jeder Amerikaner scheint instinktiv zu wissen, was dieses Konzept bedeutet. Der *American Dream* verheißt, dass jeder Amerikaner, in einem Wettstreit um die guten Dinge des Lebens, eine faire Chance hat. Diese „guten Dinge des Lebens" wurden seit Ende des ersten Weltkriegs vor allem definiert als Wohlstand, Einfluss, Sicherheit und Lebensglück und rückten bis zum Anfang dieses Jahrhunderts immer mehr in den Vordergrund. Das Versprechen des amerikanischen Traums war stets, dass alle, die bereit sind, hart zu arbeiten, Neues zu erlernen, durchzuhalten und nach den Gesetzen zu leben, in den USA eine bessere Chance auf Aufstieg und Wohlstand haben als irgendwo anders auf der Welt.

Die ursprüngliche Idee des American Dream

Die Idee des amerikanischen Traumes ist außerordentlich vielschichtig und hatte zu unterschiedlichen Zeiten verschiedene Bedeutungsschwerpunkte. Es besteht jedoch Einigkeit darüber, dass die Begriffe **Freiheit, Individualität und Gleichheit** schon lange und tief im amerikanischen Traum verwurzelt sind. Bereits in der amerikanischen Unabhängigkeitserklärung von 1776 heißt es: *„We hold these truths to be self-evident, that all men are created equal, that they are endowed by their Creator with certain unalienable rights; that among these are Life, Liberty, and the pursuit of Happiness."*

Wenn Johann Wolfgang von **Goethe** später in seinem Werk „Den Vereinigten Staaten" (1827) sagt: „Amerika, du hast es besser als unser Kontinent", dann mag er an die Unabhängigkeit von der Willkür der Kirche oder des Staates gedacht haben, die in Europa noch vorherrschte. Auch **Emma Lazarus** nennt in ihrem berühmten Gedicht *„The New Colossus"* (1883) Freiheit als wesentlichen Anreiz dafür, in die USA zu emigrieren. In ihrem Gedicht fordert der neue Kontinent den alten auf, ihm all diejenigen Menschen zu schicken, die unglücklich und unterdrückt sind: *„Give me your tired, your poor, your huddled masses yearning to breathe free"*. Die versprochene Freiheit und das Streben nach Verwirklichung persönlicher Visionen ist schließlich auch die Motivation zahlloser Einwanderer, die in den USA ein neues Leben beginnen.

Der American Dream im Wandel der Zeit

1931 subsumiert James Truslow Adams all diese Ideale und Wünsche erstmalig unter dem **Begriff American Dream**: *„The American dream [is] the dream of a land in which life should be better and richer and fuller for everyman, with opportunity for each according to his ability or achievement. [...] It is not a dream of motor cars and high wages merely, but a dream of social order in which each man and each woman shall be able to attain to the fullest stature of which they are innately capable, and be recognized by others for what they are, regardless of the fortuitous circumstances of birth or position."* (James Truslow Adams, *The Epic of America*, 1931, S. 404)

Zu Zeiten James Truslows bildet demnach immer noch die idealistische Vorstellung von Gleichheit und sozialem Aufstieg den Kern dieses Traums, doch materielle Aspekte spielen nach und nach eine immer größere Rolle. So haben viele Menschen nach den Wirren des **2. Weltkriegs** das Bedürfnis nach Sicherheit und Wohlstand. Daher stehen zu dieser Zeit materielle Güter wie Autos, Eigenheime und Fernsehapparate für die Erfüllung des amerikanischen Traums.

Als Reaktion auf dieses materiell orientierte *establishment* leben in den 60er- und 70er-Jahren des 20. Jahrhunderts viele junge Erwachsene als Hippies den Traum indvidueller Freiheit, indem sie sich von bürgerlichen Zwängen lossagen. Aus der Auflehnung gegen bestehende Ordnungen und Traditionen entsteht Raum für die **Bürgerrechtler der 1960er-Jahre**, die von der Gleichheit aller vor dem Gesetz träumen. Bis dahin hatte, beispielsweise, die soziale Unterdrückung des afro-amerikanischen Teils der Gesellschaft im krassen Gegensatz zu der gesetzlich verankerten Gleichheit aller gestanden. Der Bürgerrechtler Martin Luther King bezieht sich in seiner bekannten Rede „I have a dream" auf die Unabhängigkeitserklärung und den amerikanischen Traum, wenn er sagt: „ [...] I still have a dream. It is a dream deeply rooted in the American dream. I have a dream that one day this nation will rise up and live out the true meaning of its creed: 'We hold these truths to be self-evident: that all men are created equal.'"

2009 dürfte sein amerikanischer Traum mit der Vereidigung Barack Obamas als erster schwarzer Präsident der Vereinigten Staaten abermals ein großes Stück näher gerückt sein.

Der American Dream heute – glauben die Amerikaner noch daran?

Das Herzstück des amerikanischen Traums war stets die Verheißung, dass alle Menschen, ungeachtet ihrer Herkunft, sich auf der sozialen Leiter nach oben bewegen können. An diesem Glauben halten auch heute noch viele Amerikaner fest. Doch ist es wahr, dass alle Menschen in den USA gleichberechtigt nach der Verwirklichung ihrer Träume und Ziele streben können?

Neuere Untersuchungen belegen, dass die Frage nach der **sozialen Mobilität** innerhalb der, offziell als sehr durchlässig geltenden, Gesellschaft differenziert zu betrachten ist. Zwar sind viele Amerikaner auch heute noch davon überzeugt, dass die persönliche soziale und ökonomische Herkunft für einen Aufstieg in den USA weniger bedeutsam ist als in Europa, doch wirft man einen genaueren Blick auf „die Amerikaner" und die aktuelle wirtschaftliche Lage nach der 2007 beginnenden Rezession, wird schnell deutlich, dass der optimistische Glaube an den amerikanischen *spirit* vorwiegend auf den Teil der Gesellschaft zutrifft, der ohnehin sozial und ökonomisch wohlauf ist. Der Grund dafür mag darin liegen, dass die Aufstiegswahrscheinlichkeit der Kinder der jetzigen Elterngeneration in den Vereinigten Staaten signifikant geringer ist als in vergleichbaren Staaten Europas.[1]

Aktuellen Umfragen zufolge scheint dieses Bewusstsein der **ökonomisch-sozialen Undurchlässigkeit** und der generellen wirtschaftlichen Schieflage zu denjenigen Amerikanern durchgedrungen zu sein, die von dieser am meisten betroffen sind: 44 % aller arbeitslosen Amerikaner glauben nicht, den *American Dream* noch verwirklichen zu können **(M 9)**. Viele solcher Studien haben jedoch laut dem Wirtschaftswissenschaftler Gary Burtless und dem ehemaligen Berater für soziale Fragen des Weißen Hauses, Ron Haskins, nur einen begrenzten Wert.

Die beiden Autoren eines Buches über ökonomische Mobilität in den USA weisen darauf hin, dass vielfach **Einwanderer** in den Studien nicht berücksichtigt werden. Diese jedoch weisen nach ihrer Einwanderung in die USA einen beträchtlichen Einkommenszuwachs und damit verbunden einen erheblichen sozialen Aufstieg im Vergleich zum Status in ihren Herkunftsländern auf. Studien, die sich vor allem auf Menschen konzentrieren, deren Eltern bereits US-Bürger waren, übersehen damit die in diesem Vergleich überaus beachtliche soziale Mobilität, die zumindest für viele Immigranten aus ökonomisch schwachen Ländern immer noch den Mittelpunkt des amerikanischen Traumes bildet.[2]

Dennoch verwundert es nicht, wenn neuere Untersuchungen belegen, dass der Mythos „from rags to riches", der immer noch Tausende Migranten in die USA lockt, in Zeiten der wirtschaftlichen Krise zunehmend ersetzt wird durch **„the rich get richer" (M 9)**. 2010 verdienten die Spitzensteuerzahler, die nur ein Prozent der amerikanischen Gesellschaft bilden, 93 % des Gesamteinkommens der USA, während die anderen 99 % immer noch mühsam versuchten, sich von der Rezession zu erholen. Mehr und mehr Stimmen gegen diese soziale und ökonomische Ungerechtigkeit werden laut. So wurde 2011 beispielsweise die *Occupy-Wall-Street*-Bewegung ins Leben gerufen, bei der sich Tausende an öffentlichen Plätzen zusammenfanden, um gegen die wirtschaftlichen Unverhältnismäßigkeiten zu demonstrieren.

---

1 DeParle, Jason: Harder for Americans to Rise from Lower Rungs. In: The New York Times, January 4, 2012.
2 Burtless, Gary und Haskins, Ron: Inequality, Economic Mobility, and Social Policy. In: Schuck, Peter H. und Wilson, James Q. (Hg.): Understanding America – The Anatomy of an Exceptional Nation. New York: Public Affairs 2008. S. 516.

Die Frage: „Lebt der amerikanische Traum noch?" kann demnach nicht eindeutig beantwortet werden. Es scheint, als gelte der Traum von Freiheit und Glück vor allem für die Einwanderer, die noch immer das Herzstück des *American Dream* leben. Für die im Zuge der Weltwirtschaftskrise immer kleiner werdende Mittelschicht, scheint er sich zu der Hoffnung auf einen sicheren Job und den Besitz eines Autos dezimiert zu haben.

Didaktisch-methodisches Konzept

Zur Lerngruppe

Die Unterrichtsreihe ist je nach Kompetenzstand der Lerngruppe sowohl für einen Leistungskurs als auch für einen Grundkurs geeignet. Im Grundkurs können zum Beispiel die anspruchsvolleren Materialien M 5 sowie M 10 gestrichen werden.

Zur Methodik

Die Herangehensweise an das Thema orientiert sich vor allem an der Methode des **kooperativen Lernens**. Die Lernenden handeln dabei eine Beziehung zum Text in Partner- oder Gruppenarbeit aus, bevor die Ergebnisse dann im Plenum erörtert und gesichert werden. Die Konzeption der Aufgabenapparate richtet sich sehr klar nach der **Dreischrittigkeit der Abituraufgaben.** Zusätzlich wird zu jedem Text eine Einführungsaufgabe angeboten. Die Aufgaben weisen stets **Operatoren** auf und nutzen zudem **grafische Lernhilfen**, um optimales Lernen zu ermöglichen.

Nachhaltiges Lernen kann nur gelingen, wenn die Lerngruppe motiviert ist. Daher wird jeder Text mit einer *pre-reading* Aufgabe (**Approaching the text**) eingeleitet. Diese Aufgaben haben zum Ziel, das Vorwissen der Schülerinnen und Schüler zu aktivieren, eine Erwartungshaltung an den Text zu generieren und die Lernenden emotional zu beteiligen.

Der zweite Aufgabenbereich (**Understanding the text**) fordert von der Lerngruppe ein Verstehen auf der referenziellen Ebene (*comprehension*) und lässt sie Schlussfolgerungen ziehen.

Die Analyseaufgaben (**Studying the text**) zielen darauf, mit den Schülerinnen und Schülern die für das Abitur erforderlichen Techniken zu trainieren.

Die *post-reading* Aufgaben (**Going beyond the text**) schließlich sind unterteilt in eher textorientierte Aufgaben und solche, die sich am Reihenthema orientieren.

Zur Schwerpunktsetzung

Das Thema *„The American Dream"* ist ein Standardthema im Englischunterricht der gymnasialen Oberstufe. Die Texte dieser Unterrichtsreihe geben den Lernenden die Möglichkeit, ausgewählte Aspekte des amerikanischen Traumes klar und eindeutig zu erfassen.

Der **Einstieg** in das Thema erfolgt über die Auseinandersetzung mit **Zitaten** aus unterschiedlichen Jahrhunderten (**M 2**) und eine Internetrecherche, bei der Informationen zu berühmten Persönlichkeiten gesammelt werden, deren Lebensgeschichten Elemente der klassischen *Rags-to-riches*-Story aufweisen. Die Aktivierung von Vorwissen (Zitate) und die Auseinandersetzung mit persönlichen Schicksalen helfen den Schülerinnen und Schülern, einen emotionalen Zugang zum Thema zu finden.

In der zweiten und dritten Doppelstunde machen sich die Lernenden mit einigen **grundlegenden Gedanken des amerikanischen Traumes** vertraut. Auszüge aus Anzia Yezierskas **Kurzgeschichte** *„The Miracle"* (**M 4**) und Teile eines **Essays (M 5)** von William Faulkner zeigen vehement und sehr emotional auf, dass die Befreiung aus gewohnten Zwängen die ursprünglich treibende Kraft vieler Auswanderer war.

In den darauffolgenden zwei Doppelstunden befassen sich die Schülerinnen und Schüler mit der grundlegenden Idee des *American Dream*, dass **Bildung und harte Arbeit** der

From Rags to Riches? – The American Dream Revisited (S II)

| Reihe 6 S 5 | Verlauf | Material | LEK | Kontext | Mediothek |

Schlüssel zum Erfolg sind. So schildert Mike Rose in seinem **Reisebericht (M 6)**, wie der mexikanische Migrant Pablo spontan entscheidet, dass sich sein Leben ändern muss und mehr als nur die Erntearbeit auf den Feldern beinhalten soll. Das lyrische Ich in Martín Espadas Gedicht *„Who Burns for the Perfection of Paper"* **(M 7)** weiß rückblickend, dass Erfolg oft nur mit schmerzhaften Erfahrungen und harter Arbeit erreichbar ist.

Thema der 6. Doppelstunde ist die **Kluft zwischen Traditionen** des Heimatlandes und dem „modernen" Leben in den USA. In dem Auszug aus ihrem Roman *„Girl in Translation"* **(M 8)** beschreibt Jean Kwok aus der Perspektive einer jungen und mutigen chinesischen Amerikanerin, wie es gelingen kann, sich auch als asiatische Frau von traditionellen Rollenbildern zu emanzipieren.

Im **letzten Teil** der Reihe geht es darum, ob Amerikaner **heute** noch an den **American Dream (M 9)** glauben und ob das Erklimmen der *social ladder* wirklich für jeden möglich ist. Die Abschlussstunde wirft einen vergleichenden Blick nach **Europa (M 10)**. Hier setzen sich die Schülerinnen und Schüler mit der Frage auseinander, ob es auch einen *European Dream* gibt und wie sich dieser vom *American Dream* unterscheidet.

II/C5

Schematische Verlaufsübersicht

From Rags to Riches? – The American Dream Revisited – Eine Unterrichtseinheit für die Oberstufe (S II)

1.	**Doppelstunde**	Connecting to the topic – analysing quotations and life stories
2.	**Doppelstunde**	Immigration – living on hopes and dreams
3.	**Doppelstunde**	The original idea of the American Dream – what was it all about?
4.	**Doppelstunde**	Education – a key to the American Dream
5.	**Doppelstunde**	Hard work will get you there – realising the American Dream
6.	**Doppelstunde**	Off to new horizons! – Breaking with old traditions
7.	**Doppelstunde**	The American Dream today – does it still exist?
8.	**Doppelstunde**	Is there a European Dream?

1. Doppelstunde

Thema
Connecting to the topic – analysing quotations and life stories

Material	Verlauf
M 1, OHP	**Picture stimulus: Statue of Liberty** / Reaktivierung von Vorwissen zum *American Dream* anhand eines Bildes
M 2	**Connecting to the topic – analysing quotations** / Reaktivierung von Vorwissen zum *American Dream* anhand von Zitaten
M 3	**Presenting living examples of the American Dream** / Internetrecherche zu bekannten Persönlichkeiten, die den *American Dream* leben; Präsentation der Ergebnisse
Zusätzlich benötigtes Material: Internetzugang, um die Lebensgeschichten der bekannten Personen recherchieren zu können	

From Rags to Riches? – The American Dream Revisited (S II)

| Reihe 6 S 6 | Verlauf | Material | LEK | Kontext | Mediothek |

2. Doppelstunde

Thema
Immigration – living on hopes and dreams

Material	Verlauf
M 4	**Acting it out – an instant drama** / Einfühlen in die Situation amerikanischer Immigranten durch ein Rollenspiel
	Analysing an excerpt of a short story / Analyse ausgewählter Aspekte einer Kurzgeschichte von Anzia Yezierska

3. Doppelstunde

Thema
The original idea of the American Dream – what was it all about?

Material	Verlauf
M 5	**Working with a wordle** / Wortschatzarbeit mithilfe eines *wordle* zum Themengebiet *American Dream*
	Discussing the original idea of the American Dream / Stellungnahme zu grundlegenden Aspekten des *American Dream* nach Faulkner

4. Doppelstunde

Thema
Education – a key to the American Dream

Material	Verlauf
M 1, M 6, OHP	**Linking two pictures** / Herstellen einer *forced relationship* zwischen zwei Bildimpulsen
	Expressing a sequence / Erstellen einer Grafik zu einem Textausschnitt
	Making a statement / Begründet zu einem Textauszug Stellung nehmen
	A class discussion / Diskussion zum Thema „Auswandern"

5. Doppelstunde

Thema
Hard work will get you there – realising the American Dream

Material	Verlauf
M 7	**"No pain, no gain." Debating a saying** / Kontroverse als Einstieg in das Stundenthema
	Analysing a poem / Analyse des Gedichts „Who Burns for the Perfection of Paper"
	Finding an alternative title / Überlegungen zum Titel des Gedichts anstellen und alternative Ideen begründet äußern
Zusätzlich benötigtes Material: Büro- oder Wäscheklammern, damit die Einstellung zur Kontroverse an das Oberteil geheftet werden kann; Placemat in DIN-A3-Format	

From Rags to Riches? – The American Dream Revisited (S II)

| Reihe 6 S 7 | Verlauf | Material | LEK | Kontext | Mediothek |

6. Doppelstunde

Thema
Off to new horizons! – Breaking with old traditions

Material	Verlauf
M 8	**What's the text about?** / Überlegungen zum Inhalt einer Textpassage anhand von Bildern anstellen
	Analysing an excerpt from *Girl in Translation* / Anfertigung einer grafischen Darstellung zu der Textpassage; Analyse des Romanauszugs
	Reader's theatre / Darbietung der eigenen Interpretation des Romanausschnitts durch expressives Lesen (fakultativ)

7. Doppelstunde

Thema
The American Dream today – does it still exist?

Material	Verlauf
M 1, M 9, OHP	**Save the American Dream because …** / Deutung eines Bildimpulses und Vervollständigung von Sätzen zum Thema *Save the American Dream*
	Looking at some data / Auswertung und Vergleich von Statistiken zur ökonomischen Mobilität in den USA und zum *American Dream* heute
	Discussion: Achieving the American Dream – is it still possible for everyone? / Erarbeitung einer Position und Argumentation; Plenumsdiskussion

8. Doppelstunde

Thema
Is there a European Dream?

Material	Verlauf
M 10	**Matching words: Describing America and Europe** / Zuordnen von Attributen auf einer Skala
	The American Dream vs the European Dream / Gegenüberstellung von *American Dream* und europäischem Traum anhand eines Textausschnitts
M 11	**How to write an essay** / Nützliche Tipps für das Verfassen eines *essays*
	Homework: *Write an essay on "Is there a German Dream?"*

From Rags to Riches? – The American Dream Revisited (S II)

Materialübersicht

1. Doppelstunde:	**Connecting to the topic – analysing quotations and life stories**
M 1 (Bd)	Picture stimulus for the unit
M 2 (Ab)	About the American Dream – analysing quotations
M 3 (Ab)	Presenting living examples of the American Dream
2. Doppelstunde:	**Immigration – living on hopes and dreams**
M 4 (Tx)	Follow your dreams – a Jewish immigrant tells her story
	Excerpt from the short story *The Miracle* (1920) by Anzia Yezierska
3. Doppelstunde:	**The original idea of the American Dream – what was it all about?**
M 5 (Tx)	William Faulkner on the idea of the American Dream
	Excerpt from the essay *On Privacy: The American dream, What Happened to it* (1955) by William Faulkner
4. Doppelstunde:	**Education – a key to the American Dream**
M 6 (Tx)	A Mexican immigrant on his long path to an education
	Excerpt from the travelogue *Possible lives: The Promise of Public Education in America* (1995) by Mike Rose
5. Doppelstunde:	**Hard work will get you there – realising the American Dream**
M 7 (Tx)	*Who Burns for the Perfection of Paper* – a poem on achieving the American Dream
	Poem *Who Burns for the Perfection of Paper* (1993) by Martín Espada
6. Doppelstunde:	**Off to new horizons! – Breaking with old traditions**
M 8 (Tx)	An acceptance letter from Yale – finding the courage to break away from old traditions
	Excerpt from the novel *Girl in Translation* (2010) by Jean Kwok
7. Doppelstunde:	**The American Dream today – does it still exist?**
M 9 (Gd)	Does the American Dream still exist? – Looking at some data
8. Doppelstunde:	**Is there a European Dream?**
M 10 (Tx)	The American Dream vs the European Dream
	Excerpt from *The European Dream: How Europe's Vision of the Future Is Quietly Eclipsing the American Dream* (2004) by Jeremy Rifkin
M 11 (Ab)	How to write an essay

From Rags to Riches? – The American Dream Revisited (S II)

| Reihe 6 | Verlauf | Material S 2 | LEK | Kontext | Mediothek |

II/C5

M 1 Picture stimulus for the unit

M 2 About the American Dream – analysing quotations

In search of a better life many people from different countries and backgrounds emigrated to the USA. Those immigrants shaped the progress of the country, and created the national heritage of the American Dream. Let's have a look at some quotes about this dream.

a) "Amerika, du hast es besser […]"
Johann Wolfgang von Goethe (1749–1832), German writer

b) "There's no free lunch."
An Italian immigrant on what forty years of American life had taught him

c) "Like all people who have nothing, I lived on my dreams."
Anzia Yezierska (1881–1970), American novelist and Jewish immigrant from Poland

d) "First generation immigrants will take any kind of job and do any kind of hard work. They are the greatest believers in the American dream."
Dr. Saskia Sassen, an American sociologist, on the spirit of immigrants from the West Indies

e) "Give me your tired, your poor,
Your huddled masses yearning to breathe free,
The wretched refuse of your teeming shore.
Send these, the homeless, tempest-tost to me:
I lift my lamp beside the golden door!"
Emma Lazarus (1849–1887), American poet

f) "To seek their American dream, many Mexican Americans have given up their homes, and everything to come here. When they get here, they know that they have to get a job and an education to survive."
Carlos Fuentes (1928–2012), Mexican novelist and essayist

g) "Here was no hot running water, cold water. The water in the village was filthy … Any place with 'clean water' must be like 'the sky above the sky.' America is heaven."
Chin Moy Lee, a Chinese immigrant

Tasks

1. Work together in pairs: Choose one of the quotations and paraphrase it to explain what it means.

2. Report to the class the most important or interesting conclusions you have reached in your group about the meaning of the quotation.

3. Divide the class in two halves and compare the quotations: One half decides how the quotations are different, and one half decides how the quotations are similar.

4. Find a common theme for the texts you are going to work with in this unit.

From Rags to Riches? – The American Dream Revisited (S II)

Reihe 6 | Verlauf | Material S 4 | LEK | Kontext | Mediothek

M 3 Presenting living examples of the American Dream

The saying "from rags to riches" became true for many immigrants or their descendants. Let's have a look at four of those who were among the fortunate.

Task

- Work in groups of three: Choose one of the people below and prepare a presentation on their lives by doing some Internet research.
- In your presentation show how the person you have chosen made the American Dream come true. While scanning the websites listed below for information, focus on aspects that are related to the American Dream. All members of your group must be involved in the presentation.

Helpful websites

Jennifer Lopez: http://en.wikipedia.org/wiki

Madonna: http://www.biography.com

Howard Schultz: http://en.wikipedia.org/wiki
http://www.referenceforbusiness.com/biography

Arnold Schwarzenegger: http://www.biography.com, http://en.wikipedia.org/wiki

Jennifer Lopez – born to immigrants from Puerto Rico

Madonna – is the granddaughter of Italian immigrants

Howard Schultz – comes from a poor Jewish family

Arnold Schwarzenegger – emigrated to the United States in the 1960s

Hinweise (M 1–M 3; 1. Doppelstunde)

Ziel der ersten Stunde ist es, das **Vorwissen** der Schülerinnen und Schüler zum *American Dream* zu aktivieren. In der zweiten Hälfte der Stunde machen sie sich dann im Rahmen einer Internetrecherche mit berühmten Persönlichkeiten vertraut, deren Lebensgeschichten Elemente der klassischen *Rags-to-riches*-Story aufweisen.

Als **Einstieg** dient ein **Bildimpuls der Freiheitsstatue (M 1)**, die eines der bekanntesten Symbole der USA ist und für Freiheit und Unabhängigkeit steht. Sie begrüßte viele Immigranten, die mit dem Schiff nach New York kamen und auf ein besseres Leben in den USA hofften. Mögliche Fragen zum Bildimpuls:

- What comes to mind when you see this picture?
- What do you know about this statue?
- What does it stand for?

Alternativ kann die Lehrkraft eine **Bildertheke** vorbereiten, indem sie (laminierte) Bilder im Klassenzimmer auslegt, die Aspekte des amerikanischen Traums zeigen (z. B. die amerikanische Flagge, den Hollywood-Schriftzug, eine amerikanische Vorstadtidylle etc.). Die Schülerinnen und Schüler einigen sich zu zweit auf ein Bild, das ihrer Meinung nach den *American Dream* am besten symbolisiert. Sie begründen die Auswahl ihres Bildes entweder in einem Kugellager oder gegenüber einem anderen Schülerpaar.

Erarbeitung: Anschließend finden sich die Lernenden paarweise zusammen. Jeder erhält das **Arbeitsblatt (M 2)**, auf dem **Zitate** zum *American Dream* abgedruckt sind. Jedes Paar erarbeitet ein Zitat, indem es sich auf eine erklärende Paraphrase verständigt. Die Ergebnisse werden im Plenum genannt und in Stichworten an der Tafel notiert.

Um die Aufmerksamkeit auf unterschiedliche inhaltliche Aspekte zu lenken, wird die Klasse zur Bearbeitung der **Aufgabe 3** in zwei Hälften geteilt. Der lernpsychologische Hintergrund der Aufgabe ist es, eine erzwungene Beziehung (*a forced relationship*) zwischen verschiedenen Aspekten zu erstellen; hier: Gemeinsamkeiten und Unterschiede der Zitate, die womöglich nicht vorhanden sind. Die Ergebnisse werden im Plenum gesammelt und die Schülerinnen und Schüler fügen ihren Notizen die Ergebnisse der jeweils anderen Gruppen hinzu. Über das Thema der Reihe **(Aufgabe 4)** wird danach im Plenum gesprochen.

In der zweiten Hälfte der Stunde führen die Schülerinnen und Schüler in Kleingruppen arbeitsteilig eine **Internetrecherche** zu den Lebensgeschichten bekannter Persönlichkeiten durch, die typische Elemente des *American Dream* enthalten **(M 3)**. Um Zeit zu sparen und um zu vermeiden, dass die Lernenden zu lange im Internet surfen, sind pro Person eine bis zwei Internetseiten angegeben. Für die Recherche bekommen die Gruppen ca. 20 Minuten Zeit. Die anschließenden Kurzpräsentationen sollten nicht länger als ca. 10 Minuten dauern. Jede Lebensgeschichte wird mindestens einmal vorgestellt.

Erwartungshorizont (M 1)

Bildimpuls „Statue of Liberty":

- New York, freedom, Ellis Island, Declaration of Independence, "Lady Liberty"
- Stands at New York harbour, was given to the Americans by the French as a present in 1885, bears a burning torch, symbolising enlightenment and holds a book reading "July IV MDCCLXXVI" (July 4, 1776), wears a crown symbolising the seven seas or continents, the broken chains at her feet stand for freedom from oppression
- Symbolises liberty, stands for the hopes of millions of immigrants, represents the ideals of the USA and is an icon for the American spirit

Erwartungshorizont (M 2)

Analysing quotations:

1. a) Goethe: He was thinking of the freedom from old and useless traditions in Europe. b) Italian immigrant: Life is difficult. You must work hard to get along. c) Yezierska: Poor people have nothing but their dream of a better life. They must follow their dreams. d) Dr. Sassen: They think that through hard work anything can be achieved. e) Lazarus: There is a contrast between the poor and wretched lives in their old home countries and promising lives in the new world. f) Fuentes: A better life is not for free. Without a good education you won't get anywhere. g) Chinese immigrant: The living conditions in America are so much better than at home. Life there must be wonderful.
2. USA as land of dreams, promises, freedom and riches; destination for poor people from all over the world
3. Examples of how the quotations are different: Some quotations talk very specifically about a better life, others are vague in what they address; the quotations are from and about people with very different cultural backgrounds.

    Examples of how the quotations are similar: They all talk of better lives; most of them mention hard work as a necessary prerequisite for a better life.
4. "Dreams of a better life", "How to get a better life", "The American Dream", "Why people come to America" etc.

Erwartungshorizont (M 3)

Jennifer Lopez (*1969): – born to Puerto Rican immigrants – raised in the Bronx – parents stressed the importance of work and being able to speak the English language – encouraged her to sing and dance to make sure she stayed out of trouble – Jennifer decided to become a famous movie star when she was a teenager – moved to Manhattan to achieve her goal – financed singing and dancing lessons herself by working as a waitress – her parents disapproved, being of the opinion that no Latina would become a movie star in the USA – is a successful singer, dancer, fashion designer and actress

Madonna (*1958): – grandchild of Italian immigrants – third of six children – lost her mother at the age of five – had to look after her younger brothers and sisters and decided that she had to do something different – very ambitious: A-grade student, disciplined dancer, graduated from highschool one year earlier than her classmates – moved to New York with only 30 dollars in her pocket to further her dance career – earned money to pay her rent as a nude model, selling doughnuts and as a waitress – today she's a a singer, songwriter, dancer and actress and is the best-selling female recording artist of all time – according to *Time* she's also one of the 25 Most Powerful Women of the Past Century

Howard Schultz (*1953): – born to poor Jewish immigrants – his father had to do more than one job (taxi driver, factory worker etc.) in order to support his family – he lived in a small two-bedroom apartment in a housing project – had the plan to create a company his father never had the chance to work for – was the first in his family who had the chance to go to college where he received a degree in communications – became the founder of Starbucks

Arnold Schwarzenegger (*1947): – born to a policeman and housewife in Austria – dreamed of moving to America from an early age – finally emigrated to the USA, speaking only a little English – wanted to move forward his body building career there – was an illegal immigrant at one point after having problems with his visa – made millions in real estate – became a movie star – married the niece of former President John F. Kennedy – became Governor of California

M 4 Follow your dreams – a Jewish immigrant tells her story

The following text is taken from Hungry Hearts, *a collection of short stories first published in 1920. The author of the short story excerpt and her Jewish family emigrated to New York's Lower East Side in the 19th century.*

A. Approaching the text

1. **Instant drama:**

Work in pairs. Use the eight lines below to develop a drama scene. Create the whole scene: relationship, atmosphere, emotions, movement, pause, rhythm, intonation, gesture. You may change the order of the lines. You may not change, add, cancel or swap around anything in the lines.

Read the eight lines and rearrange them:

- "Let me explain."
- "I was sure you could do it alone."
- "You promised."
- "So I lied."
- "No! I can't! Do it for me."
- "America is so cruel."
- "But I want to make a person of myself."
- "You said, 'Come to America, it's the golden land!'"

2. Act out the scene in front of the class. The others take notes on the situation and the emotions the characters display.

3. Read the following text and decide which presentation comes closest to the emotions the narrator expresses.

Excerpt from *The Miracle* (1920) by Anzia Yezierska

Like all people who have nothing, I lived on dreams. With nothing but my longing for love, I burned my way through stone walls till I got to America. And what happened to me when I became an American is more than I can picture before my eyes, even in a dream.

[…] Nu, I got to America. Ten hours I pushed a machine in a shirt-waist factory, when I was yet lucky to get work. And always my head was drying up with saving and pinching and worrying to send home a little from the little I earned. All that my face saw all day long was girls and machines – and nothing else. And even when I came already home from work, I could only talk to the girls in the working-girls' boarding-house, or shut myself up in my dark, lonesome bedroom. No family, no friends, nobody to get me acquainted with nobody! The only men I saw were what passed me by in the street and in cars. "Is this a 'lovers land'?" was calling in my heart. "Where are my dreams that were so real to me in the old country?"

[…] For two days and for two nights I lay still on my bed, unable to move. I looked around on my empty walls, thinking, thinking, "Where am I? Is this the world? Is this America?" Suddenly I sprang up from bed. "What can come from pitying yourself?" I cried. "If the world kicks you down and makes nothing of you, you bounce yourself up and make something of yourself." A fire blazed up in me to rise over the world because I was downed by the world. "Make a person of yourself," I said. "Begin to learn English. Make yourself for an American if you want to live in America." […]

The first night I went to school I felt like falling on everybody's neck and kissing them. I felt like kissing the books and the benches. It was such great happiness to learn to read and write the English words.

Because I started a few weeks after the beginning of the term, my teacher said I might stay after the class to help me catch up with my back lessons. The minute I looked on him I felt that grand feeling: "Here is a person! Here is America!" His face just shined with high thoughts. There was such a beautiful light in his eyes that it warmed my heart to steal a look on him.

25 "Why are you so eager for learning?" he asked me.

"Because I want to make a person of myself," I answered. "Since I got to work for low wages and I can't be young any more, I'm burning to get among people where it's not against a girl if she is in years and without money."

His hand went out to me. "I'll help you," he said. "But you must first learn to get hold of yourself."
30 [...]

Often as I sat at the machine sewing the waists I'd forget what I was doing. I'd find myself dreaming in the air. "Ach!" I asked myself, "what was that beautifulness in his eyes that made the lowest nobody feel like a somebody? What was that about him that when his smile fell on me I felt lifted up to the sky away from all the coldness and the ugliness of the world? Gottunui!" I prayed, "if I could
35 only always hold on to the light of high thoughts that shined from him. If I could only always hear in my heart the sound of his voice I would need nothing more in life. I would be happier than a bird in the air."

"Friend," I said to him once, "if you could but teach me how to get cold in the heart and clear in the head like you are!"

40 He only smiled at me and looked far away. His calmness was like the sureness of money in the bank. Then he turned and looked on me, and said: "I am not so cold in the heart and clear in the head as I make-believe. I am bound. I am a prisoner of convention." [...]

"[...] I do not have bosses just as you do," he said. "But still I am not free. I am bound by formal education and conventional traditions. Though you work in a shop, you are really freer than I. You are
45 not repressed as I am by the fear and shame of feeling. You could teach me more than I could teach you. You could teach me how to be natural."

"I'm not so natural like you think," I said. "I'm afraid."

He smiled at me out of his eyes. "What are you afraid of?"

"I'm afraid of my heart," I said, trying to hold back the blood rushing to my face. "I'm burning to get
50 calm and sensible like the born Americans. But how can I help it? My heart flies away from me like a wild bird. How can I learn to keep myself down on earth like the born Americans?"

"But I don't want you to get down on earth like the Americans. That is just the beauty and the wonder of you. We Americans are too much on earth; we need more of your power to fly. If you would only know how much you can teach us Americans. You are the promise of the centuries to come. You are
55 the heart, the creative pulse of America to be." [...]

Source: Yezierska, Anzia: The Miracle In: Yezierska, Anzia: Hungry Hearts. New York: Signet Classic 1996. p. 92 ff.

4 **nu (Yiddish):** here: well – 4 **shirt-waist factory:** a factory where tailored blouses or shirts worn by women were produced. Workers were subjected to unfair wages in unsafe conditions working unbelievably long hours – 5 **to pinch:** to be very careful about how much money you spend – 15 **to bounce up:** to feel better quickly – 19 **bench:** a long seat – 21 **term:** one of the three periods of time that a school or university year is divided into – 22 **back lesson:** a missed lesson – 25 **eager for:** very excited about sth. – 26 **wage:** money you earn – 42 **bound:** (here) to be involved in a difficult situation

B. Understanding the text

1. Read the text again and work on the following tasks:
   a) Sum up what you learn about the narrator's past.
   b) Outline her dreams.
   c) Describe her working conditions.
   d) Explain why the narrator starts learning English.
   e) Describe how the teacher encourages her.
2. Compare your answers with a partner. Then share them with the rest of the class.

C. Studying the text

The climax is the point in a story when a conflict reaches its highest point of interest or suspense and where decisions are made.

1. Use the chart below to, list events from the text that lead to the moment of decision. Describe the climax and characterise the conclusion.

climax

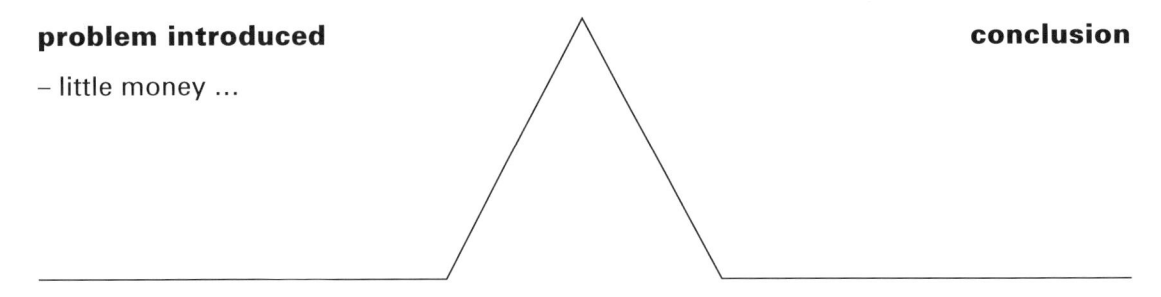

problem introduced

– little money ...

conclusion

2. Work in small groups. Use a chart like the one shown here to write a literary analysis.

	Point of view	Style	Characterisation
Examples			
Conclusion			

3. Use your notes for a written literary analysis of the text. Do not simply present your conclusions. Give examples from the text to support your ideas.

D. Going beyond the text

Choose a quote from the text you found most interesting/striking/touching ... Introduce it to your partner by reading it out loud. Paraphrase it for your partner and explain why you chose this quote.

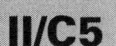

From Rags to Riches? – The American Dream Revisited (S II)

| Reihe 6 | Verlauf | Material S 10 | LEK | Kontext | Mediothek |

Hinweise (M 4; 2. Doppelstunde)

Im Mittelpunkt der Stunde steht ein Auszug aus der Kurzgeschichte *„The Miracle"* von Anzia Yezierska. Die Autorin emigrierte im 19. Jahrhundert gemeinsam mit ihrer Familie nach New York, wo sie tagsüber hart arbeitete und abends Englisch lernte. In ihre Kurzgeschichte lässt sie diese Erfahrungen einfließen und schildert so exemplarisch Hoffnungen und Träume vieler damaliger Immigranten.

A. Approaching the text

Als **Einstieg** dient ein **Rollenspiel**, das Emotionen von Auswanderern zum Ausdruck bringt und die Lernenden auf den Text einstimmt. Die Dialogfragmente stammen aus dem Vorwort zu der Kurzgeschichtensammlung *„Hungry Hearts"*, in dem Vivian Gornick dem *mainstream America* vorwirft, sich der Immigranten nicht richtig anzunehmen. Die Rollenspiele werden entwickelt und vorgeführt. Mindestens zwei Gruppen sollten ihren Dialog präsentieren, damit die unterschiedlichen Inszenierungen im Plenum miteinander verglichen werden können. Die Schülerinnen und Schüler, die nicht vortragen, machen sich jeweils Notizen zur Situation und zu den Emotionen der Personen. Vor dem Hintergrund der Rollenspiele und der Notizen liest die Lerngruppe den **Textauszug** aus *„The Miracle"*.

B. Understanding the text

Im anschließenden **Plenumsgespräch** werden die Ergebnisse des Rollenspiels mit dem Text in Verbindung gesetzt und verglichen. Anschließend lesen die Lernenden in Einzelarbeit den Textauszug erneut und bearbeiten die **Verständnisaufgaben zum Text (B.1)** stichpunktartig. In Partnerarbeit werden diese Notizen gegebenenfalls erweitert oder korrigiert **(B.2)**. Die Ergebnisse werden danach im Plenum besprochen und zwei bis drei Stichwörter an der Tafel festgehalten.

C. Studying the text

Für das Ausfüllen der **Spannungskurve (Aufgabe C.1)** ist die *Think-Pair-Share-Methode* geeignet. Unter Verwendung des Tafelanschriebs durchdenken die Lernenden die Aufgabe in Einzelarbeit, bevor sie ihre Zwischenergebnisse mit einem Partner besprechen. Die Ergebnissicherung erfolgt im Plenum. Die **Tabelle** in Aufgabe **C.2** dient als Vorbereitung der schriftlichen Textanalyse. Die Lernenden tragen hier Beispiele aus dem Text und die daraus resultierenden Schlussfolgerungen ein. Hierdurch bereiten sie eine klar strukturierte Erarbeitung von **C.3 (Textanalyse)** vor. Die literarische Analyse wird in Einzelarbeit schriftlich erarbeitet. Je nachdem wie viel Zeit in der Stunde bleibt, kann die Analyse von der Lehrkraft eingesammelt oder durch die Lernenden in Partnerkorrektur verbessert werden.

D. Going beyond the text

Die Wahl eines **Zitats** aus der Textstelle ermöglicht es den Schülerinnen und Schülern erneut, eine persönliche Verbindung zu dem Text aufzubauen und sich emotional und individuell dazu zu äußern.

Erwartungshorizont (M 4)

A. Approaching the text

2. Emotions might include: anger, frustration, despair, hope, joy, fear, mistrust, disappointment etc.

B. Understanding the text

1. a) very poor, longed for love; b) to find love, to make a person of herself, to get among people; c) long working hours in a factory, very low wages, no social contact, lonely; d) doesn't want to pity herself any longer, wants to be as American as possible, wants to be a person, wants to get an education, meet other people and get ahead, wants to control her emotions and become more sensible; e) explains how she is special, while he is bound by traditions, she is free to achieve what she wants to achieve with her energy, power and creativity.

C. Studying the text

1. <u>Problem introduced</u>: very little money, no social life, nowhere near her dreams, lonely, exhausted, disappointed; <u>climax</u>: realises she is pitying herself, sees life has been treating her badly and she has done nothing, becomes aware it is up to her to change her life; <u>conclusion</u>: get an education, begin to learn English.

2.

	Point of view	Style	Characterisation
Examples	uses "I", "me" and "my" a lot; writes about her feelings, thoughts, hopes and worries; talks to herself	informal, very personal, uses language to express ideas in a vivid imaginative way, simple sentence structure (ll. 1–3; 18–20; 12–17, 26–28; 31–37)	ll. 12–17: thoughts; ll. 26–28: words; ll. 18–24: actions; ll. 52–55: what others say about her
Conclusions	first-person narrator	shows that protagonist is very emotional, lively person and that English is not her mother tongue	indirect characterisation; very emotional character, highly motivated, ready to work hard, determined, willing to change her life

3. *Written analysis of the excerpt*

The excerpt of Anzia Yezierska's short story *The Miracle* deals with the problems a Jewish woman faces trying to make something of her life in the USA. Due to the informal and very personal language the first-person narrator uses, the reader is exposed to vivid images of the woman's everyday life. The simple sentence structure of the short story and the direct way of expressing emotions allows the reader to get a colourful insight of an immigrant's living conditions in the early part of the 20th century.

The protagonist's life is characterised by hard work at a shirt-waist factory and the isolation she feels in her private life. Working ten hours at a factory and still having to worry about "saving and pinching and […] send[ing] home a little from the little I earned" she longs for love and friendship, but she is alone in a country in which she once yearned to be: "No family, no friends, nobody to get me acquainted with nobody!" Being confronted with the reality of her American life, she is disappointed and slowly seems to lose her spirit and dreams. Two days long she lies in bed and questions her decision about having come to America: "Where are my dreams that were so real to me in the old country? […] Where am I? Is this the world? Is this America?" But two days of contemplating and pitying herself is enough for the woman who is, in fact, willing to work hard in order to make her dreams come true. She finds her strong will once again and the ambition to change her life.

Coming to the conclusion that she has to learn English if she wants to become a proper American (l. 17), she joins an English class. At school the first-person narrator not only finds joy in learning to read and write the English language, but is also thrilled by her English teacher. In him she sees all the attributes she thinks are American and wants him to teach her to be just like him: "I'm burning to get calm and sensible like the born Americans." (ll. 49–50) Her teacher, who sees the unspoiled, natural European woman in her and is attracted to her emotional manner, tries to convince her that it is not at all desirable to become an American like he is: "We Americans are too much on earth; we need more of your power to fly. If you would only know how much you can teach us Americans." (ll. 53–54) With this statement the teacher refers to the traditional idea of immigrants positively contributing to building up the new country which is America. Therefore, the reader gets the impression that both sides are potentially going to learn from each other and that there is a chance of realising the American Dream together.

M 5 William Faulkner on the idea of the American Dream

William Faulkner (1897–1962) wrote novels set in the U.S. south, portraying the lives of wealthy land-owning families and poor farmers, both black and white. In the following excerpt he analyses what the American Dream meant in the first place.

A. Approaching the text

1. This wordle contains words from a text you are going to read in this lesson. Work in pairs: Copy the word table below into your exercise books and fill in the words from the wordle. You can use a dictionary where needed.

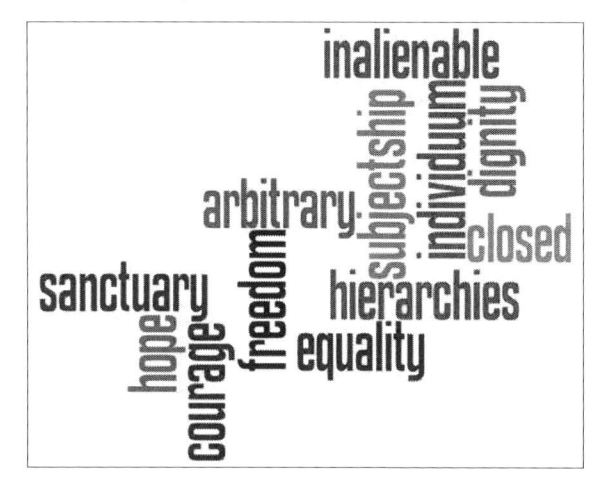

Word table:

Word	Definition	Example
hope		

2. Consider the words you have just studied and predict the content of the text you are going to read.

Excerpt from *On Privacy: The American Dream, What Happened to It* (1955) by William Faulkner

This was the American Dream: a sanctuary on the earth for individual man: a condition in which he could be free not only of the old established closed-corporation hierarchies of arbitrary power which had oppressed him as a mass, but free of that mass into which the hierarchies of church and state had compressed and held him individually thralled and individually impotent.

5   A dream simultaneous among the separate individuals of men so asunder and scattered as to have no contact to match dreams and hopes among the old nations of the Old World which existed as nations not on citizenship but subjectship, which endured only on the premise of size and docility of the subject mass; the individual men and women who said as with one simultaneous voice: "We will establish a new land where man can assume that every individual man – not the mass of men but individual men – has an
10 inalienable right to individual dignity and freedom within a fabric of individual courage and honorable work and mutual responsibility."

Not just an idea, but a condition: a living human condition designed to be coeval with the birth of American itself, engendered, created, and simultaneous with the very air and word *America,* which at that one stroke, one instant, should cover the whole earth with one simultaneous suspiration like air or
15 light. And it was, it did: radiating outward to cover even the old weary repudiated still-thralled nations, until individual men everywhere, who had no more than heard the name, let alone knew where America was, could respond to it, lifting up not only their hearts but the hopes too which until now they did not know – or anyway dared not remember – that they possessed.

From Rags to Riches? – The American Dream Revisited (S II)

A condition in which every man would not only not be a king, he wouldn't even want to be one. He wouldn't even need to bother to be the equal of kings because now he was free of kings and all their similar congeries; free not only of the symbols but of the old arbitrary hierarchies themselves which the puppet-symbols represented – courts and cabinets and churches and schools [...].

© From ON PRIVACY: THE AMERICAN DREAM, WHAT HAPPENED TO IT? by William Faulkner. © 1955 by William Faulkner. Used by permission of Random House, Inc. Any third party use of this material, outside of this publication, is prohibited. Interested parties must apply directly to Random House, Inc. for permission.

4 **to compress:** to press sb. or sth. into a small place – 4 **thralled:** subjected to bondage; enslaved – 5 **asunder:** widely separated – 5 **scattered:** disorganized – 7 **to endure:** to tolerate without resistance or with patience – 7 **premise:** a basis of reasoning – 7 **docility:** obedience – 9 **to assume:** to take for granted – 10 **fabric:** a framework or structure – 12 **coeval:** of the same age – 13 **to engender:** to give rise to – 13 **air:** here the general character or complexion of something – 14 **suspiration:** a long, deep sigh – 15 **to radiate:** to move like rays from the centre – 15 **to repudiate:** to reject as having no authority or binding force – 18 **to dare:** to have the boldness to try – 21 **congeries:** a collection of parts in one mass

B. Understanding the text

Scan the text for the information below and tick if it is true, false or not in the text.

	True	False	Not in the text
a) The old nations of Europe kept people apart and subjugated so that they could not develop and follow their dreams.	❏	❏	❏
b) A message of freedom went out from America to people from all over the world.	❏	❏	❏
c) At one time the American Dream meant people had to serve their church and state.	❏	❏	❏
d) Like air and light the American Dream was not only an idea but a necessary condition to live as a human being.	❏	❏	❏
e) In Europe the people had the dream of living in a country where they had enough land to cultivate and which could not be taken away from them.	❏	❏	❏
f) To have individual freedom was worth much more than financial security and possessions.	❏	❏	❏

C. Studying the text

1. Work in groups of three or four. Take notes on your conclusions and share them with the rest of the class.

    a) To make his text effective, the writer appeals to sentiments he knows readers have. Find parts in this text which appeal to sentiments connected with freedom, equality and oppressive forms of government.

    Example: <u>freedom</u>: arbitrary power (l. 2) ...; <u>equality</u>: one simultaneous voice (l. 8) ...; <u>oppressive forms of government</u>: still-thralled (l. 15) ...

    b) How does Faulkner contrast Europe and America? Draw a table with two columns in your exercise books. Take notes on how Faulkner describes both continents.

    c) How does Faulkner compare the terms "living condition" (l. 12) and "America" (l. 13)?

D. Going beyond the text

What do you think Faulkner means by the American Dream being free from "old arbitrary hierarchies [...] of church and state" (ll. 21–22)? Give examples to illustrate your opinion.

From Rags to Riches? – The American Dream Revisited (S II)

| Reihe 6 | Verlauf | Material S 14 | LEK | Kontext | Mediothek |

Hinweise (M 5; 3. Doppelstunde)

In seinem **Essay** „*On Privacy: The American Dream, What Happened to It*" (1955) setzt **William Faulkner** sich mit dem Verhältnis von Persönlichkeitsrechten und dem Recht der Bevölkerung auf Information auseinander. Der auf dem **Arbeitsblatt** enthaltene Auszug beschäftigt sich mit der Frage nach dem amerikanischen Traum von individueller Freiheit.

A. Approaching the text

Da der Text sprachlich recht anspruchsvoll ist, bietet es sich an, den **Wortschatz** vorzuentlasten. Dies geschieht mithilfe eines *wordle* (Aufgabe A.1), das zentrale Begriffe des Textes enthält.

Tipp: Um die Aufmerksamkeit der Lernenden auf die Aufgabe zu lenken, kann das *wordle* auch vergrößert und auf Folie kopiert werden.

In Partnerarbeit füllen die Schülerinnen und Schüler die Tabelle unter dem *wordle* (A.1) aus, die sie in ihr Heft übertragen. Die aufgeführten Kategorien (Wort aus dem Text, Definitionen, Beispiele) vertiefen das Verstehen der Lexeme nachhaltig und entlasten so das Textverständnis vor.

Im Anschluss daran formulieren die Lernenden erneut in Partnerarbeit ihre **Erwartungen zum Inhalt** des Textes (**Aufgabe A.2**). Diese können stichpunktartig festgehalten werden. Hierbei ist es wichtig, dass alle Wörter berücksichtigt werden, denn erst so entsteht ein Zusammenhang.

B. Understanding the text

Aufgrund der Komplexität des Textes geht es in **B.1** um ein **erstes Verstehen** auf der referenziellen Ebene. Die Aufgabenstellung bietet den Lernenden Paraphrasen von Informationen aus dem Essay an, deren Wahrheitsgehalt sie am Text überprüfen sollen. Die Formulierungen sind deutlich leichter als die Aussagen im Text und doch im Text wiederzuentdecken (*recognition*). Die Ergebnissicherung erfolgt im Plenum.

C. Studying the text

Die Textanalyseaufgabe C wird zunächst in kleinen Gruppen erarbeitet. Für die Aufgaben 1. b) und c) mag es hilfreich sein, noch einmal zu verdeutlichen, was die Operatoren *contrast* (How are ideas different?) **und** *compare* (How are ideas similar?) bedeuten.

Die Ergebnisse der Gruppenarbeit werden im Plenum gesammelt und in Notizform an der Tafel festgehalten. Die Tafelnotizen und das Vorwissen der Lernenden werden dann verwendet, um **Aufgabe D** schriftlich zu bearbeiten. Je nachdem, wie viel Zeit übrig ist, kann diese Aufgabe auch Hausaufgabe sein.

Erwartungshorizont (M 5)

A. Approaching the text

1.

Word	Definition	Example
hope	A feeling of wanting something to happen.	Is there any hope that we will be home by tomorrow?
inalienable	An inalienable right that cannot be taken away from you.	The rights enshrined in our laws are inalienable.
sanctuary	A peaceful place especially for people who are in danger.	A sanctuary is open to everyone.
courage	Being brave enough to do what you believe in.	The troops fought with great courage.

freedom	Being free to think, say, do etc. what you want without being controlled.	When I was younger I didn't have so much freedom compared with young people today.
arbitrary	Not being planned, based on chance.	He wanted to avoid making an arbitrary decision about where to live.
equality	Different groups of people having the same rights, social position and being treated in the same way.	Today we're going to talk about racial equality.
hierarchies	A system in which people and structures are organised according to their importance.	Some hierarchies are not balanced.
subjectship	The status of being a subject or citizen.	The British Parliament granted subjectship to people from the British colonies.
closed	not open	It might be warmer in here if the windows were closed.
dignity	The opinion that you are important and valued.	How could you behave like that? Don't you have any dignity?
individual	separated from other things in a group	Every individual person has to sign the paper.

B. Understanding the text

a) true b) true c) false (True would be: At one point the American Dream meant people could live as individuals and free from powers such as church and state.) d) true e) not in the text (In the text it says that people in Europe had the dream of living in a country where they could be free and live with rights that could not be taken from them. f) false (True would be: To have individual freedom was worth much more than having the power of kings or other state symbols.)

C. Studying the text

1. a) <u>freedom</u>: arbitrary power (l. 2), thralled (l. 4), subjectship (l. 7), air (l. 13), lifting hearts and hopes (l. 17); <u>equality</u>: one simultaneous voice (l. 8), every individual (l. 9), free of that mass (l. 3); <u>oppressing forms of government</u>: hierarchies of church and state compress (ll. 3–4), still-thralled (l. 15), docile (l. 7), king (l. 20), puppet-symbols (l. 22).

   b) To contrast Europe and America Faulkner uses a lot of charged words that are likely to produce a strong emotional response.

Europe	America
old, closed, weary, oppressed, thralled, arbitrary, impotent people, mass, subjects, puppet-symbols, hierarchies	free, responsible, courageous, citizens, individuals, with inalienable rights to dignity and freedom, sanctuary

   c) America is not just an idea or a country, it is a living condition. As people need air and light to live, they need the living condition America as in freedom, inalienable rights and individual dignity etc. America as a living condition could be anywhere on earth.

D. Going beyond the text

<u>Answers could include the following aspects</u>: If the power of states, churches and other institutions is arbitrary, an American Dream – like a living condition – cannot become true; undemocratic forms of government, religions that prevent individuals from obtaining their inalienable rights to dignity and freedom etc. are obstacles that have to be removed before the American Dream can be lived; established old social classes based on birth, money, property etc. keep people from living their American Dream.

M 6 A Mexican immigrant on his long path to an education

In his travelogue Possible Lives: The Promise of Public Education in America, *Mike Rose provides the reader with the opportunity to see how hopes and dreams can be vitalised through education. In the following excerpt from his travelogue, he describes the situation of a Mexican immigrant worker in Calexico, a city in California near the Mexican border.*

A. Approaching the text

1. Work in small groups:

   - Brainstorm possible connections between the two photographs on the transparency. Imagine the photograph on the left is the cause for the one on the right.

   - Now imagine it to be the other way around: The photograph on the right is the cause for the one on the left.

   - Share the results of your brainstorming with the class. Explain to the others which way round you'd prefer.

2. Read the text and find information associated with your earlier discussion.

Excerpt from *Possible Lives: The Promise of Public Education in America* (1995) by Mike Rose

[In] Calexico [the] attitudes toward English ranged from intimidation and resentment to admiration and a desire for fluency. There was a strong Mexican work ethic fused with an American "can do" attitude. There was despair and weariness, alcohol and violence, and a fierce commitment to the possibility of a better life: "Take care of yourself and work hard", was one old man's philosophy. "I never could have owned a home like this in Mexico," said another. There was provincialism, yet there was respect for those who went away to acquire specialized knowledge and brought it back to the community. There were communitarian bonds and a deep commitment to family, yet a strong individualist ethic as well, a belief that, as one woman explained: "You have to show what you can do. You can't be one of so many. You have to stand out." There was talk of solidarity [...], and there were class conflicts. There were a wide range of reactions to historical inequities and racism: from fury to denial, with many believing that they could effect change by entering professional and managerial and service ranks and doing things differently. [...]

[Rafael Jacinto] looked from his trousers up to me [...] explaining how this decision to go back to school had limited the hours he can work, how he and his wife have to spend so many hours studying, so he wears these old pants, and this windbreaker, staying up late, tired, the crease carefully ironed in once the kids have gone to bed.

From Rags to Riches? – The American Dream Revisited (S II)

He was telling me the story of his decision. It was made in 1985. He was working in the fields, packing cauliflowers. It was past midnight, and he was driving through the desert. Late, tired, those little hallucinatory wisps flitting in from the periphery of the beams of his headlights. "I started thinking about my life. What I had achieved so far. What I would probably achieve in the future. And just like that" – he snapped his fingers – "just like *that,* I knew I had to make a change." When he went home, he woke up his wife and told her what he wanted to do. He asked her to join him, and they began taking high school equivalency classes at the local adult school. They applied for citizenship and enrolled in ESL classes at Imperial Valley College. Five years later, with associate arts degrees in hand, they entered San Diego State. They have both passed the difficult English composition proficiency exam. Last semester, each got a 3.0. They want to become teachers.

Guadalupe Jacinto, who had been outside in the warm evening […], walked in and took a seat beside Rafael. She was polite, engaging, full of thoughts that she expressed slowly, measuring her expression, conscious of her spoken English, but gaining fluency and fervor as she spoke. She was born in Mexicali, married Rafael at sixteen, had four children. […] "My father always wanted me to go to school," she explained, "but ..." She shrugged and smiled. "She's very smart," Rafael said softly. "The English is very hard," she said, leaning forward, "but we work on it together. We study together." She looked simultaneously weary and poised, in the evening, a warm breeze, dark outside. They have about two more years to go for the bachelor's degree. Then certification. "It's like you're in a dream," she said. "I can't believe it sometimes." There was exhaustion in her voice – as though every word of English came with oppressive weight – but anticipation, too. To be a teacher. Pride and disbelief. "San Diego State University," Rafael said, pausing on each word, melodious, a Spanish lilt to his English.

© Mike Rose: Possible Lives. Houghton Mifflin Company, 1995. Reprinted by the permission of Houghton Mifflin Harcourt Publishing Company. All rights reserved.

1 **intimidation:** the state of being frightened or feeling threatened by sb. – 1 **resentment:** the feeling of displeasure – 2 **fused:** to unite or blend into a whole, as if by melting together – 3 **weariness:** the feeling of being tired – 3 **fierce:** intense – 3 **commitment:** being willing to invest your time in something you believe in – 6 **to acquire:** to come into possession – 7 **bond:** sth. that unites individuals into a group – 10 **inequity:** the lack of fairness and equal rights – 11 **denial:** disbelief in the existence or reality of a thing – 15 **crease:** the straight, vertical line produced in the front and back of trousers – 19 **wisp:** a thing that can hardly be seen – 19 **to flit:** to move swiftly – 23 **equivalency:** the same in value and significance – 24 **ESL:** English as a second language – 24 **associate arts degree:** a two-year degree, usually offered at community colleges, that shows you have completed the general education requirements necessary for a bachelor's degree programme – 25 **composition proficiency exam:** a practice essay test to prove one's command of the English language – 26 **3.0:** in the U.S. grading system a 4.0 is the best. A 3.0 is satisfactory – 28 **measured:** carefully weighed or considered – 29 **fervor:** great warmth and earnestness of feeling – 33 **poised:** self-assured – 34 **certification:** (here) a certified statement allowing sb. to teach – 36 **oppressive:** causing discomfort – 36 **anticipation:** expectation or hope – 37 **lilt:** (here) melody

From Rags to Riches? – The American Dream Revisited (S II)

| Reihe 6 | Verlauf | Material S 18 | LEK | Kontext | Mediothek |

B. Understanding the text

1. Work with a partner and show your understanding of the passage above by filling out a sequence chart like the one below. Illustrate the various steps to Rafael's and Guadalupe's teacher certification.

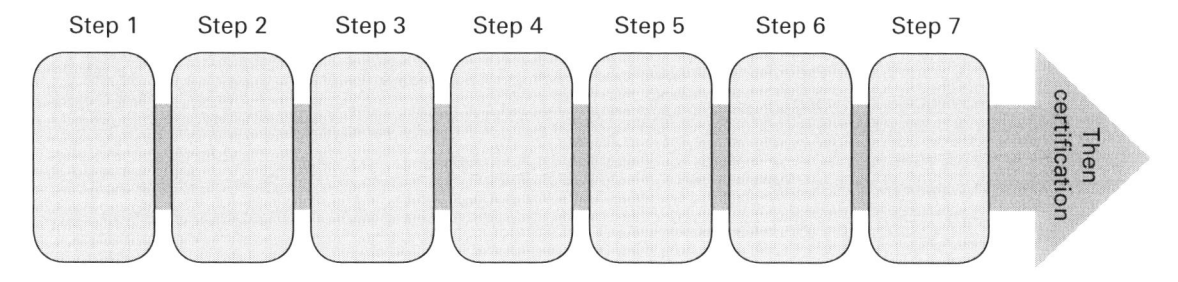

Step 1 — Step 2 — Step 3 — Step 4 — Step 5 — Step 6 — Step 7 → Then certification

2. Using the chart describe the events that led up to their teacher certification.

C. Studying the text

1. Study the text and make notes on the following tasks:

   a) Describe the atmosphere at Calexico and the attitudes of the Mexican workers towards America.

   b) Based on Rafael's experiences, explain which character traits you feel were necessary to follow his dream of becoming a teacher.

2. Find someone in your class to share your findings. Discuss similarities and differences in your answers.

D. Going beyond the text

Class discussion:

Would you have the courage and determination to leave your home to settle in a foreign country? Explain why and under what circumstances.

II/C5

From Rags to Riches? – The American Dream Revisited (S II)

| Reihe 6 | Verlauf | Material S 19 | LEK | Kontext | Mediothek |

II/C5

Hinweise (M 6; 4. Doppelstunde)

In der vierten Doppelstunde lernen die Schülerinnen und Schüler anhand eines Auszuges aus dem Reisebericht *„Possible Lives – The Promise of Public Education in America"* von Mike Rose, inwieweit **Bildung** dazu beitragen kann, den amerikanischen Traum zu verwirklichen. Der Text zeigt, welche überaus bedeutsame Rolle die Ausbildung im Bewusstsein jener Immigranten spielt, die sich dazu entschlossen haben, sich aus schwierigen Lebensumständen emporzuarbeiten.

A. Approaching the text

Als **Einstieg** dienen zwei Bilder der **Farbfolie (M 1)**. Auf dem einen Bild sind zwei mexikanische Gastarbeiter bei der Birnenernte abgebildet, das andere Bild zeigt erwachsene Schüler im Klassenzimmer. Der Zusammenhang zwischen den beiden Bildern wird von den Schülerinnen und Schülern konstruiert und anschließend im Plenum kommuniziert. Dabei gibt es kein richtig oder falsch, jede Darstellung wird inhaltlich akzeptiert. Die Sprechimpulse zu den Bildern sind auf M 6 abgedruckt. Es empfiehlt sich jedoch, zunächst nur die Folie aufzulegen und die Impulse mündlich zu geben.

Tipp: Um die Bildabfolge tatsächlich ändern zu können, empfiehlt es sich die beiden Bilder auszuschneiden. So können sie auf dem Overhead-Projektor frei bewegt werden.

B. Understanding the text

Grafische Lernhilfen (B.1) eignen sich, um mündliche oder schriftliche Äußerungen der Lernenden vorzustrukturieren. Hier lesen die Schülerinnen und Schüler den Text erneut und machen sich dann in Partnerarbeit Notizen zu den Schritten, die zur *teacher's certification* des Protagonisten führen. Die Notizen werden anschließend verwendet, um in **B.2** schriftlich eine zusammenhängende Darstellung der Ereignisse zu erarbeiten. Die Ergebnisse aus dieser Einzelarbeit werden im Plenum ausgewertet.

Tipp: Unter Umständen kann es nützlich sein, den Lernenden die folgenden *connectors* als Hilfe anzubieten. Sie können an der Tafel gesammelt und gegebenenfalls von der Lehrkraft ergänzt werden:

Expressing sequence
initially, first(ly), then, after(wards), at last, finally, once, secondly, next, subsequently, meanwhile, at length, in the end, eventually

C. Studying the text

Die **Analyseaufgaben C.1** werden individuell bearbeitet. Bei 1. b) ist es hilfreich, zunächst an der Tafel Adjektive für eine **Charakterisierung** zu sammeln. Es ist wesentlich, dass die Schülerinnen und Schüler ihre Aussagen am Text belegen.

Um einen hohen Kommunikationsanteil zu erzielen, werden die Ergebnisse zunächst in Partnerarbeit besprochen, bevor die Sicherung im Plenum erfolgt.

D. Going beyond the text

Am Ende der Stunde überlegen die Schülerinnen und Schüler, unter welchen Umständen sie selbst in ein anderes Land auswandern würden und welcher Voraussetzungen es bedarf, ein solches Vorhaben in die Tat umzusetzen. Damit eine ertragreiche **Plenumsdiskussion** ermöglicht wird, machen sie sich zunächst Notizen. Zusatzimpuls: *Find the ten best responses to the question.*

Erwartungshorizont (M 6)

A. Approaching the text

Bildimpuls *forced relationship*:

1. very hard work, harsh working conditions, low wages, insecure job, only seasonal work, no insurance etc. ——→ go back to school, attend evening classes, try to get a better education to be eligible for better jobs etc.

    very demanding classes, too tiring after long hours of work, expensive, language problems etc. ——→ find an easy job, get at least a little money, be with people who speak the same language etc.

B. Understanding the text

1.

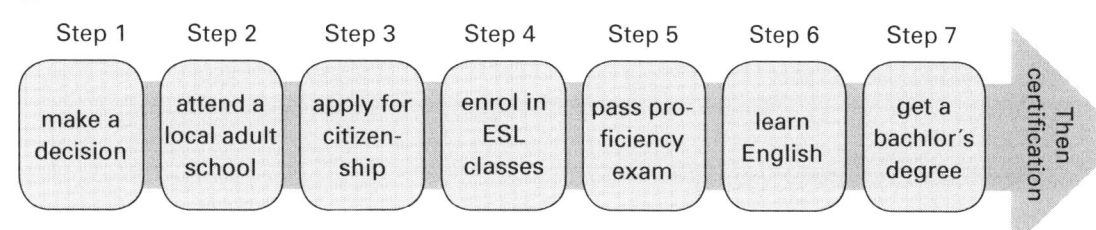

Step 1	Step 2	Step 3	Step 4	Step 5	Step 6	Step 7	
make a decision	attend a local adult school	apply for citizenship	enrol in ESL classes	pass proficiency exam	learn English	get a bachlor's degree	Then certification

2. Initially, Rafael Jacinto makes the decision to change his life while driving home from the exhausting work he was doing in cauliflower fields. His decision leads him and his wife to take equivalency classes at the local adult school. They then also apply for U.S. citizenship and enroll in ESL classes. Eventually they gain an arts degree and pass the difficult proficiency exam. In the long term they are planning on improving their English and get a bachelor's degree. Finally, they will achieve their dream of becoming teachers and therefore will work on their teaching certification.

C. Studying the text

1. a) <u>Atmosphere in Calexico</u>: provincial, affected by weariness → alcohol abuse and violence among the Mexican immigrants, fervent hope of a better life in the USA, respect for those who acquire additional knowledge and bring it back to the Mexican community, individualist ethic vs communitarian bonds and commitment to family

    <u>Mexicans attitudes towards America</u>: resentful and intimidated by the English language, but also admire it, have the desire to become fluent in English, inequities and racism, Mexican work ethic influenced by American "can do" attitude, they can have better homes than in Mexico, react to American racism with fury and denial and by working even harder

    b) dynamic, hard-working, honest, confident, visionary, serious, self-assured, risk-taking, determined, etc.

D. Going beyond the text

<u>Reasons to leave might include the following aspects</u>: be pulled away to a new home by the attraction of work, higher wages, and better opportunities, maybe also by attractive living conditions, spirit of adventure and leaving everything you know so well behind etc. <u>One would need</u>: courage, strong mentality to move from one place to another for a new start, willing to take risks, tolerance of uncertainty etc.

M 7 *Who Burns for the Perfection of Paper* – a poem on achieving the American Dream

Not many lawyers pursue simultaneous careers as poets, but, until 1993, Martín Espada (born in 1957) was an exception. In his work he concentrates on the immigrants' experiences and how they might achieve their American Dream.

A. Approaching the text

1. *No pain, no gain.*
   - Write down whether you a) agree, b) disagree or c) partially agree with this saying.
   - In pairs, tell each other which of the three options you have chosen and why.
   - Write down the statement you have chosen on a piece of paper and pin it to yourself with a paper clip. Move around the room trying to find other people who are of a different opinion.
   - Form groups of three and explain your choice to each other. Try to convince each other that your position is right.

2. Read the poem and find out which view it might take about the saying.

At sixteen, I worked after high school hours
at a printing plant
that manufactured legal pads:
Yellow paper
5 stacked seven feet high
and leaning
as I slipped cardboard
between the pages,
then brushed red glue
10 up and down the stack.
No gloves: fingertips required
for the perfection of paper,
smoothing the exact rectangle.

Sluggish by 9 PM, the hands
15 would slide along suddenly sharp paper,
and gather slits thinner than the crevices
of the skin, hidden.
Then the glue would sting,
hands oozing
20 till both palms burned
at the punchclock.

Ten years later, in law school,
I knew that every legal pad
was glued with the sting of hidden cuts,
25 that every open lawbook
was a pair of hands
upturned and burning.

© Reprinted by permission of W.W. Norton & Company, Inc. from City of Coughing and Dead Radiators. Copyright 1993 by Martín Espada.

2 **plant:** often the buildings and machinery needed to carry on any industrial business – 3 **legal pad:** a ruled writing tablet, usually yellow and measuring 8 $\frac{1}{2}$ × 14 inches (22 × 36 cm) – 10 **to stack:** to put on top of each other – 11 **to be required:** to be necessary – 14 **sluggish:** lacking in energy – 16 **crevice:** a crack forming an opening – 19 **to ooze:** to flow slowly, as through holes or small openings – 22 **law school:** a graduate school offering study leading to a law degree

B. Understanding the text

1. Explain the view the poem takes about the saying.
2. State the main message of the poem.
3. Share your ideas with the class.

C. Studying the text

1. Analyse how the speaker's use of language and structure support his message.
2. Compare the poem's message to the messages of the texts you've read before in this unit.

D. Going beyond the text

1. **Placemat activity:**
   - In groups of four, each group member thinks of a title for the poem and writes it down.
   - Rotate the placemat clockwise: Comment on the title your partner wrote or ask a question.
   - Continue rotating until you've got your own title in front of you again.
   - In your group agree on a title and write it into the field in the middle.

2. Look at the real title of the poem: Evaluate the title's relationship to the content of the poem. Is the title effective? Explain.

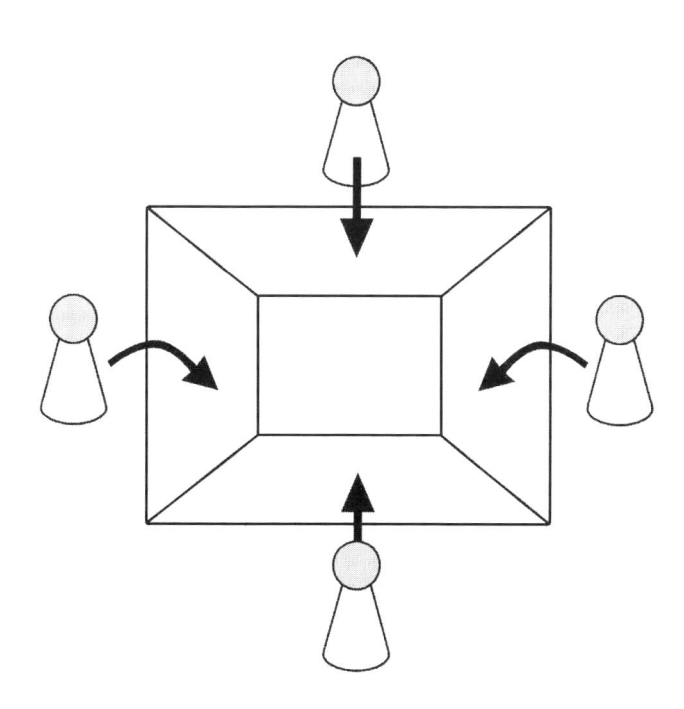

Hinweise (M 7; 5. Doppelstunde)

Das Gedicht *„Who Burns for The Perfection of Paper"* (1993) von **Martín Espada** zeigt, dass nicht selten große Mühen notwendig sind, um die eigenen Ziele zu erreichen. Der Glaube daran, dass jeder Einzelne seine Lebensumstände durch eisernen Willen und harte Arbeit verbessen kann, ist fester Bestandteil des *American Dream*.

A. Approaching the text

Einstieg: Die Lehrkraft schreibt die **Redewendung *„No pain, no gain."*** als Impuls an die Tafel. (Die Redewendung ist auch auf M 7 abgedruckt, aber es empfiehlt sich, das Arbeitsblatt erst später auszuteilen, da der stumme Impuls an der Tafel effektvoller ist.) Die Schülerinnen und Schüler besprechen mit einem Partner, ob sie dieser Aussage ganz, teilweise oder gar nicht zustimmen, und notieren dies dann jeweils auf einem Zettel, den sie sich mithilfe einer Wäsche- oder Büroklammer an ihrem Oberteil befestigen. Anschließend finden sie sich in Dreiergruppen zusammen. Jedes Mitglied der Gruppe sollte dabei eine andere Meinung zu dem Zitat haben. Aufgabe ist es nun, die Gruppenmitglieder von der eigenen Position zu überzeugen.

Anschließend wird das Gedicht in Einzelarbeit gelesen. Die *while-reading task* knüpft dabei an die vorangegangene Kontroverse an.

Achtung: Die Lehrkraft sollte das Gedicht **ohne den Titel** kopieren, damit Aufgabe D bearbeitet werden kann.

B. Understanding the text

Die Schülerinnen und Schüler stellen in Partnerarbeit die Redewendung in Beziehung zum Gedicht und einigen sich dann auf die **Hauptaussage**. Die Ergebnisse werden im Plenum besprochen.

C. Studying the text

In der anschließenden **Gedichtanalyse (C.1–2)** wird das Gedicht sprachlich untersucht und anschließend in den Kontext der vorangegangenen Stunden und der bereits behandelten Texte gesetzt. Hierbei ist es wichtig herauszuarbeiten, dass der *American Dream* durch den festen Glauben an die eigenen Stärken, ein Ziel vor Augen und harte Arbeit erreicht werden kann.

D. Going beyond the text

Bevor die Schülerinnen und Schüler die Aussagekraft des Gedichttitels evaluieren, formulieren sie in **Aufgabe D.1** zunächst selbst einen **passenden Gedichttitel**, um diesen später mit dem eigentlichen Titel vergleichen zu können. Dies findet in einer **Placemat Acitivity** statt. Der Kurs wird dafür in Vierergruppen eingeteilt. Jede Gruppe erhält ein Placemat, das wie auf der Abbildung aussieht. Jeder Lernende schreibt seinen Titel in das Feld vor sich. Anschließend kommentieren die anderen Gruppenmitglieder den Gedichttitel eines jeden Gruppenmitglieds. Zu diesem Zweck wird die Placemat im Uhrzeigersinn gedreht, bis jeder wieder seinen eigenen Titel vor sich liegen hat. Anschließend einigt sich die Gruppe auf einen Titel und schreibt diesen in das leere mittlere Feld.

Unter Rückgriff auf die Gedichtanalyse diskutieren die Lernenden die Frage nach der **Effektivität des Titels**, der zuvor von der Lehrkraft an die Tafel geschrieben wird (*„Who Burns for the Perfection of Paper"*), in Bezug auf das Hauptthema des Gedichts **(D.2)** im Plenum und gleichen diesen mit dem eigenen Titel ab.

Erwartungshorizont (M 7)

A. Approaching the text

"No pain, no gain".

Agree: I agree, people who make it to the top always have to work a lot to get there, etc.

Disagree: I disagree, some people are born rich and never have to face any major problems in their lives, etc.

Partly Agree: Sometimes hard work is not enough, you also have to be lucky, etc.

B. Understanding the text

1. The lyrical I actually goes through physical pain to achieve her/his dream of going to university and studying law. Her/his hands are cut and burn, but s/he finally escapes the paper plant, "gains" an education, and therefore knows what hard work really means.

2. Work hard and follow your dreams: Hard, sometimes painful work is necessary to achieve what you want; with hard work you can get anywhere; don't let pain keep you from going where you want to go; don't give up.

C. Studying the text

1. How language and structure support the message:

Semantic field "pain" with strong images making the reader feel the pain of hard work; incomplete sentences/breaks create sombre mood; pauses add emphasis and give the impression that narrator ponders every thought.

2. Message in comparison to messages of other texts:

Hard work to achieve goals is a common theme in all of the texts; all of the people in the texts want to learn and educate themselves, but they have to work in low-paid jobs first; they all share a strong will and endurance.

D. Going beyond the text

1. Individual results

2. Effective:

The word "burn" is used to describe the pain while working at the printing plant, so the lyrical I has to physically burn for the perfection of paper; the form of a question motivates the reader to think again, the sentence structure indicates that usually nobody "burns" for the perfection of paper as to burn for something also describes the degree of passion somebody does something with → The original title of the poem is effective because it mentions major aspects of the poem and gives the reader something to think about.

Not very effective:

The question raised doesn't get answered; it doesn't say anything about the message of the poem; burning for the perfection of paper only hints at one part of the poem → The title of the poem is not effective, because it doesn't capture the main aspects of the poem.

M 8 An acceptance letter from Yale – finding the courage to break away from old traditions

A Chinese girl and her mother emigrated to the United States. Let's have a look at how their life developed in a country so different from their cultural background.

A. Approaching the text

Task

Work in pairs. Describe what kind of conflict could arise between the two women below.

Excerpt from *Girl in Translation* (2010) by Jean Kwok

Ma and I had been waiting for the decisions from the colleges to come, so we weren't surprised when Aunt Paula called us into her office again. Her face was still and white underneath the foundation and powder. […] I was still drawn along in the wake of emotion of having been accepted by Yale. I had found a new apartment and all of the paperwork had been finalized, except for the character reference
5 for Ma. I knew we could break our ties with Aunt Paula now, and that knowledge allowed me to speak the truth.

Aunt Paula wiped her face with her sleeve, smearing her eye-liner. "Your teeth are sharp and your mouth is keen."

"Fake kindness, fake etiquette is all you've shown us."

10 "How dare you give me so little face?"

I stared at her. "Face or no face doesn't matter in America. What matters is who you really are."

"America! If I hadn't brought you here, you'd still be in Hong Kong. I even gave you another address so you could go to a better school."

"You did that because it's illegal for us to be living where we are." Aunt Paula clenched her jaw. She
15 hadn't realized how much I now knew about the way things worked.

Ma tried to intervene. "Older sister, you've helped us a great deal, but maybe it's time we stopped depending on you so much." I continued as if Ma hadn't spoken. "Just like it's illegal for you to pay us by the piece here at the factory."

"After everything I've done for you, you speak to me like this. You treat the human heart like a dog's
20 lung." But her manner was more regretful than angry, which meant she was getting scared.

I rose to my full height. I wasn't quite as tall as Aunt Paula but I was much taller than Ma by then. "You should be ashamed of yourself for putting us in that apartment all these years. And for making us work here, under these conditions. After we fell down a well, you dropped a boulder on top of us."

Ma had kept her eyes down, but now she looked up and slowly nodded in agreement. "Older sister, I cannot understand why you have treated us like this."

Aunt Paula was sputtering. "I gave you work and shelter! And this is how you repay my human currency." The currency of humanity is kindness. "I brought you here! That is a life debt, one you can never repay."

"You should think about your own life debt, to the gods," I retorted.

Aunt Paula had had enough and she pulled out her final card. "I wouldn't want to take advantage of you. If you think I've treated you badly, you can leave. Leave the factory and move out of the apartment." She said the words with gravity, then waited for us to beg her to reconsider.

Ma's hands were trembling but she managed to smile. "In fact, ah-Kim has found us an apartment, in Queens."

Aunt Paula's eyes popped.

"We've already repaid our debts to you," Ma said. When I heard her words, I knew we were freed of Aunt Paula forever. I met Ma's eyes, and saw she was ready to leave.

I spoke to Aunt Paula. "If you do anything to hinder us in any way, I will report you to the authorities."

And we walked out of there, leaving Aunt Paula gaping in her little office at the factory.

I had a blurred impression of the other workers staring at our departure as we got our things from the finishing area and then started for the exit. [My friend] Matt caught my arm as I passed by and I paused for a moment to whisper, "It's all right, come find me later," and then Ma and I were out of the factory and on the street, hurrying toward the subway. A cool breeze blew against my hair.

"Are you all right, Ma?" I had been ready for this step long before. This was what I'd been working toward. I just didn't know how Ma felt about losing her only family except for me.

She sighed. "Yes. I am afraid but I feel light too. Even if Aunt Paula bathed in grapefruit water, she wouldn't be able to wash the guilt off. It is time for us to make our own way."

I squeezed her arm. "Mother and cub."

Source: Kwok, Jean: Girl in Translation. New York: Riverhead Books, 2010. p. 266f.

3 **wake:** as a result of – 3 **Yale:** one of the most prestigious and expensive colleges in the U.S. – 7–8 **Your teeth are sharp and your mouth is keen:** Chinese idiom: The words Kimberly uses cut deeply and she knows exactly what will hurt most and where a person is vulnerable – 10 **How dare you give me so little face?:** Chinese idiom: When sb. gives sb. face they help the other person at a particular moment in a social situation that is embarrassing or unpleasant – 14 **to clench:** to close tightly – 14 **jaw:** either of two bones forming the framework of the mouth – 20 **regretful:** sorrowful because of what is lost, gone, or done – 23 **boulder:** a large rock – 26 **to sputter:** to make explosive popping or sizzling sounds – 27 **currency:** (here) money – 29 **to retort:** to reply in a sharp way – 32 **gravity:** heaviness – 39 **to gape:** to come open – 40 **blurred:** vague – 48 **cub:** (here) a young inexperienced person

B. Understanding the text

Work in groups of three or four and use this graphic organiser (the "fish bone") to show your understanding of the text.

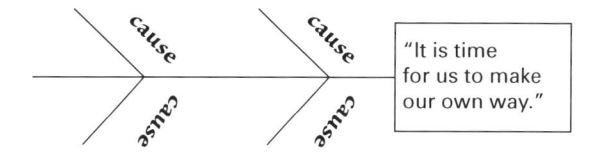

"It is time for us to make our own way."

1. Decide what the causes were for the narrator and her mother to cut relations with Aunt Paula.

2. Present your conclusions to the class.

From Rags to Riches? – The American Dream Revisited (S II)

C. Studying the text

In groups work on the following tasks. Then compare your answers with those of others in the class.

1. Identify three things you learn about Kimberly through direct characterisation.
2. Describe the atmosphere in the extract. Find examples of different moods.
3. Explain Ma's contrasting feelings, and account for the conflict in her attitude.
4. Comment on how the passage implies aspects of the American Dream.

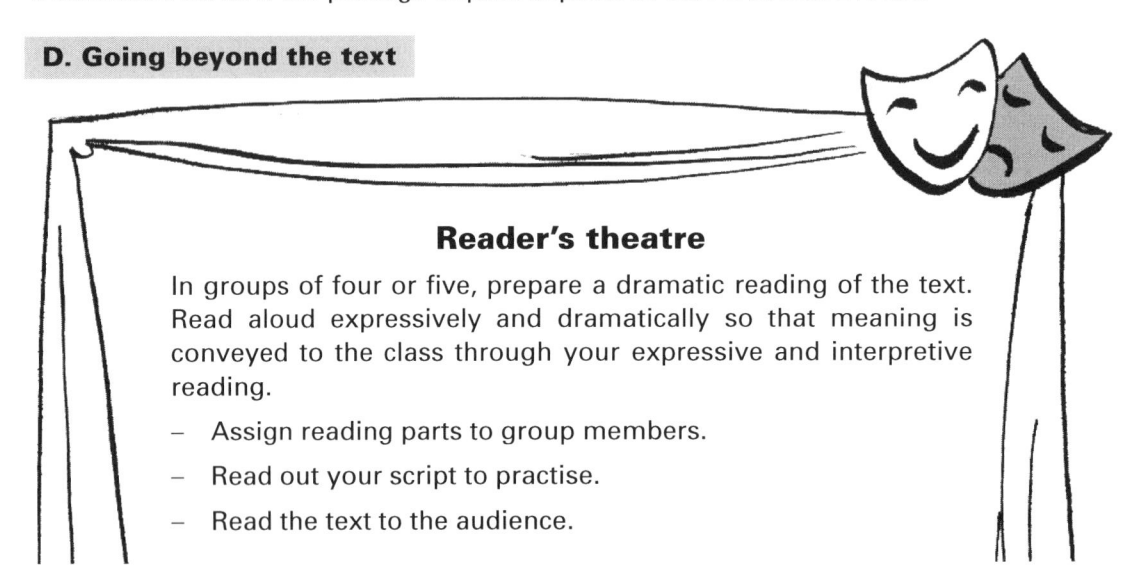

D. Going beyond the text

Reader's theatre

In groups of four or five, prepare a dramatic reading of the text. Read aloud expressively and dramatically so that meaning is conveyed to the class through your expressive and interpretive reading.

– Assign reading parts to group members.
– Read out your script to practise.
– Read the text to the audience.

Hinweise (M 8; 6. Doppelstunde)

In dieser Doppelstunde lernen die Schülerinnen und Schüler, wie schwierig es ist, als Immigrant den richtigen Weg zwischen **alten Traditionen** und Werten und der **fremden Kultur** des neuen Heimatlandes zu finden. Als 5-jährige emigrierte **Jean Kwok** mit ihren Eltern von Hongkong in die USA und lebte und arbeitete einige Jahre in einem New Yorker Slum. Später machte sie ihren Abschluss an der Harvard University und ist seither als Schriftstellerin tätig. Ihr Roman *„Girl in Translation"* (2010) verarbeitet einige dieser Erfahrungen. Anders als der Freund der Protagonistin, Matt, der auch weiterhin die traditionelle chinesische Kultur in New York leben will, ist es Kimberlys Traum, eine möglichst gute westliche Ausbildung zu erhalten. Dabei lernt sie, dass jede Entscheidung für etwas Neues auch eine Ablösung von den Traditionen ihrer Heimat bedeutet.

Dieser Textauszug zeigt deutlich, wie intensiv junge *Asian Americans* ihren amerikanischen Traum leben, auch wenn das heißt, mit einigen alten Traditionen brechen zu müssen.

A. Approaching the text

Einstieg: Die Schülerinnen und Schüler stellen mithilfe der Bilder Hypothesen an, was der Inhalt des Textes sein könnte. Durch den Aushandlungsprozess in der Partnerarbeit werden erste Erwartungen an den Text aufgebaut. In einer kurzen Plenumsphase werden die Ergebnisse genannt und in Stichworten an der Tafel notiert.

B. Understanding the text

Unter Verwendung der **grafischen Lernhilfe** machen sich die Schülerinnen und Schüler in Gruppenarbeit Notizen zu den im Text genannten Ursachen, die letztlich zum Bruch mit den Familienbanden führen. Anschließend werden diese im Unterrichtsgespräch erläutert.

From Rags to Riches? – The American Dream Revisited (S II)

| Reihe 6 | Verlauf | Material S 28 | LEK | Kontext | Mediothek |

C. Studying the text

Für den fortgeschrittenen Englischunterricht ist es unerlässlich, ausgewählte **Aspekte einer literarischen Analyse** immer wieder zu üben. In Kleingruppen erarbeiten die Schülerinnen und Schüler die Antworten zu **Aufgabe C**. Während sich **C.1–3** ausschließlich auf den vorliegenden Text beziehen, werden für die Beantwortung von **C.4** auch Bezüge zu zuvor behandelten Texten hergestellt. Die Ergebnisse der Gruppenarbeit werden im Plenum erörtert. Hier haben die Aussagen zu **C.4** einen besonderen Stellenwert, da an dieser Stelle zuvor erarbeitete wesentliche Aspekte des *American Dream* genannt werden.

D. Going beyond the text

In **Aufgabe D** (fakultativ) haben die Lernenden die Möglichkeit, ihre Interpretation durch Artikulation sowie Gestik und Mimik beim Vorlesen darzustellen. Diese Aufgabe ist zugleich ein Differenzierungsangebot, denn auch kompetenzschwächere Lernende können hier beachtliche Präsentationen erreichen.

II/C5

Erwartungshorizont (M 8)

A. Approaching the text

Possible answers: There might be a conflict between the two women: between young and old, between traditions (home country) and western ways (USA) …

B. Understanding the text

Possible solutions: She has received a letter of acceptance from Yale. She and her mother have already found a new apartment to live in. She has gained a good knowledge of how things work in America. She has uncovered Aunt Paula's true character. Family ties have lost importance for her.

C. Studying the text

Answers include:

a) She acts with great strength and courage (ll. 5–6). She will not be bound by cultural values she grew up with (l. 11). She is loyal and thoughtful regarding her mother (ll. 44–45).

b) Throughout the excerpts, the author creates different moods: tense and optimistic (ll. 1–6) aggressive and angry (ll. 7–15), appeasing (ll. 16–17), uncertain and sad (ll. 24–25), threatening (ll. 30–32), strong and powerful (l. 38), relieved (ll. 46–47).

c) Ma's conflict is internal, or inside her mind and external as well. She grew up with very traditional Chinese values which strongly demand respect for an older sister. At the same time there is her daughter who has developed a very independent mind and follows her dream of excellent education. Ma has to decide to either stay with her sister or go with her daughter.

d) In America "what matters is who you really are" (l. 11). Kimberly frees herself from traditional obligations, family ties and social dependencies to follow her dream and achieve her American Dream.

M 9 Does the American Dream still exist? – Looking at some data

Is the American Dream still alive today? And is it really possible to rise from rags to riches?

A. Approaching the topic

1. Work in small groups. Consider these sentence stems and finish each:
   - Save the American Dream because ...
   - Save the American Dream or ...
   - Save the American Dream from ...

2. From what you have already learned about the USA, choose the most appropriate sentence and write it on the board.

B. Understanding and studying the topic

Graph 1: Work in pairs or in small groups. Study graph 1 and answer the questions. Take notes.

1. Point out the key message of the graph.
2. State whether Americans still think they can reach the American Dream.
3. Explain what this graph indicates about economic mobility in the USA.

Do Americans Think They Will Reach the American Dream?

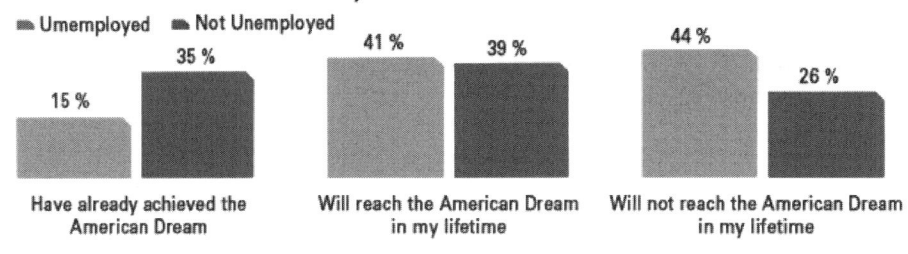

- Unemployed / Not Unemployed
- Have already achieved the American Dream: 15% / 35%
- Will reach the American Dream in my lifetime: 41% / 39%
- Will not reach the American Dream in my lifetime: 44% / 26%

Source: Pew Charitable Trusts

Graph 2: Work in pairs or in small groups. Study graph 2 and answer the questions. Take notes.

1. Point out the key message of the graph.
2. State whether it is still true today that people can move up and down the economic ladder.
3. Some people say that in the United States today it is no longer "from rags to riches" but "the rich get richer." Point out what the statistics say.

Chances of moving up or down the family income ladder, by parents' quintile

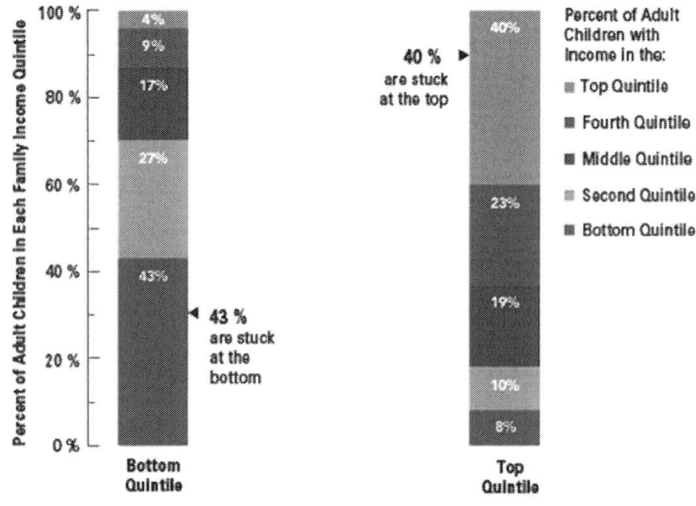

Bottom Quintile: Bottom 43%, Second 27%, Middle 17%, Fourth 9%, Top 4%
Top Quintile: Top 40%, Fourth 23%, Middle 19%, Second 10%, Bottom 8%

◄ 43 % are stuck at the bottom
40 % ► are stuck at the top

Percent of Adult Children with Income in the:
- Top Quintile
- Fourth Quintile
- Middle Quintile
- Second Quintile
- Bottom Quintile

Parents' Family Income Quintile

Source: Pew Charitable Trusts

C. Going beyond the topic

Take one of the two positions:

1. *The American Dream is dead.*
2. *The American Dream is still alive.*

Work in groups and plan how to argue effectively for your position.

– Gather relevant facts and information from the info box and from what you already know.

– Organise what you know into a reasoned position by a) arranging the information into a thesis statement, b) arranging the supporting facts, information and other evidence into a logical structure, and c) making the conclusion that the statement is true (the conclusion is the same as the original statement.) The "How to box" may help you.

– Present your position.

Info box: The USA – a dream come true?

– The American Dream still exists – it has just changed as it has changed throughout history. Most Americans still believe in it and define it as spiritual happiness and having a job.

– Mainly the rich become richer: the wealthiest 1% own more than a third of all the wealth in the USA.

– After the recession began in 2007 the unofficial unemployment rate went up to 20%. 5.5 million of Americans without a job are even without unemployment benefits.

– Many people from so-called advanced countries still emigrate to the USA. In Germany the USA is the second favourite destination when it comes to emigration.

– Martin Luther King famously fought for the rights of black Americans in the 1960s. Much has changed since then, but recent statistics suggest that the colour of one's skin still does matter: African Americans are more likely to be on the bottom rung of the economic ladder.

– Inequality can also be found in the health care system: 41% of working US Americans have problems with their medical bills.

– In 2009 the American Dream of many black Americans came true when Barack Obama became President of the USA.

– There are still examples of people who have made it: Mark Zuckerberg, the founder of Facebook, became rich and famous while still a student.

How to present the best case for your position

☑ We will begin with a strong, sincere, and enthusiastic appeal for the listeners to agree with our position.

☑ We will present several points of evidence organised in a logical way.

☑ During the presentation, we will select a few major points, four or five at the most, and expand on them by using examples, stories, and statistics.

☑ We will make eye contact with all members of the audience.

☑ We will keep our presentation within the time limit.

☑ We have developed visual aids to help make our case.

☑ We have practised our presentation. We are comfortable delivering it.

From Rags to Riches? – The American Dream Revisited (S II)

| Reihe 6 | Verlauf | Material S 31 | LEK | Kontext | Mediothek |

II/C5

Hinweise (M 9; 7. Doppelstunde)

Wie ist es **heute** um den *American Dream* bestellt? Im Zuge der **Wirtschaftskrise** haben viele Amerikaner ihre Arbeit verloren und die Zahl derer, die unter der Armutsgrenze von weniger als 4000 Euro leben, erreichte 2011 mit 6,7 % einen Rekordwert. Besonders hart trifft es auch die **amerikanische Mittelschicht**, die immer kleiner wird: Menschen mit guter Ausbildung, vermeintlich sicherem Job und Eigenheim, die plötzlich vor dem Nichts stehen und im schlimmsten Fall sogar auf der Straße leben.

Stimmen werden laut, die besagen, dass der amerikanische Traum, der in den letzten Jahrzehnten allzu oft mit finanzieller Sicherheit gleichgesetzt wurde, ausgeträumt ist. Besonders unter arbeitslosen Amerikanern sinkt die Hoffnung, dass sie diesen Traum zu Lebzeiten erreichen werden. Das amerikanische Sozialsystem gerät immer häufiger in die Schusslinie öffentlicher Kritik.

In dieser Doppelstunde untersuchen die Schülerinnen und Schüler zwei **Säulendiagramme**, die etwas über die aktuelle Realität des *American Dream* aussagen. Im Anschluss daran beziehen sie in einer **Diskussion** Position zu der Frage, ob der amerikanische Traum endgültig ausgeträumt ist.

A. Approaching the topic

Als **Einstieg** dient das **Bild einer demonstrierenden Frau (M 1)**, die auf ihrem Plakat dazu auffordert, den amerikanischen Traum zu retten. Das Bild wird als Folie aufgelegt und bietet Anlass für ein gelenktes Unterrichtsgespräch:

– *Describe the picture.*

– *Why are the people demonstrating?*

– *What is meant by "Save the American Dream"?*

Im Anschluss rekapitulieren die Schülerinnen und Schüler ihr **Vorwissen** zur aktuellen Situation des amerikanischen Traums. Als Impuls dienen **Satzfragmente (A.1)**, die die Lernenden in kleinen Gruppen vervollständigen. Der erste Satzanfang erfordert Begründungen, warum der amerikanische Traum erhalten bleiben muss. Der zweite zeigt Konsequenzen auf, falls der Traum nicht erhalten bliebe. Der dritte schließlich listet Faktoren auf, die den amerikanischen Traum bedrohen.

In einem Aushandlungsprozess einigen sich die Gruppen auf jeweils einen Satz, den sie auf Grundlage ihres bisherigen Wissensstands für besonders passend halten. Die Sätze werden an der Tafel gesammelt **(A.2)** und im Plenum erläutert.

Alternative: Die Schülerinnen und Schüler schreiben ihre treffendsten Sätze gut lesbar auf buntes Papier und laufen damit im Klassenzimmer umher. Dabei tauschen sie sich mit ihren Mitschülern aus, indem sie ihre Sätze erklären und ihre Wahl begründen.

B. Understanding and studying the topic

M 9 bietet die Gelegenheit, Ergebnisse der bisherigen Arbeit mit statistischen Daten und Fakten zu vergleichen. Die Aussagen der literarischen Texte deuten an, dass man durch harte Arbeit und Durchhaltevermögen den amerikanischen Traum verwirklichen kann. Untersuchungen der *Federal Reserve Bank of Boston* zeigen jedoch, dass in den vergangenen Jahren deutlich weniger Familien die sozial-ökonomische Leiter aufwärts kletterten als noch in den 70er- und 80er-Jahren des letzten Jahrhunderts (www.bos.frb.org/economic/nerr/rr2002/q4/issues.pdf).

Die Klasse wird zur Bearbeitung der **Aufgabe B** in zwei Hälften geteilt. Die eine Hälfte erarbeitet in Partnerarbeit **Graph 1**, die andere Hälfte **Graph 2**. Anschließend finden sich immer zwei Paare mit unterschiedlicher Grafik für die Ergebnispräsentation zusammen. Im Plenum wird der **Glaube der Amerikaner an den *American Dream*** (*Graph 1*) mit der **Realität** (*Graph 2*) verglichen. ***Graph 1*** beantwortet die Frage, ob Amerikaner immer noch daran glauben, dass sie den amerikanischen Traum erreichen können. Dabei unterscheidet die Statistik zwischen arbeitslosen Amerikanern und solchen, die berufstätig sind. Die Statistik zeigt, dass fast ebenso viele Arbeitslose (41 %) wie Arbeitende (39 %) denken, dass sie den amerikanischen Traum noch erreichen können, wohingegen deutlich mehr Arbeitslose (44 %) der Meinung sind, dass sie den amerikanischen Traum nicht mehr erreichen werden, und nur wenige dieser Gruppe denken, dass sie ihn bereits erreicht haben (15 %).

Graph 2 sagt etwas über die **ökonomische Mobilität** der amerikanischen Gesellschaft aus. Der Glaube daran, dass alle Menschen gleich sind und sich unabhängig von ihrer Herkunft nach oben arbeiten können, ist fester Bestandteil des *American Dream*. Die Statistik jedoch zeigt eine andere Realität auf: Die linke Säule zeigt die prozentuale Wahrscheinlichkeit für Kinder von Amerikanern, die dem ökonomisch schwächsten Fünftel angehören, sich nach oben zu arbeiten: 43 % der Kinder dieser Gruppe bleiben als Erwachsene im untersten Fünftel. 27 % schaffen es auf die nächste Ebene und nur 4 % schaffen es ganz nach oben. Die rechte Säule zeigt die Prozentsätze für die Kinder der Eltern an, die sich auf der höchsten ökonomischen Ebene befinden: 40 % bleiben auch dort, wenn sie erwachsen sind.

An dieser Stelle kann auch besprochen werden, welchem Aspekt des amerikanischen Traums die Ergebnisse von ***Graph 2*** widersprechen, und es kann Bezug auf die **Einstiegsaufgabe A** genommen werden.

C. Going beyond the topic

Eine **strukturierte Diskussion** führen zu können, gehört zu den angestrebten Kompetenzen des fortgeschrittenen Englischunterrichts. Die Aufgabenstellung gibt klare Anweisungen, wie die Präsentation der Argumente vorbereitet wird. Ob die Schülerinnen und Schüler sich selbst einer Position zuordnen oder ob die Lehrkraft sie zuordnet, muss aus der Klassensituation heraus entschieden werden. Die Gruppen nehmen bei der Vorbereitung Bezug auf die **Ergebnisse der Reihe** und entnehmen der **Infobox** zusätzliche Informationen. Die Infobox ist so aufgebaut, dass sie jeweils **vier Fakten für beide Positionen** enthält, die für die anschließende Diskussion verwendet werden können.

Erwartungshorizont (M 9)

Photograph "Save the American Dream":

In the picture you can see four women who are demonstrating. They look frustrated and angry. An African American woman is holding a sign in her hand saying "Save the American Dream". The sign is painted in the colours of the American flag. The initials of the request are written in red whereas the other letters are blue. So the initials form an acrostic that reads "sad". They seem to want somebody to save the American Dream. Most likely they are addressing politicians. The American Dream with its promise of material security for everyone has been in danger since the financial crisis.

A. Approaching the topic

Possible solutions:

Save the American Dream <u>because</u> that is what America is all about in the first place, … because we want opportunities for everybody, … because we want justice and equality.

Save the American Dream <u>or</u> we will fight for it, … or America will be a different country, … or the promise of the Declaration of Independence will no longer be true.

Save the American Dream from too much government in Washington, D.C., ... from the power of Wall Street, ... from people who want to cut constitutional rights.

B. Understanding and studying the topic

Graph 1:

1. The key message is that people who have a job are more optimistic about the American Dream than those who are unemployed.

2. The graph distinguishes between unemployed Americans and those who have work. Only 15% of unemployed people believe that they have already reached the American Dream which again seems to show that the American Dream is still closely connected with material security today. 44% are sure that they won't achieve the American Dream whereas 35% of the Americans who have a job believe that they have already achieved the American Dream or will sooner or later achieve it (39%). So the American Dream is still alive for both groups, but people without work find it harder to believe in it.

3. The graph hints at the fact that people seem to know that economic mobility doesn't exist in the way the American Dream promises. People without work think that it's not as likely for them to achieve the American Dream as it is for people who have a job.

Graph 2:

1. The key message of the graph is that it's extremely hard for the children of parents who are in the bottom quintile to move their way up.

2. It is possible to move up and down the economic ladder, but it does not seem very likely. Only 27% of those raised in the bottom quintile make it to the next quintile and only 4% of them make it to the top. 40% of those born into the top quintile remain there when they are adults. The chance of moving upwards is therefore limited.

3. Families at the top of the income ladder enjoy increasing advantages over those at the bottom, and those at the bottom do not seem to have good prospects of moving up. The rich get richer, the poor stay poor. The saying from "rag to riches" is becoming ever more a myth.

C. Going beyond the topic

1. The American Dream is dead:

It's much harder for people from low-income families to make their way up; some Americans work a lot and some even have more than one job, but they only earn a little and won't be able to climb the economic ladder; poor people aren't supported the way they are in other countries; people who are not Caucasian still get discriminated against in the USA (ghettos, police etc.); there's a lot of inequality in the USA ...

2. The American Dream is still alive:

It exists and has just adapted; you only have to work harder than before; you can achieve everything if you really want it; there are examples of people who made their way up after the economic crisis; there are scholarships and evening classes for those who are willing to learn and educate themselves; sometimes you can be lucky and have a really good business idea; it also depends on how you define the American Dream (Freedom is also an aspect of the American Dream and people emigrating from e.g. Cuba might find it in the USA); there are still successful branches like the computer industry which attracts immigrants from advanced countries as well ...

M 10 The American Dream vs the European Dream

Does Europe have a dream as well? And if so, to what extent is it different from the American Dream? In the extract from his book The European Dream: How Europe's Vision of the Future Is Quietly Eclipsing the American Dream *Jeremy Rifkin deals with this question.*

A. Approaching the text

1. Working individually, place the words in the list below (or their numbers) on the graph according to how you associate them with the two labels, Europe and America.

2. Now work in pairs and compare your word graphs.

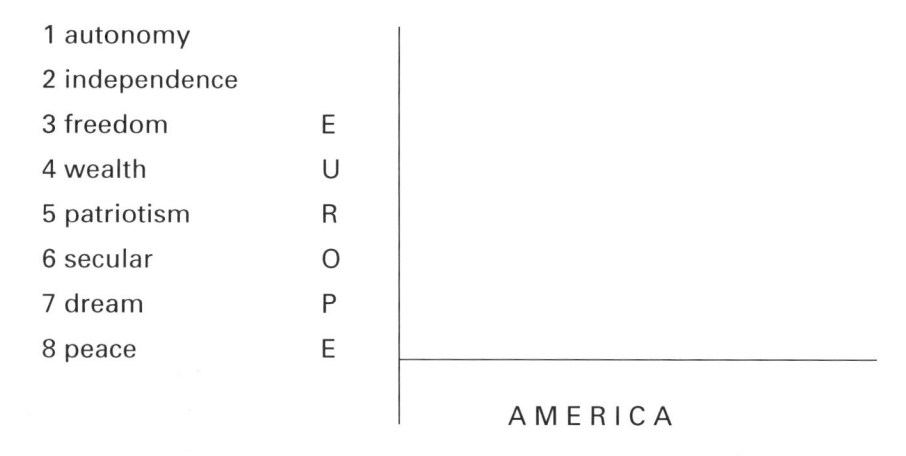

1 autonomy
2 independence
3 freedom
4 wealth
5 patriotism
6 secular
7 dream
8 peace

```
E
U
R
O
P
E
        |_____
           A M E R I C A
```

The American Dream vs the European Dream (2004) by Jeremy Rifkin

Americans hold a negative definition of what it means to be free and, thus, secure. For us, freedom has long been associated with autonomy. If one is autonomous, he or she is not dependent on others or vulnerable to circumstances outside of his or her control. To be autonomous, one needs to be propertied. The more wealth one amasses, the more independent one is in the world. [...] With wealth
5 comes exclusivity – and with exclusivity comes security.

The new European Dream, however, is based on a different set of assumptions about what constitutes freedom and security. For Europeans, freedom is not found in autonomy, but in embeddedness. To be free is to have access to a myriad of interdependent relationships with others. The more communities one has access to, the more options and choices one has for living a full and meaningful life. With
10 relationships comes inclusivity and with inclusivity comes security.

The American Dream puts an emphasis on economic growth, personal wealth and independence. The new European Dream focuses more on sustainable development, quality of life and interdependence. [...] The American Dream is inseparable from the country's religious heritage and deep spiritual faith. The European Dream is secular to the core. The American Dream is wedded to love of country and
15 patriotism. The European Dream is more cosmopolitan and less territorial.

Americans are more willing to employ military force in the world, if necessary, to protect what we perceive to be our vital self-interests. Europeans are more reluctant to use military force and instead favor diplomacy, economic assistance and aid to avert conflict and prefer peacekeeping operations to maintain order.

20 Americans tend to think locally, while Europeans' loyalties are more divided – and stretch from the local to the global. The American Dream is deeply personal and little concerned with the rest of humanity. The European Dream is more expansive and systemic in nature and therefore, more bound to the welfare of the planet. [...]

The new European Dream is powerful because it dares to suggest a new history, with an attention to
25 quality of life, sustainability, peace and harmony. In a sustainable civilization, based on quality of life
rather than unlimited individual accumulation of wealth, the very material basis of modern progress
would be a thing of the past. A steady-state global economy is a radical proposition because it challenges the conventional way we have come to use nature's resources. It does away with the very idea of
history as an ever-rising curve of material advances. The objective of a sustainable global economy is
30 to continually reproduce a high-quality present state by aligning human production and consumption
with nature's ability to recycle waste and replenish resources. A sustainable, steady state economy is
truly the end of history defined by unlimited material progress. […]

The new dream is focused not on amassing wealth but, rather, on elevating the human spirit. The
European Dream seeks to expand human empathy, not territory. It takes humanity out of the materia-
35 list prison in which it has been bound since the early days of the 18th century Enlightenment and into
the light of a new future motivated by idealism.

Of this much I am relatively sure. The fledgling European Dream represents humanity's best aspirations for a better tomorrow. A new generation of Europeans carries the world's hopes with it. This
places a very special responsibility on the European people, the kind our own founding fathers and
40 mothers must have felt more than 200 years ago, when the rest of the world looked at America as a
beacon of hope. I hope our trust is not trifled away.

Adapted from "The European Dream: How Europe's Vision of the Future Is Quietly Eclipsing the American Dream" by Jeremy Rifkin © Penguin 2004.

3 **propertied:** to possess material goods – 4 **to amass:** to collect something – 7 **embeddedness:** to be surrounded by sth. and being a part of it – 8 **myriad:** a lot of sth. – 12 **sustainable:** sth. being able to continue for a long time – 14 **core:** the most important part of sth. – 15 **cosmopolitan:** knowing sth. about people or things from different parts of the world – 17 **reluctant:** not willing to do sth. – 18 **to avert:** to avoid sth. – 26 **accumulation:** an amount of sth. collected – 27 **proposition:** a suggestion – 30 **aligning:** to bring two things into a line – 31 **replenish:** to refill sth. – 37 **fledgling:** here: the growing – 37 **aspiration:** hope – 41 **beacon:** here: symbol – 41 **trifled:** to be treated carelessly

B. Understanding the text

1. Copy the table into your exercise books. Read the article and make notes on how Rifkin describes the American Dream and how he describes the European Dream. Write captions for the different aspects he mentions.

American Dream	European Dream

2. Use your notes to write a 150-word summary of the article. Then pair up and read your partner's summary. If necessary, help your partner revise her/his summary.

C. Studying the text

1. Illustrate the different components of both dreams by finding concrete examples or explanations for them.
2. Describe what the author means when he writes that the European Dream is "new".
3. In pairs or small groups comment on the conclusion of the article. Consider what you already know about the political and economic situation in the USA and Europe.
4. The author refers to Europe as an entity. Comment on whether his assumption is true for Germany.

D. Going beyond the text

Write an essay on "Is there a German Dream?"

M 11 How to write an essay

How to write an essay	
Essay	
Essay topic:	German Dream
Essay question:	Is there a German Dream?
Introduction	
Restate question:	Interpreting the question in your own words
Define the general concept:	Identify the general question raised in topic
Thesis statement:	Brief statement of your main argument in your essay
Orientation/Outline:	Points you will make in the essay that will satisfy your argument
First paragraph	
First topic statement:	First point you intend to make
General features, details, or ideas	You first provide general information and explanation
Specific evidence:	Details that support the points you are making
Significance of the point:	and how they contribute to your argument
Second paragraph	
Second topic statement:	The second point you intend to make
General features, details, or ideas:	First provide general information and explanation
Specific evidence:	Details that that support the points you are making
Significance of the point:	and how they contribute to your argument
Third paragraph	
...	
Conclusion	Write a conclusion that effectively sums up your ideas.

From Rags to Riches? – The American Dream Revisited (S II)

| Reihe 6 | Verlauf | Material S 37 | LEK | Kontext | Mediothek |

II/C5

Hinweise (M 10 und M 11; 9. Doppelstunde)

In der **letzten Doppelstunde** wird dem *American Dream* in einem Textauszug von Jeremy Rifkin der **europäische Traum** gegenübergestellt. Jeremy Rifkin beschäftigt sich in seinem Buch „*The European Dream: How Europe's Vision of the Future Is Quietly Eclipsing the American Dream*" (2004) mit der Idee eines europäischen Traums, der langsam, aber erfolgreich den *American Dream* in seiner Bedeutung ablöst.

A. Approaching the text

In das **Diagramm (A.1)** werden in Einzelarbeit **Attribute** eingetragen, mit denen Rifkin in seinem Textauszug den *American* und den *European Dream* beschreibt. Je stärker ein Wort der Achse „*Europe*" zugeordnet wird, desto höher und weiter links wird es platziert. Je mehr ein Wort „*America*" zugeordnet wird, desto niedriger und weiter rechts wird es notiert. Anschließend vergleichen die Lernenden in Partnerarbeit ihre Eintragungen und begründen ihre Positionierung der Attribute **(A.2)**. Durch diese Zuordnungsaufgabe wird eine **Erwartungshaltung** an den Inhalt des Textes aufgebaut.

B. Understanding the text

In dem Textauszug „**The American Dream vs the European Dream**" (M 10) vergleicht der Autor beide Konzepte. Daher ist eine **Tabelle (B.1)** gut geeignet, um diese **Gegenüberstellung** deutlich zu machen und sich einen ersten Überblick über den Text zu verschaffen. Die Lektüre und das stichwortartige Ausfüllen der Tabelle erfolgen in Einzelarbeit. Die Ergebnisse werden an der **Tafel** festgehalten. Dabei muss die Lehrkraft darauf achten, eine Spalte für das Hinzufügen von **C.1** freizuhalten.

In einem zweiten Schritt verwenden die Schülerinnen und Schüler Stichpunkte aus der Tabelle, um die geforderte **Zusammenfassung (B.2)** zu schreiben. Diese Übung gilt auch als Vorbereitung auf die Klausur. Die vorläufigen Ergebnisse werden in Partnerarbeit gegebenenfalls verbessert, bevor die Ergebnissicherung im Plenum erfolgt.

C. Studying the text

Die **Fragen 1–4** werden in Kleingruppen stichwortartig beantwortet. Bei **C.1** geht es darum, Beispiele oder Erklärungen für die Behauptungen des Autors zu finden, z. B. dass die USA eher bereit seien einen Krieg zu führen, um ihre Interessen zu verteidigen (Hier kann der Irakkrieg als Beleg genannt werden.) Diese Aufgabe schärft den Blick der Lernenden für die Stützung von Argumenten und lässt sie einen Bezug zur realen Welt herstellen. In Aufgabe **C.2** überlegen sie, ob es stimmt, dass der europäische Traum neu ist, und belegen ihre Aussagen mit Beispielen. Am Schluss des Textauszugs behauptet Rifkin, dass der europäische Traum in Zukunft den amerikanischen ablösen werde. Die Schülerinnen und Schüler nehmen zu diesem Schluss Stellung und begründen ihre Meinung **(C.3)**. Abschließend wird der Blick nach Deutschland gerichtet **(C.4)**. Die Notizen zu dieser Aufgabe bereiten die **Hausaufgabe D** vor. Die Ergebnisse der Aufgabe C werden im Plenum diskutiert. Dabei können die Ergebnisse von B.1 und C.1 zu einem tabellarischen **Tafelbild** zusammengefügt werden.

D. Going beyond the text

Unter Verwendung von **M 11** (*How to write an essay*) schreiben die Schülerinnen und Schüler einen **Essay** zum Thema „*Is there a German Dream?*" als Hausaufgabe.

Erwartungshorizont (M 10 und M 11)

A. Approaching the text

1. According to the text: <u>America</u>: autonomy, wealth, independence, freedom, patriotism; <u>Europe</u>: freedom, peace, secular
2. <u>Content of summary</u>: – Rifkin's definition of the American Dream – Rifkin's definition of the European Dream – comparison of both dreams – reasons why Rifkin thinks the European Dream is more future-orientated

B. Understanding the text

B.1 und C.1: Vorschlag für ein Tafelbild:

American Dream	European Dream	Examples and explanations
freedom means autonomy autonomy = independence and wealth wealth = exclusivity exclusivity = security → **emphasis on:** economic growth personal wealth independence → **based on:** religious heritage patriotism **view on world politics:** willing to use military force loyalties are local	freedom means embeddedness embeddedness = relationships with other countries relationships = inclusivity inclusivity = security → **emphasis on:** sustainable development quality of life interdependence → **based on:** secularism cosmopolitism **view on world politics:** diplomacy loyalties are global: welfare of planet	– Most European countries have more than one border, are surrounded by other countries, they feel strong working together. vs – The USA is big, different states form one country. – Their history is relatively young and immigrants from Europe left their home countries to flee corruption and oppression→ Independence and autonomy are more important for Americans. – Wealth and religion are more important to Americans, many of their ancestors fled from poverty or religious persecution. – War in Iraq or Afghanistan

C. Studying the text: 2. Many immigrants left Europe because of wars going on between European countries. When the USA was founded and while it was developing, Europe was a continent with many independent countries which weren't linked. Some of them were even arch-enemies. It was only after World War II that Europe moved towards integration. In 1993 the European Union was formally established with the Maastricht Treaty.

3. <u>Agree with conclusion</u>: Europe's vision or dream for the future is more farsighted than the outdated American Dream. In times of advanced globalisation Europe is not merely interested in making profit but also in the environment. But the USA is mainly interested in profit and is, aside from China, the biggest polluter of the environment. Being concerned with environmental issues is essential for the future of the planet.

<u>Disagree with conclusion</u>: Rifkin talks about a dream but seems to mean power. Power is traditionally linked to territory as well as productivity and wealth. Europe is stable but has an attitude that is far too idealistic. Either the USA is going to recover from their crisis or another super power will take their position, for example China or India.

4. Germany is a founding member of the European Union. It has always played an important role in bringing forward European integration that was originally developed to bring peace to Europe. Germany, as being the latest cause for a world war, is now one of the most important advocates and believers of a united Europe and a peaceful world. It came out of the global recession very strongly and aimed at helping and advising other (European) countries. Environmental issues have always been a great concern for Germany and it has always been a pioneer in climate protection. But lately many reproach Germany for wanting to play on the global stage and leave other European countries behind and that in doing so they forgot their history and are becoming arrogant. So basically, the European Dream, according to Rifkin, seems to be the German Dream as well, but voices are being raised against this approach.

D. Going beyond the text: Is there a German Dream? <u>Yes</u>: – individual dreams of owning a house with a garden, having a spouse and two children, a job, security, stability – welfare state and financial security – peace; <u>No</u>: – social and economic mobility is not very high in Germany either – recession and fast-paced society scares young people, they lose hope – there is no individual German Dream, the European Dream is also the German Dream

The Freedom Writers with Erin Gruwell: *The first Latina Secretary of Education*

English teacher Erin Gruwell (Ms G) was confronted with a room of "unteachable at-risk" students. With a firm stand against intolerance, misunderstanding and racism she motivated her students to record their thoughts and feelings in diaries and calling themselves the Freedom Writers. *The following text is an excerpt from these diaries.*

Dear Diary,

Everyone in Ms. G's class is talking about their college application essay that was due today. The essays are supposed to be about a significant event that occurred in our lives. I thought to myself how lucky all the Freedom Writers are to be able to say, "I'm going to college." For me that statement is
5 impossible to say because of one little reason: I am an illegal immigrant.

I wish my essay could have been about the most significant event in my life; how my family immigrated to America. My mother brought her children here to provide them with a better life. My mother kept us away from my drunk and abusive father, she wanted us to have a better future, and the opportunity in life that she never had – to have a successful education. Who would have thought that getting
10 an education would be so tough? The irony is that I was brought here to get an education, yet at the same time, I feel like I am being deprived of an education in the future.

[…] The memory of my journey, or should I say my struggle to America, is buried deep inside of me. I was four years old when I was lifted into the arms of two strange men. They guided me down through the Rio Bravo in the dead of night, from Mexico to Texas. The river is called the Rio Bravo, meaning
15 the "angry river," because its huge waves are very strong. It has taken the lives of many people who have tried to cross it.

Sometimes, I close my eyes and I can hear the wind blowing against the trees surrounding the river. I remember sitting on a hard tire in the middle of cold, murky water. I was terrified that the river would swallow me alive. All I wanted at that moment was to be in the arms of my mother, who was
20 on another tire behind me with my younger sister. After my brothers, sister, mother, and I made it across the river, we were taken to a man's house. He was a "coyote" and was supposed to help us get through our second obstacle – the border, without getting caught by Immigration. I guess you could say he knew what he was doing because I am here today.

Since I'm an illegal immigrant, the obstacles didn't stop once I got across the border. My freshman
25 year, I thought I was going to be kicked out of school because [I was an Illegal]. Now I can't get a part-time job, or apply to college. On one occasion, I even blamed my mother for all of the troubles that I've had, because I don't have the necessary papers to be in this country. Blaming my mother was the biggest mistake I've ever made. She only wanted what was best for us. If she had known that in this country of "dreams" everybody talked about, things would be harder than they seemed, she
30 wouldn't have brought us here. She would have raised us in our own country to the best of her ability.

To this day I can't decide whether my journey here was taken in vain. I was brought here to have a golden opportunity, but unfortunately, it's not being given to me. I know it won't be easy, but I won't stop until I have gotten what I came here to get: my education. You know, come to think of it, my journey here was for that purpose. I must fulfill my dream of becoming an educator and helping
35 young people like myself.

[…] Growing up, I always assumed I would either drop out of school or get pregnant. So when Ms. G. started talking about college, it was like a foreign language to me. Didn't she realize that girls like me don't go to college? Except for Ms. G., I don't know a single female who's graduated from high school, let alone gone to college. […] Like they say, if you're born in the 'hood, you're bound to die
40 in it.

From Rags to Riches? – The American Dream Revisited (S II)

So when Ms. G. kept saying that "I could do anything," "go anywhere," and "be anyone" – even the President, I thought she was crazy. I always thought that the only people who went to college were rich white people. How did she expect me to go to college? After all, I live in the ghetto and my skin is brown.

45 But Ms. G. kept drilling into my head that it didn't matter where I came from or the color of my skin. […] In class today she made us do a speech about our future goals. I guess some of her madness was rubbing off on me because I found myself thinking about becoming a teacher. I began to think that I could teach young girls like me that they too could "be somebody."

I had planned to tell the class that I wanted to become a teacher, but after hearing what everybody
50 else wanted to be ... a lawyer, a doctor, an advertiser, I announced that "Someday I'm going to be the first Latina Secretary of Education." Surprisingly, nobody laughed. Instead, they started clapping and cheering. […] The more they clapped, the more I began to believe that it was actually possible. […]

© From THE FREEDOM WRITERS DIARIES by The Freedom Writers with Erin Gruwell, copyright © 1999 by the Tolerance Education Foundation. Used by the permission of Doubleday, a division of Random House, Inc. Any third party use of this material, outside of this publication, is prohibited. Interested parties must apply directly to Random House, Inc. for permission.

2 **application**: a formal request for sth. such as a job, place at a college etc. – 8 **abusive**: very rude and using offensive language – 11 **deprived**: not having things that are considered necessary – 17 **tire**: a thick, round band of rubber that fits around the wheel of a car – 18 **murky**: dark and difficult to see through – 24 **freshman year**: a student in the first year of high school or university – 31 **in vain**: without success – 39 **'hood**: here: ghetto – 51 **Secretary of Education**: der/die Bildungsminister/in

Tasks

1. Summarise the text in 200 words.

2. Choose one of the following tasks: a) Analyse how the author structures her diary entry. b) Analyse what the reader learns about the character of the narrator.

3. Based on what you have learned in this unit, do you agree with the writer's opinion that "it was actually possible" (l. 52) for her to become a Secretary of Education? Justify your opinion.

Hinweise (LEK)

Die Klausur wurde für einen Grundkurs konzipiert. Sie eignet sich je nach Leistungsstand aber auch für einen Leistungskurs. Der Zeitrahmen der Klausur beträgt **eine Doppelstunde**.

In dem **Tagebuchauszug** berichtet eine junge Frau aus Mexiko, wie sie illegal in die USA einwandert und dort versucht, die Ziele und Träume, die ihre Mutter bei der Einwanderung für sie und ihre Geschwister hatte, zu verwirklichen. Sie beschreibt, wie die Flucht aus Mexiko nicht das einzige Hindernis auf ihrem Weg zu Bildung und Erfolg bleibt. Im berühmten Land der Träume und unbegrenzten Möglichkeiten werden ihr bestehende Grenzen schnell bewusst. Die junge Frau fasst neuen Mut, als sie Unterstützung und Zuspruch durch ihre Lehrerin erfährt.

Aufgabe 1 fordert die Lernenden auf, Kompetenzen in den Bereichen Reproduktion und Textverstehen zu zeigen. Die **Aufgaben 2 a) und b)** sind Analyseaufgaben. In **Aufgabe 3** geht es darum, eine eigene Meinung zu äußern und diese unter Bezugnahme auf das zuvor Gelernte zu begründen.

Erwartungshorizont (LEK)

Task 1: The text *The first Latina Secretary of Education* is written by a girl who is about to graduate from school. Her class is writing college application essays, but the narrator can't apply because she is an illegal immigrant. She would have liked to write about the most important event in her life – her immigration to America in search of a better life. She recalls the terrifying hours when the family crossed the Rio Bravo and later the border without being detected. As an illegal, she doesn't have the necessary papers to get a job or apply for college after school. For many years now she has had the dream of becoming a teacher. Growing up, she never had much hope. She would either drop out of school, she thought, or get pregnant, because that is what usually happens to girls from her background. When her teacher in the USA speaks of the many opportunities everybody has, the narrator never believes she herself has any opportunities. But her teacher does not stop encouraging her. So finally the narrator starts thinking she can become a teacher. When the day comes and everybody talks about what they want to become, the narrator announces she wants to become the first Latina Secretary of Education. She now believes it is actually possible.

Task 2. a): After introducing the situation, the author interrupts the narration to relate events from earlier times. Each flashback opens with a phrase that takes the reader somehow back to where the specific event took place:

The family situation in Mexico: to explain why the family decided to emigrate.

The crossing of the Rio Bravo and the border: to highlight the dangers the family had to overcome to get into the United States.

No papers: to provide valuable information about the narrator's job or school situation.

Growing up: to show how the narrator dealt with racial remarks and attitudes.

Ms G's pedagogical work: to describe the encouraging influence of the teacher.

Flashbacks help the readers to understand the narrator's emotions, comments and thoughts much better. They also force the reader to take a position regarding the related events.

Task 2. b): At the beginning of the text, the narrator is in a very crucial situation. She recalls the defining moments in her life and the emotions connected with them: Realistic and disillusioned: "For me that statement is impossible […]" (ll. 4–5); Sad and disappointed: "The irony is […] I feel like I am deprived of an education in the future." (ll. 10–11); scared and terrified: "it has taken the lives of many people […]." (ll. 15–16) "I was terrified […]." (ll. 18–19 thankful and insecure: "She only wanted our best […]." (l. 28) "To this day, I can't decide […]." (l. 31); persistent: "I must fulfill my dream […]." (l. 36); hopeless: "I always assumed I would either drop out of school or get pregnant." (l. 36) "I live in the ghetto […]." (ll. 43–44); hopeful: "I began to think […]." (ll. 47–48); optimistic: "I began to believe that it was actually possible." (l. 52)

Task 3:

Agree: To achieve the American Dream, a person needs a good education, the willingness to work hard, determination, tenacity and a risk-taking mentality. The narrator has shown these characteristics throughout her life. President Obama is a clear example that it is possible for a coloured person to reach even the highest position in the United States.

Disagree: To achieve such a high-flying goal as to become a Secretary of Education one would need a degree from a very respectable college or university such as Yale or Harvard. The cost of studying there is enormous. Though scholarships are available, it is unclear whether the narrator has the necessary ability.

Not sure: As an illegal immigrant, she has to hope for an amnesty. Will she be granted permanent residency in the country? Will she get the necessary papers? To become a Secretary of Education, she will have to be a citizen. Will she become one?

East is East (S II)

| Reihe 3 S 1 | Verlauf | Material | LEK | Kontext | Mediothek |

East is East – Interkulturelle Erfahrungen im Spiegel eines Films (S II)

Björn Jörgeling und Ramin Azadian, Berlin

© defd-movies

Auf CD:
✓ PDF-Datei der Einheit

II/C7

Als zeitloses und zugleich hochaktuelles Filmdokument eignet sich *„East is East"* hervorragend dazu, verschiedene Aspekte des Themenkomplexes *„cross-cultural encounters"* zu erarbeiten. Die vorliegende Unterrichtsreihe vermittelt die authentische Welt einer *British-Asian family* im Spannungsfeld zwischen Herkunfts- und Mutterland. Handlungsorientierte Übungen zu verschiedenen Facetten ermöglichen Empathieverhalten und Abstraktion der Problemfelder. Gleichzeitig erlangen die Schülerinnen und Schüler soziokulturelles und landeskundliches Hintergrundwissen.

Klassenstufe: 12/13

Dauer: Ca. 16 Stunden

Bereich: Landeskunde Großbritannien (*cross-cultural encounters, ethnic diversity, immigration*), Film (Einführung und Vertiefung der technischen Filmanalyse)

RAAbits Englisch

Sachanalyse: Der Film „East is East"

Die (Tragi-)Komödie „East is East" aus dem Jahr 1999 vermittelt die Welt einer *British-Asian family* im Spannungsfeld zwischen Herkunfts- und Mutterland. Ayub Khan-Din, Verfasser des Drehbuchs und Autor des Stückes, auf dem das Drehbuch basiert, verarbeitet und reflektiert in dem Werk seine eigene Kindheit, die er als Sohn eines pakistanischen Vaters und einer britischen Mutter im Salford der 1970er-Jahre verbrachte.

„East is East" zeigt deshalb auch eine sehr persönliche und authentische Sichtweise der Probleme von multikulturellen Einwandererfamilien, in denen unterschiedliche Vorstellungen von Erziehung, Moral, Integration und Assimilation aufeinanderprallen. Dies geschieht jedoch nicht ohne Komik. Dabei verzichtet der Film weitgehend auf Slapstick-Elemente oder sinnfreie Übertreibungen, vielmehr beobachtet der Zuschauer die handelnden Charaktere aus einer Perspektive der Sympathie und des Mitfühlens und begleitet sie durch einen existenziellen Generationen- und Familienkonflikt bis hin zu einer vorsichtig optimistischen Auflösung.

Die Vielzahl der Betrachtungsmöglichkeiten und Themen macht den Film zu einem hervorragend geeigneten Unterrichtsgegenstand für die Sekundarstufe II.

Die Handlung

Der Film spielt im Jahre 1971 in Salford. George Khan, autoritäres Familienoberhaupt und Besitzer eines *Fish-and-Chips-Shop*s, sieht sich zunehmend Konfrontationen mit seinen sieben Kindern ausgesetzt, die keine Bestrebungen haben, seinen strengen pakistanisch-muslimischen Vorstellungen zu entsprechen. Seine englische Frau Ella, die Mutter der Kinder, fungiert als Brücke und Ausgleich zwischen den in Großbritannien geborenen und groß gewordenen Söhnen und der einzigen Tochter und dem strengen, um seine Position in der pakistanisch-britischen Gesellschaft fürchtenden George Khan.

Den Anfang des Films und der Konflikte bildet die arrangierte Hochzeit zwischen dem ältesten Sohn Nazir und einer jungen Frau. Nazir flüchtet von der Zeremonie, bevor der Bund geschlossen wird. Daraufhin wird er von seinem Vater, der sein eigenes Handeln nicht reflektiert, verstoßen. Für George steht auch in der Folgezeit fest, dass er dafür sorgen muss, dass seine Kinder zu guten Moslems erzogen werden. Autoritär kontrolliert er die regelmäßige Teilnahme der Kinder am Unterricht in der Koranschule und verabredet nur kurze Zeit später hinter dem Rücken seiner Frau und seiner Kinder die Heirat zweier weiterer Söhne, Abdul und Tariq, mit einem Geschwisterpaar eines entfernt bekannten Pakistaners.

Als die Söhne von den Plänen erfahren, kommt es zum offenen Konflikt in der Familie, in dem sich auch die Mutter ein erstes Mal direkt gegen ihren Mann stellt. Dieser reagiert mit physischer Gewalt und schafft es so, den Aufstand der Familienangehörigen zunächst zu unterdrücken. Auch Versuche, ihn im Zwiegespräch von der Falschheit und Absurdität seines Handelns zu überzeugen (er zwingt seine Söhne, Frauen pakistanischer Herkunft zu heiraten, ist jedoch selbst mit einer Britin verheiratet), scheitern kläglich.

Als sich die zukünftigen Ehepartner beim ersten offiziellen Besuch bei den Khans zum ersten Mal sehen, bricht der unter der Oberfläche schwelende Konflikt erneut auf, diesmal jedoch nützt George seine physische Überlegenheit nichts: Er muss sich seiner gegen ihn vereinten Familie geschlagen geben und räumt niedergeschlagen das Feld, nicht ohne zu insistieren, dass all das, was er getan hat, stets im Interesse seiner Familie war.

Die Schlussszene des Film bildet eine vorsichtige Annäherung eines nachdenklichen George und einer gefassten Ella.

Das Sprachniveau

„East is East" bietet den Schülerinnen und Schülern Kontakt zu authentischem Englisch der Arbeiterklasse aus der Gegend von Manchester sowie zu den dialektal stark eingefärbten Sprachvariationen der pakistanischen Einwanderer. Die Schauspieler sind nicht immer gut zu verstehen. Daher können, je nach Leistungsstärke der Lerngruppe, zur Unterstützung die Untertitel eingeblendet werden.

Didaktisch-methodisches Konzept

Zur Methodik

Die Unterrichtsreihe bietet eine Vielzahl methodischer Verfahren. Sowohl ein schülerorientierter, diskursiver Unterrichtsstil als auch produktive Methoden und szenische Interpretation wurden mit dem Ziel der produktionsorientierten Aneignung des Film- und Unterrichtsstoffes ausgewählt. Darüber hinaus findet das neue Aufgabenformat der Sprachmittlung sinnvollen Eingang in die Reihe **(vgl. M 2 und Hinweise M 2)**.

Einen Schwerpunkt der Reihe bildet das Diskutieren in der Zielsprache. Arbeitsergebnisse und kontroverse Sachverhalte werden begründet präsentiert und von einem kritischen Plenum untersucht.

Zur Vorgehensweise

Die Unterrichtseinheit wurde so konzipiert, dass die Betrachtung der Charaktere und ihre Analyse zunehmend komplexer werden. Dieses Vorgehen findet seinen Höhepunkt am Ende der Reihe, wenn die gewonnenen Erkenntnisse mit Techniken der Filmanalyse, die ebenfalls in der Reihe vermittelt werden, verknüpft werden.

Über eine erste Annäherung an den Film durch das Aufwerfen von Fragen in der ersten Doppelstunde **(M 1)** und das informative Ergänzen in der zweiten Sitzung erhalten die Schülerinnen und Schüler in der vierten und fünften Stunde zum ersten Mal die Gelegenheit, sich den Figuren durch das Darstellen der Familienkonstellation in Standbildern **(M 4)** anzunähern.

Ausgehend von ihren bisherigen Beobachtungen stellen die Lernenden in der 6. und 7. Stunde in einer szenischen Interpretation Entwicklungsmöglichkeiten der Handlung und der Charaktere dar **(M 6)**. Nachdem der Film zu Ende gesehen wurde, dienen Miniplädoyers mit anschließenden Plenumsdiskussionen **(M 8)** der Klärung von Fragen zu den einzelnen Figuren.

In der zehnten Stunde wird ein alternativer Zugang zu den Figuren geboten: Hier gilt es den jeweiligen Figuren Symbole zuzuweisen, die deren Charakter besonders entsprechen **(M 9)**. Diese Übung dient der Abrundung der Einzelbetrachtungen.

Die 11. und 12. Stunde stehen im Zeichen der formalen Analyse von Filmtechnik und der Einführung bzw. Wiederholung der entsprechenden Fachbegriffe **(M 10 und M 11)**.

Die Stunden 13–15 bilden den Höhepunkt der Reihe, an dem die gewonnenen Kenntnisse und Erkenntnisse in einem produktiven Verfahren miteinander vernetzt werden. Die Schülerinnen und Schüler entwerfen Storyboards zu einer eigenen Szene von „East is East" **(M 12 und M 13)**.

Die Präsentation und kritische Diskussion der Arbeitsergebnisse bilden den Abschluss der Unterrichtseinheit.

East is East (S II)

| Reihe 3 S 4 | Verlauf | Material | LEK | Kontext | Mediothek |

Schematische Verlaufsübersicht

East is East – Interkulturelle Erfahrungen im Spiegel eines Films (S II)

1./2. Stunde:	Introducing *East is East*
3. Stunde:	The historical background (Sprachmittlung)
4./5. Stunde:	Relationships: The first part of the film
6./7. Stunde:	The next scene: The second part of the film
8./9. Stunde:	The last part of the film: Taking sides
10. Stunde:	Characters in *East is East*: Symbols
11./12. Stunde:	Interpreting film language
13.–16. Stunde:	*East is East* ten years later: Storyboards

Minimalplan: Je nach Vorkenntnissen der Gruppe können die 3. (geschichtlicher Hintergrund) und/oder die 11./12. Stunde (Einführung in die Filmanalyse) weggelassen werden.

1. und 2. Stunde

Thema
Introducing *East is East*

Material	Verlauf
M 1	**Three scenes (1. 45:20–48:10, chapter 7; 2. opening scene, chapter 1; 3. 13:15–16:15, chapter 3)** / Annäherung an den Film, Formulieren von Fragen und Hypothesen

3. Stunde

Thema
The historical background (Sprachmittlung)

Material	Verlauf
M 2	**Gaining a deeper insight** / Erwerb von Hintergrundinformationen zum Film mithilfe von Sprachmittlung/Mediation

4./5. Stunde

Thema
Relationships: The first part of the film

Material	Verlauf
M 3	**Film (00:00–38:35, chapter 5): Personal viewing log** / Beobachtungsbogen zum Film und den Charakteren
M 4	**Focus on relationships: Freeze frames** / Darstellung von Beziehungskonstellationen im Film
M 5	**Homework:** *Muslim or Christian? Fill in the vocabulary worksheet and learn the words in bold print.*

6./7. Stunde

Thema
The next scene: The second part of the film

Material	Verlauf
M 3	**Film (38:36, chapter 5–1:00:00, chapter 8)** / Eintragen der Beobachtungen in das *personal viewing log*
M 6	**What is going to happen next?** / Aufstellen von Hypothesen für den weiteren Verlauf; Erarbeiten und Vorstellen der nächsten Szene
M 7	**Homework:** *Write Tariq's diary entry.*

8./9. Stunde:

Thema
Taking sides: The last part of the film

Material	Verlauf
M 3	**Film: (1:00:01, chapter 8–1:32:00, chapter 12)** / Eintragen der Beobachtungen in das *personal viewing log*
M 8	**True statements?** / Verfassen von Miniplädoyers zu den einzelnen Familienmitgliedern als Diskussionsgrundlage
	Homework: *Try to answer your questions of the first lesson.*

10. Stunde:

Thema
Characters in East is East: Symbols

Material	Verlauf
M 9	**Which symbol represents which character?** / Zuordnung von Symbolen zum besseren Verständnis der Charaktere

11./12. Stunde

Thema
Interpreting film language

Material	Verlauf
M 10	**Interpreting film language** / Einführung in die Filmanalyse anhand einer Zuordnungsübung
M 11	**Film analysis (07:00–09:21, chapter 2): The wedding scene** / Anwendung der neu erlernten Kategorien

13.–16. Stunde

Thema
East is East ten years later: Storyboards

Material	Verlauf
M 12	**Storyboard: *East is East* ten years later** / Vernetzung der erworbenen Kenntnisse
M 13	**Your own storyboard** / Entwurf einer Szene und Umsetzung in Storyboards; Präsentation, Diskussion und Beurteilung der Ergebnisse

Materialübersicht

1./2. Stunde — **Introducing *East is East***
M 1 (Ab) — Introducing the film: Three scenes

3. Stunde — **The historical background (Sprachmittlung)**
M 2 (Tx/Ab) — Gaining a deeper insight

4./5. Stunde — **Relationships: The first part of the film**
M 3 (Ab) — Personal viewing log
M 4 (Ab) — Focus on relationships: Freeze frames
M 5 (Wo/Ha) — Vocabulary: Muslim or Christian?

6./7. Stunde — **The next scene: The second part of the film**
M 6 (Ab) — What is going to happen next?
M 7 (Ha) — Creative writing: Tariq's diary entry

8./9. Stunde — **Taking sides: The last part of the film**
M 8 (Ab) — True statements?

10. Stunde — **Characters in *East is East*: Symbols**
M 9 (Ab) — Which symbols represent which character?

11./12. Stunde — **Interpreting film language**
M 10 (Ab) — Interpreting film language
M 11 (Ab) — Film analysis: The wedding scene

13.–16. Stunde — ***East is East* ten years later: Storyboards**
M 12 (Ab) — Storyboard: *East is East* ten years later
M 13 (Ab) — Your own storyboard

Für den Einsatz dieser Materialien wird ein DVD-Player benötigt.

East is East (S II)

| Reihe 3 | Verlauf | Material S 2 | LEK | Kontext | Mediothek |

M 1 Introducing the film: Three scenes

You will be shown three scenes from the film which we will discuss in the next lessons. Each scene is shown twice.

Viewing assignments

1. While watching the scenes **for the first time** take notes. You should be able to summarize each scene.

2. Write down questions about the film that come to mind while watching the scenes **for the second time**.

Scene 1
Content:

Questions:

Scene 2
Content:

Questions:

Scene 3
Content:

Questions:

Fold here!

Tasks

1. Talk to your neighbour about each scene. What is it about? What were the questions you asked yourselves while watching the scenes for the second time?

2. Form groups of 5 people and discuss:

   a) What might the film be about? Write down a few notes about its possible content on an A4 sheet.

   b) Compare your questions and decide/discuss: what are the 5 questions about the film or the scenes which interest you most? Write each question on a separate A4 sheet.

   c) Be ready to present your hypotheses and questions in class.

East is East (S II)

| Reihe 3 | Verlauf | Material S 3 | LEK | Kontext | Mediothek |

Hinweise (M 1)

Der Einstieg in die erste Stunde der Reihe dient dazu, die Lernenden neugierig auf den Film zu machen. Bevor sie das Arbeitsblatt **M 1** erhalten, faltet die Lehrkraft den unteren Teil um, damit sich die Schülerinnen und Schüler ausschließlich auf die *viewing assignments* konzentrieren.

Sie sehen nun drei Szenen aus dem Film:

1. 45:20–48:10 (Kapitel 7)

2. die Eingangszene mit der religiösen Prozession (Kapitel 1)

3. 13:15–16:15 (Kapitel 3)

in ebendieser Reihenfolge.

Jede Szene wird zweimal gezeigt und die Lernenden machen sich beim ersten Sehen Stichpunkte zum Inhalt der Ausschnitte. Beim zweiten Anschauen notieren sie sich Fragen zu den Szenen. Nun wird das Arbeitsblatt **M 1** aufgefaltet: Nach einer kurzen Phase, in der die Ergebnisse mit dem Nachbarn verglichen und eventuell Verständnisfragen mit diesem geklärt werden, bilden die Schülerinnen und Schüler Fünfergruppen, in denen sie zunächst Hypothesen über das Thema und den Inhalt des Filmes bilden. Anschließend vergleichen sie ihre Fragen aus *den viewing assignments* und wählen die fünf aus, deren Beantwortung sie als Gruppe am meisten interessiert. Sowohl die Hypothesen über den Inhalt als auch die Fragen werden auf leere DIN-A4-Blätter geschrieben (pro Frage ein Blatt). Anschließend stellen die Gruppen ihre Ergebnisse vor.

Tipp: Die einzelnen Blätter an der Tafel mit Magneten oder Tesafilm fixieren und von den Lernenden nach selbst entwickelten Aspekten im Plenum ordnen lassen (beispielsweise Figurenebene, Inhaltsebene etc.).

Der so entstandene Katalog kann auf einem Plakat als Wandbild fixiert oder von den Schülerinnen und Schülern abgeschrieben werden. Denkbar ist auch, dass die Lehrkraft selbst eine Tabelle anfertigt, in der alle Hypothesen und Fragen auftauchen und diese den Lernenden in der nächsten Stunde austeilt. Die Hypothesen und Fragen können entweder am Ende oder im Verlauf der Reihe sukzessive von den Schülerinnen und Schülern verifiziert bzw. beantwortet werden.

Erwartungshorizont (M 1)

Mögliche Fragen:

Characters	*Content*
Who are they?	Where and when do they live?
Who is the father?	Are they afraid of their father? Why?
Are they Muslims or Christians?	Why do they all sleep in one bed?
What is the parents' relationship like?	What do the other children discover in the mosque?
Why are they married?	
Why don't the children want to go to the mosque?	What happens to the boy who escaped from his wedding?

East is East (S II)

| Reihe 3 | Verlauf | Material S 4 | LEK | Kontext | Mediothek |

M 2 Gaining a deeper insight

Gaining a deeper insight: Text 1

Task

Your classmate has an English speaking friend who is doing a project on "Ethnic Minorities in Britain". Luckily you have come across the text below.

1. Read your text. Make notes about the most important facts in English by using the appropriate box. Use the vocabulary aids.
2. Talk to your classmate and provide him/her with the most important facts. While presenting your text, use your notes only.
3. Listen to your classmate as s/he provides you with the most important facts of her/his text and make notes.

1. Im Land der großartigen Möglichkeiten – Pakistanische Einwanderer in Großbritannien in der zweiten Hälfte des 20. Jahrhunderts

In einer Zeit wirtschaftlichen Aufschwungs nach dem Zweiten Weltkrieg schaffte die britische Regierung wegen Arbeitskräftemangel Anreize für Millionen von Einwanderern. Es gab zwei Gründe dafür, dass Einwanderer aus dem asiatischen Subkontinent diesem Ruf folgten:

Der erste war die Teilung Indiens und die damit zusammenhängende Entstehung Pakistans im Jahre 1947. Der zweite war der Bau der Mangla-Talsperre in Pakistan in den frühen 1960er-Jahren. Beide Ereignisse führten zu Vertreibungen vieler Menschen. Erhaltene Kompensationszahlungen wurden von einigen, die Freunde oder Verwandte in Großbritannien hatten, genutzt, um ihr Land in Richtung Vereinigtes Königreich zu verlassen. 1951 wurde der pakistanische Bevölkerungsanteil in Großbritannien auf ca. 5000 Menschen geschätzt, 1961 waren es 24 900 und 1966 wuchs der Anteil sogar auf 199 700 an.

Erste Erfolgsgeschichten, weitergegeben durch Freunde und Verwandte, vermittelten den Daheimgebliebenen ein Bild Großbritanniens als Land der großartigen Möglichkeiten. Bessere Verdienstmöglichkeiten in der Textilindustrie in Yorkshire und Lancashire führten zu einer Masseneinwanderung. Bis heute ist der pakistanische Anteil an Einwanderern aus dem asiatischen Subkontinent der größte.

Damals rechneten die meisten mit einem vorübergehenden Aufenthalt. 1962 verschärfte die damalige konservative Regierung die Einwanderungsbestimmungen: Es durften nur noch Einwanderer mit einer Arbeitserlaubnis einreisen. Dies führte dazu, dass viele Immigranten, die vor 1962 eingereist waren, sich entschieden, für immer zu bleiben. Darüber hinaus wünschten sich die meisten von ihnen eine bessere Zukunft für ihre Kinder. Sie waren dann auch oft die erste Anlaufstelle für einreisende Familienmitglieder.

Waren Immigranten immer auch Feindseligkeiten im Gastland ausgesetzt, so trugen sie dennoch dazu bei, dass sich Großbritannien zu einem pulsierenden multi-ethnischen Staat entwickelte. Vor allem die Stadt Bradford, eine Hochburg der Textilindustrie in der Grafschaft Yorkshire, wurde zum Refugium vieler pakistanischer Einwanderer. 1998 lebten 10 Prozent aller britischen Muslime in Bradford, der höchste Prozentsatz in ganz Großbritannien, weshalb die Stadt auch als ‚Islamabad Großbritanniens' bekannt ist.

Das Leben vieler Pakistanis hier ist geprägt von der Tradition eines patriarchalischen Familien- und Gemeinschaftssinns. Muslime der dritten Generation, von denen die meisten kein Urdu sprechen, werden von ihren Eltern zu arrangierten Hochzeiten mit ‚importierten' Ehepartnern aus Pakistan gezwungen – oft auch mit Familienmitgliedern. Viele muslimische Eltern fürchten durch eine Ehe mit nicht-muslimischen Partnern, die im sekulären Großbritannien aufgewachsen sind, einen Verfall ihrer islamischen Kultur.

(Text: Björn Jörgeling)

East is East (S II)

M 2 Gaining a deeper insight

Gaining a deeper insight: Text 2

Task

Your classmate has an English speaking friend who is doing a project on "Ethnic Minorities in Britain". Luckily you have come across the text below.

1. Read your text. Make notes about the most important facts in English by using the appropriate box. Use the vocabulary aids.
2. Talk to your classmate and provide him/her with the most important facts. While presenting your text, use your notes only.
3. Listen to your classmate as s/he provides you with the most important facts of her/his text and make notes.

2. Enoch Powell – Ein umstrittener Tory

Den meisten politischen Gegnern und Mitstreitern seiner Zeit wird er wohl durch seine berüchtigte Birmingham-Rede aus dem Jahre 1968 in Erinnerung bleiben. Als damaliges Mitglied des Unterhauses übte Enoch Powell in einer Parteiversammlung der Konservativen harte Kritik an der Einwanderungspolitik der damaligen Labour-Regierung unter Wilson.

5 Unter geschicktem Einsatz rhetorischer Mittel in Verbindung mit offenen rassistischen Äußerungen verbreitete er über Nacht im ganzen Land ein Klima der Angst. So versetzte er sich in die Rolle eines Römers und sah vor seinem geistigen Auge den „vor Blut schäumenden Tiber". In Großbritannien sah er „eine Nation, die eifrig damit beschäftigt ist, sich ihren eigenen Scheiterhaufen aufzutürmen".

10 Seine Lösungsvorschläge waren eher pragmatischer Natur. So sollte die Einwanderung hilfsbedürftiger Immigranten aus Schwarzafrika und Asien – er ging damals von 50 000 im Jahr aus – sofort gestoppt werden. Mit seiner Forderung nach einer Repatriierung derer, die sich bereits in Großbritannien niedergelassen hatten, konstatierte er zynisch, keine Politik dürfe Familien auseinanderreißen, aber es gäbe zwei Wege, sie wieder zusammenzuführen. Noch heute wird er

15 deswegen vor allem von der britischen rechtsextremen *National Front* als Galionsfigur instrumentalisiert, indem diese mit Slogans wie ‚Powell hatte Recht!' versucht, gegen Immigranten Politik zu machen.

Als Powell am 28.02.1998 verstarb, bezeichnete ihn der damalige Premier Tony Blair als „eine der großartigen Erscheinungen britischer Politik des zwanzigsten Jahrhunderts, ausgestattet mit brillantem Verstand".
20

In seiner Rede von 1968 sagte Powell voraus, dass im Jahre 2000 der Anteil an Menschen ausländischer Herkunft bei sieben Millionen liegen würde.

Die Volkszählung im Jahr 2001 ergab, dass 4,6 Millionen oder 7,9% Menschen einer ethnischen Minderheit angehörten.

(Text: Björn Jörgeling)

East is East (S II)

| Reihe 3 | Verlauf | Material S 6 | LEK | Kontext | Mediothek |

Gaining a deeper insight: Vocabulary and notes

Vocabulary Aids

1. Im Land der großartigen Möglichkeiten – Pakistanische Einwanderer in Großbritannien in der zweiten Hälfte des 20. Jahrhunderts

großartige Möglichkeiten: great opportunities – **Einwanderer:** immigrants – **wirtschaftlicher Aufschwung:** (economic) boom – **Arbeitskräftemangel:** lack of labour – **Vertreibung:** displacement – **Kompensationszahlungen:** compensation – **bessere Verdienstmöglichkeiten:** better wages – **Masseneinwanderung:** mass immigration – **Einwanderungsbestimmungen:** immigration rules – **Arbeitserlaubnis:** work permit – **Feindseligkeiten:** hostilities – **multiethnisch:** multi-ethnic – **Refugium:** refuge – **Familien- und Gemeinschaftssinn:** sense of family and community – **arrangierte Hochzeit:** arranged marriage – **sekulär:** secular/worldly – **Verfall:** corruption

2. Enoch Powell – Ein umstrittener Tory

umstritten: controversial – **Tory:** Mitglied der Konservativen Partei – **berüchtigt:** infamous – **Mitglied des Unterhauses:** Member of Parliament (MP) – **Parteiversammlung:** party meeting – **Einwanderungspolitik:** immigration policy – **ein Klima der Angst verbreiten:** to create a climate of anxiety – **der vor Blut schäumende Tiber:** the river Tiber foaming with blood – **sich seinen eigenen Scheiterhaufen auftürmen:** to heap up one's own funeral pyre – **hilfsbedürftige Immigranten:** dependent immigrants – **Repatriierung:** repatriation – **Galionsfigur:** figurehead – **gegen etw. Politik machen:** to campaign against sth. – **ausländischer Herkunft:** of foreign origin – **Volkszählung:** census – **ethnische Minderheit:** ethnic minority

1. Notes on your text:

2. Notes on your partner's text:

Hinweise (M 2)

In dieser Stunde sollen sich die Schülerinnen und Schüler mit dem historischen Hintergrund vertraut machen, der für das Verständnis des Films relevant ist. Sie erhalten einen kurzen Überblick über den britischen Politiker **Enoch Powell (1912–1998)** und die politischen Forderungen, die er in seiner Birmingham-Rede von 1968 aufstellte **(Text 2)**. Außerdem bekommen sie einen allgemeinen Einblick in die Geschichte pakistanischer Einwanderer nach Großbritannien **(Text 1)**.

Zur Methode „Sprachmittlung/Mediation": Unter Mediation versteht man die Übermittlung von Informationen von einer Sprache in die andere, die sowohl aus mündlichen als auch aus schriftlichen Äußerungen (wie im vorliegenden Fall) entnommen werden können. Im Vergleich zur reinen Übersetzung kann man Sprachmittlung als *summary* eines Textes in eine andere Sprache verstehen. Für die Bewertung (im Land Berlin ist Mediation Teil des Zentralabiturs) wurde Sprachmittlung bisher von der Muttersprache in die Zielsprache gefordert. Mediation soll den Lernenden demnach ermöglichen, für sie wichtige Informationen zu erschließen, die sie aufgrund fehlender Fremdsprachenkenntnisse nicht oder nur rudimentär verstehen.

Jeweils die Hälfte der Klasse bekommt Text 1 bzw. Text 2 ausgeteilt. Die Schülerinnen und Schüler machen sich zunächst in Einzelarbeit mit dem Inhalt ihres Textes vertraut. Wichtig für den weiteren Verlauf der Stunde ist das Vokabular beider Texte. Es soll dem Zuhörer/der Zuhörerin während der Sprachmittlung das Textverständnis durch Vorentlastung erleichtern. Daher erhalten alle Lernenden das Blatt mit dem Vokabular und den Kästen für die *notes*. Jede Schülerin bzw. jeder Schüler macht sich nun mithilfe des Vokabulars Notizen zum eigenen Text (*„notes on your text"*). Nach dieser Phase tauschen sich die Lernenden im Gespräch über ihre Texte aus. Für den Vortrag benutzen sie ihre Notizen. Während des Zuhörens machen sie sich ebenfalls Notizen (*„notes on your partner's text"*). Abschließend werden die Ergebnisse im Plenum diskutiert.

Erwartungshorizont (M 2)

1. Im Land der großartigen Möglichkeiten – Pakistanische Einwanderer in Großbritannien in der zweiten Hälfte des 20. Jahrhunderts

After WW II many immigrants from the Asian sub-continent were attracted to Great Britain due to a booming British economy and a lack of labour. They immigrated for two reasons: 1. The division of India in 1947 which led to the foundation of Pakistan; 2. The building of the Mangla dam in Pakistan in the 60s. Both events led to a high number of displaced people. Most of them received compensation and used the money to leave their country for the UK.

Thus, the number of Pakistani immigrants increased immensely. Of all those who have immigrated to Great Britain from the Asian sub-continent, the percentage of Pakistani people has been the highest until today. The first immigrants wanted to stay only temporarily. Due to stricter immigration rules implemented by the Conservative Party in 1962, most of them ended up staying for good. They also wanted to provide their children with a better future.

Immigrants have always been exposed to hostilities from the host country. Still, their presence turned the UK into a multi-ethnic state. Most Pakistanis believe in a strong sense of family and community. Arranged marriages are rather common.

2. Enoch Powell – Ein umstrittener Tory

Enoch Powell was a controversial politician from the Conservative Party who became infamous for his Birmingham Speech in 1968 in which he:

– criticised the immigration policy of the Labour Party,
– appealed to stop the influx of dependent immigrants, esp. from Black Africa and Asia,
– proposed the repatriation of those who had already entered the UK.

The right wing extremist National Front still uses him as a figurehead to campaign against immigrants. In 1968, Powell predicted that by the year 2000, seven million people living in Britain would be of ethnic minority descent. The census in 2001, however, showed 4.6 million people living in the UK were from an ethnic minority.

East is East (S II)

| Reihe 3 | Verlauf | Material S 8 | LEK | Kontext | Mediothek |

II/C7

M 3 Personal viewing log

While we are watching *East is East*, please fill out your personal viewing log.

1. Choose two of the members of the Khan family and observe them during the film. Take notes about their character traits, behaviour etc.
2. In addition, take notes about the main developments in the film. You have to be able to summarise it in the end.

The Khan family:

Character 1: _____

Character 2: _____

Saleem — Meena — Ella — George — Saleem — Abdul — Sajid — Tariq

© defd-movies

The film:

Part I → Part II → Part III

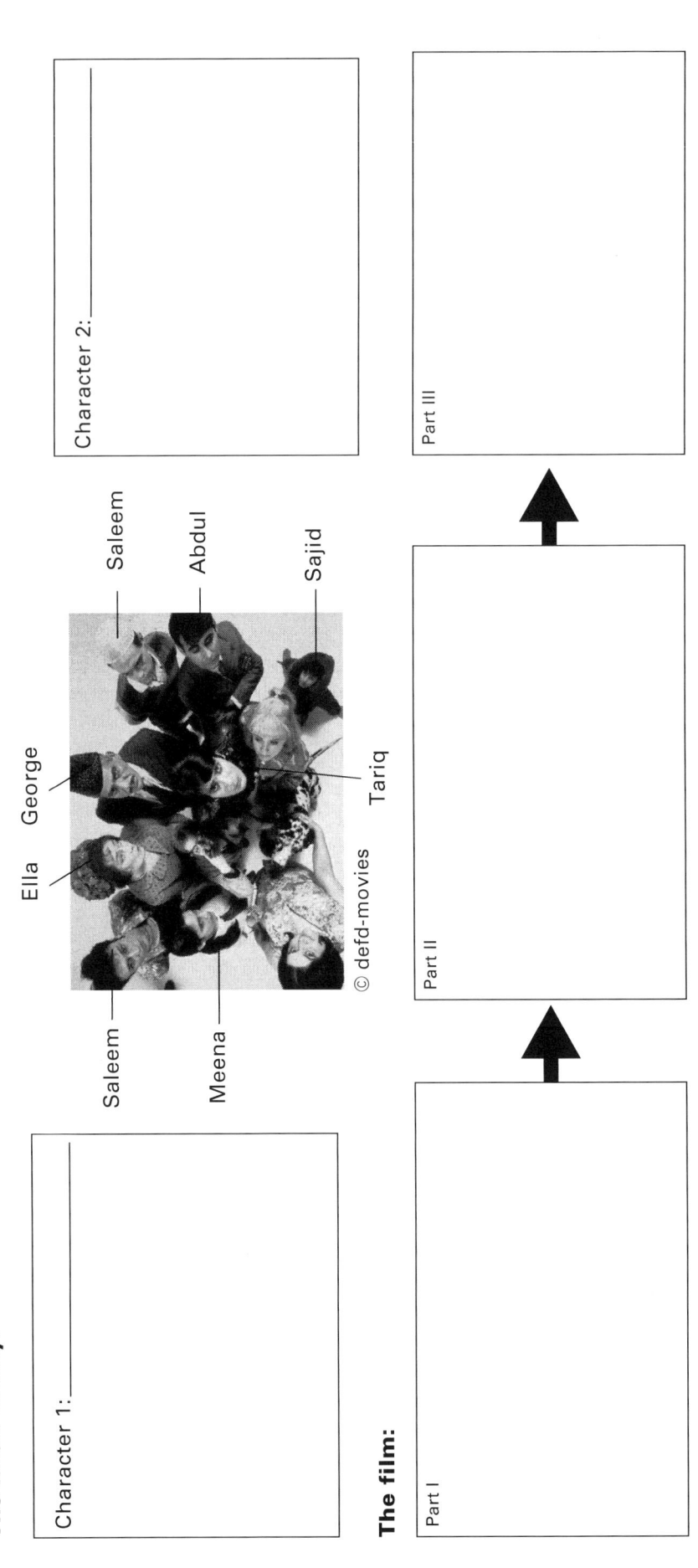

RAAbits Englisch

M 4 Focus on relationships: Freeze frames

In *East is East* relationships play a big role. The relationships between the different characters change or are perceived differently by each character.

Tasks

1. Form equally sized groups (5–7 members).
2. You are to devise a freeze frame to show the relationships of members of the Khan family, without speaking.
3. Try to focus on the *interrelationships* of the characters and **do not** present a scene from the film. Use your personal viewing log to discuss the family members' relationships.
4. Use the way the characters sit, stand and gesture to show how they feel towards each other.
5. After rehearsing, each group is to present its freeze frame and explain it.
6. Each group's interpretation of the relationships will be discussed briefly after the explanation.
7. You have 25 minutes for preparation.

Each frame consists of the following characters:

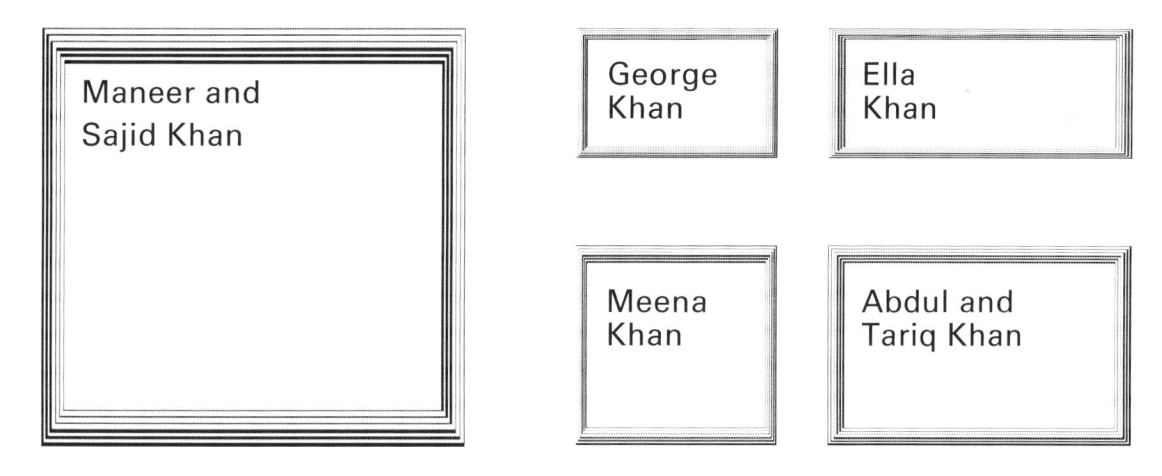

| Maneer and Sajid Khan |
| George Khan |
| Ella Khan |
| Meena Khan |
| Abdul and Tariq Khan |

East is East (S II)

M 5 Vocabulary: Muslim or Christian?

Below you find a list of words which can play a role either in a Muslim or in a Christian context. Some words could be used in both religions. Use a (monolingual) dictionary or other means of information to find out the meaning of the words you do not understand and arrange the words in the columns below.

prayer – Allah – **service** – **arranged marriage** – Rome – Old and New Testament – Mohammad – **cathedral** – Bible – parade – **ceremony** – **skullcap** – choir – church – halal – **clergyman** – cross – **dome** – **spire** – festival – holiday – Jesus – Koran – **minaret** – **procession** – **mosque** – mullah – **circumcision** – pig/pork – altar – priest – **prophet** – saint – **sari** – **veil** – turban – **vicar** – crucifix – ramadan – alcohol – Mecca – first communion – festivity – **sin** – **wedding** – chant – statue – hadj – **traditions** – mass – **baptism**

✝	↔	☪

2. Learn the words in **bold print**.

East is East (S II)

| Reihe 3 | Verlauf | Material S 11 | LEK | Kontext | Mediothek |

Hinweise (M 3–M 5)

Zu Beginn dieser Doppelstunde erhalten die Schülerinnen und Schüler das *personal viewing log* (M 3), welches sie während der gesamten Präsentation des Filmes im Unterricht bearbeiten. Dieses sollte **auf A3-Format** kopiert werden. Aufgabe ist es, sich Stichpunkte zu zwei ausgewählten Charakteren des Filmes sowie zur Handlung insgesamt zu machen. Im Laufe der Unterrichtseinheit wird verschiedene Male auf diesen Arbeitsbogen zurückgegriffen. Die Lehrkraft sollte bei der Verteilung dafür sorgen, dass alle Figuren ungefähr von gleich vielen Schülerinnen und Schülern beobachtet werden.

Im Anschluss beginnt die Präsentation des ersten längeren Ausschnitts von *„East is East"* von 00:00 bis 38:35, Kapitel 5 (Ende der Bradford-Szene). Die Schülerinne und Schüler erhalten nun **M 4**. Sie bilden Gruppen von fünf bis sieben Personen, die verschiedene Protagonisten beobachtet haben sollten. Jede Gruppe erstellt ein **Standbild**, welches die Beziehungen der Familienmitglieder untereinander darstellt, um sich so über die komplexe Familiensituation klar zu werden. Es sollte nochmals darauf hingewiesen werden, dass es nicht darum geht, eine Szene aus dem Film vorzustellen, sondern dass das Standbild auf der Beziehungsebene ausgeführt werden soll.

Die *personal viewing logs* werden in der Diskussionsphase, die dem Erstellen des Standbildes vorausgeht, benötigt und zurate gezogen. Nach etwa 25 Minuten stellt jede Gruppe ihr Standbild im Plenum vor. Die Standbilder werden kommentiert und kritisiert, aus dem Plenum können Vorschläge für die Verbesserung einiger Teile des Bildes kommen. **Hausaufgabe** ist das Bearbeiten von **M 5**.

Erwartungshorizont (M 4)

†	↔	☪
Rome	prayer	Allah
Old and New Testament	ceremony	arranged marriage
cathedral	clergyman	Mohammad
Bible	dome	skullcap
choir	holiday	halal
church	festival	Koran
cross	service	minaret
spire	procession	mosque
altar	priest	mullah
saint	alcohol	circumcision
vicar	festivity	pig/pork
crucifix	sin	prophet
first communion	wedding	sari
chant	traditions	veil
statue	Jesus (spielt als Prophet auch im Islam eine Rolle)	turban
mass		ramadan
baptism		Mecca
parade		hadj

East is East (S II)

M 6 What is going to happen next?

We are at a crucial moment in the film. Finally, the ever-rising tension has lead to an open conflict within the family. What is going to happen next?

Tasks

1. Work in groups of five people.
2. Use your personal viewing logs to discuss what the members of the Khan family think of the things that have happened and how they might react. Based on your observations and the discussion in your group, prepare the next scene of the film.
3. You will have to present your scene to the class.
4. You have 30 minutes for preparation.

M 7 Creative writing: Tariq's diary entry

When Tariq gets home that evening, his mother and brother tell him what has happened as a result of his outburst against his father's plans. Before going to bed, he decides to write in his diary. Write the entry in Tariq's diary in which he comments and reflects on the events of that day. Do not write more than 250 words.

Hinweise (M 6 und M 7)

Nach der Auswertung der Hausaufgabe (eventuell auch als Vokabeltest) wird ein weiterer Abschnitt des Filmes gezeigt **(38:36 bis genau 1:00:00)**. Wiederum machen sich die Schülerinnen und Schüler Stichpunkte in ihrem *personal viewing log*. Die DVD wird an einer Schlüsselstelle des Filmes gestoppt: als aufgrund der unterschiedlichen Wert- und Lebensvorstellungen der Familie und des Familienoberhauptes George Khan ein offener Konflikt ausbricht. **M 6** wird ausgeteilt. Ausgehend von ihren bisherigen Beobachtungen diskutieren die Schülerinnen und Schüler zunächst, wie die einzelnen Familienmitglieder wohl mit dem Konflikt umgehen werden. Im Anschluss an diese Diskussion bereiten die Lernenden die nächste Szene vor, die die Ergebnisse dieser Diskussion widerspiegelt. Nach etwa 30 Minuten Gesamtzeit werden die einzelnen Szenen im Plenum vorgestellt und kommentiert.

Hausaufgabe ist das Verfassen eines Tagebucheintrags, in dem Tariq seine Gedanken zu den Geschehnissen darlegt **(M 7)**.

Erwartungshorizont (M 7)

I just can't believe it. It seems that Dad won't ever learn anything. If I'm not mistaken (and I'm not!!!), Abdul and me are going to be the next in line to be married off to some girl my father has chosen for us ... where's the bloody point in that? Sajid was the one who broke the news and when I opened Dad's secret chest, the outrageous information was confirmed. Inside his trunk I found all the wedding garments needed to lose two sons, and Dad seems determined to lose us. Wasn't Nazeer enough? I freaked out, I broke and ripped the things apart, and I even accused poor Maneer of knowing more than he admitted. And then it was him and Mum who were hit by Dad. I don't know what to feel. I am not Pakistani, I am English. I want to do what I want to do, but I don't want Mum and my brothers or sisters to be hurt. I wish Dad had hit me. I would have hit him right back in his face. We can't continue like this. It is like living a lie. Everybody makes jokes about Dad behind his back, but everybody is afraid of him, too. I am not going to marry a girl from Pakistan unless I am in love. No, I simply won't do it, even if that means I have to leave him, too. It is my life after all.

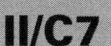

M 8 True statements?

Below you will find a number of statements in which the main arguments/points are missing.

Task

Work in pairs. Complete one of the statements below as convincingly as possible. You can add more sentences. Be ready to defend your statement in class.

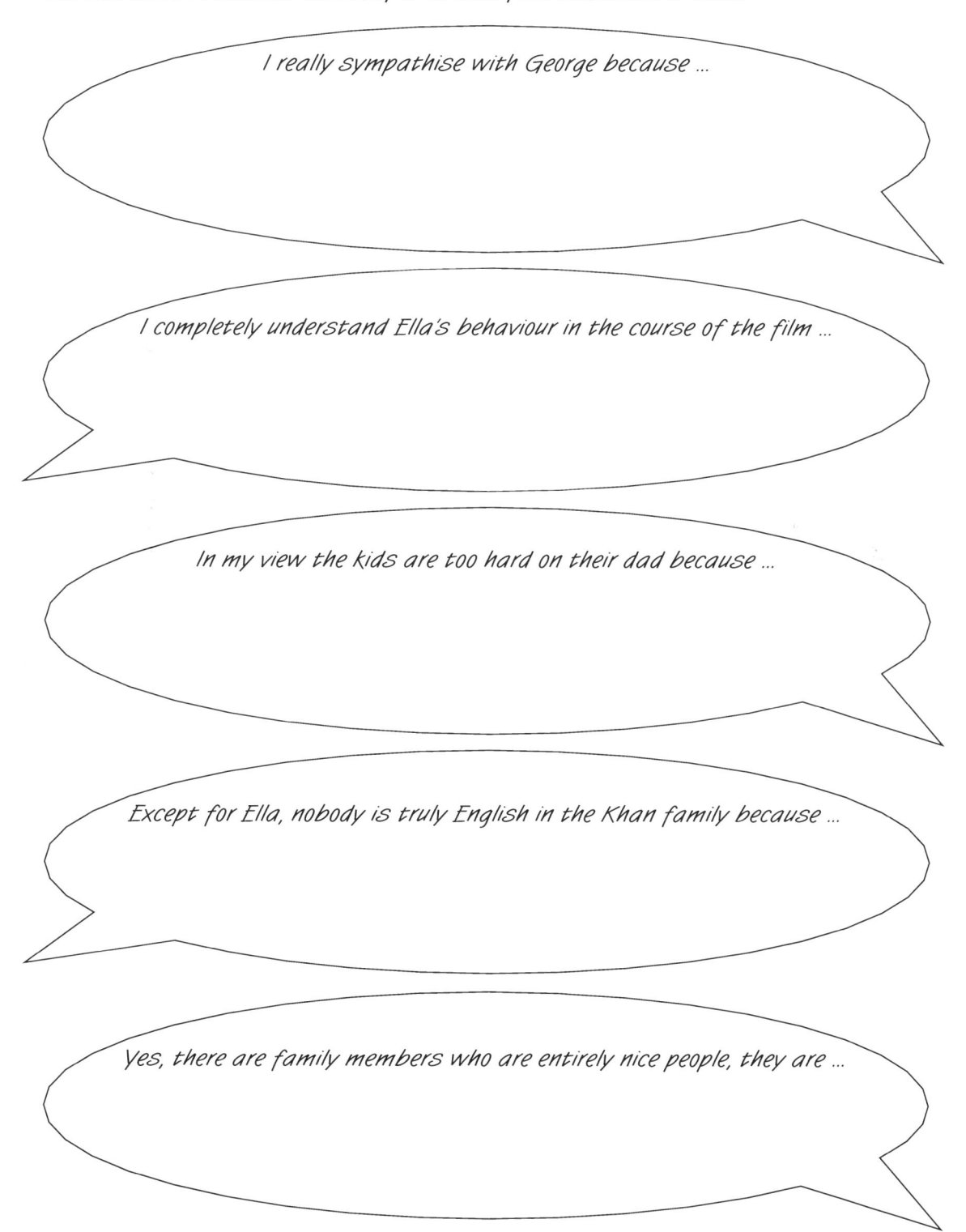

> I really sympathise with George because …

> I completely understand Ella's behaviour in the course of the film …

> In my view the kids are too hard on their dad because …

> Except for Ella, nobody is truly English in the Khan family because …

> Yes, there are family members who are entirely nice people, they are …

East is East (S II)

| Reihe 3 | Verlauf | Material S 14 | LEK | Kontext | Mediothek |

II/C7

M 9 Which symbols represent which character?

1. Choose **one** of the characters you observed during the film. Find the classmates who have chosen the same Khan family member and form a group. Then take a look at the pictures below. Discuss: which two symbols represent "your" character best? Why?
2. Prepare a presentation of your findings. Be ready to discuss your choice.

© Avenue Images GmbH

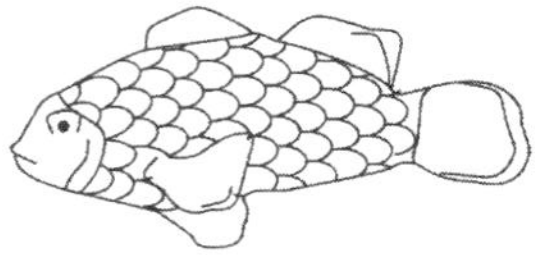

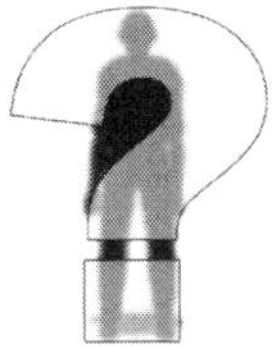

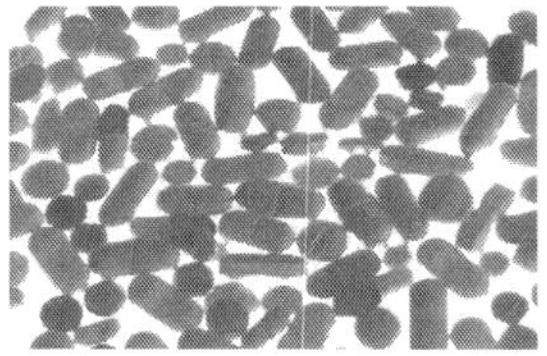

picture-alliance / dpa / Stockfood

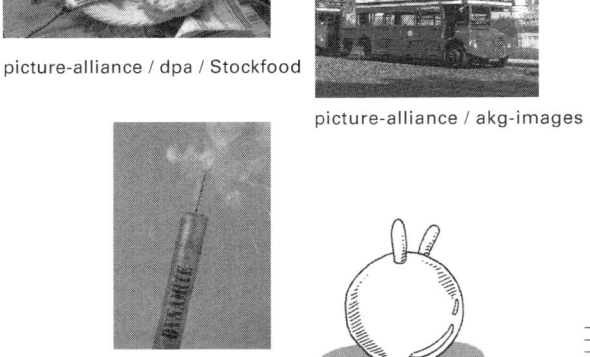

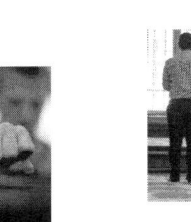

picture-alliance / akg-images

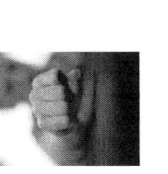

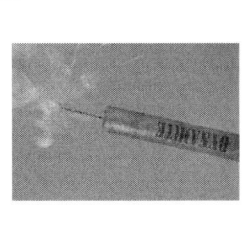

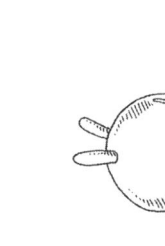

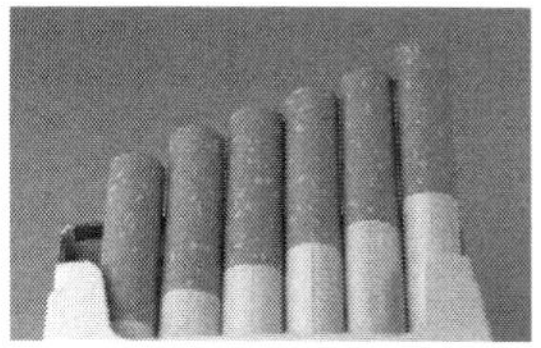

Fotos: www.bilderbox.com

RAAbits Englisch

Hinweise (M 8)

Zu Beginn der Stunde werden einige Tagebucheinträge aus der Hausaufgabe vorgelesen. Dann wird das letzte Drittel des Filmes gezeigt, d. h. die letzten 32 Minuten (1:00:01–1:32:00). Wiederum werden die Schülerinnen und Schüler dazu aufgefordert, ihr *viewing log* (M 3) zu ergänzen.

Im Anschluss an das Ende des Films bearbeiten die Lernenden in Partnerarbeit **M 8**. Hier haben sie den Auftrag, fiktive Äußerungen zu den Charakteren des Films argumentativ zu vervollständigen. Dabei ist darauf zu achten, dass die Aussagen ungefähr gleichmäßig unter den Schülerpaaren verteilt sind.

Nach einer angemessenen Bearbeitungszeit werden einige der vervollständigten Aussagen im Plenum vorgetragen. Die Mitschülerinnen und Mitschüler nehmen die fiktiven Äußerungen zum Anlass, ihre persönliche Meinung zur jeweiligen Thematik zu artikulieren. Hier kann sich eine Plenumsdiskussion anschließen.

Hausaufgabe ist das Beantworten der eigenständig erarbeiteten Fragen aus der Einführungsstunde.

Hinweise (M 9)

Nach der Auswertung der Hausaufgabe sehen sich die Schülerinnen und Schüler die Stichpunkte zu den beiden ausgewählten Familienmitgliedern nochmals an und entscheiden sich für einen der beiden Protagonisten. Anschließend suchen sie im Kurs nach Partnern, die sich für die gleiche Figur entschieden haben.

Tipp: Auch hier kann die Lehrkraft eingreifen, wenn die Gruppen unterschiedlich groß ausfallen.

Aufgabe der Schülerinnen und Schüler ist es nun, sich in einer Gruppendiskussion mithilfe von **M 9** der von ihnen ausgewählten Figur noch weiter anzunähern. In Kleingruppen suchen sie aus einer Liste mit 24 Symbolen die beiden Symbole aus, die ihrer Meinung nach den jeweiligen Charakter am besten repräsentieren. Die Bilder/Symbole wurden bewusst so gewählt, dass sie in verschiedene Richtungen interpretiert werden können. Hier gibt es kein „richtig" oder „falsch".

Die aus dem Auswahlprozess resultierende Gruppendiskussion verhilft den Schülerinnen und Schülern zu einem klarer gezeichneten Bild ihrer Figur, da sie eigene Meinungen mit denen ihrer Mitschülerinnen und Mitschüler vergleichen und kritisch dazu abwägen müssen.

Nach erfolgreicher Lösung der Aufgabe werden die Gruppenergebnisse im Plenum vorgestellt und diskutiert.

Tipp: Hierfür bietet es sich an, die Abbildungen vergrößert zu kopieren, sodass jede Gruppe sie zur Präsentation vorliegen hat.

Erwartungshorizont (M 9)

Hier sind individuelle Schülerlösungen möglich, wichtig ist nur, dass die Auswahl nachvollziehbar begründet wird.

Two possible symbols for **Tariq Khan**:

www.bilderbox.com    picture-alliance / dpa / Stockfood

Both symbols represent the way Tariq feels about himself. He doesn't want to be seen as a person of Pakistani origin but rather as a real Englishman. The Union Jack represents his identification with the country he was born in. The flag itself is a mixture of different flags (the Scottish and the English one) which can be seen as a symbol of a (more or less) successful fusion of different peoples. This is what Tariq aspires to, too.

His longing for Britishness is further emphasised by the second symbol: bacon, eggs and tea (the "typical" English breakfast). These represent the physical aspects of being part of the British/Christian culture, for example like being allowed to eat food which is not 'halal' or even drinking beer in nightclubs.

Two possible symbols for **George Khan**:

www.bilderbox.com 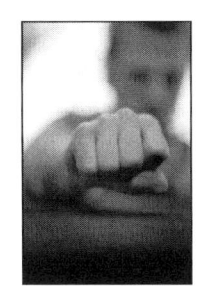   www.bilderbox.com

The symbols underline two different sides of George Khan: on the one hand he is the pious and God-fearing Muslim. He attends mosque regularly and is or wants to be a respected member of the Pakistani-British community. Religion for him is part of his identity. This is also the reason why he forces his children to attend the classes in the mosque and to follow Pakistani traditions (arranged marriage, halal food etc.).

The second symbol represents his attitude towards his family. Even though he is quite likeable in times of superficial harmony, as soon as a crisis erupts, he turns to force and even violence as the only way of pursuing his interests. Therefore, the fist, on the one hand, stands for this brutal side of his character. On the other hand, it could also be seen as a physical representation of his inner self, because, as we find out in the course of the film, George is unable to open himself up for different, new or controversial ideas.

East is East (S II)

| Reihe 3 | Verlauf | Material S 17 | LEK | Kontext | Mediothek |

M 10 Interpreting film language

a) Field size and camera movement

Tasks: Work with a partner.

1. Look at pictures 1 to 5 and describe in your own words what the camera shows of the person. Note down your findings in the boxes.
2. Focus on pictures 6 to 10 and describe in your own words the different camera movements. Note down your descriptions in the boxes.
3. Look at pictures 11 to 17 and describe in your own words the different camera movements as well as angles. Compare your findings from tasks 1., 2. and 3. with another group.
4. In groups of four, match the terms and expressions in the boxes at the bottom of the sheets with the correct pictures/explanations. Present your findings to the class.

II/C7

Field size		Camera movement	
1.		6.	
2.		7.	
3.		8.	
4.		9.	
5.		10.	
Field size		**Camera movement**	
long shot close-up full shot extreme close-up medium shot		to zoom in on/out of sth. static shot tracking shot crane shot to pan left/right; to tilt up/down	

© Ernst Klett Verlag GmbH, Stuttgart 2003: Holes Teacher's Guide.

East is East (S II)

| Reihe 3 | Verlauf | Material S 18 | LEK | Kontext | Mediothek |

II/C7

b) Camera position and camera angle

Camera position	Description
	11.
	12.
	13.
	14.

Camera angle	Description
	15.
	16.
	17.

high-angle shot   over-the-shoulder shot   eye-level shot   reverse-angle shot
overhead shot   low-angle shot   establishing shot

© Ernst Klett Verlag GmbH, Stuttgart 2003: Holes Teacher's Guide.

RAAbits Englisch

East is East (S II)

| Reihe 3 | Verlauf | **Material S 19** | LEK | Kontext | Mediothek |

II/C7

M 11 Film analysis: The wedding scene

Tasks

- As you are watching the wedding ceremony, pay attention to the wedding guests on the one hand, and the wedding couple (Nazir in particular) on the other.

- Which *field sizes, camera movements, camera positions* and *camera angles* can you identify?

- What is the effect being created by the camera work?

Hinweise (M 10 und M 11)

Diese Stunde soll den Schülerinnen und Schülern einen Einstieg in die Filmanalyse vermitteln. In Partnerarbeit erarbeiten sie anhand der Bilder die Funktionen der Kategorien *field size, camera movement, camera position* und *camera angle* **(M 10)**. Nach dieser Phase kommen sie zum Vergleich ihrer Ergebnisse mit anderen Paaren zusammen, klären eventuelle Verständnisfragen und überprüfen ihre Ergebnisse. In diesen Vierergruppen sollen dann die jeweiligen Begriffe den Bildern zugeordnet werden. Zum Schluss werden die Ergebnisse im Plenum begründet vorgestellt.

Tipp: Alternativ können a) und b) in verschiedenen Partner- bzw. Vierergruppen erarbeitet werden.

Um das Gelernte anzuwenden, analysieren die Schülerinnen und Schüler jetzt die gesamte Hochzeitsszene **(07:00–09:21, Kapitel 2)** in Hinblick auf diese Kriterien (*Kameraeinstellung, Kamerabewegung, Kameraposition und Kameraperspektive*) **(M 11)**. Darüber hinaus sollen sie untersuchen, welcher Effekt durch die Kameraarbeit entsteht. Die Lehrkraft sollte hierzu die Aufmerksamkeit der Schülerinnen und Schüler auf die Hochzeitsgäste zum einen und das Hochzeitspaar (hauptsächlich Nazir) zum anderen lenken.

Da diese Aufgabe sehr vielschichtig ist, ist es ratsam, die Szene ein zweites Mal zu zeigen. Beachtenswert an dieser Szene sind die kontrastierenden Kameraeinstellungen zwischen Nazir und den Hochzeitsgästen. Hier wird Spannung erzeugt durch die Darstellung der ausgelassenen Hochzeitsgäste und eines angespannten Nazir, der letztlich die arrangierte Hochzeit platzen lässt.

Neben der Kameraarbeit kann auch der Einsatz der Musik angesprochen werden. Im Zusammenspiel mit der Kameraführung verstärkt sie die Spannung.

East is East (S II)

Erwartungshorizont (M 10)

Field size	Camera movements	Camera position	Camera angle
1. Objects/People are seen from a very long distance. **long shot**	6. The camera does not move, it is fixed in one position. **static shot**	11. The camera gives an overview of the setting. **establishing shot**	15. A person is shown from above. **high-angle shot**
2. Objects/People are seen completely, at the centre of the picture. **full shot**	7. The camera goes up and down, left and right. **to pan left/right; to tilt up/down**	12. In a dialogue, one person is shown from behind. **over-the-shoulder shot**	16. The camera looks straight into the person's eyes. **eye-level shot**
3. The body can be seen from head to waist. **medium shot**	8. The camera is on a crane and moves flexibly in all directions. **crane shot**	13. In the same dialogue, the camera shows the opposite partner from behind. **reverse-angle shot**	17. The camera shows the person from below. **low-angle shot**
4. The person's head and shoulders are shown. **close-up**	9. The camera approaches the person and moves back. **to zoom in on/out of sth.**	14. A scene is shown from above, from a bird's eye perspective. **overhead shot**	
5. The camera focuses on the person's face, the face takes up the whole frame. **extreme close-up**	10. The camera is on a little vehicle and follows the person's movements. **tracking shot**		

East is East (S II)

| Reihe 3 | Verlauf | Material S 21 | LEK | Kontext | Mediothek |

Erwartungshorizont (M 11)

Field size

The **wedding guests** are mainly seen in **medium shot** or in **long shot**, whereas the **wedding couple** is seen in **close-up**. Ella and George are seen in **close-up**, too. At one point, when the bride approaches Nazir, the **camera zooms in on Nazir.** The camera is on the level of Nazir (camera angle: **eye-level shot**) (Timer: 08:01–08:05).

Effect: Together with the bride, the whole ceremony approaches Nazir. Tension builds up between the cheerful wedding guests, Nazir's father and his expectations towards his son, and, in contrast, Nazir's discomfort with the whole situation that eventually makes him run away.

Camera movement

The **camera is predominantly static** except for the moments when it **pans from left to right** as Aunt Annie and a male wedding guest enter the wedding hall (Timer: 07:00–07:01) and again, this time **panning from right to left**, when she has sits with another woman (Timer: 07:15–07:19) in the first row.

The camera **pans from left to right** a third time, as the Muslim teacher enters (Timer: 07:24–07:26). It **pans from right to left** a fourth time as Saleem, Maneer and two other wedding guests take their seats (Timer: 07:29–07:35). For the last time the camera **pans from right to left and tilts up** as the bride is ushered in (Timer: 07:49–07:52).

Camera position

The camera shows an **establishing shot** of the interior of the wedding hall. This makes the viewer aware of where the scene is set. It shows the very festive atmosphere which contrasts collides with Nazir's feelings of unease.

Camera angle

Mainly **eye-level shots**, especially in close-ups of Nazir, his bride, Ella and George. The camera looks from the wedding couple down to the wedding guests (**high-angle shot**).

II/C7

East is East (S II)

| Reihe 3 | Verlauf | Material S 22 | LEK | Kontext | Mediothek |

M 12 Storyboard: East is East ten years later

Design your own storyboard

Tasks

1. Form small groups. Based on the knowledge you have gained about the characters and the plot of the film (see your viewing logs and the film analysis worksheet), you should now create your own scene of *East is East*.

2. Take a look at the worksheet "Your own storyboard". It consists of the following elements:

    a) **Slug line:** Here you fill in the information about the setting of your scene. You use INT. (interior) or EXT. (exterior) to indicate where the scene takes place. The slug line is usually written in CAPS (example: EXT. BUS STATION – NEW YORK – DAYTIME). After the slug line you can add some more information on setting and character(s). This information is given in normal writing.

    Example:

    EXT. BUS STATION – NEW YORK – DAYTIME

    Sharon and David talk about their future plans. She is rather worried.

    b) **Text** (dialogue/monologue): Here you fill in the characters' words in this specific scene. (Your viewing logs should give you some guidance here. What the characters say should be consistent with your observations about them.)

    c) **Camera settings/position shot**: In this box you fill in the way you want to present the scene (Your film analysis worksheets should give you some guidance here.)

    d) **Picture**: Here you draw a little sketch of the picture that is to be presented.

    Your storyboard should be structured in the following way:

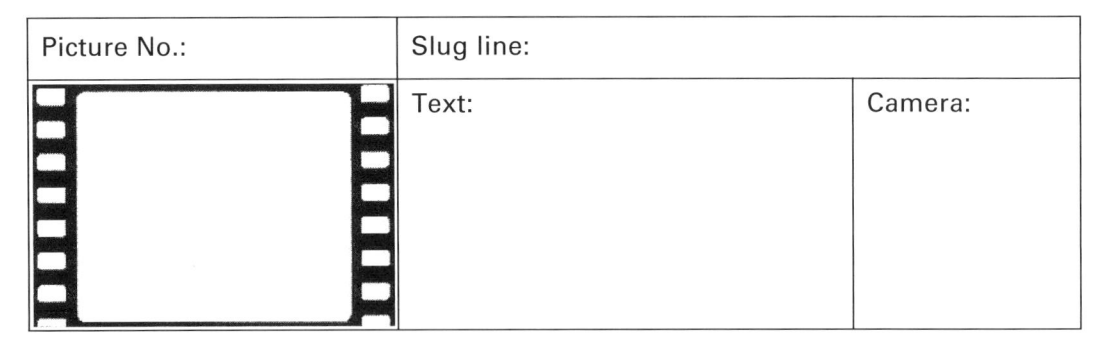

Picture No.:	Slug line:	
	Text:	Camera:

    Note: Your whole scene should not take longer than five minutes.

3. Present your storyboards to the class. Your classmates will decide on the most interesting storyboard.

M 13 Your own storyboard

Picture No.: Slug line: Text: Camera:

Picture No.:	Slug line:	
	Text:	Camera:
Picture No.:	Slug line:	
	Text:	Camera:
Picture No.:	Slug line:	
	Text:	Camera:
Picture No.:	Slug line:	
	Text:	Camera:
Picture No.:	Slug line:	
	Text:	Camera:

East is East (S II)					
Reihe 3	**Verlauf**	**Material** S 24	**LEK**	**Kontext**	**Mediothek**

Hinweise (M 12 und M 13)

In dieser Sitzung werden die Beobachtungen zu den verschiedenen Figuren (u. a. durch die *viewing logs* **(M 3)** und die *freeze frames* **(M 4)**) und die Mittel der Filmanalyse zusammengeführt. Die Schülerinnen und Schüler sollen zum einen (plausible) Dialoge zwischen den Figuren entwerfen und zum anderen Kameraperspektiven und deren Wirkung bewusst einsetzen.

Zunächst machen sich die Lernenden mit dem Storyboard-Raster vertraut **(M 12)**.

Hinweis: Für die Bildung der Gruppen ist die Zusammensetzung relevant. So sollen möglichst alle Figuren des Films in den Gruppen vertreten sein.

Danach teilt die Lehrkraft die Arbeitsbögen aus. Wichtig ist, dass die Lehrkraft mehrere (zwei bis drei) **DIN-A3-Kopien von M 13** an die jeweiligen Gruppen austeilt.

Nach Erstellen der Storyboards präsentieren die Gruppen ihre Ergebnisse im Plenum. Sie sollen begründet ihre Produkte verteidigen. Dialoge können als *stage reading* vorgetragen werden. Die Schülerinnen und Schüler entscheiden danach gemeinsam über das interessanteste Storyboard.

Fakultativ könnte das interessanteste Storyboard verfilmt werden, Equipment und Filmkenntnisse vorausgesetzt.

East is East (S II)

Reihe 3 | Verlauf | Material S 25 | LEK | Kontext | Mediothek

Erwartungshorizont (M 13)

EAST IS EAST – TEN YEARS LATER

Picture No.: 1	Slug line: INT. A CAFÉ SOMEWHERE IN ECCLES, Nazir and George sitting at a table	
	Text: A waitress (to George and Nazir): What can I get you? Nazir: I'll have a cup of tea. George: I'll have half a cup. (to Nazir) Son, I'm glad you've come.	Camera: – full shot – zooming in on Nazir and George
Picture No.: 2	Slug line: S.A.	
	Text: Nazir: What made you change your mind after all these years?	Camera: – over-the-shoulder shot – zooming in on Nazir
Picture No.: 3	Slug line: S.A.	
	Text: George: Son, you brought a lot of shame on the family.	Camera: – reverse-angle shot – zooming in on George
Picture No.: 4	Slug line: S.A.	
	Text: no words	Camera: cut to – full shot
Picture No.: 5	Slug line: S.A.	
	Text: Nazir: You've come all the way down to Eccles to tell me about your feelings!? What about me!?	Camera: – over-the-shoulder shot – zooming in on Nazir
Picture No.: 6	Slug line: S.A.	
	Text: George: I didn't mean to ... Son, things have changed ... I have changed ... Listen ...	Camera: – reverse-angle shot – zooming in on George

II/C7

East is East (S II)

| Reihe 3 | Verlauf | Material S 26 | LEK | Kontext | Mediothek |

II/C7

Ayub Khan-Din: *East is East*

1. Text

Ayub Khan-Din: Biography

"This was our Pakistani life; this is how we existed outside Salford. A life none of my friends knew or could understand ... I think in [*East is East*] I came as close as possible to understanding my father's motivation in the way he tried to bring us up," explains Ayub Khan-Din with regard
5 to his award winning play [...] The 38-year-old playwr[ight] is originally from Salford, England. He is the eighth of ten children to a Pakistani father and British mother. With one brother four years his senior and another three years his junior, Khan-Din admits: "I wasn't part of the older kids or younger kids. I lived in my own world and spent a lot of time daydreaming. It paid off in the end" [...].

10 At the age of sixteen, Khan-Din left school and worked at Lee's Salon, where he went on to become "the worst hairdresser in Manchester." Khan-Din's inspiration to become an actor stemmed from David Niven's autobiography entitled *The Moon's a Balloon*, in which Niven writes about [his] own decision to pursue a career in acting after having served many years in the army. Indeed, Khan-Din also transitioned into the acting profession. His on-screen credits
15 include *My Beautiful Laundrette* and *Sammy and Rosie Get Laid*. He remembers his acting experience to be a tumultuous one, mostly because of his bicultural background: "I had no idea after leaving drama school that I would suddenly be stamped with an invisible mark that said BLACK ACTOR! So while more of my contemporaries went off to rep, I had the added disadvantage of trying to find a company that enforced integrated casting – I didn't work for a
20 year!" [...].

Although Khan-Din wasn't "working" in the traditional sense per se, he was in process of creating what would later become his ticket to success, *East is East*. The play is based heavily on Khan-Din's own life and experiences growing up in a bicultural, working-class background: "The parents are drawn directly from my own family. The youngest boy, Sajid, is me as a child.
25 All the arguments in the film, all the theories behind the father's way of thinking are my own arguments and theories which I developed from writing the first draft of the stageplay to the last draft of the screenplay. The different issues, the different aspects of the relationships – they're all very similar to my own background" [...].

Khan-Din has received harsh criticism from more traditional members of [the] Asian society
30 for what they believe to be a somewhat derogatory depiction of Pakistani culture. In response to such comments, he claims: "It was a personal story. I wasn't writing about any specific community, I was writing about my father" [...]. Khan-Din has recently married and is currently in the process of writing two more plays called *So Soon, So Soon* and *Belmondo Sahib*. Additionally, another piece, *Last Dance at Dum Dum* started stage performances in mid-1999.
35 His latest work has received mixed reviews, but the overall consensus of critics is that *East is East* remains his most solid and compelling play.

(512 words)

http://english.emory.edu/Bahri/Khan1.html

Vocabulary Aids

4 **to bring sb. up:** jemanden aufziehen, großziehen – 5 **playwright:** author of theatre plays – 18 **contemporaries:** here: the people he studied with – 18 **rep:** repertory: a company that presents several different plays in the course of a season at one theater – 27 **draft:** version – 30 **derogatory:** abfällig, abschätzig

2. Screenshot

© defd-movies

Assignments

I   *Content*

   a) Summarise the text in no more than 180 words.

II   *Form*

   b) Briefly position the scene depicted above in the overall context of the film. Then analyse which camera technique/shot was used to film it. Comment on why this particular shot and no other might have been used.

III   *Discussion*

   c) "It was a personal story. I wasn't writing about any specific community, I was writing about my father." (ll. 31/32) Comment on this statement by Khan-Din, discussing how far this personal story goes in giving a negative image of the Pakistani community in Britain.

   d) "I think in [East is East] I came as close as possible to understanding my father's motivation in the way he tried to bring us up". (ll. 3/4) Discuss whether in *East is East* the father is shown as a villain or a victim. Justify your opinion.

East is East (S II)

| Reihe 3 | Verlauf | Material | LEK S 3 | Kontext | Mediothek |

Hinweise und Erwartungshorizont (Klausur)

Vorbemerkung: Die Einberechnung der sprachlichen Richtigkeit in die Endnote variiert stark von Bundesland zu Bundesland. Daher werden hier keine Vorschläge gemacht, wie die Sprache zu bewerten ist.

Summary

In the text "Ayub Khan-Din: Biography", published on the webpage english.emory.edu, the unknown author describes how Ayub Khan-Din's life has influenced his work and especially his stage- and screenplay East is East. He does this by giving details and quoting the playwright himself.

Khan-Din who, like the characters of East is East, is originally from Salford, Manchester. He grew up in a bicultural Pakistani-British family and after a short stint as a hairdresser, he decided to make the stage the centre of his life, after being inspired by David Niven's autobiography. The author points out how Khan-Din, even though he appeared in some major films, got fed up with always being hired as a black actor and how East is East was his breakthrough as a writer.

The playwright himself underlines that the play is highly autobiographical and therefore not to be seen as a general statement on the Pakistani community in Britain but rather as a personal investigation of his father and family. The article concludes by mentioning some other works of Khan-Din. (174 words)

Form

Context: While George is at the hospital with Ella and Sajid, the brothers and the sister eat pork in their home. When Maneer warns them that George is coming back a small panic breaks out, while the brothers and sister try to hide all traces of their feast.

Shots: static shot, medium shot, eye-level shot. By using these shots, the director makes sure we get the whole picture: we see that all three young people relish pork and that they feel very comfortable about it (body-language). (This wouldn't have been the case in an extreme close-up, for example.) Nevertheless, we are sufficiently close to them to feel a part of their little conspiracy. (This wouldn't have been the case in an establishing shot/long shot.)

Discussion

The students are expected to write structured texts: introduction, discussion, conclusion.

Introduction: introductory sentence(s), question to be dealt with, structure of discussion

Discussion: structured in itself, with clear and balanced arguments (e.g. pro/con, pro/con)

Conclusion: logical result of discussion, no new point, possibly summarising the main arguments in one sentence.

Possible arguments
c)

– Khan-Din underlines the fact the he wrote a personal story, not a story about a particular community. Therefore, he says, criticism of his work to that extent is wrong.

- However, one has to ask oneself how the story will be seen by others. We can take for granted that not even members of the Pakistani community – who should know what their lives are 'really' like – can see the film as personal and autobiographical, but rather as stereotyped and biased. Thus we could expect the same or worse could happen to other groups who don't have any real insight into the life of Pakistanis in Britain. That's why there is a danger of the film being seen as a pure and true representation of British Pakistanis.

- However: George Khan is the one truly negative example. Many other members of the community (be it the mullah, the friend in Bradford or to a certain extent the children themselves > Maneer!) are depicted positively.

- The whites are not shown in a completely positive light either: think of Earnest's racist grandfather or even passive Ella. Therefore, saying that the film paints a negative image of British-Pakistanis is a superficial and even wrong criticism.

d)

- George Khan is not a straightforwardly good or bad character.

- Even though the viewer is quickly presented with George's negative character traits, he preserves an ambiguous opinion of him for a long time as there seem to be both nice and nasty sides to him (possibly: examples).

- When George secretly plans his sons' weddings, the viewer can still understand him, as his motivation to erase the stain of Nazir's escape is clear.

- However, we get a more and more negative image of George in the last third of the film. This starts with his violent behaviour towards Maneer and then even Ella. The scene in which Tariq wants to talk to him is also full of tension and threatening violence.

- In the same scene all the sympathy we might have had for George because of his different background vanishes: Tariq confronts him with the fact that he himself married the woman he wanted to, escaping from his arranged marriage in Pakistan. George's failure to grasp this fundamental contradiction in his own reasoning makes him very unlikeable.

- His final violent outburst, when he tries to strangle Ella, seems to signify the moment in which he seems to have turned into a real villain. Nevertheless, the moments and hours of reflection which follow the open confrontation with his family indicate a possibility of hope and redemption. In the end the viewer nearly feels sorry for George.

Mediothek

Literatur

Khan-Din, Ayub: East is East. London: Nick Hern Books 1997. 96 Seiten, ISBN: 978-1854593139.

Das Theaterstück, auf dem der Film basiert und von dem parallel zum Film Auszüge gelesen werden können.

Khan-Din, Ayub: East is East: Screenplay. Houndmills: MacMillan 1999. ISBN: 978-0752218489).

Drehbuch zum Film.

Film

East is East. Regie Damien O'Donnell, 1999 nach dem gleichnamigen Bühnenstück von Ayub Khan-Din (92 min.)

Erhältlich u. a. bei www.amazon.de und www.lingua-video.com.

Unterrichtsmaterial

Bruck, Peter: East is East: Unterrichtshinweise und Kopiervorlagen. ISBN: 978-3-12-577483-4. Stuttgart: Klett 2016.

Kopierbare Unterlagen u.a. mit Szenenprotokoll, Unterrichtsideen und Arbeitsblättern zum Kultur- und Generationskonflikt und den Charakteren, Zusatztexte, Klausur- und Projektvorschläge.

Internetseiten

Filmkritiken zu *East is East* findet man u. a. bei www.imdb.com und bei www.rottentomatoes.com

Zu Enoch Powell (M 2)

http://www.telegraph.co.uk/comment/3643823/Enoch-Powells-Rivers-of-Blood-speech.html

Vollständiger Text von Powells „River of Blood"-Rede.

http://news.bbc.co.uk/onthisday/hi/dates/stories/april/20/newsid_2489000/2489357.stm

Übersichtliche Informationen zu Powells Birmingham-Rede im zeitgeschichtlichen Kontext.

Aktuelle Bezüge:

https://www.theguardian.com/commentisfree/2016/jun/16/farage-poster-enoch-powell-rivers-of-blood-racism-ukip-european-union

Artikel aus dem Guardian, in dem eine Parallele zwischen Powells Rede und einem Wahlplakat von Ukip / Nigel Farrage gezogen wird.

http://www.nytimes.com/2016/01/23/opinion/campaign-stops/donald-trump-and-the-rivers-of-blood.html?_r=0

Artikel aus der New York Times, der die Ideen von Powell und Donald Trump vergleicht.

Zu „Im Land der großartigen Möglichkeiten" (M 2)

http://www.bbc.co.uk/gloucestershire/untold_stories/asian/pakistani_community.shtml

Artikel, der die Geschichte pakistanischer Einwanderer seit dem Zweiten Weltkrieg beleuchtet.

http://www.localhistories.org/bradford.html

Ein kurzer geschichtlicher Abriss über Bradford vom Mittelalter bis ins 21. Jahrhundert.

http://www.migration-info.de/artikel/2015-01-29/vereinigtes-koenigreich-einwanderungsland-wider-willen

(Deutscher) Artikel, der GB als Einwanderungsland beleuchtet.

How to Improve Your Writing Style – Methodentraining für die Klassen 10–13

Manuela Olde Daalhuis, Düsseldorf

M 1 How to write a good text – some tips

How to write a good text

When writing a text, you want the reader to understand your thoughts. Therefore there is no sense in using complicated words and over long sentences. If you do not know what you mean to say, spend the time thinking about a new, powerful argument rather than writing a confusing or boring sentence. A good writing style starts with clear and structured thoughts.

How to choose your words

Use effective, clear words rather than pompous, long words. _____ (1)

Avoid repeating the same word in the same paragraph. _____ (2)

How to build your sentences

Keep sentences relatively short. Use subclauses, participles and gerunds. _____ (3)

How to organise your paragraphs

Avoid paragraphs that contain only one long sentence. _____ (4)
If your paragraph is as long as a page, split it into smaller paragraphs.

Use some connectives[1] to show how one sentence refers to the next one in a paragraph. _____ (5)

1 **connective:** linking word, e.g. although, therefore, yet

Task

Where do the sentences a)–e) fit in? Read the text and fill in the correct letters in the gaps.

a) Every few lines, a full stop gives the reader time to breathe before reading your next idea.

b) This way the reader can follow your train of thought and concentrate on your arguments easily.

c) This is a means to vary the sentence structure and shorten your text.

d) Why make it difficult for the reader?

e) Otherwise, the reader might find the text boring.

How to Improve Your Writing Style (Klasse 10–13)

M 2 Using the right register[1] – formal vs informal English

Good writing starts with choosing the appropriate register.

> **Who is going to read your text? – Using the right register**
>
> People you don't know very well, e.g. your teacher, your boss.
> → Use *formal* English.
>
> People you know well, e.g. your friends, your classmates, your parents.
> → Use *informal* English.

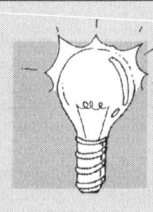

Task 1

a) What is typical of formal and informal English? Fill in the table with the correct words and phrases from the box. Some examples are given.

b) Try to find more examples for formal vs informal English and write them in the empty lines.

| child | Send it soon! | I am afraid I disagree. |
| cannot | on top of it all | to drop a line | definitely |

Formal English	Informal English
Abbreviations and contractions	
	can't
Verbs	
to send somebody a note	
Nouns and phrases	
	kid
	Rubbish!
Connectives	
Furthermore, moreover …	
Emphasis words	
	very, really
Letter and email expressions	
Please send it at your earliest convenience.	

[1] **register:** die Sprachebene

Task 2

Would you write in formal or informal English in the situations below?
Tick ☑ the correct box.

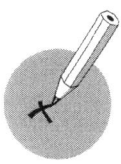

	Situation	Formal English	Informal English
a)	You would like to share how your day at school was with your best friend.	☐	☐
b)	You would like to discuss a topic in an exam paper.	☐	☐
c)	You would like to apply for a job.	☐	☐
d)	You would like to complain about the headphones you have bought.	☐	☐
e)	You would like to chat with a classmate about the latest film.	☐	☐
f)	You would like to let your parents know what is happening on the class trip via email.	☐	☐

Task 3

Olivia plans to apply for a summer job at Ms Thompson's shop. Rewrite her email in formal English.

```
Hello Ms Thompson,

I'm looking for a summer job, and my dad kept an ear open. He's told me you're looking for somebody to help out at your shop. Well, I could be in the right place at the right time! How come? I'm pretty good at being on time and giving a hand. Last summer, I was a waitress and got on well with all kinds of people. Call me if you want me to come round for a chat!

Yours,

Olivia Walker
```

How to Improve Your Writing Style (Klasse 10–13)
Einzelmaterial 195
S 4

M 3 Hero for a day – understanding an article

Find out how people in San Francisco realised a five-year-old's dream to help his superhero for a day.

Batkid saves San Francisco as charity makes a wish come true

Thousands volunteer to help five-year-old leukaemia patient battle The Riddler and Penguin on a day of realised dreams

San Francisco was beset by a wave of crime on Friday, as a woman was taken hostage and tied to cable car tracks, a criminal calling himself the Riddler attempted to rob a bank vault, and a miscreant known as Penguin generally made a nuisance of himself in the downtown area.

Happily, each incident was staged: an attempt on the part of the charity Make-A-Wish to give five-year-old Miles Scott, who is recovering from leukaemia, a memorable day assisting his favourite superhero.

Miles walks to help the tied up woman.

San Francisco's mayor and police were among thousands involved in an extraordinary day that gripped the city and caught the attention of the White House. Miles's day began with a fraught message from police chief Greg Suhr, alerting "Batkid" to the various criminal activities and pleading with him to assist. Miles acquiesced, and was collected by a man dressed as Batman who was driving a vehicle which bore a passing resemblance to the Batmobile.

With little time to waste, the pair hastened to the Grand Hyatt in San Francisco's Union Square, where an unnamed woman had been tied up on cable car tracks with what appeared to be an improvised explosive device strapped to her back.

A large crowd had gathered at the scene as Batkid arrived and sprinted over to the woman. After a tense few moments a cheer went up as Batkid managed to free the woman from her bonds. The device did not detonate.

Less than an hour later, Batkid was summoned back to Union Square, where a criminal mastermind known as The Riddler was attempting to rob a bank vault.

Batkid successfully downed the villain, despite significant disadvantages in height and strength, and The Riddler was taken away in a San Francisco police department truck. SFPD did not immediately respond to questions regarding charges against The Riddler.

Later, Batkid apprehended a known felon called Penguin before being handed the key to the city by an understandably grateful mayor. The stunt gripped the city: "This has turned into a full blown phenomenon," said Suhr, the police chief.

Miles received a made up newspaper front.

RAAbits Englisch

How to Improve Your Writing Style (Klasse 10–13)

40 The White House sent out a tweet encouraging Batkid to "Go get 'em!" In a video recording, President Barack Obama said, "Way to go, Miles! Way to save Gotham!"

Make-A-Wish grants the wishes of children with life-threatening illnesses. Miles, a Batman fan, had one wish: "To be Batkid." Make-A-Wish reached out through email and social networks, asking for help making Miles's wish come true. The charity was inundated with
45 offers to help. Volunteers formed the crowd or pretended to be villains.

The San Francisco Chronicle is among the many organisations involved, and its Friday front page was dedicated to the superhero. The headline? "Batkid Saves City".

© www.theguardian.com/world/2013/nov/15/batkid-san-francisco-charity-make-wish by Adam Gabbatt, 15 November 2013.

Vocabulary Aids

charity: die Wohltätigkeitsorganisation – 1 **the Riddler and Penguin:** comic book supervillains, the enemies of Batman – 3 **to be beset by sth.:** to have a lot of trouble with sth. – 4 **to take sb. hostage:** to take sb. as a prisoner in order to force sb. else to do what you want – 5 **cable car tracks:** die Gleise der Kabelbahn – 7 **bank vault:** a protected room in a bank used to store money safely – 7 **miscreant:** sb. who behaves badly, often a criminal – 8 **to make a nuisance of oneself:** to cause trouble – 11 **on the part of the charity:** seitens der Wohltätigkeitsorganisation – 15 **mayor:** the governor of a town – 16 **fraught:** extremely worrying – 17 **to alert sb. to sth.:** to warn sb. of sth. – 18 **to plead with sb. to do sth.:** jmndn. inständig bitten, etw. zu tun – 18 **to acquiesce:** to agree – 20 **the Grand Hyatt:** a skyscraper hotel – 26 **bonds:** ropes used to keep sb. a prisoner – 26 **to detonate:** to explode – 27 **to summon sb. back:** to order sb. back – 29 **to attempt to do sth.:** to try to do sth. – 34 **charge:** accusation – 35 **to apprehend:** to catch and arrest – 35 **felon:** sb. who is guilty of a serious crime – 42 **to grant a wish:** to realise a wish – 44 **to inundate:** to give sb. so much work or things that the person cannot deal with them all

Task 1

a) Describe what Miles Scott's dream was.

b) List the incidents Miles had to help out with.

c) Describe what people did to realise his dream.

Task 2

a) Find two examples of formal and informal English in the article and write them in the table.

	Formal English	**Informal English**
1		
2		

b) When is formal English used in the article? Explain.

c) When is informal English used in the article? Explain.

How to Improve Your Writing Style (Klasse 10–13)

M 4 Avoiding repetitions

Practise avoiding repetitions in your texts with this worksheet.

Task: Improve the writing style of the text about Make-A-Wish. Replace the words "very good", "to think" and "bad" by crossing them out and filling in the gaps with an alternative expression from the boxes. Pay attention to the context to choose an appropriate alternative and avoid repetition.

"very good" – alternative expressions
wonderful   perfect   famous   special   happy
worthwhile   successful   excellent

"to think" – alternative expressions
to believe   to expect   to maintain   to feel   to suppose

"bad" – alternative expressions
sad   painful   terrible   unwell   discouraged   downcast   unhappy   difficult

---

Make-A-Wish

Make-A-Wish is a **very good** _____ (1) charity organisation in the United States. It grants wishes to children between 2½ and 18 years, who suffer from a life-threatening disease.

A friendly team meets the child to create a vision of a **very good** _____ (2) day. A child may wish to go to a **very good** _____ (3) place (e.g. a theme park), to be somebody else (e.g. a firefighter, a superhero), to meet a **very good** _____ (4) athlete or singer or to give a present to somebody (e.g. to other children, their family, their school).

The Make-A-Wish organisation **thinks** _____ (5) it can bring back hope, strength and joy to these children's **bad** _____ (6) lives. The children can regain their confidence. Doctors **think** _____ (7) that such a **very good** _____ (8) day often is a turning point in the treatment. The experience helps the children when they are feeling **bad** _____ (9). The children turn to the **very good** _____ (10) memories they have for comfort and strength at **bad** _____ (11) moments.

Make-A-Wish **thinks** _____ (12) the wish also influences the families who no longer feel isolated and **bad** _____ (13) in their fight against the disease.

The volunteers and donors **think** _____ (14) it is **very good** _____ (15) to make the world a little better. About 25,000 volunteers work for the organisation that uses donations to realise these wishes.

---

1 **charity organisation:** die Wohltätigkeitsorganisation – 2 **to grant a wish:** to realise a wish – 5/6 **theme park:** der Vergnügungspark – 11 **to regain sth.:** to get sth. back – 12 **treatment:** die Behandlung – 19 **donor:** a person who gives money or goods to an organisation

How to Improve Your Writing Style (Klasse 10–13)

M 5 Stressing your message – intensifying adverbs

Learn how to underline your thoughts without using "very (much)" with the help of intensifying adverbs.

Task 1: Match the words listed below with the corresponding intensifying adverbs from the boxes.

affected	*disgusting*	*recommended*
ashamed	*effective*	*ridiculous*
to believe	*impossible*	*shocked*
concerned	*to influence*	*successful*
to condemn	*likely*	*wrong*
convinced	*to oppose*	

highly/extremely
(used with words with a positive connotation or words that express probability)
– likely

utterly/absolutely
(used with adjectives with a negative connotation)

very (much) [crossed out]

deeply
(used with feelings)

strongly
(used with verbs that express an opinion)

Task 2: Choose a combination from task 1 to complete the sentences.

a) The parents were _____ when the doctor told them the diagnosis.

b) The ill child _____ in the healing power of his superhero.

c) A perfect wish day is _____ to give the ill child hope again.

d) Some parents try to profit from Make-A-Wish by asking for an expensive holiday just for themselves. This wish is _____.

e) The volunteers are _____ by witnessing the children's joy and consequently feel their charity is worthwhile.

How to Improve Your Writing Style (Klasse 10–13)

M 6 Stressing your message – practise intensifying adverbs

Task 1

a) Work with a partner, cut out the cards and put them face down on the table. Choose one of the cards and on your own write down pros and cons of the wish for two minutes. Do not talk to each other.

b) Discuss: Would you grant the wish[1] on the card or dismiss it? Why? If you want to grant it, what might be the greatest challenges? Use intensifying adverbs (*highly/ deeply* etc.) to express degrees of e.g. probability or feelings. Be prepared to present your dialogue in class.

Sam, 5, would like to give cuddly toys to other patients.	**Joyce, 12, would like to have a flash mob in the hospital.**
Glenn, 14, would like to meet Lady Gaga.	**Kyra, 9, would like to offer a well-being holiday to her parents.**
Dylan, 7, would like to be a firefighter for a day.	**Brenda, 15, would like to have a large flat-screen TV and an interactive game console.**

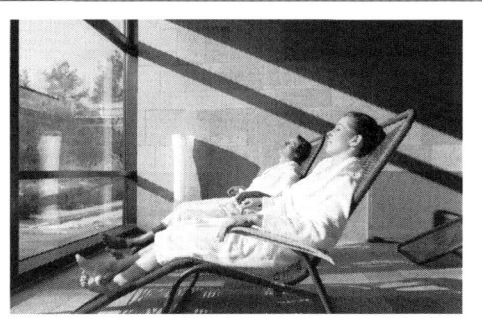

Task 2

Choose a wish from the cards and write a formal answer letter to the child's parents. Explain why you are going to grant the wish/cannot grant it. Explain the next steps or give ideas for more realistic wishes. In your letter, use at least 2 intensifying adverbs.

1 **to grant a wish:** to realise a wish

M 7 Varying your sentence structure – participle clauses

Find out how participle clauses help you to vary your sentence structure.

> A participle clause can replace a relative clause, or express two actions that are related in time or by cause and effect. It can also describe the circumstances of an action.
>
> Example:
>
> <u>When I read about girls' everyday life in Pakistan</u>, I decided to sign a petition for worldwide access to education.
>
> → **Reading** about girls' everyday life in Pakistan, I decided to sign a petition for worldwide access to education.

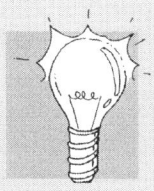

Task

Shorten the sentences by using a participle construction.

a) When I watched a documentary on girls' living conditions worldwide, I realised that education for girls cannot be taken for granted in many parts of the world.

b) Some girls who fight for the right to be educated risk physical abuse, and in some parts of the world even their life is threatened.

c) Some groups are afraid of giving girls access to equal education because they argue it does not conform to their religion or cultural tradition.

d) Girls can realise injustice and try to change it when they learn more about their rights.

e) When they have gained knowledge for several years, girls know how to create networks and can work for social change so that they may avoid poverty.

How to Improve Your Writing Style (Klasse 10–13)

M 8 Varying your sentence structure – preposition + gerund

Find out how preposition + gerund constructions help you to vary your sentence structure.

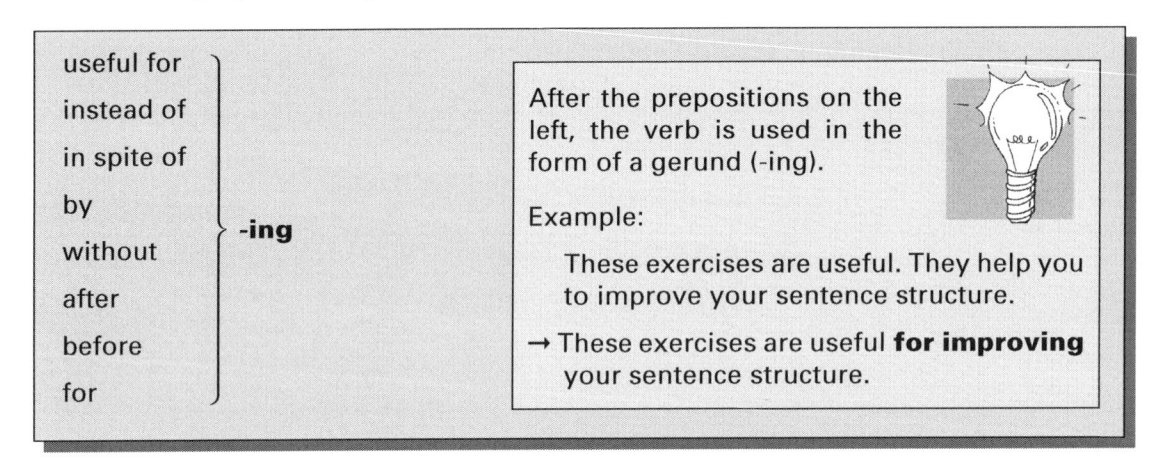

Preposition	
useful for	
instead of	
in spite of	
by	-ing
without	
after	
before	
for	

After the prepositions on the left, the verb is used in the form of a gerund (-ing).

Example:

These exercises are useful. They help you to improve your sentence structure.

→ These exercises are useful **for improving** your sentence structure.

Task: Shorten the sentences by using one of the prepositions + gerund listed above.

a) Malala Yousafzai is a Pakistani educationalist activist. In the year 2013, she was listed as the youngest candidate for the Nobel Peace Prize <u>after she fought for girls' access to education even in life-threatening conditions</u>.

b) The eleven-year-old wrote about the Taliban terrorist activities. She also described a girl's everyday life in her region <u>when she wrote a BBC blog under a pseudonym from 2009 onwards</u>.

c) <u>Before the Taliban attacked Malala's school bus</u>, they spread fear in the region because they banned girls from attending school, dance, and music. They also blew up a lot of girls' schools.

d) Many girls stopped attending school. <u>Malala did not give up</u>, she continued to go to school and learned for her exams. On 9th October 2012, the Taliban stopped Malala's school bus and asked specifically for her. After one Taliban shot her in the head and throat, she had serious life-threatening injuries. Worldwide, there was an outcry of rage.

e) <u>Although Malala is famous worldwide</u>, Malala knows that her autobiography *I am Malala* has been banned from thousands of private schools in Pakistan.

f) In Pakistan, some people blame her <u>because she has become the tool of western forces in their eyes.</u> They think the western countries use the Taliban's attack on Malala for their own political aims but fail to see the fact that many Pakistani civilians have already died from American drone attacks.

Malala Yousafzai

Malala and her family now live in Great Britain. On her 16th birthday, she spoke in front of the UN and gave them a petition with 4 million signatures asking for a universal right on education. The UN wants to realise this by 2015. To honour Malala's activism, the UN wants to celebrate her cause every year on 10th November on Malala Day.

Text: Manuela Olde Daalhuis; Source: www.bbc.com/news/world-asia-23241937, www.childrenspeaceprize.org/

How to Improve Your Writing Style (Klasse 10–13)

M 9 Applying connectives – from sentences to paragraphs

With connectives, you can show how one sentence refers to the next one in a paragraph.

To structure the text	To add ideas	To contrast
to begin with	in addition	although
secondly	moreover	whereas
another point is	furthermore	however
ultimately	likewise	yet
To give examples	**To give reasons**	**To describe results**
for example	that explains why	as a consequence
for instance	as a result of	to conclude
	therefore	to sum up
	for this reason	accordingly

Task: This text on charity organisations lacks connectives. Take a look at the table and fill in the gaps with connectives. Often, there is more than one correct answer.

_____ (1), many charity organisations focus on children's living standards and most of them need people to help by donating money to their cause.

_____ (2), there are also other ways of getting involved: You can buy products from companies who donate a part of the price to a charity (Christmas cards, _____ (3)), work as a volunteer, or organise fundraising activities.

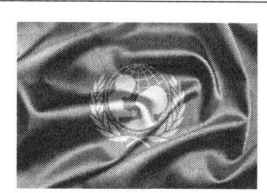

The UNICEF flag

One of the best-known global organisations around children's rights is UNICEF. This charity is a global authority, active in more than 190 countries and part of the United Nations system. _____ (4), it can put pressure on decision-makers. UNICEF is guided by the Convention on the Rights of the Child and strives to establish children's rights as enduring ethical principles worldwide.

There are many obstacles that can threaten a child's well-being e.g. poverty or violence. One goal, _____ (5), is to prevent the spread of HIV among the young.

_____ (6), UNICEF helps in cases of emergency like natural disasters by organising e.g. drinking water and shelter. _____ (7), this charity promotes education. _____ (8), it especially supports girls' education and equal rights for girls so they can take part in their community instead of being victimised.

Some people maintain that a large organisation like UNICEF is needed to lead to effective changes. _____ (9), others believe that too much money is spent on organising such a large network instead of giving the money directly to those in need. _____ (10), these people prefer small, local charities.

_____ (11), it is a question of taste whether you prefer small or large organisations. They all have one goal in common – to make the world a better place for children. What really matters is that you get active and help too.

Text: Manuela Olde Daalhuis; Source: www.unicef.org

1 **charity organisation:** die Wohltätigkeitsorganisation – 3 **to donate:** to give money or goods to sb. in order to help – 7 **volunteer:** der/die Freiwillige – 8 **fundraising:** die Beschaffung finanzieller Mittel – 12 **Convention on the Rights of the Child:** a children's rights treaty – 14 **obstacle:** das Hindernis

How to Improve Your Writing Style (Klasse 10–13)

M 10 Revising an email

Alec has written an email to his trainer to ask him if their sports club could help UNICEF. The email contains typical elements that make a text sound unclear and boring. Show your writing style competence!

Tips

a) Replace "very good" with an alternative expression.

b) Replace the verb "say" by a more precise expression.

c) Use connectives.

d) Use participle constructions.

Tasks

1. Fold the paper to hide the solution column on the right. Take a look at the tips. Revise the text passages a)–d). Check your results by comparing them to the solutions.

2. Write Mr Dean's response to Alec's email.

↓ Fold here.

a)	Dear Mr Dean, Yesterday after our training I went shopping and was attracted to a very good UNICEF information stall. It informed people about children worldwide who live in bad conditions. They suffer from hunger or violence. There were some very good brochures. Later I visited their very good website. I think we should do something in our very good sports club to help UNICEF.	an interesting UNICEF information stall excellent/informative brochures helpful/interesting/informative website famous/successful/well-known sports club
b)	The charity says they need everybody's help to protect children's rights. They say that young people can raise money in many ways. They also say that most people have a lot of fun while they contribute to a good cause.	emphasises point out/show stress/explain/add/argue
c)	We could hold a jumble sale or sell homemade biscuits. We could charge for tickets to a special sports day or a competition (table tennis). We could raise money by organising a raffle.	To begin with, we could hold … Likewise, we could charge … (table tennis, for example). Moreover, we could raise money …
d)	Many people are afraid of taking the first step. Yet, UNICEF helps fundraisers. They provide checklists that help you to prepare a project and inform people about children's rights. When you have registered your project, you can download and order fundraising materials like collection tins, posters etc. at www.unicef.org.uk. If you're interested, I could give you more info. Yours, Alec	Yet, UNICEF helps fundraisers by providing … Having registered your project, you can …

How to Improve Your Writing Style (Klasse 10–13)

Einzelmaterial 195
S 13

Kompetenzen

Lexikalische Kompetenz: Sprachliche Mittel zur Schaffung von Textkohärenz und zur Vermeidung von Wiederholungen einsetzen.

Grammatische Kompetenz: Komplexe syntaktische Strukturen, die besonders im schriftsprachlichen Englisch verwendet werden anwenden.

Schreibkompetenz: Notizen und E-Mails verfassen.

Schulung der Lesekompetenz: Einen authentischen englischsprachigen Text bearbeiten.

Auf CD:
✓ Word-Datei
✓ Zusatzmaterial

Niveau

Klasse 10–13

Dauer

1–5 Unterrichtsstunden (je nach Auswahl des Materials)

Einbettung

Die Materialien sind unabhängig vom Lehrwerk einsetzbar. Thematisch ist eine Anbindung an die Bereiche „Being young", „Being different", „Making a difference" und „Charity work" (Jahrgang 10) sowie „Globalisation" (Jahrgang 11 bis 13) möglich.

Hinweise

Die Meinung, der Schreibstil sei reine Geschmackssache, ist weit verbreitet. Aber ein prägnanter und kohärenter Stil kann trainiert werden. Die vorliegenden Materialien enthalten Übungen, mit denen die Lernenden umständliche oder unangemessene Formulierungen sowie Inkohärenz und Wiederholungen in Texten erkennen, und diese verbessern.

Zur Durchführung

1. Stunde: *How to write a good text*

Als **Einstieg** sammeln die Schülerinnen und Schüler[1] in einem Brainstorming mündlich Kriterien gelungener Texte. Die Ergebnisse werden stichpunktartig an der Tafel festgehalten.

In **M 1** lesen sie in Einzelarbeit **Schreibtipps** und ordnen in den Text ergänzende Sätze ein. Im Plenum werden die dort aufgeführten Kriterien eines guten Texts mit den eigenen vergleichen. M 1 informiert die Lernenden zugleich über die Inhalte der folgenden Stunden: Stilübungen auf der Wortebene (Wortwahl), der Satzebene (Grammatik, Satzbau) sowie der Ebene von Textabschnitten (Satzverknüpfungen).

Im Anschluss üben die Schüler in Einzel- oder Partnerarbeit, **formelles** von **informellem Englisch (M 2)** zu unterscheiden.

2. Stunde: *How to choose the right words I*

Als **Impulseinstieg** halten die Lernenden in wenigen Sätzen schriftlich fest, wie für sie ein **perfekter Tag** aussehen würde, wenn sie sich alles wünschen dürften.

Sie lesen einen **Onlineartikel (M 3)** über einen kranken Jungen, der dank der Wohltätigkeitsorganisation Make-A-Wish einen Tag lang seinen Lieblingshelden Batman begleiten durfte und beantworten Fragen zum **Textverständnis (*task 1*)**. Im Text finden sie Beispiele für **formelles** und **informelles Englisch (*task 2*)**.

[1] Im weiteren Verlauf wird aus Gründen der besseren Lesbarkeit nur „Schüler" verwendet.

How to Improve Your Writing Style (Klasse 10–13)

Einzelmaterial 195
S 14

Darauf vergleichen die Schüler, ob sich ihre Vorstellungen eines perfekten Tages ändern würde, wenn sie an einer lebensbedrohlichen Krankheit litten.

In **M 4** trainieren sie anhand eines Textes über Make-A-Wish, **Wortwiederholungen** zu **vermeiden**. Sie ersetzen „very good", „to think" und „bad" im Text durch kontextuell angemessene Alternativen. Dies kann in Einzel- oder Partnerarbeit erfolgen.

Abschließend üben die Lernenden, *very/very much* durch ***intensifying adverbs*** **(M 5)** zu ersetzen, indem sie alleine oder zu zweit passende Kollokationen bilden. M 5 kann auch **Hausaufgabe** sein.

3. Stunde: *How to choose the right words II*

Die Schüler diskutieren in Partnerarbeit anhand von **Sprechkarten (M 6)**, ob den Wünschen auf den Karten entsprochen werden soll. Dabei wenden sie die ***intensifying adverbs*** aus M 5 an **(task 1)**. Zwei bis drei Dialoge werden im Plenum präsentiert.

Tipp: Lassen Sie die Lernenden beispielhaft einen kurzen Dialog im Plenum erarbeiten, bevor sie zu zweit arbeiten. Kündigen Sie auch die anschließende Präsentationsphase an, um zu gewährleisten, dass die Lerner die Kollokationen tatsächlich einüben und anwenden.

In **task 2** beantworten sie in Einzel- oder Partnerarbeit schriftlich eine Wunschanfrage. Der **Brief** kann auch Hausaufgabe sein.

4. Stunde: *How to vary sentences and organise paragraphs*

Den **Einstieg** in die Stunde bilden folgende Impulsfragen:

– *Imagine you could not go to school for the next year for political reasons. What would you do?*

– *Would you miss school?*

Erfahrungsgemäß werden viele Schüler zunächst erfreut reagieren, sich dann aber bewusst machen, wie selbstverständlich es für deutsche Schüler ist, zur Schule gehen zu dürfen.

M 7 und M 8 enthalten Übungen zur Satzstruktur. **Participle clauses (M 7)** und **preposition + gerund (M 8)** werden in Einzelarbeit wiederholt, indem die Lernenden vorgegebene Sätze umformulieren. Inhaltlich geht es in den Texten um den Zugang zu Bildung für Mädchen und die Kinderrechtsaktivistin Malala Yousafzai.

Alternative: Die Erarbeitung von M 7 und M 8 erfolgt vorbereitend als **Hausaufgabe**. Die Schüler diskutieren nach der Ergebnissicherung in der nächsten Stunde, wie wichtig ihnen Schule ist:

– *Would you be willing to keep on going to school if this meant that someone threatened to beat or attack you?*

Tipp: Diese Frage kann anhand eines ***think-pair-share*** beantwortet werden. Jeder denkt eine Minute über den eigenen Standpunkt nach und diskutiert diesen anschließend mit ein bis zwei Partnern. Die Gemeinsamkeiten und Unterschiede werden im Plenum verglichen.

In **M 9** üben die Lernenden, ihren Stil auf der Ebene eines Textabsatzes zu verbessern. Sie fügen in einen **Lückentext** passende ***connectives*** ein, um die einzelnen Sätze sinnstiftend zu verknüpfen. Inhaltlich befasst sich der Text mit der Wohltätigkeitsorganisation UNICEF. Je nach Zeitbedarf der Lerngruppe erfolgt die Erarbeitung von M 9 zum Abschluss der Stunde in Einzelarbeit oder als **Hausaufgabe**.

How to Improve Your Writing Style (Klasse 10–13)

Einzelmaterial 195
S 15

5. Stunde: *Summing up*

Als **Einstieg** in die Stunde fassen die Schüler zusammen, was sie bislang über den Einsatz für Kinderrechte erfahren haben.

Durch die **Überarbeitung** einer **E-Mail (M 10)** wenden sie in Einzelarbeit alle zuvor erlernten Bausteine der Stilverbesserung an (*task 1*). Das Material enthält in der rechten Spalte die Lösungen, sodass die Lernenden ihre Ergebnisse **selbst kontrollieren** können. Die Lösungsvorschläge erheben dabei keinen Anspruch auf Vollständigkeit.

Differenzierung: Auf der **CD Grundwerk** findet sich M 10 ohne die Lösungstipps. Das Material kann **leistungsstärkeren Schülern** zur Bearbeitung gegeben werden.

In *task 2* verfassen die Lerner selbstständig in Einzelarbeit eine formelle **Antwort-E-Mail**. Die Aufgabe kann auch zu Hause bearbeitet werden.

Tipp: Wenn genügend Zeit zur Verfügung steht, können die Schüler zwei Mitschüler im **Partnerinterview** zu deren Erfahrungen mit Wohltätigkeitsarbeit befragen. Ein **Interviewbogen** steht auf der **CD Grundwerk** zur Verfügung.

Alternative: M 10 kann ohne die Lösungsvorschläge auch als **LEK** eingesetzt werden.

Erwartungshorizont (M 1)

(1) d; (2) e; (3) c; (4) a; (5) b

Erwartungshorizont (M 2)

1. a) Formal vs informal English

   cannot/can't; to send somebody a note/to drop a line; child/kid; I am afraid I disagree./Rubbish!; furthermore, moreover …/on top of it all; definitely/very, really; Please send it at your earliest convenience./Send it soon!

   b) More examples for formal vs informal English:

   Abbreviations and contractions: refrigerator/fridge, television/TV, as soon as possible/ASAP; **Verbs:** to bother somebody/to get on somebody's nerves, to detonate/to blow up, to increase/to go up; **Nouns and phrases:** I regret …/I'm sorry; comprehension/grasp, position/job; **Connectives:** nevertheless/anyway, to summarise/in a nutshell, however/but; **Letter and email expressions:** Yours sincerely/Love, Dear Sir or Madam/Hi, Please do not hesitate to contact me./Ring me up if you need anything.

2. Formal English: b), c), d)

   Informal English: a), e), f)

3. Example for a formal email:

   Dear Ms Thompson,

   I understand that you are looking for a reliable assistant for your shop during the summer holidays. I would like to be considered for this position because I am organised, punctual and have experience in working with various customers from my previous summer job as a waitress. Please do not hesitate to contact me if you wish to arrange an interview. Thank you for your time.

   Best regards,

   Olivia Walker

How to Improve Your Writing Style (Klasse 10–13)

Erwartungshorizont (M 3)

1.
   a) Miles Scott's dream was to assist his favourite superhero Batman for a day.

   b) Miles was first asked to free a woman tied to cable car tracks. Secondly, he downed a villain who was about to rob a bank. Finally, he helped the police to arrest the famous villain Penguin.

   c) The police asked Miles to help them fight against criminals. Actors dressed up as Batman and his enemies the Riddler and the Penguin. Many people came to see Batkid in action. San Francisco's mayor also thanked Miles and even the president encouraged Miles in his fight against the villains.

2.
   a)

	Formal English	**Informal English**
1	Long negative form: e.g. "The device <u>did not</u> detonate." (l. 26); "SFPD <u>did not</u> immediately respond" (l. 33)	Abbreviation: "Go get <u>'em</u>!" (l. 40)
2	Formal verbs e.g. "a criminal […] <u>attempted</u> to rob" (ll. 5–7)	Colloquial terms e.g. "a <u>full blown</u> phenomenon" (l. 38); "<u>Way to go</u>, Miles. <u>Way to save</u> Gotham!" (l. 41)

   b) Formal English is used for the general text of the article.

   c) Informal English is only used in quotations.

Erwartungshorizont (M 4)

(1) wonderful, excellent; (2) wonderful, perfect, special; (3) wonderful, special; (4) famous, successful; (5) believes, maintains, feels; (6) sad, painful, unhappy, difficult; (7) believe, maintain, feel; (8) wonderful, special, happy; (9) sad, terrible, unwell, discouraged, downcast, unhappy; (10) wonderful, happy; (11) sad, terrible, unhappy, difficult; (12) believes, feels; (13) discouraged; (14) believe, feel, suppose; (15) worthwhile, excellent

Erwartungshorizont (M 5)

1. <u>highly/extremely</u>: effective, recommended, successful

   <u>utterly/absolutely</u>: convinced, disgusting, impossible, ridiculous, wrong

   <u>deeply</u>: affected, ashamed, concerned, shocked

   <u>strongly</u>: to believe, to condemn, to influence, to oppose

2. a) deeply shocked; b) strongly believes; c) highly effective, highly recommended, extremely likely; d) absolutely disgusting, absolutely ridiculous, utterly wrong; e) deeply affected

Erwartungshorizont (M 6)

1. <u>Possible pros and cons for (not) granting the wish:</u>

   Sam: cuddly toys

   <u>Pros</u>: Shares the understanding of suffering; builds a bond with other patients; gives comfort to others.

   <u>Cons</u>: Too many discouraging meetings with ill children, will be preoccupied with his own condition again; older children might scorn him for his gesture or feel too old for a toy.

Glenn: Lady Gaga

Pros: A unique experience to get to know his favourite star; have an unrealistic dream finally come true as an encouragement to fight against the disease.

Cons: Too expensive to pay for flight, accommodation, security …; the singer might say no, not realistic.

Dylan: firefighter

Pros: Exciting adventure; gives him a goal for his future; many boys will admire him for his experience; easy to realise locally.

Cons: Too dangerous; might see others injured; can easily go to an "open day" activity at a firestation himself without needing the organisation's help.

Joyce: flash mob

Pros: Gives her and others the feeling of being part of a large group; the unusual meeting catches people's attention; is fun and a distraction.

Cons: Disturbs the daily routine at the hospital too much; the crowd may get out of control; might lead to bad publicity for the charity organisation or for the hospital.

Kyra: well-being holiday

Pros: Kyra can give something back to her parents, to show them how special they are, how thankful she is; lets them recover.

Cons: She does not join the holiday, she will not have any experience herself; seems as if she feels guilty although the disease is not her fault.

Brenda: flat-screen TV and interactive game console

Pros: It's flexible in use; might help her physically; might build up new friendships.

Cons: It's nothing special, just an ordinary product that anyone can buy.

2. Example for a letter to the parents:

Dear Mr and Mrs Smith,

Our Make-A-Wish organisation was deeply touched by your son's wish. We strongly believe it would be a unique opportunity for Sam to share his experiences with a life-threatening disease in a positive way.

To make Sam's special day perfect, we need to meet you and your son to discover more about Sam's interests and passions. Here are some suggested dates: 16th October, 9 a.m., 21st October, 11 a.m., 18th November, 3 p.m. Please inform us what would suit you. We are looking forward to realising Sam's dream.

Best regards,

The Make-A-Wish committee

Erwartungshorizont (M 7)

a) Watching a documentary on girls' living conditions worldwide, I realised …

b) Some girls fighting for the right to be educated risk physical abuse, …

c) Some groups are afraid of giving girls access to equal education arguing it does not conform to their religion or cultural tradition.

d) Girls can realise injustice and try to change it, when learning more about their rights.

e) Having gained knowledge for several years, girls know how to create networks …

How to Improve Your Writing Style (Klasse 10–13)

Erwartungshorizont (M 8)

a) In the year 2013, she was listed as the youngest candidate for the Nobel Peace Prize <u>after fighting</u> for girls' access to education ...

b) She also described a girl's everyday life in her region <u>by writing</u> a BBC blog ...

c) <u>Before attacking</u> Malala's school bus, the Taliban spread fear in the region ...

d) <u>Instead of giving up</u>, Malala continued to go to school ...

e) <u>In spite of being</u> famous worldwide, Malala knows that her autobiography *I am Malala* has been banned ...

f) In Pakistan, some people blame her <u>for becoming</u>, in their eyes, the tool of western forces.

Erwartungshorizont (M 9)

(1) to begin with

(2) however, yet

(3) for instance, for example

(4) therefore, for this reason, that explains why, as a result

(5) for instance, for example

(6)–(8) in addition, furthermore, moreover, likewise

(9) yet, however

(10) as a consequence, accordingly

(11) ultimately, as a consequence, to conclude, to sum up

Erwartungshorizont (M 10)

2. <u>Example of the content of Mr Dean's email:</u>

– Thanks for the email and the information.

– Helpful ideas to raise money for children in need.

– Could talk to other team members and ask for their opinion.

– If they agree, could contact UNICEF and ask for the checklist and additional material.

<u>Language in the email:</u>

– Alternative expression to "very good" and "say".

– Use of connectives.

– Use of participle constructions.

"Where's the boy for me" (Klasse 10/11)

Einzelmaterial 203
S 1

„Where's the boy for me?" – Die handlungsorientierte Erarbeitung einer Short Story unter Einführung abiturrelevanter Aufgabenformate (ab Klasse 10)

Eva Maria Schepp, Münster

V

M 1 It's complicated ...

Look at the following picture. It hints at the topic of the short story we are going to deal with.

© thinkstock/istock

Tasks

1. Describe the picture.
2. Explain its meaning.
3. State the topic of the short story we are going to read.

RAAbits Englisch

"Where's the boy for me" (Klasse 10/11)

Einzelmaterial 203
S 2

M 2 How to write a summary

Writing a summary means briefly stating the most important information of a given text in your own words. You must not include your opinion or even an interpretation but just briefly summarise the text's main aspects.

> **Task:** Give a concise (using few words, only including important information) account of the main points of a text ("Summarise …", "Write a summary").

1. Before writing

- ✓ Read the text carefully. Look up words you do not know.
- ✓ Take a pen and highlight important key words or key phrases.
- ✓ Take notes on important facts.
- ✓ Leave out information that is unimportant.

2. While writing

- ✓ Begin your summary with an introductory sentence (genre, title, author, main idea).
- ✓ Briefly summarize the content.
- ✓ Use the simple present.
- ✓ Follow your notes and use your own words.

3. After writing

Proofread your summary for mistakes. A good summary …

- has got an introductory sentence.
- is written in the simple present.
- is divided into paragraphs.
- answers all "w-questions" (who?, what?, when?, where?, why?).
- is precise but short (about 1/3 of the original text).
- uses connectives.
- does not give quotes.
- does not give any details.
- does not use direct speech.
- does not copy sentences from the text.
- does not give a personal opinion (~~I think, in my opinion~~…).
- does not use short forms (~~don't, can't, isn't,~~ …).

M 3 How to write an introductory sentence to a summary

*The very first sentence of your summary is the introductory sentence. It should contain the following information (all of it in **one sentence**!):*

- **genre** (What kind of text is it? Newspaper article, short story, film script etc.)
- *title* of the text
- **author**
- place of publication (if given, otherwise leave it out)
- **publication date** (if given, otherwise leave it out)
- ***main idea*** (central topic/message of the text)

How to form the introductory sentence

The **genre** *"title"* written by **author** and published in place of publication on/in **publication date** deals with/is about ***main idea***.

Example:

The **short story** *"Linda's love letter"*, written by **John Do** (and published in London in **2011**), is about ***a girl who, after suffering from a major heart break, tries to commit suicide***.

"Where's the boy for me" (Klasse 10/11)

Einzelmaterial 203
S 4

M 4 Self-assessment sheet: How to write a summary

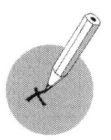

Use this feedback sheet to check if your summary meets all important criteria.

You ...	☑	Notes
have written an introductory sentence including • genre • author • title • main idea.	☐ ☐ ☐ ☐	
have answered the questions who? what? when? where? why?		
have used the simple present.		
have not copied or quoted sentences from the original text.		
have not used short forms.		
have not given your personal opinion or interpretation.		
have not given details.		
have written precisely but short.		

You ...	☑	Notes
have used **connectives**.		
haven't made many **grammar mistakes**.		
haven't made many **vocabulary mistakes**.		
Tips on how to improve your summary writing skills:		

M 5 Task sheet: Hidden thoughts

What is going on in Debbie and Helen's minds while they are talking? Let's find out!

Task

- ✓ Work in groups of four. Read the short story again up to line 51.
- ✓ Then write down "hidden thoughts" Debbie and Helen could have during their conversation.
- ✓ All of you are going to note down these thoughts on your worksheet.
- ✓ **Time allowed:** 20 minutes

Example:

Debbie: "What's wrong with me?

Debbie's thought: "I REALLY don't know! I am smart, not ugly and funny, too! Why does nobody want to go out with me?!?

When you have finished, practise reading the conversation:

- All four students need to get up.
- Two of you are going to read out the normal dialogue between Debbie and Helen. Stand in the middle of the room, facing each other.
- The other two members of your group are going to read out Debbie and Helen's hidden thoughts. Stand behind "your" character (the other group members) – depending on whose thoughts you are going to read.
- Place one hand on your group member's shoulder.
- Make sure to practise reading the whole conversation as well as your hidden thoughts at least once!

Feedback questions:

1. Which hidden thoughts were presented?
2. What do they reveal about the characters?

M 6 Worksheet: Hidden thoughts

Imagine you are Debbie/Helen now. What are you thinking during your conversation?

Task: Write down the thoughts of the characters.

[…]

"What's wrong with me?" I wailed plaintively. "Pete practically ignores me and Dave treats me like an elderly relation!"

Debbie's thoughts: _____

5 Helen grinned. "Not a thing," she replied. "You look all right to me – a bit young maybe, but …"

Helen's thoughts: _____

"Young?" I spluttered indignantly. "I'm the same age as you!"

Debbie: _____

"I know that! But, well, there's something young about you." She smiled apologetically. "I'm not
10 being much help, am I?"

Helen: _____

"Oh. I wouldn't say that," I replied, through clenched teeth. "But what exactly am I supposed to do until the years begin to take their toll? Wear a bag on my head?"

Debbie: _____

15 "It might help!" Helen giggled. "No, seriously Debbie, you could try a more sophisticated hairstyle, or revamp your make-up, but I think there's more to it than that."

Helen: _____

She paused, "You've never actually been out with a boy, have you?"

Helen: _____

20 "No!" I said glumly. "That is the whole point!"

Debbie: _____

"All right, I know! I was just thinking … boys' minds work in pretty mysterious ways, sometimes. It seems to me that the very fact you haven't got a boyfriend might be putting them off."

Helen: _____

25 I stared at her. "Eh?" I said, intelligently.

Debbie: _____

"Well, you haven't got a boyfriend, so every boy you meet thinks you're after him. And I suppose you are, really, so you seem a bit too pushy and eager, and put him off … Does that make sense?"

"Where's the boy for me" (Klasse 10/11)

Einzelmaterial 203
S 7

Helen: _____

30 "I think so." I said slowly. "But it's a vicious circle, isn't it? I need to have a boyfriend to get a boyfriend. But the whole problem is that I can't get a boyfriend in the first place ..."

Debbie: _____

Helen winked wickedly. "Well, if you're really desperate, you have got one admirer!"

Helen: _____

35 "Who?"

Debbie: _____

"That boy who lives next door to you – the one you say you can't stand!"

Helen: _____

"Oh, Danny! But I don't fancy him at all! I've known him for years!"

40 **Debbie:** _____

Helen cut me short. "Now just hang on a minute. I think I've got an idea ..."

Helen: _____

The next half-hour was extremely enlightening. According to Helen, I should agree to go out with Danny, who, fortunately enough, had been keen on me for ages. That would get me into the swing
45 of things.

"Then," said Helen triumphantly, "you can see how things work out and take it from there!"

Helen: _____

"Take what from there?" I muttered gloomily, picturing myself tied to Danny for life.

Debbie: _____

50 "Oh, Deb, you are slow! By then, lots of other boys will have noticed you and some of them are bound to ask you out. That's the way it always happens!"

Helen: _____

I marvelled at her confidence.

"Then," she finished, "all you have to do is choose the one you like best, and ditch Danny!"

55 **Helen:** _____

It seemed straightforward enough, I had to admit, but I did have a pang of conscience about the ditching bit. Helen told me not to worry – love was a tough business and only the strong survived! I grinned, and made up my mind to be a survivor.

© DC Thomson & Co. Ltd. 2014

M 7 How to write a continuation

Recreation of text | Creative writing

The terms 'creative writing' or 'recreation of text' refer to a set of tasks which involve creative writing processes. These could be writing the continuation of a fictional text or re-writing a passage from the point of view of another of the stories' characters. Also, writing a diary entry or an interior monologue (in a character's mind) can be possible tasks.

How to write a continuation

1. Content:

- Stick to the given plot and atmosphere.
- Use information from the text to write a logical and plausible continuation.
- Keep specific details (e.g. places, description of landscape or weather) that have already been used by the author to make your story more convincing.

2. Point of view:

- Use the same narrative perspective as the author (unless you are told otherwise).
- Language:
  o Stick to the given tense.
  o Imitate the author's writing style.
  o Adopt the author's register → formal, colloquial ...

Remember:

- The age, relationship between characters, their social class as well as their emotions can influence the way they speak.

DON'T ...

☹ Don't make up a completely new story – or contradict the previous plot.

☹ Don't invent illogical twists and turns.

☹ Don't use your own writing style.

☹ Don't quote.

"Where's the boy for me" (Klasse 10/11)

Einzelmaterial 203
S 9

M 8 How to write a characterisation

The characters of a fictional text bring its story to life and are a very important aspect for its success. In the text, the author describes the characters through their main features, e.g. their age, outward appearance, behaviour, direct speech, emotions and thoughts. The goal of writing a characterisation is to find out and explain in which way the author presents a character by interpreting the given information.

Task: Describe and examine the way in which the character is presented ("Characterise …").

1. Before writing

Use a pen to highlight every detail you can find out about the person you want to characterise. Helpful aspects might be:

1. name
2. age
3. outward appearance
4. social background (family, friends, education…)
5. job
6. behaviour
7. direct speech
8. emotions (can be seen by others → e.g. crying)
9. thoughts
10. feelings (feelings inside the person)

from outside → to inside

- Use a grid to note down your findings chronologically. Include the line, quote from the text and your interpretation of the quote: *What does this quote tell us about the person's character?*
- Use the priority column to categorise each of your notes. Use the numbers from the 'outside to inside' structure. *(name = 1, age = 2, outward appearance = 3, … feelings = 10.)*

2. While writing

- Start with a short introductory sentence.
- Write the characterisation by following your numbered notes.
- Arrange your text into paragraphs and link these with connectives.
- For quotes, use the English quotation marks "…" and give lines in round brackets, e.g. "…" (l. 12) or "…" (ll. 12–14).
- Write a conclusion in which you briefly sum up your main results.

3. After writing

Proofread your characterisation! A good characterisation …

- has a short introductory sentence.
- is divided into paragraphs.
- uses quotations and gives lines.
- uses connectives.
- is written in the simple present.
- follows the structure from 'outside to inside'.
- does not use short forms (~~can't, doesn't, isn't…~~).
- does not give a personal opinion (~~I think, I believe…~~).

M 9 Character grid for preparing a characterisation

This grid will help you to structure the given information before writing your characterisation. The first line has already been filled in as an example.

Tip: *Make use of the worksheet "How to write a characterisation".*

Line/lines	Quote	Interpretation	Priority
1	"I suppose I was getting a bit desperate."	she feels desperate, hopeless, sad about not having a boyfriend	10
...			

M 10 How to write an introductory sentence and a conclusion of a characterisation

When writing a characterisation you will need an introductory sentence as well as a conclusion.

1. Introductory sentence

Information which should be included in your first sentence of the characterisation:

- **character's name and his or her role** (e.g. protagonist, antagonist ...)
- genre
- title of text
- **general statement about the character**

Example:

Alex, the protagonist of the short story *"This is an example"*, **is a smart and outgoing young man who studies very hard for his test but nevertheless suffers from panic attacks right before the upcoming exam.**

2. Conclusion

In the end, wrap up your characterisation with a brief summary of your findings.

Helpful connectives: all in all, to sum it up, summing it up, as a conclusion ...

Example:

All in all, Alex is a very clever and ambitious person who, with the help of his discipline, manages to overcome his fears.

"Where's the boy for me" (Klasse 10/11)

Einzelmaterial 203
S 11

M 11 Good angel vs bad angel

Shall I do it? Or better not? Everybody's conscience is divided into two parts. You can compare these parts to a good angel and a bad angel, sitting on your shoulder and trying to pull you in different directions.

Tasks

1. Describe the picture.
2. Explain its meaning.
3. When you think of the short story which we have just read – in which way could this picture relate to the story?

M 12 Debbie's inner conflict

Let's find out more about Debbie's inner conflict ...

Tasks

Work together with a partner. One of you is Debbie's good angel, who wants her to stay with Danny as he is cute and lovable. The other one is her bad angel, arguing for ditching Danny and following the plan to get her dream boy.

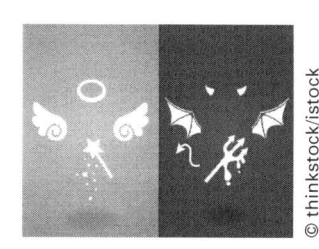

1. Put yourself in Debbie's shoes. What could be going on in her mind after the great date with Danny and the flattering reactions of the other boys at the club? Collect arguments for your role.
2. Talk to your partner and discuss your arguments. Use these to write a *"conversation of conscience"* (*Gewissensdialog*) between Debbie's good angel and bad angel.
3. Practise your dialogue and be prepared to act it out in class!

Time allowed: 25 minutes

"Where's the boy for me" (Klasse 10/11)

Einzelmaterial 203
S 12

M 13 Feedback sheet: Debbie's inner conflict

Use this feedback sheet to check whether the presentations meet all important criteria.

Feedback on	Your comment					
	Presentation 1	Presentation 2	Presentation 3	Presentation 4	Presentation 5	Presentation 6
... language						
Which opinion phrases did the presenters use?						
... content						
Did the presenters stick to their roles?						
Which argument did you like best? *(Write down one argument for each angel.)*						
Did the presenters consider the consequences of Debbie's action?						
... presentation						
How do you evaluate the presenters' overall performance?						

RAAbits Englisch

M 14 Feedback sheet: Characterisations

Use this feedback sheet to check whether your characterisation meets all important criteria.

	You ...	☑	Notes
Introduction	have written an introductory sentence which contains	☐	
	• the character's role in the story	☐	
	• his/her name,	☐	
	• the genre of the text	☐	
	• the title of the text	☐	
	• a general statement about the character.	☐	
Main part	have followed the 'outside to inside' structure.		
	have interpreted the given information.		
	have supported your interpretation by directly quoting from the text.		
Conclusion	have briefly summed up the main results of your interpretation.		
	have not included new aspects.		

You ...	☑	Notes
have used connectives.		
have used many adjectives to describe the character.		
haven't made many grammar mistakes.		
haven't made many vocabulary mistakes.		

Tips to improve your characterisation writing skills:

"Where's the boy for me" (Klasse 10/11)

Einzelmaterial 203
S 14

Zeichnung: Oliver Wetterauer

M 15 Everybody freeze!

An example of what a freeze frame could look like.

Tasks

1. Describe the picture. Mention every detail. Also talk about body language and postures!
2. Which adjectives would you use to describe the different stickmen? Justify your choices.

"Where's the boy for me" (Klasse 10/11)

Einzelmaterial 203
S 15

M 16   Freeze frame

Freeze frames help you to find out more about character relationships.

Building a freeze frame in 5 steps

Your task is to represent the relationship between the different characters of the short story – only with the help of your body, gestures and facial expressions.

Step 1: Form groups of 5–6 students.

Step 2: In your group, discuss the relationships between Debbie, Helen, Danny, Dave and Pete.

Step 3: For the freeze frames, half of the groups work on **part a)** of the story, the other half on part **b)**.

a) from line 1 up to line 51 of the story. (l. 1–"… and made up my mind to be a survivor.")

b) from line 52 ("That Saturday, Danny certainly …") to the end of the short story.

Step 4: Now build a freeze frame with the 5 characters from the story.

Step 5 (optional): Choose one sculptor & presenter. He/she positions the other characters of the story so that we get a better idea of their relationship towards each other.

Time of preparation: 15 minutes

What you should also keep in mind …

- Do the characters stand far away from or close to each other (expressing friendship/ love or distance/hate …)?
- What is your position in the room?
- Do you want to use props (tables, chairs, …)?
- What is the character's body language like?
- Which feelings towards each other do they have in your part of the story? → Use your body and gestures to show these!
- What are their facial expressions like?
- Do the characters look at each other or not? Which feelings do you want to express with your face?

Class presentation

- You will present your freeze frame. Take your position or let the sculptor of your group do final arrangements.
- Upon the **command "FREEZE!"** freeze all your movements and **stay like this for 15 seconds.** Then there will be a short pause, after which you have to freeze once more for 15 seconds.
- Afterwards, the audience will comment on what they have seen.
- Finally, the performers get the chance to talk about what they wanted to show and how they felt during their presentation.

"Where's the boy for me" (Klasse 10/11)

Einzelmaterial 203
S 16

M 17 Amanda Mandinian: *Where's the boy for me?*

Part 1

I suppose I was getting a bit desperate. Not desperately desperate, you understand, but things definitely weren't going my way and I didn't know what to do about it. What did I want? A boyfriend. Why haven't I got one? Heaven only knew – I certainly didn't!

I tried to be friendly, to join in the chat and general teasing at school, but somehow I always got it wrong.
5 Lots of boys used to talk to Helen, my best friend, but my efforts seemed doomed to failure from the start. Pete Matthews, for example, was my idea of the ideal boy, and as Helen knew him quite well, I thought all I had to do was chat him up at breaktime and leave the rest to him.

Wrong! I joined in as usual, but although I thought he seemed quite interested, he just walked off when the break bell rang, without a second glance. Later, I saw him walking home, but although I was alone
10 and there was no-one around to embarrass us, he more or less ignored me, and walked past, just as if I didn't exist. My friendly smile froze – and some girl on the other side of the street laughed. I just knew she'd seen what happened and that she was giggling at me.

It was the same at the disco. Dave was a friend of Pete's and number two on my list of fanciable males, but even though he did ask me to dance – once! – he acted as though he was just doing his duty, instead
15 of enjoying himself. By this stage, my confidence was at an all-time low. I just couldn't see where I was going wrong, but obviously was, so I decided to consult Helen about it. At least *she* seemed to know what she was doing!

"What's wrong with me?" I wailed plaintively. "Pete practically ignores me and Dave treats me like an elderly relation!" Helen grinned. "Not a thing," she replied. "You *look* all right to me – a bit young
20 maybe, but ..."

"Young?" I spluttered indignantly. "I'm the same age as you!"

"I know that! But, well, there's something young about you." She smiled apologetically. "I'm not being much help, am I?"

"Oh. I wouldn't say that," I replied, through clenched teeth. "But what exactly am I supposed to do until
25 the years begin to take their toll? Wear a bag on my head?"

"It might help!" Helen giggled. "No, seriously. Debbie, you could try a more sophisticated hair-style, or revamp your make-up, but I think there's more to it than that."

She paused, "You've never actually been out with a boy, have you?"

"No!" I said glumly. "That is the whole point!"

30 "All right, I know! I was just thinking ... boys' minds work in pretty mysterious ways, sometimes. It seems to me that the very fact you haven't got a boyfriend might be putting them off."

I stared at her. "Eh?" I said, intelligently.

"Well, you haven't got a boyfriend, so every boy you meet thinks you're after him. And I suppose you are, really, so you seem a bit too pushy and eager, and put him off ... Does that make sense?"

35 "I think so." I said slowly. "But it's a vicious circle, isn't it? I need to have a boyfriend to get a boyfriend. But the whole problem is that I can't get a boyfriend in the first place ..." I groaned.

Helen winked wickedly. "Well, if you're really desperate, you have got one admirer!"

"Who?"

"That boy who lives next door to you – the one you say you can't stand!"

40 "Oh, *Danny*! But I don't fancy him at all! I've known him for years!"

Helen cut me short. "Now just hang on a minute. I think I've got an idea ..."

The next half-hour was extremely enlightening. According to Helen, I should agree to go out with Danny, who, fortunately enough, had been keen on me for ages. That would get me into the swing of things.

"Then," said Helen triumphantly, "you can see how things work out and take it from there!"

45 "Take what from there?" I muttered gloomily, picturing myself tied to Danny for life.

"Oh, Deb, you are slow! By then, lots of other boys will have noticed you and some of them are bound to ask you out. That's the way it always happens!" I marvelled at her confidence. "Then," she finished, "all you have to do is choose the one you like best, and ditch Danny!"

It seemed straightforward enough, I had to admit, but I did have a pang of conscience about the ditching
50 bit. Helen told me not to worry – love was a tough business and only the strong survived! I grinned, and made up my mind to be a survivor.

© DC Thomson & Co. Ltd. 2014

1 **desperate:** very sad and upset because of having little or no hope – 5 **doomed to failure:** very bad events or situations that cannot be prevented – 10 **to embarrass:** to make sb. feel uneasy or bad – 13 **fanciable:** attractive – 18 **to wail:** to cry – 18 **plaintively:** having a sad sound – 21 **spluttered indignantly:** making a confused noise, feeling or showing anger because of sth. that is unfair or wrong – 24 **to clench sth.:** to set in a tightly closed position – 25 **to take their toll:** here: to make her look older – 27 **to revamp:** to improve one's looks – 31 **to put so. off:** to scare so. away – 35 **vicious circle:** a repeating situation or condition in which one problem causes another problem that makes the first problem worse – 42 **enlightening:** clearing things up – 47 **to marvel:** here: to admire – 48 **to ditch so.:** to stop seeing so.

Part 2

That Saturday, Danny certainly got the shock of his life! I hung around in our back garden all morning, sitting on the wall staring into space, attempting to look casual but purposeful. At last, towards lunchtime, he came out and cautiously, perhaps even nervously, he walked over to me. I suppose it was no wonder
55 he was worried, after the rebuffs I'd given him in the past.

I felt rather guilty about those. There was nothing actually wrong with Danny, but I'd known him so long, I couldn't take him seriously! Still, according to Helen, I had to go through with it.

"Hi, Debbie," he said, smiling shyly. "Hi, Danny," I answered. "How's things?"

"Great," he said, not sounding as if he meant it.

60 I sighed, hoping that that would convey more than words could. It obviously spoke volumes to him, because he stopped looking at his feet and asked, "Going anywhere tonight, Debbie?"

"No," I answered, truthfully enough. "Neither am I," he said. Then, after another pause, he added, "How about us going nowhere together?"

I took a deep breath. "Should certainly be cheap!" I said brightly, grinning at him.

65 "We could always try the disco."

"We could!"

"You mean – you will?"

I looked at him curiously. He sounded as if he couldn't believe his ears. I felt very uncomfortable – he was so keen to go out with me and I was only using him as a stepping stone to better things.

70 That evening, I decided to make myself look as sophisticated as I could look, according to Helen's instructions. I couldn't do much about my hair, but I really went to town on my make-up and chose a super dress I'd been saving for a special occasion.

Actually, our local disco is usually such an informal affair that any girl in a dress really stands out among all the jeans and sweaters. Still, I ought to make a bit of an effort for a change, and was pleased to notice
75 that Danny seemed suitably dazzled.

Danny the dazzled, soon to be Danny the ditched! I put the thought out of my mind and concentrated on the job in hand. Things seemed to start off well. When we got to the hall Pete was there already and even from a distance I could see that he noticed the new improved me. Dave arrived, too, just after Danny had gone to buy some drinks, and came over almost immediately, much to my satisfaction.

80 "Hi, Debbie!" he said, smiling. "You're looking rather special! Would you like to dance?" It was working! I couldn't believe everything was going so well, but it was happening a bit too quickly for me. So I just smiled and said sorry, I was with someone.

"Who's the lucky man?" he asked, looking around. "No-one you know!"

He was about to say something else, but when he saw Danny approaching with the glasses, he excused
himself and went back over to his mates, looking distinctly rattled. Later, I was chatting to Janice and
Rosemary from school, when Pete himself came over.

"You're Helen's friend, Debbie, aren't you? I remember speaking to you the other day." Speaking to me!
He'd looked straight through me!

"Like to dance?" he asked, rather too casually. I could've jumped up and down on the spot, but again, I
explained that I couldn't.

"Oh. See you around then," he said, looking down at me with what seemed very like a wistful expression.

"Oh, probably," I said airily.

"I hope so!" he replied and this time there was no doubt about the disappointment. Better than ever! In
the course of the evening one or two other boys, total strangers, asked me to dance, but I said no to them,
too, rather to Danny's surprise. But then, although Helen's plan was working so well, I'd had a surprise
too – Danny.

I'd been expecting the Danny I'd known as a child, or at least the spotty horror who'd set his dog on me
and made my life a misery. What I got was a shy, funny, interesting and incredibly lovable boy who, for
some unaccountable reason, thought I was wonderful.

© DC Thomson & Co. Ltd. 2014

55 **rebuff:** to refuse sb. in a rude way – 69 **stepping stone:** sth. that helps you get or achieve
something – 71 **to go to town:** to do something in a detailed and enthusiastic way – 76 **dazzled:**
impressed – 85 **rattled:** here: very upset – 91 **wistful:** full of longing/desire

Part 3

By the end of the evening, I couldn't remember when I'd been so happy in someone's company, especially
when he kissed me goodnight at the garden gate. Happiness right next door and I'd never even suspected
it! The Monday after, I met Helen at break to report to her on my progress. She got in first, though, and
she said she'd heard I'd had a wonderful time at the disco with Danny.

"Who told you?" I asked, curious to know who'd been talking.

"Oh, some of the boys," she replied. "Anyway, it did work, didn't it?"

"It was great! And I owe it all to you!"

"Think nothing of it," she grinned. "Which one are you going to choose then? When are you going to
ditch Danny?"

"Ditch Danny?" I repeated. "Why should I ditch Danny? He's wonderful. Absolutely wonderful!"

Helen's jaw dropped. "Well!" she gasped. "Talk about the best-laid plans! I thought he was the boy you
loved to hate?!"

"Not any more!"

I beamed at her and we both burst out laughing while I told her what had happened. We'd just about
pulled ourselves together, when Pete came over. Helen watched him chatting me up. Helen watched him
angling for a date. Helen watched me laughing, and saying no, and saw Pete walking off sulkily.

"See?" I grinned. "I do!" she replied and we burst out laughing again.

After all, things had gone according to plan, hadn't they? With a little help from Danny ...

© DC Thomson & Co. Ltd. 2014

106 **to owe:** to need to do or give sth. to so. who has done something for you

"Where's the boy for me" (Klasse 10/11)

Einzelmaterial 203
S 19

Exam: *Prom Date from Hell* by Christine John

Tasks

1. Summarise Pamela's situation and her prom date as it is presented in this extract. *(Comprehension/Context: 12 points)*
2. Characterise Pamela to show her feelings and expectations about having a date to the prom. *(Analysis: 16 points)*
3. Continue the short story and write a logical ending to it. *(Recreation of Text/Continuation: 12 points)*

Prom Date from Hell by Christine John

[...] My name is Pamela and I am seventeen years old. It was near the end of the school year and I was in my fifth year of high school. All of us students had just completed our exams and we were busy talking about the prom. Mostly all of the girls had dates and I was the only one who did not have one. The prom was the most important event in my life and I could not believe that I might end up going alone. I just
5 could not let that happen. I would be humiliated!

I walked slowly home from school one afternoon. I was so preoccupied with my thoughts of not having a date to go to the prom that I barely noticed another car parked in the driveway of my parent's home. I sighed heavily as I entered the house and paused in the doorway with a puzzled expression on my face when I saw my parents sitting in the living room with strangers- I stared blankly at each of the faces until
10 my gaze rested on a really, really cute guy sitting on one of the chairs.

"Pamela, I'm so glad you made it home early today," said Mom as she stood up and came by my side. She draped her arm around my shoulder and gave me a gentle squeeze. "Pam, this is Mr. and Mrs. Brown and their son Ben."

I glanced briefly at the couple and gave a slight nod in greeting, not that I meant to be rude or anything,
15 but Ben was so cute that I could not take my eyes off him. He gave me a lopsided grin and I could see his dark brown eyes examining my slender figure from head to toe. I suddenly felt shy and self-conscious and I wished I had ran a comb through my hair and made sure that my uniform did not have any ketchup stains before leaving school. I ran my hand through my short dark hair and decided that it probably did not look bad. At least I did not feel any stray strands of hair sticking up out of place.

20 "The Browns just moved in across the street. Their son Ben just graduated from his school about a week ago but was unable to attend his prom," Mom explained. "So I thought it would be nice if you could take Ben to your prom, especially since you were having so much trouble finding a date..." [...]

The prom was being held at a hotel. On our way there Ben put on some music and turned up the volume so high that the music was pounding in my ears. He was playing a heavy metal CD and I was not pleased
25 at all. "Ben!" I yelled. "Turn it down!"

"What?" he yelled.

"The music! It's too loud! Turn it down!" I yelled back. He slowed down the car and parked in front of a convenience store. He turned off the engine and I gave a loud sigh of relief when the music stopped. I'm pretty sure I lost about 30% of my hearing that night. "Thank you."

30 "Wait here. I'll be right back." He stepped out of the car and went inside the store. A few minutes later he came back out carrying a paper bag. I had a sneaky suspicion what he had bought and my stomach filled with dread. "Ben, that's not what I think it is, is it?" I asked suspiciously. In reply he opened the bag and took out a bottle of wine. "Hey, we can't have fun without something to drink." He popped the cork and held the bottle to his lips and took a large gulp of wine. He held the bottle out to me and said, "Here. Try
35 it. I promise you'll love it." [...]

John, Christine: Prom Date from Hell. Short Stories for Teenagers. United States: CreateSpace Independent Publishing Platform, p. 4-6

5 **humiliated:** to make so. feel very ashamed or foolish – 6 **preoccupied:** thinking about sth. a lot or too much – 8 **puzzled:** here: confused – 10 **gaze:** to fix one's eyes in a steady intent look – 15 **lopsided:** unequal – 16 **slender:** thin – 28 **convenience store:** a small store that is open for many hours of the day – 31 **sneaky suspicion:** a feeling that so. is possibly guilty of doing sth. wrong – 32 **dread:** to fear that sth. might happen

"Where's the boy for me" (Klasse 10/11)

Einzelmaterial 203
S 20

Inhalt	ANFORDERUNGEN Der Prüfling ...	Mögl. Punkte	Erreichte Punkte
Teilaufgabe 1 (Comprehension – Summary)	verfasst einen angemessenen Einleitungssatz, der die folgenden Bestandteile beinhaltet: *text type, title, author, main idea*.	4	
	nennt etwa folgende inhaltliche Aspekte: – Die 17-jährige Pamela ist verzweifelt, weil das Ende des Schuljahres naht und sie noch immer keine Begleitung für den Abschlussball hat. – Ihre Mutter arrangiert für sie eine Verabredung mit Ben, dem Sohn der neuen Nachbarn. – Pamela ist zunächst überglücklich, denn Ben sieht gut aus und scheint sympathisch. – Am Abend des Balls holt er sie mit dem Auto ab, aber auf der Fahrt zeigt der Junge sein „wahres Gesicht" – er hört laute Musik und kauft Alkohol, den er auch Pamela anbietet.	8	
	erfüllt ein weiteres aufgabenbezogenes Kriterium.	3	
	Erreichte Punktzahl Teilaufgabe 1:	**12**	
Teilaufgabe 2 (Analysis – Characterisation)	verfasst einen die *characterisation* einleitenden Satz, der die folgenden Aspekte beinhaltet: *name, role, genre, title of the text, general statement about the character*. charakterisiert die Protagonistin und nennt z.B. folgende Aspekte: – Sie heißt Pamela (Z. 1) und ist 17 Jahre alt (Z. 1). – Sie ist schlank (Z. 16) und hat kurzes, dunkles Haar (Z. 18). – Sie wohnt bei ihren Eltern, zu denen sie ein gutes Verhältnis zu haben scheint → ihre Mutter sorgt sich um ihre Ballbegleitung (Z. 22). – Sie ist im 5. Jahr der Highschool (Z. 2). – Sie ist etwas unorganisiert → Ketchupflecken, Haare kämmen (Z. 17) → legt keinen allzu großen Wert auf ihr Äußeres. – Sie sagt, wenn ihr etwas nicht passt, wie z. B. die laute Musik, die Ben im Auto hört (Z. 25). → steht für ihre Überzeugung ein – Der Ball ist das momentan wichtigste Ereignis in ihrem Leben (Z. 3/4). → typisches Teenagerverhalten – Sie ist die Einzige aus ihrem Freundeskreis, die noch kein *Date* für den Schulball hat (Z. 4). → Sie ist vielleicht noch etwas schüchtern in Bezug auf Jungs. – Sie scheint noch nicht viel *Dating*-Erfahrung zu haben, wie ihre Mutter anmerkt (Z. 22). – Sie will auf keinen Fall die Demütigung erleben, dass sie allein zum Ball muss (Z. 5). → fühlt sich sozialem Druck ausgesetzt – Sie ist fasziniert von Ben und fühlt sich sofort zu ihm hingezogen (Z. 16/17). → In seiner Gegenwart wird sie sich ihrer selbst bewusst und noch schüchterner. – Sie errät sofort, was Ben gekauft hat und fühlt sich wegen seines illegalen Verhaltens unwohl (Z. 32). → Dies zeigt, dass sie unrechtes Verhalten erkennt und nicht gutheißt. – Sie bekommt Angst (Z. 32). → Sie kann die gefährlichen Konsequenzen einschätzen und bricht nicht gerne Verbote, hat klare Moralvorstellungen. verfasst eine kurze, die Ergebnisse der *characterisation* zusammenfassende *conclusion*.	16	
	erfüllt ein weiteres aufgabenbezogenes Kriterium.	3	
	Erreichte Punktzahl Teilaufgabe 2:	**16**	

"Where's the boy for me" (Klasse 10/11)
Einzelmaterial 203
S 21

		Mögl. Pkte	Err. Pkte
Teilaufgabe 3 (Recreation of text/Continuation)	Zum Inhalt: Der Prüfling verfasst eine inhaltlich logische und plausible Weiterführung des Textes, indem er (zum Beispiel): – die Figuren Pamela und Ben beibehält sowie eventuell noch weitere Personen einführt – das weitere Verhalten der Protagonistin beschreibt und dabei schildert, welche Entscheidung Pamela trifft (trinkt sie ebenfalls Alkohol oder lehnt sie ihn ab?) sowie die weiteren Konsequenzen ihres Handelns ausführt – allgemein den weiteren Verlauf der Handlung darstellt – den Handlungsort beibehält oder einen neuen Ort einführt – die Geschichte logisch fortführt und ein Ende schreibt, das dem Titel *„Prom Date from Hell"* gerecht wird	8	
	Zur Form: Der Prüfling verfasst eine formal angemessene Weiterführung des Textes, indem er: – die Kurzgeschichte in derselben Erzählperspektive weitererzählt. – das *past tense* als Tempus beibehält. – direkte Rede verwendet.	4	
	erfüllt ein weiteres aufgabenbezogenes Kriterium.	3	
	Erreichte Punktzahl Teilaufgabe 3:	**12**	
	Erreichte Punktzahl „Inhalt" gesamt:	**40**	
Sprache	**ANFORDERUNGEN** Der Prüfling ...	**Mögl. Pkte**	**Err. Pkte**
Kommunikative Textgestaltung	**Aufgabenbezug:** richtet seinen Text konsequent und explizit auf die Aufgabenstellung aus; eindeutiger Aufgabenbezug durchgängig in allen Teilaufgaben; Beachtung der Anforderungsbereiche (ausgewiesen durch die Operatoren).	4	
	Textformate: beachtet die Konventionen der jeweils geforderten Zieltextformate. Aufgabe 1: Angabe des Genres, Titels, Autors und *main idea*; keine Zitate/Textverweise; Verwendung des *simple present*; Aufgabe 2: sachlich-neutraler Stil/Register; verdichtendes Wiedergeben, Befolgen der *Outside-to-inside*-Struktur, Verwenden von Adjektiven, um Charakterzüge zu beschreiben; Belegen durch Zitate; Aufgabe 3: adaptiver Stil/Register (angepasst an den Originaltext); Beibehaltung des Originaltempus, logische Fortführung.	4	
	Textaufbau: erstellt einen sachgerecht strukturierten Text (Geschlossenheit des Gesamttextes; sach- und intentionsgerechte Untergliederung in grafisch erkennbare Sinnabschnitte; inhaltlich-thematische Geschlossenheit der Sinnabschnitte, Herstellung deutlicher Bezüge; leserfreundliche Verknüpfung der Sinnabschnitte und Gedanken, z. B. durch gliedernde Hinweise, Aufzählung, Vor-/Rückverweise; zusammenfassende Wiederaufnahme zentraler Punkte, *connectives*).	4	
	Ökonomie: gestaltet seinen Text hinreichend ausführlich, aber ohne unnötige Wiederholungen und Umständlichkeiten (Beschränkung auf relevante bzw. exemplarische Punkte/Details/Zitate; abstrahierende Zusammenfassung mit konkreten, exemplarischen Belegen (statt langwieriger, textchronologischer Bearbeitung); Bereitstellung und ggf. Erläuterung verständnisrelevanter Informationen).	4	
	Belegtechnik: belegt Aussagen durch funktionale Verwendung von Verweisen und Zitaten (Gebrauch von Textverweisen (direkt/indirekt) zur Orientierung des Lesers; der Darstellungsabsicht angemessener Gebrauch wörtlicher Zitate aus dem Ausgangstext, Zeilenangaben).	4	
		20	

"Where's the boy for me" (Klasse 10/11)

Einzelmaterial 203
S 22

Ausdrucksvermögen/ Verfügbarkeit sprachlicher Mittel	**Eigenständigkeit:** löst sich vom Wortlaut des Ausgangstextes und **formuliert eigenständig** (keine wörtliche Wiedergabe auswendig gelernter Textpassagen, z. B. aus Sekundärliteratur; ein punktuell das Sprachmaterial des Ausgangstextes kreativ verarbeitendes Vorgehen ist durchaus erwünscht).	4	
	bedient sich eines sachlich wie stilistisch angemessenen und differenzierten **allgemeinen und thematischen Wortschatzes** (Inhalts- und Strukturwörter: treffende/präzise Bezeichnungen von Personen, Dingen und Sachverhalten, Berücksichtigung von Bedeutungsnuancen (auch Modalitäten); stilistisch angemessene Wortwahl (*register: formal, neutral, informal*); Verwendung von Kollokationen, Redewendungen, etc.; Variationen der Wortwahl, Vermeidung von „Allerweltswörtern" wie *thing, think, want, good, nice, guys* etc.).	5	
	bedient sich eines sachlich wie stilistisch angemessenen und differenzierten **Textbesprechungs- und Textproduktionswortschatzes** (Aufgabe 1: Vokabular zur Wiedergabe und Zusammenfassung von Inhalten; Aufgabe 2: Vokabular der Charakterisierung von literarischen Figuren; Aufgabe 3: Vokabular der Weiterführung von fiktionalen Texten).	5	
	bedient sich eines variablen und dem Zieltextformat angemessenen **Satzbaus** (durchgängig klare Syntax, Verständlichkeit beim ersten Lesen (Überschaubarkeit, Eindeutigkeit der Bezüge, Satzlogik); dem Zieltextformat angemessene Satzmuster: z. B. Hypotaxe (Konjunktional-; Relativ- indirekte Fragesätze), Parataxe, Aktiv- und Passivkonstruktionen, Gerundial-, Partizipial- und Infinitivkonstruktionen, Adverbiale).	6	
		20	
Sprach- richtigkeit	1. Orthografie: /4 2. Grammatik: /8 3. Wortschatz: /8	20	
Sprache gesamt		60	

Gesamtwertung	max. erreichbare Punktzahl	erreichte Punktzahl
Inhalt	**40**	
Sprache	**60**	
Gesamtpunktzahl	**100**	

Note: _____

Note	1+	1	1-	2+	2	2-	3+	3	3-	4+	4	4-	5+	5	5-	6
Punktzahl	100-96	95-90	89-85	84-80	79-75	74-70	69-65	64-60	59-55	54-50	49-45	44-40	39-35	34-30	29-25	24-0

"Where's the boy for me" (Klasse 10/11)

Einzelmaterial 203
S 23

Kompetenzen

Die Schülerinnen und Schüler[1] erweitern ihre Text- und Medienkompetenz, indem sie

- unter Verwendung von Belegen eine einfache Textdeutung entwickeln und unter Bezugnahme auf ihr Welt- und soziokulturelles Orientierungswissen Stellung beziehen.
- sich dem Gehalt und der Wirkung von Texten annähern, indem sie eigene kreative Texte entwickeln und dabei angeleitet ausgewählte Inhalts- oder Gestaltungselemente verändern oder die Darstellung ergänzen.
- Vertiefte Erarbeitung und Identifikation mit den Charakteren einer Short Story durch die handlungsorientierte Auseinandersetzung mit einem literarischen Text (*hidden thoughts, good angel/bad angel, freeze frame*)
- Einführung und Übung der abiturrelevanten Aufgabenformate der *summary*, *characterisation* und *continuation* (*recreation of text*)

Auf CD:
✓ *Word-Datei mit allen Materialien*

Niveau

Einführungsphase der S II (Klasse 10/G8 bzw. 11/G9)

Dauer

Ca. 6–10 Stunden (je nach Auswahl der Materialien) + eine Doppelstunde Klausur

Minimalplan: Bei Zeitmangel oder, falls die abiturrelevanten Aufgabenformate bereits bekannt sind, kann dieser Teil wegfallen und Sie können sich auf die Erarbeitung der handlungsorientierten Aufgaben konzentrieren. Ein Minimalplan sieht dann wie folgt aus:

Stunden 1 und 2: Der erste Teil der Geschichte wird eingeführt. Daran angeschlossen wird die Methode *„hidden thoughts"* angewandt und die Schüler verfassen und präsentieren die Gedanken von Debbie und Helen während ihres Gespräches.

Stunden 3 und 4: Die Geschichte wird weiter erarbeitet (Teil 2). Die Schüler lernen die Methode *„good angel/bad angel"* kennen und verfassen das Zwiegespräch zwischen Debbies Engelchen und Teufelchen.

Stunden 5 und 6: Die restliche Geschichte wird eingeführt. Abschließend werden die beiden *freeze frames* mit dem Kurs erarbeitet und präsentiert.

Einbettung

Die Einheit kann im Rahmen des Themas *growing up* eingesetzt werden. Anhand der Short Story lässt sich an folgende zentrale inhaltliche Themen anknüpfen: *teenage problems, first love, taking responsibility, having a guilty conscience, having an argument.*

Hinweise

Pete? Dave? Oder doch lieber Danny? Für wen soll sich Debbie, ein junges Mädchen im Teenageralter, entscheiden? Die Handlung der Short Story von Amanda Mandinian, *„Where's the boy for me?"*, besitzt durch die einfache Identifikation mit den Figuren der Geschichte und ihrem direkten Bezug zur Lebenswelt der Schüler eine hohe Motivationskraft.

---

[1] Im weiteren Verlauf wird aus Gründen der besseren Lesbarkeit nur noch ‚Schüler' verwendet.

„Where's the boy for me" (Klasse 10/11)

Einzelmaterial 203
S 24

Zum Inhalt der Kurzgeschichte

Die Ich-Erzählerin Debbie, ein junges Mädchen im Teenageralter, ist unglücklich, da sie noch nie einen Freund hatte. Ihre beste Freundin Helen vermutet, dass gerade diese Tatsache abschreckend auf das andere Geschlecht wirkt („*you seem a bit too pushy and eager*"). Gemeinsam hecken die beiden einen Plan aus, wie Debbie sich einen ihrer Traummänner – Pete oder Dave, die coolsten Jungs der Schule – angeln kann. Debbie soll sich mit ihrem Nachbarn Danny verabreden, der schon lange für sie schwärmt, um sich so für das andere Geschlecht interessant zu machen. Wenn der Plan aufgeht, soll Danny eiskalt abserviert werden. Trotz anfänglicher Gewissensbisse setzt Debbie den Plan in die Tat um – und er funktioniert. Reihenweise fordern die anderen Jungen sie in der Disco zum Tanzen auf, aber sie weist sie alle voller Genugtuung ab. Doch im Laufe des Abends lernt sie Dannys Gesellschaft schätzen und entdeckt, was für einen netten, zuvorkommenden und sie wahrhaftig liebenden Freund sie in ihm hat. So kommt es, dass Debbie von ihrem ursprünglichen Plan ablässt und von nun an glücklich mit Danny zusammen ist.

Zum Leseprozess

Um die handlungsorientierten Verfahren umzusetzen und die Aufgabenformate einzuführen, wird die Methode des *progressive reading* angewandt. Dazu wurde die Geschichte in drei Teile unterteilt, die in den folgenden Abschnitten gelesen werden:

Teil 1: "I suppose I was getting a bit desperate." (l. 1)–"I grinned, and made up my mind to be a survivor." (l. 51)

Teil 2: "That Saturday, Danny certainly got the shock of his life!" (l. 52)–What I got was a shy, funny, interesting […]." (l. 99)

Teil 3: "By the end of the evening, I couldn't remember […]." (l. 100)–ending.

> Eine **Textvorlage mit Annotationen (M 17)** ist am Ende des Materialteils abgedruckt und bereits in die drei Abschnitte unterteilt.

Zur Durchführung

1. Stunde: Mithilfe von **M 1** wird in die Stunde eingestiegen. Die Schüler beschreiben die Grafik und benennen das Thema der Kurzgeschichte. Sie erhalten dann den **ersten Teil (M 17)** und lesen diesen in Einzelarbeit. Nach der Klärung von Verständnisfragen bekommen die Schüler die Materialien **M 2** und **M 3**, anhand derer das Verfassen einer *summary* strukturiert eingeführt wird. Als Hausaufgabe schreiben sie eine *summary* des ersten Teils der Kurzgeschichte.

2. und 3. Stunde: Die Schüler präsentieren ihre *summaries*. Das **feedback sheet (M 4)** dient hierbei der individuellen Rückmeldung. Sie arbeiten nun in Vierergruppen und verfassen die *hidden thoughts*, die Debbie und Helen während ihres Gespräches haben könnten (**M 5 und M 6**). Anschießend präsentieren sie ihre Ergebnisse. Zwei von ihnen lesen den normalen Dialog zwischen Debbie und Helen. Die anderen beiden stehen jeweils hinter der Person, deren Gedanken sie vortragen. Sie legen Debbie oder Helen eine Hand auf die Schulter und lesen die versteckten Gedanken. Als Hausaufgabe bekommen die Schüler **Teil 2** der Geschichte **(M 17)** zur Lektüre und üben erneut das Schreiben einer *summary*.

4. Stunde: Die Lernenden kontrollieren ihre *summaries* in *peer correction* mithilfe des **feedback sheet (M 4)**. Zwei bis drei *summaries* können auch im Plenum nochmal präsentiert und besprochen werden. Dann wird mithilfe von **M 7** das Format *recreation of text/writing a continuation* eingeführt. Als Hausaufgabe führen die Schüler die Geschichte fort.

"Where's the boy for me" (Klasse 10/11)

Einzelmaterial 203
S 25

5. Stunde: Die Schüler stellen ihre *continuations* vor. Nun wird das Format der *characterisation* anhand von **M 8–M 10** eingeführt. Als Hausaufgabe entwerfen die Schüler das **character grid** (**M 9**) für die Protagonistin Debbie und die ersten beiden Teile der Kurzgeschichte. Sie schreiben ein direktes Zitat aus der Geschichte mit Zeilenangabe auf, interpretieren dieses und vermerken in der dritten Spalte ihre Interpretation der Charaktereigenschaften Debbies. Die vierte Spalte dient der Sortierung der Zitate nach der O*utside-to-inside*-Struktur (vgl. **M 8**) zur Erleichterung des späteren Schreibprozesses.

6. und 7. Stunde: Es werden zunächst Schwierigkeiten bei der Erstellung der Hausaufgabe (**M 9**, *character grid*) besprochen. Anschließend wird mithilfe der **Grafik** (**M 11**, auf Folie oder über Beamer präsentiert) zum Stundenthema hingeführt. Die Schüler bekommen anschließend **M 12 und M 13** ausgeteilt und haben 25 Minuten Zeit, in Partnerarbeit einen Dialog zwischen Debbies *good angel* und *bad angel* zu verfassen. Die zentrale Frage für diesen Gewissensdialog ist, ob Debbie bei ihrem Plan bleiben und Danny kaltherzig abservieren soll, da ja nun sowohl Pete als auch Dave Interesse an ihr haben – oder ob sie von diesem Abstand nehmen und mit dem treuherzigen Danny zusammenbleiben soll.

Im Anschluss an die Partnerarbeit werden mehrere Dialoge präsentiert. Dabei kann ein dritter Schüler die Rolle von Debbie übernehmen. Er sitzt zwischen den beiden stehenden Engelchen/Teufelchen, die zu ihm sprechen und sie von ihrer jeweiligen Ansicht zu überzeugen suchen

Tipp: In diesem Zusammenhang kann auch nochmal die Verwendung von *opinion phrases* geübt werden.

Der dritte Schüler darf am Ende des Dialogs entscheiden, welche der beiden Argumentationen er schlüssiger fand, und muss dies natürlich auch begründen. Anhand von **M 13** geben die restlichen Schüler den Präsentierenden Feedback. Hausaufgabe ist es dann, den **letzten Teil** (**M 17**) der Kurzgeschichte zu lesen sowie das *character grid* zu vervollständigen.

8. Stunde: Das **character grid** wird auf Folie gesichert und eventuelle Fragen und Schwierigkeiten werden besprochen. Hausaufgabe ist es nun, auf der Basis der gesammelten Notizen eine *characterisation* zu schreiben.

9. und 10. Stunde: Die *characterisations* werden in einem *correction circle* bestehend aus einer Gruppe von jeweils vier Schülern kontrolliert. Dabei lesen die Schüler alle Texte der anderen Mitglieder ihrer Gruppe und korrigieren diese mithilfe von **M 14**. Anschließend werden besonders gelungene *characterisations* zur Präsentation vorgeschlagen und besprochen.

Jetzt wird mithilfe von **M 15** zum thematischen Schwerpunkt der Stunde übergeleitet: dem Bauen eines *freeze frames*. Die Schüler bekommen **M 16** und bilden **Gruppen** von 5–6 Mitgliedern. Die eine Kurshälfte erstellt einen *freeze frame* für den ersten Teil der Geschichte (a), die andere stellt den zweiten Teil dar (b). Die Schüler erhalten 15 Minuten, um sich ein Standbild zu überlegen, das die Beziehung der Figuren zueinander widerspiegelt. Dabei sollten sie durch ihre Position im Raum, ihre Gesichtsausdrücke und Körpersprache die Beziehungen zwischen den einzelnen Figuren verdeutlichen. Danach präsentieren sie ihre Ergebnisse und nehmen dabei **zwei Mal** hintereinander **für jeweils ca. 15 Sekunden** ihre Positionen ein. Die anderen Gruppen müssen raten, welcher Schüler welche Figur darstellt. Anschließend dürfen die Präsentierenden ihre Darstellung genauer erläutern. Zuletzt werden noch offene Fragen in Bezug auf die Klausur geklärt.

Lernerfolgskontrolle (11. und 12. Stunde): Die Lernerfolgskontrolle ist für die Bearbeitung in einer Doppelstunde konzipiert und behandelt inhaltlich ebenfalls das Thema *growing up*. Dies geschieht anhand eines Ausschnitts aus einer anderen Short Story zum gleichen Thema. Alle drei im Zuge der Reihe erarbeiteten Aufgabenformate (*summary, characterisation, continuation*) werden anhand der Klausur überprüft.

"Where's the boy for me" (Klasse 10/11)

Einzelmaterial 203
S 26

Erwartungshorizont (M 1)

1. In the picture there are different hearts. An arrow passes through the heart in the middle of the picture, two other hearts are broken down the middle and the heart in the top left-hand corner has wings.

2. The picture shows that love has many faces: the heart that has been coloured in could stand for a fulfilled love; the heart with the wings perhaps wants to demonstrate that love can inspire people and give them wings. The heart with the arrow (Cupid's arrow) symbolises the fact that anyone can be hit by this arrow and fall in love. The broken hearts represent an unhappy or unrequited love or perhaps the end of a romance.

3. The short story will be about the subject of love (or falling in love or complications in a love story).

Erwartungshorizont (M 6)

Bei den Ergebnissen ist es wichtig, darauf zu achten, dass jeweils die richtige Perspektive eingenommen wird, die die Position von Debbie oder Helen widerspiegelt. Natürlich ist es auch möglich – abweichend vom Gesagten – überraschende Gedanken zu formulieren (z. B. negative Gedanken von Helen, die Debbie gedanklich mit abschätzigen Kommentaren versieht).

Beispiel:

"What's wrong with me?" I wailed plaintively. "Pete practically ignores me and Dave treats me like an elderly relation!"

Debbie's thoughts: "I REALLY don't know! I am smart, not ugly and funny, too! Why does nobody want to go out with me?!?

Helen grinned. "Not a thing," she replied. "You *look* all right to me - a bit young maybe, but ..."

Helen's thoughts: Oh boy, not THAT again .... If she only realized she needs to do something about her outward appearance ...

"Young?" I spluttered indignantly. "I'm the same age as you!"

Debbie: I don't get it. I mean – why does everybody like her, but not me??

"I know that! But, well, there's something young about you." She smiled apologetically. "I'm not being much help, am I?"

Helen: Oh well, she'll never get it.

"Oh. I wouldn't say that," I replied, through clenched teeth. "But what exactly am I supposed to do until the years begin to take their toll? Wear a bag on my head?"

Debbie: I need some more helpful advice! And she even thinks it's funny! I thought she was my best friend.

"It might help!" Helen giggled. "No, seriously Debbie, you could try a more sophisticated hair-style, or revamp your make-up, but I think there's more to it than that."

Helen: Maybe that'll help. But she also needs to stop being so shy!

„Where's the boy for me" (Klasse 10/11)

Einzelmaterial 203
S 27

Erwartungshorizont (M 10)

Line/lines	Quote	Interpretation	Priority
1	"I suppose I was getting a bit desperate."	she feels desperate, hopeless, sad about not having a boyfriend	10
2	"What did I want? A boyfriend."	the most important issue in her life	9
4	"I tried to be friendly."	she tries to be open and friendly	6
5	"… but my efforts seemed doomed to failure."	she has no luck with boys, no matter how hard she tries	6,8
10/11	"… as if I didn't exist."	boys ignore her, she is not interesting, unimpressive	3,6
15	"… my confidence was at an all-time low."	her bad luck with boys makes her feel miserable and shy	6,10
16	"… so I decided to consult Helen about it."	she has got a best friend she can talk to for advice, she takes advice	4
19/20	"You *look* alright to me – a bit young maybe."	Debbie looks young	3
26/27	"Debbie, you could try a more sophisticated hair-style, or revamp your make-up …"	her name is Debbie; according to her friend Helen she can still improve her outward appearance	1,3
28	"You've never actually been out with a boy, have you?"	Debbie has no dating experience, maybe she is too shy	4,6
37	"… you *have* got one admirer!"	but she is attractive to at least one boy	4
40	"Oh, *Danny*! But I don't fancy him at all! I've known him for years!"	Debbie doesn't fancy Danny at all, he's just her neighbour	7,8
46	"Oh Deb, you are slow!"	she needs help in matters of romance	6
49	"… but I did have a pang of conscience about the ditching bit."	she knows she does sth. immoral, she doesn't feel good about hurting his feelings	10
50/51	"I grinned, and made up my mind to be a survivor."	however, her despair outweighs her feeling of guilt	9
56	"I felt rather guilty …"	she feels guilty → has moral standards	10
68/69	"I felt very uncomfortable – he was so keen to go out with me and I was only using him as a stepping stone to better things."	she knows it's wrong to use Danny like she plans to do and she feels bad about it	10
80/81	"It was working! I couldn't believe everything was going so well…"	Debbie is surprised by her unexpected success	9,10
88	"He'd looked straight through me!"	she is unattractive to boys	3,4
89	"I could've jumped up and down on the spot…"	Debbie is thrilled about her sudden popularity – her dreams come true	10
97	"I'd been expecting the Danny I had known as a child…"	Debbie is surprised about the 'new' Danny she gets to know	9
101	"Happiness right next door and I'd never even suspected it!"	her naughty plan actually showed her the way to love – though where she'd never expected it	9
109	"Why should I ditch Danny? He's wonderful! Absolutely wonderful!"	she finally has found true love and decides to let her original plan go	7,8,10

"Where's the boy for me" (Klasse 10/11)

Einzelmaterial 203
S 28

Erwartungshorizont (M 11)

A young woman is standing between two drawings above her shoulders. On one side there is a drawing of a little devil or bad angel that appears to stand for the darker side in us. On the other side there is a drawing of an angel on a cloud, characterising the better characteristics in us like honesty or fairness. It seems that the young woman is faced with a dilemma. The two angels represent the young woman's thoughts on how to solve a problem. Perhaps the person doesn't know what to do and the good and bad angels start talking to her to give her advice.

The picture describes Debbie's situation. On the one hand, she can now date her dream boys Pete or Dave and only has to ditch Danny (that's what the devil is telling her to do), on the other hand she starts to like Danny and feels bad about hurting his feelings (the angel's position).

Erwartungshorizont (M 12)

Die Schülerlösungen sollten auf jeden Fall die Perspektive (*good angel/bad angel*) beibehalten und überzeugende Argumente für diese Position beinhalten. Im optimalen Fall gelingt es den Schülern, im Anschluss an ihre argumentative Auseinandersetzung einen Kompromiss zu schließen. Sie sollten dabei *opinion phrases* verwenden sowie die Konsequenzen von Debbies möglichem Handeln aufzeigen.

Beispiele:

Bad Angel: "I think you should ditch Danny! He is the most boring guy ever – and you have already known him for years!"

Good Angel: "I don't agree! Look at him – he really admires you and he is the kindest person you have ever met!"

Bad Angel: "Ugh ... just like I said ... boring! In my eyes, he's not good enough for you! And can't you see – you could have Pete or Dave right now!"

Good Angel: "I don't think so – they are just looking for a quick flirt, they are not really interested in you. But Danny truly cares about your feelings!" ...

Erwartungshorizont (M 15)

There are seven different stickmen in the picture. The purple stickman on the far left has a microphone in his hand. He appears to be worried or afraid because he is covering his mouth with his hand as if to stop a cry. The brown stickman next to him is holding a book in front of his face and seems to be uninterested in what is happening. In the middle, there is a blue stickman looking down on another stickman on the ground with his foot placed firmly on his back so that he appears dominant. The blue stickman has a bundle of money in his right hand and from his expression seems to be ruthless or even greedy. The grey stickman on the ground is crawling on the floor and has a collar around his neck together with a leash, making him look rather like a submissive dog. A green stickman is holding the leash but is on one knee and appears to be holding out a helping hand to the grey stickman. He makes a sympathetic or caring impression. Standing behind and to the right of the green man is a yellow stickman with his arms crossed and eyes wide open. Above his head there are two punctuation marks – suggesting that he is shocked or can't understand what is taking place. His crossed arms show us that he may feel insecure or wants to protect himself or simply does not want to get involved. On the far right of the picture a red stickman is standing a little apart from the others but looking in their direction. From his expression it is hard to judge what he is feeling. His eyes are wide open, telling us that he is attentive. He is standing a little apart which may mean that he is detached or is a neutral bystander. His hands are on his hips making him appear determined or confident.

Purple: worried, nervous, afraid; **brown:** hiding himself or his fear, shy, uninterested, not involved; **blue:** powerful, dominating, ruthless; **grey:** obedient, servile, submissive; **green:** helpful, sympathetic, caring; **yellow:** shocked, insecure, stunned **red:** detached, determined, confident, attentive. → Their body language and gestures make it possible to assign them different adjectives.

Our Blue Planet (Klasse 10/11)

Einzelmaterial 211
S 1

Our Blue Planet – Our Changing World: Materialien zur Durchführung einer mündlichen Prüfung in der Einführungsphase

Eva Maria Schepp, Münster

M 1   Prüfungsblock 1 – Partner A

Part I: Monologue – Cartoon analysis

1. **Describe** the cartoon in detail.
2. **Interpret** the cartoon and explain the environmental topics related to it and its punchline.

Panel 1: "I thought we were dining 'international' tonight?"

Panel 2: "The broccoli is from Spain, the potatoes from Portugal and the lamb from New Zealand. Send me a postcard when you've eaten!"

Spencer Hill, 12 August 2010; © www.cartoonstock.com

Part II: Dialogue – Discussion

Online shopping

You and your best friend love to go shopping at least once a week. At school you have just learned about the destruction of the earth. Thinking about your own carbon and water footprint has convinced you that you want to help protect the environment. Therefore, you have now decided to buy all your clothes online, as you think this will protect our planet better than buying in stores.

You are now talking to your best friend about it. You think he/she should also shop online, but your friend is not convinced and prefers to go to local stores.

Collect arguments that support your opinion, **discuss** them with your friend and try to convince him/her that shopping online is better. Finally, find a compromise.

You will start the discussion.

RAAbits Englisch

M 2 Prüfungsblock 1 – Partner B

Part I: Monologue – Cartoon analysis

1. **Describe** the cartoon in detail.
2. **Interpret** the cartoon and explain the environmental topics related to it and its punchline.

Ralph Hagen, 27 October 2010; © www.cartoonstock.com

Part II: Dialogue – Discussion

Online shopping

You and your best friend love to go shopping and at least once a week. At school you have just learned about the destruction of our blue planet. Your best friend has now decided to buy all his/her clothes online, as this, in his/her opinion, is the most eco-friendly way of shopping.

You do not think so. You think he/she should rather buy at local stores, as online-shopping has negative side effects on our environment. In your opinion, there are other, better ways to save the environment.

Collect arguments that support your opinion, **discuss** them with your friend and try to convince him/her that shopping at your local stores is better and that there are many other ways to protect the world. Finally, find a compromise.

Your partner will start the discussion.

Our Blue Planet (Klasse 10/11)

Einzelmaterial 211
S 3

M 3 Prüfungsblock 2 – Partner A

Part I: Monologue – Cartoon analysis

1. **Describe** the cartoon in detail.
2. **Interpret** the cartoon and explain the environmental topics related to it and its punchline.

Vocabulary
Kreisverkehr: roundabout

Chris Madden, 4 September 2015; © www.cartoonstock.com

Part II: Dialogue – Discussion

A school fair

Your headmaster wants to organise a school fair[1]. You and your best friend are members of the planning committee and are responsible for organising the food for this special event. You want to have a buffet, so you have to decide which food you want to offer and how to serve it.

After having learned about the pollution of our earth at school, you are planning to sell locally grown food from your area. Your best friend, however, just looks at the huge amount of work which needs to be done and therefore prefers to offer food that is ready to eat from the supermarket.

Collect some arguments for selling locally grown food and **discuss** why this is the most eco-friendly option for your school fair. Finally, find a compromise.

Your friend will start the discussion.

1 school fair: Schulbasar

RAAbits Englisch

M 4 Prüfungsblock 2 – Partner B

Part I: Monologue – Cartoon analysis

1. **Describe** the cartoon in detail.
2. **Interpret** the cartoon and explain the environmental topics related to it and its punchline.

[Cartoon: Top panel labeled "London Eye 2007" showing people in a gondola of the London Eye above the city skyline. Bottom panel labeled "London Eye-quarium 2057" showing the same scene underwater with fish swimming around the submerged city. Caption: "Opportunities arising from Global warming"]

Vocabulary
Gondel: gondola

Chris Taylor, 14 June 2011; © www.cartoonstock.com

Part II: Dialogue – Discussion

A school fair

Your headmaster wants to organise a school fair[1]. You and your best friend are members of the planning committee and are responsible for organising the food for this special event. You want to have a buffet, so you have to decide which food you want to offer and how to serve it.

Your best friend wants to buy only locally grown products in order to help protect the planet.

However, you are afraid that organising the buffet will be a lot of work and therefore, you'd rather sell food that is ready to eat from the supermarket. Also, you prefer to use plastic plates, cups, spoons and napkins. Collect arguments for your position and **discuss** this topic with your best friend, trying to convince him/her that there are other, better ways to help protect the planet. Finally, find a compromise.

You will start the discussion.   1 school fair: Schulbasar

Our Blue Planet (Klasse 10/11)

Einzelmaterial 211
S 5

M 5 Prüfungsblock 3 – Partner A

Part I: Monologue – Cartoon analysis

1. **Describe** the cartoon in detail.
2. **Interpret** the cartoon and explain the environmental topics related to it and its punchline.

Vocabulary
Angel: fishing rod
Abflussrohr: drainage pipe

© Mark Lynch, 21 October 2010; www.cartoons-a-plenty.com

Part II: Dialogue – Discussion

A field trip

Congratulations! You and your schoolmates have won a competition! The first prize is a large amount of money. Your headmaster thinks the money should be used for financing a field trip. You and your best friend are members of the planning committee.

You have learned at school about the destruction of the earth. Information about food miles, carbon and water footprints have convinced you that travelling by ship and plane is bad.

That is why you think that you should plan an eco-friendly trip. You think of taking the train and going camping somewhere nearby. Talk to your best friend and try to convince him/her to stay local. You could use the rest of the money for fun group activities. However, your friend does not agree at all.

Think of arguments to convince him/her and **discuss** why camping is the best way to protect our environment. Finally, agree on a compromise.

Your partner will start the discussion.

Our Blue Planet (Klasse 10/11)

Einzelmaterial 211
S 6

M 6 Prüfungsblock 3 – Partner B

Part I: Monologue – Cartoon analysis

1. **Describe** the cartoon in detail.
2. **Interpret** the cartoon and explain the environmental topics related to it and its punchline.

> *Cartoon:* A cashier at a checkout counter hands a very long receipt to a customer holding a small shopping bag. The cashier says: "GLAD TO SEE FOLKS LIKE YOU USING REUSABLE SHOPPING BAGS. WE'RE SAVING A LOT OF TREES! HERE'S YOUR RECEIPT."

Jon Carter, 24 May 2012; © www.cartoonstock.com

Vocabulary
Kassenbon: receipt

Part II: Dialogue – Discussion

A field trip

Congratulations! You and your schoolmates have won a competition! The first prize is a large amount of money. Your headmaster thinks the money should be used for financing a field trip. You and your best friend are members of the planning committee.

You would love to fly to another country. After all, you have money to spend and you see a once-in-a-lifetime chance to go to a foreign country.

That is why you think that you should plan a trip abroad. However, your best friend does not agree at all. He/she wants to go on an eco-friendly camping holiday in Germany. Talk to him/her and try to convince him/her that going to another country is better.

Think of arguments to convince your friend and **discuss** why your idea is great and that there are other, better ways to protect the environment. Finally, agree on a compromise.

You will start the discussion.

Our Blue Planet (Klasse 10/11)

Einzelmaterial 211
S 7

M 7 Prüfungsblock 4 – Partner A

Part I: Monologue – Cartoon analysis

1. **Describe** the cartoon in detail.
2. **Interpret** the cartoon and explain the environmental topics related to it and its punchline.

Vocabulary
Wohnmobil: camping trailer
Vierradantriebswagen: quads (pl)
Mülleimer: recycling bin

it is important to do our part to help the environment son....

Christine Anderson, 15 May 2012; © www.cartoonstock.com

Part II: Dialogue – Discussion

Eating meat

You know a lot about the destruction of our blue planet. Information about food miles, global warming, carbon and water footprints have convinced you that eating meat is ecologically bad.

You already are a vegetarian. Talk to your best two friends and try to persuade them to become vegetarians as well. One of them loves to eat meat and does not agree at all, but the other one wants to take it a step further and wants to try vegan living.

Think of arguments and **discuss** why eating meat damages our earth and how being a vegetarian is healthy and can be a great help for protecting our environment.

Finally, agree on a compromise.

You will start the discussion.

Our Blue Planet (Klasse 10/11)

Einzelmaterial 211
S 8

M 8 Prüfungsblock 4 – Partner B

Part I: Monologue – Cartoon analysis

1. **Describe** the cartoon in detail.
2. **Interpret** the cartoon and explain the environmental topics related to it and its punchline!

Speech bubble: "I HEARD RIDING THE BUS WAS BETTER FOR THE ENVIRONMENT... SO I BOUGHT US EACH ONE!"

Vocabulary
Schaufel: shovel
graben: to dig
Motor: engine

Published on www.cartoonstock.com

Part II: Dialogue – Discussion

Eating meat

You love meat in all its variations and tastes. One of your best friends, however, is a vegetarian and tries to convince you to stop eating meat. Your other friend even wants to take it a step further and wants to try vegan living.

You do not agree at all: Many animals are carnivorous[1] and humans originally descend from[2] animals – so why should you stop eating meat? In addition, you are convinced that only our evolution to being meat-eaters has made us the smart, big-brained human species that we are today – and that eating meat is important to our health.

Think of arguments, **discuss** with your friends and try to convince them that eating meat is part of an evolutionary master plan and that there are other, better ways to protect the environment.

Finally, agree on a compromise.

Your partner will start the discussion.

1 carnivorous: eating meat
2 to descend from: von etw. abstammen

Our Blue Planet (Klasse 10/11)

Einzelmaterial 211
S 9

M 9 Prüfungsblock 4 – Partner C

Part I: Monologue – Cartoon analysis

1. **Describe** the cartoon in detail.
2. **Interpret** the cartoon and explain the environmental topics related to it and its punchline.

Chris Madden, 3 July 2015; www.cartoonstock.com

Part II: Dialogue – Discussion

Eating meat

You have learned at school about the destruction of our blue planet.

Information about food miles, global warming, carbon and water footprints have convinced you that eating and drinking animal products is ecologically bad.

That is why you think about living vegan. Talk to your two best friends and try to convince them to also become vegans. One of them already is a vegetarian, but the other one does not want to stop eating meat or drinking milk at all.

Think of arguments and **discuss** why eating animal products damages the earth and how being a vegan is healthy and can be a great help in protecting our environment.

Finally, agree on a compromise.

Your partner will start the discussion.

M 10 Discussion phrases

English	German
Stating an opinion	**Eine Meinung äußern**
In my opinion …	Meiner Meinung nach …
In my view …	Meiner Meinung nach …
I am sure that …	Ich bin sicher, dass …
I am convinced that …	Ich bin überzeugt davon, dass …
I think …	Ich denke …
I believe …	Ich glaube …
I am of the opinion that …	Meiner Meinung nach …
It seems to me that …	Mir scheint, dass …
My personal opinion is that …	Meine persönliche Meinung ist, dass …
From my point of view …	Aus meiner Sicht …
That is why I think that …	Darum denke ich, dass …
This proves that …	Das beweist, dass …
It is obvious that …	Es ist offensichtlich, dass …
There are several reasons for this …	Es gibt mehrere Gründe dafür …
Let me give you an example …	Lass mich dir ein Beispiel geben …
The result of this is that …	Das Ergebnis davon ist, dass …
There is no doubt that …	Es gibt keinen Zweifel daran, dass …
Agreeing	**Zustimmung ausdrücken**
You are quite right.	Du hast durchaus recht.
You are absolutely right.	Du hast völlig recht.
Exactly.	Genau.
I agree.	Ich stimme dir zu.
I totally agree.	Ich stimme dir absolut zu.
I think you are right.	Ich denke, du hast Recht.
Disagreeing	**Ablehnung ausdrücken**
Do you really think so?	Denkst du das wirklich?
I don't think that's right.	Ich glaube nicht, dass das richtig ist.
I disagree.	Ich stimme dir nicht zu.
I totally disagree.	Ich stimme dir absolut nicht zu.
I am not convinced that …	Ich bin nicht überzeugt davon, dass …
I can't agree, I'm afraid.	Ich fürchte, ich kann dir nicht zustimmen.
I don't agree at all.	Ich stimme dir überhaupt nicht zu.
Clarifying	**Um Klarstellung bitten**
What do you mean?	Was meinst du damit?
Could you say that again, please?	Könntest du das bitte wiederholen?
Could you repeat that, please?	Könntest du das bitte wiederholen?
I am afraid I didn't understand what you mean. Could you explain that again, please?	Ich fürchte, ich habe nicht verstanden, was du meinst. Könntest du das bitte noch einmal erklären?

Our Blue Planet (Klasse 10/11)

Einzelmaterial 211
S 11

Kompetenzen

Die Schülerinnen und Schüler[1] erweitern ihre **funktionale kommunikative Kompetenz** und können sich an Diskussionen über das Thema „*Our Blue Planet*" beteiligen, indem sie einen vorgegebenen oder eigenen Standpunkt vertreten und begründen. Sie können ihre Gesprächsbeiträge planen und funktional umsetzen sowie auftretende sprachliche Schwierigkeiten durch die Verwendung von Kompensationsstrategien umgehen.

Sie erweitern ihre **Text- und Medienkompetenz** und können Cartoons sach- und fachgerecht analysieren, indem sie diese in Bezug auf ihre Aussageabsicht, Darstellungsform und Wirkung deuten.

Darüber hinaus erweitern die Schüler ihre **Kompetenz im Bereich soziokulturelles Orientierungswissen**, indem sie sich anhand des Themas mit globalen Herausforderungen im Hinblick auf die Aspekte „Umweltverschmutzung" und „Umweltschutz" kritisch auseinandersetzen.

Auf CD:
- Word-Datei
- alle Cartoons in Farbe
- Vorlagen für Protokollbögen
- Vorlage für Prüfungsplan

[1] Im weiteren Verlauf wird aus Gründen der besseren Lesbarkeit nur „Schüler" verwendet.

Niveau

Klasse 10 (G8)/11 (G9)

Dauer

Ein Prüfungstag (mündliche Prüfung von maximal 25 Schülern)

Einbettung

Die Prüfungsmaterialien können unabhängig von einem Lehrwerk im Rahmen des für die Einführungsphase vorgegebenen Themas „*Our Blue Planet*" eingesetzt werden.

Hinweise

Inhaltliche Vorbereitung der Prüfung

Die folgenden Themen und Umweltkonzepte sollten in Vorbereitung der Prüfung erarbeitet werden:

Methodische Vorbereitung

- Analyseschritte für die Interpretation eines Cartoons (Erklärung der *punchline*)
- Vermittlung von Diskussionsvokabular (*discussion phrases*)
- Vermittlung von Vokabular zur Bildbeschreibung
- Vermittlung von thematischem Wortschatz

Umweltkonzepte

- greenhouse effect / global warming / rising sea level
- food miles
- water footprint
- carbon footprint
- deforestation
- organic farming
- fossil fuels / renewable energies
- green travelling

Our Blue Planet (Klasse 10/11)

Einzelmaterial 211
S 12

- pollution (air, water, plastic ...)
- biological advantages and ecological disadvantages of eating meat and dairy products

Die thematische Vorbereitung kann u.a. mit den **gängigen Oberstufenlehrwerken** für die Einführungsphase geschehen:

- Green Line Oberstufe Klasse 10, Klett Verlag, Topic 3 „The Blue Planet";
- Green Line Transition, Klett Verlag, Topic 3 „Think Globally – Act Locally";
- Context Starter, Cornelsen Verlag, Topic 3: „Living in the global village".

Zur Durchführung

Informationen zu den Rahmenbedingungen

Die Prüfungsmaterialien sind für Prüfungen von **jeweils drei Schülerpaaren** mit denselben Materialien gedacht. Vorbereitungs- und Prüfungszeit betragen jeweils **zwanzig Minuten** (jeweils fünf Minuten pro Prüfling für die Cartoon-Analyse, zehn Minuten für die anschließende Diskussion). Zu beachten ist, dass das erste Prüfungspaar erst entlassen werden darf, wenn das dritte Prüfungspaar die Vorbereitung beginnt, sodass sich die Prüflinge nicht untereinander begegnen (Verfahren wie im Abitur). Während der Vorbereitungszeit sollten den Prüflingen zudem ein **zweisprachiges Wörterbuch** und **Schreibpapier** zur Verfügung gestellt werden.

Aufbau der Materialien

Die Materialien sind so aufgebaut, dass sich im ersten Teil jeweils ein **Cartoon** zu einem Umweltthema befindet (für den **monologischen Teil** der Prüfung). Der zweite Teil bietet einen **Diskussionsanlass** für den **dialogischen Teil**, in dem ein Umweltthema kontrovers diskutiert und am Ende ein Kompromiss gefunden wird.

Tipp: Es empfiehlt sich, den Prüflingen die Cartoons als **farbigen Ausdruck** auszuhändigen.

Erwartungshorizonte zur schnellen Einarbeitung

Die detaillierten Erwartungshorizonte behandeln stets alle Umweltkonzepte, die von den Prüflingen genannt werden könnten, auch wenn diese sich in den Prüfungsmaterialien zum Teil wiederholen. Dies hat folgenden Grund: Häufig hat man als Hauptprüfer über einen gesamten Prüfungstag unterschiedliche Mitprüfer, die zwischendurch wechseln. Diese bekommen die Prüfungsteile – eventuell auch nur einen Teil davon – vorab zur Kenntnisnahme und Einarbeitung. Die Erwartungshorizonte helfen ihnen, einen schnellen Einblick zu gewinnen, falls sie selbst gerade nicht im Thema „drin" sind.

Zusatzmaterialien auf der CD Grundwerk

Auf der beiliegenden **CD Grundwerk** finden sich alle **Cartoons** noch einmal **in Farbe**, sodass nach Belieben darauf zurückgegriffen werden kann. Dort gibt es außerdem **Vorlagen für Protokollbögen (ZM 2, ZM 3)** und ein Muster für einen **Prüfungsplan (ZM 4)** mit Zeitangaben. Außerdem enthalten ist das **Prüfungsmaterial für den Block 4** im Fall einer **Zweiergruppe**.

Gerade vs. ungerade Schüleranzahl

Block 4 ist in dieser Einheit für eine **ungerade Anzahl** von Prüflingen als Dreiergruppe konzipiert. Eine Alternative für eine Zweiergruppe ist auf der **CD Grundwerk** enthalten.

Our Blue Planet (Klasse 10/11)

Einzelmaterial 211
S 13

Bewertung

Vorschläge für Bewertungsraster und Bewertungsvorgaben finden sich auf den Seiten der Ministerien, z. B. für Nordrhein-Westfalen unter: https://www.standardsicherung. schulministerium.nrw.de/cms/muendliche-kompetenzen-entwickeln-und-pruefen/ angebot-gymnasiale-oberstufe/.

Praxistipps zur Organisation – Was ist wann zu tun?

Vor der Prüfung

- ✓ **Termin** für die Prüfung festlegen. Da die Noten noch am selben Tag feststehen, ist eine Prüfung z. B. kurz vor dem Termin der Notenabgabe möglich.

- ✓ Rechtzeitig die **Stundenplaner** informieren.

- ✓ **Prüfungs- und Vorbereitungsräume** blocken (idealerweise nah beieinander).

- ✓ **Kollegen** zur Prüfung und zur Aufsicht im Vorbereitungsraum freistellen, Vertretungen planen. **Tipp:** Zwei Prüfer für einen ganzen Tag als Prüfungsteam einsetzen. So haben beide Prüfer den Vergleich aller Schüler des Tages und es bleibt mehr Zeit für die Besprechung, da keine „Einarbeitung" eines neuen Kollegen nötig ist.

- ✓ Klären, wer im „Notfall" einer **Nachprüfung** einspringt. Diese sollte bei Prüfungen, die sich über zwei Tage erstrecken, erst im Anschluss an den zweiten Prüfungstag angesetzt werden (wegen der Prüfungsmaterialien). Ist ein Schüler am Tag der Prüfung krank (mit Attest!), wird er bei Wiedererscheinen in der Schule geprüft – mit einem **„Springerkandidaten"**, der freiwillig die Prüfung ohne Bewertung erneut absolviert.

- ✓ Einige Tage vor der Prüfung: **Materialienübergabe** an alle mitprüfenden Kollegen. Diese sollten das Prüfungsthema und die Materialien sowie die Bewertungsraster bereits kennen, damit diese vom Prüfungsvorsitzenden nicht ständig neu erklärt werden müssen und eventuelle Fragen vorher geklärt werden können. Materialien (falls möglich farbig) ausdrucken und sortieren.

- ✓ **Prüfungspaarungen** zusammenstellen. **Tipp:** Erfahrungsgemäß macht es keinen Unterschied, ob die Prüfungspartner gleich oder unterschiedlich leistungsstark sind. Losen ist die gerechteste und meist auch einfachste Auswahlmethode.

- ✓ **Dreiergruppen** immer an das Ende eines Prüfungstages setzen, da der Hauptprüfer hier während der Diskussion zwei Protokolle gleichzeitig schreiben muss (dies gelingt leichter, wenn man schon etwas Übung hat). Außerdem müssen eventuell am Prüfungstag noch Änderungen am Prüfungsplan vorgenommen werden, sollte ein Schüler erkrankt fehlen.

- ✓ **Prüfungszeitplan** erstellen, Schüler durch Aushang informieren. Auf Pausen im Zeitplan achten – nach jeweils drei Prüfungen wird die Bewertung vorgenommen, danach noch weitere Zeit für eine Pause für die Kollegen einplanen (siehe Beispiel für einen Zeitplan auf der **CD Grundwerk**).

- ✓ Die Schüler sollten sich fünf Minuten vor der Vorbereitungszeit **am Sammelpunkt** einfinden, damit der Ablauf reibungslos klappt.

- ✓ Das **Bewertungsraster** sollte den Schülern im Unterricht vorher transparent gemacht werden.

Während der Prüfung

✓ Jeder Kollege **protokolliert** den jeweils vor ihm/ihr sitzenden Prüfling. **Tipp:** Innerhalb eines Blocks darauf achten, dass der Schüler vor einem immer denselben Cartoon bzw. dieselbe Rolle hat.

✓ Hilfreich ist es zudem, während beider Prüfungsteile jeweils die **Zeit** zu **stoppen**, um zu sehen, wie lange die Prüflinge gesprochen haben. (Dies dann auch auf dem Protokollbogen vermerken). Sollten sie länger als die für den Diskussionsteil angesetzten zehn Minuten sprechen, ist die Diskussion von der Lehrkraft kurz zu unterbrechen, mit dem Hinweis, dass nun langsam ein Kompromiss gefunden werden sollte.

✓ Am Ende jeder Prüfung alle **Prüfungsmaterialien** wieder einsammeln. Dies garantiert die Wiederverwendbarkeit der Materialien.

Nach der Prüfung

✓ Die **Notenbekanntgabe** empfiehlt sich in der nächsten regulären Stunde im Kurs. Sie noch am Prüfungstag durchzuführen, ist nicht sinnvoll.

✓ Die **Durchführung** der mündlichen Prüfungen (Wie hat es geklappt? Was kann eventuell beim Ablauf verbessert werden?) sollte mit den Schülern **evaluiert** werden. Dies kann z. B. in der Stunde der Notenbekanntgabe durchgeführt werden.

✓ Die Schüler erhalten bei der Bekanntgabe der Noten das **Bewertungsraster in Kopie**, die Protokollbögen dienen nur der Referenz und eventuell notwendigen Begründung einer Note, sie verbleiben bei der Lehrkraft.

Erwartungshorizont (M 1)

Part I: Cartoon analysis

a) **Description**

- Cartoonist: Spencer Hill, publication date: 12 August 2010, place of publication: www.cartoonstock.com
- The cartoon is divided into 2 pictures.
- In the left picture, you can see an old man sitting at a table. In front of him, there is a plate with food – broccoli, potatoes and a lamb chop. It looks ready to eat.
- The man looks irritated and points at the food saying "I thought we were dining 'international' tonight."
- In the right picture, the setting is the same: the man is still sitting at the table, in front of him the plate with food. However, a voice coming from the side is saying, "The broccoli is from Spain, the potatoes from Portugal and the lamb from New Zealand. Send me a postcard when you've eaten."
- The man's face shows surprise, his mouth is wide open and he covers it with his right hand. He has not expected this answer.

b) **Interpretation**

Explanation of environmental topics:

- **Food miles:** The way your food travels from its place of production to your plate, thus creating CO_2 emissions. Nowadays, however, one knows that the production process is environmentally much more important than the distance the food travels.
- **CO_2 emissions:** They pollute our atmosphere and increase global warming by influencing the greenhouse effect.

Our Blue Planet (Klasse 10/11)

Einzelmaterial 211
S 15

- **Greenhouse effect / global warming:** Actually, the greenhouse effect is a normal phenomenon. Solar radiation passes through the atmosphere and warms the earth's surface. The greenhouse gases in the atmosphere filter the radiation into space and, thus, keeping the earth's temperature at an average of 14°C, making life for humans, animals and plants possible.

- The **greenhouse effect in the 21st century**, however, is influenced by our massive air pollution with greenhouse gases such as CO_2 and methane. As a result, the sunrays cannot – after being reflected by the earth – pass through the atmosphere as easily as before and, thus, more of them are reflected and bounce up and down between the earth and the atmosphere. This increases the earth's temperature and leads to **global warming**, which again influences the melting of the poles and leads to a rising sea level.

Explanation of the punchline / joke:

- The joke of the cartoon is in the different notions of 'international dining'.

- The man probably had international cuisine – such as Italian, Mexican, Chinese etc. – in mind, when he thought of dining internationally.

- However, the food – which to him looks perfectly 'normal' and not at all international – actually is very international, as it has travelled from countries far away to his plate (food miles). Therefore, the other person ironically suggests sending a postcard once he has eaten, like you do when you travel to a foreign country.

Part II: Discussion – Online shopping

Partner A / Pro online shopping:

- **Carbon footprint:** The amount of carbon emissions which are generated by the production of every single item we use. The more items and people that can be transported in one vehicle, the fewer carbon emissions. Therefore, it is not environmentally friendly for single persons to drive in one vehicle.

- **Energy use:** Stores are heated in winter or cooled down in summer. This costs a lot of energy.

- **Fair trade:** Many fair trade sellers like to sell online in order to keep the prices reasonable and save the extra-money for the store's profit – thus, more fair trade clothes are sold as they are not too expensive.

- **Packaging:** Most packages are nowadays made of recycled paper and can be recycled again; therefore they do not pollute the planet and the argument against excess packaging is weakened.

- **Plastic pollution:** When you buy at stores, very often you will get a plastic bag to carry your new clothes home. This is very bad for the environment.

- **Possible compromise:** Buy some fair trade clothes online, ride your bike into the city, do not accept plastic bags at stores.

Erwartungshorizont (M 2)

Part I: Cartoon analysis

a) **Description**

- Cartoonist: Ralph Hagen, publication date: 27 October 2010, place of publication: www.cartoonstock.com

- The setting of the cartoon is outdoors, obviously at a farmers' market.

- There are four people in the picture, two adults (a woman and a man, the latter one is the farmer) and two children (a boy and a girl).
- On the right, there are gigantic pumpkins set next to each other. They are nearly as tall as the children. One of the children is hugging a giant pumpkin and looks happy.
- The woman is also holding a pumpkin, but this one is much smaller than the other ones. She looks a little puzzled and surprised, while the farmer tells her "That one is 100% organic." He looks a little bored or even annoyed.
- The little boy is looking up at the pumpkin in his mother's hands.

b) **Interpretation**

Explanation of environmental topics:

- **Organic farming:** Growing crops without using pesticides or fertilizers or antibiotics as well as genetically manipulated seeds.
- **Buying local / food miles:** Buying locally grown food at a regional farmers' market minimises food miles, a concept which refers to the way your food travels from its place of production to your plate, thus creating CO_2 **emissions**. Nowadays, however, one knows that the production process is environmentally much more important than the distance the food travels.

Explanation of the punchline / joke:

- The joke of the cartoon is that a woman wants to be environmentally friendly and, therefore, buys locally grown food at a farmers' market.
- However, at some local farms, the using of pesticides, fertilizer and genetically manipulated seeds is also quite common. As everything needs to be 'bigger and better' these days, the pumpkins the farmer has grown with the help of chemicals are gigantic.
- The only pumpkin, which has not been treated with anything, however, looks ridiculously small in comparison. The woman is shocked and cannot believe how small a pumpkin naturally is, if not treated with chemicals.
- The picture uses irony to show how our behaviour (the little girl absolutely loves the giant pumpkins) changes nature.

Part II: Discussion – Online shopping

Partner B / Against online shopping / Pro local stores:

- **Water footprint:** Online shopping is bad for the environment as you tend to shop much more than you would in a store. This increases your water footprint (the amount of water which was used in the production of the clothes).
- **Excess packaging:** Everything you buy online is packed in a single box, which creates excess packaging and pollutes our environment.
- **Plastic pollution:** Very often, your clothes are once again wrapped in plastic to protect them against dirt or damage. Plastic, however, does not disintegrate into smaller pieces and, therefore, pollutes our environment and oceans.
- **Job market:** If you buy only online, smaller local stores might have to close and, thus, jobs are destroyed.
- **Carbon footprint:** At a store, you can try the clothes on and see which one fits and which colour you like best. If you shop online and you don't like it, you have to send the purchase back and reorder, which creates a lot of pollution and a very high carbon emission, increasing your carbon footprint.

- **Green travelling:** You do not have to drive a car into the city – you can also ride a bike to get to the stores.
- **Possible compromise:** Buy some fair trade clothes online, ride your bike into the city, do not accept plastic bags at stores.

Erwartungshorizont (M 3)

Part I: Cartoon analysis

a) **Description**

- Cartoonist: Chris Madden publication date: 4 September 2015, place of publication: www.cartoonstock.com
- The setting of the cartoon is outdoors. In the middle of the picture, there is a roundabout. The flowers planted in the middle form the shape of the continents, so that the whole roundabout looks like our planet earth.
- A man is standing on the left. He is wearing a vest and is holding a gardening tool.
- In the background, you can see a truck driving away. On its back it says: "Delivered to your door." The truck emits clouds of fumes and pollutes the air.
- The truck has not used the roundabout correctly, but has driven across it and therefore destroyed the plants. Its tyre tracks can be seen in the grass.
- The gardener just stands there and looks helplessly at the truck.

b) **Interpretation**

Explanation of environmental topics:

- **Carbon footprint: CO_2 emissions** produced by cars that pollute our atmosphere and increase global warming by influencing the greenhouse effect.
- **Greenhouse effect / global warming:** Actually, the greenhouse effect is a normal phenomenon. Solar radiation passes through the atmosphere and warms the earth's surface. The greenhouse gases in the atmosphere filter the radiation into space and, thus, keeping the earth's temperature at an average of 14°C, making life for humans, animals and plants possible.
- The **greenhouse effect in the 21st century**, however, is influenced by our massive air pollution with greenhouse gases such as CO_2 and methane. As a result, the sunrays cannot – after being reflected by the earth – pass through the atmosphere as easily as before and, thus, more of them are reflected and bounce up and down between the earth and the atmosphere. This increases the earth's temperature and leads to **global warming**, which again influences the melting of the poles and leads to a rising sea level.

Explanation of the punchline / joke:

- The irony of the cartoon is hidden in the roundabout, which metaphorically stands for our blue planet.
- The truck driver carelessly destroys it by driving across it, which has a double meaning here. The carbon emissions of the truck increase the greenhouse effect and, therefore, negatively influence climate change.

Part II: Discussion – A school fair

Partner A / Pro locally grown food:

- **Organic farming:** Growing crops without using pesticides or fertilizers or antibiotics as well as genetically manipulated seeds is very environmentally friendly.

- **Buying local / food miles:** Buying locally grown food at a regional farmers' market minimises food miles, a concept which refers to the way your food travels from its place of production to your plate, thus creating **CO_2 emissions**.

- **Carbon footprint:** The **CO_2 emissions** of the food miles pollute our atmosphere and increase global warming by influencing the greenhouse effect.

- **Greenhouse effect / global warming:** Actually, the greenhouse effect is a normal phenomenon. Solar radiation passes through the atmosphere and warms the earth's surface. The greenhouse gases in the atmosphere filter the radiation into space and, thus, keeping the earth's temperature at an average of 14°C, making life for humans, animals and plants possible.

- The **greenhouse effect in the 21st century**, however, is influenced by our massive air pollution with greenhouse gases such as CO_2 and methane. As a result, the sunrays cannot – after being reflected by the earth – pass through the atmosphere as easily as before and, thus, more of them are reflected and bounce up and down between the earth and the atmosphere. This increases the earth's temperature and leads to **global warming**, which again influences the melting of the poles and leads to a rising sea level.

- **Excess packaging:** Everything you buy at a supermarket is wrapped somehow, which creates excess packaging and pollutes our environment.

- **Plastic pollution:** If you buy something at the supermarket, very often it is wrapped in plastic to protect it against dirt or damage. Plastic, however, does not disintegrate into smaller pieces and therefore pollutes our environment and oceans. Also, instead of plastic cups and plates, washable porcelain plates can be used and the amount of waste will decrease.

- **Possible compromise:** Only serve vegetarian food (thus reducing CO_2 from meat production); buy at the supermarket – but only seasonal food.

Erwartungshorizont (M 4)

Part I: Cartoon analysis

a) **Description**

- Cartoonist: Chris Taylor, publication date: 14 June 2011, place of publication: www.cartoonstock.com

- The cartoon is divided into 2 pictures.

- The setting of the cartoon is London – as you can see by the landscape and buildings as well as the caption of the cartoon "London Eye 2007".

- In the foreground of the upper picture is the river Thames, in its background you can see Big Ben and the Houses of Parliament.

- On the right side you can see a gondola of the Millennium Eye, London's famous Ferris wheel. There are three people standing in it: a man, a woman and a boy. All three of them look happy and are obviously enjoying the view.

- The lower picture shows the same setting: it again shows Big Ben, the Houses of Parliament and also a gondola with the same people in it. However, its caption says: "London Eye-quarium 2057" and the whole scene is 'flooded' by water. The gondola is underwater and there are fish swimming around it. The two grown-ups do not look happy anymore.

b) **Interpretation**

Explanation of environmental topics:

- **Greenhouse effect / global warming:** Actually, the greenhouse effect is a normal phenomenon. Solar radiation passes through the atmosphere and warms the earth's surface. The greenhouse gases in the atmosphere filter the radiation into space and, thus, keeping the earth's temperature at an average of 14°C, making life for humans, animals and plants possible.
- The **greenhouse effect in the 21st century**, however, is influenced by our massive air pollution with greenhouse gases such as CO_2 and methane. As a result, the sunrays cannot – after being reflected by the earth – pass through the atmosphere as easily as before and, thus, more of them are reflected and bounce up and down between the earth and the atmosphere. This increases the earth's temperature and leads to **global warming**, which again influences the melting of the poles and leads to a rising sea level, which can be seen in this cartoon as London is flooded.

Explanation of the punchline / joke:

- The cartoon shows the same setting within a time difference of 50 years. One picture is set in the future. This picture shows that London will be flooded by then, due to climate change and global warming.
- People who now take a ride on Millennium Eye Ferris wheel to get a good view of London will then have the feeling as if they are were at an aquarium (cf. pun of words: Eye-quarium).

Part II: Discussion – A school fair

Partner B / Pro food from supermarket:

- **Saving water:** By not having to wash cups and plates, you do not waste so much water.
- **Cheaper:** If you offer food from the supermarket, you can save a lot of money and, therefore, can buy more food and offer more variety.
- **Vegetarian:** You could make the buffet vegetarian, but then you would have to offer a great variety. You only get that at the supermarket!
- **Easier:** It is easier if you sell the food ready to eat.
- **Convenience:** Plastic cups are more convenient.
- **Other ways to help save the planet:** Green travelling on holidays, saving energy, eating less meat etc.
- **Possible compromise:** Serve only vegetarian food (thus reducing CO_2 from meat production); buy at the supermarket – but only seasonal food.

Erwartungshorizont (M 5)

Part I: Cartoon analysis

a) **Description**
- Cartoonist: Mark Lynch, publication date: 21 October 2010, place of publication: www.cartoons-a-plenty.com
- The cartoon is set outdoors.
- In the foreground, there is a river. A man is sitting on the bank of the river and is fishing.
- In the background, you can see factories, which are emitting a lot of smoke and fumes.
- On the left, there is a drainage pipe discharging dirty water into the river.
- There are some fish in the water, which are obviously dead.
- The other ones, which are still alive, are all clinging to the fishing rod, in order to get out of the polluted water.
- The man looks surprised, his eyes are big and his mouth is pointed.

b) **Interpretation**

Explanation of environmental topics:
- **Water pollution:** Many factories discharge their wastewater contaminated with chemicals into rivers and seas and, thereby, pollute the water and destroy the habitat of animals.
- **Carbon footprint:** The CO_2 **emissions** of the food miles pollute our atmosphere and increase global warming by influencing the greenhouse effect.
- **Greenhouse effect / global warming:** Actually, the greenhouse effect is a normal phenomenon. Solar radiation passes through the atmosphere and warms the earth's surface. The greenhouse gases in the atmosphere filter the radiation into space and, thus, keeping the earth's temperature at an average of 14°C, making life for humans, animals and plants possible.
- The **greenhouse effect in the 21st century**, however, is influenced by our massive air pollution with greenhouse gases such as CO_2 and methane. As a result, the sunrays cannot – after being reflected by the earth – pass through the atmosphere as easily as before and, thus, more of them are reflected and bounce up and down between the earth and the atmosphere. This increases the earth's temperature and leads to **global warming**, which again influences the melting of the poles and leads to a rising sea level.

Explanation of the punchline / joke:
- The joke is that the fish would rather cling to the fishing rod (and thus are in danger of being eaten) than stay another second in the water, their natural habitat, which is contaminated and polluted.

Part II: Discussion – A field trip

Partner A / Pro camping / staying local
- **Carbon footprint:** The CO_2 emissions of planes pollute our atmosphere and increase global warming by influencing the greenhouse effect.

Our Blue Planet (Klasse 10/11)

Einzelmaterial 211
S 21

- **Green travelling:** Travelling by bus or train reduces our carbon footprint.
- **Greenhouse effect / global warming:** Actually, the greenhouse effect is a normal phenomenon. Solar radiation passes through the atmosphere and warms the earth's surface. The greenhouse gases in the atmosphere filter the radiation into space and, thus, keeping the earth's temperature at an average of 14°C, making life for humans, animals and plants possible.
- The **greenhouse effect in the 21st century**, however, is influenced by our massive air pollution with greenhouse gases such as CO_2 and methane. As a result, the sunrays cannot – after being reflected by the earth – pass through the atmosphere as easily as before and, thus, more of them are reflected and bounce up and down between the earth and the atmosphere. This increases the earth's temperature and leads to **global warming,** which again influences the melting of the poles and leads to a rising sea level.
- **Cheap and environmentally friendly camping:** Camping is not expensive and also very environmentally friendly. The money saved can be spent on fun group activities.
- **Possible compromise:** Go abroad to a country like Italy or France by bus or train. You experience another culture, can go to the beach, but travel green and stay at a youth hostel.

Erwartungshorizont (M 6)

Part I: Cartoon analysis

a) **Description**
- Cartoonist: Jon Carter, publication date: 24 May 2012, place of publication: www.cartoonstock.com
- The cartoon is set inside a store.
- A man is standing in front of the checkout. He is carrying a reusable bag in his hand.
- A woman is standing behind the cashier and obviously has just printed out his receipt.
- The receipt is very long and covers several metres of the floor. The man looks down unhappily, eyeing the receipt with discomfort.
- The woman, however, happily hands him his receipt and says: "Glad to see folks like you using reusable shopping bags. We're saving a lot of trees! Here's your receipt!"

b) **Interpretation**

Explanation of environmental topics:
- **Deforestation:** Many trees are cut down and rainforests are destroyed in order to produce paper and also to create farmland for planting corn or breeding cattle. Trees, however, turn CO_2 into O_2, the oxygen we breathe and diminish the greenhouse gas carbon dioxide, which contributes to the **greenhouse effect** and therefore causes **global warming.**
- **Plastic pollution:** When you buy something at a supermarket, very often it is wrapped in plastic to protect it against dirt or damage. Plastic, however, does not disintegrate into smaller pieces and, therefore, pollutes our environment and oceans.

Explanation of the punchline / joke:

– The cartoon is highly ironic: the woman is happy that the man uses a reusable shopping bag and comments on how they saved a lot of trees; on the other hand, she prints out an incredibly long receipt made of paper and thus contradicts herself without realising it.

Part II: Discussion – A field trip

Partner B / Pro travel abroad

- **Convenience:** Flying is much more convenient than travelling by car, bus or train. It is much faster and you get food and drink.
- **Broaden your horizon:** By going abroad, you can learn more about other cultures. For some students, this might be a once-in-a-lifetime chance.
- **Safe travelling:** Flying is the safest way to travel.
- **Other ways to protect the environment:** Eat less meat, use your bike instead of your car, car pool, reduce your plastic waste, eat seasonal food, buy locally grown food.
- **Possible compromise:** Go abroad to a country like Italy or France by bus or train. You experience another culture, can go to the beach, but travel green and stay at a youth hostel.

Erwartungshorizont (M 7)

Part I: Cartoon analysis

a) **Description**

– Cartoonist: Christine Anderson, publication date: 15 May 2012, place of publication: www.cartoonstock.com

– The cartoon is set outdoors. In the foreground, there are a man and a boy, obviously father and son. In the background, there is a forest and in front it, there is a red truck pulling a camping trailer. On top of the camping trailer, there are several jet skis and quads and behind the camping trailer is a motorboat.

– The truck emits a lot of fumes.

– The father throws a can into a recycling bin and says: "It is important to do our part to help the environment, son …"

b) **Interpretation**

Explanation of environmental topics:

- **Carbon footprint:** The CO_2 **emissions** of the truck and other vehicles pollute our atmosphere and increase global warming by influencing the greenhouse effect.
- **Recycling:** A way of reusing items (bottles, paper, plastic).
- **Greenhouse effect / global warming:** Actually, the greenhouse effect is a normal phenomenon. Solar radiation passes through the atmosphere and warms the earth's surface. The greenhouse gases in the atmosphere filter the radiation into space and, thus, keeping the earth's temperature at an average of 14°C, making life for humans, animals and plants possible.
- The **greenhouse effect in the 21st century**, however, is influenced by our massive air pollution with greenhouse gases such as CO_2 and methane. As a result, the sunrays

therefore cannot – after being reflected by the earth – pass through the atmosphere as easily as before and, thus, more of them are reflected and bounce up and down between the earth and the atmosphere. This increases the earth's temperature and leads to **global warming**, which again influences the melting of the poles and leads to a rising sea level.

Explanation of the punchline / joke:

- The father is telling his son to protect the environment and recycles a can, but he also drives a truck and many other vehicles that emit a lot of carbon dioxide and, thereby, contribute to global warming and climate change.

- Therefore, his advice seems very hypocritical and ironic.

Part II: Discussion – Eating meat

Partner A / Pro vegetarian

- **Air pollution / global warming:** Animals produce methane and, thereby, contribute to greenhouse gases → global warming.

- **Greenhouse effect / global warming:** Actually, the greenhouse effect is a normal phenomenon. Solar radiation passes through the atmosphere and warms the earth's surface. The greenhouse gases in the atmosphere filter the radiation into space and, thus, keeping the earth's temperature at an average of 14°C, making life for humans, animals and plants possible.

- The **greenhouse effect in the 21st century**, however, is influenced by our massive air pollution with greenhouse gases such as CO_2 and methane. As a result, the sunrays cannot – after being reflected by the earth – pass through the atmosphere as easily as before and, thus, more of them are reflected and bounce up and down between the earth and the atmosphere. This increases the earth's temperature and leads to **global warming**, which again influences the melting of the poles and leads to a rising sea level.

- **Fresh water consumption:** Animal agriculture uses 70% of all fresh water. If you do not eat meat, you will not waste so much water.

- **Deforestation:** Agriculture is responsible for 80% of deforestation worldwide. The land is used to grow food for cattle.

- **Antibiotics:** Animals are fed with antibiotics to be resistant to diseases – when we eat meat, these antibiotics end up in our bodies.

- **World hunger:** Instead of growing grass and corn for cattle, land could be used to produce food for people in developing countries.

- **Save money:** Meat is expensive: you can save money by going veggie!

- **Possible compromise:** Eat meat only 1–2 times a week, as this already minimises your carbon footprint. Buy locally produced/organic meat from grass-fed cattle. Eat seasonal vegetables. Eat and drink fewer dairy products.

Erwartungshorizont (M 8)

Part I: Cartoon analysis

a) **Description**

- Cartoonist: Guy & Rodd, publication date: 23 March 2012, place of publication: www.cartoonstock.com

- In the foreground, there are four people. One man is facing the others and is talking to them. He is pointing at four buses, which are in the background, all wrapped in huge bows. The man says: "I heard riding the bus was better for the environment ... So I bought us each one!"
- The other people look at him rather unhappily.

b) **Interpretation**

Explanation of environmental topics:

- **Air pollution / global warming:** Animals produce methane and therefore contribute to greenhouse gases → global warming.
- **Greenhouse effect / global warming:** Actually, the greenhouse effect is a normal phenomenon. Solar radiation passes through the atmosphere and warms the earth's surface. The greenhouse gases in the atmosphere filter the radiation into space and, thus, keeping the earth's temperature at an average of 14°C, making life for humans, animals and plants possible.
- The **greenhouse effect in the 21st century**, however, is influenced by our massive air pollution with greenhouse gases such as CO_2 and methane. As a result, the sunrays cannot – after being reflected by the earth – pass through the atmosphere as easily as before and, thus, more of them are reflected and bounce up and down between the earth and the atmosphere. This increases the earth's temperature and leads to **global warming**, which again influences the melting of the poles and leads to a rising sea level.
- **Green travelling:** Travelling by bus or train reduces our **carbon footprint.**

Explanation of the punchline / joke:

- Obviously the man in the cartoon has heard and thought about ways to protect the environment (i.e. riding buses) and wants to support this idea.
- However, he gets it completely wrong: instead of using public transportation or car-pooling as a means of travelling in a "green" way, he has bought a bus for each of his family members. As a result, his good intentions are reversed, because buses driven and ridden by only one person are of course even bigger producers of CO_2 than normal cars.
- The man wanted to do something good, but has not understood the problem and, therefore, even worsens the environmental situation. The sceptical look on the faces of the other two people show they understand the situation – in contrast to the man, who still does not comprehend, which makes the cartoon funny in a sad way.

Part II: Discussion – Eating meat

Partner B / Pro eating meat

- **Evolution:** Evolution made us meat eaters (teeth, stomach).
- **Brainpower:** Eating meat contributed to making us smarter (bigger brains), it triggered evolution and therefore made us what we are today.
- **High quality protein:** Meat provides us with high quality protein and is therefore really important to our health.
- **Healthy body:** Bone and muscle growth is supported. Meat helps us to get a healthy body.
- **Vitamins:** There are a lot of vitamins in meat that you cannot get from vegetables.

- **Job market:** The meat industry offers many jobs – without it, there would be much more unemployment.
- **Locally grown:** You can reduce food miles by eating locally grown meat.
- **Reducing the amount of meat:** You do not have to stop eating meat completely: a reduction is already an environmental help.
- **Eat meat ethically:** You can be an ethical meat-eater: buy free-range chicken and beef from grass-fed cattle.
- **Possible compromise:** Eat meat only 1–2 times a week, as this already minimises your carbon footprint. Buy locally produced/organic meat from grass-fed cattle. Eat seasonal vegetables. Eat and drink fewer dairy products.

Erwartungshorizont (M 9)

Part I: Cartoon analysis

a) **Description**
- Cartoonist: Chris Madden, publication date: 3 July 2015, place of publication: www.cartoonstock.com
- The cartoon is set on the sea. In the middle of the picture, there are two men in a boat.
- The boat is shaped like half of a globe, the southern hemisphere of our earth. On it, you can see Australia and a part of Africa.
- The two men are holding shovels and are digging in their boat, the earth, in order to get resources (like coal) to keep their boat's engine running.
- One of the men, however, has cracked a hole in the earth's mantle, as he has dug too deep. The engine emits dark and thick smoke. The punchline reads: "Overexploiting the earth's resources."

b) **Interpretation**

Explanation of environmental topics:
- **Fossil fuels / renewable resources:** Fossil fuels like oil, coal etc. are used to produce energy. However, renewable energies like wind or solar power are much more sustainable and should be used instead in order to prevent an overexploitation.
- **Air pollution/ global warming:** Animals produce methane and therefore contribute to greenhouse gases and global warming.
- **Greenhouse effect / global warming:** Actually, the greenhouse effect is a normal phenomenon. Solar radiation passes through the atmosphere and warms the earth's surface. The greenhouse gases in the atmosphere filter the radiation into space and, thus, keeping the earth's temperature at an average of 14°C, making life for humans, animals and plants possible.
- The **greenhouse effect in the 21st century**, however, is influenced by our massive air pollution with greenhouse gases such as CO_2 and methane. As a result, the sunrays cannot – after being reflected by the earth – pass through the atmosphere as easily as before and, thus, more of them are reflected and bounce up and down between the earth and the atmosphere. This increases the earth's temperature and leads to **global warming**, which again influences the melting of the poles and leads to a rising sea level.

Explanation of the punchline / joke:

- The men dig into the earth (metaphorically, their boat) in order to use its resources to produce energy. They do not realise, however, that overexploitation means cracking the earth's mantle and, therefore, the sinking of their ship. In addition, the carbon emissions of their engine contribute to global warming and thus, a rising of the sea level – the earth will drown/be flooded.

Part II: Discussion – Eating meat

Partner C / Pro vegan:

- **Fresh water consumption:** Animal agriculture uses 70% of all fresh water. If you do not eat meat, you will not waste so much water.
- **Air pollution / global warming:** Animals produce methane and therefore contribute to greenhouse gases and global warming.
- **Deforestation:** Agriculture is responsible for 80% deforestation worldwide. The land is used to grow food to feed cattle.
- **World hunger:** Instead of growing grass and corn for cattle, land could be used to produce food for people in developing countries.
- **Food variety:** Nowadays, there is a huge variety of foods. Getting enough food is not a problem in the modern developed world.
- **Dairy products hurt animals:** Dairy (= milk) products and the egg industry harm millions of animals.
- **Antibiotics:** Animals are fed antibiotics to be resistant to diseases (especially chickens) – when we eat meat, these antibiotics end up in our bodies.
- **Protein:** Studies show: you can get enough proteins from plants (e.g. soy).
- **Possible compromise:** Eat meat only 1–2 times a week, as this already minimises your carbon footprint. Buy locally produced / organic meat from grass-fed cattle. Eat seasonal vegetables. Eat and drink fewer dairy products.

Let's talk – Mit *speaking cards* die Sprechfertigkeit fördern (S II)

Einzelmaterial 215
S 1

Let's talk! – Mit *speaking cards* die Sprechfertigkeit fördern (S II)

Martina Angele, Friedrichshafen

M 1 Presenting a picture and talking about the topic

Healthy lifestyle(s) – healthy eating */**

1. Tell your partner about the cartoon.
2. In your opinion, what is a healthy lifestyle?
3. "There's lots of people in this world who spend so much time watching their health that they haven't the time to enjoy it." (Josh Billings, 1818-1885, American humorist). Comment on this statement from today's point of view.
4. Discuss the advantages and disadvantages of being vegan.

"How much longer do I have before I have to change to a healthy lifestyle?"

Useful words:

doctor's surgery: die Arztpraxis – **treatment table:** die Behandlungsliege – **to follow a healthy lifestyle:** gesund leben – **to abstain from smoking/drinking/fast food:** auf das Rauchen/Trinken/Fastfood verzichten – **social pressure:** der soziale Druck – **vegan:** vegan; der/die Veganer/in – **vegetarian:** vegetarisch; der/die Vegetarier/in – **malnutrition:** die Mangelernährung – **ecologically sustainable:** ökologisch nachhaltig

Men's and women's jobs */**

1. Describe the pictures.
2. In your opinion, what is a "typical" men's/women's job? Explain.
3. "The man goes to work and the woman stays at home and looks after the children." Comment on this statement.
4. Talk about your future career plans.

Useful words:

gender related: geschlechtsspezifisch – **motor/car mechanic:** der/die KFZ-Mechaniker/in – **cosmetician/beautician:** der/die Kosmetiker/in – **to put make-up on sb.'s face:** jmndn. schminken – **stereotypical gender roles:** stereotype Geschlechterrollen – **outdated:** überholt/veraltet – **to work part-time:** Teilzeit arbeiten – **parental leave:** die Elternzeit – **equal pay for equal work:** gleicher Lohn für gleiche Arbeit

RAAbits Englisch

Let's talk – Mit *speaking cards* die Sprechfertigkeit fördern (S II)

Einzelmaterial 215
S 2

Political issues in GB/the USA: War against terrorism **

1. Describe the photo.
2. Could you imagine joining the army or responding to a recruitment campaign for the police force in order to fight terrorism?
   – **Yes:** Explain.
   – **No:** Give reasons.
3. Discuss reasons for terrorism and how one could try to stop it.
4. "Terrorism is the war of the weak and war is the terrorism of the strong." (Martin Bell, *1938, British UNICEF Ambassador and former broadcast war reporter). Comment on this statement.

Useful words:

sniper: der Scharfschütze – **battle dress:** der Kampfanzug – **sniper rifle:** das Präzisionsgewehr – **to menace sb./sth.:** jmndn./etw. bedrohen – **humanitarian:** humanitär/menschenfreundlich – **peacekeeping:** die Friedenssicherung – **to protect/secure liberal and democratic values:** freiheitlich-demokratische Werte schützen/sichern – **to reject the use of violence:** den Einsatz von Gewalt ablehnen

Equal rights **

1. Describe the picture.
2. Which specific human rights do you know? Explain what they stand for.
3. Would you support a human rights campaign (e.g. one addressing the rights of LGBT people)?
   – **Yes:** Which one would you like to support? How would you do it?
   – **No:** Why not? Which other campaigns would you like to support?
4. Talk about values and rights that are important to you in your life. Give reasons.

Useful words:

(a piece of) cardboard: (ein Stück) Pappe/Karton – **minority:** die Minderheit – **to be discriminated against:** diskriminiert werden – **equal opportunities:** die Gleichberechtigung – **basic/fundamental right:** das Grundrecht – **human dignity is inviolable:** Die Würde des Menschen ist unantastbar. – **LGBT people:** lesbian, gay, bisexual and transgender people – **to advocate sth.:** für etw. eintreten – **prohibition of torture:** das Folterverbot – **freedom of expression:** die Freiheit der Meinungsäußerung – **freedom of belief and religion:** die Religionsfreiheit – **electoral freedom:** die Wahlfreiheit

Let's talk – Mit *speaking cards* die Sprechfertigkeit fördern (S II)

Einzelmaterial 215
S 3

Cosmetic surgery */**

1. Describe the picture.

2. "It is totally acceptable to use modern medicine to optimise your looks." Comment on this statement.

3. Could you imagine having a cosmetic operation?
   - **Yes:** Under what circumstances? Explain.
   - **No:** Why not? Under what circumstances might an operation be useful?

4. Do you think cosmetic operations should be forbidden for teenagers under 18? Discuss.

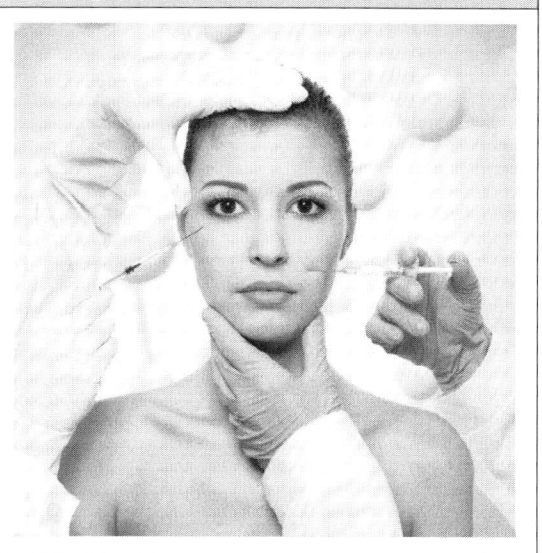

Useful words:

to inject Botox: Botox spritzen – **syringe:** die Spritze – **glove:** der Handschuh – **to fight wrinkles:** Falten bekämpfen – **to pursue the ideal of ageless beauty:** das Ideal alterloser Schönheit verfolgen – **to have high/low self-esteem:** viel/wenig Selbstbewusstsein haben – **unpredictable risks:** unvorhersehbare Risiken – **reconstructive medicine:** die Wiederherstellungsmedizin – **to interfere with nature:** (störend) in die Natur eingreifen

Utopia and dystopia **

1. Say what you can see in the picture.

2. Explain the terms *utopia* and *dystopia* and give examples.

3. Discuss whether you would like to live in a world as shown in the picture.

4. There are many literary works and films with a utopian or dystopian setting. Name some examples and discuss why this topic is so fascinating for many people.

Useful words:

futuristic shuttle trains: futuristische Pendelzüge – **to float:** schweben – **utopia (*adj.* utopian):** derived from the Greek words for 'no-place' and 'good-place'; a desirable imaginary society – **dystopia (*adj.* dystopian):** a threatening, anti-utopian society – **to be set in ...:** spielen in – **to be a warning against ...:** eine Warnung vor ... sein – **to establish a totalitarian system:** ein totalitäres/antidemokratisches System errichten – **surveillance:** die Überwachung

Let's talk – Mit *speaking cards* die Sprechfertigkeit fördern (S II)

Einzelmaterial 215
S 4

Family life – then and now */**

1. Describe the pictures.
2. "A family, that's mother, father and children." Discuss.
3. Talk about values in the past and in today's time. What has changed? Why?
4. Who is more important to you – family or friends? Discuss.

Useful words:

the change in values in society: die Veränderung von Werten in der Gesellschaft – **to uphold values:** Werte vertreten – **to cheat on sb.:** jmndn. betrügen – **to split up with sb.:** sich von jmndm. trennen – **to be separated:** getrennt leben – **to suffer from (a divorce):** unter (einer Scheidung) leiden – **same-sex marriage:** die gleichgeschlechtliche Ehe – **surrogacy:** die Leihmutterschaft

Globalisation – outsourcing **

1. Describe the picture.
2. Explain the term *outsourcing* and give examples.
3. Talk about possible ways of improving working conditions, e.g. in sweatshops.
4. "If you buy very cheap clothes produced in developing countries, you support the exploitation of workers." Comment on this statement.

Useful words:

garment/textile factory: die Textilfabrik – **sewing machine:** die Nähmaschine – **sweatshop:** a small factory with poor working conditions and only little payment – **trade union:** organisation that fights for workers' rights – **exploitation:** die Ausbeutung – **(un)skilled worker:** der/die (un)gelernte Arbeiter/in – **domestic production:** die Produktion im Inland – **fair trade:** a way of selling and buying goods that ensures fair prices for the workers – **to boycott a product:** den Kauf eines Produkts verweigern

Migration / Refugees */**

1. Describe the photo.
2. Give reasons why people might leave their home countries to seek refuge in countries such as the UK, Germany or the USA.
3. Tell your partner what you know about problems migrants are often confronted with and about (German) initiatives to help refugees.
4. What steps would you recommend in order to prevent illegal immigration?

Useful words:

to escape poverty/a disease/war: der Armut/einer Krankheit/dem Krieg entfliehen – **to persecute sb.:** jmndn. verfolgen – **to flee from (fled, fled):** fliehen vor – **to seek asylum/refuge:** Asyl/eine Zufluchtsstätte suchen – **to stay in hiding:** sich versteckt halten – **to smuggle immigrants:** Immigranten schmuggeln – **desperate:** verzweifelt

Cyberbullying */**

1. Tell your partner about your photo.
2. Explain what the term *cyberbullying* means and give examples.
3. What might happen to the victims of cyberbullying? Talk about possible consequences.
4. "[...] Everybody gets bullied – whether it's cyber[ ]bullying or to your face or behind your back." (Sammi Hanratty, *1995, American actress). Comment on this statement.

Useful words:

to remain anonymous: anonym bleiben – **instant messaging:** das Chatten – **to insult sb.:** jmndn. beschimpfen/beleidigen – **to offend sb.:** to hurt sb.'s feelings (e.g. by rude behaviour) – **derogatory comment:** die abwertende Bemerkung – **to cut sb./oneself off:** jmndn./sich isolieren – **to suffer from ...:** unter ... leiden – **to develop suicidal tendencies:** to consider killing oneself – **to defend oneself against sb./sth.:** sich gegen jmndn./etw. wehren

Anxiety about the future */**

1. Talk about your photo.
2. Have you ever been in a situation like this?
   - **Yes:** Describe the situation and your feelings.
   - **No:** Describe the experiences friends have had in such a situation.
3. What steps would you recommend and take in order to help?
4. "It is living in our modern, globalised and highly technological world that makes young people feel more and more insecure." Comment on this statement.

Useful words:

anxiety (*adj.* anxious): die (starke) Besorgnis – **to be confused:** verwirrt sein – **insecurity:** die Unsicherheit – **to upset:** aus der Fassung bringen – **to be in a desperate situation:** sich in einer verzweifelten Lage befinden – **to be shaky:** wackelig/unsicher auf den Beinen sein (auch *fig.*) – **to be paralysed with fear:** vor Angst (wie) gelähmt sein – **lack of perspectives:** der Mangel an Perspektiven

Homeless people */**

1. Say what you can see in the picture.
2. Do you think homeless people should be supported financially?
   - **Yes:** Give reasons.
   - **No:** Explain why not and talk about alternatives.
3. Do you know other outsiders in society? How could they be helped?
4. Discuss the following statement: "Even nowadays everybody can get a job if they really want to work."

Useful words:

social security: die soziale Sicherheit – **upper/middle/lower class:** die Unter-/Mittel-/Oberschicht – **to provide a safety net:** ein Sicherheitsnetz bereitstellen – **indifference:** die Gleichgültigkeit – **on the top/bottom rung:** am oberen/unteren Ende der Gesellschaft – **class distinctions:** Klassenunterschiede – **to receive public aid/assistance/benefits:** öffentliche Hilfe/Unterstützung bekommen – **increase in poverty:** die zunehmende Armut

Science and technology: GM food **

1. Describe the photograph.
2. Imagine you have just eaten a delicious salad at a restaurant. Then you find out it had GM ingredients in it. Do you mind?
   - **Yes:** Explain why.
   - **No:** Give reasons why not.
3. Try to explain why people in Europe and in the USA show different attitudes towards GM food.
4. Do you think GM ingredients should be indicated to the consumer when the product is sold? Give reasons.

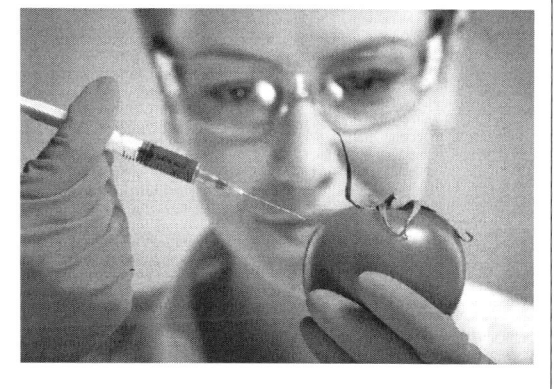

Useful words:

GM food: genetically engineered or genetically modified food – **to engineer genes:** to insert foreign genes into genetic codes – **to select and pass on desired traits:** gewünschte Charaktereigenschaften auswählen und übertragen – **selective breeding:** die Auslese (bei der Tier-/Pflanzenzucht) – **soybean:** die Sojabohne – **maize (AE corn):** der Mais – **stem cell:** die Stammzelle – **to convert into:** umwandeln in – **laboratory:** das Labor – **to spray pesticide:** Schädlingsbekämpfungsmittel sprühen

Capital punishment in the USA **

1. Describe the picture.
2. What do you know about capital punishment in the USA? Talk about it.
3. Name arguments often given in favour of capital punishment. Do you agree? Discuss.
4. Turkey has also been considering a (re-)introduction of the death penalty recently. Germany and most European countries, on the other hand, express different attitudes towards capital punishment. Try to explain why.

Useful words:

prison cell: die Gefängniszelle – **to be on death row:** im Todestrakt sitzen – **to sentence the accused to death:** den/die Angeklagte/n zum Tode verurteilen – **lethal injection:** die Todesspritze – **execution:** the act of killing sb. as a legal punishment – **hangman:** the person who executes a death sentence – **to act as a deterrent:** als Abschreckung dienen – **to show mercy:** Gnade zeigen – **irreversible:** unwiderruflich

Let's talk – Mit *speaking cards* die Sprechfertigkeit fördern (S II)

Einzelmaterial 215
S 8

Shakespeare **

1. Describe the picture.

2. Summarise what you know about Shakespeare (biography, Elizabethan Age, the Globe Theatre, works …).

3. Have you read one of his works?
   - **Yes:** Which one? Talk about it.
   - **No:** Would you like to read one work of this famous poet? Explain.

4. Do you think it is still contemporary to read and to talk about Shakespeare at school? Give your opinion.

Useful words:

to persecute sb.: jmndn. verfolgen – **Elizabethan Age:** the age associated with the rule of Queen Elizabeth I in England (1559–1603) – **the "Great Chain of Being":** Elizabethan belief that there was a (social) order for everything in the universe set out by God – **predetermined fate:** das vorherbestimmte Schicksal – **playwright:** der Dramatiker – **audience:** das Publikum – **to be on stage:** auf der Bühne sein – **timeless themes/leitmotifs:** zeitlose Themen/Leitmotive – **to coin words/ expressions:** Wörter/Ausdrücke prägen

The British Empire and the Commonwealth today **

1. Describe the picture and the situation the people are in. Who are they?

2. Summarise what you know about the British Empire.

3. Explain what legacy the British Empire still has today? Refer e.g. to India as a Commonwealth country.

4. Do you think the British Empire is an interesting and important school subject? Explain.

Useful words:

at its height: auf dem Höhepunkt – **to cover:** einnehmen/abdecken – **trade:** der Handel – **curiosity:** die Neugier – **the right to self-rule:** das Recht auf Eigenherrschaft – **to suppress customs of the indigenous peoples:** Bräuche der einheimischen Bevölkerung unterdrücken – **decline:** der Untergang/Niedergang – **legacy:** *here:* lasting effects – **an association of nations:** eine Gemeinschaft von Nationen – **to consist of:** bestehen aus – **to pay allegiance to the British Crown:** der Britischen Krone Treue geloben

Let's talk – Mit *speaking cards* die Sprechfertigkeit fördern (S II)

Einzelmaterial 215
S 9

M 2 Discussing a topic

In your summer holidays, you would like to travel to a Commonwealth country with a friend. The problem is that one of you would like to see Canada whereas the other wants to explore South Africa ...

Task: Work with a partner. He or she is your friend. Discuss your travel plans and come to an agreement.

A journey to a Commonwealth country */**

Partner A	Partner B
You would like to spend your holiday **in Canada**. Look at the pictures and talk about your holiday plans. You start.	You would like to spend your holiday **in South Africa**. Look at the pictures and talk about your holiday plans. Your partner starts the conversation.
Talk about ... – which city/cities you would like to explore. – how you would travel around. – what you would like to visit and do there (sights, activities, places ...). – where you would sleep. – why you are particularly fascinated by Canadian history and culture.	**Talk about ...** – which city/cities you would like to explore. – how you would travel around. – what you would like to visit and do there (sights, activities, places ...). – where you would sleep. – why you are particularly fascinated by South African history and culture.
Useful words: **to explore urban attractions:** städtische Sehenswürdigkeiten erkunden – **to go hiking in the mountains:** bergwandern – **to go kayaking:** Kajak fahren gehen – **an anglophone:** someone whose first language is English – **a francophone:** someone whose first language is French – **Quebec's French heritage:** das französische Erbe der Provinz Quebec	**Useful words:** **to explore the landscape:** die Landschaft erkunden – **to go on a guided safari:** an einer geführten Safari teilnehmen – **to go whale watching:** Wale beobachten – **to visit archaeological sites:** Ausgrabungsstätten besuchen – **Afrikaans:** one of South Africa's eleven official languages – **the overcoming of apartheid:** die Überwindung der Rassentrennungspolitik in Südafrika

Let's talk – Mit *speaking cards* die Sprechfertigkeit fördern (S II)

Einzelmaterial 215
S 10

Protect the environment */**

Partner A	Partner B
While walking in the park, you **notice a person leaving some rubbish under a bench**.	After your lunch break in the park **you are in a hurry**. As there aren't any bins nearby, you **decide to leave your rubbish under a bench**.
You are shocked about this behaviour. You start a polite conversation to make the person take the rubbish to a bin.	Another person starts talking to you as you start hurrying back to work.
– Act out the conversation with your partner and find arguments to convince him/her that the environment has to be respected. Reach a compromise.	– Act out the conversation with your partner and find arguments to convince him/her that you usually respect the environment. Reach a compromise.

Useful words:

bottle bank: der Flaschencontainer – **bottle deposit:** das Flaschenpfand – **to be careful with sth.:** behutsam mit etw. sein – **to be concerned about sb./sth.:** sich um jmndn./etw. Sorgen machen – **to separate waste:** Müll trennen

Social networks */**

Partner A	Partner B
Social networking platforms, such as Facebook, are very popular. Nonetheless, there is a lot of criticism because some of them threaten or violate personal privacy on the web.	**Social networking platforms**, such as Facebook, are very popular. Nonetheless, there is a lot of criticism because some of them threaten or violate personal privacy on the web.
You are a strong critic of social networking. You do not have an account and you see a lot of disadvantages.	**You are totally committed to the idea of social networking** and you see only the advantages.
You want to make your friend, a social networking addict, aware of the dangers of such sites.	Your friend does not have a Facebook account yet. You want to gain him/her as a new member.
– Act out the conversation with your partner and find arguments to convince him/her that it is not necessary to be a Facebook member.	– Act out the conversation with your partner and find arguments to convince him/her that it is important to be a member of Facebook. Reach a compromise.

Useful words:

to become a victim of ...: ein Opfer von ... werden – **to threaten sb.:** jmndn. bedrohen – **to violate (sb.'s personal privacy):** (jmnds. Privatsphäre) verletzen – **to be obsessed with sth.:** von etw. besessen sein – **to make sb. aware of sth.:** jmndm. etw. bewusst machen – **to be behind the times:** hinter dem Mond leben (*fam.*)

The British Monarchy **

Partner A	Partner B
You participate in a discussion about the value of the British monarchy: Should it be abolished or not?	You participate in a discussion about the value of the British monarchy: Should it be abolished or not?
You are of the opinion that **the British monarchy should not be abolished**.	You are of the opinion that **the British monarchy should be abolished**.
You start the conversation. Give reasons to convince your partner.	Your partner starts the conversation. Give reasons to convince your partner.
Advantages you see: – The constitutional monarchy is an effective political system and has a symbolic role for national unity. – The monarchy is an important factor for the UK's revenue from tourism. – …	**Problems you see:** – The monarch plays only a ceremonial role without any political power (only head of state). – There are unjustifiable costs of monarchy (e.g. maintenance of the Royal family's luxurious lifestyle with the help of tax money). – …

Useful words:

to sustain: (aufrecht)erhalten – **constitutional monarchy:** a system in which the monarch's power is considerably limited in favour of the politicians forming the government – **to inherit from:** erben von – **heritage:** das Erbe – **revenue from tourism (sg.):** die Tourismuseinnahmen (Pl.) – **to be critical of sb./sth.:** jmndm./ einer Sache gegenüber kritisch eingestellt sein – **to live at the taxpayer's expense:** auf Kosten der Steuerzahler leben – **to serve as an example for sb.:** jmndm. als Vorbild dienen

Let's talk – Mit *speaking cards* die Sprechfertigkeit fördern (S II)

Einzelmaterial 215
S 12

Police violence in the US */**

Partner A	Partner B
You are a **police officer** working for the NYPD. You have been **confronted with a lot of anger and protest** after the series of police shootings across the US that led to the deaths of (unarmed) African Americans.	You are a **black teenager** taking part in a protest march in New York. You are really **outraged after recent incidents of police violence** that led to the deaths of often unarmed African Americans.
You are of the opinion that **the police sometimes have to use violence** in order to protect people's lives and to maintain law and order. A young black protester starts talking to you during a protest march you help to protect.	You address a police officer who is protecting the protest march asking him/her for explanations.
Comment on the arguments your partner presents. Express sympathy for the victims but, on the other hand, defend your colleagues' actions.	Comment on the arguments your partner presents. Express your frustration and concern and try to convince your partner that excessive police brutality can never be a solution. You start the conversation.
Talk about … – your commitment to fighting crime and securing peace under challenging conditions. – your colleague who was shot during a gang fight in a black neighbourhood. – the fact that officers from different ethnic backgrounds work for the NYPD. – …	**Talk about …** – your feelings of helplessness and anger after the recent injustices against the black community. – your impression that many police officers have racial prejudices. – your belief that it is not a matter of race, but of social discrimination whether teenagers become criminals or not. – …
Useful words: **NYPD:** New York City Police Department – **to maintain law and order:** Recht und Ordnung aufrechterhalten – **law enforcement:** der Gesetzesvollzug – **to be committed to doing sth.:** sich einer Sache mit vollem Einsatz verpflichten – **challenging:** (heraus)fordernd – **to act in self-defence:** in Notwehr handeln	**Useful words:** **to be outraged:** entrüstet sein – **concern:** die Besorgnis – **grief:** a deep feeling of sadness (at sb.'s death) – **to tend to overreact:** zu Überreaktionen neigen – **to be defenceless against sb./sth.:** jmndm./einer Sache gegenüber wehrlos sein – **to be biased:** voreingenommen sein

Let's talk – Mit *speaking cards* die Sprechfertigkeit fördern (S II)

Einzelmaterial 215
S 13

Sharing a flat *

Partner A	Partner B
You have just started your studies at Bristol University and found a two-bedroom flat there. Now you are **trying to find someone to share the flat with**. You live in the flat with your cat and turtle. You hate noise, alcohol and cigarettes and you have to get up early in the morning. Your flatmate should help in the household, feed your pets and be able to pay 350 pounds for the room. – Act out the dialogue. You start the conversation. Reach a compromise.	You have just finished school in Germany after stressful exams and are **looking forward to your year abroad** in Bristol – with lots of new people, parties and friends visiting from Germany. After reading an advert for a two-bedroom flat, you are now on location. You ask about using the kitchen, bathroom and the TV in the living room, and inviting guests. Start by ringing the bell at the door. – Act out the dialogue. Your partner starts the conversation. Reach a compromise.

Useful words:

roommate/flatmate: der/die Mitbewohner/in – **to move in with sb.:** mit jmndm. zusammenziehen – **to share the rent:** (sich) die Miete teilen – **to observe rules:** Regeln beachten – **to be considerate towards sb.:** auf jmndn. Rücksicht nehmen

Intellectual property on the Internet */**

Partner A	Partner B
You **often download free songs from the Internet**. Now your friend tells you to save YouTube videos on your computer as private copies. Your mum/dad overhears this conversation and seems worried. You only download MP3s from websites where young artists promote their songs for free. You have never watched films on illegal streaming sites. – Act out the dialogue with your partner. Find arguments to convince him/her that not every free download means copyright infringement.	You overhear your teenage son/daughter talking to a friend about downloading free songs and videos from the Internet. Now **you are worried that might be illegal file sharing**. In order to protect your child from possible difficulties, you decide to share your concerns with him/her. – Act out the dialogue with your partner and find arguments to convince him/her that one has to be very careful on the web in order to not commit e.g. copyright infringement.

Useful words:

intellectual property: das geistige Eigentum – **copyright infringement:** die Urheberrechtsverletzung – **parental responsibility:** die elterliche Verantwortung/Aufsichtspflicht – **supervision:** die Beaufsichtigung/Überwachung – **written warning:** die Abmahnung

The UK after the Brexit referendum **

Partner A	Partner B
You are an **elderly British citizen** and in the Brexit referendum you **voted in favour of the UK leaving the EU**.	You are a **British teenager** and you would like to study and work abroad in the future. You **voted in favour of the UK staying in the EU**.
At a local workshop on politics, you start a conversation with a teenager who does not share your views.	At a local workshop on politics, an elderly person with opposite views starts a discussion about the Brexit result with you.
Comment on your partner's arguments and try to convince him/her that there will only be advantages for British society after the Brexit.	Comment on your partner's arguments and try to convince him/her that Britain's leaving the EU will only cause problems for its people.
Advantages you see:	**Problems you see:**
– More independence from European politics and economy – Decrease in immigration – Return to "British" values – …	– Britain's political and economic isolation in Europe – Limited freedom of movement – Less opportunities for young people and people of non-British origin – …

Useful words:

referendum: a vote on an important political or social issue involving all the people in a country/area – **the European Single Market:** der Europäische Binnenmarkt – **the four freedoms, i.e. free movement of people, of goods, capital and services:** legal permission for workers, goods, etc. to leave one country and enter another without any restrictions – **to feel restricted:** sich eingeschränkt fühlen

Let's talk – Mit *speaking cards* die Sprechfertigkeit fördern (S II)

Einzelmaterial 215
S 15

The American Dream – is it still valid today? **

Partner A	Partner B
You have been invited to participate in a discussion about the importance of the **American Dream** nowadays.	You have been invited to participate in a discussion about the importance of the **American Dream** nowadays.
You are of the opinion that **this concept is still valid today** and that its promises can come true for everybody who is willing to work hard enough.	You hold the opinion that **this concept is outdated** because, at present, American society is facing many more problems than chances.
Comment on the arguments your partner presents and convince him/her that the American Dream is still alive. You start.	Comment on the arguments your partner presents and convince him/her that the American Dream is over. Your partner starts the conversation.
Talk about …	**Talk about …**
– America's attractiveness for many immigrants, e.g. from Mexico or Asia, because of economic reasons. – many people's ongoing fascination with the 'American way of life'. – biographies of success, such as Barack Obama's, Arnold Schwarzenegger's or Mark Zuckerberg's. – …	– America's decreasing attractiveness due to economic problems, rising unemployment and high cost of living (health care, education, …). – the huge gap between rich and poor. – persisting inequalities between the different ethnic groups. – …
Useful words:	**Useful words:**
to firmly believe in …: stark an … glauben – **to cling to dreams:** an Träumen hängen – **to achieve success through personal effort:** durch persönliche Anstrengung zum Erfolg kommen – **fundamental human/civil rights:** grundlegende Menschen-/Bürgerrechte – **the notions of freedom, liberty and individuality:** die Ideen von Freiheit, Unabhängigkeit und Individualität	**persisting:** ongoing – **to (not) enjoy the benefits of material success:** (nicht) die Vorteile materiellen/finanziellen Erfolgs genießen – **the struggle to make one's way up:** das Ringen um sozialen Aufstieg – **low-income family:** die Geringverdienerfamilie – **to be discriminated against:** diskriminiert werden

Globalisation **

	Partner A	Partner B

Partner A	**Partner B**
You are **in favour of globalisation** and have a positive view on changes in society. You have been invited to participate in a TV discussion about globalisation.	You are **against globalisation** and have critical views on current global developments. You are invited to participate in a TV discussion about globalisation.
Talk about the advantages of globalisation.	**Talk about the problems** connected with this topic.
Comment on the arguments your partner presents. Convince your partner that globalisation makes a positive contribution to societies all over the world. You start the conversation.	Comment on the arguments your partner presents. Convince him/her that globalisation has also negative side-effects. Your partner starts the conversation.
Advantages you see:	**Problems you see:**
– Wider range of available products at very low prices – Growing interaction and exchange between economies and cultures worldwide – Financial support for developing countries (e.g. debt relief) and international peacekeeping – …	– Increasing ecological problems – Persistent poverty and growing inequalities (destruction of local markets in developing countries/low wages for workers) – Increase of international conflicts and terrorist attacks – …

Useful words:

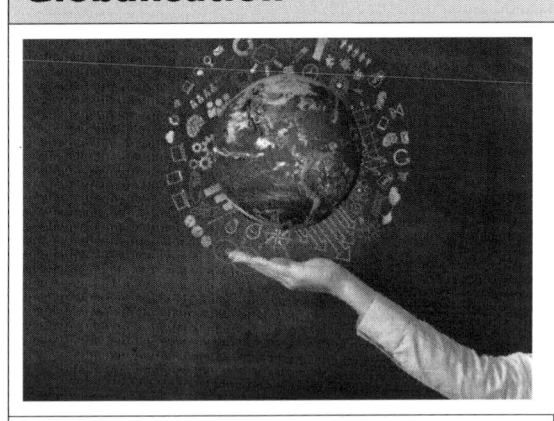

to lead to economic growth: zu wirtschaftlichem Wachstum führen – **to raise the living standard:** den Lebensstandard erhöhen – **to grant debt relief:** to not make poorer countries pay back the money they owe to wealthier nations – **to close down local enterprises:** heimische Firmen schließen – **to compete with sb./sth:** mit jmndm./etw. in Wettbewerb treten – **manufacturer:** der Hersteller – **at the expense of …:** auf Kosten von … – **developing country:** das Entwicklungsland – **to undermine workers' rights:** die Rechte der Arbeiter untergraben – **to threaten domestic labour:** den inländischen Arbeitsmarkt bedrohen

Let's talk – Mit *speaking cards* die Sprechfertigkeit fördern (S II)

Einzelmaterial 215
S 17

M 3   How to use the speaking cards

Erste Übungsform *** / ******** *für* speaking cards *mit einem oder mehr Bildimpulsen*

(***M 1***): *Immer ein Schüler äußert sich zu jeweils einer Bildkarte/einem Thema nach Wahl. Alternativ äußern sich beide Schülerinnen und Schüler zu derselben Karte.*

What to do with the speaking cards

1. Work with a partner.
2. Choose one of the cards or work on the card handed to you.
3. Look at the picture and read through the questions/tasks.
4. Take 3–5 minutes and make notes so that you can answer the questions and work on the instructions.
5. Present your results to your partner. Talk for about 5 minutes. (You can also talk about further ideas if you want to.)

Zweite Übungsform *** / ******** *für* speaking cards *mit unterschiedlichen Positionen*

(***M 2***): *Immer zwei Schülerinnen und Schüler äußern sich zu jeweils einer Bildkarte/ einem Thema nach Wahl und handeln einen Kompromiss aus bzw. überzeugen ihren Partner.*

What to do with the speaking cards

1. Work with a partner.
2. Choose one of the cards or work on the card handed to you.
3. Look at the picture and read through the tasks.
4. Take 3–5 minutes and make notes so that you can work on the instructions.
5. Then start the discussion.

   Discuss your ideas for about 10 minutes.

   (You can also talk about further ideas if you want to.)

Let's talk – Mit *speaking cards* die Sprechfertigkeit fördern (S II)

Einzelmaterial 215
S 18

V

Kompetenzen
- Förderung der monologischen und dialogischen Sprechfertigkeit
- Schulung der Argumentations- und Diskussionskompetenz
- Vertiefung der interkulturellen Kompetenz bezüglich englischsprachiger Lebenswelten

Niveau
Klasse 10–12 (G8) bzw. 11–13 (G9)

Dauer
Je nach Einsatz der Karten für die Übungsform M 1 pro Karte ca. 10 Minuten und für die Übungsform M 2 pro Karte ca. 15 Minuten.

Einbettung
Die *speaking cards* können im Rahmen der Behandlung des jeweiligen Themas als Stundeneinstieg oder Vertiefung eingesetzt werden. Sie eignen sich außerdem dazu, gezielt auf **mündliche Prüfungen** vorzubereiten. Inhaltlich wurden gängige Themen des Englischunterrichts der S II (ab Einführungsphase) ausgewählt. Der thematische Wortschatz der jeweiligen Lehrbucheinheit sowie Redemittel zur Bildbeschreibung und Meinungsäußerung werden vorausgesetzt.

Auf CD:
✓ *Word-Datei*
✓ *alle Bilder in Farbe*

Hinweise

Zum Einsatz der speaking cards *im Unterricht*

Vorbereitung: Die Lehrkraft kann die Karten beliebig oft kopieren, gegebenenfalls laminieren und auslegen, sodass die Schülerinnen und Schüler nach Interesse und Lernstand auswählen können. Der Motivations- und Aufforderungscharakter zum Sprechen ist hoch und in der Regel wird beim ersten Betrachten klar, was zu tun ist.

Einsatz: Die Karten für die **Einführungsphase** sind neben dem jeweiligen Titel der *speaking card* mit einem * gekennzeichnet, die für die **Qualifikationsphase** mit **.

Unterhalb der einzelnen Karten befinden sich *useful words*, die in leistungsschwächeren Kursen eingesetzt werden können. Bei leistungsstärkeren Kursen oder bei einem erneuten Durchgang kann die Hilfe nach hinten umgeknickt oder abgeschnitten werden.

Arbeitsauftrag: Bevor die Karten das erste Mal eingesetzt werden, kann die Lehrkraft die Arbeitsaufträge **(M 3)** auf Folie kopieren bzw. über Beamer präsentieren, gemeinsam besprechen und anschließend im Klassensatz austeilen.

Zur Durchführung

Der Kartensatz ist in **zwei unterschiedliche Übungsformen** unterteilt. Bei der **ersten Übungsform (M 1)** beschreiben die Schülerinnen und Schüler ein Bild und beantworten anschließend Fragen bzw. reagieren auf Sprechimpulse. Diese Karten werden in Partnerarbeit bearbeitet. Dabei werden die Fragen und Sprechimpulse dem Partner vor dem Beantworten vorgelesen.

Die Karten der **zweiten Übungsform (M 2)** beinhalten Bildimpulse und geben Situationen vor, die in einem Rollenspiel zu zweit umgesetzt werden. Die Lernenden wählen gemeinsam eine Karte und verteilen die Rollen. In Einzelarbeit bereiten sie dann ihre Rollen vor, indem sie Argumente sammeln. Anschließend treten sie miteinander in einen Dialog. Ziel dabei ist es, gemeinsam einen Kompromiss zur vorgegebenen Situation zu finden oder den Partner von der eigenen Meinung zu überzeugen.